After reading this book, I was shocked at how in your face it is. This is a serious financial-planning tool that opens your eyes WIDE.

E. J. Long, President, Long Financial Group

A must read for anyone who wishes to avoid the possibility of creating havoc and heartbreak among and within their loved ones. You say you would like to "control" the really important things in your life. Well … guess what? You can actually have some "control" over the most profound occurrences in life … but only if you act … *between now and then*.

A. T. "Al" Benelli, CFP®
Owner/Founder, The Merlin Group

This book has a wealth of knowledge and recommendations about a part of life that we all share, written by a woman who has a vast knowledge of how to deal with these decisions.

Sherrie P. Schoen, Owner, Signature Gallery

Jeanne has taken the knowledge from her work experience and put it all together in one place to show how those important decisions are interconnected. She translates the language of the professionals into easy-to-understand words to enable people to make these informed life choices.

James J. Heffernen, BS-Econ.; JD; LL.M.-Tax (retired)

As an Estate Tax Attorney for almost 40 years, I found Jeanne's book a wonderful primer for one's life – it is informative, entertaining and most of all gently directs the reader to consider serious alternatives that we all need to address, but are reluctant to do so. A worthwhile read.

Stephen H. Frishberg, CPA, JD, LL.M-Tax

As someone who has already had to face many landmarks and landscapes of aging, I look back and wish this book had been there to guide me.

Barbara M. Christy
The Library of Congress (retired professional librarian)

Read this book … and leave this life without regrets.

Jerry Spinelli,
Newbery Medal-winning author of 'Maniac Magee'

Between now and then is informative, easy to comprehend, and at times even fun to read despite the seriousness of the subject. Relying on her vast experience, research, and interviews, Jeanne Hoff delivers the goods on pretty much everything one needs to know about planning for those events that everyone is destined to face. It's not likely one will find so much information in just one book and where more is needed, Hoff points the way to obtain the best professional advice.

Richard D. Bank, Esquire

Between now and then is a well-organized, clearly written guide for everyone who is now or will eventually face those difficult, often confusing end-of-life decisions. An essential read!

Donald A. Young (retired)

Jeanne's attention to the details she has garnered over many years as a legal professional make this book a must read for anyone who hopes to retire with any comfort at all.

Dr. James J. McKeown, Jr.

We all know we cannot avoid "Death and Taxes" No question this book is a great reference to help us plan for now and for our future. A must read.

Suzanne B. Shank, Owner, Atlas Travel Agency

...between now and then

What do you plan
to do with your time
between now and then?

A Common-Sense
End-of-Life Planning Guide
for Baby Boomers
(and the Rest of Us)

Jeanne C. Hoff

Copyright © 2013 by Jeanne C. Hoff
Library of Congress Control Number: 2013907162

ISBN 978-0-7414-8495-6 Paperback
ISBN 978-0-7414-8496-3 eBook

Printed in the United States of America

Published July 2013

INFINITY PUBLISHING
1094 New DeHaven Street, Suite 100
West Conshohocken, PA 19428-2713
Toll-free (877) BUY BOOK
Local Phone (610) 941-9999
Fax (610) 941-9959
Info@buybooksontheweb.com
www.buybooksontheweb.com

TABLE of CONTENTS

FOREWORD

Jeanne Hoff is an anachronism. She is a genuine throwback to the days when the title of executive secretary or administrative assistant meant something of substance. People who held those positions in a firm were expected to have an array of competencies from postal physics to punctuation. They were usually the last line of defense preventing some highly paid, graduate-educated big shot from looking like a real bonehead to his clients or colleagues as a result of the all-too-ubiquitous dumb mistake... the one we all make at one time or another.

I met Jeanne as the result of our search for the "Holy Grail" of office staff. Years earlier I had founded The Merlin Group, a full-service financial planning firm with a rare, but not totally unique business plan ... bring values-based, life planning & financial services to the public with a "fiduciary" standard of competency, commitment and communication. I wanted to make my training as a Certified Financial Planner Practitioner and my personal values work for our clients in an industry riddled with greed and corruption. Our customers made us a success. We were growing like a weed. We desperately needed an office manager who could pull it all together... do practically anything with little or no supervision... and clearly reflect our commitment to competency. Like I said ... the Holy Grail!

Jeanne's resume ... documenting vast experiences running her own business, working in key Philadelphia and Montgomery County law firms, personally assisting some near-celebrity estate attorneys led me to ask ... "Why do you want to work here?" She was, obviously, way overqualified for what we thought we were able to afford. Someone like her would likely shock our salary budget. Her answer was equally shocking. "I'm not sure that I do want to work here", she replied. Who was interviewing who, I thought. It became obvious real soon. "I want to be a part of something special. I don't need to be a chief... but I don't want to be just an Indian either. Challenge me ... make it worth my time and talent ... not so much in what you pay me ... but how you make use of what I know and what I can do!" Like I said ... the Holy Grail. And she was to become a big part of our enterprise. Her undying passion for conveying the need and implementing the details of estate planning made her an invaluable asset to us and our client base. She brought a goldmine of knowledge and experience to the table. She had "been there" and "done that" so many times before and now she was part of our planning team. Thus, I feel uniquely qualified and deeply honored to introduce this treasure of a book to you.

Nothing is more certain than death and taxes. Actually I've witnessed some folks who, legally or otherwise, have managed to avoid the latter. I know of no one who has successfully made provision to avoid the former ... and therein lies the undeniable need for what's in this book. Our passing will (hopefully) be sad enough to those we've left behind without the added insult and injury of not having made proper arrangements for our orderly departure. Unlike a hotel, check-out times for life are seldom posted behind the door.

Much like the biblical Parable of the Sower, the information contained in the pages that follow ... like the seed of the farmer planting his field ... will fall on ground of varying fertility.

Some readers will simply ignore it, failing to see any need to act ... letting it pass all their eyes and register not within them. They will, by default, adopt the belief that their lives will continue forever ... or that they need not care for anyone or anything they leave behind when their time is up ... a textbook quality definition of selfishness.

Another class of reader may admit to the need to plan out the remainder of their stay here on earth ... they may even feel within their insides a bit of a disturbance or a discomfort at the conscious realization that they have done little to secure their legacies. What will happen, unfortunately, is that some element of human nature will put these poor folks into a state of "denial"... something that has been a supreme puzzlement to me for most of my adult life. I don't know if it's a fear or an unwillingness to face our own mortality. What I do know is that I have seen so many families deeply wounded by the reality of what one or more of their members left undone for the sake of comfort or convenience. In our office was a sign that read "You can't fix stupid". It was there to remind our staff that some folks were not to be cured of their "denial" no matter how hard we tried to educate them.

Others will fall into a group I'll call the "amicable agreeable"... or A.A. They will recognize the need that the issues illuminated in this book be addressed ... but not necessarily by them (quasi AA people) or ... that there is no rush or urgency about the whole thing. These folks will likely promise to get around to it. Not the most intelligent of options. It calls immediately to mind the case of my 47 year old doctor client and friend who ... after nearly two years of my persistent nagging ... finally went to see his lawyer to get his crucial documents and plans in proper order ... only to have his life come to an untimely end before the process could be completed. The only post-life certainty I can attest to is that the state of his final affairs is anything but what he had wanted. It could easily be said that his apparent lack of urgency was the cause of what became a family tragedy that compounded the loss of his young life.

And then there are those for whom this book will ultimately provide the greatest total return. These people will allow their intellect to not only recognize the need to "plan" but will act on the epiphany as well. To them, this book will be more than just a good starting point. They may not appreciate it now, but by implementing what Jeanne has laid out in a simple, easy to follow reference guide today, they will be giving themselves and their family a gift of infinite value to be appreciated fully at some indeterminate ... but guaranteed to occur ... point in future time. For a more immediate return on your investment, consider the fact that if you were to acquire this information from an attorney or a fee-paid planner, rather than from this book ... you would likely be out a small fortune. In fact, I deeply regret not having had this book to give ... free of charge ... to our clients as a way to demonstrate how we much truly cared for them and their families. It's in your hands now ... and so the question becomes ... What will you do "Between Now and Then"?

A.T. "Al" Benelli, CFP®
Owner/Founder, The Merlin Group

EPIGRAM

Cassandra was a prophetess who foresaw the doom of Troy.
She was cursed so no one would ever believe her predictions.

Robert Fagles in his translation of *The Aeniad*, page 439

PREFACE

I invite you to come along with me on a journey of a lifetime ... your life, that is. It is an important journey that everyone will take, so pay attention along the way, ask questions, make wise choices, speak your own truth, keep an open mind, and most of all, enjoy the trip.

I believe now is the time to make conscious choices about what route you want to take. When you consider that the ultimate destination of life's journey is the cemetery, I recommend that you enjoy every day of this trip that life has to offer you.

This journey is one of both time and distance. It requires some preparation on your part ... as does any journey ... but the rewards will be worth it. It also requires that you begin to think about what you will do with the rest of your life and then take steps to make those things happen. It is especially important that such plans are made while you are still young and healthy enough to be in charge of your own life, because there may come a day when you are no longer in charge of your personal choices. That being said, it puts some degree of urgency on the choices you make right now.

I urge you to fill your "Bucket List" with everything you want to do, establish priorities for each, and then begin working through your list. If you are fortunate, you will live a long, healthy, vibrant life, and can benefit from having a guide, a map, some planning tips, and some suggestions to smooth your path and give you some comfort for your journey *between now and then*. After all, it could be a journey of 20 or 30 years. When you hit a bump in the road, remember that there are always detours that you can choose to take to help you reach your destination.

By 2009, I had not worked for several years, had just experienced the death of my former husband, and was beginning the work of being his executor. When I completed the administration of his estate, I looked at my life and what I wanted to do with the rest of it. There are many things I enjoy doing, but I was not focused on any one thing.

That's when I began working with an acupuncturist. We talked a lot before we got to the truth of what I wanted to do with the rest of my life, but once it was revealed, there was no turning back. Her skills, commitment, understanding and compassion helped me focus on giving birth to this book which I had been thinking about for more than 20 years. The time was right. Although I am passionate about the subject of end-of-life planning and everything it includes, I needed her counseling to keep me focused and committed to the completion and publication of this book.

The name of this book came out of a conversation I had years ago with a man who said that he wasn't afraid of dying; he was afraid of what was between now and then. In retrospect, I see that his words were to become the title of this book, and one of the sources of my inquiry into the question:

*"What do you want to do with the rest of your life **between now and then**?"*

When I tell people I have written a book about end-of-life planning, I often get the same reaction: *"Don't you think that's a pretty morbid subject?"* They are referring to the fact that end-of-life planning sounds like it is about funerals and death. Well, yes, end-of-life planning does include those things, but also much more. It also includes important legal, financial, medical, and personal decisions that some people would prefer to ignore indefinitely ... until *later*, whenever that is.

After people hear my perspective of the importance of planning, most people generally, *even if reluctantly,* agree that end-of-life planning makes perfect sense. It was an entirely new concept for them to consider. Baby Boomers, in particular, have an admirable, forever-young philosophy of life that has served them well up to now; however, if they continue to make the choice to ignore the various aspects of retirement and aging, there will be problems ahead. I want them to at least be prepared for the potential consequences of their choice to ignore end-of-life planning, and do their best to make wise choices and avoid problems.

In this book, readers will gain perspective and knowledge that will prepare them to face the challenges of the future squarely and intelligently, as opposed to being caught off guard by events that had a certain degree of predictability.

Why Baby Boomers? Why now? Because Baby Boomers (i.e., persons born between 1946 and 1964), are reaching age 65 at the rate of 10,000 each day, and that will keep happening every day for the next 20 years. They are moving full-speed-ahead toward two of the biggest challenges of their lives: retirement and old age. *There, I said it.*

Retirement and old age are unfamiliar territory for which many Baby Boomers are generally unprepared. No matter how you define retirement and old age, both carry with them an implication of a decline of some kind. Old age, disability and a reduction in lifestyle are not things Baby Boomers like to think about, let alone talk about and plan for. They are busy living life in the moment. Nevertheless, they, too, will someday pass away.

The contributions of this group of people in America are enormous. Much has been written about Boomers because of this milestone birthday some of them will be celebrating, and there isn't much I can add to all the statistics.

What I can do, however, is point out things Baby Boomers should consider doing with the rest of their lives **between now and then** … that is between today and their last day on earth … things that will benefit them in significant ways.

Between now and then, ready or not, you will find yourself having to make many (choices) (decisions) (plans) about things both large and small, urgent or merely important, insignificant and consequential. As you read this book, you will begin to _think_ about your life as it is today and as you want it to be in the future. The secrets to making responsible choices that can help you enrich your life and achieve your goals are:

- to have as much relevant information as possible,

- to have a basic understanding of the potential benefits and consequences of your decisions,

- to take actions that have predictably positive results.

In each of the five chapters of this book, choices are required. Well, actually, that's not true. Choices are presented for consideration, but you are not obligated to make the suggested choices, as long as you understand that making _no choice_ is, in fact, making a choice, and that every non-choice comes with its own set of consequences.

Should you choose not to follow any of the suggestions in this book, I do ask you to at least evaluate the suggestions on their respective merits and then compare each suggestion against the potential benefits or consequences for you and your loved ones if your choice is to do nothing.

The stories I relate in this book are true. You will read about real people, some of whom made real mistakes, many of which could have been avoided had there been some timely, appropriate planning beforehand. Are there lessons to be learned from them? I certainly hope so. Right now, you probably have many questions. There are answers and ideas and stories and suggestions in this book for most of your questions … and lots more. You may recognize yourself in some of the stories. You may recognize your parents and your children in some of the stories, and find that some of my suggestions will apply to them, too.

What I do know, and what I have confirmed for myself as a result of writing this book, is that I want to be in charge of my life **between now and then**. I want to be the person making the decisions about what I will do and will not do with my time and my life. I want to be the person making the plans. I want to be fully responsible for my life to the greatest extent possible. I do not wish to settle for anything less. I absolutely do not wish to have important life decisions made for me by someone else, and I certainly don't want other people assuming they know what I want. How can anyone possibly know what I want if I don't tell them? I believe in making my own choices about how I live, so that I can die with few regrets.

Having said this, and knowing that people are not mind readers, it is therefore my responsibility to tell people what I want and do not want. If this sounds like the kind of life you want, too, this book is for you. If you are a person who wants to be in charge of your own life **between now and then**, then there are things you must do before it is too late.

While we can agree that no one can know what the future will bring, there are certain predictable events and consequences that should not be ignored … notice, I did not say they _cannot_ be ignored … because the truth is, they can be ignored … as long as the people making the choices are willing to pay the price of their choices. The point is to be able to at least anticipate the potential consequences of every choice. Much of life, from the very small events to the very large ones, is about choices and consequences.

By now, you may be wondering why you should believe me. You do not have to believe me. You are free to ignore everything I say. There is absolutely no reason to do anything suggested in this book unless you clearly see the benefits and are willing to do what is necessary to bring about the desired changes and results in your life. You are free to make your own choices about your days **between now and then.**

Each person must walk the path of his/her own life. Don't beat yourself up because these tasks seem too hard or the decisions too difficult to make, even if you understand and agree that the consequences might be dire. While you are deciding whether or not to follow some suggestions in this book, I want you to forgive yourself if it is your choice to skip the entire matter. You will not be a failure for making that choice.

Reading this book may bring up certain emotions for you, especially fear: fear of the unknown; fear of taking risks; fear of change; fear of running out of money; fear of speaking your own truth; fear of the disapproval of others; and the big one, fear of dying. It is natural that you would experience such emotions. You won't be alone in having those feelings. But, when you consider that feelings of fear live only in your head, it is entirely possible for you to rethink those emotions when you have information to guide you. I hope that what I have written will enable you to make wise choices for yourself to live the rest of your life **between now and then** your way.

What would happen if you were to make the choice to do nothing that has been suggested in this book? You will live out the rest of your days, one day at a time, and when your last day arrives, your family will do what is necessary. But, before you decide whether to do any end-of-life planning or not, think about your family and how they might struggle to deal with things you should have handled while you had the time, and think about whether you would have regrets for "*words left unspoken and deeds left undone*." Now is the time to begin your "Bucket List."

If you have chosen to accept my invitation, allow me the privilege of being your guide on this most important journey **between now and then**.

Jeanne C. Hoff

INTRODUCTION

> *A truly good book teaches me better than to read it.*
> *I must soon lay it down, and commence living on its hint.*
> *What I began by reading, I must finish by acting.*
>
> Henry David Thoreau

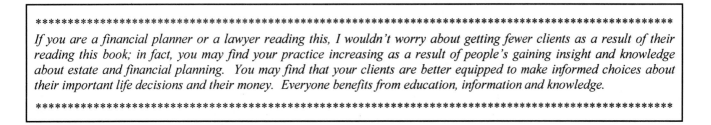

If you are a financial planner or a lawyer reading this, I wouldn't worry about getting fewer clients as a result of their reading this book; in fact, you may find your practice increasing as a result of people's gaining insight and knowledge about estate and financial planning. You may find that your clients are better equipped to make informed choices about their important life decisions and their money. Everyone benefits from education, information and knowledge.

An investment in knowledge always pays the best interest.

Benjamin Franklin

"What do you plan to do with the rest of your life
between now and then?"

Having just read the question above, what immediately comes to mind? Do you have an immediate answer? Or are you thinking who cares? What does it matter? I'm too busy to think about that now? Are you annoyed or worried? Keep in mind that there is no right or wrong answer to the question. All that matters is YOUR answer.

The purpose of this book is to introduce you to the idea of planning. "*Planning what?*" you may be wondering. Planning what you will do with the rest of your life such that you will have no (*few*) regrets on your last day. This planning process asks you to do certain things: THINK, DECIDE, SPEAK, and ACT.

- <u>Think</u> about what? What you plan to do with the rest of your life. Let your imagination run free.

- <u>Decide</u>? Investigate options and choices, what works for you and what does not. Then decide.

- <u>Speak</u> to whom, and about what? Share your decisions, wishes, plans, intentions, fears, directions with the people in your life who will be going on the journey with you.

- <u>Act</u>? Once you have made decisions for yourself, and have talked about those decisions with your loved ones, then you must take action to make those things happen.

An idea not coupled with action will never get any bigger than the brain cell it occupied.

Arnold H. Glasow

If you are a Baby Boomer, the time *between now and then* can be another 20 or 30 years ... it could be 1/3 of your entire life! That's a whole lot of hours and days and years to fill with activity. Ask yourself: (1) are the activities worthwhile? And (2) do they produce the results you want? Planning will help you focus your energy in the direction of things that are important to you, even figuring out, for what may be the first time in your life, what is <u>really</u> important to you. This is the time in your life when planning can make the difference between whether you achieve your goals or not.

*In all things, success depends upon previous preparation,
and without such preparation, there is to be such failure.*

Confucious

I empathize with the struggles you may have in making decisions. I know all too well the results of people's making poor choices. Many of the stories are from my own family situations that resulted from poor decision-making. If it feels to you like I am delivering a bitter pill, or that I am stuck in "repeat mode," I apologize in advance. It is not because I get pleasure out of telling you what to do; it is because I believe that the things I recommend are important and bear being repeated for emphasis.

While this is not a textbook or a "do-it-yourself" manual, this book can be thought of as a self-directed course guide … *written in easy-to-understand language* … to help you navigate the often unfamiliar territories of the five end-of-life planning categories listed below. You could even think of it as a prep course similar to an SAT prep course, designed to prepare you to meet with professionals as each of you will do at some time in the future, so that you will know the right questions to ask. I'm referring, of course, to lawyers, financial planners, medical professionals, and funeral directors.

The lists I have prepared are to make you take a close look at things you may never have thought about before, so that you can do something about them before it's too late. As you read this book, you may find yourself thinking, "*Wow, I didn't know that,*" or "*I better take care of that right away.*"

HOW TO USE THIS BOOK

I recommend you read through the book once, not with the intention of retaining what you read as if for a test, but just to get a sense of the information it contains. You can skip around and read what interests you at a given moment. Don't let the large amount of information frighten you into putting the book aside. Once you have a sense of the total of what is here, you will be able to direct your attention to the topics that matter the most to you right now, and establish priorities for where to begin your own end-of-life planning process. While I do suggest you take notes for yourself, there will be no test at the end. Granted, there is a lot of information between the two covers, but it is all connected in one way or another.

I personally believe Living Wills and Healthcare Powers-of-Attorney are of a very high priority, and recommend that you educate yourself about these two documents <u>first</u>; but if you find something of more interest to you, go with it.

Sooner or later, you will find yourself having to meet with the professionals in some or all of these fields, and armed with the information you will get from reading this book, you will be prepared to fully engage them in conversations about your future. What conversations?

- When a lawyer asks you what you want in your Will.
- When a financial planner asks you what you want your money to do for you.
- When a funeral director asks you what you want for the funeral of a loved one.
- When your doctor asks you what kind of end-of-life treatment you want for yourself.

These are not questions with immediate one-word answers, or fill-in-the-blank answers, or multiple choices. These questions require thought and conversations, and if you are prepared by knowing the right questions to ask, you can expect to achieve the results you seek. In this book, you will find the questions, and then find some answers so that you will be able to make *informed* choices when the time comes. There is much to think about in each of the situations, and not much time in which to come up with your answers if you haven't given them any prior thought.

End-of-life planning, as I have defined it, falls into five categories: (1) Legal; (2) Financial; (3) Funeral and Burial; (4) Record-Keeping, and (5) Personal. Each of these categories requires attention, and all of them overlap each other in one way or another.

It has been suggested to me that instead of writing a single book that includes all five topics, I write five separate books. I chose not to do that. The reasons that were given to me were that some people might become frightened by the size of this book, or that others might become bored reading.

- If I wrote, and you read, only the book that contained the legal manuscript, you would not then have had the opportunity to see how matters of a legal nature connect to financial and personal matters. If you were to buy only the book about funerals, you would miss the connection between that transaction and others in your life of a legal, financial and personal nature.

I chose to give you as much information as possible ... *all in one place* ... to enable you to make the best possible decisions for yourself and your family *between now and then*. If you find yourself getting weary as you turn the pages, take a break. To take a break or not to take a break ... it is one of the many choices available to you as you read this book.

I believe it is important for you to know how the decisions you make relative to each of the five chapters in this book connect to the others in various ways, and the best way to introduce you to that idea is to give you all the information at one time. The following examples illustrate some of the connections between the five topics.

a. If you decide not to sign a Living Will and a Healthcare Power-of-Attorney, that is a **legal** decision that could have serious <u>personal</u> consequences for you and your loved ones, and possibly major <u>financial</u> consequences as well.

b. If you decide to spend most of your money before you retire, that **financial** decision could have both <u>personal</u> and <u>legal</u> consequences if it causes you to run out of money before you run out of time.

c. If you make the **personal** decision to re-marry without consideration of your family and financial situation, the consequences will not only be very personal, but <u>financially</u> and <u>legally</u> costly.

d. If you decide that it is too hard to think about making your own **funeral** plans, so you just skip it, your family will be affected <u>personally</u> and <u>financially</u>.

e. And last, but certainly not least, if you choose to keep your personal **records** and important papers in a messy, unprotected way, you will be leaving your family with the problem of sorting it out after your death, and that could have both <u>legal</u> and <u>financial</u> consequences.

In reading this book, you will learn ways in which to accomplish your goals in each of the five categories. You may be thinking that some of these categories don't apply to you. But, don't be too quick to judge. You will see, by many examples, where situations and questions come up in your life where you could use some direction, where it would be beneficial to you to be able to understand the details of each category necessary to make wise choices, where it would be useful to have an understanding of the language spoken by the professionals in each category. You will find answers to many questions, and guidance in the process of planning for the rest of your life *between now and then.*

Individually and collectively, decisions require:

- thought (ideas)
- commitment to completion
- time
- money
- communication (conversations)
- action

THOUGHTS (IDEAS): Every action, be it large or small, begins with a thought. How many thoughts and ideas have you had that you instantly believed were stupid, a waste of time? How many ideas have you relegated to the part of your brain where you store unworthy ideas? What if those thoughts and ideas turned out to be significant in your own life? I'm not talking about inventing the light bulb or sending a man to the moon ... I'm referring to the ideas that pertain to you and the lives of those close to you. In the big scheme of things, your thoughts and ideas matter ... *they really do.*

Thoughts and ideas come before conversations and actions. If you think you can do something, and if you hold fast to that thought for a long time, and then have conversations for possibility and take actions, there is no telling what kind of success you may achieve.

Possibility – now there's an interesting word. Are you a person who quickly, almost automatically, dismisses an idea as having no chance for success? What if you could change your thinking to one of possibility that your plan will succeed ... the belief that your ideas are worthy, if only to you? What difference would that make in your life and the lives of others? Who knows? Anything is possible.

Progress is impossible without change, and
those who cannot change their minds cannot change anything.

George Bernard Shaw

PERSONAL CONVERSATIONS: IN WRITING THIS BOOK, IT HAS BECOME CLEAR TO ME THAT THE SINGLE MOST IMPORTANT THING THAT CAN MAKE THE DIFFERENCE BETWEEN WHETHER YOU ACHIEVE YOUR LIFE'S GOALS OR NOT, WHETHER YOUR DREAMS COME TRUE OR NOT, AND WHETHER YOU LIVE OUT YOUR LIFE WITHOUT REGRETS OR NOT, IS COMMUNICATION! HONEST, SENSITIVE, TIMELY CONVERSATIONS. THAT'S IT.

Oh, already, I hear some of you saying, *"Sounds too easy. It can't be that simple."* Trust me about this. Go with me on this journey ***between now and then,*** and learn about the benefits of good communication between you and your loved ones and friends, your lawyers and financial planners, your funeral director, even your doctor.

People have difficulty successfully conversing with others in ways that make their intentions understood. Talking to another person seems easy enough, except when it isn't. And, apparently there are things that go against successful conversation that require thought and understanding; for instance, the fact that men and women speak differently to each other. Neither is right or wrong. They are simply different. And the differences can significantly interfere with communication and understanding.

In order to try to minimize the problem communicating with a loved one, I recommend you read the following books. I have read them and have used many of their suggested conversational tips. They work!

- *Men are from Mars; Women are from Venus; A Practical Guide for Improving Communication and Getting What You Want in your Relationships,* by John Gray.

- *You Just Don't Understand; Men and Women in Conversation*, by Deborah Tannen.

- *That's Not What I Meant; How Conversational Style Makes or Breaks Relationships*, by Deborah Tannen.

- *Life-Changing Conversations; 7 Strategies for Talking About What Matters Most,* by Sarah Rozenthuler.

Sometimes, the conversations require preparation. Conversations do not happen by themselves, or in your mind, or by accident. Someone must begin the conversation. If that person is you, don't wait too long. Often, the "hard conversations" never happen. If you want to have the high-stakes conversations ... *you know the ones I'm referring to* ... you may have to be the person to bring up the subject. It will depend upon how important it is to you. It may be risky, and only you can determine if the risk of speaking your own truth is worth the price you may pay for keeping silent.

> ***Any feelings of anxiety you may have talking about these things now,
> are tiny compared to the feelings of regret you'll have if you don't.***
>
> Dr. Phillip C. McGraw (Dr. Phil)

Sometimes, the "conversation" must be done in writing, and if that is the only way you can see to communicate your most important thoughts to someone else, then do it. But be careful of putting things on paper. First, written communication does not allow for two-way discussion of what is probably a highly sensitive, very important matter to you. And, you can be bound by your written words, sometimes in ways you may regret. *Just something to think about ...*

As you are reading this section, begin making a list of important things you would like to talk about with people in your life. Don't put pressure on yourself to come up with questions at one sitting. Just write them down as they come to you. *"What things?"* you may ask. Oh, I don't know. For starters --

- You may want to ask your parents if they have a Will and a Living Will, and where they keep their documents and important papers.

- You may want to ask them what arrangements they want for their funeral.

- Ask them what they want and do not want in extreme medical situations.

- Tell your family what <u>you</u> want and do not want in those same medical situations.

- If you are adopted, you may want to ask about your biological parents.

- You may want to ask your parents or grandparents to tell you about their childhood.

- You may want to express your gratitude to your parents for all they have given you ... before it's too late.

- You may want to tell your parents that you are gay.

- You may want to tell your spouse that you want a divorce.

- You may want to be able to speak with a lawyer with confidence and knowledge of the process of estate planning.

- You may want to tell your children you cannot afford to send them to college.

- What conversations to you want to have before you run out of time? What are you waiting for?

> ### *Only those who will risk going too far can possibly find out how far one can go.*
> T. S. Eliot

Are you beginning to get the idea? The list of "hard" conversations is endless. Those mentioned above are just to get your mind working. As you begin having the conversations, do it with genuine sensitivity to the other person(s), without the need to be right, without an attitude of punishment or revenge. Stay focused on what you are trying to achieve in the conversation. Keep in mind that the other person may be frightened to speak with you about the subject. Don't push them at first. Just slowly, carefully impress upon them your genuine need to know, and why you are asking. These are people you care about and love, so don't hurt them as you have the "hard" conversations.

Does any of this really matter? I don't know.
It only matters if it matters to you. So, what do you think?

> ### *The greatest problem with communication is the illusion that it has been accomplished.*
> George Bernard Shaw

I did not say that having these conversations was going to be easy, just that it is essential that you have them. You will learn ways to ask the right questions of the right people at the right time, to speak your own truth, to ask for what you want and need. Right now, you most likely can't think of the things you want to say or the questions you want to ask, but they will come to you as a benefit of reading this book.

Since the time when my parents passed away years ago, I have thought of so many questions I wish I had asked them, conversations that we should have had but did not, and now it is too late. For every single human being, there will come a time when it is too late for the important conversations. What you learn from this book may inspire you to take action to make those "hard" conversations happen sooner rather than later. These are important, sensitive subjects, and require commitment, empathy, and good use of words to convey your intentions. Failure to have complete communication is the source of many problems. The book contains examples of flawed communication that caused serious upset (not the least of which is the loss of money), as well as some hints on how to make the conversations happen.

> ### *The bitterest tears shed over graves are for words left unsaid and deeds left undone."*
> Harriet Beecher Stowe

"Words left unsaid and deeds left undone." Those are powerful words. That quotation has always been a favorite of mine because it speaks to the urgency of your saying and doing things before it's too late. It points to words and actions that are important to you so you can leave this life without regrets. So many people live their lives without ever saying things they want to say because they are afraid to say them? In your own defense, you may say, *"It's easier that way."* Who said anything about easy? What I want for you is to have no (few) words left unsaid and no (few) deeds left undone on your last day, so you can leave behind no regrets. Isn't that what you want for yourself? For your loved ones?

CONVERSATIONS WITH PROFESSIONALS: Now I want to move those conversations in a different direction. Now it is time to consider other conversations you will want to have in order to forward your intention to live your own authentic life to the greatest degree possible. I'm talking about having the "hard" conversations with professionals whose language you do not speak: Lawyers, financial planners, funeral directors and medical professionals, for example, so that the things you want to happen, do, in fact, happen.

Have you ever found yourself meeting with a lawyer who is quietly, politely speaking to you in a foreign language ... *legalese*? It happens every day in every lawyer's office. Having worked with lawyers for 40 years, I'm not sure they know they are doing it ... it is just how they speak. In a situation like this, are you comfortable asking questions, asking for explanations of words you don't understand? Or are you afraid you will look "stupid?" I don't like the use of that word in situations like this; I prefer "uninformed." You are not educated about their field of specialization. Don't feel you should be expected to speak their language. It is <u>their</u> job to educate you. Sometimes they do. Sometimes they do not.

As you read this book, you will benefit from my years of working with legal and financial professionals. You will find translations for some legalese. You will learn ways in which to ask the important questions so that the legal and financial professionals you are paying can assist you in accomplishing your goals, exactly as you want them to happen.

If it is true what AARP says (that 98% of all estate plans fail), the failures often begin with incomplete conversations between clients and lawyers, and between clients and financial planners, and with clients who are unprepared for those meetings and are hesitant to ask questions. You will read about estate plans that failed, and how it happened. My hope for you is that after you have read this book, you will feel confident to meet with those professionals when the time comes.

What about conversations between you and a funeral director? That is one place where it is necessary to *get it right the first time* ... where you want to be able to say what you mean in clear, understandable words. Funeral Directors may sometimes perform magic, but they are not mind readers. They can only do their job based upon what you say. You will find many questions and answers about funeral planning that may make it less stressful when you are in a situation of having to plan a funeral for a loved one.

What about conversations with your doctors about the kinds of care you want and do not want if you are ever in an extreme medical situation? Have you expressed your intentions with your doctors and your families? And, if not, why not?

Some of the most important conversations about end-of-life planning relate to your Living Probate documents: *i.e.,* your Living Will and Healthcare Power-of-Attorney. These documents will take effect during your lifetime, as opposed to a Will which does not go into effect until after your death. By the wording of those two documents, you will state, as clearly as possible, what you want and do not want for your healthcare, and exactly who you want to be in charge in the event you cannot speak for yourself. In order to do this well and wisely, there are certain conversations and choices you will face. In this book, you will learn ways to best achieve success in this important area of your life.

Talk about important conversations! These conversations take place between you, your lawyer, your doctor, and your family. You must be willing to not only take the action to have the documents prepared, but to speak with the people in your life who have the need to know about them. You will learn how to navigate the sometimes muddy, often rough waters of these kinds of conversations so you will have peace of mind knowing that you will have been heard and understood.

Have you successfully communicated your wishes for your Living Will to your spouse, parent(s), sibling(s)? When you try to have the conversation with them, do they say, "*Not now. You're such a worrier. Nothing's going to happen. We can talk about it later.*" Oh, yeah! It's not their life you're talking about. Their words are spoken out of their own fears, and are ignoring your need to speak with them about some of the most important things you could ever talk about. How long are you willing to wait to make those "hard" conversations happen? *Until it's too late?* If you say you can wait until some other time, people sometimes mistakenly believe the conversations are not really important to you and can be put off until later. I say they cannot.

In an episode of the TV show, "*The Closer*," the main character's mother asked her daughter, Brenda Leigh Johnson, the Police Chief, for a few minutes of her time to talk to her about something important, but Brenda did what she always did ... she put off her mother, saying, "*Oh, not now, Mama. I'm really busy. We can talk about it when I get home.*" And guess what happened? That night, the mother died without the two women ever having that important conversation.

How would you feel if that were your mother? *Just asking ...*

Any problem, big or small, within a family, always seems to start with bad communication. Someone isn't listening.

Emma Thompson

Of all the things you will be doing *between now and then,* don't you think that telling your family what you want and do not want in your future health care is on the top of the list of "hard" conversations? If it is important enough, you will find a way to have the conversations. And if not, consider the potential consequences. These are life-altering conversations, possibly the most important you will ever have.

I recommend you read *Last Wish* by Lauren J. Van Scoy, MD. In her book, Dr. Van Scoy beautifully illustrates, by the use of real stories about real patients, what can happen in extreme medical situations. It is a "must read" for everyone interested in making their own choices about end-of-life care.

If you continue to put off having the "hard" conversations until later, has it occurred to you that you could run out of time? Then what? Of course, you can always choose to avoid the conversations altogether and allow Fate to make the decisions for you. Somehow, I think you might not like the way things turn out if that is your choice. Still, you are free to make it.

COMMITMENT TO ACTION: All action begins with a thought, an idea. Whether or not you bring that idea into existence is entirely up to you. Many people have lots and lots of excellent ideas that they never voiced for many reasons, fear being the most obvious. If you have an idea or a thought that can enhance your life, make you happier, healthier, wealthier, more peaceful, what are you waiting for? *Someone's permission to speak?* The years are long gone when you had to raise your hand to ask the teacher for permission to speak. You are an adult. Speak your own truth before you run out of time.

None of the conversations described above happen by spontaneous combustion. You must commit to taking the action of speaking the words that you believe are necessary. If there are conversations you must have, then have them. If there are documents you must sign, sign them. If there are things you want to do, you must do them. No one else can do these things for you.

There are things you know you should be doing and saying, but how, when, and where do you begin? This book can help you learn to establish priorities and take action to complete your own personal "Bucket List." It may seem difficult at times, but it is probably not impossible.

TIME and MONEY: As you begin to contemplate what you will do *between now and then*, there are two important questions to ask yourself:

    (1) Will you live long enough to accomplish your goals?
    (2) Will you have enough money?

> *Many people take no care of their money till they come nearly to the end of it,*
> *and others do the same with their time.*
>
> Johann Wolfgang von Goethe

If you are a Baby Boomer, it is possible you have already lived 2/3 of your lifetime. I encourage readers to regularly ask themselves what they plan to do with the remaining 20-30 years, especially in relation to money. Baby Boomers have historically spent too much and saved too little, and may be facing their "golden years" in dire financial situations.

It is not easy to comprehend a block of time as huge as 20-30 years all at once, but it could turn out to be the amount of time you have remaining in your life between your 65th birthday and your last day on earth. What about planning for your personal life, what you will do every day? Once you retire, you may find that you are really enjoying doing nothing for a little while; but, sooner or later, you will get bored. That would be a good time to answer the question, "What do you plan to do with the rest of your life *between now and then*?"

Do you want to enjoy those years to the fullest, or just cross the days off on a calendar, one day at a time, for many years, until that last day? You are now the boss of your own life. Every day is like a Saturday. You get to choose what to do and what not to do, to make your life happy and fulfilled. Isn't that what you have been waiting for?

> First man says to another: *"Do you have a retirement plan?"*
> The other man, lying on the couch, replies, *"You're looking at it."*
> Ouch!

Consider the possibility that a long "Bucket List" can give each day purpose and excitement. I am not recommending rigidly structured days. I am recommending thinking and planning about how you will use your time. And, don't forget to think and plan about making your money last for the rest of your life. Again, in order to do the things you want to do, you need <u>both</u> time and money … *and a plan.* Well, now you have the time, we're working on the plan, and hopefully, you will have the money.

What if it turns out that you don't have the time? I stress the importance of attaching a sense of urgency to your planning such that you will accomplish the things that are really important to you before you run out of days. It is entirely up to you what you plan to do *between now and then*.

Having said that, there is nothing that says you must do any of the things suggested in this book. But, my hope is that you will see the benefits from being proactive with the use of your time, learning ways in which to make wise decisions for yourself, and living your own authentic life until your last day.

> *It is only when we truly know and understand that we have a limited time on earth –*
> *and that we have no way of knowing when our time is up –*
> *that we will begin to live each day to the fullest, as if it (were) the only one we had.*
>
> Elizabeth Kubler-Ross

It is important to recognize one significant fact that relates to the time left *between now and then* … and that is, that there will come a day in the future that will be your last day on earth. This is a universal truth, and yet, so many people choose to ignore it, and just let their days run out, one day at a time, wasting that precious commodity called time, until that final day … when they may be faced with regrets for *words left unspoken, and deeds left undone.*

There is nothing inherently wrong with ignoring the fact that your life on earth will someday come to an end. The day will come, whether or not you are ready, whether or not you have chosen to live your life to the fullest, whether or not you wish for more time, whether or not you have completed everything you wanted to finish, whether or not you have had the "hard" conversations, whether or not you have taken care of your own personal business during your time *between now and then*.

20 GOOD REASONS WHY YOU SHOULD READ THIS BOOK

As you read this book, you can begin to see that it is possible for you to:

1. See the benefits of planning, one being peace of mind.

2. Save time, aggravation, and money, and reduce potential mistakes by becoming educated and informed.

3. Know that you have an unlimited number of choices available to you.

4. Improve the ways you handle money.

5. Understand the benefit of saying "no without guilt."

6. Protect your assets for yourself and future generations.

7. Reduce worry and fear when making decisions.

8. Understand the benefits of good, complete communication.

9. Know what can happen when you do-it-yourself.

10. Recognize the price to be paid for avoiding decisions until later.

11. Appreciate the importance of details.

12. Gain a basic knowledge of personal, legal, and financial planning.

13. Be empowered by knowing the right questions to ask.

14. Reduce family squabbles about money and "stuff."

15. Live your life <u>your</u> way, with honesty and integrity.

16. Do the things that are important for you before it's too late.

17. Learn how to use your time wisely.

18. Once and for all, know that your days are numbered.

19. Leave your family a legacy of love, harmony, and peace.

20. Leave this life without regrets.

<u>MANY OF YOUR QUESTIONS WILL BE ANSWERED IN THIS BOOK</u>

<u>LEGAL:</u>

Who do you want to inherit from you? Who do you NOT want to inherit from you? Who will ultimately inherit from you if you don't have a Will? Where and how do I find a Lawyer? Do I need a Lawyer specializing in estate planning? What happens if I die without a Will? What is the difference between a Will and a Living Will? Why do I need them? What is probate? Why is it so expensive and why does it take so long? Why do I need a Healthcare Power-of-Attorney? Should I keep my Will and other legal documents in a safe deposit box at the bank? Who besides me should know where they are? What happens if the documents and the box can't be found in an emergency? Couldn't I save money if I download forms from the Internet and do them myself? How can I decide who to name as my Executor? What will happen to all my possessions?

<u>FINANCIAL:</u>

What did I learn from how money was handled in my family of origin? How can I make my retirement funds last for the rest of my life? What if I lose my job, or become ill or disabled and cannot work to pay my bills? How should I prioritize the repayment of all my debts? What would be the consequences for my children if I were to marry for the second time without a PreNuptial Agreement? When should I begin taking Social Security? How would I ever recover financially if I have to go into bankruptcy or foreclosure? What are the consequences for me if I co-sign for a loan for someone else? Do I have enough insurance? Are my beneficiaries exactly as I want them to be? Will I have enough money to afford to keep my dog and cats? Why do I need a 12-month emergency fund? Why did I have to pay all those penalties when I tapped my 401(k)? What can potentially happen if I decide to do things by myself?

<u>FUNERAL AND BURIAL:</u>

Do you know that the number of things that are required to plan a funeral and burial in 3-4 days is almost exactly the same as those required to plan a wedding in 12-18 months? If your funeral and burial arrangements are important to you, have you communicated your wishes to someone who will ultimately be responsible for making those arrangements? In writing? If you have not told your loved ones what you want, how do you expect them to know? Have you put aside money for your funeral and burial? Have you made pre-arrangements? Who knows about them? What kind of service do you want, if any? Do you want in-ground burial or cremation? Where is the deed to your cemetery plot? Do you intend for your organs or body to be donated? Have you made the arrangements for that to happen? What do you want to wear for your viewing? Do you even want a viewing? Would you like to be buried in a cemetery or a memorial park? Do you know the difference? Who else besides you knows these things?

<u>RECORD-KEEPING:</u>

If you were to fall off the face of the earth tomorrow, would it be easy for someone to locate your Will, your assets, and insurance policies? In an emergency, could someone quickly and easily locate your Living Will and Healthcare Power-of-Attorney? Where is the deed to your house, the title to your car? Where are your tax returns, passports, and birth certificates? Where is your safe deposit box and the key? Are your important papers safe from fire and water damage? If they are in a safe in your home, who else has the combination? Are there piles of papers on your kitchen counter or desk top? Where is your list of the people in your life, including family, friends, doctors, insurance agents, lawyers? Why does it matter whether or not I keep my personal papers in order?

<u>PERSONAL:</u>

What will you do with your time after you stop working? Where are all those books you want to read? Do you want to volunteer, and if so, where? Do you have a hobby to keep you busy and relaxed? Are you happy in the work you are presently doing, such that you might continue working there indefinitely? Are you happy in your marital situation, or is a major change long overdue? Are there things you should be doing to improve your health? Are there classes or lessons you have wanted to take for years, but never made them a priority? What about that Caribbean cruise you always wanted to take? What about all your stuff? Have you thought about down-sizing? Relocating? Do you have a family emergency plan? What have you been ignoring for years that you will finally have the time to address? Who will care for your pets if you are ever disabled or when you die? Are you always "*very busy?*" Doing what? Do you live your life with honesty and integrity? Have you ever had to navigate the sometimes muddy waters of major personal changes in life, including unemployment, serious illness or disability, financial crises, divorce and remarriage, and death of a loved one? How will you pay for the things you want to do *between now and then*?

> *Time is more valuable than money.*
> *You can get more money, but you cannot get more time.*
>
> Jim Rohn

WHAT KIND OF LEGACY DO YOU WANT TO LEAVE BEHIND?

Baby Boomers have already left a mark in the world by doing things in a big way. Although Boomers are only in their 60s, it's time for them to think about what kind of legacy they want to leave behind. People generally want to be remembered fondly, with happy, loving memories. How do you want to be remembered? Will it be different from how you _will_ be remembered? *Just asking...*

Legacies of love and happiness are _created_ by the total of little events lived over a lifetime. Legacies of unhappiness and abuse are created the same way: One little memory at a time, that add up to a lifetime of memories, some good, some not so good.

Everyone leaves a legacy behind after they die, whether or not it was their intention to do so. A legacy can be one of happy memories, or dysfunction and conflict. Some people work to create a legacy that represents how the person wants to be remembered, even if their legacy is only money. Others don't even think about the legacy they leave behind. Many don't care one way or the other. No matter, there will be a legacy of one kind or another. There are stories about such family situations in this book.

> *It's not what you take when you leave this world behind you.*
> *It's what you leave behind you when you go.*
>
> Randy Travis

Although "legacy" generally carries with it an implication of money passing from one generation to the next, it can be something other than money. Here is the true story of one woman's intention to leave behind a legacy for her only child.

> *Once upon a time, a financial planner had a weekly radio show into which people could call their questions. A woman called and said that she was poor, barely making ends meet, but she wanted to leave her son (her only child) a legacy of $500 dollars when she died.*
>
> *Her question was, "How could she manage to save $500 considering how little extra money she had?" The financial planner first asked the woman what she thought her son would do with the money when he got it. She said he would just spend it because it wasn't really very much money.*
>
> *The financial planner then suggested instead that this woman write a letter to her son, telling him about her life, her family history, things she loved, things she did, things she wanted to do but never got around to doing, how she survived and managed to raise him by herself, in poverty. The financial planner suggested that this letter be her legacy, and that it would be a priceless gift to her son far exceeding the value of five hundred dollars.*

If the amount of money you leave behind causes your loved ones to fight over it, what then is your legacy? History and the courts are full of true stories of rich people fighting over money when a member of their family dies. It makes for good books and movies.

March 2012: According to the *New York Times*, the estate of Brooke Astor, New York socialite and philanthropist, has finally been settled after a bitter 5-year legal battle among her son and various charities named in her Will. She died in 2007 at the age of 105, leaving behind a legacy of $198 million and much legal fighting and bitterness. In 2009, her son was convicted for trying to use his mother's mental state to bilk her out of her own money. Even so, he ended up with more than $14 million.

This kind of case is what lawyers refer to as an annuity … it just keeps on paying and paying. Reminds me of the Energizer Bunny.

Could her legacy have been different? I don't know. Maybe. Maybe not. What do you think?

If you could attend your own funeral luncheon or reception *(I know it's a stretch, but keep reading)*, would you see people truly sorry for your loss, people quietly crying, sharing loving memories of your life and times with them?

Or would you see people angry and upset with you because you left behind hurt feelings, debt, and messes for your loved ones to clean up now that you have passed on. Which kind of legacy do you want to leave behind?

CAN YOU LEARN FROM THE MISTAKES OF OTHERS?

I certainly hope so. You may see yourself in some of the situations described in this book. I tell those stories in the hope that you can save yourself time, money, stress, and aggravation by avoiding similar mistakes in the first place.

Don't beat yourself up if you have already made some of these mistakes. You will not be alone. Mistakes happen. When you realize you have made some of the same mistakes, that would be your opportunity to begin to fix them, and to do what is necessary to go forward.

WHAT IS IMPORTANT IS WHAT HAPPENS ***AFTER*** YOU RECOGNIZE THE MISTAKE.

> *The greatest mistake you can make is to be continually fearing you will make one.*
>
> Elbert Hubbard

People don't know what they don't know. They cannot be expected to know. It is up to the professionals to educate them, and I see that as an area that is fertile for miscommunication, misunderstanding, and mistakes. My goal is to explain some of the subtleties of estate and financial planning and funeral planning in understandable language.

> *Education is learning what you didn't even know you didn't know.*
>
> Daniel Boorstin

While there are many questions about end-of-life planning, there are no right answers - - only YOUR answers. Your life is about YOU, your choices. Of course, there are other people in your life to consider, and it is essential that you learn to communicate with them about important matters. Still, it is not absolutely necessary. You can skip the conversations, but I don't recommend it. So many mistakes happen because of the tendency of people to avoid having the "hard" conversations about things like money, for example, and Wills, and death and dying.

> *Knowing is not enough; we must apply. Willing is not enough; we must do.*
>
> Goethe

I do not want you to become frightened at the prospect of making plans for the rest of your life. Many of your fears can be eliminated with information that will empower you as you learn to make wise decisions for yourself and your family. How you perceive life and how you live it are up to you … right until your last day. You can choose to experience life as frightening, or you can see it as thrilling. So, since you have a choice about which to call it, I urge you to choose **thrilling**.

> *When you are afraid, keep your mind on what you have to do.*
> *And, if you have been thoroughly prepared, you will not be afraid.*
>
> Dale Carnegie

NOW WHAT?

You can see that there is much to do *between now and then.* Some things can and should be addressed quickly; others can be put off, but not indefinitely, and not until that undetermined time, "later." It is important that you have a basic idea of what you need to do, then establish priorities and expected completion dates. If you are feeling overwhelmed by what you see ahead of you … all the things that need to be done … there is a secret I'll share with you that works for me in every situation.

THE SECRET IS LISTS -
Making, Prioritizing, and Updating Lists.

It doesn't matter what I am planning, I always work from a list. Lists keep me organized, prepared, on time, and eliminate unpleasant surprises . I make lists for everything, whether I'm going to the grocery store or planning a party. The simple truth is that lists keep me focused and make my life easier, and they can do the same for you. The concept works perfectly if you surrender to the idea. You might actually find that you not only enjoy the process and the benefits, but that you are becoming an expert at list-making. *Why not?*

Keep your list book handy at all times so that whenever you get an idea, you can immediately write it down. As you really get into the process of making plans of every sort, you may need to keep a pen and a tablet beside your bed, because ideas will wake you up and keep you awake until you write them down. *Trust me on this one … I know it well.*

I know a man who keeps a tiny tablet and pen in his pocket all the time just in case he sees something … *anything* … or gets an idea that peaks his interest in the moment. What he writes on that tiny tablet today just might be something really important in the future. *Who knows? It can't hurt.*

OK, already, do I hear you whining? *"Who has time for making lists? What kind of lists?"* Being organized is really easy if you don't over-think the process. Be patient, because you will learn how and what to do to write a list and make it work for you.

> *Order and simplification are the first steps toward the mastery of a subject –*
> *the actual enemy is the unknown.*
>
> Thomas Mann

NOTE: Keep in mind that this list-making is an evolving process. It is not a one-time thing. Your lists should grow and change as you learn and change. It can help you to clearly see the options available to you, the potential for success or failure, the results and benefits of each, and ultimately reflect the end-of-life plans and choices you make.

> *Perseverance is not a long race; it is many short races one after another.*
>
> Walter Elliott

READY OR NOT, IT IS TIME TO BEGIN.

If not now, when? What are you feeling right now? Fear? Annoyance? Upset? Well, yes, they would be honest feelings. Once you notice what you are feelings, step back, take a deep breath, relax, and you may see that this is all about YOUR LIFE and what you will do *between now and then.*

What about feeling <u>excited</u> about the journey you are about to begin? Can you at least think about that possibility, and how good you will feel each time you accomplish one of your goals, each time you check it off your "Bucket List?" Relax a little. Enjoy the trip. You will reach your ultimate destination soon enough.

> ### *The greater the obstacle, the more the glory in overcoming it.*
>
> Moliere

NOW ARE YOU READY?

It's important to have some fun along the way. Try not to look at this journey as a burden, something you think that someone is making you do, like when you had to study for a test. This time, you are in charge of your life and you get to say what happens, choose how and when those things happen, and what's important to you. Maybe for the first time in your life, you become "*the Decider.*"

Now you have some knowledge and information you may not have had before. Even so, there are three more things I want you to have so you can get more enjoyment from your trip into your future and to keep some humor and fun in the process:

1. A Choice Ticket
2. A Permission Slip
3. A Round Tuit

---

1. A CHOICE TICKET

It appears to me that many people are under the false assumption that they are born with a limited number of choices in this life, as if on the day of their birth, they are given a ticket that specifies the exact number of choices they have before they die. And, so, they believe they must be careful how they use them so they don't run out of choices too soon. *Sound silly?*

I, on the other hand, believe the number of choices in a person's life to be infinite ... and firmly believe that if you make a (bad) choice that doesn't work out, you can make another and another and another until you get it right, because no one is keeping score or punching your ticket like a train conductor.

What follows are two different tickets. Which ticket will you choose?

<u>YOUR LIFE CHOICE TICKET</u>

This TICKET issued to _____ on this ____ day of _____, _____, the day of his/her birth, whereby she/he is hereby granted 25 choices to be made in his/her lifetime. As each choice is made, the ticket will be punched, and there will be no more choices after the last choice is punched. It is recommended that the choices be made sparingly so they will last for your entire life.

1 2 3 4 5 6 7 8 9 10 11 12 13 14 15 16 17 18 19 20 21 22 23 24 25

OR

MY LIFE CHOICE TICKET

This TICKET issued to _____ on this ____ day of _____, _____, the day of his/her birth, whereby she/he is hereby granted <u>un</u>limited choices to be used in his/her lifetime. Any choice that is considered bad can be immediately replaced with another choice, and another and another, in an effort to get it right. There is no limit to the number of choices granted to the holder of this ticket.

1 2 3 4 5 6 7 8 9 10 11 12 13 14 15 16 17 18 19 20 21 22 23 .... *ad infinitum*

---

2. PERMISSION SLIP

Do you need permission from someone else to begin the important life work you know that you want to do ... that you know that you *must* do? Of course, you do know that a permission slip is not necessary for you to begin, because, it is YOUR life. After all, you are an adult, free to make choices by yourself, for yourself. Why do you think you need permission from someone else? What does their permission (opinion) matter to you? The way I see it:

   (a) every person (including you) has opinions;

   (b) someone else's opinions may not be the truth for you;

   (c) every person is free to express his/her opinions;

   (d) you do not have to believe them.

   (e) you do not have to act upon them.

A man cannot be comfortable without his own approval.

Mark Twain

Just in case it will make it a little easier for you to make your own decisions, here is your own personal Permission Slip. You can photocopy it and carry some copies around with you for the times when you feel you need permission from someone other than yourself. And, finally, if you need to get permission from yourself, simply sign the Permission Slip yourself. No big deal.

PERMISSION SLIP

   I. _____, hereby give to _____, permission to do the following: _____. The task shall begin on _____ and be completed by _____. This permission slip expires on _____ and is not renewable.

_____

(date)_____   (signature) *

(*) parent, sibling, friend, teacher, priest, doctor, etc.

---

3. A ROUND TUIT

Many people think the subject of end-of-life planning can be put off until later. *When is later?* Do you often find yourself saying that you will do this or that *as soon as you get **around to it**?*

So that you never have to use that excuse again, I am going to show you how to make **A ROUND TUIT**. You can copy it and carry it with you for the times when you find yourself inclined to say "*I'll do it when I get around to it.*" From now on, you will be ready to make decisions because you have your own personal ROUND TUIT for the times you find yourself needing it.

Here are the instructions for making A Round Tuit

Using a black marker, draw a 4-1/2" circle around the words. Photocopy. Cut out the Round Tuit, make some copies, and carry several with you to use as necessary. No more excuses!

A

ROUND

TUIT

- Your first choice was to buy this book, and I hope you will find this to be just the first of many choices that provide you with positive benefits for the rest of your life.

- For your next choice, choose to take this journey with me. It is time to begin planning your life *between now and then*. What do you have to lose except more time?

ONCE AGAIN, I ASK YOU:

"What do you plan to do with your time *between now and then*?"

It's not what we intend but what we do that makes us useful.

Henry Ward Beecher

End-of-life planning is a marathon not a sprint. If you commit to run the race to the finish line, you will have to do certain things in order to be prepared for what the race requires of you. Sure, there will be days when you don't feel like it, and wonder why it seems so hard. When those moments happen, try not to think only of yourself. Other people in your life will benefit from your finishing this race I call end-of-life planning. If you need help in this marathon, get it. Marathon runners have trainers. There is no shame in asking for help.

When you feel like quitting, think of the joy and pride you will get from finishing. There is no satisfaction from quitting in the middle of a race, no matter what kind of race it is. You could look at end-of-life planning as the race of your life as you decide what you will do with your life and your time *between now and then.*

Set your course and commit to stay that course to the finish. If you believe you cannot finish or will not finish, you might be right. On the other hand, if you say you will finish … *if you see the value in succeeding* … then you will finish. If you have lived your life up to this time with the habit of quitting when the going gets tough … you know those times, when the stress and aggravation exceed the satisfaction and reward, when you know you are close to achieving your goal, but you are tired … this could be your once-in-a-lifetime opportunity to prove to yourself that you have what it takes to keep your word. Think how good that will feel.

End-of-life planning is not required, but it is important. Only you can decide how important it is to you and your family. If you find yourself feeling upset at something you have to do, and if you are thinking about quitting, remember that "this, too, shall pass." When the fatigue overtakes you, take a break, and do something you love for a short time, something that will renew your spirit and your commitment. And soon, pick up where you left off with renewed energy and focus.

Appreciate every moment of this race, because that is all there is. NOW! You will reach your destination soon enough, whether or not you choose to do any end-of-life planning.

Success is not final, failure is not fatal. It is the courage to continue that counts.
Never, never, never give up.

Quotes by Winston Churchill

- You have much to do and an unknown amount of time in which to do it.
- Don't rush the process, but at the same time, keep your eye on the calendar.
- Make time for the "hard" conversations.
- Make lists. Enjoy the pleasure of crossing things off your list when you finish them.
- Assign a priority to everything you <u>have</u> to do.
- Assign a priority to everything you <u>want</u> to do.
- Have fun along the way.
- Enjoy the journey. You'll get to the final destination soon enough.
- Don't forget about the people who are important to you.
- Be good to yourself.
- Laugh at yourself at least once a day.
- You have things to do before you sleep. Only you know which things are important.
    If it matters to you whether or not you finish them, then you must begin today.

NOW YOU HAVE EVERYTHING YOU NEED

- **YOUR TICKET FOR UNLIMITED CHOICES**

- **YOUR PERMISSION SLIP**

- **YOUR OWN PERSONAL ROUND TUIT**

- **A BOOK WITH END-OF-LIFE PLANNING STRATEGIES**

- **A GUIDE FOR YOUR JOURNEY (that would be me)**

If you choose to accept my invitation,
allow me the privilege of being your guide on this most important journey
between now and then.

Tempus Fugit

THINGS TO DO   *   IDEAS   *   FOLLOW-UP

#	Priority A,B,C	Description	Start Date	Completion Date
1				
2				
3				
4				
5				
6				
7				
8				
9				
10				
11				
12				
13				
14				
15				
16				
17				
18				
19				
20				

Chapter I

LEGAL

*If a man dies and leaves his estate
in an uncertain condition,
the Lawyers become his heirs.*

Edgar Watson Howe

Chapter I – LEGAL

If you are reading this book, you are interested in making estate-planning decisions. Estate planning is generally done by lawyers and is considered a legal transaction; but not all of it. There is much to consider that is not necessarily legal in nature, and as I have said before, many things in this book intertwine and overlap in various ways, and they connect by way of conversations. Estate planning involves many financial and personal considerations before the documents are prepared and executed. If your estate plan is ever to exist, questions must be asked and answered, conversations must be had, actions must be taken. An estate plan does not happen by itself.

In this chapter, you will learn many of the questions to ask of your lawyer when you finally meet to discuss formalizing your estate plan. In her newspaper column of January 20, 2013, ("Estate Planning, once and for all."), Jill Schlesinger said: *"To keep your costs down, make sure you know how you want your assets distributed before you set foot inside the lawyer's office."* Good advice.

When asked if they have a Will, many people say yes. Those same people often think that's the end of it, that they have made all of the end-of-life legal preparation necessary. And, while it is generally better to have a Will than not to have a Will, it doesn't stop there. There are other legal documents required in order to have a complete estate plan.

- It's interesting to note that when asked if they have a <u>financial</u> plan, most people say no.
  When you consider that a Will is a plan for distributing your assets after your death, and the financial plan relates to your life today, why do so many people do it backwards? *Just asking …*

In my opinion, estate planning is good; no estate planning is not so good. One way to determine if your plan is a good one is to ask yourself the following question:

Will your plan produce the results you intend?

The way to get the results you seek is to prepare yourself with information and knowledge to enable you to make wise decisions. I want to show you ways to achieve the results you are seeking.

> ### *In all things, success depends upon previous preparation, and, without such preparation, there is to be such failure.*
> Confucius

Estate planning, if it is to succeed as you desire, requires that you think about what you want, gather information, ask questions, have conversations, and ultimately take appropriate actions to bring about a successful plan. What happens as a result of your reading this book is up to you. At times, the going may seem difficult, but know that estate planning is not impossible when you are prepared.

If you think it is difficult to do your estate planning now, think of how difficult it will be for the person(s) who have to administer your estate after your death *without your assistance* – without the knowledge and help of the very person who owned the assets and knew more about them than anyone else. YOU!

Whether or not you make estate plans is entirely up to you. Life will go on, day by day, one after the other, until that final day. When that day arrives, will you be happy if your choice was to do nothing? Will your family be happy that you chose to do nothing? Will you have regrets? Only you know the answers to these questions.

Just be clear that choosing to do nothing is, in fact, a choice that has its own set of consequences, some of which you will not like.

What do you really want to do with the rest of your life
***between now and then*?**

In this chapter, you will read about real people and real situations. I tell these stories as examples of what can happen when people do things without benefit of legal counsel or when people choose to skip the hard conversations. I hope that the examples may cause you to think twice before you leap into a legal situation that could backfire and cause you harm of one kind or another.

Estate planning is serious business, and I believe it deserves to be treated seriously. Let's begin at the beginning.

WHAT IS AN ESTATE?

An estate is everything a person owns in his/her name or with another person including, but not limited to, your residence, cash, stocks, bonds, other investments, businesses you may own, retirement plans, life insurance and death benefits, personal property such as household furnishings, jewelry, vehicles, collectibles, and other treasured items.

WHAT IS ESTATE PLANNING?

Simply stated, it is the process of taking specific steps to manage your assets in the event of your incapacitation or death, and to see that your assets go to the people you want to have them, when you want them to have them, and by what process after you die. If it is important to you, make your estate plans now, while you are still healthy and aware of what you are doing. In addition, it is prudent to reevaluate your estate plan over time as your life and family situation changes. Sounds simple enough, doesn't it? Yet, there is much evidence that many estate plans fail.

There are two primary areas of estate planning:

1. <u>While you are alive</u> Proper estate planning to protect yourself while you are alive can include (but not necessarily be limited to):

      a. Durable (General) Power-of-Attorney
      b. Specific Power-of-Attorney (for specific purpose only)
      c. Power-of-Attorney for Healthcare
      d. Living Will
      e. Pre-Nuptial Agreement (optional)
      f. Co-Habitation Agreement (optional)

2. <u>After you die</u> If you do proper estate planning to transfer ownership of your possessions to the people you want to have them after you die, it can include (but not necessarily be limited to):

      a. Last Will and Testament
      b. Revocable Living Trust (optional)
      c. Irrevocable Trust (optional)

WHAT IS ESTATE ADMINISTRATION?

What is the difference between estate planning and estate administration. The most obvious difference is in the timing:

- Estate Planning is done while you are alive
- Estate Administration takes place after your death

When you are alive, you can do anything you want with your possessions. But, after your death, ownership of your assets must be legally and appropriately transferred to others. How your heirs get your "stuff" is up to you, and can be determined by the steps you take (or do not take) today. This is where estate planning comes in.

In the process of administering your estate, someone else will be responsible to see that your assets are gathered, your bills and taxes are paid, and the rest is then passed out to your heirs according to the directions you stated in your Will or Trust, or according to the laws of the state in which you reside if you did not leave a Will.

Your "stuff" will be taken care of by your Executor or Administrator. How your "stuff" gets to the people you want to have it after your death can happen in several ways:

- You could already have given your "stuff" to people while you are alive; or,

- You can have your assets in financial vehicles that have designated beneficiaries, and at your death, the assets will then pass directly to those beneficiaries. Such financial vehicles (e.g., life insurance, IRAs,) do not pass your assets to your beneficiaries through your Will, but directly to them; or,

- You can write a Will and give your "stuff" to people through probate, with an Executor named by you; or,

- You can write no Will and make no estate plans, and the state will give your "stuff" away according to a list of people prescribed by state law, still through the probate process. This situation is referred to as being intestate. Your assets will pass for you through an Administrator appointed by the court to function in much the same way as an Executor; but the appointed person may not be a person you would have chosen had you made the choice yourself.

- You can write a Revocable Living Trust and give your stuff to people through your Successor Trustee, who you name. Your assets will not go through probate.

Sounds simple. Maybe. Maybe not.

It may depend on whether or not you have taken care of your personal legal business in a timely, appropriate and legal manner.

One major difference in having an estate plan or not having an estate plan lies in WHO makes the decisions: You, or the state in which you live? Does it matter to you? Most people do not want the state deciding who gets their "stuff;" but, again, it's entirely up to you to see that it doesn't happen that way if it matters to you. After all, it's just "stuff," or is it?

WHY DO I NEED ESTATE PLANNING?

YOU DO NOT NEED ESTATE PLANNING.

Estate planning is optional. It is absolutely legal and perfectly all right for you to live and die without making any plans. The "estate police" will not seek you out and put you in jail for not taking care of your personal business while you have the time ... that is, before it is too late.

Having said that, I warn you, however, that if you do not have an estate plan, the state in which you reside has a plan for you, and I'm pretty sure neither you nor your heirs will like it.

Let's say that it is possible that reading this book will make you think you **do** need some estate planning. That would be good. While estate planning is not necessary, it is certainly a good thing to do if you are interested in protecting your assets for the remainder of your life and for your loved ones after you pass away. It might also be a good thing for you to have certain documents to protect your own health and well-being while you are still alive.

SO, DO YOU HAVE AN ESTATE PLAN OR NOT?

Over the years, I had several conversations with a colleague about why people do not do what is necessary to get estate and financial plans in place for themselves before it is too late. It was <u>my</u> position that people simply <u>*do not*</u> understand the choices and consequences that are available to them. It was <u>his</u> position that they <u>*do*</u> understand, but are unwilling to take the steps necessary to make the plans happen. So, which is it?

- People don't understand? <u>or,</u>
- People do understand but choose to take no action?

WE AGREED THAT IT IS A COMBINATION OF BOTH.

> *It is not knowledge of ways and means we lack;*
> *it is the will to put them into effect.*
>
> Alfred Vanderbilt

It is well known that people like "how to" books about everything from how to lose weight, how to decorate your home, how to invest money. Even this book offers "how to" tips. While we say we want "how to" suggestions, what we really want is to fast-forward from A to Z, skipping over actual problems without having to do anything that might cause us to experience any form of discomfort, upset, or aggravation.

We the people don't like to be uncomfortable – we want quick fixes to our problems. We want help, and we want it now! Yet, in solving our problems, we don't want to have to think about them, we certainly don't want to talk about them, and we especially don't want advice. We are struck dumb when it comes to speaking our own personal truths, as if we are not worthy to express our deepest needs and wants.

CONVERSATIONS and COMMUNICATION

The easy way to live life is to skip over the hard stuff, bury your head in the sand, and ignore whatever is causing upset or discomfort … especially avoiding the hard conversations. But life doesn't always work that way, until the time when there are subjects that can no longer be ignored, that force us to address them, like it or not. While collectively, we say we want to change, to "fix" problems, to learn and grow, is that the truth? *Really?*

The truth is that we cannot move forward without doing the work. Of course, we can ignore end-of-life planning until our very last day. But, realistically, wouldn't it be better to learn to talk about the things that get in the way of our living the life we want? And, if we are honest about it, if we want to accomplish our goals, we are going to have to talk about things we don't want to talk about, do things we may not want to do. A thought is just a thought, and without action, a thought has no life. So, thinking about end-of-life planning, by itself, is not enough, not now, not ever. The thinking must be followed by actions, like it or not.

Complicating this is the fact that we already know many of the "how to" solutions. We just choose to ignore what we know in favor of putting things off until that undetermined time known as "later." We are masters at the art of procrastination, living our lives as if we expect to live forever. We use Scarlett O'Hara's solution: *I'll think about it tomorrow* … thinking that tomorrow may not come. Even that excuse will one day lose its effectiveness. What if you wait too long?

Most of you reading this book already know something about end-of-life planning. You may not think you do, but trust me, you do. If nothing else, you know what to avoid doing … signing a Will, for example. You already know which choices will produce desired results and which choices will not. Yet … you continue to seek more information, while avoiding the actions required to accomplish your goals. You say you're not ready yet, all the while knowing that you simply don't want to do what is necessary … all the while knowing that no one can force you to do something you do not want to do.

6

So, which is it?

- People don't understand? <u>or</u>,
- People do understand but choose to take no action?

Are you one of the people who know what to do, but don't do it? *Just asking …*

WHAT DOES A CAR HAVE TO DO WITH ESTATE PLANNING?

Just for comparison sake, let's consider the similarities and differences between a car and estate planning. (*I know, I know … it's a stretch, but stick with me a while longer.*)

It is important to know and trust that your car will take you from one place to another when you want to go. You don't need to know how to build it or repair it. Of course, it helps if you have faith in the company that manufactured the car.

In this respect, estate-planning documents are not all that different. You need to know and trust that they will do what you need, when you need it. You don't have to know the exact language to create the document or the details that make it legal. Of course, it helps if you have faith in the Lawyer who drew up the documents.

<u>For your CAR, you want to know:</u>

That it is built by a reputable company.

That it has a solid reputation of being well-built.

That it will provide you with safety.

That it will meet your personal needs.

That it will safely get you from one place to another.

That you have a basic understanding of the way it is manufactured.

That you know and understand the features of this particular car.

That you are able to adequately describe your car to others.

That you know how to start the car.

That you know how to drive the car.

That you know how to maintain the car.

That you do not repair the car yourself.

That you have competent maintenance personnel.

That you maintain an on-going relationship with them.

That you find new maintenance personnel if you are not satisfied.

That you know how to get a different car if it no longer suits you.

That someone other than you knows where the keys are.

KEEP READING ……

For your ESTATE-PLANNING DOCUMENTS, you want to know:

That they are prepared by a reputable, knowledgeable attorney.

That the documents are legally and technically correct.

That they will meet your individual needs.

That they will provide you with safety in the time of need.

That you have a basic understanding of the contents.

That you know and understand how the contents apply to you.

That you can describe your documents knowledgably.

That you know when and how to use the document(s).

That you must safeguard the document(s) until the time of need.

That you know how and when to change a document if necessary.

That you need a new document when circumstances change.

That you do not prepare or modify the documents yourself.

That you maintain an on-going relationship with your Lawyer.

That you can change Lawyers when appropriate or necessary.

That someone other than you knows where you keep the documents.

CAN YOU SEE THE BASIC SIMILARITIES?

Never worry about theory as long as the machinery does what it's supposed to do.

Robert Heinlein

In this chapter, I point out some of the important aspects of estate planning that, if chosen, can make a big difference in your life and the lives of your loved ones, and if not chosen, point out some possible consequences. Remember that every choice has consequences, either for better or for worse, and that "no choice" has its own set of consequences, too.

NOW WHAT?

It is time for you to seriously consider doing some timely and appropriate estate planning. I am going to take you on a journey through some parts of the legal maze known as estate planning.

You may be wondering who am I to offer suggestions to you and to Lawyers about how to better communicate, and why do I think it is important that clients and Lawyers learn to speak to each other in language they both understand?

I am the person who, for 40 years, worked with Lawyers who specialized in estate planning and administration. I prepared documents for clients, witnessed and notarized hundreds of them. I am the person who for those same years, organized the messy papers people left behind, and kept the estate administration files. I prepared the bills that the Lawyers sent to their clients. I speak "*legalese*." I am the person who was given the opportunity to learn about estate planning from successful, experienced professionals who were generous with their time and knowledge to teach me a portion of what they know and do. It may be only a small portion, but I genuinely believe that what I know can be the communication bridge between clients and Lawyers.

I listened and learned from the Lawyers when they gave their clients advice which the clients chose to ignore. I understand the difference between certain language in a Will that could cause your estate plan to fail, and language that will bring about a successful conclusion to your estate. I would like you to also be aware of certain specific language and situations that can affect your own estate plan for better or for worse.

In addition, I was the person who did much of the work of administering decedents' estates, and saw the costly messes people left behind for their families to sort out. I would like you to know what consequences can result from poor communication and poor record-keeping, and from the refusal to seek advice and to make wise choices. I want to share my knowledge with you so that you, too, may have a better, *albeit* a layperson's understanding of estate planning.

> You won't find such information on forms you download from the Internet.
> And you certainly won't find stories about estate plans like the true stories I relate in this book.

A sad fact is that the person whose estate plan failed, has already passed away and will never know their plan failed. They would be upset to think that it were even possible, and that they didn't correct the plan in time so that things went the way they wanted them. It is just one of the many possible consequences of waiting too long to take care of your personal business.

Having worked around the environment of estate planning for so long, I am of the opinion that the primary reason why estate plans fail, when they do fail, is because of poor communication. Another major deficiency that I believe causes estate plans to fail is the clients' lack of understanding of the intricacies of the language of the various documents. A client should not be expected to understand the definition of every word in a legal document. They also cannot be expected to know that the lack of a particular word or clause *here*, or the insertion of another word or clause *there*, can make the difference in whether or not the client's intentions happen after their death or not.

I cite many examples that show what can happen in such cases. It is the Lawyer's job to educate the client about options, choices and consequences. That being said, it has been my observation that Lawyers take very little time explaining such language intricacies to clients. I believe that Lawyers feel clients don't need to know such details. I disagree.

Take Wills, for example. Many Wills can be thought of as "cookie cutter" Wills; that is, they all read pretty much the same. In my experience this is a true statement, and by itself, there is nothing wrong with such a document if it is legally and technically correct, and if it accurately and completely expresses your intentions regarding distribution of your assets after your death. If the required basic terms and conditions of a Will are present, as well as the necessary signatures and witnesses, the document can successfully be entered for probate and the administration of a decedent's estate may proceed. But, what if the Will does not adequately and appropriately address the specific assets of the person making the Will? You will read about situations like this. It happens all too often.

As you read this book, you will see that I am strongly opposed to what I call the "do-it-yourself" practice of law, and I cite examples of why it is not usually a good idea. So, don't hurry to your computer, look up "Will forms" and press the "print" button. Of course, some of you will follow my suggestion and some of you will not. And, that is all right with me if it is all right with you.

WHY DO SOME ESTATE PLANS FAIL?

Before we begin, I want to talk about how and why many estate plans fail so you will have some idea of certain things to look out for as you think about your own plan, talk with your family, and finally when you meet with your Lawyer to put the plan in place.

It concerns me that so many estates fail, because it doesn't have to be that way. I believe that the chances of estate plans succeeding can be significantly increased with some effort and commitment on the part of individuals to learn about estate planning choices and consequences, hand-in-hand with a willingness to do what is necessary to protect yourself and your loved ones.

Before we look into what it takes to create a successful estate plan, let's first look at some estate failures.

What does your estate plan look like, that is assuming you have an estate plan? If you do not, the next step is to *decide* to create an estate plan. And, if you are going to go to the trouble of creating an estate plan in the first place, you want to know that it has every chance of succeeding, don't you? This sort of action does not happen by itself.

It would be in your best interests to work with a lawyer who specializes in estate planning because it is a complicated specialty in the law. That offers you the best opportunity to get an appropriate estate plan for yourself and your family.

An estate plan is much more than a Will. It is a *plan* … a series of steps … whereby you determine when and how you want your assets to be passed to your heirs, after which your wishes are committed to a formal writing such as a Will or a Trust. For your plan to succeed, it requires thinking, communication, education, commitment, and action. Are you willing to do what is necessary to see that your estate plan succeeds?

In this book, you will find information to assist you in creating your estate plan exactly as you want it to be. You will learn about subtle choices for you to make that can be the difference between your heirs getting what you want them to have after your death, or not.

It isn't enough for a person to be told they need a Will (or any other estate document). Most people already *know* they should have a Will, but, not knowing where to begin, they put it off until "later" … until that unknown date in the future. It is not as simple as filling out a form from the Internet. A Will form, downloaded from the Internet, does not constitute an estate plan.

Of course, there will always be people who choose not to do any estate planning. They have every right to make that choice. Choosing to ignore end-of-life legal and financial, even personal, matters could have serious consequences in your own life and the lives of your loved ones. The choices are yours to make or not.

AARP has said that 98% of all estate plans fail. Why do you suppose that statistic is true, assuming it is? Even if that percentage is wrong … *let's say, for example, it's only 85%* … that's still a whole lot of failed estate plans. Does that statistic disturb you? It should.

In a recent newspaper column, I read the following comment by Deborah Jacobs, a Lawyer, business journalist and author. Referring to estate planning, she said, *"We're heading into a world where there will be a lot of people who haven't done what's necessary."*

Will you be one of those people? If your answer is yes, or probably, the next question you must ask yourself is, *"Why would you make that choice?"* I know, I know, you're *very* busy.

You may be wondering why estate plans fail, considering the time and effort that go into the planning process. You would be surprised how easily and how frequently estate plans fail. There are many reasons why, including, but certainly not limited to:

- Poor communication
- Poor record-keeping
- Refusal to take appropriate and timely actions
- Indifference
- Practicing do-it-yourself law
- Not understanding your money
- Not connecting your financial-planning actions with your estate-planning actions
- Refusal to take appropriate advice from professionals
- Refusal to ask the right questions of the right people at the right time

If you want your estate plan to succeed, you must take action. In the LEGAL and FINANCIAL chapters of this book, you will learn things you can do to see that your estate plan succeeds, and read about some estate plans that failed, and the reasons why.

Believe it or not, on the Oprah Winfrey TV network (OWN), there was (in 2012) a show titled *THE WILL – Revealing Family Secrets, True Stories About Real People Whose Estates Failed Big Time.* I heard the following said on one of those shows: *"Where there's a Will, there are relatives."* Very funny … if it weren't so true.

In the television series, two specific family situations stood out for me. One was a family of French Canadians named Dumaine. The other was Doris Duke (the poor little rich girl). The principles in each case did not do one specific thing that was necessary to accomplish their estate goals. Why not? Who knows. Refusal to believe and follow advice from professionals? Lack of trust? Belief that only they knew what was best for them and their family? A belief that they were going to live forever?

It is amazing how far people will go if they think they are about to inherit money. If a TV network has spent the money and put forth the effort to have a show that describes failed estates, it must be representative of a trend, don't you think? *Just asking...*

Of the stated reasons for failure of estate plans, it is my firm belief that the <u>one</u> that can make the difference between success and failure is <u>communication.</u>

When a person has thorough two-way communication with their Lawyer, the chances for success of their estate plan are exponentially increased. Such communication allows the opportunity to express details that are important, as well as to ask pertinent questions. It is also essential to establish good communication among you and your family members. This book is my contribution toward increasing the chances of your estate plan's success.

The following is one man's true story of his brother's estate plan that failed because of a single oversight.

Once upon a time, Harry, a widower, died at the age of 92, leaving his brother Alan as Successor Trustee. Harry had repeatedly assured Alan that his estate details were in order, and because Harry had all of his documents (including a Revocable Living Trust) duly signed and witnessed, Alan believed Harry; that is, until Harry died, and Alan went to his brother's bank to close out a checking account.

The bank clerk told him that he needed a Short Certificate. Alan was under the impression that as a Successor Trustee, he would not be probating a Will, and would therefore not need a Short Certificates. Still, the bank clerk insisted.

Guess what? It seems that Harry never bothered to change the ownership designation on that one bank account into the name of the trust, and consequently, Harry's estate would not pass easily and quickly under the trust, which had been his original intention. Instead, Alan, as Trustee, was required to get a lawyer, get appointed as Executor, and take his brother's estate through the entire probate process for one single mistake: failure to title a checking account into the trust.

All it takes for an estate plan to fail is one oversight, one mistake, one incorrect assumption.

FAMOUS ESTATE PLANS THAT FAILED

Let's take a brief look at some very famous people who failed to do appropriate estate planning for themselves. These people were intelligent, wealthy, well versed in the ways of the world, supposedly represented by advisers and specialists who had their best interests (both personal and financial) first and foremost. Still, things went terribly wrong!

Let's begin with **Elvis Presley**'s estate. When he died in August 1977, his gross estate was valued in excess of $10 million. The probate process of his estate took 12 years, and reduced the value of his estate by 73%. His estate was reduced by debts, administrative expenses, attorney's fees, Executor's fees, and state and federal estate taxes. What was left after all the probate expenses? Only $2.8 million. Keep in mind that all of the transactions involved in his estate administration were open to the public because of probate.

John D. Rockefeller's estate was reduced by 64%. **Walt Disney**'s estate was reduced by 30%. **Franklin D. Roosevelt**'s estate was reduced by 30% ... that is, the estates of these famous men were reduced by the expenses of administering their estate, and for the lack of appropriate, timely estate planning.

Wouldn't you have thought they would have availed themselves of the finest advice money could buy, because money was certainly not lacking in their lives? Still, they didn't do what was needed to preserve their assets for their families. Even the super-rich can fail to get their affairs in order. In the end, these famous people were just like everyone else.

Let's take a brief look at the estate of **Jacqueline Onassis**, who was a very benevolent lady. Her estate plan was praised because her assets would eventually belong to her grandchildren, mostly free of estate tax. There was, however, a hitch in the plan. She had established a charitable lead trust, the existence of which was subject to Caroline's and John's disclaiming their bequests. (Translated, that means they would be surrendering their right to inherit from their mother's estate). They didn't do that.

To make things worse, she left everything to her two children as tenants-in-common. (Translated, that means that her children were joint owners of the things they inherited from their mother's estate. Caroline was given 50% ownership and John was given 50% ownership of all of the assets they inherited from their mother.) When John, Jr., died, it meant that his estate presumably owned his half, with his sister owning the other half.

Can you see the potential for family infighting and enormous attorney's fees to sort things out? There are many ways in which Jackie's estate could have been set up to avoid such a mess, but they were either overlooked or ignored for whatever reasons. She had the advice of seasoned professionals. Why did this happen?

When **Charles Kuralt** died in 1997, he left a handwritten note in his Will stating his intention to leave some Montana land to a long-time secret mistress. His heirs rebelled ... keep in mind this kind of rebellion always ends up in court and lines the pockets of Attorneys, who may be fighting in court for years! While it originally appeared that his family would win the court battle, a judge ultimately awarded the real estate to his sweetheart, saying that he clearly meant for her to have it. The lesson here is that your private life is nobody's business ... that is, until you die.

When **Philip and Helen Wrigley** both died in 1977, as the owners of the Chicago Cubs, Wrigley Field, and the Wrigley Company, they left an enormous Federal Estate Tax burden of some $40 million. As is often the case, they were asset rich and cash poor, and their only son was forced to liquidate all those assets simply to pay the tax. Had their financial and legal advisors suggested (insisted is a better word) that the Wrigleys get life insurance funded into an Irrevocable Life Insurance Trust, there would have been money to pay the tax, and their son could have kept those extraordinary assets his father had worked for all his life. This sort of thing happens all the time. Why? Failure to act somewhere along the way.

What do these people have in common: **Pablo Picasso, Howard Hughes, Sonny Bono,** and **John Denver?** They all died without Wills, and for years, people fought over their right to inherit. **Tony Curtis** disinherited all of his children, guaranteeing a long court fight among his estate and at least some of his six children from six marriages. Such litigation provides a nice income for lawyers for years to come. I've heard cases like this referred to as lawyers' annuities. It's not funny if it's your family and your inheritance.

The bottom line is that these estates should not have failed, but they did.

The only sure bets are:

(1) that complications will arise to question the intentions and/or competence of the deceased person; and

(2) that the Attorneys may end up with more money than the heirs.

> *On Friday the 13th of July, 2012, at Laurel Hill Cemetery in Philadelphia, there was a screening of an old reel of film that a man bought at a flea market 20 years before. It shows the exhumation of the body of Henrieta Edwardina Schaefer Garrett, a reclusive woman who died on November 16, 1930, leaving an estate worth in excess of $17 million and no heirs. [Today, her estate would be worth $200 million.]*
>
> *It appeared that Mrs. Garrett had not taken her husband's advice to have a Will prepared for herself ... and, after years of searching for her Will, a member of her household hinted that her Will might be in her casket? What? So, on September 24, 1937, the court ordered that her body be exhumed to conduct a Will search, and it turns out there was no Will in the casket.*
>
> *Ultimately in 1951, the estate was settled when three legitimate heirs (first cousins Mrs. Garrett had never met) split the $21 million estate in three shares. After taxes, each heir received between $2 and $3 million.*
>
> *What happened to the rest of the money? It ended up paying for the exhumation, the legal costs of trial, and the administration of her estate.*

All of those events took place because one woman didn't sign a Will. It wasn't as if this woman was young, or that she couldn't afford a lawyer. What was she waiting for? *Just asking...*

YOUR ESTATE PLAN COULD FAIL, TOO

It doesn't *have* to fail, but it *might* … if the wrong documents or words are used in the wrong places for the wrong reasons. Consider the following scenarios:

1.   Your plan is to leave all your assets to your children, in equal shares, so you sign a Will stating that goal. The reality is that all of your assets are jointly owned with your husband, their stepfather. What that means is that, because you own nothing in your own name to leave to your children, your husband inherits everything when you die, and your children get nothing.

2.   Your plan is to leave all your assets to your children, in equal shares, so you sign a Will stating that goal. The reality is that your one major asset is an IRA wherein you named only one of your children as your beneficiary (you said it was just for convenience sake). An IRA does not pass to your heirs under the terms of your Will, so the reality is that all the money in your IRA will pass directly to that one child, and the others will get nothing.

3.   Your plan is that certain people inherit specific assets of yours (personal property and cash), so you signed a Will that included those specific bequests. Your Will, however, did not specify who will inherit those assets in the event that any of those people predecease you. As it turns out, most of those people do predecease you. Who then gets their stuff?

4.   Your plan is that your brother be your Executor, and you stated this in your Will, but he predeceased you. Because you did not prepare an updated Will, and, because your original Will did not specify an alternative Executor, the reality is that his wife (who you do not trust and who you always disliked) applied for and was appointed by the court to be Administrator of your estate.

5.   Your plan is that all of your assets should pass to your heirs by way of a Revocable Living Trust. The reality is that your Revocable Living Trust failed because it was not complete funded; thus, your estate will go through probate (which is exactly what you wanted to avoid).

6.   You named friends to be your Executors because your children were very young at the time and you never updated your Wills. Your wife died in her early 50s, and you died only a few years later. By that time, your children were educated, intelligent young adults, and could easily have handled the responsibility of being Executors. They asked the friends to renounce as Executors, and the friends refused. Your children ended up fighting with your friends in court for the right to become your Executors.

7.   Your Will names both of your children as Co-Executors. They do not live in the state in which you reside and, in fact, they each live in different states, and they do not like each other. Neither would renounce as Executor, even for convenience purposes. Because of their long-established contentious relationship, they end up fighting in court … an expensive, divisive, difficult situation. I doubt that was your intention. In fact, you said you appointed both your children so they would feel that you had treated them fairly and equally.

8.   You had a one-million dollar life insurance policy on your life, with your wife named as beneficiary. Your plan was to provide for your family in the event of your death. The reality is that you and she divorced, you never changed the beneficiary, and your now-former wife received an insurance payout of one million dollars when you died.

9.   Your Will leaves your entire estate to your children, Robert, James, and Suzanne; however, some years after you signed the Will, you had another child, Barbara, and you never signed an updated Will. What about her? Did your Will contain language that provided for after-born children?

10.   Your plan is to leave your entire estate to your son and daughter, in equal shares. But, your estate had no assets except your house, which you have already put into the name of your son to help you pay the bills. Your plan was that your children would each inherit one-half of your estate. The reality is that your son got it all, and your daughter got nothing.

11.   Your plan is to leave your entire estate to your son and daughter, in equal shares, so you leave one house to your son and one to your daughter. The problem is that the value of one greatly exceeds the value of the other. How fair is that? There are ways to get around this so your children can be treated equally, but you must have a conversation with your lawyer to make sure that your children are provided for on an equal basis … not one house/one child.

12.   And, here's a worst-case scenario. Your plan was to get around to signing estate-planning documents sooner or later, but you never got around to it. You had good intentions, but the reality is that you never signed a Living Will or a Healthcare Power-of-Attorney, and now you are in a persistent vegetative state and it's too late. Without instructions from you in an appropriate legal document, what do you think happened when it came time to make medical decisions on your behalf? Remember Terry Schiavo?

13. Well, maybe this scenario is even worse than that: You <u>did</u> take care of your personal business and signed all of the appropriate estate-planning documents, including a Living Will and a Healthcare Power-of-Attorney. Your plan was to see that if you were ever in a serious medical situation, you wanted a specific person to speak for you. The reality is: (a) you never told this person that you appointed them as your Agent; (b) you never told anyone where your documents were kept. So, in an emergency, your family acted as if you didn't have any documents at all, and found themselves fighting in court over who should be appointed your Guardian. Lawyers made a lot of money on this mess.

14. And, to carry this scenario just a little bit farther, your plan was for a specific person to act as your Agent. The reality is that you didn't name a Successor Agent, and the person you did name predeceased you. This means that there was no one designated to speak for you when you could not speak for yourself. Another courtroom situation.

15. You and your husband are Baby Boomers in your early 60s. You each have 3 children from previous marriages. You ask your lawyer to prepare Wills for you, wherein you leave your entire estate to each other, and when the second one dies, the estate is to be equally divided among your six children. Sounds OK, doesn't it? What if the second spouse to die changes his/her Will to leave his/her entire estate to his/her own children, and nothing to yours? It happens.

16. You spent your life working hard to build a successful business which supported you and your family for many years. Your plan was always to pass the business on to your children. The business was owned by you and your wife as tenants-by-the-entireties. When she, as surviving spouse, died a few years after your death, there was a huge Federal Estate Tax bill due, and her estate had no money to pay it. Had you purchased a large insurance policy and properly funded it into an irrevocable life insurance trust, there would have been money specifically for the purpose of paying that tax. But, you said you didn't believe in life insurance. What are your children supposed to do now?

17. You chose a Revocable Living Trust rather than a Will as the means by which to pass your estate to your heirs; nevertheless, your estate plan failed because the trust was not fully funded.

Now, do you see how estate plans can fail?
If you think these things can't happen to you, think again.

Does the above list disturb you? I hope so, because it may make you give serious thought to how you express your intentions to your lawyer and your family, so that your estate-planning documents not only match your intentions, but match your assets as well. The situations described above DO NOT have to happen. A properly written Will or Trust, reviewed periodically, can make the difference between your estate plan failing or succeeding.

All that you have to do to ensure that your estate plan fails is:

- give your attorney incomplete instructions and incomplete information;
- don't follow good advice from trusted advisors;
- don't ask the right questions of the right people at the right time;
- skip the "hard" conversations;
- keep putting the whole thing off until it's too late;
- keep practicing do-it-yourself law;
- surrender to pressure (influence) from someone in your life;
- do nothing.

Once upon a time, there was a man who, as the family story goes, "stole" a beach house from an elderly woman shortly before her death! Legally, that is not the truth, but it is the way people spoke about it.

*As the story goes, this woman (friend of the family from their church) was dying, and somehow (who knows how?) the man **influenced** her to rewrite her Will to state that she gave her beach house to him. I have no idea how it all came about, but after this woman died, her family challenged her Will and sued the man.*

He prevailed, and this beach house became one of the best parts of his family's history ... a cottage by the beach that his grandchildren thought was a little piece of Heaven.

The man had a good Lawyer.

That house belonged in one family, yet it ended up in another. How do things like this happen? There are probably as many reasons as there are people who didn't take care of their own personal business in ways that protect their property for their heirs. That other family was right to sue, and the question of how the court decided in the man's favor will remain unanswered forever because there is no one left to ask.

If a family believes that an elderly person has been unduly influenced by someone to change their Will, it is time to ask serious questions. Is your relative displaying any kind of cognitive decline or health problem that could interfere with their ability to make good choices for themselves? It could be the time to go with your relative to the doctor's visit and ask pertinent questions.

When a man dies with secrets, people begin to show up to claim their right to inherit. If you are such a man, take care of your personal business quickly, privately and legally, with the advice of wise counsel, before it's too late! It is not beyond the realm of possibility that people from every walk of life – *not just the rich and famous* – may have secret family members (e.g., a child fathered out of wedlock many years ago). Everybody knows that DNA can accurately determine paternity, or a life-long mistress nobody knows about.

If you don't want your survivors to hate you, or worse, spend their inheritance fighting in court for years, TAKE CARE OF YOUR PERSONAL BUSINESS WHILE YOU STILL HAVE TIME. Of course, when the situation explodes, you'll be gone, and may not care. Believe me, your relatives will care.

Keep in mind that all of the information about the estates of the rich and famous … *and people just like you* … is available for public inspection because of PROBATE. Maybe that doesn't matter to you. Maybe it does. Either way, have lengthy discussions with your Lawyer about estate-planning options that can avoid probate, and to determine if those options are appropriate for you and your family. Pay attention. Take notes. Ask questions until you understand what you're doing.

Sound estate-planning may prevent some unwelcome post-death publicity, but keep in mind that the media scours court records every day looking for "juicy gossip" about famous people who die! Even your neighbor could go to the local court house to look at your inheritance tax records to see how much money you had. That would be a pretty "nosey" neighbor, but people like that do exist, and it is perfectly legal to look into the court records.

Sometimes, though, there are good reasons to check on estate files in the office of the Register of Wills.

> *Once upon a time, a Lawyer represented a woman who tripped on some broken sidewalk damaged by tree roots. The woman was elderly, and was seriously injured and disabled for quite some time.*
>
> *The Lawyer representing the injured woman brought suit, and the owners of the property with the damaged sidewalk claimed there was no damaged sidewalk. Fortunately, the injured woman's niece had taken photographs of the sidewalk immediately after the accident occurred, so there was proof that the sidewalk had, at the time of the accident, been in poor condition.*
>
> *During the course of the litigation, the owner of the property in question died. How do you suppose the injured woman's lawyer finally prevailed? She went to the local court house to review the inheritance tax return of the recently-deceased property owner. It revealed that $8,000 had been spent to replace all of the sidewalks only days after the injured woman's fall, in a poor attempt to claim the sidewalk had been in good condition all along. Case closed!*

Do you think Lawyer's fees for writing Wills are too expensive? *Just asking…* While you may be complaining about his fee, remember that you are paying him for his knowledge and expertise in a complicated area of the law about which you know very little. Do you also complain about the fees your plumber charges, or your dentist? Sometimes, you have to pay people to do that which you, yourself, cannot do. After all, your Lawyer isn't running a charity.

What I recommend is that you make your Lawyer earn his fee by taking the time to educate you about the contents of each document, so that you have a good understanding of what every document says, and what each can and will do for you, and importantly, what they cannot and will not do for you. When you feel comfortable in the knowledge about your estate plan, then your Lawyer can prepare appropriate documents for you. It is, after all, YOUR estate plan, not your Lawyer's.

COMMUNICATION

You will find this word repeated many times in this book. Having done the work of administering decedents' estates for many years, it is my opinion that the weak link in the entire estate-planning process is poor communication: between clients and Lawyers; between spouses and/or partners; among parents and children; between people and their medical and financial professionals; among people in general. Good, honest, complete communication is an essential component of estate planning.

It's very easy to skip the conversations because they seem too "hard," or painful. While you have every intention of having those conversations "later," be careful not to wait too long ... *you know what I mean.*

I know of so many situations where no communication, poor communication, or miscommunication caused hurt feelings among family members who were unequally or inappropriately disinherited. I'm not speaking about a person's being intentionally left out. I'm referring to situations where people had Wills (or Trusts), and still, their children did not inherit what the writers of the documents really wanted them to inherit. It happens all too often.

Many people are willing to put off having the "hard" conversations until later, or until they get around to it. Other people don't even want to talk about estate planning, probably because of its association with death and dying, let alone take the steps necessary to see that their estate plan is appropriately and timely completed.

It seems that communication among people tends to be more **in**complete than complete, more implied than specific, often misunderstood. People often speak in some sort of code, assuming that the listener heard and understood. I don't believe that is a fair assumption.

In many counseling sessions, two people are guided to conduct an exercise in speaking to each other. First, one person speaks, then the second person is supposed to state what they heard. It is seldom the same ... sort of like that child's game which seems to have followed us into adulthood: *"Whisper Down the Lane."* It was funny then. Not so funny now.

If there are things you want to say and do, you, yourself, must take the initiative required to make those things happen while you are still vibrant and healthy enough to take charge of your personal business before it is too late. There may very well come a time when you are no longer physically or legally able to make decisions for yourself. While you are procrastinating, be careful you don't wait too long. Life goes quickly, and it gets complicated, no matter what choices you make. As a friend once said, *"Life is short, and you're dead a long time."*

The following scenario is but one example of how and why an estate plan failed from what appears to have been an incomplete communication between the client and the lawyer. The woman had a Will. She took the actions she thought were appropriate and necessary; nevertheless, her Will did not ... *and, under the law, could not* ... do what she expected it to do. While her Will matched her intentions, it did not match her assets. Thus it failed.

Scenario

Widow with three adult children asked her Lawyer to prepare a Will for her that included the following bequests:

- Her beach house to her daughter.
- Contents of the beach house to be divided equally between her 2 sons.
- Rest, residue and remainder to be divided equally among her three children.

What happened?

Lawyer prepared a Will that divided her estate as woman requested.
Woman signed the Will.
Woman died, believing that her estate would be equally divided.
Will probated by daughter, who was the Executrix.
Daughter got the beach house.
Sons got the contents of the house.
Daughter got <u>all</u> of the woman's money? *What?*
Children are left confused, bitter, and fighting with each other.

How and Why Did it Happen That Way?

Because all of the woman's money was in three IRAs, with the proceeds payable to her daughter as beneficiary on all three accounts; thus, her daughter got all of the woman's money. IRAs pass to beneficiaries in the same way that life insurance passes to beneficiaries … that is, outside of the Will.

Could This Situation Have Been Prevented? Absolutely.

Whose Fault Was it That The Estate Plan Failed? What do you think? Was it the woman, who, in her own defense, would say that she told her lawyer what she wanted? Was it the lawyer who would say that he did what she wanted?

In a perfect world, a conversation would have taken place to cause the woman to revise the beneficiary designations of her IRAs to provide for a more equal distribution of her estate to her children. As things turned out, her intentions didn't matter. Neither did the fact that her Will was legally and technically perfect and contained language that divided her estate equally.

Nevertheless, it appears that a communication failure occurred somewhere between the woman and her lawyer, although there is no evidence of that statement, only the fact that her estate did indeed fail.

Think how upset the woman would be if she knew that she failed her children.

Can you see the problem?

What was missing? Complete communication.

Why did I tell you this story? So the same thing doesn't happen to you.

What might the woman have done to ensure equal distribution of her estate?

- She could have specified in her Will that the beach house and contents be sold and the net sale proceeds divided equally among her three children.

- She could have given the beach house to her daughter if her daughter really, really wanted it, and then would have given each son something of relatively equal value.

- She could have retitled her IRAs to provide for relatively equal distribution of her money.

There are ways in which you can actually provide for equal distribution of your estate, but they may be ways you don't know about. Just know that in order for equal distribution to happen *if that is really your intention*, you must have conversations with your Lawyer so your Will can be prepared to include the specific language to make it happen. It will not happen automatically or by magic. Your Lawyer is not a mind reader. He can only know what you tell him.

Can the success or failure of an estate plan (or any other plan)
really be caused by something as simple as communication?

YES, IT CAN.

TIP:

If you already have a Will, you might want to make an appointment with your lawyer to educate yourself about the contents. Ask questions to see if your Will should be updated or revised, and determine if your Will will, in fact, do everything you want it to do when the time comes. Pay the lawyer's fee if there is one. It just might turn out to be one of the best investments you ever make.

The woman described above died believing that she did the right thing for her family. And, even though she didn't know her plan failed, that's what happened. Her children had to clean up the mess she left behind. It happens all the time. People trust that their Will is going to do exactly what they want it to do, but if they don't understand the language and the workings of the document, that may not be a reasonable expectation.

Who benefits when estate plans fail? Lawyers do! They earn a living assisting family members clean up the messes left behind by otherwise loving, well-intentioned people whose estate plans failed. Wouldn't you rather leave your money to your family instead of to your lawyer? *Just asking...*

Oh, dear - I hear you already: *"That's ridiculous. How is it possible that poor communication can cause an estate plan to fail?"* How? It's so easy it will frighten you. Oversights and mistakes. Do-it-yourself practice of law. Poor communication. Waiting too long. Making excuses that it is too much to think about, and that you'll do it when you get around to it. Or that you have other things more important to do right now. Being unwilling to sign the appropriate documents out of fear of the unknown ... etc. Are those words you, yourself, have occasionally used when putting off something you know you should be doing, but don't feel like it?

In her book, ***Life-Changing Conversations; 7 Strategies for Talking About What Matters Most,*** Sarah Rozenthuler offers valuable tools to help you learn how to have conversations for possibility, especially the ones that people find most difficult. I highly recommend this book for everyone who is dreading a "hard" conversation with someone.

It is important that you understand that your estate plan does not have to fail. There are things you can do to see that your estate plan succeeds, but, that success will not happen automatically or by accident. Sooner or later, decisions must be made, important conversations had, actions must be taken ... even when you don't feel like it.

The people who made the plans that failed have since passed away, and cannot answer our questions. So, estate plans will succeed or they will fail, and this being said, wouldn't it be in the best interests of everyone to take steps to see that your estate plan succeeds?

Many mistakes can be eliminated by virtue of good communication.

- Lawyers could take more time to understand and discuss their client's intentions.

- Lawyers could take more time to advise clients of options.

- Lawyers could take the time to inquire deeper into the client's intentions when the clients seem uncertain themselves.

- If a client is elderly, the Lawyer must pay close attention to try to determine if the client is experiencing cognitive decline, such that the client's ability to sign legal documents might be questioned in the future.

- Lawyers could provide at least a brief translation of "legalese."

- Lawyers could better explain consequences of omissions or mistakes in estate planning, and the harsh realities of not having proper documents.

- Clients could be more willing to listen, learn, ask questions and require answers of their Lawyer.

- Clients could clearly and completely express themselves and state their intentions.

- Clients could educate themselves before meeting with their lawyer, so as to make their time together more meaningful, and allow themselves to feel more confident when speaking with their Lawyer.

- Clients could be entirely forthcoming with their Lawyers about their assets and their debts.

- People could have important conversations with loved ones.

- There could be better listening between Lawyers and clients.

- There could be better communication between a client's Financial Planner and Lawyer.

Once upon a time a widow had two adult children and two houses. In her Will, intending to divide her estate equally between her two children, she left one house to her son, one house to her daughter. Two children – two houses. Sounds equal, doesn't it? So, you may ask, what's the problem?

*The problem, as I see it, was the **unequal** distribution of her assets to her children pursuant to the terms of her Will. The house left to her son was of a value much greater than the house left to her daughter. [I'm not going to go into any psychological opinions I have about the relationship issues, here. Just know that this is how it happened.]*

The house which the daughter inherited was in another state, where additional probate was required; and, because the value of the house had seriously depreciated because of a decline in real estate values, it will be extremely difficult to sell. So? Keep reading.

Looking back, I can see the widow meeting with her Lawyer, saying that she wants to treat her children equally, and the Lawyer making notes of names, addresses, etc. But, what I don't see is the Lawyer suggesting another possible option for more equal distribution of the widow's assets.

For example, might it not have been better (more equal) if the Lawyer had suggested to the widow that her Will contain language specifying that both of her houses be sold, and the net sale proceeds equally divided between her children? Do I know for a fact that that conversation never took place? Of course not.

But, I do believe that the widow intended to treat her children equally, and actually thought she was doing that by giving each a house. But, by giving houses to her children instead of money, she did not accomplish her goal of treating her children equally. It was up to the Lawyer to point out the inequity. Did that happen? Apparently not.

The children didn't really want those houses. They would have been much happier with equal distribution of sale proceeds.

But, you see, the Lawyer would say that he did what the widow asked him to do. So what's so terrible about that? Maybe nothing. Maybe everything. People who go to Lawyers to have their Wills prepared don't know the law. They may think they do, but they don't understand how they can state their intention to leave a fair (equal?) inheritance to their children, and then fail to accomplish that goal. They don't know that certain words included, and certain words left out, of a Will, can mean the difference between accomplishing their goals or falling short.

News Flash

It has occurred to me that many of the true stories I relate in this book are about mistakes made by widows. Could that be a weak link in the estate-planning process? Maybe. The weak link, as I see it, is the fact that many husbands, before their deaths, did not educate their wives about how to handle their money and their estate. They would justify this by saying it was their job to handle the money, which they did while they were alive … but then they died, and it was too late.

If men don't show their wives how to handle their own money, how can the widows be expected to manage after the death of their husbands? *Just asking…*

If a man dies before his wife, and he has no Will, it might not even create a problem for the widow if all of their assets were jointly owned with right of survivorship and will pass automatically to the widow. But, if *she* (by then a widow) later dies without a Will, that's when problems can occur.

The bottom line is that it is up to women to educate themselves to the greatest extent possible about all things relating to their money and their assets, and ultimately, to their estate planning.

<u>If you are a wife reading this,</u> have you insisted *(demanded?)* that your husband show you everything you need to know about your money before it's too late?

<u>If you are a husband reading this,</u> are you guilty of this sin of omission? Is it OK with you that you might die leaving your wife unprepared to handle her own money without you?

Don't wait too long, because there will come a day when it will be too late.

HOW WE COMMUNICATE IS A MYSTERY

There are various ways in which people communicate with others. The obvious ways are written and verbal. Also, there is imagined or misunderstood communication. We have not yet reached the place of mind reading, although some people live as if they believe the people in their lives can read their minds.

Verbal communication always leaves the possibility that the listener did not accurately hear or understand the speaker's words. Although verbal communication is not usually considered to be a valid "contract" in a court of law (if you don't believe me, just watch "*Judge Judy*" on TV), there are times when a verbal communication will stand up to legal scrutiny. But, it is not good to rely on *he said/she said* conversations or "whisper down the lane," where there is a high likelihood of misunderstandings.

> *In the Philadelphia "Inquirer" of June 24, 2011, there was an article stating that Anna Nicole Smith's heirs lost their bid to benefit from the Will of her husband whose estate was valued in the billions of dollars. Before her death, Anna stated that her husband told her that he would leave her one-half of his estate, but he never documented that in a legal writing such as a Will.*
>
> *The Will contest took some 15 years, countless hours of preparation of legal documents, many court hearings, and thousands of dollars in Lawyers' fees. Ultimately, Anna's "he-said/she-said" communication did not hold up under legal scrutiny.*
>
> *And, once again, who benefitted from all that litigation? Lawyers.*

Why did I tell you this? Because, if you told your family that they would inherit something specific from you when you die, and if you never took the time to preserve your statement and intentions in a valid Will or other legal writing, your family may be disappointed when they do not inherit that which they believed would be theirs someday ... an all-too-common example of failed communication.

And, for example, if you promised someone your coin collection after your death, and it was so stated in your Will, but you sold the coins before you died and never told anyone and never changed your Will, someone will be looking for those coins after your death, and maybe even blaming your executor or someone else of stealing them.

> ### The greatest problem with communication is the illusion that it has been accomplished.
>
> George Bernard Shaw

Do you want your family fighting in court, paying legal fees for years, just because you didn't take care of your own personal business? Do you want that to be your legacy? You may be thinking that by the time your family discovers that you didn't take care of your personal business, you will already have passed away, and won't be around to answer questions, so what does it really matter? Trust me, it will matter. Lawyers get rich trying to decipher your undocumented intentions and helping your family fight about who is right and who is not. The obvious way to prevent verbal miscommunication is by signing estate-planning documents that very specifically state your intentions.

Here is a story about an estate that is destined to fail, and if it fails, it will not be because of any of the usual reasons. I say that the estate "is destined to fail" in the future tense because the estate has not yet been settled and will no doubt be in the courts for a long time.

> *Once upon a time, there was a family that consisted of a father, a mother, and two young adult sons. One of the two sons viciously murdered both of his parents and his brother, and is now trying to be declared the beneficiary of his mother's estate so that he can use the money for his medical treatment and legal defense. The law does not generally allow for a person who murders someone to benefit from that person's estate. The young man is currently being treated for a mental illness, and if an insanity defense prevails, he may never see a day in prison. It is probable that lawyers will make a lot of money on this case.*

WHAT ABOUT COMMUNICATION WITH YOUR LAWYER?

In my opinion, it is absolutely essential that you give your Lawyer exact details of what you want and do not want. Remember, Lawyers may be smart, but they are not mind readers.

You can sit by and allow him to speak to you in the foreign language of *legalese*, or you can engage your Lawyer in a dialogue that will help to educate you about the documents you are about to sign. The documents can have life-or-death consequences. Does knowing that increase their level of importance? I hope so.

Many times, a Lawyer will ask you how you want your Will written, and will then prepare it exactly that way. I hear you already: *"What's so terrible about that?* In my opinion, and from what I observed from many years of preparing Wills and other estate-planning documents, and observing estate plans that failed, the problem is that there may be options that a client does not know about, that may be available and appropriate for their situation, and I believe it is necessary for the Lawyer to tell the client about those options. How else is a client supposed to know that such options even exist?

Some Lawyers gloss over the *legalese*, rush through the explanation of the terms and conditions of estate-planning documents, all the while trying to assure the Clients that there is nothing to worry about, that the Lawyer has taken care of everything. Some lawyers will bristle at this statement, but maybe they should think a moment before reacting.

I strongly believe it is the responsibility of the Lawyer to tell clients that there may be better, more appropriate alternatives to what the client says they want … alternatives that the clients cannot possibly know about … and then, having given the client information, allow the client to decide. After all, the clients are not Lawyers, but they are the people whose estate is being discussed … and, don't forget that they are also the people paying the Lawyer's fee.

Let me tell you about my grandmother's Will. Of course, I was not with my grandmother when she signed her Will, so I don't know the exact words her attorney said to her, but I do have a copy of her Will, and I know the consequences of that document. She was another one of those widows I mentioned above, whose husbands had not educated their wives about their money and estate plans.

My grandmother's Will was prepared by one of the most prestigious Lawyers in our county, and she had complete faith in him because he had been my grandfather's Lawyer for many years. He could probably have told her the moon was made of green cheese, and she would have believed him ... that is how strong her faith was in this Lawyer.

Several years after our grandfather's death, she asked the Lawyer to prepare a new Will for her, wherein she left her entire estate in equal shares to two of her three sons, thereby disinheriting my father, her oldest son. I believe my grandmother had valid reasons for disinheriting him.

One of the choices available to her relates to the share of her estate which she did not give to my Father. Instead of dividing her estate into two equal shares for her other two sons, which is what she did, she could have, instead, divided her estate into three equal shares; that is, her Will could have been written to include language that gave our Father's one-third share to my sister and me. But, that is not what happened.

You may be wondering, "Why did she not divide her estate into three equal shares so that her only grandchildren could inherit their Father's share?" Did she even know that she had such an option available to her? Although I have no evidence to support this claim, I say she did not, because I believe her Lawyer never mentioned it.

I believe it was his responsibility to have at least suggested this alternative to her so that she, herself, could make an informed decision. It appears that what her Lawyer did was prepare the document the way she asked him to, and if anyone complained, he would simply have said he was doing his job.

Did she intentionally leave us out of her Will? My sister and I choose to believe that she would NEVER have intentionally left us out of her Will had she known she had the option of giving us our Father's share. Perhaps we are wrong about this. Perhaps not, but, we will never know for sure, will we?

In case you are wondering, I have copies of both grandparents' Wills, so I know what each document said. Our grandfather's Will left his estate his wife, and upon her death, to their three sons in equal shares. It appears that during the final years of her life, our grandmother decided, on her own, to disinherit her oldest son, and thus, she needed a new Will. No matter who said what, the reality is that my grandmother's estate was divided equally between her two other sons.

Ask yourself:
How was this elderly widow supposed to know that there was another option
available to her if her Lawyer didn't tell her?
Can you see the problem?

It would be a mistake for you to <u>mis</u>interpret this example as,
"Oh, poor Jeanne, she's unhappy that she didn't inherit from her Grandmother."

Although I cite this only as an example from my own experience, things like this do happen.

There is no malice intended on the part of the Lawyers; it is simply how they speak to Clients. I do believe some Lawyers tell Clients what they think Clients can understand and handle, and may gloss over some of the more subtle details of estate planning. I don't believe Lawyers even know they sound that way. Unless the Client is unusually and genuinely interested in engaging the Lawyer in a meaningful two-way conversation and asking lots of questions, with the goal of understanding the documents, Lawyers sometimes forget that the clients do not speak *legalese.*

I want you to be Clients who are informed and comfortable asking questions, even if they seem like dumb questions to you! Keeping in mind there is no such thing as a dumb question, slow your Lawyer down, insist that he speak to you in understandable language so that you will have a basic understanding of the documents before you sign them.

Often when they are finished, the Lawyer will say, *"Now, Mr. and Mrs. Client, do you understand these documents as I have explained them to you?"* What do you suppose the Clients' reply is going to be? Of course, they would say yes, because they don't want to feel stupid, or are too shy or embarrassed to ask questions, or don't even know how to form an intelligent question to ask, because *legalese* is not a language they speak.

Legalese is not that difficult if you understand it, but it may as well be hieroglyphics to the average Client. My intention is to translate some of the *legalese* for the average person who does not speak the language.

WHO SAYS YOU ARE ENTITLED TO INHERIT ANYTHING FROM YOUR PARENTS or GRANDPARENTS?

I do. As a person whose family members were guilty of multiple sins of omission in regard to their estate planning, I do. As a person who, with my sister, has been "disinherited" four times, I do. Oh, we were not disinherited intentionally. We were left out because of lack of understanding, incomplete communication, and failure to take appropriate action.

Once upon a time, a woman repeatedly said that she wanted "her half" of her house to go to her two daughters. Every time she said it, her daughters told her it was not a possibility because she owned the house jointly with her husband (their stepfather), and he would inherit the house after her death; and if she wanted her daughters to inherit "her half" of the house, certain legal steps were necessary to make that happen.

What you should know about this woman was that by the time she spoke those words, she had been damaged by years of verbal abuse from her husband. She had lost confidence in herself and her abilities. Although she was beautiful, intelligent, a talented musician, a college graduate, after years in this abusive marriage, she had shut herself off from the world and didn't always hear what was being said to her anymore. Her husband's weapon of choice was words.

This woman reached the place where she was no longer willing or able to do the legal things that would have been necessary for her daughters to inherit one-half of that house because she was too afraid of what her husband would do if she even brought up the subject.

I only know that her daughters inherited nothing from her. Her entire estate passed to her husband, even though that was not her intention.

This woman was our mother.

CAN YOU SEE HOW IT HAPPENED?

I believe most parents intend to leave some kind of inheritance ... *a legacy* ... for their children, no matter how large or small. Yet, many times, that intention is not carried out correctly.

TEMPUS FUGIT

If you agree that life is short, and you're dead for a long time, what do you plan to do with the time you have left on earth?

What if you were told that at noon in exactly S-E-V-E-N (7) days, you would die. What would you do ***between now and then***?

There are important legal matters that you know should be handled. If you haven't taken care of them by now, do you think you would take care of them during that 7-day period? Or would you just throw in the towel, and thinking that it's too late!

If you knew, with absolute certainty, that you had exactly 10 years (approx. 3,650 days) left on earth, what would you do with the time ***between now and then***? If you still had all that time remaining, would you then handle all your important legal and personal matters?

Do you think that *time* has anything to do with whether or not you take care of your personal business before it's too late? Is time a motivator or an excuse? *Just asking ...*

You could choose to make valuable use of the time you have left, or you could choose to simply let your days run out, one day at a time. Do you think you would find it useful to know exactly how much time you have left on earth? Or would you be too upset, confused, frightened to do anything about the things you have left undone? Would you be thinking of this quotation as you attended the funeral of a loved one?

> ***The bitterest tears shed over graves are for words left unsaid and deeds left undone."***
>
> Harriet Beecher Stowe

HOW DO YOU FEEL ABOUT ADVICE?

When someone makes a suggestion to you about how you might do something, do you automatically say NO, or do you think about it first? Do you hear your mother's voice? Can you hear her love and good intentions, or do you just hear her nagging you, bossing you around, always telling you what to do? What if her suggestion has life-altering consequences? Would *that* make a difference in how you listen to her?

Is it that you don't like to be given advice, no matter what the source? Would you be more inclined to pay attention if the word "advice" were changed to information, suggestion, idea, recommendation, counsel, guidance, opinion, or any other substitute word (euphemism)? (*A rose by any other name is still a rose ...*) Or is it that you simply don't like to be told what to do no matter what you call it?

Information is not the same as advice. Both carry with them, by definition and implication, a choice of whether to follow them or not ... sort of like an invitation which you may accept or decline. Is the idea more worthy if you are paying someone a lot of money for that information? I don't know. Does it depend on who is giving the suggestion whether or not you pay attention to it? What if it is being said by a teacher? Or a doctor? Or your plumber? Or your spouse? Or a loved one? Or your Financial Planner or your Lawyer?

What do you think?

Unless you are in the military or prison, where you have no choice but to do as you are told, most advice can be ignored. But, some advice deserves thought and consideration before quickly dismissing it. Are you able to distinguish between advice that will benefit you and advice that will be a waste of your time and/or money? Are you automatically inclined to kill the messenger? Are you coachable?

If someone makes a suggestion to you that can save you a whole lot of aggravation, heartache or expense, do you hear it as someone trying to boss you around, and so you ignore it on general principles? Or do you consider it first to see if it has valid points, and *then* quickly reject it? What if that person really cares about you? Does *that* make any difference in how you listen? Can you get out of your own way long enough to consider the possibility that the advice might be good?

Remember -- it is entirely up to you whether or not you choose to pay attention to suggestions freely given ... or suggestions you get from professionals whose advice you pay for. There is no police squad that will hunt you down if you choose to ignore good information. You get to make the choice, and you get to deal with the consequences of that choice. Oh, yes, maybe your loved ones will also pay if you choose to ignore a suggestion (information, advice, whatever). Does *that* alter your thinking at all?

Consider the following scenario:

You are on a plane headed for a long-awaited vacation, and the flight attendant is standing in the front, giving instructions on emergency procedures. Do you ever listen, or have you heard it so many times that it bores you? You just want to settle into your seat, listen to some music, read a magazine, and relax. ("Why doesn't she just shut up?") So, you stop listening.

What if you knew, with absolute certainty, that the plane was going down in the middle of the ocean, and that the chances were very good that you would die? Would that change how you pay attention to that flight attendant's advice?

Tell me how this is different from the way you listen to suggestions and information about estate planning? After all, you do know, with absolute certainty, that you will die someday, don't you?

That fact is not arguable.
The only part that is arguable is the date.

What if you may have been able to survive this plane crash had you paid attention to the flight attendant's speech you found so boring? If you die in that crash, your loved ones will never ask if you listened to that speech, so what does it really matter?

I say it matters. What do you say?

So, knowing that death is certain to happen someday, somehow, don't you think it would be wise for you to pay attention and take care of your personal business while you still have the time? When that plane is descending into the ocean, that is not the time to try to recall the words of the flight attendant. So, it is the same with dying. Don't wait until the time when you might be physically or mentally incapable, or legally incompetent, and thus unable to ask questions and make estate-planning decisions or sign legal documents.

There seems to be a common thread among human beings to not want advice, whether solicited or uninvited. Many people even choose to ignore good advice that they, themselves, asked for. Some people seem to be unable to objectively weigh one piece of advice against another? Why do you suppose it is that way? Could it be because:

- they think they know more than the person they asked?
- they hate being told what to do, plain and simple?
- they question the advice that was given, so they ignore it?
- they knew in advance that they weren't going to do what was suggested?
- they just wanted to hear what the other person had to say to compare it to their own ideas?
- they don't like the style in which the advice was presented?
- they believe that if they take someone else's advice, they might lose control of their own life?
- they want to decide for themselves whether the advice given was good or bad, even if they are not qualified to know the difference?
- that some people are afraid to make decisions by themselves, so they choose to make no decisions at all, even when presented with appropriate, valuable advice?
- that some people think if the advice costs a lot of money, it therefore must be good advice, and vice versa?

I ask you these questions because I want you to <u>think</u> about whether you are inclined to pay attention when someone is offering you a good suggestion or idea, and whether or not you always seek the opinion of someone else before making up your own mind? Why would you suppose a friend or relative knows more about estate-planning than you do … that is, unless that person happens to be an estate Lawyer? Who do you know whose opinion would help you make estate-planning choices?

The truth is that I don't know the answers to any of these questions because each is based upon a person's individual style and way of living their life. There are no right or wrong answers, only YOUR answers.

While I am not an expert in human psychology, I am an observer of human behavior, and I have seen many people make mistakes because they chose to ignore good advice. So, let me ask you another question?

- Do you think people are more inclined to seek, and possibly take, advice after they have experienced some kind of trauma or serious upset that makes them rethink how they make decisions?

When it comes to making estate and financial plans and/or funeral and burial plans, you already know that men, in particular, don't like to talk about such things?

Do you think a heart attack would get their attention?

Maybe. Maybe not.

A good scare is worth more to a man than good advice.

E. W. Howe

DOMICILE

Let's begin at the beginning. When creating estate-planning documents, it is essential that you have established "domicile;" that is, the exact legal location of your permanent residence. You will recall that I told you my experience is in Pennsylvania. Always keep in mind that while the forms and procedures and laws vary from state to state and jurisdiction to jurisdiction, <u>in concept</u>, estate planning is not all that different no matter what the jurisdiction.

Let's say that you own three houses in three different states. Basically, two of them are vacation homes because one of those houses is your primary residence. If you want to consider your primary residence as your place of "domicile" as it relates to estate-planning, the following things must be considered:

1. Do you vote in that town and state?
2. Do you live there more than 50% of the year?
3. Are your major religious and social activities there?
4. Do you have a valid driver's license in that state?
5. Is your vehicle registered in that state?
6. Do you file your Income Tax returns in that state?

Let's take this one step further. You recently heard that there are better tax advantages in one of the other two states where you own a home, and you want to take advantage of the better tax situation. How would you go about doing that? If you want to be sure that you understand the situation, consult with a tax attorney. Don't believe what you have read or heard on TV or the Internet or from your friends. Spend the money; consult with a tax attorney. Think of it as an investment.

It is possible to have your attorney construct your Will and/or other estate planning documents to contain language which would allow you to select the law of another state which would give you the best tax advantages under the terms and conditions of your documents. BUT … DO NOT ATTEMPT TO DO ANY OF THIS BY YOURSELF.

ESTATE PLANNING IS
LEGAL, FINANCIAL, and PERSONAL

Estate planning is generally considered to be a legal matter, done with the assistance of a Lawyer experienced in this field of the law. And, while it is true that the factual and documentation parts of estate planning generally require consultation with a Lawyer, there are also aspects of estate planning that are both financial and personal as well.

Whether you have substantial assets or only a few, if it is your intention to pass these assets to your heirs after your death, you must take certain steps to see that it happens the way you want it to happen.

Before you actually sign any estate-planning documents, you should understand as much as possible about your finances so that your Lawyer can prepare documents that will allow for the transfer of your assets after your death to the persons you want to have them. This may require your having a consultation with a Financial Planner before you meet with your Lawyer.

In addition to estate planning being both a legal and a financial transaction, it is also a very personal transaction, requiring careful thought, communication, and commitment to doing what needs to be done to produce the results you desire. After all, what is more personal than the transfer of all of your possessions to others after you die? You won't be around to see that things are done your way, so you must leave carefully crafted instructions, and legal estate-planning documents are a good way to make it happen.

And what could possibly be more personal and important than signing the appropriate legal documents to see that you receive the medical care you want and do not want for yourself?

SEEK PROFESSIONAL ADVICE

Am I being idealistic to believe the best way to be certain that your documents are technically perfect is to have an experienced Lawyer prepare them; and to believe that the best way to see that your assets are distributed after your death the way you want them, to whom, and when, is by having an a Lawyer prepare documents that contain your exact intentions? Maybe, but, I don't think so, having worked with estate Lawyers for many years.

Sometimes, the documents an estate Lawyer prepares fail to accomplish the client's objective. It happens. Do I believe that it could be legal malpractice. Maybe, but seldom. Or could it be due to incomplete communication between the client and the Lawyer? The sad reality is that:

- some clients are not entirely honest with their Lawyers;

- some Lawyers don't ask the right questions to elicit the answers from uninformed clients.

Do I believe people intentionally set out to create an estate plan that would ultimately fail? Absolutely not. (Well, there is that movie, *Body Heat*, to which I refer later in this chapter, where you will read about a woman who intentionally created a Will she knew would fail. But, it is the exception.)

As you read further, you may think I am being critical of how Lawyers interact with clients. Sometimes. But know this: my purpose is to encourage Lawyers and clients to communicate at a deeper level for the ultimate good of the clients and their families, and provide people with information and knowledge so that they can accurately and completely understand their options and fully express their wishes to their Lawyer, thus allowing the Lawyer to prepare documents that will accomplish the clients' goals.

Having said that, I also believe that clients have a responsibility to fully express their intentions regarding the distribution of their assets after their death. And, I especially do not want clients to hide behind the excuse that (a) they didn't understand what the Lawyer said to them; or (b) the Lawyer didn't understand what they, themselves, said. Like it or not, SUCCESS REQUIRES COMMUNICATION.

THE DO-IT-YOURSELF PRACTICE OF LAW

I am not unaware of how many places a person can go to get information and printed forms to prepare estate-planning documents without the help and expertise of Lawyers. I just saw a TV ad for *LegalZoom* which offers complete estate-planning packages on disc so you can prepare your own documents. The ad clearly states that they will save you money. Even Suze Orman offers a package of estate-planning information and documents.

LOOK AT THE LAWYER'S FEE AS AN INVESTMENT, NOT AN EXPENSE.

I have no facts to explain the exact reason for people's trying to practice do-it-yourself law except that maybe they are naturally inclined to be do-it-yourself people, or they simply don't want to pay the Lawyers' fees, and besides, the Internet encourages do-it-yourself "everything." *Just my opinion ...*

I also think many people are intimidated by Lawyers. While you keep in mind that Lawyers know the law, and you do not, never allow yourself to be made to feel inferior. After all, you're paying the bill. In truth, however, maybe Lawyers could work a little harder to remove this perception on the part of the average person. After all, "perception is everything." *Just another opinion ...*

Later on in this book, you will read about some actual situations where people made the choice to take legal matters into their own hands, with serious, irreparable consequences. I cite examples of what happened in situations about which I have personal knowledge when certain persons practiced do-it-yourself law.

Question: "Would you do your own dental work, or perform surgery on your own body?"

No. You would seek the services of an experienced professional in the field. Why is this any different?

Could it be that the fees of experienced medical professionals are paid by health insurance, and the fees of a Lawyer are paid by the client? *Just asking...*

> **I've said it before, and I'll say it again:**
> **DO NOT PRACTICE DO-IT-YOURSELF LAW.**

WHAT ARE THE TERRIBLE CONSEQUENCES THAT CAN HAPPEN IF YOU TAKE LEGAL MATTERS INTO YOUR OWN HANDS?

How bad can they possibly be? Pretty bad. As unrealistic as some of the situations in this book may sound, the facts have not been exaggerated. While you are thinking about the do-it-yourself approach to estate planning, there are a few things to consider:

- Your Will could be declared invalid, and as a result your assets may not be distributed as you want them to be.

- Do you believe that the form you download from the Internet or purchase from a stationery store, will really be specific to the state in which you reside?

- Do you really believe that the form will explain the myriad of distinctions that are required for you to understand before you express your intentions regarding the distribution of your assets after your death?

- Do you think a Living Will form or a Healthcare Power-of-Attorney form will explain why it may not be a good idea to name two people to represent you in a life-threatening healthcare situation?

- Do you really believe that the forms are kept current with the laws of all 50 states? How would you even know if the printed form is the most recent version?

- What if you have a question while you are filling out the form? Who will you ask? There is no one sitting across the table from you to answer your questions. No form supply company and no website can provide the information you need to really know what you're doing.

OK, I have seen some of those forms. They look "legal" enough. They have blank spaces for you to fill in what you want to happen to your assets at the time of your death. There is room to include your name, the name of your personal representatives, the names of your beneficiaries, and places to sign for you, and witnesses and a notary public. Some of you may already have signed such forms and believe them to be satisfactory. Maybe they are, but the real question is: Are you <u>sure</u>?

If you have not already used printed forms, STOP and THINK about the consequences if the form turns out to be invalid. Some of you will use the pre-printed forms and may actually accomplish your desired results. Others will not. Are you willing to risk a mistake because you don't want to spend the money for a Lawyer's fee, or because you have a compulsion to do things by yourself? The following is an example to consider:

Once upon a time, a woman (a widow) copied the language from her sister's Will which her sister had prepared on a form obtained from a stationery store, and prepared her own Will. Afterward, the woman had her Will signed, dated, notarized and witnessed by two people. (The sisters, by the way, lived in different states.)

When the woman died and her Will was entered for probate, it was declared invalid, because her Will did not have the required three witnesses as required in her state. Not knowing that in her state, three witnesses were required on Wills, the woman had copied her sister's Will exactly the same; that is, with two witnesses.

This woman's estate was therefore administered as if she had died intestate (that is, without a Will). This was not her intention, but this is what happened because she practiced do-it-yourself law.

See how easy it is to make a mistake if all you are trying to do is save a Lawyer's fee.

Are you thinking to yourself: *"So what does it matter?"* So what if the woman's estate was distributed according to the intestate laws in the state in which she resided and not according to the specific terms in her Will? The state's distribution of her assets, as it turned out, was very different than the distribution her Will had specified. Of course, this is another situation in which the woman had already passed away and never knew what happened. All she knew is that she saved a few dollars by not paying a Lawyer to prepare her Will.

How would you FEEL if you were this woman's son and Executor of her estate, when you got to the Register of Wills' Office, only to find out that your own mother's Will was declared invalid because she didn't want to pay a few dollars for a Lawyer's fee? How much more will it cost you and your family because of her poor choice?

And, if you are so firmly convinced that you can fill out a form from the Internet and have it accomplish your estate-planning goals, then just go ahead and do it. But, you should tell your family of your choice not to pay a Lawyer to prepare your estate documents. And they should be prepared for the consequences if you make a mistake, because, when the mistake is discovered, you will already have passed away and won't even know. But your family will know, won't they? How understanding and forgiving will they be?

What good is it to incorrectly or incompletely fill out a form you got from the Internet if all you did was save a few hundred dollars for a Lawyer's fee, and then the document does <u>not</u> do what you want it to do for you, and ultimately costs your family a lot more money? Likewise, what good is it to have your Lawyer prepare a technically perfect legal document that will not accomplish your goal because you didn't tell your Lawyer the whole truth about your assets and what you really want?

I will go so far as to say that a blank Will form downloaded from the Internet can be filled in, and if properly dated, signed, witnessed and notarized, may be better than no Will at all, and may satisfy the requirements of probate,

B-U-T ...

<u>DO</u> <u>NOT</u> MISINTERPRET WHAT I JUST SAID AS YOUR
"GET OUT OF JAIL FREE" CARD
TO MAKE YOU THINK IT IS ALL RIGHT TO PREPARE SUCH A DOCUMENT BY YOURSELF.

I did <u>NOT</u> say that!

Maybe a Will form like this will produce the results you intend. Maybe not.
Are you willing to take the risk just because you're feeling especially "cheap" today?

WHAT I AM ADVOCATING IS GOOD, HONEST, COMPLETE COMMUNICATION
BETWEEN CLIENTS AND THEIR LAWYERS, AND CLIENTS AND THEIR FAMILIES.

I KNOW IT ISN'T ALWAYS EASY, BUT I BELIEVE IT IS ABSOLUTELY NECESSARY.

HOW TO FIND A LAWYER

If you agree with me that it is not a good idea to play Lawyer and prepare your own estate-planning documents, begin by making an appointment with a Lawyer to discuss and prepare your estate-plan. Look for a Lawyer who specializes in estate planning and/or estate administration. It is, of course, permissible for you to have your own Lawyer prepare your estate documents, even if he does not specialize in estate planning, if that makes you more comfortable; just be sure that the documents prepared by your Lawyer satisfy all the things that are important to you.

Now, it is time to pull out that ROUND TUIT found elsewhere in this book, and make that appointment with a Lawyer. Do it today! If not today, when? The longer you put it off, the more likely you will never do it.

1. Ask person(s) you know and trust to recommend a Lawyer who specializes in estate planning and estate administration with whom they have had satisfactory results. I recommend such a specialist, because estate law is complicated. You wouldn't go to a cardiologist for a foot problem; likewise, you don't want a personal injury Lawyer preparing your estate documents.

2. If you have a divorce Lawyer or a real estate Lawyer you have used for other legal transactions, you might ask them to recommend an experienced estate Lawyer with whom they themselves have worked in the past.

3. Call the local Bar Association and ask for names of Attorneys specializing in estate planning and estate administration. Once you have the names of the various Lawyers practicing in this specialty, you may want to ask around for word-of-mouth referrals.

4. The Internet. Most Lawyers have Web sites, if not for themselves individually, then for their law firm. You will find a great deal of information this way.

5. The Martindale-Hubbell Law Directory is a good source of information to assist you in finding a Lawyer in your area. You will find this Directory in many libraries, all law libraries, and the Internet.

6. The Yellow Pages and TV ads (least recommended). No matter how visually attractive those ads may be, they are no indicator of competence of the attorney. In my opinion, all it says is that the lawyers can afford the ads.

LAWYERS' FEES

NEVER call a Lawyer and begin the conversation by asking:

"How much do you charge for a Will?"

You might as well call a Porsche dealer and ask how much he charges for a Porsche. Just as there are different kinds of Porsches, there are different kinds of wills and different fee structures. Ask questions, but don't begin with this one.

It is important that you, the client, know and understand how you will be billed for the work your Lawyer does for you. If you don't know how you are going to be billed, how can you know whether or not the Lawyer is billing fairly and correctly? You won't.

Lawyers' fees are calculated differently, depending upon the kind of case. Before the lawyer begins the work of representing you in a specific legal matter, he will present you with a Fee Agreement for you to sign; or, in the alternative, will send you a Letter of Confirmation, with the request that you sign the copy and return it to the Lawyer for the case file. Don't be put off by the request. It is good business practice for the protection of both parties.

The Agreement and the Letter describe the terms and conditions of the legal representation which the Lawyer will be providing for you, including the fee arrangement. This would be your opportunity to begin to formulate questions to ask of the Lawyer.

Never lose sight of the reality that a Lawyer is running a for-profit business. The Lawyer may present himself as kindly, caring, genuinely interested in helping you, while, in the back of his mind is that new Mercedes convertible he saw over the week-end. You get my drift? Do not hesitate to ask questions.

Would you hire a contractor of any sort to do work in your home without their first giving you a written estimate of what they will do and how much it will cost, and without first getting references? Of course not. Why, then, would you not require at the very least, specific details of how the Lawyer is going to bill you. For instance:

- How will you be billed for photocopies? Sadly, there are law firms that contract the work out to a copy center that charges 35¢ per page, then bill clients $1 per page. Their profit is enormous!

- What about postage? What about expensive overnight delivery such as Express Mail or FedEx? Make it understood between you and your Lawyer that you will not pay for overnight delivery of anything that is not absolutely urgent and which could have been delivered by ordinary mail of the U. S Postal Service. Make it also understood that you will refuse to pay for those amounts unless you have been notified in advance, and have given your approval, for that delivery service. In the alternative, you could suggest that if the "package" is urgent, you would pick it up yourself at his office (if that is a possibility).

- Will you be billed monthly? Are you expected to pay each bill in full upon receipt? Or can you pay when the case is concluded? And, if you don't pay the bill in 30 days, will a finance charge be added to the bill?

- What is the Lawyer's hourly rate? What are the hourly rates of his Associates and Paralegal?

- How will you be billed for phone calls? Some Lawyers charge in increments of $1/10^{th}$ of an hour (translated, that equals 6 minutes). Others may use different fractions ($1/6^{th}$ or $1/4^{th}$, for example). That means that a 2-minute conversation with your lawyer could be billed as 6 minutes, or 10, or 15, and, depending upon their hourly rates, will cost you hundreds of dollars. Don't skip this conversation.

- Come to an agreement about phone calls. Can you expect a return call from your Lawyer that same day? Or if the Lawyer will be in court and unavailable for a day or two, will the Lawyer's Assistant tell the client not to expect a return call right away? And, if the Lawyer calls you and you are not available, will you be expected to return the call right away? It's a 2-way street. Remember how many times I have elsewhere said it's all about COMMUNICATION.

- If the Lawyer will be working with an Associate, ascertain that Associate's legal experience. The least expensive Associate may also be the least experienced, and may thus require substantially more time to do the work. So don't be fooled by a low hourly rate for the Associate.

- Ask if you will be billed double or triple for multiple Lawyers' fees when they meet in an inter-office conference to discuss your case. Even if the meeting is specifically about your case, why should you be expected to pay for one Lawyer to serve as a sounding board for another Lawyer you are paying in the first place? *Just asking...*

- Will your Lawyer be sending you copies of all relevant correspondence relating to your case? It is good business practice for both the Lawyer and the client, because it keeps the client current on the activities of the case, and eliminates phone calls from clients wondering what's happening. And, make it understood that you don't want to be billed for these copies. They are part of doing business.

- Ascertain in advance if there are things that you, yourself, can do to keep the fees down. For instance, if there is a lot of copying to be done, you might take it to a local copy center and pay a whole lot less for each copy. Or if something needs to be hand-delivered (to the court house, for example), ask if you could do it. Be creative. Think of ways that you can keep the bill down.

- If your Lawyer will be sending you a monthly invoice, check it as precisely as you check your bank statement or credit card bill. (*You do check them, don't you? Just asking...*) Question the bill if something jumps out at you as excessive or as not being correct. The best way for you to have a basis for understanding (or questioning) your monthly invoice is to keep your own time log of phone conversations, copies received, postage, etc. Be proactive in the process. Never lose sight of the fact that it is your money that is paying the Lawyer's fees.

For general legal representation, a lawyer will generally bill by the hour, and will often submit a detailed bill to you every month for as long as the legal representation goes on. That bill will include both the lawyer's fee and the various costs associated with that representation (again, including, but not limited to, photocopies, postage, fax, overnight mail, special reports, and reimbursement to the lawyer for all costs advanced by the firm on behalf of the client).

Estate Planning: Lawyers often charge a flat fee for preparation of estate-planning documents, depending on the complexity of the documents. At the first meeting with your lawyer, you should ask how much the fee will be, and exactly what that fee includes.

Estate Administration:

Ask if the Lawyer's representation might be governed by statute in the state where the estate will be administered, and if so, ask for an explanation. For representation of an Executor (or an Administrator) in the administration of a decedent's estate, the lawyer may calculate the fee on a sliding scale, depending upon the value of the estate. The lawyer's fee and all costs are expenses of the Estate, deductible on inheritance and/or estate tax returns.

Another way of charging a fee for a decedent's estate would be based upon the time the lawyer and his legal assistant spend working on the estate. The lawyer's hourly rate and the assistant's hourly rate would, of course, be different. Feel free to ask the lawyer right up front what those fees will be. The bill would also include costs for things such as photocopies, postage, and all administration and court costs advanced by the lawyer, etc. The lawyer and his assistant will keep accurate records of the amount of time they spend working on the estate.

For a small estate for which there will be very little legal work, a lawyer may quote a flat fee.

If the administration of an estate becomes litigious, complex and lengthy, and/or ends up in court, the lawyer would have to redefine his billing terms. If there is anything you, personally, can do to prevent such extended administration of a decedent's estate (for example, family fighting), I recommend that you do it.

Guardianship Proceedings:

A lawyer will generally charge a flat fee to represent you in a Guardianship Proceeding. If, however, the guardianship proceeding becomes lengthy and complex, with preparation of many legal documents and court appearances, the lawyer may bill differently.

If you retain the services of a lawyer for this purpose, thoroughly discuss the fee arrangement in advance, and again, be prepared to sign a Fee Agreement.

If the Decedent Died in an Accident

If you retain the services of a lawyer to represent you in the administration of an estate in which the decedent died in an accident, the fees will most likely be calculated very differently.

An estate like that would most likely require the services of one lawyer to do the work of administering the decedent's estate, and another lawyer (or a team of lawyers) to handle the personal injury case. You would probably be asked to sign separate Fee Agreements for each case.

It is possible that the Lawyer's fees would be a combination of billing methods, including (but not necessarily limited to) both hourly and contingent. Billing on a contingent basis means that if the lawyer wins your case, then he gets a fee; otherwise, there is no fee. But, be careful – there are important distinctions for you to know and understand about contingent fee arrangements. Ask questions, and expect answers until you are satisfied that you understand the billing arrangement.

But, know this about contingent representation: You, yourself, (or the decedent's estate) will be responsible for the payment of all costs of the litigation, including photocopies, postage, medical reports, specialists' fees including court appearances of expert witnesses, court costs, etc. Remember that Lawyer's fees are separate from litigation and court costs.

If the Decedent died as a result of Medical Malpractice

If the decedent died having a probate estate, you will need an attorney for the administration of that estate. And, if you were to pursue medical malpractice litigation, you would need another lawyer (or a team of lawyers) to handle that law suit.

There is no easy way to handle such an event. It is my sincere recommendation that you slow down and give serious thought about whether or not to pursue a medical malpractice case, for several reasons.

- First, the person's death may have been a result of natural or even extreme medical circumstances that do not qualify as malpractice, as it is legally defined. Of course no one wants to think that their loved one passed away as a result of some medical "mistake" that is truly malpractice, but it can be difficult to define the circumstances that make it malpractice. So, don't be too quick to jump to conclusions without facts. Discuss the definition of medical malpractice with your attorney to be certain you understand it before proceeding.

- The best thing you can do is to give yourself some time to grieve for your lost loved one until you can be a little more relaxed and able to think and react clearly. There is a Statute of Limitations on medical malpractice, so, if you actually end up pursuing such litigation, you will have time to think about it before jumping into the whitewater that such a medical malpractice case could turn out to be.

- I do want to caution you not to casually talk about medical malpractice with your friends and family. It brings up all sorts of negative feelings that may interfere with the grieving process. If you think you have a malpractice case, before making a final decision, you will need to thoroughly discuss the circumstances with a lawyer specializing in that kind of litigation, which is often very painful, very upsetting, very expensive, and sometimes fails. You might also wish to first discuss the matter with a personal or religious counselor.

When my former husband died, there was absolutely no question that the medical malpractice condition known as "failure to diagnose" was present; however, I discussed the matter thoroughly with a healthcare lawyer who happens to also be a nurse, and we decided that the diagnosis, even if it had been earlier, would not have prolonged his life, and might, in fact, have caused him to suffer.

The costs of such litigation can be enormous, in particular, medical records and the cost of testimony of medical experts who are willing to say it was malpractice. His estate did not have sufficient funds to pay for the costs of such litigation, and besides, even a win in court, many years later, would not have brought him back to life.

Sometimes, the best thing you can do is nothing ... except deal with your personal loss of someone you loved.

A few final words about contingent fees.

- First, your Lawyer cannot authorize a settlement of any case without first obtaining your consent. Some Contingent Fee Agreements provide language that states that if you refuse to approve a settlement recommended by your lawyer and the case goes to trial, you must pay the Lawyer's fee based upon an hourly rate should you lose.

- Second, you must know the manner in which the Lawyer's percentage is calculated. It can be between 25% and 50%, and varies based upon certain circumstances; for example, the fee might be 25% if the case is easily and quickly settled; a higher rate if the case is settled out of court, but after a longer time; and a still higher rate if the case goes to trial.

To make sure you are being charged fairly, require that the Contingent Fee Agreement clearly states that the final percentage is reached only if the case is actually tried in court. It's all in the details. Read the small print and verify the facts.

TIME RECORDS

Lawyers' keep daily time records that accurately reflect the amount of time dedicated to your case (or estate). One lawyer I know dictates a description of his every act in relation to his clients' cases into a recorder, and his secretary/assistant transcribes the tapes, entering the information into the computer billing software every day before she does anything else. This kind of timely precision billing gives both the lawyer and the client accurate and complete information about every transaction relating to each case (estate).

When you receive your Lawyer's bill, check it out to see if it is correct; and if there are things you question, call him right away.

When I worked for one particular attorney, I kept a running time sheet in my computer for each individual estate on which he and I worked, such that when it came time to bill the estate, there was a complete record of all the time devoted to the administration of the estate.

I am so accustomed to keeping such records that I even did it when I was Executor of my former husband's estate. And, if you are ever an Executor, I recommend that you do the same. Your time records will justify your taking the Executor's commission in the event that some unhappy heir questions what you did to earn the commission. Since an Executor is in a position that carries with it both legal and fiduciary responsibility, I believe it is important to pay attention to details such as keeping accurate time records.

BILLING FOR CLIENT/LAWYER COMMUNICATION

In addition to billing for meetings with clients, Lawyers bill for the time they spend on the phone, for the time they devote to writing and reading correspondence, and for preparation and reading of legal documents relating to your case (estate). Of course, their time for court appearances, if required, would also be included in the bill.

In this day of advanced electronic forms of communication, however, there is much email contact directly between the client and the lawyer, and between lawyers. I've known situations where the client was upset when the lawyer billed for his time to read and write emails. If you think about it for a moment, you'll understand that when the lawyer reads and writes email, he is giving of his professional time and expertise, for which the client will be billed. I understand that email communication may not require the time of a secretary/assistant, and the communication is not on paper and sent by the U.S. Postal Service; but email communication is, nevertheless, a pertinent and necessary form of communication, and will be billed to the client.

> *What's said's air. What's writ's there.*
>
> Author unknown

The lawyer will print out every email relating to your case (estate), to be placed into the file, no differently than filing a copy of every letter or legal document relating to your case (estate). An email, when printed, is a form of written communication even if it is transmitted electronically, and must therefore be retained as part of the file.

Knowing that your lawyer will also bill you for all phone conversations relating to your case (estate), I recommend that you do not make a habit of calling your lawyer (or sending short emails) every day or every time you have a quick question, or you may find yourself upset when you get your monthly statement. If you think you need to be in touch with the lawyer by email or phone, try to make the communication time worthwhile.

A WORD OF CAUTION

I believe it is essential that you establish a relationship of mutual respect and trust with your lawyer. It may be all right if you don't particularly "like" him, but you must trust his professional and personal ethics and expertise and feel confident that you are working with a lawyer who will do for you what needs to be done.

If there should come a time when you feel you do not trust your lawyer, have an open, honest, non-critical conversation with him to express your dissatisfaction and try to find the source of it. Also try to see if it is possible you have misunderstood or misinterpreted something, and see if the bond of trust can be re-established. If it cannot and you determine it is necessary to get another lawyer, be sure you are making the right decision, and then go about finding another lawyer. Just try to make the separation in a dignified, respectful manner. Don't burn any bridges.

One thing you must know at that point is that you must pay your first lawyer's fee in full before your first lawyer will release the file to another lawyer. That is just how it works. Just because you had a change in heart about the lawyer does not necessarily mean he did not do a good job for you. Lawyers deserve to be paid for the work they did for you up to the time of your changing Lawyers.

Of course, if there is a possibility of legal malpractice, that's another story entirely. And know this – there is a big difference between legal malpractice and unsatisfactory results according to a client's opinion. So, be careful before you begin pointing (legal) fingers at a Lawyer if you are dissatisfied with the results. Once again, it may be that you didn't entirely understand the process or the path the Lawyer was taking. That would be another opportunity for you to open up a dialogue between you and the Lawyer to ask questions, listen, and see if the situation can be remedied to your satisfaction.

Be careful of talking about the situation with friends and family who also probably don't understand the legal process. They have opinions which they are entitled to voice, and probably have your best interests at heart. Just don't let your judgment be clouded by comments about your lawyer's abilities spoken by people who don't understand. *Just my opinion ...*

TIPS FOR WORKING WITH YOUR LAWYER

If you do not have a Lawyer, **contact two or three Lawyers to discuss your estate-planning needs.** You will want to have your appointments with Lawyers who specialize in estate-planning and estate-administration, or even tax law.

Call for an appointment for a consultation once you have chosen the Lawyer with whom you intend to work. Ask if the consultation is complimentary, or will there be a fee for the consultation; and, if so, will that consultation fee be applied to the actual fee for preparation of the document(s)?

Do not expect a Lawyer to grant you a long interview for the purpose of your deciding whether or not to retain their services to prepare your estate plan. As the consultation appointment moves along, decide whether you and the Lawyer are a "good fit," and whether or not you wish to retain that Lawyer. If not, pay the consultation fee (if any), and find another Lawyer.

After you make the appointment, the Lawyer may send you an **Estate-Planning Worksheet**, with the request that you complete the form and bring it with you to your first meeting. **JUST DO IT!** Many people do *not* complete the worksheet. Why do you suppose that is? *Just asking...*

I've actually heard people complain that the Lawyer is just being nosey. *Excuse me?* **Do not assume the Lawyer is being nosey by asking questions about your family and your finances.** This information is necessary for him to prepare proper documents for you. Don't show up in his office with preconceived notions of how you think a Lawyer should perform his duties. You will recall that previously, I said that it is important that your communication between you and your Lawyer be complete. Don't start out on the wrong foot.

How do you expect a Lawyer to prepare appropriate documents for your situation if the Lawyer doesn't know anything about you, your assets, your family, or your estate-planning needs and goals? As I said previously, Lawyers may be smart, but they are not mind readers.

Do not be intimidated by the Lawyer. Having said that, keep in mind that you and your Lawyer are attempting to create a partnership arrangement of comfort, trust, and mutual respect, in which you work together to accomplish your estate-planning goals. So, be fully engaged in the process.

- If you are married or in a committed relationship, both parties should attend all meetings with your Lawyer.

- Be prepared to ask questions, and remember, there is no such thing as a *stupid* question.

- Take detailed notes, including dates.

- Discuss the Lawyer's fee structure and fee agreement. If you are asked to sign a fee agreement, read it carefully, ask questions about it, then sign it. It is for your benefit as well as the Lawyer's.

- Ask what the Lawyer's fee will be for your estate plan, and exactly what the plan includes.

- Ask about the fee for paralegals. They do much of the actual work, especially when the work is estate administration.

- Ask when the Lawyer will have your documents ready for your signature.

Be prepared

When you first meet with your Lawyer, be prepared to give him the following information, and be ready to discuss it all:

1. If the Lawyer sent you an Estate-Planning Workbook, take the completed workbook with you. (*You did fill it out, didn't you? Just asking ...*)

2. A current and complete list of all your assets and debts.

3. Names (including exact spelling) of all your beneficiaries, plus their addresses and phone numbers, and your relationship to each.

4. Names (including exact spelling) of all your contingent beneficiaries, plus their addresses and phone numbers, and your relationship to each.

5. If you have a special-needs child, provide all information relating to that child so your Lawyer can appropriately include that child as a beneficiary under your Will.

6. Specific bequests: include exact description of each item, name and relationship of the person(s) to receive the item(s), and who should get the items if the person(s) predecease the writer of the Will.

7. Personal Representatives: Exact name and correct spelling of the names of the person you designate to be your Executor and your Substitute Executor, your Agents and substitute Agents, and your Successor Trustee(s). Also, give your Lawyer their phone numbers and addresses for his file.

8. Guardian for minor children: Exact names and correct spelling of all persons into whose hands you entrust your children's lives and finances. Specify substitutes. Also give your Lawyer their phone numbers and addresses for his file.

9. Domicile. Where have you established your primary residence?

10. Simultaneous Death: In the event you and your spouse die under circumstances that make it difficult or impossible to determine the order of your death, your Wills must specify who shall be determined to be the survivor. This is a complicated subject that varies from state to state, and if not correctly spelled out in your Will, can cause your estate (heirs) to pay taxes they might not otherwise have to pay and to pass on your assets to people you might not want to inherit from you. This is an important subject to thoroughly discuss with your Lawyer.

11. Specific Omissions: Exact name(s) of person(s) you intend to formally disinherit.

12. Residuary estate: Specify the name(s) and exact spelling of the names of all person(s) and the relationship you have with all person(s) who will inherit your entire estate after all taxes and expenses have been paid, and after all specific bequests have been distributed. If the beneficiary of your Will is a trust, specify all the details of the trust. Specify the percentage each person is to receive. Specify who will inherit the portion of a deceased beneficiary.

13. If you intend to establish a trust, whether revocable or irrevocable, your lawyer needs to know this right away so that the documents can be prepared appropriately.

14. Your intentions regarding your Living Will and Healthcare Power-of-Attorney.

15. Your General Durable Power-of-Attorney.

16. Your need for a business succession plan if you own a business.

17. Trust agreements, including life insurance trust, revocable living trusts, special needs trusts.

18. Any marital agreements you have, and the basic terms and conditions in each (i.e., a Pre- or Post-Nuptial Agreement, a Co-Habitation Agreement, a Divorce Settlement Agreement). Your Lawyer might ask you for copies of each, which you could provide after the meeting.

19. If you have a blended family, be sure to tell your Lawyer the circumstances so that the people you want to inherit from you, and only those people, do inherit from you. Estate-planning documents must contain specific language precisely spelled out to avoid potential hard feelings among members of blended families. *Something else to think about ...*

20. The Three A's:

    - Abatement: This is about what happens if you die and, for whatever reason, there is not enough money in your estate to honor the gifts you specified in your Will. One way to avoid this problem is to state that each beneficiary receives a percentage of your net estate, and not a specific dollar amount. Discuss this with your Lawyer to determine how your state's abatement statutes work.

    - Ademption: This applies to situations where you identify certain items of personal property to be given to certain people under the terms of your Will ... but, when you die, you no longer own those things. Those things that are considered to be missing (i.e., adeemed) are then subject to the ademption statutes of your state. This can be a real source of hard feelings among your heirs if someone is expecting to receive something from you (your coin collection, for example), and when you die, there are no coins. *Something else to discuss in detail with your Lawyer ...*

- Antilapse: This is the situation when someone named in your Will dies before you, and there is no one named to receive that person's gifts. One way to avoid this situation is by naming contingent beneficiaries for every specific bequest. If you don't specify contingent beneficiaries, and if your state has an antilapse statute, your possessions will be distributed according to the laws of your state.

ARE YOU BEGINNING TO SEE WHY IT DOESN'T PAY TO WRITE YOUR OWN WILL?

It's all in the details

*Once upon a time, I **typed** a Will for a Client of the Lawyer for whom I was working. I emphasized the word "typed" because that is exactly how I did it ... on an IBM typewriter, the workhorse of all typewriters. In those days, Wills were typed on 8-1/2" x 14" legal paper, and there were no editing or self-correcting options on the typewriter. A Will could have absolutely NO corrections whatsoever: no erasures, no cross-outs, no lift-offs, and no "Wite-Out." The document had to be perfect in every respect.*

The Lawyer I worked for required precision in the preparation of Wills, which always included a line at the bottom right-hand corner of every page (except for the actual signature page) on which the Client was to sign his/her name. Underneath the line was the typed name of the Client ... on every page.

This particular Will was for a man whose first name was John. Or, was it? When the Lawyer presented this perfectly typed Will to the Client, his immediate reaction was, "This isn't how I spell my name. My name is JON." I had to retype the entire Will.

Here again, incomplete communication played a part. Should the Lawyer have asked his client how he spelled his name, or was it safe for the Lawyer to assume that "J-o-h-n" was how the client spelled his name in the absence of any information to the contrary? After all, the client's name was "John," which is a pretty common name.

Should the client have told the Lawyer that his name was spelled in an unusual way? Of course.

I do know that ever since this incident, that Lawyer ALWAYS asks Clients to spell their names, no matter how familiar they may be. And, today, with the trend to spell popular names in unusual ways, it will become an absolute necessity for people to spell their names in every transaction of their lives.

When parents give their children oddly spelled names, they doom their kids to a lifetime of having to spell their names. OK, that's just my opinion, since my name is spelled in a way that has required me to always spell it. I know. It's annoying, but necessary.

GOOD ESTATE PLANNING REQUIRES THE EXPERTISE OF A LAWYER <u>AND</u> A FINANCIAL PLANNER

Estate planning is so much more than just writing a Will. The field of estate planning has become very sophisticated and complex over the years. In a perfect situation, especially if you have significant assets, you will do your estate planning with the assistance and advice of both a Lawyer who specializes in estate planning <u>and</u> a Financial Planner, all of you working together to achieve the best possible estate plan for you and your loved ones.

<u>DO YOU REALLY NEED TWO ADVISORS?</u>

Again, you do not, although I recommend it. As I said before, you can skip the estate planning process entirely. Or, you can use the services of one without the other. You can even do it yourself! [*Elsewhere, you will read the story of two sisters who did their own estate planning, and the extreme consequences of their decision.*]

It is very possible that if you were to ask your Lawyer if you should also have a Financial Planner, he might say no. Having worked with both estate-planning Lawyers and Certified Financial Planners, **I absolutely believe you need both.** I have seen how their combined expertise helps people achieve their goals.

Be careful! Do you honestly believe you know what is required to make a proper estate plan for yourself and your family, or how to wisely invest for the future? Maybe you do. Probably, you do not. Why risk it?

I believe Clients will get the best possible results if their Lawyer and Financial Planner talk with each other and work together. What might even be better is if the Clients were to meet simultaneously with their Lawyer and their Financial Planner so they can together talk about the many issues that are involved in creating an estate plan that is right for them. Such a combined meeting will probably not happen unless the client requests such a meeting (<u>insists</u> might be the appropriate word). *Just so you know ...*

Should you ask your Lawyer for advice about financial planning? Should you ask your Financial Planner for advice about estate planning? Technically, the answer is no. But, there is a lot of overlap in the areas of expertise of these two professionals. In my opinion, the best way for clients to obtain desired results is to have both professionals working together and with the clients to achieve the best possible estate plan that will include planning for your wellbeing while you are alive, and planning for distribution of your estate after your death.

Open, honest, timely, complete communication among these people is essential if you want your estate plan to succeed. Also, it's important for both advisors to know your intentions regarding the distribution of your estate at the time of your death, whether it be to your spouse and children, or a charity, or otherwise, and for them to work together to reduce taxation to the greatest degree possible. Believe it or not, it is possible to reduce taxes!

Using football as an analogy, after you have met with the Financial Planner and the Lawyer, the Financial Planner would thoroughly analyze your assets, and would then hand off the information to your Lawyer. After your Lawyer completes his work of preparing appropriate estate-planning documents, and after you have signed them all, it would be wise for the Lawyer to pass the clients back to the Financial Planner so the Financial Planner can meet with the clients, discuss the assets they have, and what should and should not be funded into a trust if there is a trust. (Read more about funding trusts later in this text.) It is also an opportunity for the Financial Planner to establish other appropriate investments that will accomplish the estate plan they discussed with Lawyer ... everyone working together toward the same goal.

ESTATE PLAN LETTERS

What exactly is an estate plan letter, and to whom should such a letter be addressed?

After you have executed all of your estate-planning documents, it is important that you tell your family what you have done, and that you also communicate your thoughts, wants, needs and priorities to your loved ones. They are not mind readers. And besides, I believe it is valuable for you to know that you have done your best to express yourself to your loved ones.

One way to do that is by writing Estate Plan Letters. You may want to write several individual letters, some (but not all) of which you designate to be opened only after your death.

This purpose of estate plan letters is to communicate specific information to your family, things that are not included in your formal estate-planning document. Such a letter is of a personal nature and is not intended to have any legal effect on the kinds of treatment you receive or how your property is to be distributed after your death.

    1.   You might consider writing a letter to your family expressing how strongly you feel about certain aspects of your end-of-life health care. Even if you have executed a Living Will and a Healthcare Power-of-Attorney, they are written in "*legalese.*" I believe it is important for you to honestly and completely tell your family what you want and do not want, and to ask them to honor your wishes, even if they are contrary to their own. This is one letter that you <u>do not</u> want to put in an envelope marked "to be opened upon my death."

        - Exactly when you give this letter to your family is entirely up to you, but I don't recommend that you wait too long. Let them have time to consider your requests and instructions, ask questions, have conversations with you. These could turn out to be some of the most meaningful conversations you will ever have with your family.

2.   You might want to write a letter to your children to explain how and/or why you selected the person to be your Executor, or how you determined the person you named as Agent under your Living Will and Healthcare Power-of-Attorney. You might also want to state why you gave certain assets to certain people and not to others.

3.   You might also write a very specific letter explaining your wishes about how your pets are to be cared for in the event of your incapacity or death.

4.   You may wish to write a letter to your Executor to include information about the location of your assets and personal property, including real estate, bank safe deposit box(es) and keys, for example. Your letter might also specify how your Executor should distribute your jewelry or cherished collectibles to members of your family. You may wish to include the names and phone numbers of your attorney, accountant, and financial advisor.

Once you have written these letters, put them with your other estate planning documents. It is up to you whether you choose to mark the envelopes *"to be opened upon my death"* or not.

Remember, these letters are to express your feelings to people you love, and who love you. Be careful what you write, such that your written communication lovingly and accurately expresses your thoughts and feelings and what you want them to know and understand about you and your intentions.

YOUR ESTATE-PLANNING DOCUMENTS SHOULD BE REVIEWED EVERY FEW YEARS

When you receive a letter from your Lawyer, suggesting you make an appointment to review your estate-planning documents, it would be a mistake to automatically assume your Lawyer is just trying to drum up more business and get another fee from you.

The Lawyer is trying to determine if your life circumstances have changed such that you need new, more current documents. A divorce, for example, would require you to have a new Will; likewise, death of a spouse. Relocation to another state would require a new Will, Living Will and/or Healthcare Power-of-Attorney. Or, your Lawyer may feel that your estate plan should be reviewed because of a recent change in the law.

Writing a Will, for example, one time does not eliminate the probability that you will have to write another at a later date to accommodate the changes in the law or in your life circumstances. One reason estate plans fail is because people don't give a priority to updating their estate-planning documents when it is appropriate to do so.

Would you believe that there are people who won't sign a Will in their younger years, because they think they will have to write another in later years, and then they will have to pay the Lawyer a second fee! *What*? Where do people get these ideas? Do they forget the possibility of death by accident?

MORAL OF THE STORY: When your Lawyer contacts you to get together to talk about updating your estate-planning documents, make the appointment. Take care of your personal business. Your loved ones will thank you.

Once upon a time, a couple took care of their personal business early in life, when their children were very young. The husband and wife signed their Wills, and named friends (a married couple) to be Co-Executors, because at that time, their children were too young to assume that role.

Both parents died relatively young. By the time the second spouse died, their children were well educated, self-sufficient young adults, more than capable of acting as Executors for their parents' estates. But, because the parents never updated their Wills over the entire time of their marriage, when the second spouse died, their friends became Co-Executors. What followed was a lengthy legal battle with the children's requesting that the named Co-Executors renounce, and the Co-Executors refusing. That could have been avoided had the parents simply reviewed their Wills periodically.

<u>Moral Of The Story</u>: Review your Will when your life circumstances change. (In this case, their children grew up.) And, if you have no major changes in your life circumstances, review your Will with your Lawyer every few years anyway, even if you think there is no reason. Your Lawyer may know of a new law that could have a significant impact upon your estate. And, don't wait for your Lawyer to call you. Call your Lawyer yourself. Be proactive ... after all, it's your estate and your life.

CHANGES IN YOUR ESTATE-PLANNING DOCUMENTS

Before I go any further, there are a few things about your estate-planning documents that you must know.

<u>First</u>, they are not carved in granite! They can and should be changed periodically; for example, if you change your mind, or if you move to another state, or if you change your life circumstances (marriage; divorce; children; death of a spouse, win the lottery) to name just a few.

<u>Second</u>, they should absolutely be changed formally, prepared by your Lawyer in a manner consistent with your original document.

    - If you change your Will by virtue of a Codicil, the new document must be signed by you, dated by you, and properly witnessed and notarized. And, it must be kept with your original Will, or how else would you expect anyone to know that you had made a change? And at the time your Will is entered for probate, the Codicil must be attached.

    - Rather than prepare a Codicil, it has become common practice today, with the use of word-processing equipment, for Lawyers to completely rewrite a client's Will, thus creating an entirely new document which would be signed, witnessed and notarized just like the original Will.

<u>Third</u>, if your attorney prepares an entirely new Will for you, your previous Will should be voided or destroyed. At the time of your death, you would not want any confusion as to which Will is the correct one. I recommend shredding, but, if you cannot bring yourself to destroy your old Will, at least write VOID on every page of the document in large bold letters, followed by the date and your initials or signature.

    - And, for example, if there were two different Wills, it would be entirely possible for someone to destroy the most recent Will if it contains language that makes them unhappy. These things happen!

<u>Fourth</u>, do not hand-write changes on the original documents! No inserts, no cross-outs, no doodles, no Wite-Out, no marks of any kind in the margins. NO NOTHING! A single hand-written mark could invalidate your Will.

    - This is not to say, however, that a <u>separate</u>, hand-written modification of one of your documents would not be acceptable for probate, because if it contains the necessary elements that make it a legal document (including signature, date, notary and witnesses), it *might* be acceptable; however, you already know it is never a good idea to practice do-it-yourself law, so why risk it?

So, if or when the time comes to make a change to one or all of your estate-planning documents, call your Lawyer, and have the document(s) prepared the right way. If you want to make changes, go ahead and do it! Just be sure the replacement document will have all the elements required to validate it. After all, you've come this far. THIS IS NO TIME TO MAKE A MISTAKE.

Remember the following story the next time you hesitate to sign your Will or other estate-planning documents.

Once upon a time, there was an elderly woman (a widow) who didn't have any of her estate-planning documents signed, her stated reason being: "I don't have to worry; my son will take care of everything when the time comes." When she was asked if her son was a Lawyer, her very quick reply was, "No. He's a surgeon, but he's very smart."

While this woman was justifiably proud of her son, she was blind to his shortcomings. A son who is a surgeon is generally not well versed in the practice of law, too. Believe me when I tell you that being smart isn't enough. Would you go to a (smart) Lawyer for surgery; would you go to a (smart) surgeon for legal work?

> *When this woman dies without a Will or a Trust, her son, who, by the way, lives in a different state, will have to administer his mother's estate by long-distance through an attorney. The legal fees will be high, and you might say that's all right because, if her son is a doctor, he must have money, right? Maybe. Maybe not. What if he's only a resident, not yet making the big bucks?*
>
> *Another question is: does he have the time and availability? If he is a busy doctor, does his mother really think he has time to fly back and forth across the country to administer her estate? Maybe the son should have sat down with his mother and asked her to remove her rose-colored glasses when it came to her vision of him. He was a very busy man with a life elsewhere, and he would be enormously inconvenienced by having to deal with his mother's estate long-distance.*
>
> *If the woman had been willing to open her mind long enough to listen and consider the facts about a Revocable Living Trust, for example, that her son could have easily handled upon her death, the son's life might have been made easier.*
>
> *As it is, her son will have to go to the state where his mother lives, apply to be Administrator at the court house, and hire a Lawyer. Oh, and I can hear you already, "So what's the big deal? He'll have to go to his mother's state for her funeral anyway, so he might as well take care of her estate administration while he's there." Sorry, that's not how it works. Estate administration is a <u>process</u> that can take months, if not years, to complete. It cannot be completed in a day or a week's visit for a funeral.*
>
> *Let's take this scenario one step further. With this woman's not having a Living Will or a Healthcare Power-of-Attorney, and were she to become ill or disabled, it would be extremely difficult for her son to take care of her needs from across the country.*
>
> *Just something else to think about while you are putting off signing your estate-planning documents.*

WHAT HAPPENS IF YOU NEVER WRITE A WILL?

Of course, you already know that nothing will happen to you, personally, because you will have already passed away. The consequences of your not having written a Will, will be passed on to your heirs who may or may not inherit from you as you intended. Your family may be seriously disappointed to learn that you didn't put forth the effort to take care of your personal business. And, remember, we agreed elsewhere that you do not have to write a Will. You will die anyway.

Why do a majority of people die without a Will? Take your answer, multiply it by thousands, and you still couldn't come up with a better answer than this: They don't want to think about anything that has to do with their death, even when they know, in their heart of hearts, that someday, they will die. They believe it is safe to ignore the situation until "later." It may be safe, but is it reasonable and responsible?

This situation of dying without a Will is known as *intestacy*, which, translated, simply means that a person died without a Will. Dying without a Will is, in fact, a method of estate planning, although most people wouldn't think of it this way. If you die without a Will, you have given the state the right to decide who will receive your property and who will not. If you don't want that to happen, just sign a valid Will and be done with it. It will not kill you.

There are good reasons why you should take steps to ensure that you do not die intestate; that is, why you should have a valid Will.

- **The first thing you should know is that the intestate laws are different in every state, and the laws must be applied rigidly.** You will have no say in the matter.

- All children will be treated equally. There is no provision for a special needs child for whom you might want to set aside a larger portion of your estate. The intestate laws will not allow for such special circumstances.

- The share that each of your heirs will receive is set by law, so you will not have any say about who gets what, or how much, or when.

- If you have minor children and no Will, a guardian will be appointed for them by the court, and it may well be someone you would never have chosen had you, in fact, named a guardian for your children. It might even be someone you and your children wouldn't want. This fact alone should spur you to take steps to sign a Will.

- The intestate laws of most states have no provisions for domestic partners or other non-family members … or even for your pets.

- There will be no provision for any of your estate to be donated to charity.

- Estate/Inheritance Taxes might be higher because your estate property will be distributed by law, and that distribution may not take advantage of laws available to minimize your taxes.

- Without a Will, there will be no Executor whom you designated to handle your affairs after your death. Instead, there will be a court-appointed Administrator, who could very well be someone you would never want to handle your affairs, but, hey, if you didn't bother to write a Will, you have no say in the matter. The automatic operation of the law will go into effect, and it will be too late for you to do anything about it.

- Your assets will still have to go through the probate process, with all the same requirements as if you had written a Will.

ARE THESE ENOUGH REASONS TO MOTIVATE YOU TO WRITE A WILL?

UNDER WHAT CIRCUMSTANCES MIGHT A PERSON DIE INTESTATE?

If you die intestate (that is, without a Will), your estate assets will be distributed according to the laws of the state in which you had established permanent residence. Although the laws of every county of every state vary, the priority for distribution of your assets may (*but may not necessarily*) be something like this, in declining order:

- Your spouse
- Your children
- Your parents
- Your siblings
- Your nieces/nephews
- Other people

Under what circumstances might a person die intestate?

1. Plain and simple, they thought they were going to live forever, and didn't bother to write a Will.

2. They really wanted to write a Will, but they were busy, and simply never got around to writing a Will. Too bad, because there is "A ROUND TUIT" elsewhere in this book that might have influenced them to take care of this personal business before they ran out of time.

3. They practiced do-it-yourself law, and wrote a Will that was declared invalid. This would be discovered at the beginning of the probate process, when the Register of Wills would find some legal flaw in the construction of the document itself. It could be something as seemingly simple as not having the proper number of witnesses. Some states require a Will to have two witnesses plus a notary acknowledgement; others do not. If you make a mistake like this, it doesn't matter what your Will says, if it is structurally incorrect, your Will may not be accepted for probate, and your estate will be administered under the intestate laws.

4. Maybe the witnesses could not be found, and the Will therefore will not be accepted by the Register of Wills as valid. Years ago, when a Will was entered for probate, the people who witnessed it would be required to go to the Register of Wills and sign a form stating that they had been present when the Will was signed. It was even done by a process known as reciprocity … if a witness lived far away, they could go to their local court house, sign a form, and the form would be forwarded to the court house where the Will was to be probated. This process became increasingly difficult as time went on, because witnesses couldn't be located or had predeceased the signer of the Will. Worse, their signatures may have been illegible, and it could not be determined who actually witnessed the document.

- Today, a Lawyer will generally structure your Will such that it is "self-proving." What does that mean? It means that it has all of the legal requirements necessary to prove that you were the person who signed the Will, that you were a competent adult at the time, and it will include your signature; your printed name; the date; signatures of the required number of witnesses; printed names and addresses of the witnesses; all signatures on the same page; and notary acknowledgement for your signature and those of your witnesses. Everyone present at the same time. Signed, sealed and delivered!

5.   There could be language in the Will that would make the Will invalid. This could be for one of several reasons: (1) you wrote the Will yourself, and didn't understand what was required to make the Will legal and valid; (2) your Lawyer made a mistake (it happens); or (3) the Will was intentionally (or accidentally) written in such a way that it was declared invalid because of some particular language not considered legal, even though the Will was structured perfectly.

What follows is a true story of a man who died without a Will, owning a house in his own name. All of his other assets were jointly owned with his wife.

> *Once upon a time there was a man who owned a house in his own name. Ownership of the house was never put into joint names with his wife, as were all his other assets. Why not? Because the actual "owner" of the house (that is, as compared to the "legal" owner) was a deadbeat, with a long history of bad credit practices, low credit score, and an enormous list of judgments against him, but he nevertheless wanted a house to live in. He could not legally buy it by himself, although he did have the money to buy it. He was a very nice man in every respect other than how poorly he handled his own personal finances.*
>
> *The man who occupied the house was paying for it by giving the legal owner money every month, as if it were a real mortgage payment. (Let's not speculate as to the source of his income.)*
>
> *This good friend (that is, the legal owner of the house) suddenly died without a Will. He left behind a wife and several adult children. What a mess it created in his family! His wife knew about this other house, but had absolutely no idea of the legal consequences of her husband's ownership of that house.*
>
> *Of course the husband wanted the house to pass to the man who occupied it; <u>but he never wrote a Will saying so.</u> Worse, that house became a taxable asset of the husband's probate estate?*
>
> *Oh, you thought there was no probate when one spouse died, leaving behind a surviving spouse? Sometimes, yes. Sometimes, no. In this instance, the ownership of that one single asset (that house) required that the probate process be started. His wife was appointed Administrator, although, sadly, she had no idea what that meant to her personally, legally, and financially.*
>
> *The wife, not having even the most basic understanding of the probate process, thought she had inherited the house because she was the surviving spouse. But, under the intestate laws of her state, she only inherited a portion of the ownership of the house. Her children inherited the rest! What?*
>
> *Ultimately, the children "disclaimed" their right to inherit under their father's estate, and that still left the wife to complete the probate process for her husband's estate. It also left the wife owning a house she didn't buy, couldn't afford, and didn't want. She had <u>no</u> agreement with the man as to terms of his continued residence in the house, or who would pay the taxes, or how much he would pay to her every month toward a mortgage that she now owed. She didn't even seem to understand that she could have sold the house and made him move out. It was an enormous emotional and financial burden for this woman who still was grieving the sudden loss of her husband.*
>
> *The wife couldn't understand why she owed inheritance tax on the value of this house. After all, didn't the house "technically" belong to that other man? Why shouldn't he be made to pay the inheritance tax?*
>
> *The fault lies with the husband who thought he would live forever, thought that he had plenty of time to take care of his personal business, including writing a Will. Also, he did not include his wife in any discussions about the details of his ownership of that house. She was left mourning, upset, angry, confused and financially damaged. She incurred substantial income loss when her husband died, to say nothing of the expenses of his funeral and estate administration, for which NO planning had been done.*
>
> *In order to avoid the expense of a Lawyer for the entire probate process, from the very beginning, starting at the date of her husband's death, she began doing things by herself, and made terrible mistakes. In a very short time, she incurred a Lawyer's fee of $11,000 for work he did for her after she realized she was in over her head. It was money she did not have. And, there was still much more to be done! She was left grieving, confused and angry. It will take years before this mess is resolved, if it ever is.*
>
> **See what can happen when a man thinks he's going to live forever?**

WILL SUBSTITUTES

Although most people would not think of the following as "Will substitutes," they do, in fact, provide ways for you to pass your assets on to your heirs without a Will.

- Joint tenancy with right of survivorship
- Living trusts
- Tenancy by the entireties
- Payable-on-death accounts (PODs) and Transfer-on-death accounts (TODs)
- IRAs
- Life insurance
- Annuities
- Other assets paid to named beneficiaries

The things listed above describe ways in which you can title ownership of your assets, including everything from a simple savings or checking account to ownership of real estate.

>*In this chapter and in the FINANCIAL chapter, you will read descriptions of true situations where one or more of the above ownership designations determined "who got what" after a person died ... not always with the desired results.*

Ownership designations as stated above are valuable ways to pass your assets to your heirs as long as you understand the ways in which they work and what they will do for you <u>and</u> what they will not do. While each has its own benefits, each also has its own potentially negative consequences if not used properly. I recommend that you have conversations with both your Financial Planner and your Lawyer before titling your assets in any of the above ways to be sure they will accomplish your goals. Too many times, they do not.

DO NOT MISINTERPRET WHAT I JUST SAID AS YOUR
"GET OUT OF JAIL FREE" CARD TO MAKE YOU THINK YOU DON'T NEED A WILL.

I did NOT say that!

WHAT HAPPENS IF NO ONE APPLIES TO THE COURT TO BE APPOINTED ADMINISTRATOR OF AN ESTATE?

Most likely, this situation would only happen if a person has no living family or friends who could step up and be appointed Administrator. But, *someone,* sooner or later, will have to do it if the decedent owns assets at the time of death. The estate will have to be administered one way or another and brought to its legal completion.

In fact, anyone can apply to the court to be appointed Administrator. It could be a creditor of the decedent's. It could be a neighbor. It could be a realtor who is trying to sell the decedent's home.

This is not an easy question to answer, and if you really want to know the answer, your Lawyer can give you a complete explanation.

WHAT IF YOU DON'T HAVE ASSETS SUFFICIENT TO JUSTIFY COURT-SUPERVISED ADMINISTRATION OF YOUR ESTATE?

At some point soon after your death, the Department of Revenue of the state in which you resided will send a form to your last-known address which basically says, "*We know (name) died. Tax is due.*" If you are wondering how the state even knew of your death, remember that computers talk to each other during the night while you're sleeping!

Receipt of this form usually upsets the family, but if there is no tax due, all that is necessary is to say so, sign and date the form and send it back. (*Of course, you will keep a photocopy, right?*) There would probably be no tax due if all of your assets were owned jointly with your spouse, for example, or if you had no assets at all (or very limited assets).

Are you still wondering how the state knew about your death?

> *My mother died at 5 p.m. on a Wednesday. At 9 a.m. the next morning, my sister and I went to our Mother's bank to do a Will search in her safe deposit box; and before we could utter a syllable, the bank clerk saw us and quickly approached us, saying, "We already know your Mother died, and you can't touch her bank box." So much for good customer relations.*
>
> *Excuse me? Both my sister and I were signers on the box, which gave us legal permission to enter the box at any time. Also, the law permits the box to be searched for a Will.*
>
> *But, you ask, how did the bank clerk know our Mother had died so soon after her death? Computers speaking to each other in the night. That's how!*

DON'T FORGET THE DOCUMENTS THAT CAN AFFECT YOU WHILE YOU ARE LIVING

> *Before I get into the subject of Healthcare Powers-of-Attorney and Living Wills, I apologize in advance if suggestions I make, especially relating to these two documents, appear insensitive to the wide spectrum of emotions involved in estate and end-of-life planning. I can understand how you might see it that way.*
>
> *In my life, I am a straightforward person, focused on the task at hand, and I am pretty much able to put my emotions on hold until the task is completed. It is how I survive in the world. You may not be this way. I am saying this to alert you to the fact that your emotions may take over as you think and talk about these documents. I ask that you do your very best to think realistically and practically, to focus on the business aspect of estate planning, while never losing sight of the personal. It may sound difficult, but it can be done.*
>
> *My goals for this book are to make you THINK about the legal, financial and personal situations that are involved in estate planning; to help you navigate the often complicated waters of the legal field known as estate planning in order to accomplish certain tasks which I believe are important, and to try to FEEL the anguish your family will experience if you fail to do what is necessary ... so that you can and will do all things necessary to execute appropriate documents in a timely manner.*
>
> *As I said before, I am not a Lawyer and I am not a psychologist trained in the ways of emotions and the mind. I am, however, an observer of human behavior, and I have seen the good results from careful, thoughtful estate planning, as well as the often predictable, undesirable results from no estate planning.*

To quote Eleanor Roosevelt:

"It is not fair to ask of others what you are not willing to do yourself."

I have taken care of my estate planning.
Now, it's your turn.

So far, the only estate-planning document I have mentioned in regard to estate plans having failed is a Will. But, what if the document that fails is your Healthcare Power-of-Attorney or your Living Will?

Besides a Will, there are other estate planning documents that are even more personal because they may affect you <u>while you are still alive</u>. These include your **Living Will**, your **Healthcare Power-of-Attorney**, and your **Durable Power-of-Attorney**. The instructions you leave for the care you want at the end of your life are about as personal as anything you will ever have to do.

This is where serious personal conversations are needed. Without the conversations, things may not happen as you want them to happen, and the consequences of avoiding the conversations could be dire. It's about COMMUNICATION. *Here's that word again.*

HEALTHCARE POWER-OF-ATTORNEY and LIVING WILL

<u>Caution:</u> It is important that you know and understand that the laws regarding Living Wills, Advance Directives, and Healthcare Powers-of-Attorney vary from jurisdiction to jurisdiction. These are not documents you should prepare by yourself, no matter how many blank forms you can get. You do not want to make any mistakes with these documents.

It is important that you know and understand that a Health Care Power-of-Attorney and Living Will just might be of significantly greater importance to you than a Will. Why?

Because they are documents that may go into effect <u>while you are still living</u> if you should become terminally ill, injured or in a persistent vegetative state – that is, as compared to a Will, that does not go into effect until after your death.

Many people find these documents extremely difficult to think about, let alone talk about or sign; and, because of their discomfort, some people will bury their head in the sands of time or hide behind every excuse in the book in order not to sign them. Believe me, people are very creative with excuses of why they won't do something

---

Do you think it has something to do with dying?
People are born, they live and die. You know that is true.

So, what is it about dying that you are so afraid of?

The fear of death follows from the fear of life. A man who lives fully is prepared to die at any time.

Mark Twain

Still the question remains:

"What are you going to do with the rest of your life *between now and then*?"

Of course, the perfect scenario is that you will never have occasion to use either a Living Will or a Healthcare Power-of-Attorney. But, Life doesn't always work out that way. You NEED those documents.

And, if your choice is to do nothing, the consequences could be dire, even life threatening. Be wise about these documents, make good choices, and protect yourself and your loved ones, because these documents are all about <u>your</u> life, no one else's life. YOUR LIFE!

Are you thinking that maybe you don't need these documents in the first place. After all, you are a careful person. You take care of your health, you take vitamins, your exercise regularly, you don't drink or smoke or "do" drugs, you don't drink-and-drive, you get your cholesterol and blood sugar checked regularly. After all, what could possibly happen? Did you ever hear of auto accidents? Random acts of terrorism? Does the name Terry Schiavo sound familiar?

45

> *Terry Schiavo was a young woman when she collapsed in her home in full cardiac arrest in February 1990. As a result, she suffered massive brain damage due to lack of oxygen.*
>
> *Her husband and her parents fought in court for* **6 years** *about whether to remove Terry from life support, or, praying for a miracle, to leave her languish in a persistent vegetative state indefinitely.*
>
> *This poor woman's face was splashed all over the covers of magazines, newspapers and TV. Talk about invasion of someone's privacy! As her family publicly fought about who was right, it appeared no one cared about her personal dignity?*
>
> *Ugly charges and accusations were thrown back and forth between Terry's husband and her parents. Terry ultimately died at the age of 41 in March of 2005, after years of ugly, time-consuming, expensive, painful, very public humiliation and litigation.*
>
> *Is this what you would want for yourself, to live the last years of your life as Terry did?*
>
> **All it takes is for you to do nothing.**

If you are about to have a Healthcare Power-of-Attorney and a Living Will prepared, there are a few things to think about. The first is DO NOT PREPARE THESE DOCUMENTS YOURSELF! Oh, yes, I know you can download forms from the Internet, and they may even be state-specific. DON'T DO IT!

Oh, wait, I keep forgetting. You <u>can</u> download these forms yourself. Go right ahead. No one is going to stop you. But, you better pray they are the right forms if and when the time comes to use them, because, by then, it will be too late for you to sign.

If you meet with your Lawyer to have the documents prepared, this would be a perfect time for open and honest communication, the time when you tell your Lawyer what you want and do not want in extreme healthcare situations. The documents should reflect you and your wishes. Complete communication is the best way to see that it happens.

In these documents, you will designate the person(s) who will speak and act on your behalf in the event that you can no longer speak and/or act for yourself. The name for this person(s) is your Agent. You cannot afford to select the wrong person for the wrong reasons, because, for you personally, it could turn out to be a matter of life and death.

- In her book, *Last Wish,* Dr. Lauren Van Scoy provides information about end-of-life situations in clear, understandable language from the perspective of a medical professional, yet, at the same time, she clearly explains the connection between these two documents and the medical treatment you may or may not receive.

THINGS TO THINK ABOUT BEFORE APPOINTING AGENTS UNDER YOUR HEALTHCARE DOCUMENTS

I want to point out some things for you to consider as you make the appointments necessary in each of the documents that you will be signing, so that when you meet with your Lawyer, you will already have given these appointments serious thought, and you will be prepared to ask questions and thoroughly discuss the various aspects of your choices with your Lawyer. Each appointment you make could ultimately make an enormous difference in <u>how</u> or even <u>if</u> your wishes are carried out.

Conversations are necessary before you sign your documents. I understand that these conversations are not easy, and I would never imply that making decisions like this is simple or easy; but I do recommend that you don't over-think the process. **Decisions must be made, and you are the person to make them**, so commit your time and energy until you are completely satisfied with your decisions, and until you have taken care of your obligation to document your wishes.

If you do not speak with your family about the kind of care and treatment you want, and <u>do not want</u>, how are they supposed to know? They are not mind readers. If you do not speak the right words to fully express yourself, how do you suppose things will go the way you want them when the time comes? If you choose not to make your wishes known, you may be cared for and treated according to the wishes of your spouse, or your children, or other family members who have completely different points of view, or by medical professionals, or the courts. Is that what you want?

Even if you have signed all the proper legal documents, that doesn't exclude the possibility that your family will squabble about your care, but at least the document provides direction and guidance for the care you want and do not want. In fact, even if you have stated your healthcare wishes in a Living Will, your family could technically (and legally) override that document. YOU MUST MAKE THEM UNDERSTAND THAT YOU NEED THEM TO HONOR YOUR WISHES, that this is about YOUR life, not theirs, and to dishonor your wishes is nothing but pure selfishness on their part.

I realize this sounds harsh, but think about it for a moment before you react.

> *Once upon a time, a woman asked her sister if she would be able to "pull the plug" (as it is euphemistically known) when the time came, and her sister said NO! Her reason was that her religion would not permit it. She was unwilling to put her own beliefs aside and do what her sister was asking her to do. It is a good thing this conversation happened before the document was signed, or worse, before the need arose and the sister refused to act, although she was the designated Agent.*

The person you appoint must be able to stand up to pressure from the medical professionals and even your own family when they disagree with your legally documented wishes … a person who can clearly and firmly say, with conviction, "*No, this is what he or she wants, and this is what he or she does not want,*" and make it stick! The person you appoint must be able to feel what you are feeling, to put themselves in your position, and be willing and confident that they are speaking for you, and not for themselves.

What is required for you to make a good choice in your appointment of an Agent under your Healthcare Power-of-Attorney is for you to choose a person who is willing to speak for you when you cannot speak for yourself, a person who is capable of making serious decisions on your behalf when necessary and appropriate, and is willing to take into consideration your wishes about your own life, and put aside their own beliefs and prejudices … a pragmatic person, a person who thinks with reason, common sense, and logic, a compassionate person who will want only what's best for you, and is willing to see that your wishes are honored to the fullest extent possible, a person who considers their promise to you as sacred. In short, a person who will fight for your rights, even if it is the right to die on your own terms.

There are many factors to be considered before legally designating anyone to act on your behalf at the time when you are no longer able to do so for yourself. In addition, I believe it is essential that you discuss these factors in advance with your Lawyer, before you sign any documents, so that you will be well versed on the consequences of the choices you are making.

Before preparing your legal documents, your Lawyer will ask for the names and addresses of the person(s) you will be naming as your Agents and Substitute Agents, and after you provide the Lawyer with that information, that might be the end of that conversation. It reminds me of the TV show, *Dragnet*, with Joe Friday saying, "*Just the facts, ma'am.*" If you still have questions to ask, ask them. It may be your only opportunity. **Do not allow your Lawyer to brush you off** when you attempt to have an in-depth conversation about your appointments.

Each of these appointments carries with it a lot of responsibility and even liability, so you should not make these choices carelessly or frivolously. You cannot predict the behavior of anyone in an extreme situation. Today, they might say they completely agree with you. Then, when the time comes, they may no longer agree. Again, this is where COMMUNICATION and trust come into play.

As you read further, you will see some examples of why conversations are so important. Before you actually sign the documents, think about the following things:

- Come right out and ask that person if they are willing to act on your behalf or not. Don't be shy. This is the time for you to be strong in standing up for yourself, even if you have never done it before, and even if you are not comfortable doing it.

- It is important that you ask their permission before naming them, to see if they are willing to assume such a responsibility for you.

- It is important for you to give serious thought about the person(s) you intend to appoint, so you can be confident they are up to the task(s) you are assigning to them. Before you make your choices, think about their life situations. Are they in good health themselves? Do they drive and have access to a vehicle at all times? Do they have young children whose care might distract them from your needs? Do they have important jobs or careers that require them to travel regularly? Do they own and operate a business that requires their attention every day? Would they be able to assist you in a moment's notice were you to be suddenly stricken by serious illness or injury? Would they be comfortable meeting and speaking with legal and medical professionals?

- Tell them what will be required of them in a time of need, and let them know that they may consult with your Lawyer if necessary. There are many personal and emotional ... *even religious and spiritual* ... reasons why a person might not want this responsibility, and which would render them unable to honor your wishes. If they express any fear or anxiety about their ability to speak for you if the time comes, you need to know this in advance, and select someone else.

- Give the person the option to decline for any reason whatsoever. Thank them for considering your request.

    - If the person expresses hesitation or unwillingness for any reason whatsoever, you may wish to have a lengthy discussion of why you are asking them, and what your wishes and expectations are, and they will see your point of view and agree with you ... *or not*.

    - If you are unable to convince them to willingly act for you, thank them for considering your request and choose someone else. And, if the next person says no, keep on asking until you find the person you believe and trust to do what you want done. Only then should you sign your name to a Healthcare Power-of-Attorney and a Living Will. To choose the wrong person could mean much difficulty and suffering for you later on. This is no place to make a mistake, so it is important that you get it right.

- Avoid naming two people to serve as joint Agents, even if those two people are your children. If there is disagreement between them, who is there to break the tie? Your Lawyer can construct your documents in such a manner that requires your Agent to consult with other people you designate, but the document can also clearly state that your Agent will make the final determination about any care you receive or do not receive, based upon your expressed wishes as stated in the documents you yourself sign.

- If and when you actually do appoint them, give them a copy of the document, and let them know where you keep the original if it is needed at some point in the future. Also give them the names, phone numbers and addresses of your Lawyer and all your medical professionals.

- Let your Agent know that if, at some point in the future, after you have appointed them, they may resign if they change their mind. Their resignation must be done formally with your Lawyer, but the appointment is not for life.

- And, if your Agent has already begun serving in such capacity, and he/she finds it too difficult, too time-consuming, or too stressful to continue, or if they are no longer able to act due to illness, relocation, change in family circumstances ... *any reason whatsoever* ... they can resign. Be sure to ask your Lawyer how to go about formally and legally resigning so that someone else can be formally appointed as your successor.

- It is my opinion that it is absolutely essential that you appoint a Successor Agent for your Living Will and Healthcare Power-of-Attorney. There are many situations that could arise to make your originally appointed personal representatives unable or unwilling to act or continue to act on your behalf. If you want them to represent you firmly and honestly, you must offer them the comfort of knowing there is a back-up person you selected in the event that your originally appointed Agent feels unable to act.

- Be sure that your primary Agent knows how to get in touch with the Successor Agent in the event that it becomes necessary.

- Generally, a husband will appoint his wife, and *vice versa.*

- If you should find yourself single by virtue of the death of one spouse or by divorce, you may want to appoint one of your adult children. It is not good to appoint two or more children because of potential conflicts among them.

- When considering one of your children, and before signing any documents, know for a fact that he/she is in complete agreement with your intentions and beliefs regarding your end-of-life choices and decisions. Before you sign these documents, you must determine if they are *not* in agreement with you, and will they therefore be able to set aside their own opinions and do only what you ask them to do? If you are not completely confident that they will honor your choices, choose someone else.

> *It would be a good idea to write a letter to your children to clearly express yourself*
> *as to why you made the choice you made. Ask them to honor your wishes and*
> *respect you enough not to fight with each other about the decision you made.*
> *Remind them how much you love them.*

- Do not appoint your first-born "just because," or because his/her feelings would be hurt if you appointed someone else ... unless you are certain your first born is the right person for the job.

- If you are a single adult, you may wish to appoint a sibling; or, if you are a <u>young</u> single adult, you may wish to appoint a parent.

- A single adult may wish to appoint a close friend if they believe the friend knows them well and cares for them enough to take on this responsibility. At the same time, it is essential that you know, beforehand, that that person could withstand pressure from your own family if your friend takes steps they don't approve. This requires in-depth conversations beforehand.

- If you are in a committed relationship, but unmarried, whether heterosexual or otherwise, you may wish to appoint your significant other. On the other hand, you may NOT want to appoint this person for many reasons. This decision requires good, clean, honest communication and decision-making.

- Be sure that your Agent(s) know the names and all contact information for your family, your medical providers, and your legal advisors.

<u>If you are the legally appointed representative of another person</u>, you will be acting on behalf of that person in matters of great importance, possibly in extreme or even life-and-death situations. If you feel, for any reason whatsoever, that you will not be able to perform the duties of your appointment, speak up immediately. Be honest with the person about why you believe you will be unable to fulfill your duties, and ask them to appoint someone else. There is no shame, blame, or guilt that is appropriate in this situation as long as you are honest with each other.

WHAT IF YOU DON'T HAVE
a HEALTHCARE POWER-OF-ATTORNEY or a LIVING WILL?

As previously stated, if you don't have a Will, the law makes provisions for distribution of your estate. But, if you don't have a Living Will and/or Health Care Power-of-Attorney, it gets much more complicated.

Sometimes, a Healthcare Power-of-Attorney and a Living Will are separate documents, but not always.

Under the legal statute of Pennsylvania, the directions in a Living Will are specifically for the purpose of determining the healthcare of a person who has been declared, by medical professionals, to be in a persistent vegetative state with no medical hope of recovery, or to be terminal in the short term. **The law in every state may be different, so it is essential that you have this document prepared by a Lawyer in the state in which you reside.**

If your Living Will specifies that you want no chemo or radiation therapy, it is really saying that if you are in a persistent vegetative state or otherwise terminally ill, no treatment for cancer shall be administered to you.

The document is not to be used to make medical decisions for a person in any other (relatively routine) medical situations, although, in my opinion, the check-list in Living Wills does provide some intention on the part of the person who wrote the document. This is where COMMUNICATION becomes essential; that is, communication between patient and doctor, between patient and family members. The people in your life who will have something to say about your medical care are not mind readers, no matter how well you think they know you, no matter how smart you think they are. They can only know what you want and do not want if you tell them. Once again, COMMUNICATION.

If your spouse or adult child were to become injured and sick, and if they failed to sign these documents to appoint someone to speak for them, you may find yourself applying to the court to be appointed guardian for your spouse or young-adult child. Worse, someone else may want to be guardian, and then you can fight it out in court. It can get ugly and expensive.

In the absence of these documents, the law requires that someone take the legal steps necessary to be appointed as the legal guardian for the injured or ill person. What this can mean is that you will have to hire an attorney and go before a judge to be appointed to take care of your loved one.

Applying for appointment as a legal guardian can be a very public, painful, expensive, degrading legal process that will cost you money for an attorney and court costs, and will probably delay the immediate treatment your injured/sick loved one needs. It will cause upset to everyone involved.

Who is the priority in such situations? NOT YOU! There is a loved one who is in an extreme situation who needs you to take care of them. This is no time to think of yourself. This is no time to delay their treatment by fighting with family, in court or otherwise.

I just asked a Lawyer friend of mine what is the average legal fee for a simple, uncontested guardianship proceedings, and it is $2,500-$3,500 in southeastern Pennsylvania. Guardianship proceedings like the lengthy court contest that Terry Schiavo's family engaged in would cost many thousands of dollars more. Often, the cost is much more than money.

These public court fights serve to satisfy certain fears and needs of the people who are doing the fighting. In my opinion, the person requiring the medical care doesn't benefit all that much, because, in the end, *someone will* be appointed guardian, and that person may not be the person you would have chosen. And, when all the court proceedings are over (even if it is after many years, as in the Terry Schiavo case), that disabled person will eventually pass away, and no one will ever really know what kind of suffering they experienced.

Do you want to spend your life fighting in court?
It could happen, you know.

In my opinion,

- **Worst-case scenario No. 1** **is that you become terminally ill and don't have a Health Care Power-of-Attorney and/or Living Will, thus there is no one you appointed to speak for you when you cannot speak for yourself.**

- **The No. 2 worst-case scenario** **is that you become terminally ill and you DO have these two documents, but no one knows about them, and if they do, they cannot find them!**

- **The No. 3 worst-case scenario** **may be that your family doesn't even know your documents exist in the first place. If you went to the trouble and expense of having your Lawyer prepare a Healthcare Power-of-Attorney and/or a Living Will, and before it's too late, you MUST TELL your loved ones that they exist, and where you keep them! You don't want them to begin court proceedings to get someone appointed as your guardian if you have already done it. It's about communication, remember!**

And, no matter what the reason for the *absence* of the appropriate legal documents,
someone *will* be put through the anguish of applying for legal guardianship in order to take care of you.
Is this what you want?

I know a Lawyer who represents a nursing home where there are many very old residents who have no Healthcare Powers-of-Attorney or Living Wills, and their medical conditions sometimes decline such that a feeding tube is required to sustain their lives. Since the patients have no living relatives, a guardian must be appointed for them to give legal permission for the doctors to insert the feeding tube. It is too late to ask what that person wants, because they are no longer legally competent to state their wishes in a legal writing.

Why do I tell you these things? Because of the situations, family messes, and legal battles that can occur in the absence of these two documents.

Many of you will remember the Terry Schiavo case because it received extreme nationwide media attention a few years ago. The Karen Quinlan case also received widespread attention, but about 20 years before. Both women were young and vibrant when they were rendered comatose (what is now called "persistent vegetative state") because of different circumstances.

Karen Quinlan slipped into a coma at a party in 1975. Her case revolved around the fact that her body was entirely dependent upon machines to sustain life. Her parents decided to remove her from the respirator to allow her body to die in "God's time." The doctors refused to comply with her parents' wishes because Karen was legally an adult and did not have a Living Will or a Healthcare Power-of-Attorney. In those days, these documents were rarely used.

Karen's father had to be appointed her guardian through legal proceedings that lasted more than a year. In March 1976, Karen was removed from the respirator as a result of a unanimous decision by the New Jersey State Supreme Court. The surprise was that she did not immediately die as expected, and so she was moved to a nursing home, where she

> *lived in that persistent vegetative state until June 1985 ...if that can be called living. The family never sought to have the feeding tube removed during those long years while her body remained alive after being removed from the respirator.*
>
> *Karen's family incurred huge debt for her health care, and the loss of control of their own family disrupted and strained the lives of the entire Quinlan family for years.*

Need I say more than the names, Terry Schiavo and Karen Quinlan, to get your attention?

Do you think that either Karen Quinlan or Terry Schiavo intended for their families to suffer this way? Of course not! WHAT WAS MISSING WERE SOME "HARD" CONVERSATIONS WITH FAMILY AND A FEW PIECES OF LEGAL PAPER. The women had been young and healthy, and never dreamed that their lives, and the lives of their respective families, could be turned upside down in a split second. But, it happened.

The medical costs to keep these two women alive were in the millions of dollars. Who do you think paid the bills? *Just asking...*

> *In the Philadelphia "Inquirer" of December 11, 2010, there appeared a very sad story about a 40-ish woman who suffered cardiac arrest while sitting on a park bench in mid-August. When she was found, she had no identification on her except several tattoos, which were photographed and sent to many media outlets in the hope that someone would come forward to identify her. Yes, you read that correctly! No one knew who she was. For quite a while, all attempts to identify her produced no information about her identity.*
>
> *Jane Doe remained unconscious and unresponsive, with no possibility of recovery. She did, however, remain in stable medical condition, and could potentially live in a persistent vegetative state for years. The cost of her care, as of early 2011, was over $250,000, with another $2,000 per day additional expense anticipated. The bill for her care was being paid by the Hospital of the University of Pennsylvania, which agreed to continue to pay for her stay in the hospital or another facility as long as necessary, according to a Hospital spokesperson.*
>
> *Jane Doe could not, however, be placed in residence in a nursing home, because the nursing homes will not accept a patient without a guarantee of payment, which requires a Social Security number, which requires a name. Social Security Administration was unable to issue a "temporary" Social Security number for her without proper identification.*
>
> *Can you see the merry-go-round effect of this terrible situation, to say nothing of the personal, medical, legal and financial consequences.*

This "Jane Doe" case is extreme in that this woman was not quickly identified. It turns out that Jane Doe has a name and a family who had been looking for her. They were upset about the fact that her fingerprints did not show up on any law enforcement system. Although I do not know her present whereabouts, I did read that she and her family were reconnected, although under these tragic circumstances.

What if she did have a wallet and cell phone on her person when she had the heart attack, that would have made it easy to identify her, and while sitting on that park bench, someone robbed her? What if she did not have either in her possession while she was in that park?

I realize that when you are walking or running, it may be cumbersome to have a wallet and a cell phone with you, but if you take only this one incident as an example, it points out the necessity to carry a cell phone and some form of identification on your person AT ALL TIMES. I've stated elsewhere that some people believe everyone should carry a cell phone on their person AT ALL TIMES, "just in case." If you believe these are good ideas, just do them.

HIPAA NOTICE OF PRIVACY PRACTICES

Oh no, not another form! Doctors may now ask their patients to sign this Privacy Notice, which describes how doctors and other medical professionals may use and disclose your protected health information to carry out treatment, payment, or healthcare operations and for other purposes that are permitted or required by law. In this document you will state the names of all persons to whom your personal healthcare information may be disclosed.

Each time my former husband and I went to his doctors' offices, he was given a HIPAA Notice to sign, which allowed his doctors to disclose his medical records to me. Remember, I was not his wife, I was his former wife. But know this: It may not have even mattered if I had been his wife at the time, because, without the HIPAA Notice having been signed by him, the medical professional would not release his information to me. READ THAT AGAIN: The fact that you may be married to the patient does not necessarily entitle you to their medical information unless they have signed a HIPAA Privacy Notice. Be safe, not sorry.

WHERE AM I SUPPOSED TO KEEP MY LIVING WILL and HEALTHCARE POWER-OF-ATTORNEY?

I have heard it suggested that if you have a Living Will and Healthcare Power-of-Attorney, you keep a copy with you <u>at all times</u>: In your car, in your desk, in your briefcase, in your purse, on your person. I once heard it suggested that copies of your documents should be hung on the side of your refrigerator with a clip so that if you ever require emergency assistance, the EMT's can easily find them. Not a bad idea!

The ICE (in case of emergency) cards my husband and I carry in our wallets and in our cars state clearly that we have such documents in our home.

It occurred to me some years ago that I should wear some kind of Medic Alert jewelry AT ALL TIMES so that, if I required emergency assistance, the EMT's would see the Medic Alert symbol, and act accordingly. What I did get is a dime-size round gold charm, with the Medic Alert symbol on one side, and the words "living will" on the other side. Will it stop EMT's or at least slow them down? I certainly hope so!

I feel so strongly about not wanting heroic life-support measures if I am in a terminal condition , that I have even entertained the extreme thought of having the letters DNR tattooed on the back of my hand near the base of my thumb. In a medical facility, it is widely known that DNR means "do not resuscitate," ... but what if the EMT mistakenly thought, on first glance, before locating any form of ID, that the DNR tattoo letters represented my initials instead? It could happen, you know. It is not beyond the realm of possibility. So far, I haven't gotten a tattoo ... I hear it hurts a lot!

In the summer of 2012, there was an article in the newspaper about seniors having tattoos put on to their chests stating that they do not want cardiac resuscitation or other life-saving measures. Although there may come a time when emergency personnel honor such instructions, as of this time EMTs are not legally required to be guided by the tattoos. So, anyone inclined to get such a tattoo had better have the documents to back up their request.

The intention, of course, is to keep overzealous emergency workers from taking heroic life support measures to keep you alive if you do not want that. Keep in mind that medical professionals are obliged to do everything possible to keep you alive **in the absence of written, legal documentation to the contrary**. They are just trying to protect themselves from law suits. Be smart about this. It's about protecting yourself.

There is no time to be running around your house looking for your documents in an emergency!
You must be able to put your hands on them in a moment's notice!
NO KIDDING!

DO YOU GET IT NOW?

Or do you need more information to support my claim that it is absolutely necessary for you to sign a Healthcare Power-of-Attorney and/or a Living Will, and take all the legal steps required to put them into effect?

HOW MUCH LONGER WILL YOU AVOID DOING THIS BEFORE IT'S TOO LATE?

> **Procrastination is one of the most common and deadliest of diseases,**
> **and its toll on success and happiness is heavy.**
>
> Dr. Wayne Dyer

You can see that I've given this a lot of thought ... *maybe too much* ... but then, how much is too much if the Jane Doe situation could happen to anyone?

> *Once upon a time, a woman had her very elderly mother (a widow) living with her for several years. Her mother was not ill in any respect, just quite old and fragile, and she generally got around in a wheelchair.*
>
> *This woman took her mother with her when she went to the gym, or to the "Y" for swimming lessons, or to her book club at the library, and to many restaurants, art galleries and concerts, and she provided her mother with a very lively, interesting last few years, spent with interesting, stimulating people. She was always mentally alert and enjoyed socializing with and meeting new people.*
>
> *The woman, herself in her 70s, realized that a situation could happen that she, herself, might became injured or ill, and worried about what would happen to her mother in such a situation when there might be no time to scramble for her mother's documents in an emergency.*
>
> *So she had a copy of her mother's Living Will reduced, and along with copies of her mother's Medicare card, and a few other important papers, placed those photo reproductions in a small pouch designed for carrying cash on your body when you are traveling. Her mother thereafter always had this pouch on her person AT ALL TIMES.*

It only takes an auto accident, or a non-predictable medical event to thrust you and your family into the courts to sort out the details of the rest of your life.

IS THAT WHAT YOU WANT?

Of course, everyone knows that the cost of medical and residential care for people in these situations is exorbitant! But what about the incalculable cost to their families in anguish, fear, stress, financial damage, and family conflicts.

Nobody goes out in the morning thinking today is the day I'll be injured in a car accident, or that lightning will strike me today and render me in a persistent vegetative state for years! BUT THESE THINGS HAPPEN. Everyone knows this is true. These occurrences are, for the most part, completely unpredictable, as random as any terrorist attack.

Jane Doe, Terry Schiavo and Karen Quinlan had certain things in common when they were stricken with life-altering medical situations. They were young. They were healthy. They had no expectation that such a terrible thing could happen to them. All three women found themselves in a most horrific place ... caught between the worlds of the living and the dead. And, you must remember that they are not the only three people who have experienced such tragedies. It could happen to you or someone you love. It could happen to one of your kids when they do drugs or drink-and-drive. It can happen to anyone, any time, any place. You already know this, don't you, so why am I telling you this?

BECAUSE I WANT YOU TO BE <u>DISTURBED</u> ENOUGH
TO SIGN THE DOCUMENTS BEFORE IT'S TOO LATE!

One can only imagine the difference in their lives and the lives of their families if these three women had signed a Healthcare Power-of-Attorney and a Living Will before they were stricken.

> ***What if Jane Doe left a cat or a dog behind in her home?*** *Just asking...*

I REPEAT:

A <u>HEALTH CARE POWER-OF-ATTORNEY</u> and a <u>LIVING WILL</u>
MAY TURN OUT TO BE THE MOST IMPORTANT DOCUMENTS YOU WILL EVER SIGN.

**I feel so strongly about Healthcare Powers-of-Attorney and Living Wills
that I believe that every person 18 years of age and older NEEDS THEM!**

Why? Because I have read about and personally seen the legal and financial messes that result when a young adult does not have these documents.

> *Note: In the FINANCIAL chapter, you will read about what happened after a college student was injured and comatose for months before he died. He had outstanding student loan debt for which his parents co-signed, but he did not have a Durable Power-of-Attorney. A very sad tale.*

You may be that child's parent, but, without that appropriate legal piece of paper, you may or may not be authorized to make medical decisions for that child because he/she is at or over the age of consent. The laws about this kind of medical situation vary from state to state. Just know that **your young-adult child needs his/her own Healthcare Power-of-Attorney and Living Will, and that's that**! You can agree or disagree with this opinion, but in the end, if your child does not have the properly executed documents, you may find out what must be done to take care of your own child. And you won't like it!

Having said that, however, the law in some places changed several years ago that allows for parents to have some say in the care of their young adult (unmarried) children. But, don't count on this as your "get-out-of-jail-free" card ... as your excuse to put it off until LATER. Talk with your Lawyer to see what is required, and do it today.

Chances are good that your child is not going to college locally. Were that child to become seriously ill or injured while away from home, it would mean that you have to travel some distance, to a place with which you are unfamiliar, deal with Lawyers and doctors you don't know. How would you go about finding a competent Lawyer if your child's medical emergency occurs in another state? At night? On a week-end? How would you accomplish all of this in time to see that your child received the proper emergency medical attention in a timely fashion?

If your child had signed a Healthcare Power-of-Attorney and/or a Living Will before leaving for college, you could have kept the original with your important papers such that you could put your hands on it in a moment's notice. And, your child could have carried a card the size of a credit card in his/her wallet, stating that he/she executed a Healthcare Power-of-Attorney (and a Living Will), and stating the whereabouts of those original documents, and who is to be contacted in an emergency. Medical decisions are regularly handled by phone, FAX, and overnight mail. All it takes is your child's having this one piece of paper, legally signed, and safeguarded in the event of need.

**What is so difficult about this,
such that you have not taken care of this one piece of your family's personal business?**

When I see all the shopping parents do for their kids to go off to college, getting all the electronic stuff the kids need, all their clothing and furnishings for their dorm room, getting all their health certificates and shots, I have to ask why parents don't take care of this one particular part of the personal legal business of their child who is about to live away from home for the first time.

<u>YOU READ IT HERE</u>

YOUR 18+ YEAR OLD UNMARRIED CHILD NEEDS A HEALTH CARE
POWER-OF-ATTORNEY AND A LIVING WILL **PERIOD. END OF SENTENCE.**

You are free to AGREE OR DISAGREE, DO IT or NOT DO IT!
IT'S ENTIRELY UP TO YOU.

You know that your job, as a parent, is to see that your children are legally protected in the event of a medical emergency. If you don't do it, who will? Without these documents, you may find yourself dealing with the consequences, and the consequences are time-consuming, degrading, painful and expensive.

CALL YOUR LAWYER TODAY AND MAKE AN APPOINTMENT TO TAKE CARE OF THIS!

WHAT DOES A HEALTHCARE POWER-OF-ATTORNEY DO FOR YOU?
HOW DOES IT WORK?
WHY DO YOU NEED ONE?

I have said in certain instances that you really do not need a particular document.
In this case, I say the opposite.
I say you need this one, like it or not.

Of course, you already know that you can die without it. The question for you to think about is how will you be cared for if you don't die suddenly. Everyone hopes for a quick, pain-free death. Unfortunately, it doesn't happen that way for many people.

In your Healthcare Power-of-Attorney, you will choose the person you want to make some medical decisions for you, and speak for you when you cannot speak for yourself; for example, if you were to become seriously injured, unconscious, or in a persistent vegetative state.

This is an enormous responsibility to place on the shoulders of another person, but the burden can be lightened by your having good, timely and honest communication between you and that person, and then signing the proper legal documents to see that your wishes are carried out. You may even want to have a joint meeting with your Lawyer to better explain every aspect of this document, in particular, the responsibilities of your Agent when the time comes.

Once you, yourself, know what you want and do not want for your care and treatment if you become seriously or terminally ill, you must have appropriate and timely conversations with your loved ones before it's too late. Thus, the family meeting mentioned hereinafter.

If you hesitate, or worse, if you fail to have these important conversations, you must realize that you are choosing to put your welfare into the hands of others who may not think as you do, may not want the things you want, or may not even have the faintest notion of what you want because you did not COMMUNICATE your wishes. COMMUNICATION is absolutely necessary, whether you like it or not! In your whole life, you may never again be called upon to have such serious talks. Keep in mind this is all about YOUR LIFE and the lives of your loved ones! That counts for something, doesn't it?

If, after appropriate consultation with your medical providers, it is determined that you will not recover, your Agent is the person who would ultimately instruct the medical professionals to discontinue life support for you because that is what you stated you wanted in your Healthcare Power-of-Attorney and Living Will.

Talk about a burden! But you must keep in mind that your Agent is **not** responsible for making the actual decisions. You already made the decisions and preserved those decisions in your documents. **Your Agent is there to see that your wishes are carried out and to speak for you when you cannot speak for yourself.**

You must be honest with yourself, and know whether or not you would want to be kept on life support indefinitely … *as in years* … with medical evidence suggesting no possibility of recovery. And, having made your decision for yourself, can you make this person (your Agent) understand what you would want, and ask them if they can see that life support is terminated for you if the time comes and if that is your choice?

BELIEVE IN MIRACLES,
BUT DO WHAT IS NECESSARY ANYWAY.

Once upon a time, before Healthcare Powers-of-Attorney, there was woman who fought a courageous 2-year battle against cancer. She and her husband had many important conversations about her treatment, care, and ultimate death. She told her husband and four adult children that she would know when it was over, and she asked them to respect her wishes when the time came. They all agreed.

Sadly, things didn't go as well as they probably should have, because when it came time to terminate her life support, two of her children balked and their refusal to accept their mother's death caused very bad feelings in the family. This is exactly what their mother did not want to happen, and that is why she talked with them beforehand. Still, they felt they could not let her go. A vote among them was 3-2 in favor of terminating life support, and soon she died.

> *No one wants to see their mother leave them forever. It is understandable that the two children who balked did not want to lose their mother. Neither did her husband or her other two children. The two who resisted were only doing what was natural ... they were fighting to keep their mother alive. She believed (and her husband and her other children believed) she had suffered more than her fair share in this lifetime.*
>
> *When a loved one understands their need to let go of this life, who are you to be so selfish as to keep them from the journey their spirit must go on?*

What I always hope is that the patient is not aware of their own circumstances, or that they are not aware of the family fighting, but that is not something we can know with certainty.

> What if you were either terminally ill or comatose, with very little hope of recovery, or worse, in a persistent vegetative state, and lying in a hospital bed, hooked up to all sorts of machines to keep you alive ... <u>and you can hear everything that is said in the room, but you cannot respond!</u>
>
> All you can hear is your family fighting over your care, hasty, unpleasant words shouted back and forth among people who are supposed to love you! To me, this would be HELL on earth! I'm sure you have heard it said that there are worse things than death. This might just be one of those things!

When family members act this way, they are speaking out of their own emotional pain, fears, and anxiety, refusing to face the loss of their loved one. But, are they speaking in the best interests of the loved one, whose life is ebbing away, possibly in pain every minute? I don't think so, but then again, it's easy for me to say, because it is not my loved one lying in that bed.

At that point, it may be an act of loving and compassionate generosity to set the person free ... that is, to let them die as pain free and peacefully as possible. This is where palliative care and hospice come into play, coupled with good, honest, sensitive conversations among family members.

When the family is not yet ready to contemplate this possibility, it may be time for some counseling. The Hospice staff will be able to recommend counselors for you.

As with Terry Schiavo's situation, the patient's family may insist that their relative is getting better every day, even in the face of overwhelming medical and scientific evidence to the contrary. So they put loud, unreasonable demands on the medical staff to take all possible heroic efforts to keep their loved one alive **at all cost**, including <u>threatening to sue</u> if their demands are not met.

It is at this point that many medical professionals will give in to the demands of the family and keep the patient alive indefinitely. Why? Because they don't want to get sued. It's that simple. Ever wonder who pays for such expensive hospitalization and litigation? *Just asking...*

And before we finish with the subject of what can happen in the absence of a Healthcare Power-of-Attorney, consider what can happen to a person in your family who steps up and volunteers to be your court-appointed guardian in the situation where you had no Healthcare Power-of-Attorney. Because they never had a serious discussion with you about your wishes, they could make a decision on your behalf that other members of your family don't like, or worse, make a decision for you that you would never have wanted for yourself? Will this person require court intervention to protect themselves from being sued by your family. IS THAT WHAT YOU WANT TO HAPPEN? Do you really want to leave a legacy of family feuding over your care, just because you refused to take care of your own personal business?

If you can, even for a split second, see the possibility of one member of your family suing another over a decision about **<u>your</u>** care that they don't like, you MUST PREVENT THIS FROM HAPPENING by signing a Healthcare Power-of-Attorney and a Living Will. And, you must tell them they are not to fight about your care, and to honor your request. It is your life, not theirs.

By now it probably sounds to you like I am a broken record, stuck in repeat mode, but I am trying to impress upon you the absolute need to take care of this aspect of your own personal business ... NOW!

Most of this kind of pain and suffering can be avoided if you just sign a Healthcare Power-Of-Attorney. What are you waiting for? Call your lawyer today, and just do it! Who knows? You could be injured in a car accident on the way to the lawyer's office.

LIVING WILL

A Living Will may be considered a companion document to a Healthcare Power-of-Attorney. They are usually, but not always, separate documents, although I have seen the two documents combined into one.

- In the Healthcare Power-of-Attorney, you choose the person(s) who will speak for you if you are unable to speak for yourself.

- In a Living Will, you state your wishes regarding the kinds of medical care <u>you</u> <u>want</u> and <u>do</u> <u>not</u> want. It is essential that you know and understand that the directions you give under a Living Will are not for routine medical conditions or treatment. They are for extreme end-of-life situations where you may not want to be kept alive by artificial means for any additional length of time if there is no hope for your recovery.

What follows is an example of a common version of a Living Will (a/k/a Advance Directive):

I, _____, being of sound mind, willfully and voluntarily make this declaration **if I become incompetent** (*emphasis supplied*). This declaration reflects my firm and settled commitment to refuse life-sustaining treatment under the circumstances below.

I direct my attending physician to withhold or withdraw life-sustaining treatment <u>that serves only to prolong the process of my dying</u> if I should be in a terminal condition or in a state of permanent unconsciousness (*emphasis supplied*).

I direct that treatment be limited to measures to keep me comfortable and to relieve pain, including any pain that might occur by withholding or withdrawing life-sustaining treatment.

In addition, if I am in the condition described above, I feel especially strongly about the following forms of treatment:

I do(_____) do not(_____) want cardiac resuscitation.

I do(_____) do not(_____) want mechanical respiration.

I do(_____) do not(_____) want tube feeding or any other artificial or invasive form of nutrition .

I do(_____) do not(_____) want hydration (water).

I do(_____) do not(_____) want blood or blood products.

I do(_____) do not(_____) want any form of surgery.

I do(_____) do not(_____) want any form of invasive diagnostic tests.

I do(_____) do not(_____) want kidney dialysis.

I do(_____) do not(_____) want antibiotics.

I do(_____) do not(_____) want chemotherapy, radiation, or other form of cancer treatment.

Once you have made decisions for yourself, you will check the boxes of your choice, sign and date the document, have it witnessed and notarized, and have your Agent's Acknowledgement form attached.

> - You can <u>choose</u> to find this list *terrifying*, <u>or</u>
>
> - You may <u>choose</u> to find it *liberating*, as it removes the fear of decision-making
> when the time comes and emotions are running high.

I've seen people so frightened by this list that they refused to sign the document! They were generally unwilling to be educated beyond their fear as to what the various choices mean and do not mean. If you are uncertain, check with your medical professional before you sign the document, but do not be one of those people whose choice is not to have a Living Will. The items on the check-list are not for routine health problems; they are for a time if/when you become terminally ill or disabled with no possibility of recovery. Get past your fears, ask questions, educate yourself, and sign the document. Your family will thank you.

In her book, *Last Wish,* Dr. Van Scoy gives first-person examples from the medical perspective, of what can happen if a person has a Living Will, and what can happen if a person does not. She points out that if you have checked the box saying you do not want CPR or a breathing tube, for example, remember that you are saying that for the time when you are in a terminal condition and not expected to recover. It does not mean that you might not receive CPR if your medical condition warrants it in order to help you recover, or it has not yet been determined that you are terminal. This being said, if you NEVER want life support under any circumstances whatsoever, then you must clearly say so in your Living Will; and if that is your decision, the language of the document must be changed accordingly.

A Living Will is not a document to be taken lightly. It is a life-and-death piece of paper, and requires that you get it right the first time, as you define "right" for yourself.

If you think that checking off your choices is difficult, think about the families of Terry Schiavo, Karen Quinlan, and some of the people written about in Dr. Van Scoy's book, and consider what those families were put through because those people did not have Healthcare Powers-of-Attorney or Living Wills. The families did their best to say what they *believed* their loved ones would have wanted for themselves, but without the legal paper to back it up, it was only speculation.

You can forgive those two young women to some degree because they were healthy and not expecting to find themselves in a persistent vegetative state, and the documents were not in common use at the time. Or, can you? Even without the documents, a person could always talk about their wishes with their family, to at least give them some guidelines. Talking about such things will not bring on sudden death. And, as I have said elsewhere, it is my genuine belief that every person 18 years of age or older needs these two documents.

By signing a Living Will <u>*now*</u>, you will be making your wishes known while you are still vibrant, healthy, and competent. You do not want to wait until you become seriously ill to make these decisions, because your judgment may be clouded by drugs, pressure from your family, or your own fears and anxieties. Also, it is possible that you could wait too long, until a time when you would be considered "legally incompetent" and therefore unable to sign a legal document giving instructions for your care. WHY WAIT?

Remember that the person you appoint as your Agent to speak for you must clearly know and understand your wishes, and be strong and able to stand up to pressure from family and medical professionals to see that your wishes are carried out. Choose this person wisely! This person will be assisting you in making possible life-and-death decisions for you while you are still alive (that is, as opposed to your Executor, who will be handling your affairs after you have passed away).

The person you appoint as your Agent under your Healthcare Power-of-Attorney should be the same person designated to act for you under your Living Will. The worst case would be if you named two different people, and they have opposing opinions and ultimately, a serious disagreement about your care. Who do you think will be in the position to make the final decisions? Maybe the courts. Is that what you want? No, it is not what you want.

Healthcare Powers-of-Attorney and Living Wills are documents that are only effective during your lifetime, and EXPIRE WHEN YOU DIE. The person(s) you appoint under these two documents will have no authority or responsibilities whatsoever after your death.

IF YOU HAVE AGREED TO ACT AS AGENT FOR SOMEONE

I believe when someone agrees to be Agent under the Healthcare Power-of-Attorney and Living Will of a loved one, they have made a sacred promise to carry out the wishes of another person. It may be very, very hard to keep your word, but keep you word you must.

If you have agreed to act as Agent for someone and if there has been a Successor Agent also appointed to act in the event that you, yourself, cannot, there are two things you must do while you are acting as Agent:

No. 1:   Firmly and completely honor the wishes and instructions of the person who appointed you, to the best of your ability.

It is entirely possible that you may find yourself in the middle of a family feud, whether or not you are a member of the family. In fact, if you are *not* a member of the family, it could be even worse if there are others in the family who disagree with what you are doing. They will only remember that their loved one asked *you*, and not them, and all of their negative feelings will be focused on you. It can be very unpleasant. I speak from experience.

You must do your best to make them understand that you are doing what you were asked to do, having had sufficient conversations with the person who appointed you, wherein you talked about what that person wanted and did not want. The family may not like what you are saying and doing, and may even take legal steps to have you removed as Agent. Notwithstanding what they say or do, keep in mind that you are the person who was trusted to do what someone asked you to do, you are the person in the position of authority until you resign or until a court orders you to renounce your position.

The wishes of the person may be in direct conflict with what the family wants for them. Keep in mind that they are suffering, afraid of the loss of their loved one, and may be handling their emotions badly. If the only emotion they know is anger, it may be pointed directly at you. What I am saying is to be prepared to deal with very difficult people and decisions, even while you, yourself, are in the midst of your own suffering at the anticipated loss of this person you care about enough to assist them in taking care of their personal business at what could turn out to be the end of their life.

When I was the Agent for my former husband, in the final weeks of his life, I put my emotions aside in order to accomplish the tasks at hand. He trusted me to do what he asked me to do, and I did, to the best of my ability. His family disagreed publicly and ruthlessly, and made it difficult for me at several levels. Still, I never lost sight of what had to be done, and of the fact that he trusted me to do the things that were necessary and important to him. So, I say to you, be prepared for nasty words and accusations, disagreements, differences of opinion, misunderstandings, hurt feelings, etc. Remember that they, too, are suffering, and you are an easy target for their very strong emotions. Don't take it personally! (Easier said than done.)

Maybe you will be fortunate and never have to experience any of those negative situations or deal with the extreme emotions that can arise when someone you love is injured, ill, or dying. I pray that will be your experience, because it is hard enough to be in emotional pain yourself, let alone have to deal with all that negative emotion coming at you like poisoned arrows all the while you are just trying to honor your word to a seriously ill or dying person.

There may even be times when you have to stand up against the medical (or legal) professionals, and remind them of the stated wishes of the person who appointed you to speak for them. Be strong and stay focused on the wishes and instructions of the person who appointed you.

No. 2:   Take good care of yourself physically, emotionally, and spiritually.

In my opinion, the things listed below are absolute musts! You cannot allow your own health and wellbeing to suffer during this difficult time when someone is counting on you to do for them what they cannot do for themselves … or you will not be able to do the tasks that you have agreed to do.

- You must *try* to eat well. I say that gently, remembering how easily I succumbed to donuts while sitting with my former husband in a hospital room as he lay dying. Try very hard not to live on junk food; BUT, *and it's a big but,* if it helps you to manage your stress level to eat donuts or ice cream or pizza every now and then, give yourself permission to do it! You can't allow yourself to go to pieces for want of some junk food. You can go back to healthy eating when the crisis has passed.

- <u>Try to get enough sleep</u> … naps are wonderful! Relax whenever you can steal a few moments.

- <u>Showers and bubble baths</u> provide relief and restoration for a tired body and spirit.

- If you are accustomed to regular <u>exercise, yoga, massage, or chiropractic adjustments,</u> do your best to fit them into your schedule, but recognize it may not be possible for a little while.

- If you are the kind of person who turns to <u>prescription medication</u> to handle stress, you may have to speak with your doctor in order to be able to function, but <u>do not allow yourself to become dependent upon such medication.</u> There are better ways to handle stress, and you know that is true.

- <u>Give yourself permission to cry</u> if that's what you feel like doing. Crying will relieve some of the pressure you are feeling. It is not a sign of weakness, but of self-expression, and, in this case, may even be self-preservation.

- While this may sound like a tall order, do your very best to <u>surround yourself with positive people, pleasant situations, soothing music, and beauty.</u> Do not feel that you are being self-indulgent! Depending on the time of year, actually *see* the snow or the brilliant colors of autumn. Relax to the soothing sound of rain. Enjoy the colors of the sunset and the beauty of spring flowers.

- <u>Treat yourself to a bunch of flowers</u> every now and then.

- <u>If you have a cat or dog, pet them as often as possible.</u> The simple act of petting them will reduce your blood pressure and your stress level.

- <u>If you need emotional support, get it!</u> You agreed to do a job for a person who is unable to do it for themselves, and if you need help doing it, ask for it.

- <u>If you need spiritual counseling,</u> or if you need help praying, you know where to go to get it.

- If you need a break … a few hours, a day, a week-end … ask for help. There are people who are willing to help, but need to be asked. This is no time to be shy. Someone is counting on you.

- And, if the time comes when you are absolutely, without a doubt, no longer able to function as Agent, you must step aside and allow the Successor Agent to take over where you left off. It is not a crime to have reached the end of your tolerance level. You're only human after all!

- At all times throughout these difficult days, be aware of what is happening to you, and be good to yourself.

WHAT IF THOSE TWO DOCUMENTS ARE THE ONLY THINGS THAT SEPARATE YOU FROM A LIVING HELL OR A GOOD DEATH?

Be honest, and ask yourself if you want to live out whatever few days you may have left, hooked up to machinery keeping you alive? Do you want to put your family into emotional pain and conflict and financial ruin, and cost the American taxpayers untold millions for your end-of-life care (*remember Terry Schiavo and Karen Quinlan*)?

If you answer is NO, then call your Lawyer TODAY and get a Living Will and a Healthcare Power-of-Attorney prepared, and when the documents are ready, SIGN THEM immediately. Other than actually signing the documents, the most important thing you can do for yourself (and, ultimately for your family) is to TALK ABOUT THESE THINGS BEFORE IT'S TOO LATE, to tell them how you feel and what you <u>expect</u> of them when the time comes for you to require extreme end-of-life medical care. Those conversations may make the difference between whether or not your family fights with each other and with the medical professionals when the time comes.

> **Any feelings of anxiety you may have talking about these things now,**
> **are tiny compared to the feelings of regret you'll have if you don't.**
>
> Dr. Phillip C. McGraw (Dr. Phil)

Follow the suggestions I've made about selecting the right person to see that your wishes are carried out, and then go live your life to the fullest degree possible.

The primary question for me is how well a Living Will and a Healthcare Power-of-Attorney will hold up against pressure from family and the medical and legal establishment. I choose to believe that signing these two legal documents, in particular, will give me the best chance to have my end-of-life healthcare issues handled my way …

I urge you to be proactive in contacting your Lawyer at least once every year to see if there are any changes in the laws regarding Living Will and Powers-of-Attorney that could affect you and your family. There is no benefit to sitting around and worrying if a conversation with your Lawyer can put your mind at ease.

And, should your Lawyer contact you first, requesting an appointment to update you on the laws regarding these two important documents, make the appointment, show up, and pay his fee if he sends you a bill. Does your plumber ever do anything for nothing? *Just asking...*

BREAKING NEWS!

In *The Philadelphia Inquirer* of May 6, 2011, there appeared an article by D. J. Tice, commentary editor of the Minneapolis Star Tribune, entitled: "Health Care's Ugliest Truth." The main point in his article, as written in the following sentence, is:

"HEALTH CARE ALWAYS FAILS IN THE END."

In my opinion, that is the most straightforward, honest statement I know about what really happens at the end of life. EVERYONE DIES SOONER OR LATER, no matter what medical procedures were used to keep them alive.

Remember that line I put elsewhere about Humpty Dumpty and how all the king's horses and all the king's men couldn't put Humpty together again? Well, Mr. Tice's comment is similar:

> *"Even Bill Gates and Warren Buffet, with all their billions,*
> *will eventually be unable to buy another day of wellness or life."*

AGENT'S ACKNOWLEDGEMENT

You'll recall that the term, Agent, is the name for the person you choose to act on your behalf under the terms and conditions of your Living Will, Healthcare Power-of-Attorney, and Durable Power-of-Attorney. Successor Agent is the term for the person you designate to act if the originally named person is unable, unwilling, or unavailable.

One of the things that I like about a Living Will and a Healthcare Power-of-Attorney is the fact that they have attached to them a separate page known as "Agent's Acknowledgement." The Agent's Acknowledgement is a form which the person you designate to be your Agent signs (with appropriate witnessing and a notary seal), stating that they formally agree to serve as your Agent.

Before that person signs the Acknowledgement page, you will effectively have been FORCED to have a conversation with that person in which you ask them to be your Agent. This conversation between you and that person requires open, honest, timely communication between the two of you. This is where COMMUNICATION comes into play. And, as I have said elsewhere, if that person so much as "blinks," choose someone else.

It is also essential that you ask your Successor Agent if they are willing to act in the event that your appointed Agent cannot or will not, for any reason whatsoever. It would help if they knew each other, but I don't suppose that's absolutely necessary.

Your Lawyer will insert the name of your Agent and the Successor Agent into each document, so you should have their verbal agreement to serve before you give their names to your Lawyer … that is, unless you don't mind paying the Lawyer another fee to re-draft your documents if there is a change in your designated Agents.

TIME TO TAKE A BREAK!

If you aspire to the highest place, it is no disgrace to stop at the second, or even the third, place.

Cicero

It's good to take a break every now and then. It gives you time to rest, to look at what you've accomplished and give yourself a pat on the back for a job well done. Breaks refresh your body and spirit, and help you renew your commitment to accomplishing your goals. But before we get too far into the subject of a break, let me ask you:

"What have you done to deserve a break? Have you met with your Lawyer and signed the 4 major documents, or at least, is your Lawyer in the process of drafting them right now?"

"NO," you say.

"Why not? When are you planning to meet with your Lawyer and get this process started? And, don't give me some lame excuse that you'll do it later. This is ME you're talking to!"

"I just didn't get around to it."

"Oh, no, that excuse won't work either. Have you at least begun organizing your important papers? and reducing the 'piles' to put them into your BIG BOOK?"

- [The BIG BOOK is described in detail in the RECORD-KEEPING CHAPTER.]

"NO!"

"Why not?"

"Because I think the BIG BOOK is a stupid idea." [Ouch!]

"OK! I never said you had to use <u>my</u> system, but you <u>will</u> need a system of some kind, don't you agree? Do you have a different system in mind, one that will accomplish the same things as the BIG BOOK, only by a different route?"

"Well, no I don't. I just find the whole process boring and overwhelming."

"So, you just stopped. Is that what you are saying?"

"Yup, that's pretty much it."

Most people never run far enough on their first wind to find out they've got a second.

William James

"And you think you deserve a break? I don't agree. What have you done to earn a break? Before you take a break, will you agree to call your Lawyer, make an appointment, and gather all the information the Lawyer will need to draft your documents."

"All right. I suppose I can at least do that much."

"Will you agree to begin again after you do take an EARNED break?"

"All right."

I never said you have to complete your end-of-life planning in a particular amount of time. There is much to do, and it requires a lot of thinking, talking and action. Take a deep breath, relax, give yourself credit for what you have done so far, and begin again. As I said before, estate planning may seem difficult, but it is not impossible.

> ***If you do anything for too long, it starts to lack edge, it becomes too easy.***
> ***Easy** is the kiss of death.*
>
> Julia Ormond

This is no small task before you. So, allow yourself to take a break. It's not a bad thing. JUST DON'T STOP BECAUSE IT'S TOO HARD OR BORING (or for any of those other easy excuses you regularly use to get out of doing something you don't feel like doing).

So, go ahead, take a break when you need one. Relax and enjoy the journey, always keeping the goal in mind. Were you to accomplish all the things suggested in this book, it would be amazing, because I'm not even sure it is possible. Doing this work is a _process_, not a single event. There are some very big steps and decisions that will take time. Just don't let "*time*" be your excuse for putting things off until that day when it really is too late.

After you have a **reasonable** break, begin again. The break could be one day, a week, maybe even a month if your life's activities require that you put aside this work that long … that is, as long as you have the really important things taken care of before giving yourself permission to slack off.

You know what you have already accomplished, and you know what remains to be done. Focus again on the priority items and make the hard choices. **They won't kill you!**

> **Of course, there is always that one possibility that cannot be ignored.**
> **You can do nothing!**

NO WHINING!

My Fitness Trainer has a sign in his studio that says NO WHINING. Why do you suppose it doesn't say NO COMPLAINING? Because he doesn't want Clients who whine; they are usually not serious about accomplishing their goals.

> How serious are you about accomplishing your goals about planning for the rest of your life?

His sign is written this way because he knows there is a big difference between complaining and whining! A legitimate complaint says that something is wrong, and requires correction or improvement, or at the very least, some discussion. WHINING is the way 3-year old children express unhappiness at having to do something they don't want to do.

Is that why you are **whining** … because you are starting to feel like you don't want to do the things suggested in this book? Are you starting to feel pressured to do things you don't want to do? Do you hear your mother's voice again? [*"Do your homework; pick up your socks; take out the trash."*] Eee-gad! *"Will she never stop nagging me?"*

Excuses, excuses: *"It's too hard. It will take "forever" to finish, so why even bother? What does it really matter? I don't feel like doing it. I need more time. I have to think about it?"*

What was that last one? *You have to think about it?* Are you kidding me? **You've been thinking about it for years.** When you say you need more time to think about something, is that your way of saying you really don't want to do it? Gotcha!

Some things require thinking, and some things do not. If your house were on fire, would you rush to put it out, or would you want time to think about it first? If a car was speeding toward you, would you quickly move out of the way, or would you want more time to think about it first? When something is important to a person, he/she acts immediately, does what must be done. People always find time to do the things they want to do, no matter how busy they are. That's probably the source of the saying, "*If you want something done, ask a busy person.*"

It's simple. When it comes to end-of-life planning, there are two types of people: those who do it, and those who don't. People who want more time to think about it are people who don't, because they're too busy thinking about ways to put it off.

That makes me think of kids who keep putting their book report off, having all sorts of excuses of why they haven't done it, how it's too hard, how they don't feel like doing it now, how they're planning to do it next week … until all of a sudden, it's due tomorrow! Now what? They say they work best under pressure. For some people, that may be true. But, sometimes in the rush to complete something, you might leave out an important fact or step? Think about these things before you dismiss the idea of estate planning because you find it too hard.

Is whining how you express your unhappiness at facing the prospects presented in this book? Why are you so unhappy about these things in the first place? You bought this book. What did you think was in it? Recipes? Travel tips?

THIS BOOK IS ABOUT END-OF-LIFE PLANNING.
You know this, so tell me again why are you *whining*?

Let's break for a little humor

A wife says to her husband: "*Do you realize that most of our problems are caused by a lack of communication?!! Did you hear what I just said?*"

Husband's reply was, "*No, were you talking to me?*"

Genderspeak

In my experience, whining is something that adult men do (more so than adult women) when they perceive they are being pressured to do something they don't feel like doing. (Remember, that's just my experience and opinion.) It's seems to remind them of the times they heard their mother's voice telling them to do something they didn't feel like doing.

Men seem to have a scrambler in their ears or brains that make what you say to them sound like what their mother said to them years ago. Men hear suggestions and follow-up as "nagging," and don't seem able to distinguish between your voice and their mother's voice. It's annoying for women who are trying to communicate something ... big or small ... with men. I'm curious to know what mothers do to their sons that causes men to stop hearing our voices?

Does the man in your life whine when you suggest you need to take care of your end-of-life planning? Does he do everything possible to put it off?

There is something annoying about a man's whining to get out of doing something he doesn't feel like doing, even simple things like when you ask him to get the mayonnaise out of the refrigerator, and he whines that there is no mayonnaise there. So you say, "It's right there on the shelf. Just keep looking." He will whine again, and actually believe it's not where you say it is. You ask him if you have to come over there and find it for him. He again whines that there is no mayonnaise in the refrigerator ... that is, until you walk across the kitchen, reach into the refrigerator, and immediately put you hand on the jar of mayonnaise. "Oh, yeah, I guess I didn't see it." Excuse me? Are you having vision problems?

What he is really saying is that he didn't feel like getting the mayonnaise in the first place, that it was too much trouble ... so he chose the very annoying, very dishonest, childish way of trying to get out of doing that which he didn't want to do in the first place – that is, get the mayonnaise out of the refrigerator.

Is this what happens when the subject of end-of-life planning comes up for discussion?

Doing the things suggested in this book are not the same as finding mayonnaise in the refrigerator.

These things relate to life and death – YOUR LIFE AND DEATH. Maybe that's the problem. You don't want to think about these things, let alone do anything about them. It's bad enough that you have to die, isn't it?

I hear your mind screaming, "*I can't do this,*" so you stop reading, turn on the TV, get a snack, zone out, hoping to make this all go away, hoping to escape from a fate worse than death. ***Is estate-planning really worse than death?***

Remember when your grade-school teachers taught you the difference between CAN and WILL. You <u>CAN</u> do these things. You know this. You are physically able.

Are you saying that you WILL NOT do them, that you refuse? Be honest.

While you're having your meltdown, keep in mind that there could come the day when you absolutely CANNOT do these things because of some physical condition that renders you incapable, or some mental condition that renders you legally incompetent.

So, if you're looking for a way out, sit back and wait. Just do nothing. Maybe something will happen to you in the meantime so that you don't have to do what you don't feel like doing, something like a stroke or an auto accident?

Somehow, I don't think you'll be so happy having to be physically or mentally incapacitated, and incapable of communicating your wishes. Or dead.

Remember Terry Schiavo and Karen Quinlan?

I recently heard Suze Orman ask a man on her TV show if this is what he is thinking – that if he just waits long enough, something terrible will happen to him, and he won't have to do what he doesn't want to do in the first place. *WHAT*? Are there really people like that? Apparently there are, or this man would not have been used as an example on a national TV show. Don't tell me that you're one of those people, too?

In different words, are you saying that you
CHOOSE <u>NOT</u> TO DO THE THINGS THAT I'M SUGGESTING?

That is perfectly all right with me, if it's all right with you. Perhaps before you make the final decision NOT to do these things, you should first ask your family if it's all right with them.

REMEMBER THAT YOU HAVE MY PERMISSION
TO CHOOSE TO <u>NOT</u> DO ANY OF THE THINGS IN THIS BOOK

Remember that every choice has consequences. Have you weighed the negative consequences of doing nothing against the positive benefits of taking care of your own personal business before it's too late? If you're in charge of your own life, it is up to you to do the right things, at the right time, for the right reasons. No one else can do them for you. But, you already know this, don't you? Why do I sense that I need to keep reminding you?

Whew, that was a close one! For a minute, there, you really believed I could make you do something you don't want to do, didn't you? And, after all, you're an adult, you don't have to do anything you don't want to do. Right. I agree.

WHAT ABOUT DYING?

You don't want to do that either, but you will have to do it someday,
whether or not you want to do it,
whether or not you're ready,
whether or not you have finished your personal business.

Oh, you say, but that's not the same thing. It's different.

Is it?

BESIDES, WHAT ARE YOU SO AFRAID OF?

While you're whining, take a minute to think about somebody else for a change. Think of your family who will be left standing beside your grave, grief stricken, confused, afraid that you left a mess behind for them to clean up. After all, you hadn't done any funeral planning. It is only natural for them to worry about what other things you had left undone.

So, instead of hearing the comforting words of the clergy, their brains are racing to figure out what other messes await them at home … JUST BECAUSE YOU DIDN'T WANT TO HAVE TO DO CERTAIN THINGS! Is this the behavior of a mature, responsible adult, or a 3-year old child?

Why do you think this book is called ***between now and then***?
Because there are things you <u>must</u> do, *for others, if not for yourself,*
between now (today) and ***then*** (last day of your life).

So stop whining and get back in the game, finish this book, and, at the very least, sign the 4 most important legal documents, check the beneficiaries on your retirement accounts and insurance policies, and clean up your messy files. Is that asking too much? What else do you have to do that is so important that you can ignore these matters any longer? You knew you were going to run out of time someday, didn't you?

The Green Bay Packers never lost a football game. They just ran out of time.

Vince Lombardi

LAST WILL AND TESTAMENT

Picture a Lawyer sitting behind a gigantic desk, with the family of the decedent seated in his office, each one expecting to be named in the Will, and the Lawyer begins to read the Will: *"Being of sound mind, ...?* These scenes only happen in the movies.

I always liked this version better: *"Being of sound mind, I spent my children's inheritance while I still had the chance."* Just a little estate-planning humor to begin with. Of course, if you don't do appropriate and timely estate planning, there won't be much laughing in your family.

> <u>MYTH</u>: When you sign a Will, you will die.

> <u>FACT</u>: Signing a Will probably will not cause your death.

It has occurred to me that there should be a WARNING at the beginning of every Last Will and Testament, similar to the ones you see on medications or on power tools. Everyone knows those warnings are meant to keep you safe from situations that could potentially cause you harm; some warnings, however, go from the sublime to the ridiculous. One that immediately comes to mind is the warning on electric hair dryers, instructing you not to use the appliance in the shower. *Excuse me?* Are there people who actually do that? You know what I mean … warnings like that.

So, why a WARNING on a Will? Because it appears that some people are so afraid they will die after they sign a Will, that they refuse to sign the document, never considering the potential for negative consequences of not having a Will. Here is an example of such a hypothetical warning:

<u>WARNING:</u>
Give careful thought to whether or not you should sign this document,
because it is a known fact that you will die after you sign it.

SCARY?

I don't think so. Let's take a closer look at the words.
The WARNING does ***<u>NOT</u>*** say that you will die ***<u>when</u>*** you sign the Will.
It says that you will die ***<u>after</u>*** you sign the Will.

IN RELATION TO TIME, HOW COULD IT BE OTHERWISE?

First you sign, then, on some unknown day in the future, you die (just not immediately). You do understand that it cannot be the other way around; that is, first you die, and then you sign. That's ridiculous!

REMEMBER:

    - You <u>CAN</u> die without ever having signed a Will.

    - You <u>WILL</u> die, with or without signing a Will.

Statistics say that a majority of Americans die without a Will. Could it be that they believe the myth? *Just asking…*

Your Will is the written document in which you specify who inherits your estate (your assets), under what circumstances, and when. In your Will, you also designate the person(s) to be your Executor(s). In some jurisdictions, the term used for this position is Personal Representative.

SPECIFIC BEQUESTS

In your Will, you can list the names of people to inherit specific things from your estate. But be careful about listing specific bequests. What you DO NOT want to do is make it a long list of names of people and items. There are valid reasons why you do not want to do that, even though at first glance, you think it is a good idea, and a fair and equitable way to pass your assets and/or personal property to certain individuals. This is something you want to discuss in detail with your Lawyer before he prepares the Will.

Once upon a time, a woman asked her Lawyer to prepare her Will to include a list of about 25 specific bequests. The Lawyer told the woman all the reasons why it is not a good idea to list such things in her Will, but she insisted. So, the Lawyer prepared and sent a draft to her for her review.

When the woman got the draft, she was quick to respond that the specific bequests were not correct. The Lawyer again took notes about the things she said were not right, and sent her a revised draft. Still, it was not to her satisfaction.

So, the Lawyer sent his legal assistant to the woman's home to sit with her and carefully list all of the woman's specific bequests, and the Will was ultimately prepared to the woman's satisfaction, notwithstanding her Lawyer's advice. Included were specific bequests such as, "my collection of porcelain birds," "my emerald ring," etc. As it turned out, none of her cherished possessions had any monetary value whatsoever.

When the woman died and her Executor presented her Will for probate, the estate Lawyer had to prepare and send letters to every beneficiary, stating that they had been named in the Will of this woman. Some of the beneficiaries could not be found, others had predeceased the woman, which was a problem … because the woman had named no contingent beneficiaries. All of her things would have to be distributed under the Residuary Clause of her Will, but which things to which people? Can you see the problem?

A copy of her Will had to be attached to the Inheritance Tax return, and at that time, the state Department of Revenue would see the long list of specific bequests and would ask for a written appraisal stating the value of each specific item on her date of death. What value, you may ask? There was none. Nevertheless, the Lawyer for the Estate and the Executor would have to get an appraisal stating that the value of the personal property was minimal … maybe even zero.

Because the woman insisted her Will be written her way, against the Lawyer's advice, she significantly increased the costs of the probate of her estate. The Lawyer charged for every letter sent to every beneficiary. The Appraiser charged for the Appraisal, although he/she probably wasn't too happy to discover that the value of the items was just about zero. And I doubt that the Dept. of Revenue was very happy about not getting any tax for that long list of items because they were worthless.

<u>Morals of the story</u>:

Do not include a long list of specific bequests in your Will.
Pay attention to your Lawyer's advice.

<u>CHARITABLE GIVING</u>

If you wish to leave money to a charity, whether by virtue of a specific bequest or otherwise, be sure to thoroughly investigate the charity for legitimacy before naming them in your Will or Trust. And, as time passes, and each time you review your Will (*you do review your Will every few years, don't you?*), do another check-up on the charity to see if they are still in existence and if they are still worthy of your gift, or if you want to give your gift to another charity.

Also, unless you are very wealthy, it would be wise to specify a certain percentage of your estate to be donated to the charity, as opposed to giving them a specific amount of money.

This is another area that you should thoroughly discuss with your Lawyer before preparation of the documents.

APPOINTING YOUR EXECUTOR

It could be said that one of the primary reasons to sign a Will is, in fact, to name your Executor. If you don't sign a Will, who will be your Executor? NO ONE.

Choices and consequences. If you choose not sign a Will, and thus, not name an Executor, one consequence might be that the sister-in-law you never trusted or liked, will apply to the court and be appointed your Administrator? It could be your deadbeat brother who has bad credit history. It could be *anyone*. Is that all right with you?

And, as with any other suggestion in this book, you can ignore this responsibility. But why would you choose to ignore something this important? Oh, I know. I forgot how easy it is to come up with reasons (*excuses*) why you haven't done what needs to be done.

The responsibilities and liability of an Executor are serious matters. As the person appointing your Executor, it is important that you recognize that the choosing of that person is not to be taken lightly; and, if you are appointed as Executor under a person's Will, the same thing goes for you as well. The appointment of your Executor should not be made without forethought and conversations.

Your Executor is the person you designate to be responsible for closing out your life, the person to whom you will entrust your lifetime's assets to legally and responsibly handle them according to the terms and conditions of your Will. Don't you want to be the person who specifies who that person will be?

Q: What's the difference between an Executor and an Administrator?

A: The Executor is appointed by you in your Will. The Administrator will be appointed by the Court in a situation where you have not named an Executor (as when you die intestate), or where the Executor has predeceased you or refuses to act, and you have not appointed a Substitute Executor.

Q: What is the difference in their job descriptions?

A: Almost nothing.

Before you decide on the person to name as your Executor, give serious thought to whether that person is capable of doing everything that is necessary to close out your life. That is the Executor's job. I know. I just did it.

Before you make the appointment in your Will, you must first ask the persons you intend to appoint if they are willing to serve as your Executor and Substitute Executor. Graciously allow them to say no if that is their desire. It is a big responsibility that some people find daunting and would rather not assume.

If one or both accept your appointment, it is valuable (but not absolutely necessary) to educate them as to what their responsibilities will be so that when the time comes for them to act, they will be prepared. You may even want to have a joint consultation with them and your Lawyer. You should pay the legal fee (if any) for this meeting, which could turn out to be a good investment.

Many times, a person selects or chooses not to select their Executor for the wrong reasons. I know people who are in their early 60's, own a successful business, an expensive house, and refuse to write a Will because they say they don't know who to appoint to be their Executor. *Excuse me*? Are they saying they don't know a single person who could/would do the job? They could always appoint their Lawyer for now, and when they do finally make the decision, their Wills can always be changed. But, to live, owning assets, without a Will is foolhardy on their part. *Just my opinion ...*

I won't say that the decision of whom to appoint as Executor is necessarily easy, but it must be done, and you are the person to do it. If you don't make the selection and you die without a Will, the court will appoint *someone* to be your Administrator. You will have no say in that decision. After all, someone has to be responsible to see that your estate is handled. Would it be all right with you if it were someone appointed by the court and not by you, especially if it should turn out to be someone you don't like or don't trust?

Be responsible and do what is necessary.
Take the time to think about it, discuss it with your spouse, your children, your Lawyer or anyone else you trust. Just do it.

While you are deciding who should be your Executor, you must also decide who should be your Substitute Executor to take over ... even in the middle of probate ... if the Executor can no longer act, for any reason whatsoever.

Before you decide who should be your Executor and Substitute Executor, give serious thought to whether those persons are willing and capable of doing everything that is necessary to see your estate through the probate process which may take as long as two years.

- Do they have time to commit to the process?

- Do they live geographically close to where you lived and close to the court house where your Will will be probated?

- Are they capable of doing the job?

- Do they handle their own finances responsibly?

- Do you trust and respect them?

- Do they have personal integrity?

- Are they organized and diligent?

- Will they be able to work well with a lawyer as needed?

- Are they good at resolving conflicts?

- If they are not a member of your family, do they know your family, do they get along well with your family such that there should be no anticipated conflicts among them?

- Will they do the job until completion of the estate, no matter how long it takes?

- Once your Executor has been named in your Will, it is necessary that you tell the Executor where your Will is kept for safekeeping. With your Lawyer? In your home? In a bank safe deposit box? You might even ask your Executor to keep the document for you. The point is that at the time of your death, your Executor must be able to locate your original Will.

- Tell them also where you keep your other important papers, assets, etc. If you have a bank safe deposit box, tell them the name and address of the bank and the branch office, as well as the box number, and where you keep the key.

- Some people believe that they must name their oldest son as their Executor, or "*his feelings will be hurt*." Except, that they know their oldest son is an irresponsible person, unable to handle money, not capable or willing to intelligently handle his own affairs, let alone your affairs after your death. "*But,*" you say, "*he will be hurt if I don't choose him*." Still, not a good choice.

- And, further, in pleading his case, you may say that he will be assisted by your Lawyer during the administration of your estate, so how much damage can he cause? That is a negative, back-door reason to appoint your son, especially when you already know his capabilities. Still, you are free to name him if that is your choice.

• It is recommended that you rethink your appointment of Executor(s) every few years to determine if those persons are still willing to act for you. Their personal lives may have changed such that they would not be able to devote the amount of time and effort required of an Executor. If this were to be the case, your Executor would welcome such a conversation with you, and if they request to be excused, thank them, see that their renunciation is done formally through your Lawyer, and find someone else.

• You may wish to appoint two people to act as Co-Executors. While it is not forbidden by any law that I know, it is generally not a good idea to appoint two people. Before you make your final determination, consider:

- what if they don't know each other?

- what if they live in different places?

- what if they have different lifestyles that will require one to do most of the work?

- who will have the final say if they cannot agree on an important aspect of the administration of your estate?

- what if they are of different religions with conflicting beliefs that could interfere with their responsibilities?

- what if the disagreements between them require intervention by the estate Lawyer or the court, and it increases the legal fee for the estate?

- what if one person is a beneficiary under your Will and the other person is not?

- what if you select two of your children who have a history of not getting along?

- what if you select two of your children and not any other(s)?

"But," you say, *"you only have two children. How could you ever choose one over the other?"* Ask them. Maybe one of them would be happy <u>not</u> to be appointed. Maybe they are extremely compatible and work well together. Only you know their personalities and situation. The secret to successful appointments is good, clean, open, timely, honest and complete COMMUNICATION. There's that word again.

Once upon a time, there was a divorced man who intentionally named both his son and daughter as his Co-Executors, knowing full well that they live in different states, don't like each other, and don't get along. His reason was, "They'll just have to work it out this time."

- Do you think it was fair of that man to appoint his two children to work together, when he already knows they don't like each other? This man put his children in a very difficult situation. And, they may or may not work out their differences … but they will most assuredly require the assistance of at least one Lawyer … and all the while, the man's estate will be incurring legal fees.

- Of course, there is always the option that one of them could renounce. This can be problematic if they don't trust each other. Which one should renounce, and which one should act? And what if the one who acts as Executor wants to take the Executor's commission? That means the Executor will technically be getting more money from their father's estate than the other child, but, after all, the Executor did all the work of administering their father's estate. CAN YOU SEE THE POTENTIAL FOR PROBLEMS?

- At the time when they will be grieving the death of their father, both will have to travel not only for his funeral, but to be present when his Will is probated, whether or not it was convenient for them, whether or not they had sufficient funds for such travel.

- And, who will be responsible for disposing of his personal property (all his stuff) and selling his house? Someone has to be available to take care of all the details of closing out his life. That is the responsibility of an Executor, but two people from different states?

- And, the signatures of both will be required on every estate document, including checks. It is not impossible to get both signatures, just inconvenient, and expensive.

But, hey, that's how the man wanted his Will written. As he said, his children will just have to work it out this time. Maybe he should have appointed his Lawyer or a more neutral party. What do you think?

Because he knows the problems that will arise, a lawyer I know recently refused to write the Will of a widow who <u>insisted</u> that he prepare a Will in which she named all three of her children as Co-Executors, saying that she wanted to treat them equally. Maybe she'll find another lawyer who will write her Will her way; maybe not.

If you want something in your Will that your Lawyer knows will create problems in the future, at the very least, listen and learn from what he has to say to you. Maybe you will change your mind. Maybe not. But, at least you will have been advised of the potential problems.

- If your Executors would be your children, chances are they would want to waive their right to collect the Executor's commission because they are probably going to inherit most, if not all of your entire estate anyway. If they were to take the commission, that amount of money would be taxable for U. S. Income Tax. I'm pretty sure they would not want that to happen, but <u>don't</u> <u>assume</u> <u>anything</u>. Suggest that they discuss this with their Lawyer(s).

- If one person believes they did more work than the other, they might think they are entitled to the commission, and the other is not. It can be a problem that can be solved in advance if there are appropriate conversations among you and your children, even if you must include your Lawyer in the conversation to provide better explanations of the consequences of taking the fee or waiving it.

- If there are two persons appointed as Executor, both must sign every paper relating to your estate (unless one person renounces). This could be a significant inconvenience for both or either of them, and can cause a delay in completing some of the tasks of the administration of your estate. It is not an impossible situation, but things will go more smoothly if you have only one Executor working with the Lawyer. And, having two Executors could potentially increase the legal fee for your estate because of the duplication of effort. *Just something else to think about ...*

• Your Executor should know, in advance, what you expect of him/her. If the person agrees to being appointed, you must have conversations about your intentions, specifically about the disposition of your personal possessions. Of course, your general intentions will be carefully spelled out in your Will, but there will be nothing in your Will as to who gets your Limoges china, your emerald necklace, or your fly-fishing equipment.

- Pay particular attention to a discussion of the distribution of your personal property in order to prevent any upset or fighting among your heirs. Your Executor may not be willing to act if there is any hint of anticipated problems among your heirs.

- A good way to prevent problems about distribution of your "stuff" is to prepare a list of the possessions you want to go to specific people. That should keep your heirs from complaining, but if it does not, your Executor must be able to resolve the conflict to the satisfaction of everyone, even if it requires the estate Lawyer or the court to intervene.

- Your list would be very meaningful to your family if it were in your own handwriting. It could be in the form of an estate letter as previously described, wherein you explain how you made your decisions as to who gets your things. In your letter, you can come right and ask them not to fight about your "stuff." Invite them to follow the Suze Orman rule: First, people; then money; then things.

• If your Executor is one of your children, or if not, is this person capable of managing disagreement among your family members to the satisfaction of all parties?

• If you own real estate in more than one state, your Executor will be required to go to the court house in the county of each state in which you own real estate. Is your Executor in the position to do that? What if they have family and job obligations, or health problems that would keep them from the traveling that is necessary to administer your estate in different states? *Something else to think about ...*

• You should know that there is both legal and financial liability associated with the appointment, so you want to be sure that your Executor understands that, and will be able to meet the high standards of personal integrity required to do the job. If you know that your Executor has difficulty handling his/her own money, will he/she be able to handle your estate assets honestly? *Just asking...*

• Will you expect your Executor to handle any aspects of your funeral and burial? If so, you must discuss this in detail so there are no mistakes made at that time of your death, and so that things will be done as you wish them to be done. If your Executor is not a member of your family, this can create problems if your Executor makes decisions of which your family does not approve. (The best way to avoid such problems is to make your own funeral and burial arrangements in advance, but that's another subject for Chapter III of this book.)

- Is the person you named as your Executor capable of standing up to the pressure of other heirs or family members? Here is a true story to illustrate what can happen.

Once upon a time, there was a woman named Executor of her father's estate. She was the oldest of four children. She expressed pride in being named as her father's Executor, and decided to do the work of administering his estate by herself (that is, without benefit of legal counsel) so she could make her father proud of her (those were her exact words) and to avoid a legal fee.

Unfortunately, she was guilty of some sins of omission ... things she did not do in a timely way because she didn't know they were required. For example, more than a year after the deadline for filing, she had not yet filed a state Inheritance Tax Return because she didn't know she had to do that.

There remained other incomplete tasks relative to the administration of the estate which she had not done and which she said she didn't even know they were required, even though she had been given a complete package of instructions from the Register of Wills.

She did not realize she had missed some important steps in the probate process until she retained an Accountant to prepare her father's final U. S. Income Tax Return. Since it was also necessary to file an Inheritance Tax Return, she had the Accountant prepare it because she didn't know how to do it herself. Of course, she had to pay a fee to the Accountant. She hadn't counted on that.

When she found out that the Inheritance Tax due was approximately $7,000, she asked, "Where will I get that money?" Well, before his death, her father had owned a house that had no mortgage, and he had a few small bank and investment accounts. She had sold the house and closed out the accounts, so there was *money to pay the tax. Or, was there?*

The sad truth is that she had been pressured by her siblings to give them their inheritance ... and she made the choice to cave in to their pressure. She had passed out nearly every cent of the money to her siblings. When she made this choice, she exposed herself to legal and financial liability.

Technically, in order to pay the tax, she had the right to go to her siblings and ask them (and expect them) to give back enough of the money she had given them from their father's estate to pay the taxes and the attorney's fees the estate ultimately incurred. But, they had already spent the money.

She did not know there would be consequences for premature distribution of her father's estate funds. She just wanted her siblings to stop pressuring her. This choice of hers left no money to pay the tax. And, who do you think was responsible for paying the inheritance tax?

Had she retained a Lawyer to handle the administration of her father's estate, she would still have been his Executor, but she would not have been proceeding alone, in the wilderness of do-it-yourself law. Her attorney would have advised her of the consequences of early distribution of estate assets, and would have, if necessary, explained it to her siblings so that they would stop pressuring her.

At that point, it was an absolute necessity that she retain a Lawyer to complete the work of administering her father's estate, to file the appropriate settlement papers with the court, and to be legally discharged as Executor.

This woman's choice to practice do-it-yourself law cost her big time. And, her reasons for not retaining the services of an attorney to guide her in administering her father's estate were selfish and personal: (a) she didn't want to pay a Lawyer's fee; and (b) she wanted to make her now-deceased father proud of her.

<u>*Moral of the story*</u>*: Resist the temptation to practice do-it-yourself law!*

JOB DESCRIPTION OF AN EXECUTOR

Disclaimer

Let me state up front that I am writing this in the firm belief that an Executor requires the services of experienced legal counsel in order to complete the job. You may agree or disagree. While it is not absolutely required by law in every location, as you can see from the above example, it is not a good idea to try to administer a decedent's estate by yourself. There are other true stories elsewhere herein that give excellent examples of what can happen if you, as an Executor, make the choice to do it yourself. You, as Executor, are not paying the Lawyer's fee, the estate is.

Do what is necessary and appropriate. Get a Lawyer.

Listed below, in no particular order, are some of the things an Executor and Substitute Executor must consider while doing the job.

1. The most important thing for your Executor and Substitute Executor to know is that he/she has been appointed. Knowledge of such appointment is not to be sprung upon a person at the time of your death without their having prior knowledge of their appointment.

2. Remember that elsewhere, I told you it is _not_ an honor to be appointed as an Executor; it is a _job_ that may require your time for as long as two years, depending on the complexity of the estate. Knowing this, if you feel that you will be unable to fulfill your duties, you must say so before the Will is prepared. If you change your mind after the Will is prepared and signed, it will be necessary for the writer of the Will to incur an additional legal fee to have the Lawyer prepare a new document.

3. If you decide you do not want to fulfill your obligations as an Executor at the moment you must probate the decedent's Will, or, having already begun your work as Executor, you can renounce your appointment in favor of the Substitute Executor, assuming there is one. If there is no Substitute named in the Will, it will be necessary for someone to be appointed Administrator of the Estate instead. I recommend that if you have any misgivings about being an Executor, you be honest about it and renounce well before the time to probate the Will.

4. Your Executor may choose to work with your Lawyer or may select another. If your Executor has trouble making the decision, you might arrange an appointment with your Lawyer so they can get to know each other.

5. Your Executor must be able to locate your original Will. Soon after your burial, your Executor will meet with the estate Lawyer to prepare documents to enter your Will into probate. The Lawyer will explain what is necessary, and will go to the court house with your Executor; but first, he will need your Will.

6. Your Executor should also know the name of your Accountant or anyone else who has prepared your tax returns over the years, and should know where you keep your tax returns. You don't want your Executor to begin serving, only to find out that you have some pending business with the IRS or other taxing authority.

7. It is necessary that a checking account be set up for your estate expenses. This is done through the Lawyer, who will generally prepare all of the checks for the Executor's signature. As assets are sold, the proceeds will be deposited into this estate checking account to await payment of taxes and final distribution.

> *Occasionally, an Executor with a do-it-yourself approach, will go to a bank and open an estate checking account. Having done the work of assisting executors administer hundreds of estates over the years, I urge you not to do this. While you, as executor, are responsible for the payment of estate bills and for signing every check, let the lawyer and his staff do the work of handling the money and the bank account. There are good reasons for this, including giving them the opportunity to track all income and expenses so the information will be readily available to them when it comes time to prepare the tax returns.*

8. If there are large amounts of money placed in the estate checking account, the Executor (through the Lawyer) may want to set up a money-market account or short-term CD or investment account so that money can earn interest.

9. It is the responsibility of the Executor to locate all of your assets to present documentation about them to the Lawyer so the administration of your estate can begin. Do him/her a favor … make your assets easy to locate.

10. Once the Will is probated, it is the responsibility of the Executor to notify every beneficiary that they have been named in your Will, and that they may be receiving an inheritance. (Of course, whether or not they actually receive that inheritance is based upon whether or not there are sufficient assets in the estate after the payment of all of the decedent's bills and taxes.) This notification is done by a form provided by the court, and prepared by the Lawyer. Along with this notification, each beneficiary will be given a copy of the Will.

11. Sometimes, an Executor is unable to locate a beneficiary. While you are familiarizing your Executor with your Will, it may be a good time to provide the current address and phone number of all of your beneficiaries. If your Executor and estate Lawyer have to engage the services of others (a private investigator, for example) to locate a beneficiary, it will take time and increase the legal fee for the estate.

12. As you select the person to act as your Executor, give serious thought to whether the person has the capacity to address the special needs of any beneficiary. Your Executor should be familiar with that person and their individual situation and needs. This requires a high degree of understanding and compassion on the part of the Executor, so choose wisely. Your death may cause a serious upset to your special-needs child, and your Executor may be the person who has a large part in arranging your child's transition to living without you.

13. If a charity is named as a beneficiary, be sure your Executor knows the name and address of such charity, and what you would want to happen to the bequest in the event that charity no longer exists at the time of your death; that is, your Will should contain language that specifies a substitute beneficiary for the charity's bequest.

14. If you anticipate the possibility that anyone you know might contest your Will, it would be wise to discuss the situation with your Executor well in advance of your death. Discuss with your Lawyer what you can do in advance to be prepared in the event such a situation happens.

15. Although the Lawyer selected to represent the Executor and your estate will be handling all of the legal and financial matters (and most of the paperwork) of administering your estate, the Executor will have many things to do separate from the legal things. There is the matter of distributing your possessions and having meetings with the Lawyer and/or Accountant, and possibly a realtor. If your Executor is employed full-time, being an Executor may be burdensome. This is another reason to ask in advance if your Executor is able to do the job.

16. The Executor will be responsible to contact the decedent's pension/retirement services and the Social Security Administration to notify them of the decedent's death. In addition, if certain amounts of money must be returned to any of those organizations, the money will be returned from the decedent's estate.

17. The Executor can contact the decedent's insurance agent(s) to put in claims for all insurance policies. In the alternative, the Executor can notify all the beneficiaries of the decedent's policies and give them information about how to contact the appropriate insurance agent to put in a claim by themselves. It is not absolutely necessary that the Executor and the estate be part of this transaction, but often, the beneficiaries don't know what to do, and the Executor can provide direction as a courtesy.

18. If the decedent was on hospice, the Executor should contact them and make all appropriate arrangements to terminate their services and return all medical equipment and medications to them. If the decedent was not on hospice, the Executor can donate medical equipment no longer necessary and can contact the decedent's physician and/or pharmacy to find out about properly disposing of any unused medications.

19. One of the big things an Executor must handle is the sale of your house(s) and appropriate distribution and disposal of the contents. The job is especially big if you own more than one house in more than one geographical location. Getting the house(s) ready for sale is a big, time-consuming job, possibly requiring meetings with realtors, movers, auctioneers, appraisers, clean-out persons, code-enforcement agents, repair persons, etc. Will your Executor have the time to spend with all these people? Will your Executor be a person who makes wise choices regarding all that must be done to sell your house(s)? Having been an Executor in the recent past, I will tell you that emptying and selling the house was the biggest job of all, and it required a huge amount of my time.

> *My former husband died in the middle of the night. Upon the advice of counsel, at 8 a.m. that same day, I had the locks changed on his house. His brothers and sister were furious with me, but as an executor, it was my responsibility to protect his assets, and that included changing the locks on his house. Don't overlook this task. [Things have a way of disappearing (if you get my drift).]*

20. If the decedent rented an apartment, condo or home, the Executor will have to do many of the things listed above in Item 16 in order to vacate the premises and terminate the Lease, make final payment, and return keys to the landlord.

21. One of the hard things will be to make provisions for all pets the decedent owned at the time of death. It will be necessary for you to know what the decedent wanted for care of his or her beloved pets, and you must agree to follow his or her instructions. For me, it was the hardest thing I had to do, and you will read about it hereinafter.

22. The Executor will be responsible to return leased (or rented) vehicles, library books, or other borrowed items to their rightful owners if you know who they are.

23. If the decedent owned a car that had not yet been completely paid for, the Executor must determine the best way to get rid of that car. First, contact the bank that holds the loan and determine the pay-off amount. If you can locate a person willing to buy the car from the decedent's estate at the then-fair-market value, you could sell the car privately through the estate attorney. If you cannot find a buyer, you can make arrangements for the bank to repossess the car, and ask what will be the remaining balance of the loan. The bank will arrange for the vehicle to be picked up at an agreed-upon date and location. It will be the Executor's responsibility to verify that the people who show up to pick up the vehicle are, in fact,

representatives of the bank. At that time, the Executor will turn over the owner's card and keys. The decedent's estate will be responsible to pay off the balance of the loan to the bank.

24. An Executor must keep all estate assets and funds separate from his/her own. This should not be a problem if a Lawyer is handling the estate account(s).

25. An Executor must maintain regular contact with all of the beneficiaries. Such on-going communication can often prevent problems from happening. People who are due an inheritance are always anxious to get it, so keeping them up to date should help them understand any perceived delay. If they are pressuring the Executor, it might be necessary to have the Lawyer send them a letter explaining the timeline of the distribution of estate assets. (See the above story of the woman who *did it herself* for an example of what can happen if an Executor caves in under family pressure.)

26. The Executor is responsible to gather and pay all of the decedent's bills (including, but not necessarily limited to) the funeral bill, unreimbursed medical bills, and appropriate taxes. It is also necessary to determine if the bills are legitimate or duplicates of bills the decedent already paid before their death. The Lawyer will submit legal notices for publication in the appropriate periodicals for this purpose.

27. An Executor is responsible to collect all monies owed to the decedent. (An explanation of what is necessary is explained elsewhere.) The Lawyer will submit legal notices for publication in the appropriate periodicals for this purpose.

28. An Executor of an estate is entitled to a fee for serving. That fee could be several thousand dollars, usually based upon a percentage of the value of the probate estate. The fee is considered taxable income for purposes of U. S. Income Tax. Executors can waive their right to the fee, and should discuss with the Lawyer under what circumstances it may be appropriate to waive their right to the fee.

29. At the end of the administration of the estate, the Executor, with the assistance of the Lawyer, will prepare an informal Account of the transactions of the estate. If it is decided between the Executor and the Lawyer that it would be wise to submit a formal account to the court, the Attorney will prepare such a document and present it to the court for review and approval.

30. At the end of the administration of the estate, the Lawyer will prepare a document for signature by all beneficiaries wherein they acknowledge receipt of everything to which they are entitled, and which will discharge the Executor. Such a document will then be filed with the court, and your work as Executor will be complete.

APPOINTING GUARDIANS FOR MINOR CHILDREN

If you are a Baby Boomer reading this, you may choose to skip this section if you do not have minor children. But, if you have adult children who are married with children, or will be in the not-too-distant future, you may want to consider some of the following information.

There are two separate but distinct guardianship positions relating to minor children.

GUARDIAN OF THE PERSON

The guardian of the person of your minor children is the person your children would live with after your death.

It has been my observation that people give little thought to the appointment of persons who would raise their children in the event of their death. Most young people think such a terrible thing can never happen to them, so they put off making the decision and getting the appropriate documents signed until later. And what if "later" turns out to be too late? The decision is often based on emotions, not the reality of the situation and the individuals you intend to appoint.

And, while I'm really on a roll here, do you have adequate life insurance?
If not, and if you die, where is the money supposed to come from to care for your children?

Are your beneficiary designations the way you want them?
If not, the wrong person might end up with the proceeds of your life insurance policy,
which is supposed to be for your children.

Keep in mind that every time you and your spouse get into the car together, you are at risk of serious injury and death. If you have minor children, you had better do what is necessary and proper to provide the best possible protection for them in the event of your deaths, including the choice of who you would want to raise your children if the unthinkable were to happen. This choice requires serious thought, conversation, agreement, communication, sensitivity, and a basic understanding of things that can happen.

The following are specific things to consider when appointing guardians for minor children.

• If both parents were to die suddenly, never expecting to die at a young age, and let's say the couple had not put forth the effort to write Wills naming Guardians for their minor children, what then?

- One possible scenario is that the husband's family ends up fighting in court with the wife's family for custody of your children? Is that what you want?

- What if you want to choose a sister or brother, but they are not sufficiently established in life to take on the role of parent to your kids?

- What about your parents, who are in their 60s? Do they have the physical stamina and financial resources to raise a second family? They are in their "golden" years, looking for some time for themselves. Do you want to burden them with the emotional and financial responsibilities of parenting a second family?

• If a couple is divorced, and if the custodial parent were to die, the court would most likely grant custody to the other parent. If you are the custodial parent, you may not have much (if any) say in this matter, depending on the law where you live.

- If you believe there is good reason for your former spouse not to get custody of your children after your death (if he or she were in jail, a known drug offender or child molester, financially unstable and living in less-than-acceptable housing, living in another state, etc.), you must have a serious talk with your Lawyer before signing your Will. This conversation, and your ultimate decision, may be of the highest degree of importance for your children.

- Notwithstanding the laws that determine that the children's other biological parent would get custody if you, the custodial parent, were to die, I think it would be wise for you to have your Will written such that it states the name of the children's other biological parent, and designates someone else to get custody of your minor children if your former spouse were to predecease you or be found unfit to raise the children. It would provide guidance to assist the court in making a final determination of who should raise your children if you were to die and your former spouse were unable to raise them for any of the reason whatsoever.

- If your kids say they would not want to live with their other parent after your death, for lots of reasons, you might want to have a heart-to-heart talk with them to ask them a lot of questions and alleviate their fears. Mostly, you want them to know they will be taken care of if/when you should die while they are still young children (but old enough to have a basic understanding of the circumstances).

- This would be a good time to have a serious discussion with your former spouse about what would happen to your children in the event of your death. Even if you have to have such a discussion through your Lawyers or with their assistance, the legal fees would be an investment in the protection of your children's future. I also recommend that somehow, you and your former spouse find a middle ground by constructive negotiation, with the focus on your children for once, instead of yourselves. The two of you have argued enough for two lifetimes already, and this conversation is not about you. It is about and for your children's future in the event of your death. Don't chicken-out on them.

> *Remember when Christopher Reeves died after years with paralysis after falling off a horse? And, then in a short time afterward, his wife died, too, leaving behind a young boy. Unless in an accident, it isn't often that both parents die, leaving behind young children; but, as you can see, it does happen. In short, it can be a mess, personally, legally and financially.*

During the years when other people are raising your children, they may face some or all of the problems that you would have faced had you lived. Do a mental exercise for your own sake to think about whether the person(s) you intend to appoint could manage some of the following for your children:

• What if your children need counseling to recover from the loss of you. Will these people see that they get it for as long as necessary?

- What if your children seriously act out and get in trouble in school (even with the law)? What if your children begin drinking and/or doing drugs? What if your children's shenanigans incur big legal fees to "rescue" them?

- What if one of your children becomes seriously ill, or is injured in an auto accident?

- Will there be sufficient money to pay for problems such as these?

How happy will your Guardians then be about the agreement they made with you to raise <u>your</u> children? It is one thing to have to deal with all these personal situations and legal issues for your <u>own</u> children; but it is entirely different when the kids are someone else's.

THE GUARDIAN OF THE ESTATE

The person who will handle your minor children's money after your death is known as the guardian of the estate.

Minor Children Cannot Inherit

Before moving on, let me say that minor children cannot inherit. Not money. Not the proceeds of life insurance policies. Not investments. Not a house. Nothing -- that is, without the benefit of a trust that has been set up for the purpose of protecting the child's money (assets) until they reach a pre-determined age which is specified in the trust.

This is just one more place where you need to consult a Lawyer experienced in this kind of estate planning. And, once again, let me state that you must not do it yourself, especially if you care about your children if there should ever be a time when you are no longer living and cannot care for their money yourself.

YOU <u>CAN</u> SPECIFY THE SAME PERSON FOR BOTH GUARDIANSHIPS, but there are reasons why this may not be a good idea:

- What if the person whom you appoint to raise your minor children after your death spends that money for themselves?

- What if they get into financial trouble and think they'll just "borrow" some of your children's money. Legally, as Guardian of the estate of your children, they would be operating in what is known as a fiduciary capacity; that is, they are responsible for someone else's money. The guardian(s) cannot legally spend that money, but it could happen in the heat of a desperate financial moment, when they may forget all about their promise to you and their legal obligations and liability to your children. I realize they agreed to do this for you, but what if the temptation is just too great? It is a crime for someone acting in a fiduciary capacity to use the other person's money for their own personal use, but desperate people sometimes do desperate things.

IT IS POSSIBLE TO APPOINT A DIFFERENT PERSON AS GUARDIAN OF THE ESTATE OF YOUR CHILDREN so that their money will be wisely protected and invested for their future. The person could be a trusted lawyer, a bank officer, an accountant, or a financial planner. It may be necessary and appropriate for you to establish a trust for your children, and to name a financial professional as the Trustee. But, unless this other person knows you and your children well, they may be somewhat detached and strict in giving your children needed attention and money; and what if this person is stingy, or very, very busy, and can't be bothered dealing with the financial "trivia" of your children? How well do you know this person? Is this person acquainted with the person who will be raising your children? Do they communicate well?

- You could also appoint someone you know very well and trust completely to be Guardian of the Estate of your minor children – a close friend, another sibling. But, it is essential that the two persons you appoint as Guardians are compatible and have only the best interests of your children foremost in their minds.

- What if they reach a point of serious disagreement that they are unable to amicably resolve, and they require intervention by a Lawyer or the court? Such legal intervention will cost money. Whose money will pay for it?

IT IS NEVER A GOOD IDEA TO NAME A MARRIED COUPLE (for example, your sister and brother-in-law) to be Guardians of your minor children's person or their estate. Why not?

- If they were to have custody of your children after your death, and then they get a divorce, your children could end up in the custody battle of their divorce. This is not something you ever want to happen.

- What if one of your children is developmentally disabled, and your sister and brother-in-law are not able to handle the special needs of your precious child? What then?

- What if your sister and brother-in-law live in a small house, and there really isn't room for your children to live with them? Then what? If your children put their children out of their respective (bed)rooms, there could be serious upset and anxiety among the children that could cause your children to feel very unwelcome and unhappy. What if their kids simply don't like your kids, or vice versa?

- Your sister and brother-in-law are two people. What if they seriously disagree on matters involving your children. Who is there to break the tie?

- What if you didn't have any life insurance to provide money for a trust fund to raise your children? Where do you expect the Guardians to get the money for the added expense of raising your children?

- What if the extra added expense of having your children live in their house causes them serious financial distress, even bankruptcy? Then what?

- What if your sister or her husband should die, and the survivor finds him/herself unable to honor their promise to raise your children? Then what?

- What if they never wrote a Will specifying the people who would raise your children after their death. Then what?

- What if your children, as they get a little older, become behavior problems for your sister and her husband? What if they fight with your sister and her husband over issues like homework, friends, outside activities, chores?

- What if your children, as they get older, don't like their aunt and uncle, and wish you had appointed someone else to take care of them? You must talk about this with your children way in advance.

- What if one of your children becomes seriously ill, injured or disabled (whether in the short term or permanently)? Are you sister and brother-in-law up for the challenge of caring for your child in such an extreme situation? Where would the money come from?

- If your children are old enough to understand the concept of their having to live with others in the event of your death, take the time to compassionately and thoroughly explain things to them. Assure them that they will be loved and taken care of. Encourage them to ask questions, and give them ample time to express their feelings and fears. Give them permission to cry if they need to; and if they absolutely would not want to be raised by your sister and her husband, you must then find someone else.

I recommend that you see the movie, "*Stepmom*," starring Julia Roberts and Susan Sarandon. Susan Sarandon's character is divorced and dying, and her ex-husband is married to a younger woman, Julia Roberts' character. Susan's character is really upset to learn that her children actually like their stepmother, and over time, the two woman create a peaceful, loving, mutually beneficial arrangement where the children will be loved, allowing their mother to die in peace. Keep the Kleenex box nearby.

- And, before your Lawyer prepares your Will, be sure to ask the **one** person you designate for each position if they are willing to do this for you and your children. If they so much as "blink," maybe you should ask someone else.

- And, if your children are very young when your Will is prepared, ask the people every few years to see if they are still in agreement about caring for your children as described here.

- Every few years, as your children begin to grow up, ask them if they are comfortable with your choice.

- What if those people are on the verge of divorce?

- What if they are facing bankruptcy?

- What if they plan to relocate to another city or state?

- What if one of them develops a drinking or drug problem?

- What if the person you have appointed becomes physically disabled or seriously ill, and cannot manage raising your children?

- What if one or both of them become unemployed in the long term?

- What if they lose their house to foreclosure? Where will your children live?

CAN YOU SEE HOW COMPLICATED AND MESSY IT CAN GET?
I'M TRYING TO GET YOU TO THINK BEFORE ACTING.

It is your responsibility to protect your children and their money for their future if you won't be around to see that they are cared for. It is ABSOLUTELY NECESSARY that you have the hard conversations with the person(s) you intend to name as Guardians for your minor children. Don't chicken out, and think that things will be all right. Maybe they will. Maybe not. For your children's sake, make this a priority.

I hear you already: *"OMG! Why does it have to be so complicated?"* Well, considering that no one has a crystal ball to see into the future, all you can do is your very best to protect your children and their money, and this may require the assistance of both a competent attorney and a financial planner well versed in such matters.

COMMUNICATION is what is required: between you and your spouse or former spouse; between you and your children; between you and your parents and siblings; between you and the person(s) you appoint as Guardians. Ignoring the conversations will only make things more difficult were the unthinkable to happen.

Do not allow your Lawyer to brush you off with vague comments like, *"Don't worry, I'll take care of everything."* Insist that your Lawyer explain every detail of the guardianships, such that you thoroughly understand them.

THIS IS YOUR *CHILDREN* WE'RE TALKING ABOUT HERE!
What could possibly be more impor tant?

DO NOT PREPARE THE DOCUMENTS YOURSELF … even if you can.

Even if there is no law denying you the right to prepare your own documents, it's still not a good idea. If it is important to you that the documents be appropriate and accurate, you might consider the possibility you could make a mistake that will have irreversible consequences.

Laws vary from state to state and jurisdiction to jurisdiction. Always keep this in mind.

If you think you'll be saving the attorney's fee, you might just be causing yourself and your heirs a great deal of heartache and costing them a lot more money by mistakes or omissions on your documents. Resist the temptation. Spend the money for the Lawyer's fee.

I know a Lawyer who told me that he is regularly retained by people who have made serious mistakes practicing "do-it-yourself" law. The following true story illustrates how the mistakes made by people who practiced "do-it-yourself" law earned big fees for the Lawyer who cleaned up their messes.

A TALE OF TWO SISTERS
or
What Can Happen If You Don't Want to Pay a Lawyer $75 to prepare a Will

Once upon a time, there were two elderly sisters who wrote their own Wills because they didn't want to pay a Lawyer $75 to do it for them.

Neither sister had ever married, neither had any children, and they had no living relative except for each other. The sisters were very old when they died, only 2 days from each other.

The sisters believed they had included everything necessary to see that, after they died, their possessions and assets would pass to the people they wanted to have them; however, they made mistakes that had consequences the sisters did not and could not have anticipated when they practiced "do-it-yourself" law. In writing their own Wills, the mistakes they made had a significant, negative impact upon the administration of their respective estates. Had a Lawyer prepared their Wills, the results would have been very different.

While their Wills were legally and technically correct, they were insufficient and inappropriate for their personal circumstances. Here's why.

Each sister's Will included most of the basic provisions, as well a long list of specific bequests. For example:
- *I give and bequeath the sum of $1,000 to my friend, Mary;*
- *I give and bequeath my cherished grandfather's clock to my cousin, Jane;*
- *etc.*

What was missing was language specifying who gets the money and the clock and their other specific bequests if Mary and Jane and some of the others were to predecease the sister who wrote the Will ... which is exactly what happened. Many of the people named in the Wills of both sisters died before the sisters, and the money and other assets designated for those predeceased persons had no place to go! Do you see how that happened?

The sisters named each other as Executor. I can hear you asking, "So what's wrong with that?" Technically, nothing. But, when you consider that they were very old, it would have been wise for them to specify the name of a person to step into the position of Substitute Executor in case the designated Executor predeceased them or was incapacitated. In fact, this is exactly what happened. The scenario went something like this:

Monday: Sister No. 1 died.
Thursday: Sister No. 2 was appointed Executrix of the estate of Sister No. 1.
Friday: Sister No. 2 died.

In the brief span of only a few days, both sisters died. Now, let me explain the consequences of this unfortunate series of events.

First, even though Sister No. 2 had been certified as Executor of the estate of Sister No. 1 at the time of probate, the estate of Sister No. 1 had no Executor after Sister No. 2 died because her Will had no one named as Substitute Executor. A hearing before the Register of Wills was required to appoint an Administrator, dbncta, for the estate of Sister No. 1. (Technically, "dbncta" means that an Administrator had to be appointed in an estate where there was a Will, but where no one had been named as Substitute Executor.)

Second, when Sister No. 2 died just days after Sister No. 1, who was there to enter the Will of Sister No. 2 for probate? No one, because Sister No.1 (originally named Executrix) had already passed away. Remember that her Will also had no Substitute Executor. If Sister No. 2 had lived longer, she would probably have had a new Will prepared, but that is not how things happened. Sister No. 2 simply did not live long enough to sign a new Will. This necessitated another hearing to appoint an Administrator, dbncta, for her estate as well.

The same woman applied for and was appointed Administrator of both sisters' estates, ultimately providing her with a hefty fee. When the administration of the estates was finished, she bought a big new house with the money she was paid as Administrator of both estates, and she furnished it with much of the furniture from the sisters' home.

And, the same Lawyer represented this woman in both estates, providing him with a hefty fee as well. Oh, and by the way, if the only work he did was administer the two sisters' estates, his fee would have been large; but, because of the fact that the sisters left out so many things in their respective Wills, the lawyer was required to represent both estates in court several times over the course of several years. Those court appearances significantly increased the Lawyer's fee.

So, how much money did the sisters save by doing it themselves? Wouldn't it have been better for the sisters to have paid the $75 each to a Lawyer to write their Wills correctly, rather than have huge sums of their money ultimately go toward court fees, Administrators, and Lawyers? Of course, they never dreamed that such a mess could happen. But, it did. And, keep reading, because it gets worse.

The entire estate of Sister No. 1 was, of course, taxable for Inheritance Tax. But, because she had left nearly her entire estate to Sister No. 2, who died only days afterward, the estate of Sister No. 2 was significantly larger than it would have been if she had died first, by virtue of the fact that she inherited the estate of Sister No. 1. So, the assets of Sister No. 1 were technically taxed twice: Once in her own estate; and again in the estate of Sister No. 2 who had inherited from Sister No. 1.

By now, I'm sure you're scratching your head, wondering what you just read. But, don't stop reading yet. It gets worse.

Because their Wills did not provide names of persons to inherit specific bequests designated for deceased persons, and because their Wills did not contain residuary provisions (that is, who gets what's left over after all distribution is made and all expenses and taxes paid), all of the assets for whom there were no named contingent beneficiaries went into a lump sum that was claimed by the State by virtue of a process known as escheat, which, in layperson's language means that if there is money left over in a decedent's estate after payment of all bequests, taxes and fees, and there was no one left to inherit, the money goes directly to the State in which the decedent resided.

Their Estates took years to complete, incurring huge legal fees.

So, who benefited by the "thriftiness" of the sisters?

(1) the woman who was the court-appointed Administrator of both estates; and
(2) the Lawyer who represented both estates; and
(3) the Commonwealth of Pennsylvania.

The sisters died without knowing the mess they left behind.

This is just one example of what can happen if you choose to write your own Will.

Because they chose to write their own Wills, the intentions of the women were never carried out because of the deficiencies in the documents. While their Wills were structurally satisfactory, there were, nevertheless, three things the women left out of the Wills that would have made all the difference:

1. Substitute Executors
2. Contingent Beneficiaries for specific bequests
3. A Residuary Clause

Maybe they should have paid a Lawyer $75 to write their Wills.

PROBATE

I believe probate is seriously misunderstood. It seems to bring out fears and misinterpretations among people who don't know what it means or how it works, and the people who know the least seem willing and eager to share their misinterpretations with others, who, in turn, pass it along. (Again, *"Whisper Down the Lane."*)

There is nothing wrong with probate. While there may be valid reasons for wanting to avoid it, avoiding probate is not like avoiding the plague, although to hear some people, you would think they were the same thing! Not true.

Probate is simply the court-supervised process of administering your estate. It begins when your Executor presents your Will to the Register of Wills, and ends when the administration of your estate is complete.

If you have no Will, the process would begin when someone applies to the Register of Wills to be appointed your Administrator. The responsibilities and liabilities of an Executor and an Administrator are pretty much the same.

Once upon a time, a 70-year old widow had her attorney prepare her estate-planning documents, including a Revocable Living Trust. Before her husband's death seven years earlier, the couple owned all of their assets jointly, and after his death, she was the lawful owner of those assets by right of survivorship.

A short time after her documents were prepared, she was organizing her personal papers and found a small investment account statement among her husband's things. The account was in her husband's name only. In relation to the money it ended up costing this woman to close out that account, the actual worth of that investment was insignificant.

Still, she figured that she had taken care of her other personal business, so she might as well take care of this one account. She called the company to see what was necessary to obtain the proceeds, and the friendly company representative told this woman to send her a Short Certificate. Not knowing what a Short Certificate is, she asked and was told that all she had to do was to go to the Register of Wills, and they would give her one.

The woman drove to the county seat and went to the office of the Register of Wills and asked for a Short Certificate. This woman had absolutely no idea what a "Pandora's Box" she was opening. The clerk (who, in her own defense, would say she was just doing her job) began asking questions about the woman's deceased husband, starting with, "Where is his Will?" The woman had not brought her husband's Will with her because she was just going to get a Short Certificate. It never occurred to her that she needed her husband's Will. She did not make the connection between probate and her husband's Will. Why would she? She trusted someone who gave her advice, and had no way of knowing in advance that the advice was incorrect. A Will is only needed for probate, and he did not have a probate estate. But, I'm getting ahead of myself.

Moving right along, the clerk said, "No problem. We'll just open the estate and have you appointed Administrator and not Executor." Because the woman did not know what was meant by all those words, she nodded her approval based on her simple desire to get a Short Certificate.

The clerk prepared formal Letters of Administration and gave the woman the Short Certificate which she had requested. What this woman did not know was that she had just opened up the door to the entire probate process for her husband's estate, which did not need to be probated in the first place.

See what happens when you don't know what you don't know.

The clerk had no idea that this woman's husband's only asset was a tiny little investment account, and assumed (fairly, I believe) that the woman knew what she was doing by asking for a Short Certificate. It isn't every day that a person appears before a clerk at the Register of Wills asking for Short Certificates, and has no clue what they represent.

Pleased with herself for handling this transaction by *herself, she paid the fee and took the Short Certificate home with her, sent it to the investment company, and soon received those few dollars from her husband's account. That mistake ended up costing her a lot of money*

"What mistake, you ask?" First of all, her husband did not have a probate estate, and there was never a need for a Short Certificate. As I said before, all of his assets (with the exception of this one small account) were jointly owned with his wife. Probate was not necessary until the death of the wife.

"But, you say, there was the matter of that little investment account, and what the representative at the investment company told her." True. Had this woman called her Lawyer first, she would have been advised that she did not need a Short Certificate, and the Lawyer would have explained why not. This woman could then have explained to the representative at the investment company that her husband did not have a probate estate, and thus, upon the advice of her Lawyer, she was submitting a formal request letter and a Death Certificate. But, this required the woman to (1) UNDERSTAND what was happening in this transaction, which she did not, and (2) ASK her Lawyer for direction, which she also did not.

This woman could even have asked her attorney to do this for her and the fee would have been well worth it. **But, she didn't ask, did she. She wanted to do it by herself!**

Again, feeling proud of herself for handling this transaction by herself, this woman went about her business for a few months, and then she received a letter from the court, advising her that she had not sent Notices to the Beneficiaries, as required. The woman went into a panic, not having the slightest notion what the letter meant. All she knew was that she was frightened by the formal legal language of the letter, which said something about "imposing sanctions."

When she called her Lawyer, she was told that when she asked for a Short Certificate and agreed to be appointed Administrator of her husband's estate, she had inadvertently and unnecessarily begun the probate process. And, having done it, she was legally obligated to see the process through to completion, and she needed a Lawyer to complete the process for her.

This woman ended up paying a Lawyer to probate an estate that did not need to be probated ... all because she thought she knew what she was doing, all because she thought it was a simple transaction, all because she did not know the connection between a Short Certificate and probate, all because she wanted to do it herself.

DO YOU SEE WHY I KEEP TELLING YOU NOT TO DO IT YOURSELF?

TO PROBATE OR NOT TO PROBATE? THAT IS THE QUESTION.

It's really very simple. If a person dies owning taxable assets in their own name:

- the estate goes through probate if there is a Will;

- the estate goes through probate even if there is NO Will;

- the estate will not go through probate if there is a Revocable Living Trust.

DOES THAT HELP TO CLEAR IT UP FOR YOU?

WHAT ARE THE COSTS OF PROBATE?

People often complain about the costs of probate. What, exactly, are they?

- There is a small fee to record a Will at the county office of the Register of Wills.

- There is the cost of legal advertising, the purpose of which is to locate persons who may owe money to the decedent or to whom the decedent may owe money at the time of his/her death.

- The Register of Wills will charge a small fee for photocopies.

- The Register of Wills charges a small fee for filing some other documents necessarily associated with the probate of your Will and administration of your estate.

- Technically, the total of the <u>actual</u> <u>court</u> costs of probate may not even reach $500.

So, what ***are*** those "probate fees" people complain about so loudly?

They are the fees and costs of the Lawyer who represents your estate, and the fee of your personal representative (i.e., your Executor or Administrator). *I know, I know*, they're not referred to as "probate costs," but if your estate goes through the probate process, a Lawyer will most likely be retained to handle the administration of your estate, and the Lawyer will charge a fee. Don't you agree that the Lawyer is entitled to be appropriately compensated for the work he/she and their staff do to complete your estate administration?

> *(And, just having completed my work as an Executor of an estate,*
> *believe me when I tell you I earned every cent.)*

Whether an estate goes through probate or is settled through a Revocable Living Trust, the estate may incur all sorts of costs, fees, and expenses relating to the sale of the decedent's property, including appraisal fees, inspection fees, repair permits, realtor's commission, township and homeowner's association fees, repair bills, etc. All of these expenses would happen with or without probate. They are the costs of closing out the life of a person who died.

Why am I telling you this? Because of the misinterpretation of the definition of probate and "probate fees."

One more thing you should know about probate as you are discussing your estate-planning documents with your Lawyer: If you own real estate in more than one state, and if your primary estate-planning document is a Will (that is, not a Revocable Living Trust), your estate will have to be probated in every state in which you own real estate.

WHY DOES PROBATE TAKE SO LONG?

Another question people regularly ask. Probate is a _process_, not a single event. Having been responsible for much of the work of administering the estates of many people, let me say that it is all in the details.

Besides the requirements of the court to file certain papers for certain reasons at certain times, it takes time to close out the life of a loved one. There are many tasks which an Executor (or Administrator) must complete before the probate process is finished, not the least of which is the sale and/or distribution of all of the decedent's assets, keeping accurate records of every transaction, communication with the attorney and family of the decedent, some of whom are very anxious to receive their inheritance. Earlier, I told you what happened when a woman, acting as Executrix of her father's estate, prematurely distributed money (their inheritance) to her brothers and sisters.

Sometimes, an estate will require intervention by the court, which will naturally prolong the process and increase the legal fees. Consider that it is not worth fighting in court, especially if you find your family fighting over "stuff."

At the time of probate of a Will, the Register of Wills provides the Executor with forms and a complete package of instructions. If all things are in place, the probate process generally runs smoothly, and if everyone is doing their jobs in a timely fashion, the process may take 18-24 months to complete (more if your estate is complicated).

<u>ALERT</u>

One thing that can delay the probate process is not having a Death Certificate when one is needed. Death Certificates are ordered when funeral arrangements are made, and so often, people skimp on the number of certificates they order. OK, so they cost a <u>few</u> dollars each, but they never expire, they don't take up much room, they don't go stale, and there will be occasions in the future when it would be useful or necessary to have a Death Certificate. You will want enough Death Certificates to provide one to every financial institution, insurance company, and credit-reporting bureau to provide verification of the death of someone and to close out every such account quickly. My recommendation is that 25 Death Certificates be ordered and safeguarded for future use.

In the absence of an original Death Certificate, one must be ordered from the State Dept. of Vital Statistics, and it often takes weeks to get it.

Moral of the story: Order extra Death Certificates right from the beginning. The cost will only increase the funeral bill by a few dollars. This is no place to try to save money.

Want to save your estate some money and speed up the probate process?
KEEP GOOD RECORDS!

There _is_ something that you, yourself, can do beforehand to keep the fees down. Whether the fees are high or low depends, in great part, on how your keep your personal records before your death. This is one area where you, personally, can make a big difference.

If you choose to allow your personal records to be messy and disorganized, you will not only be responsible for delaying the probate process (and thus, the distribution of your assets to your heirs), but you will be significantly increasing the fee for the attorney who handles your estate.

If your records are messy or poorly organized, it is entirely possible that one or more of your assets could be overlooked by your Executor, or worse, lost or forgotten, in which case, your hard-earned asset could end up in the hands of the state by escheat.

When your heirs complain about how long it takes to settle your estate, and how high the Lawyer's fee will be, will they take into consideration that you were, in large part, the cause of this because you didn't keep good records? Probably not. They will just blame the Lawyer and the process.

One could think of sorting through your messy papers as a legal scavenger hunt on the part of those persons left behind, and who now find themselves in the unenviable position of having to figure out all the mysteries and clues you left behind.

This is one place where the delay can happen … in the time it takes to sort through your papers and documents and locate your assets! I included an entire chapter in this book about record-keeping because I want you to understand the importance of it, and that you have a responsibility to keep your personal papers and records organized. To do so will significantly reduce the costs of probate.

As in all things mentioned in this book, YOU DO NOT HAVE TO DO WHAT I SUGGEST. But, believe me, your heirs will thank you if you do. Keeping the Lawyer's fee low will leave more money for them! Isn't that what you (and they) want? So, it's up to you to do your part!

Many times, the Executor has no idea what to do with all the papers you left behind, and so they gather them, throw them into a big cardboard box, and deliver the box to the Lawyer.

What do you think the Lawyer does with them? Gives them to his paralegal, who will sort through them, keep the important papers, and throw away the "junk" (that is, all the envelopes, advertising, etc., that you saved for no particular reason, except that you just couldn't part with them). Trust me, the paralegal will part with them, and your estate will be charged for every hour of his/her time to clean up the mess you left behind.

If your personal filing system consists of PILES of papers (that is, instead of Files), it will be necessary that every paper you leave behind be investigated and documented by the people responsible for administering your estate. And, each will cost your estate a fee, whether it be for the Lawyer or a paralegal. These legal fees can be significantly reduced by your keeping good, simple records such that if you were to die tomorrow, someone could easily figure out what needs to be done.

WHY LEGAL ADVERTISING?

After a Will is entered for Probate, the Rules of Court require that an advertisement be placed in the local Bar Association journal and a newspaper of local distribution where the decedent lived. The cost of this advertising will be borne by the decedent's estate, and the publications will provide Proofs of Publication for the estate records.

Once again, the rules regarding publication of such a notice vary from state to state, jurisdiction to jurisdiction. The attorney handling the estate will know in which publications the ad should be placed.

Where I live, the advertisement must be placed for three (3) consecutive weeks. It states the name of the decedent and the personal representative (that is, the Executor, the Administrator, or the Trustee) and/or the attorney representing the estate, as well as addresses for each.

The purpose of the advertising is to give persons who owe the decedent money, notification of their death so they can pay back the money. It also provides an opportunity for persons who may be owed money by the decedent to submit a bill to the estate for payment.

Sometimes, an Executor finds it necessary to attempt to collect a debt owed to the decedent. It is not always easy, and the attempts to collect the money don't always succeed. The following story will give you an example of the expenses that an estate may incur while the Executor was doing his best to perform his duties.

> *Once upon a time, a woman died after having been a widow for 5 years. Among her papers was discovered a Promissory Note indicating that her son owed her and her deceased husband (now, her estate) $15,000.*
>
> *Through his Lawyer, her Executor made several attempts to collect this money on behalf of her estate, to no avail. The woman's estate executed judgment on the Note, incurred court costs and other miscellaneous costs related to attempts to garnish assets, repossess his car, etc.*
>
> *The son who owed his mother the money was very smart and clever and figured out that he could avoid paying the money back by declaring bankruptcy, which he did. His own mother's estate was depleted not only by the $15,000 he owed her, but by the legal fees and costs associated with collection attempts.*

Why have I told you this story? Because, as an Executor, you must take reasonable steps to locate people who owe the decedent money, and then make every legal attempt to collect the debt(s); however, it may be counterproductive if the person who owes the debt is a deadbeat and judgment proof. This is a subject to be thoroughly discussed between the Executor and the Lawyer for the estate. The best decision might be to simply let it go if it is going to cost as much or more for collection than the original debt.

If you are owed money by anyone, you should keep detailed information about the transaction, such that when you die, your Executor can collect that money for your estate. If you don't document details of this transaction, including name, address, phone number of the person who owes you money, how do you expect anyone to know about it, let alone collect it?

Was there an oral or written agreement between you and the person to pay the money back? Or does that person think you gave the money as a gift? Did the person sign a promissory note? And, if so, where is that note?

You might also want to include some "hint" about whether, in your opinion, this money is collectable or not. Your Executor will still look into pursuing the collection of the money, but if you loaned money to someone not inclined to repay it, your Executor should know this. After consultation with his/her Lawyer, your Executor may decide not to waste valuable money and time searching.

WHEN THE DOCUMENTS ARE READY, SIGN THEM.

Do you have any idea how many Wills have been prepared by Lawyers for Clients who never show up to sign them? Way too many!

If I were a Lawyer, I would give the Clients one month after notifying them that the documents were ready to be signed, and if they hadn't made an appointment to sign them, or have a very good explanation why they are not available to sign in that amount of time, I would double the fee. But, hey, that's just me.

What did you think, the Lawyer was running a charity?

Once upon a time, there was a widow whose daughter was a legal secretary, and who will ultimately be responsible for taking care of her mother's personal business in the future. Her daughter arranged for an attorney to prepare the appropriate documents for her mother, and when the time came, the woman saw all the places where she had to sign her name and had a meltdown.

She cried, and said there were "too many signatures." EXCUSE ME? To (almost) quote the character of Mozart in the movie, "Amadeus:" "There are precisely the number of signatures that are required, no more, no less."

The woman refused to sign anything, and gave no explanation. She was not concerned about the fact that a Lawyer prepared all her documents, and was entitled to a fee for legal services, or the situation she was putting her daughter into if she (the woman) were to become disabled and need the benefit of a Living Will and a Healthcare Power-of-Attorney. The woman could not see past her own distress, and no amount of talking could motivate her to sign the documents. She was stuck in her own fear, whatever that fear happened to be. She never did say. And she never did sign.

Do you think it was selfish of this woman to act like this?

Don't wait. You will not die the minute you sign the documents. Death doesn't happen that way. Worst of all, you might die before you sign them, and leave behind a mess for your family to sort out. Is this how you want to be remembered?

He heard his mother's voice

Once upon a time, there was a Lawyer who asked one of the paralegals in his firm to prepare a Will for someone in his family. He gave her the information needed to prepare the Will, and when she asked when he needed the Will, he said to just fit it into her work schedule.

Several days later, the paralegal told him the Will was completed. He said he wasn't ready for it yet.

After several more days, she asked him if he had forgotten about the Will, and again, he said, he was busy.

A week later, she reminded him that the Will was completed and ready to be signed, and, in a very angry tone of voice, using strong language unprintable here, told her to stop bugging him.

All the paralegal was trying to do was her job, which is called follow-up. Instead, he heard her <u>nagging</u> him. He heard his mother's voice, reminding him to take out the trash, do his homework, clean up his room.

Too bad, too, because several weeks later, his relative died, never having signed the Will. What followed was a lengthy, expensive, messy law suit among family members that would never have happened had he not heard his mother's voice.

<u>MORAL OF THE STORY:</u>

Even Lawyers mess up regarding Wills ... especially when they are not paying attention to what's really important, or what's really being said. The big difference is that they are supposed to know better.

DO NOT CALL YOUR LAWYER 3 DAYS BEFORE YOU TAKE A PLANNED VACATION AND SAY THAT YOU NEED A WILL IN A HURRY!

*I have always thought that a Lawyer should charge <u>double</u> his usual fee
for preparation of documents in the above-described rush scenario.
Once again, just my opinion ...*

This is an absolute NO-NO! Why would you expect your Lawyer to drop everything and do this for you when there are other clients waiting for work ahead of yours?

• Even if the Lawyer agrees to prepare the documents in such a short time, when you are notified that the documents are ready for signature, schedule an appointment, be ready to go to his/her office and sign the documents! And, absolutely DO NOT say that you are too busy with vacation preparations to sign them. After all, you asked for them in a rush.

• Besides, it may not be sufficient time in which to adequately discuss and prepare appropriate documents for your situation. Do not operate under the theory that <u>any</u> Will is better than <u>no</u> Will. *Ain't necessarily so!* Remember the story about the Wills the elderly sisters wrote for themselves?

• Keep in mind that, even if the Lawyer agrees to prepare the documents for you in that short time, those documents, after you sign them, may (and probably should) be considered valid but "temporary;" that is, they <u>may</u> be better than nothing, but still may not be completely appropriate for you.

- After you return, it may be necessary to have another appointment with your Lawyer to thoroughly discuss more appropriate documents to address your specific estate-planning needs. Be sure to discuss this with your Lawyer in advance, and be prepared to have another set of documents prepared if the Lawyer deems it necessary ... all because you were in such a hurry. And, be prepared to pay another fee. It's only right!

<u>**MORAL OF THE STORY**</u>

You do not need a Will because you're going on a vacation.

You need a Will <u>JUST</u> <u>BECAUSE</u>!

Your need for a Will is just as great when you go to the grocery store as when you go on vacation.

THINGS TO THINK ABOUT BEFORE YOU SIGN A WILL

If it is important that your Will specifically states who gets what when you die, ASK YOUR LAWYER TO THOROUGHLY EDUCATE YOU ABOUT THE FOLLOWING DISTINCTIONS.

1.	It is usually wise to designate beneficiaries by <u>category,</u> as well as by individual names. For example, your Will could say: *I give, devise and bequeath my entire estate to my <u>children</u>, John, Mary, and Susan, in equal shares,* that is, as opposed to inserting their individual names. Now, though, as I write this, I can see that even this could cause a problem.

- What if you do not name your children individually in your Will, but, instead, say: *I give, devise and bequeath my entire estate to my <u>children</u>, in equal shares …* and then an illegitimate child shows up to contest your Will? Of course, you will have already passed away and won't know about this happening, but your family will know? See how easy it is to mess things up if you don't think about the details?

2.	What if you were single, had only one child, and that child predeceased you? If that child has children (your grandchildren), you might want to insert language such that your grandchildren (not your deceased child's spouse) would inherit your child's share. Why? Because that spouse might remarry, and your grandchildren might not benefit from any inheritance from you.

3.	What if were single, and you die leaving minor children? You might want your Will to state that the children's respective share be held in trust until they reach certain age(s). It is generally not thought to be a good idea to leave a large sum of money to an 18-year old, for example, because they might be inclined to squander their inheritance. You could, in the alternative, specify that they receive their inheritance at an older age, or in portions when they reach the ages of 25, 30, and 35, for example. Think about this, and discuss it with your lawyer.

> *On the Suze Orman TV show of January 5, she received a call from a 23-year old girl who had inherited $560,000 from her grandparents. That call prompted Suze to talk about why it is not a good idea to leave such a large amount of money directly to a young person, who, in this particular instance, wanted Suze's approval to buy a $42,000 car that "better reflected her personality."*

4.	If your Will were to say, *I give, devise and bequeath my entire estate <u>to my children, in equal shares,</u>* and one of your children should predecease you, would you want your deceased child's share to pass to his/her children (that is, to your grandchildren), or be divided equally among the surviving siblings?

- And what about that "*per stirpes*" (or "*per capita*") language? What do those words mean in plain English? Well, I'm not going to define them for you, because there seems to be some room for interpretation in various situations, different states, etc. What I will tell you is that you must tell your Lawyer how you want your estate passed out after your death, and let the Lawyer figure out the proper words to use.

5.	What follows are other examples of how an estate plan can go wrong by virtue of a Will that does not accurately state your intentions (for example, a Will you were to write by yourself):

a.	If your Will were to say, *I give, devise and bequeath my entire estate <u>to my children, in equal shares,</u>* does that include step-children? Illegitimate children? Adopted children?

- Would that language include or eliminate illegitimate, adopted, and/or step-children who are not named in the Will? Could they challenge your Will?

b.	If your Will were to say: *I give, devise and bequeath my entire estate <u>to my children, John, Robert and Mary, in equal shares.</u>*

- Would that mean that any later-born children would not receive an inheritance? It is important that your Will contain language to provide for after-born children to receive an inheritance if that is your intention.

d.	If your Will were to say: *I give, devise and bequeath my entire estate <u>to my then-living children, in equal shares</u>* (meaning your children still living when you die), does that mean that if one of your children has predeceased you, their respective share would not pass to a contingent beneficiary?

- If that is NOT what you intend, you must say so in time for your Lawyer to specify your wishes in the language of your Will. Who would you want to inherit the share of a child who predeceased you? No one? Or, would you want their share divided among their living brothers and sisters? Or would you want their share to pass to their children, or not? Or do you want their share to become part of your Residuary Estate? So many questions, and they all require thinking and discussion with your Lawyer.

d.	If your Will were to say: *I give, devise and bequeath my entire estate <u>to my grandchildren, Amy, Mark, Susan, Jennifer, Michael and Beth, in equal shares.</u>*

- What if there were other grandchildren born after the date on which you signed your Will. Will they get anything under your Will? Would it be OK with you if they didn't?

Can you see the absolute necessity of having lengthy discussions with your Lawyer so that your documents can be written in a way that will express your EXACT INTENTIONS so that the people you want to inherit from you actually do receive their inheritance.

ALL I CAN SAY TO YOU IS THAT IT IS UP TO YOU TO TELL YOUR LAWYER, IN CLEAR, PRECISE LANGUAGE, EXACTLY WHO YOU WANT TO INHERIT FROM YOU. It's not up to you to figure out the perfect legal words to accomplish your goals. On the other hand, it's not up to the lawyer to try to interpret what you are NOT telling him. You can contribute to the successful preparation of your own documents by being completely honest with the lawyer and allowing him to decide what words to use. That's what you are paying your Lawyer to do.

DO YOU BELIEVE THAT WHATEVER YOUR WILL SAYS IS WHAT WILL HAPPEN?

It is generally a fair assumption if you understand the language and the operation of the document. But, if the statistic is true that 98% of all estate plans fail, this assumption could be a problem.

Have you ever heard your Lawyer or your Financial Planner use the words, *"These assets pass outside of your Will?"* Do you know what that means? *(Remember the widow who intended for her estate to be divided equally among her three children, yet her daughter got the bulk of it because she was the beneficiary of her mother's IRA?)*

- It means that the only assets that you can give away after your death through your Will are those assets which you own at the time of your death.

At the time of your death, assets which you own jointly with someone else sometimes automatically pass to the other surviving joint owner(s), depending on the language in the ownership documents. Assets for which there is a named beneficiary pass directly to that beneficiary after your death. That is, they *"pass outside of your Will."*

- If you own assets jointly with your spouse, when you die, your spouse will automatically inherit those assets.

- If you own assets jointly with another person (other than your spouse), as tenants-in-common, in your Will, you can pass your one-half ownership to anyone you want to have it after your death. Your heir would then become joint owner with the person with whom you originally established ownership of the asset.

- If you own assets jointly with someone other than your spouse as <u>tenants-in-common, with the right of survivorship,</u> ownership of that asset will automatically pass to that other owner after your death.

Example

You (John) jointly own a hunting cabin with your friend, Bob. The deed provides that the two of you own the cabin as *"tenants-in-common."* Each owns fifty per cent (50%). The deed does <u>not</u> contain the words, *"joint tenants with right of survivorship."* This means that when you die, Bob does not automatically inherit your share of the cabin, such that he would then become the sole owner.

In your Will, you should state who inherits your one-half share of the ownership of that cabin. If you pass that ownership to your wife, she and Bob then become the new joint owners. If you pass that ownership to your 4 children, those 4 children then own one-half of the cabin, and Bob owns the other half.

If the deed were to contain the words *"with the right of survivorship,"* your portion will automatically pass to Bob at your death.

If you own asset(s) jointly with a person who is not your spouse, have a discussion with your lawyer about the workings of the law in relation to ownership of the asset(s) after your death. Keep in mind that joint ownership does not mean that your estate will not be responsible for paying appropriate inheritance or estate taxes. Tax would be due on the share you own.

WHERE SHALL I KEEP MY WILL AFTER I SIGN IT?

There are several things to consider before you make the final decision of where to keep your estate-planning documents. Many Lawyers recommend that you leave the original documents with them. Why?

- Does your Lawyer think you will lose them? Do *you* think you will lose them? Why would you allow a Lawyer to hint (*suggest*?) such a thing? After all, you safeguard the deed to your house, the titles to your cars, your marriage certificate, your birth certificates, your children's birth certificates, don't you?

    - The important thing is that the whereabouts of your estate-planning documents are known by your spouse (partner) and Executor and Agent, or other people in your life who may have a need to know the location of such document at some time in the future.

    - And, if you take the original documents home with you, be sure your Lawyer keeps copies of a complete set of your fully executed documents in his office in case yours are ever lost or destroyed.

- Maybe the Lawyer who wrote your Will wants to be the Lawyer who represents your estate after you die. Actually, there is absolutely nothing wrong with that, except that maybe your Executor will have his/her own Lawyer when the time comes, and doesn't want to work with your Lawyer from years past. This, too, is all right.

- If the Lawyer changes firms, retires, relocates to another state, or dies, what happens to your <u>original</u> Will (which, by the way, is the ONLY Will that the Register of Wills will accept for probate … no photocopies)? So, consider keeping the original documents in your possession with all your other important papers, just as long as someone else knows their whereabouts. (More about this in Chapter IV – RECORD KEEPING.)

- I recommend that your estate-planning documents be kept in individual page protectors in a large 3-ring notebook, which you will keep in the safe in your home. I also recommend that you buy a fire-proof/water-proof safe to be kept in your home in a private, but accessible, location, and that someone you trust knows the combination.

- If you have any concerns about your Executor's changing your Will without your permission *(I know it's a stretch, but it happens)*, you may not want your Executor to have access to your original Will. In some jurisdictions (<u>but not all</u>), it is possible for you to file your original Will (in advance of your death) with your local probate court for safekeeping. After your death, your Executor can simply present your Death Certificate to the court, and your original document will be there and ready for probate.

SHOULD I KEEP MY ORIGINAL DOCUMENTS
IN A BANK SAFE DEPOSIT BOX?

No. You may want to place <u>photocopies</u> of your important papers in a bank safe deposit box, but <u>I do **not** recommend keeping your original documents there</u>. There are several common-sense reasons why this may not be a good idea, which I have explained in Chapter IV – RECORD-KEEPING.

The subject of bank safe deposit boxes bridges several of the chapters in this book (namely, LEGAL, FINANCIAL, RECORD-KEEPING and PERSONAL). To eliminate duplication, I chose to explain the use of bank safe deposit boxes in Chapter IV – RECORD KEEPING.

PROVIDING FOR A SPECIAL-NEEDS CHILD

One of the most important things to consider when providing for a special needs child after your death is how to pass on an inheritance to that child without causing their disability benefits to be discontinued. THIS IS NO EASY TASK, and it requires the advice and direction of both legal and financial professionals.

If you have a child with special needs, you will want to be completely informed about the best way to leave your child an inheritance that will adequately provide for him/her after your death, and will enable you to take all necessary steps to see that your wishes are carried out. For this to happen, it will require serious conversations with your Lawyer, your Financial Planner, your family members and counselors to see that the assets you designate for your special-needs child actually end up being used for that specific purpose after your death.

THIS IS NO PLACE FOR DO-IT-YOURSELF LEGAL AND FINANCIAL PLANNING

I don't have to remind you that the day will come when you will no longer be here to see that your child's needs are being met, and mistakes in the planning process can have serious consequences.

IS THIS NOT YOUR WORST FEAR?

Once upon a time, there was a divorced woman with <u>four</u> adult children. One daughter has special needs, and, although she is high-functioning, she is unable to live alone and care for herself without assistance.

The woman intends to divide her estate into <u>three</u> equal parts, making no provision for an inheritance to her special-needs child in her Will because she is afraid an inheritance will cause her daughter to lose her benefits. It is a very real fear, but, as with every fear, the facts can generally eliminate your worries.

She believes that her other three children will take care of their sister for the remainder of her natural life. After all, they have been very good to their sister all her life. But, will they be able to care for her as their mother did? Are they even able and willing to do so, financially, emotionally? Maybe. Maybe not.

What if no one of her siblings has room in their home for another adult, especially one with special needs?

What if all of your other adult children work full time? Who will provide the necessary daily care for their sister?

What if one of the siblings agrees to care for her, but does not have the financial resources to do so?

What if the disabled sister's needs create serious disruption in the home of the sibling who agreed to take care of her? Where will she live then?

What if there are not enough bedrooms in the home, such that the disabled sister puts a child out of their own bedroom. How will that kind of upset be handled?

What if a sibling offers to take care of her for the rest of her natural life, but it turns out to be too much to handle. She had good intentions, but it was too much for her to handle. Then what?

What if the sibling who agreed to care for their sister gets a divorce? What if having this disabled sister living in their house was the final straw in an already fragile marriage?

What if the sibling taking care of the disabled sister (or her spouse or child) becomes ill, such that she can no longer provide for her special-needs sister?

What if the sibling taking care of the disabled sister runs into serious financial trouble, such that her house is lost to bankruptcy or foreclosure? Where will her sister live after that?

What if_____? (fill in the blank)

What if _____? (fill in the blank)

CAN YOU SEE THE POTENTIAL FOR PROBLEMS?

There are ways to provide an inheritance for a special-needs child, but the way described above is probably not good. If you have a special-needs child, you have spent many years learning about the child's needs, how to obtain financial assistance, and how to provide proper care. Now is not the time to stop asking for information and assistance for the time after your death.

None of this is easy, and thinking about the future of a special-needs child can be the source of much unhappiness, worry, and anxiety as the parent ages. Of course, you know these are important decisions, so do not rush to make them. It's complicated. If you make mistakes, the price could be very high. Give this matter a high priority in your life.

And, remember that decisions made can always be changed when appropriate and necessary, as long as they are made well in advance of an emergency or your death, and are made with appropriate legal and financial advice.

What follows is a sad but true story about a failed attempt to provide for a special-needs adult son. It is a story about the joint efforts of a highly reputable Certified Financial Planner and an equally reputable Lawyer to create an estate plan for an elderly man and his special-needs adult son. The plan was brilliant, designed to care for the son for the rest of his life after the death of his father, to provide living accommodations for others with disabilities, and to ultimately give a charitable organization a lot of money to continue their good works upon the death of the son. Unfortunately, all their good intentions could not make this plan succeed. Actions that were necessary did not happen. Read on.

Once upon a time, there was a man, a widower in his middle 80's, who had a son who was in his 50's. The son had severe learning disabilities, and the father and son were inseparable, lifelong pals, especially after the man's wife passed away. This was the man's only child, and he wanted to be assured that his son would be personally and financially secure after he, himself, died.

So, he consulted with financial and legal advisors to put into place an extremely safe, very original estate plan to care for his son after he, himself, died. The father's estate plan gave his home and all of his money, in trust, to a local organization that provided group housing for disabled adults, with the agreement that his son would continue to live in the family home for the remainder of his life, and upon the son's death, the organization would then become the sole owner of the house and any money that was left over.

You see, although the financial planner came up with the plan, he could not prepare the documents. Only the lawyer could do that. Despite the repeated urgings of the financial planner to his client to keep reminding the lawyer to put the plan on paper, the client always said, "Oh, I don't want to bother him. He's a busy man." He apparently lost site of the fact that the plan was only an idea until it was committed to paper. He thought there would always be more time. The man also apparently lost sight of the fact that he was then 80 years of age, and his son was 50, and that time was of the essence.

It doesn't really matter why he didn't <u>insist</u> that the lawyer prepare the documents; the fact is that the man died without the plan ever having been formalized. The son ended up living in an assisted living residence (also known as a nursing home), which is exactly what the father did NOT want to happen. The son did not adjust well to the unfamiliar surroundings without his father, and was obliged to move to a different facility once or twice. Neither the son nor the organization ever got the opportunity that the father intended. The son died only a few years later.

What happened to the plan, you ask? Nothing. Absolutely nothing. Why? Because the father's Lawyer never prepared the documents necessary to bring this plan into being.

Whose fault was this?

This story also appears in the FINANCIAL chapter of this book for emphasis and because it reflects the work of both legal and financial professionals.

This story didn't have to turn out that way. The estate plan created by these two professionals was brilliant, and had it succeeded, it would have made an enormous difference in the lives of many people, not the least of which was that man's son. Yet it failed because of the sins of omission by a man and his lawyer. Ouch!

Whose responsibility was it to see that the Lawyer did his job? One would ... *should* ...expect more of a trusted legal advisor. Who was there to bring a malpractice action against that Lawyer after the son's death? No one. Once again, a failure to communicate changed the course of action from one of planned success to one of doomed failure.

DURABLE (GENERAL) POWER-OF-ATTORNEY

Basically, in this document you choose a person to make decisions and take actions <u>unrelated</u> to health care, for you when you are unable to do so for yourself. That person might be called your agent or your attorney-in-fact.

Oh, I know you can download this form from the Internet. Go ahead if you think you know as much as or more than your Lawyer, but beware of the consequences of playing do-it-yourself Lawyer with this document.

You will also want to appoint a successor Agent in the event the person you originally choose cannot serve, or having served, resigns because he/she can no longer serve for you in this capacity or any reason whatsoever.

STRUCTURE OF THE DOCUMENT

There are several kinds of Powers-of-Attorney generally unrelated to your health care, and you should ask your Lawyer to discuss each in detail as each relates to your particular situation, needs and wishes. The Power-of-Attorney can be simple and specific, or very general and broad.

- In one form, you designate a person to represent you in a single, specific personal business transaction, and for no other reason; for example, to attend a real estate closing in your absence because you'll be out of town on the date of closing. The term of this Power-of-Attorney is limited to the time it takes to complete the transaction, nothing else.

- Another version of the form can be so complete that the designated person will basically be taking care of all your business in your absence, possibly for a long time. Let's say you will have to spend a year or longer disabled, unable to transact your own personal business. It would be valuable if you were to have executed this document well before need. This document can either (1) state the specific kinds of personal business transactions your Agent will handle for you; or (2) have your Lawyer compose the document to give your Agent wide berth to handle a great deal of your personal business transactions in your absence.

  - The document contains a long list of general powers granted to your Agent, including your formal authority to write checks from your account to pay your bills, negotiate contracts, and other areas of your personal business, and many other things if the maker of the document cannot do these things.

- Another form of the Power-of-Attorney only becomes effective when and if one or more doctors certifies that you are no longer able to handle your affairs, as stated in the document. The Power-of-Attorney may be specific or general in terms of what conditions might prevent you from being able to handle your affairs, so discuss this thoroughly with your Lawyer before signing.

TERM (DURATION) OF THE POWER-OF-ATTORNEY

- You can have your Lawyer prepare a Power-of-Attorney which will go into effect immediately upon your signing it.

OR

- You can have your Lawyer prepare a document that only goes into effect under specifically stated situations.

These are **not** minor decisions, and should be made only after careful consideration and thorough discussion with your Lawyer before you sign any Power-of-Attorney. Be sure to ask your Lawyer the benefits and consequences of each form of the document so that you will be making informed choices.

The best advice I can give you is to schedule an appointment with a Lawyer of your choice, and proceed.

THIS IS <u>NOT</u> A DO-IT-YOURSELF DOCUMENT!

OPTIONAL ESTATE-PLANNING DOCUMENTS

Because a basic estate plan generally consists of a Will, a Durable Power-of-Attorney, a Living Will and a Healthcare Power-of-Attorney, the following documents are deemed optional, though often appropriate and useful under certain conditions and situations:

- Revocable Living Trust
- Irrevocable Trust
- Trusts for Minor Children
- Marital Trusts
- Special Needs Trusts
- Pre-Nuptial Agreements
- Co-Habitation Agreements

- Divorce Settlement Agreements

Language used in the last three documents named above can have an effect upon your estate, depending on the terms and conditions contained in each document. If you want more information about these documents, a discussion with your estate lawyer is warranted. Also, the collaborative efforts of your estate lawyer, your divorce lawyer, and your financial planner will provide you with the best possible benefits from the documents.

REVOCABLE LIVING TRUST

The idea of passing your estate to your heirs by way of a Revocable Living Trust ("RLT") is worth your consideration, but it is important that you know and understand all that is involved for yourself, your heirs, and your Successor Trustee. While the goal of the Trust is the same as the goal of a Will (that is, to pass your assets to your heirs after your death), there are significant differences that you must consider.

The idea of using a RLT as the vehicle to pass your assets to your heirs is relatively new to me. The work I did with Lawyers was administration of decedents' estates through the probate process. Probate makes sense to me from the perspective that the process has a beginning, middle and end, and flows with a certain degree of predictability. Of course, there are lots of baby steps in between that must be handled, but, with the guidance of an experienced Lawyer, the process usually goes smoothly.

In writing this book, I have had to think long and hard about if and why an RLT is sometimes a more desirable vehicle to pass your estate than probate. On first glance, an RLT offers significant benefits, including relief from the probate process and expense, a quicker, sometimes easier passage of your assets to your heirs, it is private, offers benefits in the event of incapacity of the Grantor(s), and comfort that the document is difficult to challenge by unhappy heirs. These are all valid reasons to consider an RLT; nevertheless, the idea of using an RLT requires closer examination.

First, I believe that the biggest selling point, particularly to seniors, is the matter of avoiding probate ... more like, saving the costs of probate, generally, saving Lawyers' fees, specifically. Seniors, collectively, seem to think that probate is something like the plague, to be avoided at all costs. I don't happen to agree that avoiding probate, in itself, is reason enough to use an RLT rather than a Will to pass your assets after your death.

If you have already executed a Will and you are satisfied with the terms contained in the document, you may want to leave things alone unless and until there are valid reasons to either replace or modify your Will, as determined by you and your Lawyer.

If you have already executed a Revocable Living Trust, I recommend that you thoroughly educate yourself about what the document can do for you and what it cannot do. You might even consider making an appointment with an estate attorney for this purpose. I also recommend that you give serious thought to whether or not the person you designated as your Successor Trustee is the right person for the job. Think of whatever fee your lawyer charges as a good investment in your future.

- Does the person know all that is involved in acting as Successor Trustee?

- Is the person willing to handle all that is involved in administering the trust to completion?

- Did you just pick a person to fill in the blank on the form, without actually thinking about the reasons why you chose that person?

- Is that person capable and available to handle all of the responsibilities?

One of the features of the RLT that is strongly promoted at the luncheon seminars is that no Lawyer is needed to administer a trust. <u>I disagree completely, and it frightens me to think of what an uninformed person named Successor Trustee faces if they attempt to go it alone.</u>

How many times have I suggested that you do not engage in the practice of do-it-yourself law?

If you have not yet executed either a Will or a Revocable Living Trust, I suggest you take the time to educate yourself about the workings of both documents. If it means that you have to pay a Lawyer a fee for a consultation, it may be money well spent. And, if you are considering the RLT, if you are not prepared to fully fund the trust, or at least pay your Lawyer to do it for you, stick with the Last Will and Testament or your estate may have to go through probate anyway.

Whichever vehicle you select (that is, the Will or the RLT), do it NOW. It is possible to procrastinate until the time comes when you are no longer able to execute such a legal document.

> *Once upon a time, there was a woman who was a widow for more than 20 years. She has only one child who lives several states away. When she was asked if she would consider executing a Revocable Living Trust to make it easier for her child to handle her estate after her death, her response was firm and immediate: "I don't want a trust."*
>
> *When asked what she knew about a trust that caused her to not want a trust, she said she knew <u>nothing</u> ... <u>except that she didn't want one.</u>*
>
> *Excuse me! Did I miss something? She knows nothing about trusts, cannot say why she doesn't want a trust, but knows she doesn't want one. Doesn't sound reasonable to me. What do you think?*

WHAT ARE SOME OF THE BENEFITS OF A REVOCABLE LIVING TRUST AS COMPARED TO A WILL?

1. A Revocable Living Trust, when fully funded and administered properly, can enable your assets to be passed quickly and easily to your heirs without going through probate.

- A Will guarantees that your estate will have to go through the probate process, which has specific tasks, forms and deadlines that must be followed.

2. A Revocable Living Trust may make it possible to exclude people from your estate, and makes it extremely difficult for the document to be contested.

- Anyone can contest a Will.

3. A Revocable Living Trust may need only minimal representation by a Lawyer, thus keeping the expenses of the estate low.

- If your estate goes through the probate process, a Lawyer is generally needed, and the estate will incur appropriate court and legal fees and costs.

4. A Revocable Living Trust allows for your estate to be completed in a short time, thus passing your assets to your heirs quickly.

- The probate process takes time to complete. An average would be 18-24 months for a simple estate.

5. A Revocable Living Trust is not a public document to be filed in any court. No one gets to see your estate information.

- On the other hand, if a Will is probated in a court house, *anyone* can look at the estate documents, which contain names, addresses, social security numbers, investment and bank account numbers. Those documents have become a source of identity theft. *Something to think about.*

6. A Revocable Living Trust will usually "travel" with you if you relocate to another state.

- A Will is specific to the state in which you have established permanent residence.

7. A Successor Trustee will not have to travel from out of state to go to the court house of the county in which the decedent died in order to be formally appointed, as does an Executor. The trust document, itself, appoints the Successor Trustee ... but,

- just like an Executor, a Successor Trustee may have to travel to handle the administration of the trust, including getting rid of the decedent's personal property, possibly selling a house and all that goes with those transactions. How will a person appointed as Successor Trustee take care of all that from out of state?

If you are considering a Revocable Living Trust, it is important that you discuss these and other relevant points with your Lawyer to verify if they are appropriate in your situation, and whether or not the document will accomplish your goals.

So, here's the question: IS A LAWYER REQUIRED TO ADMINISTER A TRUST <u>or NOT?</u>

<u>**YOU READ IT HERE:**</u>

IF YOU ARE THE APPOINTED SUCCESSOR TRUSTEE OF ANYONE'S TRUST, TO ACT UPON THE DEATH OR INCAPACITY OF THE GRANTOR, I RECOMMEND THAT YOU GET YOURSELF A LAWYER IMMEDIATELY.

DON'T WAIT UNTIL THERE IS A PROBLEM.

I say this with confidence, knowing all that is necessary to administer and close out a trust, and having done this kind of work for 40 years. A person who finds himself suddenly in charge of doing the work of administering and closing a trust for someone is probably unprepared for the task, while at the same time, wanting to do a good job. Having the guidance of an experienced estate Lawyer will be of great value to the Successor Trustee.

It may help if you think of a Successor Trustee in the context of an Executor ... each has a fiduciary responsibility to handle the financial and personal affairs of someone who has passed away. While, ultimately, they have the same destination, they will travel different routes to get there.

And, if you think about it, if you need a Lawyer to administer an estate, why wouldn't you need a Lawyer to administer a trust?

If you have ever attended a luncheon seminar where Revocable Living Trusts are highly recommended, you may recall that their primary selling points were: (1) avoidance of probate; (2) no need for a Lawyer; (3) quick; (4) easy; and (5) private.

Little was said about the responsibilities of the Successor Trustee. The responsibilities are serious, as are the consequences of making mistakes. I personally do not believe the average person is capable of handling the responsibilities without the assistance of a Lawyer specializing in estate and trust administration.

You may find information on the Internet and in book stores, to show you what a Successor Trustee's job really involves. Keep in mind, however, that those books, like this book, are guides, and are not intended to replace the advice of an experienced Lawyer. What they will do, however, is give you, as the Grantor of the trust document, some idea of the enormous task you have given to the person you named as your Successor Trustee. Those books can also benefit a Successor Trustee by giving them an understanding of the task before them.

While it is not an absolute necessity for the Successor Trustee to hire a Lawyer to administer and close a trust, it would be foolhardy, in my opinion, to try to do it without benefit of counsel.

APPOINTING YOUR SUCCESSOR TRUSTEE

You are the Trustee of your own Trust. The Successor Trustee is the person who will handle your affairs after you, the Trustee (a/k/a Grantor) pass away.

While I have generally agreed that the apparent benefits are worthwhile reasons to consider when deciding whether or not to use the Revocable Living Trust, there remained something about the trust that did not satisfy me. I finally realized that the weak link in the chain of Revocable Living Trusts is the enormous amount of responsibility and liability imposed upon the Successor Trustee ... the person who will handle your affairs after you, the Grantor, pass away ... especially if you and the Successor Trustee believe no Lawyer is needed.

The selection of the person to be your Successor Trustee is not to be made without careful consideration of several factors. I know people who just named someone ... *anyone* ... without giving the selection much thought, without investigating what will be required of that person in order to perform their respective duties. Can you see the potential for problems?

Being a Successor Trustee is no small task, and carries with it enormous responsibility and legal and financial liability. You must consider whether that person is capable of doing everything that is necessary to close out your life through the document known as a Revocable Living Trust. If you tell your Successor Trustee that their job will be easy, and that no Lawyer will be needed, you are not telling the whole story.

There are so many reasons why it would be easy to select the wrong person for the job, for the wrong reasons, especially if you believe that naming a person to be your Successor Trustee is an honor. It is not an honor. It is a big job.

The idea that the average person can function as a Successor Trustee without benefit of legal counsel is ridiculous, and is actually setting that person up for the possibility of personal liability and legal problems in the process of administering the trust. Why? Because the Successor Trustee is generally not knowledgeable about how to do the job.

JOB DESCRIPTION OF A SUCCESSOR TRUSTEE

Let me list for you, in no particular order, some of the things a Successor Trustee must consider while doing the job. While you are reading this list, think if you, yourself, would be willing or able to do all these things without legal assistance.

1. The first thing for you to do is give serious thought to whether or not you are willing to act as Trustee, considering all that will be required of you.

2. If you have been appointed a Successor Trustee, your first duty is to read, understand and follow the terms and conditions of the trust document. Your authority, as Successor Trustee, comes directly from the trust document itself, with which you should be intimately familiar. It is recommended that you read the document several times during the course of your work so that you stay familiar with the terms contained therein.

3. The appointment as Trustee is not for life. You can decline the appointment right from the beginning, or resign at any time during the process of administering the trust by virtue of a formal Resignation form prepared by a lawyer and appropriately signed, dated and witnessed.

4. If you ever wish to stop serving as Trustee once you have actually begun, you can resign, but it is important that you know that your job responsibilities and liability do not end until a replacement Successor Trustee is appointed and until all of the assets of the trust are transferred from you to your replacement.

5. Once you have accepted the appointment as Successor Trustee, you are the person responsible for the administration of the trust. Are you sure you want to proceed?

6. It is important to know that as a Trustee, you will be operating as a fiduciary, that is, as a person responsible for taking care of something that belongs to someone else. This responsibility carries with it personal liability for mishandling trust assets or mistakes that you may make during the administration of the trust. The primary responsibility of a Successor Trustee is to act responsibility in relation to the circumstances.

7. You have a duty to seek competent legal advice all through the process of administering the trust, notwithstanding the suggestion that no Lawyer is needed for a Successor Trustee to complete the job. If you should choose to act without benefit of legal counsel, you could end up paying out of your own pocket for any failure to consult with a Lawyer when it was necessary and appropriate to do so, and you chose not to. You could find yourself vulnerable to litigation for mismanaging the decedent's trust assets.

8. Discuss the work which the Lawyer will be doing for you, and the fees which the Lawyer will be charging. Know that the trust will pay those fees. You do not have to retain the Lawyer who prepared the trust, but it is recommended that you retain the services of a Lawyer with a lot of experience in estate and trust administration.

9. A Successor Trustee must be prepared to keep accurate records of every single transaction relating to the administration of the trust. In addition, the Trustee must keep detailed notes about every meeting with legal counsel, beneficiaries, and all other advisors. Such notes should include the date, the names of persons attending, the subject(s) discussed, and your signature. Keep these notes organized, in a safe place, and available if needed.

10. You must keep complete files of all correspondence and communication with everyone associated with the administration of the trust. This includes printing out every email and keeping them in chronological order with letters, phone messages, etc.

11. Just like an Executor, you are entitled to reimbursement for reasonable expenses you may incur while acting as Trustee. Keep accurate records of all out-of-pocket expenses so that the trust can periodically reimburse you.

12. If there is more than one Trustee, know that a high degree of cooperation and mutual acceptance of the responsibilities is required, and that each Trustee will be held accountable for any breach of fiduciary duty by the other.

13. A Successor Trustee is required to show absolute loyalty and honesty to the trust, and to be impartial to the beneficiaries.

14. As Successor Trustee, you should sign documents on behalf of the trust with your name, followed by the word, Trustee (that is, *John Doe, Trustee*).

15. You will need to rely on experienced professionals to give you appropriate direction in matters relating to the administration of the trust; advisors such as your Lawyer and accountant, for example. All fees associated with such professional advice will be paid from the trust.

16. You should know that the penalty for breaching any of the duties of a Successor Trustee is that you could be held personally liable, and could have to pay any damages as a result, from your own money, not from the trust funds.

17. Practicing do-it-yourself law while acting as a Successor Trustee is dangerous because it can potentially expose you to personal liability if something goes wrong. And, if something does, in fact, go wrong, your reliance on the advice of an experienced professional can be a reasonable defense against a charge that you breached your fiduciary duty.

18. You must never mingle the funds of the trust with your own. You will have to establish bank accounts for trust monies, separate from your own.

19. You must provide periodic accounting to the beneficiaries, who are entitled to know the progress of the trust administration and when they are likely to receive their inheritance. The best suggestion I can give is to stay connected to the beneficiaries and establish good relationships with them that include mutual respect and trust.

20. It is important that you have each beneficiary sign a written approval of your accounting, and if they do not approve, you have the option of asking a court to review and approve your accounts.

21. You must protect the assets of the trust until they are distributed to the beneficiaries.

22. You must avoid any appearance of impropriety. Judges and juries are not very sympathetic to a Trustee who appears to have acted in a manner that appears to be inappropriate, whether or not it is true. Your actions must be above reproach at all times.

23. It is recommended that you keep a time-log to document exactly how much time you spend as you fulfill your duties as Successor Trustee. The log should include the date, exact amount of time spent in the activity, and a brief description of each activity (phone call; write and/or read email; go to the lawyer's office or the bank, etc.).

24. You are also entitled to a reasonable fee for the services you render to the trust. Know that you are not required to take the fee, but know that if you do, it may be taxable for U. S. Income Tax.

25. It is important that you have beneficiaries individually sign detailed receipts for all distributions made to them from the trust assets.

26. It is recommended that you retain the services of a CPA to prepare tax returns, although I do recommend that your Lawyer prepare Inheritance Tax and/or Estate Tax returns.

27. When you conclude the administration of the trust, you should provide a lengthy, accurate, detailed accounting of every transaction of the trust, after which each beneficiary will sign as evidence of their approval of the information on the account.

28. This document should also contain language wherein the beneficiaries waive any claims against you and promise to pay any trust expenses that show up after they have received their respective inheritance.

29. It would be in your best interests to be certain that there are no stones left unturned in completing the administration of the trust such that the beneficiaries would have to return some of the money. If they choose not to sign your accounting, you can submit it to the court for review and approval.

30. It is recommended that you have your Lawyer prepare a document to be signed by the beneficiaries, whereby you are formally released from your responsibilities as Successor Trustee.

? ? ?

1. Having read the job description, do you honestly believe that the person you named as your Successor Trustee is capable of handling the job without the assistance of a Lawyer?

2. And, if you are to act as a Successor Trustee, do you really want to take on all that responsibility and liability by yourself, for as long as it takes to complete the administration of the trust?

When a person is named Executor to administer an estate after someone's death, the Executor customarily hires a Lawyer to handle the process from beginning to end. The Lawyer's fee is one of the "costs of probate" that people complain about and try to avoid by executing a Revocable Living Trust in the first place.

Having done the work of administering decedents' estates through the probate process for many years, I tell you that the Lawyer and staff earn their money. There is much to be done to complete administration of a decedent's estate, and it is important that the steps be completed in a timely, accurate manner, or the Executor could be held liable. There is much comfort offered to an Executor (and to the family of the decedent) knowing that an attorney is handling the administration of the estate.

What comfort and assistance are there for a Successor Trustee without a Lawyer? What protection from liability? What assurance they are doing everything necessary and appropriate if they don't know what's needed in the first place? *Just asking...*

While the above list is a basic job description of a Successor Trustee, it is also a general list of the things your Lawyer and staff would do for you in exchange for a fee <u>during the probate process</u>. Lawyers have experienced staff to keep accurate records; they have copy machines, postage meters, FAX machines, computers, files and cabinets to safeguard the estate and trust documents, a staff of people knowledgeable of the workings of administering a decedent's estate.

I believe their work is worth the fee.

On the Suze Orman TV show of Saturday, September 3, 2011, a young woman called to ask for help in getting her parents to address the matter of their not having any estate planning documents. The caller stated that her father was one of those men who refused to talk about Wills or anything having to do with his death, and her mother was being completely passive (her words) about it all because she didn't know what else to do.

Suze, in her forceful way, displayed disgust at the way men refuse to talk about what is an inevitable event in their lives, and how willing they are to leave behind a wife who may be unprepared to live alone, emotionally and financially.

Suze suggested that the elderly couple immediately have a Lawyer prepare a Revocable Living Trust that includes an incapacity clause which will protect each of them in the event that the other becomes unable to sign his/her own name.

In order to get this process started, Suze suggested that the caller speak with her mother alone, and ask her one question: "If Daddy needs to go into a nursing home because of dementia or worse, and cannot sign his name, and you need to sell your house which you and he own as joint tenants with the right of survivorship, will you be able to sell it?" The answer is yes and no.

The answer is NO because the woman needs her husband's signature on the deed in order to sell the house, and if he were unconscious or legally incompetent, he would be unable to sign his name.

The answer is YES because the woman could retain the services of a Lawyer to have her appointed as her husband's legal guardian, an expensive, invasive, degrading, emotionally devastating process, which requires court supervision thereafter for expenses relating to the husband's nursing home care.

Now, if you are a man reading this, are you really willing to put your wife through all that when all you have to do is sign a few legal documents that will protect her?

> *Even if the reverse were to happen (that is, if the wife were to become unconscious or legally incompetent and unable to sign her name), the husband would then have to go through the same guardianship process.*

> *Who knows whether this young woman will be able to get her parents to understand their situation such that they will take steps to avoid its happening.*

The choice to pass your assets to your heirs by way of a Revocable Living Trust may sound quick, easy and inexpensive. If all goes well, that is what will probably happen; but, sometimes, things are not always what they seem to be.

> If you go to the trouble of executing a Revocable Living Trust, at least be 100% certain that all of your assets are correctly and completely funded into the trust, or your Successor Trustee may have to go to court and be named your Executor and take your estate through the probate process, which is exactly what you were trying to avoid in the first place.

WHAT DOES IT MEAN TO FUND THE TRUST?

In my opinion (*and it is just MY opinion*) the use of "fund" (a noun) as a verb is an unfortunate use of the word. One might even call it *legalese*. Maybe way back in the history of the law, there is a good reason why "fund" was used this way, but it is very confusing to the average person. The word is not used in general conversation as a verb, and since "funding" usually applies only to a trust (or other financial vehicles), most people do not have occasion to use the word very often.

So, what exactly does it mean to fund the trust?
- Funding the trust is the paperwork process whereby the formal ownership of your assets is legally transferred from you, as an individual owner, to the trust as the owner.

Funding a trust is an ongoing process, not a single transaction. It takes time, attention to detail, good record-keeping, and a commitment to complete the process. And, as you acquire new assets (other than vehicles), you must also title them in the name of the trust.

It would be wise to have the funding completed within 90 days after signing the Revocable Living Trust. Some companies and their respective forms and procedures take longer than others. Someone must regularly monitor the process to see that it is completed in a timely manner, and that nothing is overlooked.

For some people, changing the ownership designations on their assets is frightening, because they are afraid they are giving up the right to own and handle their assets as they choose. Not so. As the Trustee of your own trust, you can handle your assets and money as before, you can add or remove property any time, and you can change or amend the trust when it is appropriate and necessary. Remember it is called a *Revocable* Living Trust.

> Note: As with Wills and other estate documents, do not attempt to amend the Trust document yourself. It will require the expertise of a Lawyer to do it properly, and it wouldn't hurt if it were the same Lawyer who wrote the Trust document in the first place. And, do not write on the original document! No inserts, no cross-outs, no Wite-Out, no doodles. No nothing!

And, know that having your assets funded into the trust can help the maker(s) of the trust by protecting assets if he and/or she were to become disabled, and by providing assurance that their estate assets will be distributed to loved ones according to the wishes of the trust maker(s) upon their death. These are good reasons to consider executing a trust.

You can still handle your own personal business as before. Having your assets titled in the name of your trust should not negatively affect your life in any way. There is nothing to fear from a Revocable Living Trust. But, I strongly recommend that you take the time to learn about what the trust can and will do for you now and after your death. If that means you should have a consultation with your Lawyer to give you a working understanding of the document, then do it; it would be worth the legal fee in peace of mind.

TAX Id. NUMBER

You may not have to get a new tax identification number for your trust. During the life of the trust maker(s), a Social Security Number can be used, and in the case of a married couple who are Co-Trustees of a trust, the husband's Social Security number can be used. Any income earned on trust assets will be reported on the trust maker's individual tax returns. It would be wise to verify this with your attorney.

HOW DOES THIS CHANGE OF OWNERSHIP HAPPEN?

You or your Attorney (or his/her paralegal) will obtain all of the forms required to change the ownership of all of your assets. If you do not fund the trust yourself, you will have to provide your Lawyer with a very complete list of names, addresses, account numbers … all of the information that is needed to contact the various companies where your assets are currently held.

- Let's use your checking account as an example of what happens when you change the title on the account. You will go to your bank, provide identification, and an Affidavit of Trust from your trust document to verify the existence of the trust, sign the forms to change the ownership of your checking account, and the next time your receive a bank statement, the account will be titled in the name of the trust.

  - For example, if your checking account is presently owned by John and Mary Doe, after you change the title, the account will be owned by The Revocable Living Trust of John and Mary Doe dated 1/2/2013. That's it. Unless your bank requires it, you may not even have to get new checks to reflect this change (that is, your checks can continue to say John and Mary Doe), and you can sign your checks as before.

WHAT HAS TO BE CHANGED?

In order to fund your trust, you will need to sign papers necessary to change the ownership of all your assets, including, but not necessarily limited to, all your bank accounts and investment accounts and U.S. Government bonds. You will need to have a new deed prepared for your house(s), and the new deed(s) must be recorded in the office of the Recorder of Deeds where the real estate is located.

You do <u>not</u> want to change the ownership designation on your car(s), insurance policies, or your individual retirement accounts.

YOU COULD DO THIS BY YOURSELF, BUT, AS USUAL
I DON'T RECOMMEND THAT YOU DO

If you were to miss just one bank account, for example, your estate will have to go through probate. *(Remember Alan's story from earlier in this chapter.)* So, precision and attention to detail are basic requirements to complete the change of ownership and get the trust completely funded.

Funding the trust is really only a paperwork process, but to the average person, it can seem extremely complicated. It <u>*is*</u> complicated. I believe the Lawyer who prepared the document should fund the trust, and that work should be included as part of his fee, but, that is <u>not</u> how it usually happens.

So, you may ask, if not the Lawyer, then who? The answer is easy: YOU! But, you say, "*I don't know how.*" Therein lies one of the big problems.

SCENARIO

Mr. and Mrs. Client meet with Lawyer to discuss estate planning. As a result of that meeting, for an agreed-upon fee of $2,500, Lawyer agrees to prepare the following nine (9) documents: Revocable Living Trust; Pour-over Wills; Durable Powers-of-Attorney; Medical Powers-of-Attorney; Living Wills.

Lawyer sends drafts to Clients for their review, with the request that they make a list of all questions they may have. Clients are asked to call Lawyer with questions, and if necessary, to meet with Lawyer again to have in-depth conversation about their questions. Once Clients and Lawyer have completed the discussion phase, final documents will be prepared.

Clients meet with Lawyer to execute documents, and the originals of each are given to Clients as they direct. At this point, Clients assume their estate plan is complete, having no information to the contrary.

In fact, at that point, the Trust is NOT complete because it is **_unfunded_**. After all the documents had been signed, the Lawyer might say: ***"The only thing left to do is fund the trust."*** The Lawyer has told Clients this fact, but has failed to inform the Clients of exactly what it means to them. *So, now what?*

QUESTIONS:

1. Do the Clients **understand** that the Trust document they signed is **in**complete? They heard the Lawyer say that the trust still needed to be funded, but without additional explanation, the clients assumed the work on that document was complete. Even if they really understood that the plan was not complete, it's pretty certain they assumed their Lawyer would do what was necessary to complete the plan. Was that a fair assumption?

2. On what basis would Client even think that Trust was <u>not</u> complete?

3. Did the Lawyer explain the definition of "funding the trust" to Clients in understandable language, such that Clients could accurately and completely explain it to their friends or family over dinner?

4. Do the Clients know what "unfunded" means to them?

5. Do the Clients know the consequences of an unfunded trust? What if the Trust is only partially funded?

6. Do the Clients know that if the trust is not completely funded, all assets which were not put into the name of the Trust will go through probate, thus defeating one of the main purposes of the Revocable Living Trust?

7. Did the Lawyer tell the Clients about the implications and/or consequences of this happening in language understandable to the average person?

8. Do the Clients know that there may be some unconscious intentionality on the Lawyer's part to have that happen, so Lawyer gets to represent their estate after their death? Of course not. They trust their Lawyer to do what needs to be done to protect them. But, Clients didn't ask, did they? Why would they? It would never occur to them that there are consequences for not funding the trust (whatever that means).

9. Do the Clients know that the Lawyer is not going to automatically fund the trust? Do the clients even know what needs to be done?

10. Do the Clients know that the Lawyer assumes they are going to fund the trust themselves?

11. Was any of this discussed?

12. Do the Clients have any idea how to go about it?

13. Did the Lawyer give them sufficient information for them to make an *informed* choice about who will fund the trust and how it will be accomplished?

14. Would the Clients ever choose to fund the trust themselves if they knew what it means and how to go about it?

15. Is it reasonable for Clients to assume that Lawyer is going to fund the trust? Clients trust Lawyer to do the job they asked their Lawyer to do. Why would they ever assume their Lawyer had not completed the job? After all, the Lawyer did not say that for $2,500, he would only prepare the documents. The Clients did not know that there was an additional step.

16. And, don't you think the Lawyer should have stated right at the beginning that the preparation of the nine documents would cost $2,500, but to fund the trust, there would be an extra fee of $_____?

   - If Lawyer had said that, Clients may have asked what it means to fund a trust, how much more it would cost for the Lawyer to do the paperwork, and a conversation would have ensued wherein Clients and Lawyer would have discussed the process of funding the trust, explain what that means in language understandable to the Clients, and at that time, a decision would have been made either to:
     (a) increase Lawyer's fee to include the work; or,
     (b) clients would fund the trust themselves .

17. Is it reasonable to assume that Clients have no idea of what is involved in funding the trust?

18. Whose job is it to inform them?

19. Why didn't the Lawyer tell the clients that:

(a)   After they signed the Trust Agreement, the Trust was **in**complete?

(b)   The Lawyer will do the work to fund the trust, but it will cost more?

(c)   The Clients can do the work themselves if they want to?

(d)   The Lawyer will advise them of what is necessary and how to go about doing it?

(e)   That the work is very detailed and requires a lot of time and preparation of other documents, contact with banks, insurance companies, investment firms, Recorder of Deeds, follow-up, etc. … and that, while the process is time-consuming and possibly hard for the Clients, it is not impossible.

HAS LAWYER COMPLETELY FULFILLED HIS OBLIGATIONS TO CLIENTS?

WHAT HAPPENS IF A TRUST IS NOT FULLY FUNDED?

At the time of your death, if you own assets that are not funded into the Trust, those assets will have to go through the entire probate process, and avoiding probate was one of the reasons why you executed a Revocable Living Trust in the first place, wasn't it?

One way or the other, your Revocable Living Trust must be fully funded, or the entire intention in establishing the trust will be for naught.

WHAT ABOUT TAXES?

Oh, somewhere did you hear that if you execute a Revocable Living Trust, there will be no taxes to pay? Wrong!

Once upon a time, I sat across the table from a woman at a party, and she was telling the group about the young female attorney who gave an estate-planning presentation at her local senior center. This woman seated at the table stated unequivocally that there was no Inheritance Tax due if you have a Revocable Living Trust. The others at the table were very interested in what the woman had to say, that is, until I chimed in.

I told her that statement was not true. She asked me if I was a Lawyer, and I told her that I was not. She then asked me why she should believe me ... after all, the woman at the senior center was a Lawyer, and she ought to know. My response was this:

First, I told her she doesn't have to believe me. Second, I said I didn't hear what that Lawyer said. Third, it is possible the woman had incorrectly heard what the Lawyer said. Fourth, no matter what she believes, someday her estate (heirs) will have to pay Inheritance Tax on the value of her estate if she dies owning taxable assets ... Revocable Living Trust or not.

The fact is that executing a Revocable Living Will does not remove the possibility of paying Inheritance or Estate Tax. Unfortunately, this is another one of those "whisper down the lane" tales that travels the senior circuit. I have heard it many times. And, whether or not she believed me, one day, after she has passed away, her estate (heirs) will probably have to pay Inheritance Tax.

CAUTION

Whether you are acting as an Executor or a Successor Trustee, there will be times when you have to transact business with people who are not Lawyers or legitimate financial advisors. I'm referring to transactions in banks, investment companies, etc., where you deal with clerks, either in person or by phone. Sometimes, those people are highly knowledgeable and the information they provide will be appropriate, accurate, and reliable. Other times, it is just the opposite. Somehow, you must be able to distinguish which it is.

One thing I want to impress upon you is to be careful not to challenge the competence of the person you're speaking with. I learned years ago that they may be the keepers of the information I needed, so you want to get on their good side. I found that asking them, "*What do you recommend?*" works wonders. Give it a try.

"I'll just put your name on the account for convenience" is a statement you may expect to hear from a bank clerk when you attempt to open an account as Agent under a Power-of-Attorney. If you allow your name to be put on the account **just for convenience** (*whose convenience?*), you will end up joint owner of the other person's money. That is not your intention. Your intention is to act as an agent for a person who may not be able to write his/her own checks or handle money some day in the future, for any reason whatsoever. You must be firm with the bank clerk, and insist that the account be opened up as a Power-of-Attorney account, not a joint account.

"Just send/give us a Short Certificate" are words often used by clerks who have no idea what a Short Certificate represents. A Short Certificate is evidence of the formal appointment of an Executor in the probate process of a decedent's estate. Where the problems arise is when there is no probate, thus, no Short Certificate, and you must convince a clerk that they don't need what they think they need (that is, a Short Certificate).

- Remember the story you read above, about the widow who wanted to close out her deceased husband's little, tiny investment account, and opened a Pandora's box when she got a Short Certificate she didn't need. Let this one example cause you, at the very least, to ask questions.

"Just go to the Register of Wills and you can get a Short Certificate from them" are other words often used by clerks who are uninformed. Wouldn't you think that a person sitting at the front desk of a bank or on the phone from an investment company would be more knowledgeable? *Just asking...*

"You need a Short Certificate to transact the business of the Trust." When you attempt to close out a bank or investment account, sell real estate, or do all of the other transactions necessary and appropriate to wind up the affairs of a deceased person, you will often be asked for a Short Certificate by an <u>un</u>informed clerk. You must impress upon them that <u>there is no Short Certificate and there will be no Short Certificate because you are not an Executor, you are a Trustee</u> operating under a specific trust agreement that gives you the authority to act. Be ready and willing to provide the clerk with proof of your appointment contained in the language of the trust agreement and with a Death Certificate, and you should be able to complete the transaction.

- If the bank clerk (or other person) insists that you go to the Register of Wills and get a Short Certificate, you will have to ask for that person's manager. But, in any event, do not go to the court house to get a Short Certificate if you are a Trustee. You will just aggravate yourself, waste time and gas, attempting to get something you don't need in the first place.

In the FINANCIAL chapter, there is information about company-sponsored retirement plans, and your need to make a choice of whether to take your money or leave it behind when you terminate your employment with that company. If you were to decide it was much easier to just leave it with the company than to have to deal with that big package of information you will be given, you would be avoiding a genuine examination of your options. If you leave the money with the company, you surrender control over it, and you would thereafter have to deal with "clerks," who are not financial planners. Their understanding of your financial situation is often incomplete, and advice they give you may or may not be correct and appropriate for your situation. Be careful.

"You just need a Short Certificate <u>and</u> a Death Certificate" are other words you may hear from clerks. For many years, I had to speak with bank clerks to impress upon them that they don't need both, they only need the Short Certificate. When you think about it, you will see that when a Will is entered for probate, a Death Certificate is given to the Register of Wills to prove that the person died, and then Short Certificates will thereafter be issued by the Register of Wills. It's all very sequential. The fact that there is a Short Certificate is proof, by itself, that the person died and a specific person is appointed Executor (or administrator). There is no other reason on earth why a Short Certificate would be issued. So, why does the bank clerk need a Death Certificate, too? Usually, they do not.

- Note that on a Death Certificate, at least in Pennsylvania, there is a notation at the top of the page, stating that the document is not to be photocopied. If you need additional certificates, you will have to order them from the state or the Funeral Director.

I know of other situations where people were given incorrect advice from bank clerks and clerks at investment organizations, and when they followed that advice, they ran into problems. The advice caused a great deal of distress to the people who could not determine for themselves if the advice was good or bad. Assuming the clerk knew what he/she was talking about, some people simply do what the clerk tells them to do. Make no assumptions about your money. Verify information at every step of the way.

If you are trying to sell a decedent's car, and the decedent does not have a probate estate, you would probably only need a Death Certificate to prove that the owner is deceased. You would probably not need to open an estate in the probate court just to sell a car; but these rules may vary from state to state and jurisdiction to jurisdiction, so verify the rules beforehand.

**What Is The Difference Between
A DEATH CERTIFICATE and a SHORT CERTIFICATE?**

Death Certificate: **evidence that a person died.**

Short Certificate: **evidence of the appointment of an executor or administrator of a probate estate.**

- **Both certificates cost a few dollars each.**

- **Death certificates never expire and cannot be photocopied.**

- **Short certificates expire, but can be renewed for a small fee.**

IRREVOCABLE LIVING TRUSTS

As the name implies, an irrevocable trust cannot be altered or amended without court approval. Trusts of this nature should be used only in certain circumstances after careful consultation and planning discussions with your Lawyer who should be well versed on the workings of such a document.

An Irrevocable Living Trust can be thought of as an advanced estate planning tool, used most often by persons whose gross estates are taxable for Federal Estate Tax purpose … that is to say, wealthy people. These documents are not usually considered to be the foundation of an estate plan, but a supplement to it.

Sometimes, this kind of trust holds a large life insurance policy as its only asset. The proceeds of that insurance policy will be used to pay Federal Estate Tax which, in certain situations, can be millions of dollars. The following is an example of a situation when the use of such a trust would have been advisable.

Once upon a time, a man and his wife built and operated a very successful business, so successful, in fact, that their sons were employed in the business and were able to support their families in so doing. The business did not operate as a corporation, a limited liability corporation, a partnership, a fictitious name, or any other possible legal entity for the ownership and operation of a business.

All of the assets of the business, including the real estate, were jointly owned by the man and his wife, as tenants-by-the-entireties; and, when the man died at the age of 81, his wife (as surviving spouse) inherited all of their assets, including the business. There was no Inheritance or Estate tax due at the time of the husband's death.

The sons wanted very much to keep the business operating, and they realized that changes had to be made if the business was to survive the death of their mother. She, now 80 years old herself, was not willing to discuss any possible succession-planning options or estate-planning options with her sons, saying that if her husband didn't see any reason to do it, why should she. What do you think happened when she died?

She had an enormous estate which included personal property, real estate and the business, the value of which was mostly taxable. The problem was that the assets of the business were not liquid ... that is, the assets did not include sufficient money to pay the tax. The assets of the business were in real estate, vehicles, merchandise, good will, customer lists, etc. The family nearly lost the business paying the death taxes.

> *If there had been an Irrevocable Life Insurance Trust, it would probably have covered the Federal Estate Tax liability, and the sons would not have had to sell assets of the business and dig into their own personal funds to pay the tax.*
>
> *The time for arranging this trust would have been when the husband was still living, when there was time for discussion among the family members of the financial consequences of doing inappropriate (or no) estate planning.*

OTHER TRUSTS

Most of the trusts mentioned in this book are used in situations of fairly simple estate planning. There are other trusts and various other legal strategies which estate-planning Lawyers use when a client owns complex assets or has family situations which would require specialized planning documents. The list includes (but is not limited to) trusts created for minor children, marital trusts, and special-needs trusts.

If you believe your estate plan warrants discussions about these other advanced planning steps, speak with your Lawyer.

ESTATE PLANNING FOR THE BLENDED FAMILY

The dictionary defines "blend" as thoroughly mixing together. That may be a good definition for a recipe or for blended whiskey, but it doesn't accurately define the blending of families. While blending families may be the intention of two people who marry, bringing with them children from a previous marriage, I tell you from personal experience and observation that it seldom turns out as expected. All sorts of emotions get in the way. Good communication may ease the transition, but I'm not even certain that can make it work, and you know how much I value good communication.

When two people with children from previous relationships marry, their estate-planning focus should include protecting the inheritance rights of their own children. This kind of estate-planning requires some serious conversations between you and your intended spouse/partner, and will have a better chance of succeeding if you also include your financial planner, your divorce lawyer, and your estate-planning lawyer in the process, all working for the highest good of your family.

This is a place where the Pre-Nuptial Agreement becomes valuable, important, even necessary. It is doubtful that most couples marrying for the second or third time sign Pre-Nuptial Agreements, but I believe that those who do will have a better chance of creating a successful life and ultimately, an estate plan. Let's take a brief look at an example of basic estate-planning of a man and woman in a second marriage.

> *Scenario*
>
> *Husband and wife, both previously married, both with children from the previous marriage, have mirror-image Wills ... that is, husband's Will leaves everything to his wife; wife's Will leaves everything to her husband. What this means in lay terms is that if the husband dies first and the wife survives, she inherits everything from him, and his children inherit nothing from their father at that time.*
>
> *The wife's Will is still legally valid, and technically, does not need to be rewritten unless she wants to make changes.*
>
> *The Wills originally executed by this woman and her now-deceased husband express their mutual intentions that, upon the death of the surviving spouse, everything is to be divided equally among ALL of their children ... that is, her 3 and his 4 children ... the survivor's estate being divided into seven equal shares.*
>
> *But, wait a minute. After the first spouse dies, what is to prevent the surviving spouse (in this example, the wife) from having a new will written, leaving her estate to her 3 children, and not to her 4 stepchildren? It happens.*
>
> *Also, after the husband dies, the wife might re-marry, maybe even to a person with children. Now, the estate of the wife becomes more complicated by the fact that there are now her 3 children, her deceased husband's 4 children, and her new husband's 2 children.*

> *DO YOU SEE HOW COMPLICATED IT CAN GET?*

So, who inherits what? Much depends upon the intentions and the integrity of the two people, whether or not they take the time to thoroughly talk with each other about the benefits of pre-nuptial planning, whether or not they consult appropriate professionals, whether or not they take the advice of those professionals, and whether or not they actually execute the appropriate estate-planning documents.

While estate planning for a blended family is complicated, it can be sorted out if two people are willing to be honest with each other, and are willing to take appropriate, timely actions. There is a lot riding on all of these contingencies, and, in many cases, who do you think experience the greatest loss when the two people do not do serious pre-nuptial planning? Their children.

OPTIONAL ESTATE-PLANNING DOCUMENTS

The following three documents (Pre-Nuptial Agreement, Cohabitation Agreement, and Divorce Settlement Agreement) are not ordinarily considered as integral parts of estate planning; however, they can and often <u>do</u> directly affect estate planning, for better or for worse.

Generally, the expertise of lawyers experienced in the practice of matrimonial and family law is required in order to prepare the documents, and to help you fully understand and execute such documents.

What follows is information to get you <u>thinking</u> about questions to ask your attorney and to help you be prepared for situations you may not have known about previously as they relate to both estate planning and family law. Once again, know that these laws vary significantly from state to state and jurisdiction to jurisdiction, and you should not make decisions regarding these documents without the advice of appropriate counsel.

PRE-NUPTIAL AGREEMENTS

PreNuptial Agreements are legal documents executed by two people about to be married. The document, among other things, spells out how their respective assets will be divided in the event of a divorce or death. These agreements are an important piece of both divorce settlements and estate planning. I firmly believe in each individual's protecting themselves legally and financially, and executing a PreNuptial agreement can provide that protection if the document is carefully crafted to accurately match your situation.

This is, however, an area of planning that may not seem like an easy fit into the category of estate planning, but which definitely fits into end-of-life planning in situations where it is appropriate to use such documents.

Since they are both legal documents to be prepared by a Lawyer well versed on the subject, I have included these Agreements in the LEGAL chapter of this book; however, it is important that you know that the subject of PreNuptial Agreements and Co-Habitation Agreements bridges the legal, financial and personal aspects of end-of-life planning.

Where these two particular documents fit into estate planning is in the way they can provide for the protection and distribution of your assets in the event of death, divorce or break-up. The failure of these documents may be simply the absence of them … that you won't know the benefits they can provide for you because you wouldn't sign one, and, in fact, you wouldn't even discuss the possibility.

Why was that? Out of fear? By now, you should have some insight into what happens when a decision is based upon fear. In specific instances, fear might be a good motivator, but that is not generally the case with estate planning, where the fear is usually about dying. In other instances, it can be the fear of not naming the right person to speak for you if you are seriously ill, so you don't bother to name anybody. Now, *that's* something to be afraid of. With marital documents, the fear may be that if you even talk about the document, your relationship will break up. If that discussion breaks up the relationship, you must question the value of that relationship in the big picture of your life.

OK, I get it. You are afraid. But, have you ever noticed that the moment you do something you are afraid to do, the fear goes away?

You must do the things you think you cannot do.

Eleanor Roosevelt

A Pre-Nuptial Agreement is not just for young people approaching marriage. In fact, these documents may be of significantly more importance to Baby Boomers contemplating re-marriage after a divorce or death of a spouse, because chances are high that one or both parties have personal assets and children from a previous marriage. If you care about your children, you will protect their inheritance rights by discussing this document with your Lawyer, and insisting that your intended (marriage) partner sign.

If you want a PreNups, be open and honest with your soon-to-be spouse about why you want it, and try to discuss it calmly. And, the sooner the better! You probably know that a conversation about a PreNups is going to open Pandora's Box and let out some unpleasant reactions and words. All I can say is to do your best to calmly and fully express yourself, listen to your intended spouse, and try not to damage your relationship while getting the Agreement signed. And, if it turns out to be a "deal breaker," maybe it should be.

Know this: You can have both: that is, <u>both</u> the marriage and the PreNups.

There are many things to be considered before signing a Nuptial Agreement, not the least of which is to ask yourself the question of whether your love for each other will survive the signing of the document? It will depend on how important the Agreement is to you, and in reality, has little to do with love. It is a business agreement between two people who plan to spend the rest of their lives together *"for better and for worse."* If the couple cannot survive this important conversation, they should rethink their marriage plans.

- *"If you really loved me, you wouldn't ask me to sign,"* is probably the most common response when one individual asks the other to sign.

- One could just as easily turn the statement around to say, *"If you really loved me, you would see the benefits for both of us and sign the Agreement."*

- Some people are outraged at the idea of putting the terms of their relationship into a legal document, but if and when they dissolve the relationship, they will be glad they did. And, if you don't like the idea of "putting the terms of your relationship into a legal document," what do you think a divorce decree does? *Just asking...*

Also, it is necessary and appropriate for each person to discuss the matter with both their personal, respective Financial Planner and Lawyer to learn about the benefits of having such documents, and the consequences of <u>not</u> having them.

So, let's just say that in order to do good estate- and end-of-life planning, you must be open to legal, financial and personal conversations about your life, your assets, your end-of-life care, and your death. And, at the same time, you must understand both the benefits of having those conversations in a timely manner, and the consequences of waiting until it is too late.

Although a Pre-Nuptial Agreement is signed before the wedding, and a Post-Nuptial Agreement is signed afterward, both can be considered valid. In the case of the Post-Nuptial Agreement, however, Attorneys will look carefully to see that the Agreement is being willingly executed by both parties and that there has been no undue pressure imposed upon one party by the other to influence them to sign the Agreement.

It has occurred to me that a Pre-Nuptial Agreement may be one of the very best end-of-life planning tools ever designed! It covers so many important areas of the life of two people, including (*but not limited to*):

- Planning for your divorce settlement before your wedding
- Revealing all of the assets and debts of each party
- Revealing your credit history
- Discussing the sharing of future earnings and expenditures

- Determining how assets acquired during the marriage will be titled, shared, owned, etc.
- Determining rights of inheritance
- Protecting your respective children's inheritance
- Revealing differences in assets and debts of each party
- Planning for serious health problems
- Planning for the funding of nursing home care
- Planning for your funeral and burial

In addition, in order to get such agreements signed by both parties, important conversations between the parties are required. Those conversations may well turn out to be a good foundation for their relationship in the future.

Once upon a time there was a couple contemplating marriage. Neither had been married before, and neither had children. The man had $125,000 in financial obligations. The woman had approximately $250,000 in liquid assets.

The woman wanted to pay off the man's debt out of her liquid assets so they could begin their life together "with a clean slate," and wanted advice from Suze Orman about whether or not it was a good idea.

Suze asked: Did she expect (ask?) him to repay the money? Was the woman going to ask for a promissory note or a repayment plan? Did he agree to pay that money back to her? In what amount of time? How long had she known this man? Did she love and trust him? Did she plan to live with him for the rest of their lives? What if they were to marry, and even though he promised to pay her, he made no effort to repay the money? How would she then feel about him? Questions ... so many questions ... to be asked and answered. Often, they are not even asked.

Suze's basic answer was this: If you were to divorce someday, without this man's having paid back that money to you, how would you feel about that? The woman replied that she loved this man and trusted him, and had every expectation that they would live happily ever after. Suze pointed out that, even though 50% of all marriages fail, most women approach marriage that same way. She recommended that the woman remove the rose-colored glasses.

This would have been a good opportunity for that woman to have a discussion with her Lawyer to see if this money matter should be part of a Pre-Nuptial Agreement, so that, in the event of their divorce, there would be clear agreement about who owes money to whom.

So, what's the big deal about these documents? The big deal, in my opinion, is that the preparation of a Pre-Nuptial Agreement requires (*forces?*) two people to have the hard conversations, to confront issues they would rather ignore. Most couples don't discuss much of importance before saying "*I do*" -- an unfortunate reality that keeps bridal shops, caterers, photographers, florists, bakeries, travel agents and divorce Lawyers in business. It is a huge mistake to skip the PreNups conversations.

Why Lawyers? Divorce! That's why. Remember the divorce rate is over 50%, in part because of the failure of most couples to have the important conversations before the wedding.

I once heard Dr. Phil ask a young married couple on the verge of divorce: *"What the hell did y'all talk about when you were dating?"* Based upon the divorce rate, apparently they didn't talk about things that really mattered, the things that make a marriage and not a wedding "day."

If you think that the PreNups conversations are hard, what do you think the divorce conversations will be like? And, keep in mind that divorce conversations that take place through Lawyers cost money-by-the-minute.

If two people can come up with a PreNuptial Agreement that is mutually satisfactory, they have accomplished an enormous feat that could make the difference in predicting whether their marriage succeeds or fails. It can actually strengthen the relationship because the process of discussing the content of the Agreement reveals a great deal about each person, about their level of maturity and sense of responsibility, and their ability to negotiate and compromise ... all of which are personal skills required within the context of a good marriage.

A Pre-Nuptial Agreement is not intended to be a deal-breaker ... that is, it's not supposed to cause two people to cancel the wedding. It is to cause them to carefully examine the things that will ultimately matter in their life together, far beyond the wedding day, the dress, and the honeymoon ... and bring two people closer together, each having a good understanding of who the other person really is.

In every relationship, whether or not you ever marry or divorce, sooner or later you will find yourselves having to talk about money: his money; her money; your joint money; your children's money; your parents' money, your estate money. Suze Orman says that <u>fighting</u> about money contributes to many divorces. It doesn't have to be that way.

How many people do you know that can or have had the hard conversations about their assets and debts, their Wills, where they want to be buried? I know very few. People usually "chicken out" as soon as the questions and issues become emotional or upsetting ... or even sooner, when the questions are asked.

Can most people do what it takes to execute a Pre-Nuptial Agreement that satisfies both parties?
Can they go through all the emotional ups and downs of the necessary conversations,
without damaging the relationship?
What do you think?

Cartoon

Scene: Front of a church. Clergyman standing and waiting for the bride and groom to come before him to begin the ceremony, but the bride and groom are sitting across a large conference table beside their respective Lawyers. One Lawyer says: "My client agrees to 'love,' but needs clarification on 'honor,' and 'obey' is a deal-breaker."

Whether or not the two of you love each other is not the pertinent issue. The object of a PreNuptial Agreement is the safeguarding of your own personal assets. Safeguarding you assets from what, you may ask? From losing them in a divorce settlement, or having your assets pass to a spouse instead of to your children when you die ... *just as examples*.

If you are inclined to mix love into the equation, you may be muddying the waters and causing potentially irreparable damage to your financial future. Take a deep breath and a step back, think about the need for this document, and examine the benefits it offers you, from a logical, common-sense perspective, then consult with your Lawyer, and see if it is appropriate for you.

And, if you need pre-marriage counseling, get it. It could make all the difference in your future. Don't wait until after the wedding to get counseling, or wait until you are at the point of divorce. Think of the process of talking about the PreNuptial Agreement as if it were a preventative well-ness check-up with your doctor.

Be smart and be informed! Ask questions. Understand the choices available to you, as well as the benefits and consequences of each. And, most important, *at least in my mind*, is to understand the consequences of doing nothing. If you take the easy way out (that is, do nothing), think of how your children will feel if their mother's estate passes to her husband and not to them because she had no PreNuptial Agreement.

Having a Pre-Nuptial Agreement will cause a couple to give careful thought to how they title assets they acquire during the years of their marriage. This subject requires the guidance and assistance of your Lawyer and/or Financial Advisor so you don't make any mistakes.

Suzy Orman regularly advises women, in particular, to "*demand*" a Nuptial Agreement before marriage in order to protect their rights in the event of a divorce. With the divorce rate above 50%, it's not such bad advice, do you think? Her firm position on the subject is that you should prepare for your divorce before you say "*I do*."

Many couples come to marriage with very unequal assets, debts, and/or uneven credit scores ... even young people marrying for the first time can have assets they might not want to divide with a spouse in the event of a divorce.

It is not uncommon for one (or even, both) of the two people to have student-loan debt, outstanding mortgages and home-equity loans, car payments, and/or credit card debt that must be considered. On the Suze Orman TV show of July 2, 2011, she talked with a couple that still has $200,000 in student loan debts. They are already in their 40s, rent their home, have 3 children, and see no way out of this debt. What kind of conversations did they have before the wedding about money?

Pre-Nuptial Agreements are no longer just for the rich and famous; in fact, a person who has managed to save $25,000 may be more interested in protecting that money than someone else who has millions, because it is likely that person worked really hard to accumulate that $25,000. And, when one of the two people has high credit-card debt and a bad FICO score, the financial health of the other can be damaged.

You should consider having a PreNups if any of the following situations apply to you:

- You own assets such as a home, investments, or retirement funds.

- You own all or part of a business.

- You anticipate receiving an inheritance.

- You have children and/or grandchildren from a previous marriage.

- One of the two of you is significantly wealthier than the other.

- One of the two of you has significant debt and/or bad credit.

- One of you will be supporting the other through college.

- You have loved ones who need financial support from you, including, but not limited to, children still in college, a disabled child, or elderly parents.

- You have or are pursuing a degree in a potentially lucrative profession such as medicine or the law.

Even though Pre-Nuptial Agreements are mostly about money, they are legal documents to be prepared by your Lawyer. I hear you already: *"I can download a form from the Internet. Why should I pay a Lawyer to do something I can do by myself."*

**I have only three words for you:
DON'T DO IT!**

OK, go right ahead. Do it yourself.

I keep forgetting that you <u>can</u> prepare your own PreNups . . .
as long as you are prepared for the consequences of something you left out or a mistake in the language.

The stakes are high. A Pre-Nuptial Agreement is not exactly a fill-in-the-blank or true-or-false test. It is the <u>content</u> that is important, not the form. The content of every PreNups is specific to the two persons for whom the document is prepared, and will have a direct effect upon their future life. If that isn't reason enough to do this correctly, I don't know what is.

Think of the Lawyer's fee for preparation of this document as an INVESTMENT in your future, or just one more expense of the wedding. And, believe me when I tell you that your lawyer's fees for a divorce will be much higher than the lawyer's fee to discuss and prepare a PreNuptial Agreement.

One reason why you want your PreNups prepared by a Lawyer is to have it drafted in such a way that it will hold up in court years later. No doubt, you have read about the PreNups of well-known personalities that were considered air-tight when they were signed, only to be challenged later by the Lawyer for one party. Often, the challenge succeeds, and the terms and conditions of the original Agreement are either voided or altered.

Where should you go for this advice? A Pre-Nuptial Agreement falls in between the realm of financial planning and estate planning. This means that you really need to consult with your Financial Planner <u>and</u> your Lawyer. I recommend you first speak with your Financial Planner to prepare a complete list of your assets and debts, and once you are satisfied that the list is complete, then you would contact your matrimonial Lawyer to prepare the document for you.

And, remember, you don't have to do any of this.

**You will not be asked for your Pre-Nuptial Agreement before the wedding ceremony
the way you will be asked for your marriage license.**

<u>SIMPLY PUT:</u>

<u>Divorce:</u> If a couple executes a Pre-Nuptial Agreement before their wedding, they have, in effect, settled most, if not all, of their financial issues in the event they divorce later on. There will be no fighting about who gets what, and there will be no huge Lawyer's fees to pay for the Property Settlement Agreement. Much of that will already have been decided and agreed upon in the PreNups. All the divorce Lawyer will have to do is prepare and file the papers to get the couple divorced.

Your Estate: If you and your spouse executed a Pre-Nuptial Agreement before your wedding, and stay married until one of you dies, the PreNups will have spelled out the disposition of the estate of the spouse who dies first. If either or both of you have children from one or more previous marriages, a PreNups will allow you to pass on your assets to your children, and not to your spouse or to his/her children.

COHABITATION AGREEMENTS

Many couples are choosing to create a life together without benefit of a formal, legal marriage. It makes perfect sense in many situations. These documents establish the terms and conditions of the relationship by which each party agrees to be bound. It is a legal agreement between two people that is mostly about the business of their life together, as opposed to being about the emotional and moral aspects of their arrangement.

If two people choose to establish life together with a Co-Habitation Agreement as the basis of their relationship, their break-up can be just as traumatic and expensive as any divorce.

As recently as June 2011 in the AARP Bulletin, there was an article titled *"Marriage and Money,"* by Jane Bryant Quinn. She speaks directly to the issue of Pre-Nuptial Agreements and Co-Habitation Agreements because it is important for two seniors establishing life together to have certain rules and boundaries in place before they begin living together.

It is important that they share *proof* of income, assets, credit history, debts and other obligations. It is important for them to discuss the benefits each may be receiving by virtue of a pension and/or Social Security. Frequently, a marriage will cancel out some benefits, and if you need the money, be smart and discuss the situation with a Financial Advisor before you call the caterer. The author stressed *"proof"* because, as she said, *"estimates have a funny way of being 'off.'"*

And, don't forget to share information about your family, your health history, your health insurance coverage and long-term care insurance, your family, your estate-planning , your plans for the future (including your funeral and burial preferences) … everything else that two people discuss before marriage … that is, of course, assuming they do talk about those things.

And, don't forget to talk about pets … the ones you have, the ones you might get in the future. Don't let anyone tell you that you cannot have pet(s), or force you to give up a beloved pet, in order to become partners with that person. If a person would force you to choose between them and your pet(s), think about what that says about that person.

One thing from that article that surprised me was a statement by Lauren Klein of Klein Financial Advisors in Newport Beach, California, who says that she sees older couples holding "weddings" for appearances only. They were taking the vows before family and friends, but not signing the documents. *EXCUSE ME? Did I miss something?*

While they were worried about what people would say if they saw this unmarried couple "living in sin," I ask the question: *"What happens when your family and friends find out the real truth?"* Are we to believe the people doing this don't tell their children or grandchildren that they aren't legally married so they won't be a bad influence? *WHAT?*

- I would be curious to know what happens when the first one dies, and the respective families try to sort out the estates of these two people who purport to be married, but who are not? Can you see why situations like this make Lawyers wealthy?

I personally do not care if couples live together by virtue of clergy or otherwise. What I am trying to point out is that the relationship should be based upon personal integrity and financial compatibility … way beyond their relationship and feelings for each other. It is entirely possible to love a person who is poor, a deadbeat, someone who is judgment-proof, and in serious debt. But, if this is the person you love, be sure to protect yourself from what could turn out to be a life-altering, negative personal, legal, and financial experience. *Suze Orman and I could tell you stories ...*

If there comes a time when the two people who established residence together without benefit of marriage, and who signed a Co-Habitation Agreement, decide to separate, it is important that they do it legally, in ways that protect themselves. If their Co-Habitation Agreement was property written, it will contain provisions for the separation of the parties.

Of course, when they entered into the Agreement, they were not contemplating separating, but it happens. Sometimes it is amicable; other times, it is not. The parties must decide if they need additional legal assistance to separate, and if they do, my suggestion is that you just meet with your respective Lawyers, do what is necessary, and part as friends. Life is way too short to break up with anger and animosity. *Just my opinion ...*

DIVORCE SETTLEMENT AGREEMENTS

The terms and conditions set forth in your Divorce Settlement Agreement can affect your estate planning and ultimately your estate. The best way to see that you are protected to the fullest extent of the law is to have your divorce lawyer work together with your estate-planning lawyer and your personal financial planner.

It is very easy to leave things out of Divorce Settlement Agreements, things that were simply forgotten, or things that seemed irrelevant at the time. Things that are often overlooked include ownership of cemetery property, life insurance policies, and Individual Retirement Account beneficiaries to name a few.

While you are caught up in the emotion of a divorce of break-up of a relationship, try very hard to maintain your balance when it comes to important legal and financial matters. You don't have to do it by yourself. You have advisors who can direct you and ultimately protect you.

VETERANS' ESTATES

In *The Philadelphia Inquirer* of November 27, 2010, there appeared an article titled, "*State is looking into policy that taps veterans' estates.*"

The article is about the fact that families of veterans who die in any of Pennsylvania's six state-owned nursing homes for veterans and their spouses may be in for an unwelcome surprise when the state attempts to recover funds for caring for these residents before their death. The nursing homes charge fees to residents based largely on their income, not on their assets. They then attempt to recoup the full cost of care (if possible) after a resident dies.

Some veterans' family members have been under the (apparently mistaken) impression that the assets in their deceased relative's estate at the time of their death, would be distributed as part of the administration of that person's estate (whether by virtue of a Will or otherwise). Apparently, the State wants its money first. In some cases, the amount the State wants may exceed the amount in the decedent's estate, leaving nothing for the family. The State does not seek payments until after burial costs are deducted from the estate.

Attorneys and representatives of the State have made it clear that they are not "seizing" assets, but attempting to collect for actual services that were rendered to the veterans before their death. They said they use a systematic process that involves notice to the families and the opportunity to participate or object to the collection.

The weak link appears to be faulty communication (*there's that word again*), and the State representatives have said they will work to improve notices to families when the veterans are admitted to the nursing homes, and will work to improve communication at the time of their death.

If you have a family member residing in a veterans' home, no matter in what state the facility is located, do your homework at the time (or well before) they are admitted. Everyone knows how complicated nursing home rules and regulations are, and how complicated medical coverage has become, and how frequently the laws and regulations change. This is another one of those situations where you can easily be blindsided simply by not knowing what you don't know.

Before admitting a veteran (or anyone else) to a nursing home, consult with a Lawyer specializing in elder law. There may be legal ways to preserve the veteran's estate assets for distribution to their loved ones when they die; but, decisions like this should be made well before being admitted to the nursing home, and not without expert advice and guidance.

This is not the place for making mistakes or trying to "do it yourself." A mistake could mean the loss of significant assets.

BUSINESS SUCCESSION PLANNING

If you are a business owner, it is important at some point to establish a business succession plan for the time when you want to retire, or if you should become disabled, ill, or when you die. If you, and/or your parents, spent years building a successful business, you may want to pass the business to your children, especially if your children have been working in the business with you. A succession plan is a vital part of passing your assets to your heirs, and there are important things you must consider. To do this well, you will need the assistance of a Lawyer well versed in the subject, plus a Financial Planner, an Accountant, and a Psychologist.

First, I suggest that you speak with your children … *that is, have the hard conversations with them* … to see if they even want the business. These conversations can be especially difficult if some of your children are in the business and others are not, and when the owner of the business owns real estate that is leased to the business.

If they are not in agreement, or don't really understand what you are trying to do, you may want to sit down with your Lawyer and your children, and together, discuss the options available to them.

It is also important to understand the many aspects of the succession plan as it relates to how you have legal ownership of the business. Is your business operating as a corporation, a limited-liability corporation, or under a fictitious name with you as the sole owner? Is your ownership interest held in your name alone or with your wife or someone else? You will want your Lawyer to advise you about the best way of passing the business to your children *if that is what they want.*

"Wait a minute. Did you say I'll need a psychologist, too?" Well, yes I did.

Once upon a time, a man established a business that over the years became very successful, so much so that he employed his sons to work with him in the business. The business thus supported four families.

When the time came to have a discussion among the father and his sons about how he wanted to pass the business on to them, the father ran into strong resistance and disagreement with them. When the succession plan was presented to them by their father's Lawyer, the father was shocked and disappointed at their lack of enthusiasm. In fact, at that point, he learned about some feelings his sons had been keeping from him for years:

- one son felt he had been overworked and undervalued for years;

- one son felt that he had never been paid what he was worth;

- one son believed that his father favored the other two over him;

- one son never wanted the business in the first place and didn't want it now;

- one son wanted money to represent his fair (equal?) share;

- one son's wife was threatening divorce because she didn't like his working long hours to run his father's business;

- on and on it went.

In spite of the father's best intentions, and his having hired qualified professionals to assist him in passing this business on to his sons, which he believed was something his sons also wanted, it got very ugly. This is where behavioral finance and psychology come into play. The members of this family were operating on pure emotion, ignoring facts.

How does a mess like get sorted out? Often, it doesn't.

You can see from the above that opinions among the children differ greatly, and your feelings may be hurt by the reactions and comments you get from your family when you present them with your succession plan. You must get past the disappointment. Remember this quote from "The Godfather:" *"This isn't personal, it's just business."* It may be really, really hard, but do your best.

If you have a family business that you wish to protect and preserve for your family in the future, you must have the hard conversations with them about what they want. I personally know several families where the younger generation wants no parts of the business their parents or grandparents worked so hard to build for them. Part of the reason is that they saw how many hours and days and years their relatives spent just working the business, and this younger generation does not choose to live that way. For most of these business owners, their work (that is, their business) was their life. Their children want more balance in their lives, and you can't blame them.

If you and your family cannot reach a reasonable plan that satisfies everyone, you may have to think about selling your business while you are alive and in good health, and before you really need to sell it. If your health were to seriously decline, and a potential buyer sees that you are desperate to sell, it may compromise your ability to get the best price for this business you devoted your life to building.

You could also do nothing. Leave things the way they are for as long as possible. When you die, if your business is still operating and successful, your family will have to deal with the business as best they can. It won't be easy for them, but it will happen, one way or the other.

One way you can smooth things over for them and assure them that the business could continue after your death, if that is what they want, is to consult with your tax Lawyer and/or Financial Planner about an Irrevocable Life Insurance Trust designed to pay Federal Estate Tax. I would not presume to advise you in this regard except to say that you should really take the time to investigate this option. Without it, it is highly likely your family could lose the business to taxes, or they could personally go broke paying them.

WHAT LESSONS CAN BE LEARNED HERE?

- Have the hard conversations with the people that matter well before a time of need.

- Consult with professionals in time to protect and/or transfer your assets in the best ways possible.

- Don't wait until it's too late.

And, if it is your intention to protect and preserve the asset known as "your business," be sure to protect it from possible divorce settlements by executing (and having your children execute) an air-tight Pre-Nuptial Agreement (or Cohabitation Agreement) before you (or they) marry or re-marry. This, too, is just good business, not personal.

FAMILY MEETING

Elsewhere I discussed the benefits of having a family meeting to plan for emergencies. I believe you should also have a separate meeting to talk about your estate plans. I don't recommend combining both subjects into one meeting, because of the large amount of information to talk about, and because the span of attention of your family members may be short.

Once you have completed your estate planning, it would be a good idea to get your family together to tell them what you have done. I realize it may be hard to get everyone together at the same place at the same time, but do your best. A family meeting can be a source of comfort or a source of upset. It is up to you to see that everyone who is supposed to be there, is there, and it is up to you to set the tone.

If there are babies or little children, it would be good if there could be a "babysitter" designated to care for them during the meeting in another part of the house or elsewhere. You don't want the meeting time interrupted or cut short because of the immediate needs of a crying child. The subject of the meeting is serious, and the children's activities will be a distraction. If you want the meeting to be worthwhile, and you want to be heard during this meeting, I recommend "adults only."

Begin by asking them,

> *"What if I had died late last night, and this meeting was being held right now, except one person was missing: me? What if you had the advantage of being able to ask me questions at that meeting? What would you want to ask me?"*

In beginning, you might attempt to keep the atmosphere light, injecting a little humor when and if possible. The idea is to educate your family, not upset them, although some people may become upset anyway.

This meeting may be emotionally uncomfortable for some members of your family, so be prepared for that. Be prepared to be honest with your children and listen to their questions, comments, complaints, suggestions, etc. Do not try to talk them out of any strong emotions that may show up. Allow them the opportunity to express their emotions while speaking about your death. But do <u>not</u> allow them to put you off by saying, "*Oh, Dad, nothing's going to happen to you,*" or something to that effect.

Be particularly aware of comments from your children's spouses (if any). They could be a source of upset, especially if there is a family history of disagreements among them. Now would be a good time to ask them to put aside their differences *forever*! I realize what I'm asking. I come from a family of people who fought to the bitter end, never reconciling. It is such a waste of time and energy, and family fighting never produces good results.

When the meeting eventually settles down to business, tell your children where you keep your important papers, and how to get access to them if they are in a safe or bank box. Show them where you keep the names and addresses and all contact information for your advisors (Lawyer, accountant, financial planner, insurance agent, investment advisor, etc.) Tell them about the PEOPLE TO CALL list, and where to find it.

While you're showing them where they can find information, don't forget to include information you keep on your computer. Someone will need to have access to that information at the time of your death anyway.

You might want to get into a discussion about the disposition of your furnishings, artwork, jewelry, collectibles, etc. Or you may not. Only you can know if this is a worthwhile way to spend your time together.

If you can keep them seated long enough, try to discuss your funeral and burial wishes, especially if you have already made plans, or if you know what you want and do not want. Show them the chapter from this book with the list of things to do, and show them your notebook about Funeral and Burial Arrangements. Those things may grab their attention.

And, believe me when I tell you that one of the greatest gifts you can leave for your family is to have everything spelled out and organized.

INTELLECTUAL PROPERTY & COMPUTERS

Where to begin on this extremely complex, ever evolving subject? Before we leave the subject of Wills, take a moment to consider what will happen to all the information you have stored in your computer. What happens to your blog? Your Facebook account? Your Twitter, eBay, MySpace, and eHarmony accounts? These and other popular sites and email services have varying policies on who, if anyone, gets access to your accounts after you die.

What about all that personal information you have online … your bank account numbers, Social Security number, your investments, etc.? Remember how easy it was to pay your bills online? Maybe it was easy for you, but what about your Executor?

Who knows all your user ID's and passwords? Are they written down in a safe place where your survivors or Executor can easily find them and take care of shutting down your accounts as part of administering your estate?

If you have made no provisions in your Will for your computer accounts, you should update your Will to include very specific provisions for who will take ownership of your intellectual property and the data that you leave behind.

What about the stuff you have online that nobody knows about … things that could come back and upset or harm your loved ones? *I know ... I know...*maybe I've watched too many episodes of "*Law & Order,*" but these are things to think about.

What about all those emails that are "*personal*" and you would die of shame if anyone else ever read them? And, worse, what if you were checking out pornography sites? Is this something you would want your family to know about you after you die?

If there are things about you that you would not want anyone in your family to see or know about, you should think long and hard about the consequences of this information getting in the hands of people you would not want to see it. Think about how you want to be remembered, and if there is one single thing on your computer accounts that would shame or embarrass you or your family, get rid of it NOW!

Remember, stuff you put on your computer will live in cyberspace long after your death! Life will go on without you, even when you are no longer here to make minute-to-minute "tweets" to your "friends." They, too, will survive without you!

In three words I can sum up everything I've learned about life.
IT GOES ON.

Robert Frost

Speak to your attorney about what to do about this subject as it relates to your Will and/or other estate-planning documents. This is one area that you should not overlook.

KEYS and OTHER THINGS

Try to put yourself into the position of being your Executor, and try to imagine that person going on a scavenger hunt to locate all of your "stuff" without any clues. Have you left sufficient information so that your Executor will be able to easily locate your possessions and deal with them appropriately?

Do you have secret hiding places for some of your "stuff?" By the time you have passed away, your secret hiding places should already have been revealed to someone you trust, especially to the person responsible for closing out your life … your Executor.

KEYS

If you were to become incapacitated and when you die, your Executor and your family members do not want to find unidentifiable keys in your home. If you have keys in all sorts of places, it would be good if you were to spend some time identifying every one of them right now, and leaving something in writing about what each key is for. Maybe you should get a duplicate set of keys so you can individually identify each. If you think this will take you a lot of time and money, think of how much time and money your Executor will spend trying to figure out the places where each key belongs.

You may have all sorts of keys in your possession, and *you* know what each one goes to, don't you? But who else knows? You may have keys to your house, your cars, cars you no longer own, the glove compartment in your car(s), your vacation house, the storage barn in your back yard, luggage, your bank safe deposit box(es), your fire-proof box, your desk, your jewelry box, your bowling locker, your Post Office box. You may have keys to your parents' house, their vacation house, your children's home or car(s), your neighbor's house … you get the idea. Right now, put identifying tags on every single key in your possession.

ENTRY CODES

If you use numerical codes for the security system on your house and your garage door opener, someone you trust should also have the numbers; also, if you use entrance code numbers for your car, your briefcase, your luggage, your parking garage, your storage locker, someone else also needs to know these codes. Where else do you use such codes?

ACCESS CARDS

If you have access cards to your office building, an apartment building, or any other place, someone else must know about these cards, where you keep them, how to shut them down after your death. In this category, don't forget your ATM card.

PASSWORDS

You may have various passwords for your computer and your ATM card. If you shop online, do your banking or investing online, you will have passwords. If you have cable TV, you have a password. Take the time to write down every password and keep the list beside your computer and with your important papers, or some other place where it will be easily accessible to your Executor or someone else you trust. All of these accounts must be shut down after your death.

STORAGE LOCKER

If you have possessions in a storage unit, someone else should know about it and have complete information about the location, the phone number, the unit number, the contract you have with them, any keys or code numbers required to gain access to the unit, and a description of the contents, especially if they are valuable.

- If the "stuff" is <u>not</u> valuable, why are you paying monthly rental charges in the first place? *Just asking…* I know a woman who down-sized her home after her husband died, and rented a storage unit for the "stuff" that didn't fit into her new house. That was 10 years ago, and as she tells the story, she has never once visited that storage unit? *What?*

What would you want your Executor to do with all that "stuff" after you pass away, especially if the contents are valuable, and especially if you want certain items given to certain people? *Just more things to write down and keep with your important papers.*

Give some thought to whether or not you really need that storage unit and the "stuff" you are storing there, and if you could eliminate it now, do it. Lots of people spend money every month to store "stuff" they don't really care about, and their rental money is being wasted; however, if what you are storing there is valuable and if it is the only place where you can house those things, perhaps you should think about parting with all those things right now.

If you store large things (a boat and trailer, snowmobile, jet ski or wave runner, or an RV) at one of those storage units, this is also information an Executor will need to know about. What should your Executor do with those things after you pass away? [Question: Where is all of the owner's information, including insurance, for those things? *Just asking…*]

IS YOUR ESTATE PLAN COMPLETE?

- It is entirely possible that some of you who are reading this book have already completed both your estate and financial planning, and are well on your way to achieving your goals. If you are one of these persons, you deserve high praise. This is a huge accomplishment, and you should be proud of yourself.

- Still, you find yourself reading this book, maybe even wondering what more could you possibly learn that you don't already know. Maybe some good ideas will come to light. Maybe not. Maybe it's time to make changes. Either way, my philosophy is that there is always something new to be learned, and I try to keep an open mind, especially about matters as complicated as estate and financial planning, where the laws and regulations change frequently.

- Others of you may have your estate-planning documents signed, safeguarded and available in case of need. Congratulations to you! This is no small accomplishment. But, have you addressed your financial needs, with a focus on your retirement years?

- Are both you and your spouse or partner equally informed about your assets and debts, and about your estate plans? Are you in agreement about how they should be handled? Are you plans complete, or are you procrastinating because you can't come to an agreement about certain details?

- Some of you may have carefully watched your finances throughout your lifetime, with a particular focus toward your retirement years, and feel comfortable that you have achieved your financial goals and will be providing a nice inheritance for your family. But, have you executed estate-planning documents that will allow you to pass on your estate to family members after your death, when and how you want them to get it, and with as few taxes as possible?

    Remember that I pointed out how the legal and financial elements of estate planning overlap?

- Have you organized and safeguarded all of your estate-planning and financial documents in a place that is not only safe, but accessible in time of need by someone other than yourself?

> ***One never notices what has been done; one can only see what remains to be done.***
>
> Marie Curie

The following CHECK-LIST is to help you evaluate your progress.

- Give yourself credit for tasks accomplished
- Don't beat yourself up for things still to be done
- Just keep on keeping on …

CHECK-LIST
(in no particular order)

____ My estate planning is complete and up-to-date.

____ My estate planning documents were prepared ____ years ago and need to be reviewed by my attorney.

____ My life circumstances have changed, and I should consult with my attorney to review the documents to see if they are still valid, or if I need new ones.

____ I have a financial plan in place that satisfies my current and future needs.

____ I have no idea of whether or not I am adequately insured, so I need to discuss this with my financial planner and my insurance agent.

____ I should have my finances reviewed by my Financial Planner to see what (if any) changes should be made.

____ I am regularly contributing the maximum amount to my retirement fund.

____ I have enough immediately available cash to handle eight months' personal needs in an emergency.

____ My life circumstances have changed, and I should consult with my Financial Planner to see what changes are necessary.

____ I regularly save a certain amount every month.

____ I do not use my emergency fund for ordinary expenses.

____ I have taken money from my retirement accounts (IRAs and/or 401(k) accounts) to use for other expenses, and I intend to repay it.

____ I have repaid none of it.____ I have repaid _____% of it.

____ No matter what, I do not touch my retirement accounts for other expenses.

____ I have named beneficiaries (and contingent beneficiaries) on all my legal, financial and insurance documents that require them, and all are current.

____ Others in my family know the intimate details of my estate plan and financial plan.

____ Others in my family know where my important documents and records are kept, and how to get access them in a time of need.

____ I know how much capital it would take for me to live in retirement at my present standard of living.

____ I have no idea how much money I would need in retirement.

____ I know how much capital and income I would need in the event of:
    ____ loss of investment money.
    ____ long-term unemployment.
    ____ disability (whether long or short term).
    ____ death of one spouse.

____ My Attorney, Financial Planner, and Accountant work together for my greater good.

____ Others in my family know the name and address of my
    ____ Attorney
    ____ Financial Planner
    ____ Accountant

____ My Attorney and Financial Planner don't know each other.

____ I plan to arrange a joint meeting with them within the next month.

____ My Family Meeting is scheduled for _____. Everyone will be there.

____ Several family members think it's ridiculous, and several stated they will not attend.

____ I will not let that stop me from completing my estate plan.

____ I have done no estate planning.

____ I have done no financial planning.

____ I need an appointment with my Lawyer soon.

____ I need an appointment with my Financial Planner soon.

____ I need an appointment with my Accountant soon.

Are you satisfied with your answers, _or_ do you still have some work to do?

On what date do you plan to begin?

When do you intend to be finished with all these details?

IN CONCLUSION

I have written about many things in this book. While each is important in its own right, legal things connect to financial things which connect to personal things. They are not completely separate, and operate best when consideration is given to the big picture, which is YOUR LIFE.

As in every other place I've written, you do not have to DO anything I suggest. You don't even have to AGREE or even LIKE the things I've suggested. I do, however, ask you to THINK about them if you want the best chance of having things go the way you really want them to go. I want you to get in touch with what it would FEEL like if you were facing death, having left much of this work undone. And, then, consider the feelings of your family.

REMEMBER: REGRET IS WORSE THAN FEAR.

Choice of attention—to pay attention to this and ignore that –
is to the inner life what choice of action is to the outer.
In both cases, a man is responsible for his choice and must accept the consequences.

W. H. Auden

- **NEVER PRACTICE DO-IT-YOURSELF LAW.**

- **NEVER** sign a legal document of any sort without having at least a basic understanding of how it works, what it does and does not do for all parties. Better yet, have your Lawyer's blessing before signing.

- **ALWAYS ASK** your Lawyer to explain things to you in plain, understandable language if you are not clear about any aspect of your estate planning. And, if necessary, ask again.

- **NEVER MAKE ASSUMPTIONS** about anything relating to a legal document. Ask questions.

- **NEVER WRITE ON YOUR ORIGINAL DOCUMENTS!** No hand-written changes, no arrows, no inserts, no Wite-out, no cross-outs, no doodles! No Nothing!

- **ALWAYS SAFEGUARD** all of your important papers against fire or water damage, loss or theft, and let someone else know where to easily find them.

- **MAKE THE TIME** for the hard conversations.

- **ALWAYS COMMUNICATE** with the people who have "the need to know"

- **ALWAYS BE WILLING TO QUESTION, LISTEN AND LEARN.**

- **PAY ATTENTION TO YOUR INSTINCTS.**

- **ALWAYS** think about whether you will regret doing something, or not doing something, so that on your last day, you will be able to leave this life peacefully with no regrets at all.

<u>**REMEMBER**</u>

LIFE IS SHORT and YOU'RE DEAD A LONG TIME!

If you don't take care of your personal business now, who else will do it for you?

NO ONE. ONLY YOU.

We say that the hour of death cannot be forecast, but when we say this, we imagine that hour as placed in an obscure and distant future. It never occurs to us that it has any connection with the day already begun, or that death could arrive this same afternoon, this afternoon which is so certain and which has every hour filled in advance.

Marcel Proust

Tempus fugit

THINGS TO DO   *   IDEAS   *   FOLLOW-UP

#	Priority A,B,C	Description	Start Date	Completion Date
1				
2				
3				
4				
5				
6				
7				
8				
9				
10				
11				
12				
13				
14				
15				
16				
17				
18				
19				
20				

Chapter II

FINANCIAL

> *Time is more valuable than money.*
> *You can get more money, but you cannot get more time.*
>
> Jim Rohn

WHAT IS FINANCIAL PLANNING, AND WHY DO YOU NEED IT?

Let's be clear about this right now. Technically, you don't need Financial Planning.

You can live out the rest of your days without any financial planning, and let the financial chips fall where they may. After all, you're smart. You don't need anybody's help or advice to tell you how to handle your money ... or do you? The truth is that you really don't like to be told what to do with your money, or that you don't trust anyone else with your money management. Does this describe you?

The subject of money for Baby Boomers in retirement is complicated, and sometimes mistakes cannot be fixed. Can you at least consider that planning makes good common sense, or that planning could provide you with peace of mind and reduce your worry about running out of money before you run out of time, or that it can actually enhance the quality of your life? Establishing your life and financial goals requires thinking, communication, learning, planning, and taking calculated risks. The planning process won't kill you, but running out of money might.

Traditionally, financial planning has been regarded as "retirement planning," or as a complicated process only for the rich and famous. Some people don't think they need to do any financial planning until they retire. Even <u>you</u> can benefit from the process, so I ask you to keep an open mind before you completely reject the idea.

Financial planning is not a one-time event. It is a process, a marathon, not a sprint. It isn't as if you make a plan one day, and follow it for the rest of your life. Your plan must be a living, evolving commitment to addressing your financial needs over time. The plan must leave room for appropriate changes as your family changes, as your needs change.

For example, in your younger years, which are generally your years of highest earnings, you wanted to accumulate money, with the goal of retiring with funds adequate to sustain your living standard in your "golden" years. When you reach those highly anticipated "golden" years, after you have accumulated as much money as possible, you want to preserve those assets.

ACCUMULATION. PRESERVATION.
Both necessary.
Very different.

How will you know if you have accumulated enough money to retire, and whether or not your money is safe from the effects of the stock market fluctuation, inflation, taxes? Start by determining whether you are in the accumulation phase of your life, or you are in the preservation phase. Once you have made this determination, you will want to work with a financial planner who can best assist you with your goal of (a) accumulating, or (b) preserving your money.

Financial planning (i.e., financial decision-making) is only one part of the puzzle; it is connected to the subjects of the other chapters in this book.

What do you want to do with the rest of your life *between now and then* that may cost you money?

Many people put off planning for their life *between now and then* because the process seems too complicated, too hard, too painful to even think about. And, besides, they're simply not ready. What does being ready have to do with it?

- Ready for what? Ready to retire? Ready to "not work" for 30 years? Ready to be short of money to pay your living expenses 20-30 years from now? Ready to move into a retirement home? Ready to not have health insurance and be unable to take care of their health for 30 years? Ready to die?

Baby Boomers feel young, they look young, and they act young, and wonder why so many people are talking about the end of life. They especially don't want to talk about their death. They say they'll do it later.

WHEN IS LATER? When they get around to it.

REMEMBER:
I ALREADY GAVE YOU A ROUND TUIT. NOW WOULD BE A GOOD TIME TO USE IT!

WHAT ARE YOU SO AFRAID OF THAT IS KEEPING YOU FROM DISCUSSING YOUR FINANCES SO THAT YOU CAN HAVE A HAPPY, SECURE, PEACEFUL RETIREMENT?

YOU KNOW WHAT I MEAN.

WHAT IS YOUR RELATIONSHIP TO MONEY?

- How do you feel about money in general?

- How do you feel about your own money?

- Do you spend a lot of time worrying about your money?

- What do you EXPECT your money to do for you?

- What do you WANT your money to do for you?

- Do you spend money to calm your anxieties? To make yourself feel good?

- Do you play the lottery, hoping against hope, that you'll win?

- What problems does your money cause you?

- What problems do you have because you don't have enough?

- How much money would be enough?

- Do you handle money like your parents did? Or just the opposite?

- What would you do with $20,000,000 lottery winnings?

- Have you ever contemplated suing someone (or some big company) in anticipation of a huge settlement that could be a retirement fund?

NEVER THINK MONEY IS ONLY ABOUT MONEY.

Too many people spend money they haven't earned,
to buy things they don't want,
to impress people they don't like.

Will Smith

There are many emotional components to the subject of money, some of which are listed alphabetically below:

- addiction;
- anger;
- anticipation;
- anxiety;
- depression;
- disappointment;
- entitlement;
- euphoria;

- excitement;
- fear;
- pleasure;
- regret;
- resentment;
- uncertainty;
- upset;
- worry.

"But," you say, *"it's **only** money."* RIGHT!

Tell that to people who lost 30% of their retirement money in the most recent stock market crash, have been unemployed for a year, have no health insurance, have student loans they cannot eliminate through bankruptcy, or who lost their home to foreclosure.

WHAT DO YOU WANT YOUR MONEY TO DO FOR YOU?

Up until now, you may have used your money to pay your living expenses and to make you happy. Would you say that's a fair assessment of what you have wanted your money to do for you until now? What about in the future?

- Do you want your money to help you pay off debt?
- Do you have adequate income, savings and investment money to last you for 20-30 years?
- Do you want your money to provide you with a comfortable life during your retirement years?
- Do you want your money to pay for your healthcare *between now and then?*
- Do you want to have a little extra money every now and then to take a vacation, even if it is a mini vacation?
- Do you want to know that you will have enough money to pay for unexpected expenses like car or house repairs, or illness or death of a loved one?
- Have you sacrificed your own standard of living in your retirement years by spending too much and saving too little?
  and by going into debt for your children? or,
  so you can leave money to your children or grandchildren after you pass away?

These are only a few of the many questions that you should begin to address as your approach retirement. Now is the time for action, the time to do whatever it takes to be sure you have enough money to support you until your last day.

> **Having enough money for your living expenses during your retirement years allows you to have the freedom to make CHOICES!**
>
> **If you run out of money, you may also run out of choices.**

Of course, you are disappointed in yourself when you realize you could have saved more money, but then, look at all the fun you had with your money. And, besides, look what happened to saving accounts earning near-zero interest. Forgive yourself for what you didn't know you didn't know, and then make a conscious choice to move FORWARD, to make plans for your future.

As I write this, I am aware that my words may have no effect upon you. You could say that you have no need to save your money for retirement, or that you're not in a hurry to retire, and that you don't see the point of saving money if you're going to die anyway. You may come up with all sorts of excuses about why you choose to ignore any or all of the suggestions I've made. And, you are free to make your own choices and continue doing exactly what it is you have been doing all along … just pay attention to the consequences of your financial choices before you decide.

And, so, I ask you:

ARE YOU READY TO BEGIN EXAMINING YOUR FINANCES?

As you are making financial plans, remember that they go hand-in-hand with your estate planning, record-keeping, and personal life plans. Don't wait until you are facing a crisis to make end-of-life decisions. Think about the process while you are healthy and vibrant, and while you still have time. Enjoy the journey. You will arrive at your final destination soon enough.

FINANCIALLY, YOU NEED HELP, AND YOU NEED IT NOW!

There is no shame in asking for help. Maybe it isn't too late. Maybe there are things you can do right now that can make a big difference in what your retirement years will look like.

I strongly suggest that you do not try "do-it-yourself" financial planning, because, at this time in your life, you cannot afford to make mistakes. You may not live long enough to recover the money you could lose by making mistakes. This is the time when the harsh realities must be examined, not avoided.

The counseling from a financial professional can put you on track to begin a plan for your retirement. Maybe you'll have to work a few years more than you really want to, but when you see the financial benefits, you may look upon those working years more as a blessing than a curse.

FINANCIAL PLANNING FOR RETIREMENT

Financial planning is good for everyone, and the need for it, and the planning itself, are different for different stages in life. It becomes especially important as you approach retirement.

In the December 2010 AARP Bulletin, the writer of a financial column said that **now** is the time, if ever there was, when people (particularly Baby Boomers) should be consulting with financial planners.

1. **Before making any serious decisions about whether or not to collect Social Security** early and whether or not to keep working, have a discussion with your financial planner or a tax lawyer. Many Baby Boomers will continue working past retirement age. Some because they must. Some because they realize it is an opportunity to accumulate money for their retirement years. Others because they enjoy working. Be careful, though, because the salary from your job, when combined with the Social Security you are collecting, could create an undesirable tax situation. It is important to look at the numbers.

2. Before you retire, especially if you are considering early retirement, **don't forget the cost of health insurance**. You may find yourself in the "never-never land" between your employer's health insurance plan and Medicare. Be very careful.

3. **Work up two Budgets.** Be brutally honest with yourself, and as you work on the numbers, be sure to factor in inflation and something for unexpected expenses such as job loss, relocation, illness, death, emergencies:

    *   Budget No. 1: List actual expenses for your life today. It helps to see the numbers on paper, and realize how much money you have and exactly where you spend it. Don't leave anything out.

    *   Budget No. 2: List anticipated expenses for your life in retirement. Compare those expenses with your anticipated income. Don't leave anything out. And, be aware that your expenses in your retirement years will not be significantly lower than your current expenses unless you make changes in your spending habits, living arrangements, or other things that cost money you may not have anticipated.

If Your **OUTGO**
Exceeds Your **INCOME,**

> ## Your UPKEEP
> ## Will Be Your DOWNFALL.

4.   Working with your financial planner, **develop a plan that will provide you with an income stream** that will not be affected by market conditions. <u>You will need to supplement your Social Security</u> and pensions. Remember that your retirement may be for 20 or more years, and the date of your death could easily be 20-30 years from now. You don't want to run out of money. And, don't stuff your money in your mattress because you are afraid of the stock market! Educate yourself. Partner with your financial planner to provide you with the good life you always wanted for your "golden years."

5.   **Be smart with your money.** Learn to distinguish between WANTS and NEEDS. "Immediate gratification" spending will cause you to put off retirement savings, because it seems so far in the future? IS IT REALLY? You may think you need that new car right now, but do you really NEED it, or do you just WANT IT. If what you really need is affordable, reliable transportation, you can get that from a good used car. You don't need that new car if the payments keep you from saving money for your retirement years. How will you feel about that car when you run out of money? IT'S JUST A CAR! What you NEED is money for retirement. And don't keep fooling yourself that you are spending money buying gifts for your family. This is the time you must begin to think about your own needs first. Your grandchildren don't need another toy ... *you get the idea.*

6.   **Don't be among the large group of people who are not likely to have enough money to maintain the lifestyle they are accustomed to in their retirement years.** Your financial planner can help you calculate your anticipated income and expenses. You may be pleasantly surprised when you see the numbers, or you may be shocked. It would be better to be shocked now than later.

7.   **Banks don't give loans to seniors to buy food, fill gas tanks, or pay electric bills and real estate taxes.** It is up to you to plan wisely for your financial needs in those "golden years."

8.   **If you choose to ignore specific advice** given to you by your financial planner, be ready and willing to sign a release that legally absolves him of the responsibility for your choice. Be willing to take responsibility for your own choices.

9.   **Cut up your credit cards.** Paying with plastic removes the sensation of actually parting with your money, as happens when you pay with your own hard-earned cash.

Every financial choice comes with the possibility of increasing or decreasing your financial situation; however, your choices about money are not just about money. Each choice you make about your money could affect you legally and personally as well. Remember that I told you that the categories in this book are interconnected one way or the other. This is one example

If you don't believe me, think about the effect of bankruptcy on your family's wellbeing ... especially if the bankruptcy is the result of your having poor money habits and making poor financial choices. Think about how fighting about money can be the cause of the breakup of your marriage. How about your choice to buy a house you could not afford? And, let's not forget that poor choices about money can put you in jail. These are but a sampling of the financial choices that carry with them serious legal and personal consequences.

Money is not just about money. What does it matter if you have lots of money and find out that your money hasn't made you happy, as you define happy? There are a lot of lonely, unhappy rich people. On the other hand, there are a lot of lonely, unhappy poor people. Money requires thinking, planning and action. You are free to disagree. But, there is truth in that old saying that money doesn't grow on trees. Money will not mysteriously show up at your door or in your bank account. You must take action to make it happen, to earn, invest and save wisely. *Or not.*

> *In the 1950s, there was a TV show called The Millionaire. In each episode, a man rang a person's doorbell and said: "My name is Michael Anthony, and I am here to give you one million dollars." Each episode was about what happened to the person who received the gift. Often, things did not turn out very well.*
>
> *As a child, I loved thinking about what I would do with all that money. The show was a fantasy, and if you are sitting around waiting for Michael Anthony to ring your doorbell, that would be a fantasy, too.*

How much money would be the right amount of money to make you happy? I've heard that when John D. Rockefeller was asked that question, he answered, *"Just a little bit more."* There must be something wrong with a person who has as much money as JD, and still wants a little bit more. Granted, he gave away zillions of his money to charity, but still …

- Do you live your life as if you are waiting for some unknown date when you will have enough money to retire and be happy?
  Are retirement and happiness the same thing? Just asking ...

- Are you expecting to receive a large inheritance?
  What if money isn't what you need to be happy?

- Are you buying lottery tickets every week, hoping to score a big win?
  Remember that buying lottery tickets is not financial planning.

WHERE DID YOU LEARN ABOUT MONEY?

If you haven't already read the book, *Rich Dad, Poor Dad*, by Robert Kiyosaki and Sharon Lechter, I recommend it. The subtitle is, *"What the rich teach their kids about money that the poor and middle class do not."* Mr. Kiyosaki had two dads when he was a child: his own dad, a teacher, who advocated that his son go to college, get a job, and work until retirement; and his friend's dad, who advocated getting rich by buying and selling real estate, among other things. The education he received was very valuable, because it was from two extremely different points of view, and he was able to see which one suited him the best. Turns out, the advice he received from his "other" dad fit him perfectly.

The book describes what happens when a child hears a parent's suggestions about their future, and knows that the message does not fit them, but, because it comes from their parent, they follow it anyway. What if Mr. Kiyosaki had only had the benefit of his biological father's advice, and he followed that advice into some dead-end desk job, when he, the son, had the free spirit of an entrepreneur? This sort of thing happens all the time.

A Little Bit of Financial-Planning Humor

Teenage son, speaking to his father: *"Dad, I think I'm ready for our little talk about the bulls and the bears."*

Parents usually have good intentions when they provide their children with career advice, but sometimes that advice is inappropriate, and is only focused on the potential earnings of a given career; e.g., doctor, lawyer. What if you are not all that interested in selling your soul for the money? What if you want to raise organic vegetables and live frugally, without the trappings of wealth? Would your parents express disappointment at your choice? Would you be upset if they were upset? Would their potential upset cause you to sacrifice your dreams?

Once upon a time, there was man who had 1 daughter and 4 sons. He drove a truck all his life. He made no provision for any of his children to go to college; in fact, when the subject of college was brought up, he said, *"What's the matter, isn't driving a truck good enough for you?"* End of conversation. A real dream killer.

Sometimes, a parent's words are not heard the way the parent intended. It happens all the time in conversation, when the listener assigns a meaning to the speaker's words that are not what the speaker meant. Here's an example of how that works:

- This is what my mother said to my sister and me about our careers:
  "I don't care what you girls do when you grow up as long as you are always able to support yourself."

- The meaning I assigned to what I heard:
  There's no point in going to art school because I'll never be able to support myself.

My mother never told me not to go to art school. My actions were based upon the meaning I assigned to her words, not to her actual words. Her words were spoken out of her fear of not being able to earn a living to support herself and us after her divorce in the 1950s, even though she was college educated, and her words had a major influence on the career my sister and I chose. We were always able to support ourselves, but we were not doing work we love.

> ### *Choose a job you love and you will never have to work a day in your life.*
> Confucius

It is my experience and observation that there has never been much learning or education taking place around the subject of money for the average person. Schools don't generally include classroom studies about money; that is, how to save it or how to manage it. It seems that even college education is not making young people smart about money. Witness the following scenarios from recent Suze Orman TV shows:

> #### 1.
>
> *A young woman in her late 20's, educated and employed as an accountant, graduated college with $95,000 in student loan debt from two federal loans and two from individual banks. She is drowning in debt and now sees that she will be paying this debt for many years. She is afraid she will never be able to marry, have children, buy a house ... you know the drill, it's called "the American dream."*
>
> *Excuse me? Did I miss something in grade-school arithmetic class? Payments on $95,000 for 30 years at 8% are around $700/month. A monthly payment like hers could instead have been used to buy a house, a car, or even better, fund a Roth IRA that would provide for her future.*
>
> *Couldn't she have done that calculation before going to college and incurring the debt? What good is her classroom education if she can't even figure out her own finances? If I were her, I would be embarrassed to tell anyone I was an accountant if I had that kind of debt. But, hey, that's just me.*
>
> #### 2.
>
> *A 50-year old wife and mother of 2 children is well employed as a Vice-President of Finance of a mid-sized company, earning $185,000/year. Her husband makes less than that, but she doesn't really know how much less. Why is that? Because they don't talk about their money. They have no joint accounts. They have "her" money and "his" money. She spends nearly all of her income buying things to give to other people.*
>
> *Although she did not say so specifically, it would appear that her husband's income is for the expenses of their family life and home, and she honestly believes her money is hers to do with as she sees fit. She has no emergency fund, no retirement or investment accounts. She says she figured that she would always make good money and it would always be there for her. She was completely out of touch with the possibility that she might be unable to work and earn a living at some point in the future, or that she would need that money in her old age. I suppose she's one of the people who thinks they will live forever.*
>
> *What good was her education that enabled her to get a job as a VP-Finance, but not enable her to handle her own money? Just asking ... Considering that she is already 50 years old, wouldn't you think that common sense would have kicked in before now?*
>
> *In both of these scenarios, the women were financial professionals.*
> *What does that tell you?*

Unless you pursue the specific study of money and finance in college, there appears to be a lack of education about money for the average college student, as well. If young people graduate from college with thousands of dollars of credit card debt and student loan debt into the 6 figures, there wasn't any learning about money taking place there, either.

Did we learn about money from our families? Gosh, I hope not, although the answer is probably yes. Even words casually spoken by our parents about money had an impact on how we think about money, how we spend money, and whether or not we save money. We might not even be aware of how we were influenced by our families about money.

I'm sure you have all heard this statement: ***"Money is the root of all evil.*** Sorry, no matter how many times you may have heard it said that way, not only is the wording incorrect, but the thought as well. The exact quotation is from the First Book of Timothy 6:10 in the Bible, and it says:

"For the <u>LOVE</u> of money is a root of all kinds of evil."

Notice the inclusion of the word "love?" <u>Money</u> is NOT the root of evil, the **<u>love</u> of money** is. There is a big difference.

If you have been taught by frugal or very poor parents that money is the root of evil, you may have difficulty connecting to money in a healthy, natural way. In fact, you may even sabotage your own financial situation so that you don't have money, subconsciously believing it is evil. The message can be very subtle.

When I was in 7th grade, I was selected from the whole student body to be the Banking Officer. I have no idea how they chose me, but what it meant was that every Tuesday morning, I would get out of class and sit with a man from a local bank as he collected money from students to put into their own savings account at the bank. Each student had a passbook, and it was my job to record the figures in the book. (It was the time before computers!) Some students put as little as five cents into their account each week. Others brought one or two dollars. It was a valuable learning exercise for them.

Where did those students get the motivation to do that? At home. Where else would it have come from? There was no TV at the time. Most of those kids were not from wealthy families … in fact, probably none of them were, as I think back. But, somewhere, they learned that saving money was important, and they actually took steps to save money for later, even if the amounts were very small.

Guess who didn't learn a thing about saving money from this experience? That would be ME! It never even occurred to me to open a savings account of my own. How could I have missed such a good opportunity? Could it be that saving money was never talked about in our home?

When my sister and I were young girls, before the ages of 6 and 9, we lived in a happy family, in a beautifully furnished home, had a beautiful new car, and went to private school. Our school friends came from wealthy families. I thought our family was wealthy, too, considering the life we lived until I was nine. After all, wasn't my father a doctor, too?

All of that came to an abrupt end when our parents divorced around 1950. My father took the car, didn't pay child support, left our mother with the big house and all the debt. He regularly failed to pay child support and our tuition, but somehow, our mother found the money to see that we both graduated. In order to see that the tuition was paid, it usually required the services of a lawyer. I don't even know how she managed it all … she never talked about money, but it was obvious to my sister and me in subtle ways, that she was hurting financially. The divorce left our mother financially and emotionally devastated, and her focus was on survival. Just surviving, however, is not a good education for how to handle money.

Our mother had come from a well-to-do family where all her needs were met. Her father was a prominent doctor. She went from that family into the family she and my father created, and I'm pretty sure she believed he would take care of her, as her father had done. But, that isn't how it tuned out. Suddenly, by virtue of divorce, she was thrown out into the world, wounded and unprepared, at a time when divorce was social death. She was in no position to educate us about money because she had never before had to handle her own money.

Both of our parents came from families that were wealthy, but lived conservative lives. Our grandparents had sufficient money to send each of our parents to Ursinus College in Collegeville, Pennsylvania, starting in 1933 – that is, during the Great Depression. So, you can see, there was no lack of money.

Despite the fact that both of our parents were college educated, there was never even a conversation about our going to college. The fact that we didn't go to college was as much from a lack of conversation, as from a lack of funds. Here was a situation where communication was required, but did not happen. We could have asked our grandparents to help us financially, but we didn't ask, and they didn't offer … *important conversations that didn't happen.*

Our father made no contribution, either emotional or financial, toward our education, or our survival. He could have stepped in to help my sister and me, but he did not. He spent money frivolously, in dysfunctional ways, and he never wanted for anything that money could buy. We had no car for 4 years. He had an expensive new car every year.

All through school, my sister and I had taken all the college-prep academic courses and had an A- average. I actually thought that, by some miracle or other, we would go to college like our friends did. But, after graduation, it was clear there was no college in our future, so, after high school graduation, I worked for 18 months and saved all the money I needed to attend business school.

<u>Never</u> <u>once</u> was there a conversation in my family about <u>saving</u> money. My sister and I had no education around the subject of money, except what we learned from watching our mother struggle when she couldn't make ends meet. You see, her formal education was in music, but not as a teacher, as a performer. So, it was virtually impossible for her to earn a living to support us in the 1950s. Thus, four years after her divorce, she married a man to help her pay the bills. Of course,

she never said it in so many words. Her actions, however, told the real truth. That's what women did in the 50s. My mother jumped from the frying pan (my father, who was a doctor) to the fire (a blue-collar 8th-grade drop-out, used car salesman).

> *One of the few conversations about money in this new family of mine occurred when I got engaged. After my small family engagement party, my stepfather raged at me about how did I expect them to pay for my wedding when I had never paid any room and board? WHAT? Did I miss something? Room and board? Was he kidding? No, he wasn't. Nobody I knew paid room and board ... that was something foreign to me, and had never been brought up before. He said that if I had been paying room and board since high school graduation, he and my mother would have put that money into a separate savings account for me, and that money would be there to pay for my wedding. Excuse me, isn't that the same as if I were paying for my own wedding with my own money? Just asking ...*
>
> *The essence of that one-way conversation was that he and my mother were not going to pay for my wedding. My reaction to that was that I had no intention of paying room and board, and my fiancé and I would pay for our own wedding, thank you very much. And so we decided to save our own money to buy furniture instead of paying for a big wedding. Would I do things differently today? Absolutely.*

THIS WAS <u>MY</u> LEARNING EXPERIENCE AROUND THE SUBJECT OF MONEY.
HOW and WHERE DID <u>YOU</u> LEARN ABOUT MONEY?

HOW WAS MONEY HANDLED IN YOUR FAMILY?

If you are a Baby Boomer, and you find yourself facing retirement with insufficient money and large debt, you somewhere learned to spend money frivolously and not save for the future. Did you ever hear your parents talk about saving money for their retirement or for their "golden years? Were you influenced by the times (that is, the 60s), or by the Viet Nam War that made you think there was no future? Was it that "free-love" culture that encouraged you to live recklessly for today, and the hell with tomorrow? Are you one of those people who think you're going to live forever, and you don't have to take care of your personal business (including saving money) until LATER? Where did you get that idea?

From Suze Orman's book, *The 9 Steps to Financial Freedom,* here are some numbers for you to ponder the next time you charge something on your credit card.

- If your average balance on one credit card is $1,100, and the credit card company charges 18.5% interest, and you pay only the minimum 1.7% every month, and you never charge another thing, it will take you 12-1/2 years to pay off the balance, and it will have cost your $2,480.94 in interest. Do you think you really got that "stuff" on sale if you ended up paying this kind of interest?

WHAT FOLLOWS IS NOT A TEST

These are not questions for you to answer, but things to recall about the way your family of origin handled money. Look to see if some of these things influence how you now handle money. The questions are being asked so that you will begin to THINK about how and where you learned your money habits.

Notice whether you have followed in the footsteps of your parents, or, as a reaction to the way they handled your family money, have you gone in the opposite direction. That is, if they saved money, do you now save money, or do you spend it as a reaction to their frugality (if it can be called that)?

Relax and take your time reading this list.

- Who was in charge of money in your family?

- Did your father believe that only he needed to know the working of your family's money, and that it wasn't necessary to "bother" your mother with such things?

- Do you remember hearing your parents fight about money? Who usually won?

- What financial knowledge did your father pass on to you?

- Was your family wealthy? Did you know you were wealthy?

- Was your family poor? Did you know your family was poor?

- Was there ever a bankruptcy in your family?

- As a child, were you ever afraid that there wasn't enough money for the basic necessities of life?

- Were your utilities ever shut off, or a car repossessed?

- Were you taught the value of saving money?

- Did your family blame the Great Depression for their financial woes?

- Did you begin earning your own money when you were 10 or 12? A paper route, or cutting grass or babysitting?

- Were you allowed to keep all the money you earned, or were you expected to give some or all of it to your parents?

- Did you pay room-and-board? At what age did that begin? How did you feel about it?

- Were you encouraged to save and pay for your own education?

- Did your parents buy your first car, or did you pay for it yourself? Who paid for the gas, maintenance and insurance?

- Did you, personally, save money as a child; i.e., money you got as gifts for your birthday, or from odd jobs, or did you spend it as quickly as you got it?

- Did you have your own savings account in a bank, and if so, did you regularly put money into it?

- At what age did you have a job that gave you walking-around money?

- Did your parents own or rent your home?

- Did you move around a lot for reasons other than job transfers?

- Did you go to private or public schools?

- Did you know the cost of that private school tuition?

- Did your parent(s) ever throw it up to you how they were sacrificing to pay your tuition?

- Did you often hear your parent(s) speak about not having enough money to pay the bills?

- When you asked your parent(s) for money to buy something for yourself, were you generally told no, and if so, were you given a reason for the no.

- Did you live in a nice home, nicely furnished, in a nice neighborhood?

- Did your family always have a car? More than one?

- Was there always enough food on the table?

- If you needed a birthday gift for a friend's party, who paid for it?

- As a child, did you make up your mind that when you grew up, you would handle your money differently than the way your parents handled money? Did you even give this any thought?

- Were you taught/encouraged to donate money to charity?

- Were you taught to feel gratitude for what you did have?

- Or, did your parent(s) bitterly complain about what they didn't have?

- Was your father always employed? What kind of job(s) did he have?

- Do you know how much money your father earned?

- Did your parents shop with credit cards or cash? How do you shop today?

- Was there a general sense of financial well-being and abundance in your home?

- Were you part of a "blended" family where your parents' income had to cover expenses for two or more families?

- Was there a divorce in your family that left your mother (and you kids) in a very poor financial situation?

- Did your mother complain about your father's not giving her enough money to support you kids?

- Did your father pay child support, regularly and on time? Through the courts, or directly to your mother?

- After the divorce, was your family's standard of living diminished?

- Did your mother have go to work after the divorce just to pay the bills? Was she bitter about this, and did she blame your father?

- Did your family take vacations together? Did you ever go to Disney World or a theme park, even for a day?

- Did you have pets? Or were you told you couldn't afford them?

- Was there money sufficient to pay for piano or dancing lessons, little league uniforms, school trips?

- What was Christmas like in your house? Visiting with family and friends? Gifts? Joy? Sharing?

- Did your parents give you socks and underwear for Christmas; that is, basic necessities instead of fun toys?

- Was Christmas a time when your parent(s) spent money for you kids way beyond what they could afford? If they overspent, did they throw it up to you later on?

- Were you given money by one parent to buy gifts for your other parent and siblings? Or did you use your own money from a job or savings to buy gifts for family members (birthday, Christmas, etc.)?

- Were you given gifts and/or parties on your birthday?

- Did your family operate out of a budget?

- Did your parents show you how to budget or write checks?

- Did you receive an allowance? Were chores tied to it?

- Do you think your parent(s) hid money in places in the house?

- If your parents are deceased, did you and your siblings receive an inheritance?

- Did either/both of your parents suffer from alcoholism or drug addiction that caused a shortage of money?

- If you needed braces on your teeth, were you told there wasn't money for them? When you began earning your own living as a young adult, did you then pay for your own braces?

- When you graduated from high school or college (if you did), did your family give you gifts or a party?

- Did your parents take pictures of your family events?

- Were you and your siblings photographed at professional studios as you were growing up? Sears? JCPenney? Wal-Mart?

- Did you have plenty of age-appropriate toys, or way too many?

- Were you encouraged to give toys you no longer wanted to charity or a thrift shop? Or to sell them at a yard sale? And if you did sell them, were you allowed to keep the cash?

- Did you parent(s) pay for your college education? wedding? divorce? If not, what did they say was the reason for not paying?

- Growing up, did you regularly hear your parent(s) say that money is the root of all evil?

- If your father predeceased your mother, did he leave her financially well-off for the remainder of her life? Did he educate your mother about how to handle money? Or did she struggle with being unable to handle money, or with insufficient money for the remainder of her life?

- Did your parents (or grandparents) require you to clean your plate because if you didn't, you were wasting money?

- Did your family tithe or otherwise regularly contribute to a church? Only in good times, or all the time?

- Were you taught to respect money or fear it?

- Was your family burdened by bills they couldn't pay because they bought too much stuff they didn't need?

- Were both parents employed? Was that necessary to pay the bills?

- What did you ever want very badly, that your parents told you that you couldn't have because they didn't have enough money?

- What was the first thing you bought for yourself when you began earning your own living as a young adult?

WHAT WAS THE POINT OF THAT TRIP DOWN MEMORY LANE?

The point was to learn from the inquiry, see where mistakes were made, where you can take different routes than those your parent(s) took in an attempt to avoid making the same mistakes. As adults, we tend to do one of two things:

-We do things the same way our parents did them,

or

-We do things the opposite of how our parents did them.

Now that I have dug up all those memories (good and bad) from your family life, what are you supposed to do with them, if anything?

- Think about how you have been influenced in the way you handle money *today* by the conversations or behavior of your parents around the subject of money, and to what extent you have benefited or suffered as a result.

- If you saw that you are generally handling money the way your parent(s) did, how is that working for you?

- If you saw that you are intentionally handling your money differently than the way your parent(s) did, is your way producing the results you anticipated or not?

- Are there things you can do to change and/or improve your way of handling money?

- If you have seen any tendencies toward poor financial habits, are you willing to seek help from a professional financial advisor?

Think of those questions as a money physical exam … like a physical you would get from a doctor. The doctor would ask you questions to determine certain facts about your health in order to establish an accurate diagnosis of your medical problems. Likewise, a financial planner will want to examine your history and habits regarding saving, spending, investing and planning before making a diagnosis and prognosis of your financial health.

If reading the list frightened you into taking action, let it be that you pick up the phone and make an appointment with a qualified financial professional. Just don't be so frightened that you do nothing, which is, of course, always an option.

WHAT ARE YOU WILLING TO DO ABOUT YOUR ADDICTIVE SPENDING HABITS?

Shopping, that is, using spending to provide mood-altering relief, can be an addiction, plain and simple. And you know that recovery from an addiction of any kind is not a quick-fix, and has a very high rate of failure.

Dr. Phil says that past behavior indicates future behavior. For your sake, I hope that is not 100% true, but there is evidence that points to repeated failures.

You also know that you can't wave a magic wand and wake up one morning debt free! That isn't how it works. It takes effort, focus and commitment to get out of debt, and you probably cannot do it by yourself. Ask for help, but be careful to ask the right people. Unfortunately, in the current economic situation, there are unscrupulous people taking advantage of people in debt, and actually causing their financial situation to become worse.

Take a hard look at the numbers. See what your addiction is costing you. Get professional counseling to address the addiction aspect of your spending.

If you find yourself at the age of Baby Boomers and in debt, you have made mistakes along the way. Did you even know they were mistakes that would cause you distress at this time in your life? Were you paying attention to all of those articles about Baby Boomers and the impact of their financial needs on the rest of the country?

Giving you tips on how to get out of debt is insufficient. I recommend that you start today to find a financial planner who will work WITH you to establish a plan you are willing to stick with in the long term. And, I'm not talking about one of those investment or insurance salespeople posing as financial planners. I'm talking about the real deal: financial planners who have the appropriate credentials, expertise, experience, and reputation.

IMAGINE WHAT YOUR FUTURE WOULD LOOK LIKE WITHOUT MONEY

If you are 60 years old, you can easily anticipate living another 30 years. Whether or not you live those 30 years in good physical and financial health is mostly up to you … *not entirely, of course* … but you have to do certain things to see that your life turns out the way you want it to turn out. If you want to be able to live until your 90s with enough money to sustain even a modest lifestyle, you are going to have to take a serious look at your financial situation NOW, and make some changes, like it or not!

ONCE AGAIN, THIS IS MY SUGGESTION.
YOU CAN AND WILL DO WITH IT WHAT YOU CHOOSE.

On June 25, 2011, Suze Orman had a young adult woman and her parents as her guests. The young woman and her two adult siblings wrote to Suze to request an intervention with their parents, who were 52 and 57, and have gotten themselves into extraordinary debt and have no savings. The children were helping their parents financially, but it was like giving a drink to an alcoholic. All the parents got from their children's financial assistance was the momentary fix that any addict gets from a little bit of the substance they crave so much.

In that family, the parents craved money ... so much so that the father was scheduled to go to Iraq for one year as a civilian mechanic to repair vehicles, for which he was going to be paid $90,000 tax-free. And, what do you think he planned to do with that money? Buy himself a new truck!?! His family and Suze were outraged at his financial irresponsibility. Suzy, in her forceful way, said, "ARE YOU KIDDING ME?"

Neither parent seemed upset or genuinely concerned with their situation. So, to jolt them out of their fog, Suze came right out and asked the man: "Are you hoping that you won't live long enough to have to worry about paying your debts? Is that why you're going to Iraq?" WOW! Talk about a pregnant pause. What do you think was his reply? He admitted it was true. EXCUSE ME? **The man actually said he would rather die than face his financial mess?** *This man, at some level, understood that he has compromised his financial future in such an extreme way that he sees no possibility for resolving the problems short of dying. Seems pretty extreme to me.*

Suze suggested some steps to help them, and told them that they still have time before their retirement years to fix their mess, but told them it would not be easy. Her first suggestion: the man had to stop smoking: (a) for his health; and (b) to save money. Second, she told him not to go to Iraq, and, under no circumstances, should he buy a new truck! She told the wife to get a "real" job ... she was only working part-time in retail, making $13,000 annually. She also told the children to stop giving their parents money. I hope there is a follow-up show to see how these people are doing in 6 months.

BABY BOOMERS' FEAR OF RUNNING OUT OF MONEY IS GENUINE.

The years went by so fast! Wasn't it just yesterday when they were young? And, now, they are reading about themselves (that is, the group known as the "Baby Boomers") in connection with retirement.

It can't be true!
Oh, but it is.
But, you say, you're not ready!
Ready or not, here it comes.
Get ready, get set, go!

A recent newspaper article states that due to a combination of procrastination and bad timing, Baby Boomers find themselves facing personal financial disaster at the very time they were planning (*more like hoping*) to retire. I used the word "planning" loosely, because it is apparent there wasn't much *planning* taking place.

Collectively, in their adult years, Baby Boomers have spent too much and saved too little. Throw in the possibility of a job lay-off, heavy debt, no health insurance, foreclosure, forced retirement, and a recession, maybe even a divorce or a health crisis, combined with a self-indulgent lifestyle and loss of invested assets, and it could be said that many Baby Boomers have all the ingredients for a financial time bomb about to explode.

DO YOU SEE THE POTENTIAL FOR PROBLEMS?

In January 2011, more than 10,000 Baby Boomers turned 65 years old, and that pattern will continue for nearly 20 years. Baby Boomers have not saved for retirement, have huge debt, and are retiring too early. Mistakes have been made along the way, not intentionally, but mistakes, nevertheless. Some can be corrected easily; some can be corrected with some direction and advice from qualified professionals.

But, SOME MISTAKES ARE LIKE HUMPTY DUMPTY! They can't be put back together again.

Never before have so many people faced the prospect of their retirement years with so many questions, so much confusion and fear, and so many choices. Collectively, Baby Boomers are moving full-speed ahead toward retirement and old age, and many are unprepared.

By failing to prepare, you are preparing to fail.

Benjamin Franklin

There is a not a day that goes by without someone writing or speaking about Baby Boomers and money. For the last several years, there has been a conversation among financial professionals about the enormous transfer of money from one generation to another. Baby Boomers were looking forward to inheriting from their parents. The sad reality is that it probably won't happen because their parents lived longer than expected and will need their money for their own living expenses.

This leaves Baby Boomers in a place they never expected to find themselves. They are in debt -- serious debt. And, now, instead of forecasting and focusing on the anticipated inheritances of Boomers, the focus is on how to get them out of debt and how to help them recover investment losses in order to save for retirement before it's too late.

In December 2011, student loan debt was estimated to be between $865 billion and $1 trillion, and is greater than credit card debt. Who is going to pay all that money back? How? If you are a Baby Boomer who has both student loan and credit card debt, it's easy to see that you have a serious financial problem.

Common sense would help. So, would removing the rose-colored glasses. Budgeting would be valuable, along with tracking every cent you spend every day. Consultation with a financial planner would be extremely helpful. And you already know that there are many, many books with information and tips about your money: how to make it; how to invest it; how to save it; how to stop spending it; how to plan for your financial future.

18

There are also all those money shows on TV. My favorite is Suze Orman. I know that some people find her style aggressive and abrasive, but since when is it all right to kill the messenger? She speaks a lot of truth to anyone who really pays attention. I especially like her mantra:

FIRST <u>PEOPLE</u>; THEN <u>MONEY</u>; THEN <u>THINGS</u>.

No one says that a person must believe every word Suze speaks, or do everything she recommends, but you have to admit that some of her ideas make good common sense. And, I like her no-nonsense style – tell it like it is, no matter how it hurts. After all, whose mess is she trying to fix? Not hers! YOURS!

**One or two financial missteps with your retirement savings,
and you could find yourself PAYING for them well into later life, *in terms <u>other</u> <u>than</u> <u>money</u>.***

WHAT CAN BABY BOOMERS DO NOW
TO RESCUE THEMSELVES BEFORE FINANCIAL DISASTER?

1. **STOP SPENDING!**

2. **GET OUT OF DEBT!**

3. **START SAVING!**

4. **FINISH READING THIS BOOK!**

5. **MEET WITH A QUALIFIED FINANCIAL PLANNER**

HOW TO INTERPRET THE VARIOUS
PROFESSIONAL DESIGNATIONS OF FINANCIAL PLANNERS

It has been said that the financial industry is drowning in credentials, and that there are more than 100 different credentialing agencies for financial planners. Which ones are legitimate? Which ones will do for you what needs to be done, with integrity and honesty? What about all those "financial planners" who created Ponzi schemes and stole millions of dollars from clients? What about those financial advisors who offer you a free lunch? How are you supposed to tell one from the other?

Well, it may be that there is no one way to tell if a financial planner is running a Ponzi scheme until it is too late. Does the name Bernie Madoff sound familiar? He was intelligent, charismatic, well known and respected in the financial community. His friends trusted him with millions of dollars of their money. But, you remember what happened? Who saw it coming?

As a client (or potential client) of a financial planner, do your homework and investigate the planner before working with him, to the best of your ability. Check with the websites of professional organizations. Check with your local police department or Better Business Bureau to see if there have been any complaints. Visit the website www.finra.com to see what the broker's credentials are, and if there are any complaints on file for the broker,

And, pay attention to your instincts and that old, familiar saying that goes like this: *"If something sounds too good to be true, it just might be."*

Knowing the professional designations is only one piece of the information you need when looking for a financial planner for yourself, but it will at least give you some idea of their education and experience. You want to work with someone who has been in the business long enough to have a track record of success and a list of satisfied clients.

A WORD OF CAUTION.

There are people presenting themselves as financial advisors who do not have genuine, measurable training, ability, credentials or experience. Usually, they are trying to "sell" something in the nature of an investment product, often to a target market such as seniors or veterans. Such behavior is highly unethical and, while it may not be illegal, it is nevertheless up to you to protect yourself because little has been done from a regulatory standpoint to protect the consumer from such "bogus" credentials.

You should insist that such advisor possess at least one of the legitimate professional designations and demand from them a "Letter of Fiduciary Responsibility," indicating (in writing) the advisor's status and commitment to act "in the best interests of the client."

Be really, really careful if the advisor brushes off your request for such documentation, and/or if you sense an urgency in their professional demeanor, such that you are uncomfortable and feel pressured to make a decision you are not ready to make, or do not choose to make in the first place. Learn how to say NO without guilt. It is, after all, your money, and chances are good you cannot afford to lose it.

If you feel pressured, at least put the offer on hold until you have had the chance to check out the person and the organization he/she represents. If the deal is good today, it will be good tomorrow. Remember that some mistakes made under pressure cannot be fixed. Be careful.

What follows is a brief description of some of the most common designations:

1. **Certified Financial Planner (CFP®).** A person who has achieved the CFP® designation is specially trained to offer full-service financial planning. To get this designation, a person must undergo 675 hours of study and have at last 3 years of relevant experience. As a client, you can expect that the Certified Financial Planner® will provide you with services that are conducted ethically, with integrity, objectivity, honesty and diligence, and will put your interests ahead of his own, as noted at www.cfp.net, the website for the CFP® Board.

2. **Chartered Financial Analyst (CFA)** is trained in investments and investing philosophy. This designation requires that a person complete 900 hours of study and have at least 4 years of relevant experience. CFAs are committed to professional ethics and investor protection through professional codes of conduct, guidance and outreach. See www.cfainstitute.org for more information.

3. **Certified Life Underwriter (CLU)** means the person holding this designation is trained in advising clients on life insurance products and related financial needs such as estate planning. The CLU designation dates back to the late 1920s. The CLU must have 3 years of relevant experience, complete 5 core courses and 3 elective courses, and successfully pass all 8 of the 2-hour, 100-question examinations. See www.designationcheck.com/learn-more-about-credentials/details/clu.

4. **Chartered Financial Consultant (ChFC)** designation means the person is trained as a full-service financial-planning expert. This designation requires more courses than any other financial planning credential. ChFC candidates must complete 9 college-level courses, with a curriculum that covers all aspects of financial planning, income taxation, investments and estate and retirement planning. The candidate must also have 3 years of full-time relevant experience. For more information, visit www.designationcheck.com/learn-more-about-credentials/details/chfc.

5. **Certified Public Accountant - Personal Financial Specialist (CPA/PFS)** A person with these designations is trained in full-service financial planning and tax planning. A PFS is more than a financial planner, though; he also is a CPA. To attain these designation requires approx. 2,000 hours of study, plus two years of pertinent experience. See www.findapfs.org.

6. **RIA (Registered Investment Advisor).** Some brokers are registered as only an RIA. Some brokers have dual registration. What does that mean to you? A broker with only an RIA designation will have minimal supervision regarding his transactions with clients. Bernie Madoff was an RIA. An RIA is only audited every 17 years, whereas an investment professional who has a broker-dealer is audited every year. Annual audits allow for the possibility of quickly seeing fraudulent activities.

7. **CSA (Certified Senior Advisor).** Be careful of people with this designation on their business cards. They could be very nice people just trying to earn a living, but, in order to get the CSA designation, all they had to do was sit in a classroom for 3 days, pass a test, and pay a small sum of money. That's it. Compared with authentic financial

planners who spent years learning their business, these people are not knowledgeable about the law and finance, and do not have the credentials to back up a claim that they do.

What you want is a professional who will evaluate your present financial situation, and together with you, will <u>help you establish a PLAN for your future</u>. Remember, this book is all about planning for your future, and making plans for your money is high on the list of priorities for what to do with your time ***between now and then***.

- Begin by making an appointment with a financial planner <u>for a consultation</u>. You can find a local financial planner by asking for a referral from people you know and trust, or from the various websites mentioned above. I don't recommend the Yellow Pages (that is, if they even exist anymore). Of course, many financial planners will have Websites, but they are filled with printed words, not words spoken by people you trust, by people who have had successful results with particular financial professionals.

Before I go any further, I want you to know that almost anyone can print business cards identifying themselves as financial advisors; however, <u>no one</u> can present themselves to the world as a CFP®, a CFA, a CLU, a ChFC, or a CPA/PFS without having studied and passed the examinations, and without taking periodic Continuing Education classes. Be careful. Do your own research about the person and organization who will be handling your money.

- A financial planner will generally meet with you once or twice for consultation. When you make the appointment, ask what the fee is for the consultation. When you meet with him, ask how he charges for his time and services. It can be fee-based, commission, or a combination of the two. Ask about the differences and benefits of each. You will probably be asked to sign a fee agreement. Don't be put off by this request; it is for the benefit and protection of both of you.

- Feel free to ask about the education and experience of the financial planner, and how he keeps current on changes in the law and the various investment products. Ask when he last attended continuing education classes.

- A financial planner will usually begin by asking you a question like this: *"What do you want your money to do for you?"* Most people have no answer to this question, and because of this reason, the financial planner will spend quite a bit of time with you, trying to assist you in finding your own answers to the question. There are no right or wrong answers. There are only "your" answers. Armed with the information and knowledge you will get from reading this book, you will be prepared for that meeting.

- Make a clear determination if you are still in the financial accumulation phase, or whether you have passed into the preservation phase. If you are uncertain, discuss it with your financial planner. This is an extremely important distinction.

- Be prepared to ask questions and take careful notes, including dates of your meetings and any telephone conversations you have.

- Are you coachable? Are you able to take direction from someone who specializes in financial planning? Are you able to weigh choices vs. consequences? Or are you a "right-fighter," someone who will argue with the financial planner to justify, explain or rationalize the way you've been (mis)handling your finances?

Once upon a time, a widow met with a financial planner. It was the first time she had consulted with a professional about her money. After one or two meetings, the financial planner made suggestions about how she should invest her money with a particular focus on protecting money she already had.

She argued that she had seen an advertisement in the local newspaper for a company that was offering a 13% return on investments ... this, around 2005, when there weren't many companies promising that high rate of interest on any investments. She disagreed with the financial planner, but reluctantly allowed him to invest a small portion of her money. The rest she invested with the company from the newspaper ad.

So, when that company went out of business, who do you think she called first in a vain attempt to recover her lost money?

- If, during or after your consultation with the financial planner, you decide that you are not going to work well together (for any reason, including instinct), talk with him about your misgivings and try to find agreement. If you cannot, then find another financial planner with whom you feel comfortable. Feel free to explain, but do not feel the need to apologize.

• If you are married or in a committed relationship where the two of you share your money, it is essential that both parties attend every meeting with the financial planner. This is especially good if you are in a second marriage or have some "financial baggage" that needs to be addressed.

Meeting simultaneously is the best way for both people to have the opportunity to ask questions in the moment, to decide together if they trust (or like) the financial planner, and speak honestly in front of each other about their individual and mutual financial goals, past mistakes, etc. There is no law saying it is required, but that way, both parties hear the same thing at the same time. It lessens the possibility of misinterpretation.

Financial decision-making requires honest self-assessment, establishing priorities, and creating a plan for achieving your personal and financial goals, a plan either made by yourself individually or as a couple, or with a financial planner. But, you already know this, don't you?

Once upon a time, a married man met with a financial planner several times by himself. When asked about his wife, he said she was unable to attend the meetings because of poor health, but he felt sure she would support whatever decisions he made. That is, until one day, they both showed up to meet with the financial planner.

Things went from bad to worse when the wife heard what her husband had been discussing with the financial planner. Not only did she disagree with her husband, but she stormed out of the office, and they never came back.

Do you think their ride home was pleasant?

The husband had been less than honest in his discussions with the financial planner, and worse, less than honest in reporting to his wife what he and the financial planner had talked about. He really thought he knew what he was doing, and didn't need any advice from a stranger. Why didn't he tell the truth about his wife, or talk about his mistakes? Pride, embarrassment, shame, guilt ... because he realized he didn't know as much as he thought he knew? Remember I mentioned how many emotions are involved in financial planning?

Don't automatically assume you know what your partner thinks about money, or what they want their money to do for them and for the two of you, or what their fears are about money. Allow them the respect to speak for themselves.

On the Suze Orman TV show of March 3, 2012, a young married woman called to ask what she should do with $115,000 she had recently received in settlement of a personal injury case. She had both student loan and credit card debt, as did her husband. The woman was inclined to use the money to pay off her own debt, and then put the remainder in an investment account for her own future ... after all, she was the person who had suffered from the accident from which she got the settlement. Her husband, however, disagreed, and was putting pressure on her to pay off his debt first, because it was at a higher interest rate.

Suze asked the woman what she was worried about with her husband's pressuring her. She sadly admitted that she was afraid he would withhold his love for her in some way, or call her selfish, or even break up with her. Suze's advice was to NEVER act out of fear. She recommended that the woman have a serious conversation with her husband, assure him of her love, and try to make him understand that the money was really hers. Suze also pointed out that if the woman put that cash settlement into a joint account with her husband, then half of it would belong to him. What that could mean is in the event they divorce in the future, one half of her money would go with her husband. Suze told her to go with her gut.

See how money and emotions can get all tangled up?

• Be prepared to be completely honest and confess your financial sins. Believe me when I tell you that the financial planner does not care about your mistakes. It is not his job to give you absolution. He really only wants to know your financial history so he can help you <u>plan</u> your financial future.

**Confession of errors is like a broom which sweeps away the dirt
and leaves the surface brighter and clearer.**

Mohandas Gandhi

- Do not begin a conversation with a financial planner by asking him to *sell* you a particular investment product. That is not "financial planning." Don't go "shopping" for a particular investment product you just read about in a magazine, heard about on TV, or from a friend. The financial planner is not running a retail store!

NOTE: The intention of a financial planner is not to "sell" you something, especially something you might not need, but to set in place a planning process. If you ask him to "sell" you a specific investment product, be prepared for him to say no. If the financial advisor quickly directs you to a specific product he recommends that you buy, RUN! It is doubtful that he is a genuine financial planner if he is attempting to sell you something.

- Be sure that your financial planner is not one of those insurance or annuity salespeople masquerading as a financial planner, and who has no credentials to back up their claim … you know the kind that offers you a free dinner in exchange for some (questionable) financial product you may or may not need. Their only real interest may be in selling you an insurance or investment product on which they earn a high commission.

DISCLAIMER:

Having said that, it is important that you know and understand that there are many highly qualified, very reputable financial professionals who market their business through lunch or dinner seminars, while at the same time providing information and education. It is a relaxed environment in which to present often highly complicated subject matter. Don't be afraid to attend. Relax and enjoy the food and sociability. Know that those seminars are a good place for you to begin to learn about estate and financial planning, so long as you just listen and take notes so you can ask questions later. "Later" is where there can be a problem.

Be forewarned that there is an enormous amount of information presented at one of those seminars, which leaves no time for individual questions; therefore, the presenter will want their representative to meet with you, in your home, to answer your questions. If you invite them into your home, be prepared for the representative to attempt to sell you something you may not want, may not need, may not be able to afford, and may not be appropriate for your situation. They may also want you to show them information about your assets. Be very careful to whom you bare your financial soul.

Remember, you are permitted to say "NO." You don't owe them anything because you did not ask them for that free dinner. If you are the kind of person who responds to pressure, even subtle pressure induced by guilt, be very careful before you say yes to anything, and especially before you sign anything.

What you must do is learn to distinguish the difference between those people and organizations you can trust and those you cannot. Mistakes are very costly and sometimes cannot be fixed. Remember the Humpty Dumpty mistakes?

- The financial planner may ask you to do some "homework" before your second meeting, because, at some point, he will want to review your existing investments (for example, IRAs, 401(k), stocks and bonds, life insurance, long-term care insurance, CDs, assets and debts). If he sends you a work-book before your first meeting, take the time to fill it out. Don't just think of it as "busy work." The information you put in that workbook will be valuable in the process of making financial plans for your future.

He is not being nosey, but a financial plan cannot be appropriately prepared for your life and situation if you only tell him part of your financial picture. If you have made mistakes in the past, or have certain fears, experiences or assumptions, talk with the planner about those things. Be upfront and keep communication open and honest. The idea is to develop rapport and trust between you and the planner.

Understand that a financial plan appropriate for you cannot be prepared without your working *together* with the financial planner. It takes time to develop a rapport and trust between you and him. Don't try to rush the process.

- Do you rely on your emotions to guide you in making financial decisions? If your instincts are good, and if you are accustomed to paying attention to them, you may get good results from relying upon them. But, get to know the difference between your emotions and your instincts.

Q.   WHEN YOU ARE LOST, WHAT IS THE MOST IMPORTANT THING FOR YOU TO KNOW?

A.   EXACTLY WHERE YOU ARE AT THE MOMENT.

- Statistically, women are more inclined to seek out and use the services of a financial planner than are men (more about Women and Money later in this chapter.)

- Men generally won't ask for directions. They often apply this same mentality to financial planning. Men believe they don't need help and can do it by themselves. It is valuable for you to understand that good financial planning is not a do-it-yourself business; however, that doesn't stop people from doing it. It also doesn't stop them from making some serious financial mistakes. There are some things in the world for which consulting a qualified professional makes sense. You can no more expect good results from do-it-yourself financial planning than you can from do-it-yourself doctoring or lawyering . . . or plumbing!

- In many marriages, the husband handles the money and the wife just goes along with it, never asking how their joint money is handled, where it is, how much they have. Your husband has put your financial future in jeopardy. If you, the husband, have kept your wife in the dark about your money, stop it today! If you, the wife, have allowed this to happen, take steps today to educate yourself about your money.

- If you enjoy the process of checking your investments every day in the newspaper or on the Internet, discussing the stock market with their friends, etc., you should know that you won't necessarily have to give up these activities when you consult a financial planner. Just be careful what you believe from these other (often questionable) sources.

- Recognize also that the financial planning needs of people approaching retirement, or already retired, are different from those of a single person in their 30's or those of a young married couple raising children and saving for their education. A financial planner will help you navigate the complex waters of investments that will be appropriate for your life situations as they exist and as they change and evolve over time.

- The plan a financial planner will prepare for you is an evolving process, basically with a beginning and an end. It is important, however, for you to understand that using the services of a financial planner can and probably should be a process over time, and not a one-time event. That process might, in fact, include assisting you with the sale of investment products that you already have, or the purchase of other investment products that will move you toward your financial goals. Keep your eye on the target.

> Be careful of any financial planner who presents you with a 50-60 page plan. It will contain way too many variables, will be confusing, and may even be out of date by the time it gets to you. And, besides, you probably won't read the whole thing anyway.

- You may want to work with a financial planner who is an independent broker not employed by any one particular company (for example, Merrill-Lynch, Janney Montgomery Scott, etc.). As an independent broker, he can consider many investment and insurance options, as compared to simply selling you something from the company that employs him.

- If, after working with your financial planner for a while, you find that the goals you had expected are not happening, consider that it may not be the fault of the financial planner *per se*. The number of variables is enormous! If you don't believe me, watch the financial TV channels around 4 o'clock every day. Financial planning is a complicated field that in many cases offers no guarantees. If you find yourself unhappy with the financial **results**, first discuss it with your financial planner, but DO NOT go around bad-mouthing him to your friends. Consider the possibility that you don't know or understand the details. Be fair and reasonable. And listen. You just might learn something.

> *When I owned and operated a flower shop, a young woman came in to order flowers to be sent to someone in the hospital. She was newly married, and mentioned the name of the flower shop where she had gotten her wedding flowers, and how horrible they were, and how unhappy she was with them.*
>
> *I asked her if she had ever spoken to the flower shop owner about her upset and her complaints, which, in my opinion, may or may not have been genuine. The flower shop she was bad-mouthing had an impeccable reputation over many years, and I know that the owner would have done everything in her power to satisfy this young woman, even at that late date. The woman said she didn't see the point of telling the flower shop owner about her upset.*
>
> *I pointed out to her that by not mentioning it, she deprived the owner of ever having an opportunity to explain things, or to remedy the situation. The young woman remained adamant that it was too late, her wedding had been ruined, and besides, what could the owner do to remedy the situation anyway? Well, maybe, if the owner were so inclined, she could have given the bride a refund, or arranged to send her a dozen roses every month for a year, or something else that was mutually satisfactory.*

But, because this young woman remained stuck in her anger, she was not open to the possibility that maybe her complaint was not reasonable in the first place, and that some agreeable remedy did exist. She did not understand the difference between a legitimate complaint and whining. It appeared that she was getting a lot of mileage out of playing the victim.

And, so, she will spend more time bad-mouthing that flower shop every chance she gets. Having been a florist, I know that there are people (brides, in particular) who really don't know much about flowers, are not open to suggestions, and often confuse facts with emotions.

I believe the same thing can be said of the general knowledge the average person has about financial planning. They have opinions that may or may not have anything to do with the facts.

I know people who have done the same thing with financial planners when they didn't understand what their financial planner was trying to do for them, and were not willing to ask questions and engage in a conversation for possibility. And, rather than bring a complaint to the financial planner that would enable them to have a rational discussion and maybe even learn something, they just storm away and tell all their friends what a terrible financial planner that person is. So, whose loss is it, really?

If you don't like the financial planner you are working with, don't sit around and worry or complain to your friends. And, don't just waste time wondering how things will work out. The statement that time is money has merit. Take action to find a financial planner you like, one with whom you feel comfortable working. And, don't allow fear to make your decision, and absolutely, don't make the choice to do nothing. After all, it's your money and your life.

As you work out your financial plans, don't ignore the cost of your health care, including insurance premiums, medications, co-pays, and expenses not covered by insurance, including hearing aids and holistic practices like acupuncture, for example. You want your quality of life to be as good as possible. Healthcare, in this country at this time, is a big deal. Do your very best to take care of your own personal healthcare expenses without total reliance on the government or insurance. Figure out what is the amount of money you need, and how to get it … just in case the program benefits are reduced or go away altogether. *Just one more thing to think about.*

In all of this planning, do not leave out possible discussions with a tax attorney about the taxability of inheritances, sale of assets, gifting, etc. Making the wrong choices regarding taxes can cost you big time!

A financial planner can help you get from here to there … to achieve your financial goals; he knows you and cares about you and your family, what you want your money to do for you, how you plan to spend your "golden years," and the financial legacy you want to leave behind for your children and grandchildren.

Why would you jeopardize the benefits of sound professional advice? Because that's what people do. Plain and simple. People don't like to be told what to do, or how to do it. They may politely listen to good advice and go home and do the opposite, or completely ignore it, or worse. Some people actually believe they can ignore good advice and expect good results by doing it themselves. Some people do the same thing with estate-planning advice. Somehow, I don't think that's a coincidence. *Do you?*

Others believe that when things turn out badly, that is, as they themselves describe "badly," they can blame the financial planner (or their mother, or their lawyer, or the government, or the weather). *Do you get the idea?*

Whether you decide to manage your money yourself or with the assistance of a financial planner, or a combination of the two, it is up to you to know exactly how your money is doing at all times. You must learn to read the statements, trust yourself to ask questions, and respect your money.

NOW WHAT?

Some people leave the initial meeting with a financial planner all excited about the possibilities ahead. If that's you, great! But, haven't you experienced that kind of excitement in the past?

- Did you take the actions recommended?
- Do you have a history of sticking with the decisions and the plan?
- Or do you quit when you feel pressured, or anxious, or any one of those other emotions and excuses you allow to stop you from getting in the game?

- Have you reached your financial goals? Or are you at least on your way to achieving them?

- Was this just one in a long line of start-and-stop ideas?

- Did you stay on course? *"No, you say, but I wasn't far off!"*

> **There is no more time to waste. You are already in your 60s!**
> **Get with the program!**

> ***Procrastination is one of the most common and deadliest of diseases,***
> ***and its toll on success and happiness is heavy.***
>
> Dr. Wayne Dyer

Involve yourself in the continuing process of working with your financial planner toward achieving your financial goals. Be one of the few people who actually begins and completes a plan.

And, once and for all, give up that DO-IT-YOURSELF mentality!

Is it going to be easy? Maybe not easy, but probably not impossible, either. It will depend on your situation. If you have money in investments, you may only need to examine those investments, how well they have been doing, make a few changes, and then take steps to protect that money. But, if you have spent yourself into serious debt, it will require an entirely different approach to rescue you.

Do you really want to be rescued or are you contented living the way you have been living for the last 25 years? Can you project to where you will be in 25 years from today if you continue living the way you've been living, spending the way you've been spending? Who do you think will pay your bills after you run out of money?

> **The real bottom-line necessity for you to bail yourself out of this mess is COMMUNICATION!**
> **Here's that word again.**

Are you willing to talk about the financial mess you're in … real, honest conversations to examine where you went wrong and to find the way out? These may be some of those "conversations you don't want to have" that I mentioned at the beginning of this book. But, if you look at the past, and how many failed attempts you have made to curb your spending and start to save for your future, you may see that you can benefit from such conversations with a professional who is neutral, who can examine the numbers with fresh eyes.

It's interesting that money is one of the things people still don't like to talk about. It used to be sex, politics and religion, but those conversational taboos seem to have disappeared. Now, talking about your money is the last conversational taboo. No one wants to admit the financial mistakes they made, so they "fudge" the truth to make things sound better than they are.

WILL YOU DO WHATEVER IT TAKES?

You say you will, but sometimes when the going gets tough, and you are not enjoying the process, you quit. If you set your compass toward retirement, and if you allow yourself to easily get off course, even by a little bit, you have only yourself to blame when you run out of money. Ask any sailor what happens when the ship gets only 2 degrees off course – the ship does not end up at its designation, that's what happens! And, it could happen to you.

For many Baby Boomers, it may not be too late; it will, however, require that they put forth a conscious, focused, committed effort to the long-term recovery and planning process. Even if you have not saved enough money during your primary working years, it doesn't necessarily mean that you can't put forth a big effort toward retirement saving in the last 5 years of working. Will you do that to secure your financial future?

Many Boomers are caught up in lifestyle expenses now that the kids are educated and gone from the home. Boomers believe they are entitled to finally relax and have a little fun, buy that new house on the beach, buy that new car they have longed for. Do Baby Boomers ever ask themselves if they can really afford it or not? And, even if they ask the question, do they ever say NO to themselves?

If you find yourself short of retirement funds, forgive yourself, seek professional guidance, and move forward into the golden years you have anticipated for so long.

You can do this … you are the Baby Boomers, the movers and shakers, the people who have changed the way things are done, have made history … have made the difference in so many areas since they were born.

THIS IS NOT THE TIME TO QUIT.

"NO."

"No" is a complete sentence. It requires no other letters or words to amplify or convey its meaning. It requires no explanation. "No" means "no." It doesn't mean "yes," or "maybe," or "I'll think about it." Saying "no" skillfully can save you a lot of time, aggravation, upset, and money.

Learn to say "no." Better yet, learn to say "no" without feeling guilty about it. If it is said well, appropriately, and with intentionality, a polite "no," spoken with a firm voice and a smile on your face, will prevent you from getting into what could turn out to be a financial disaster.

Learn to say "no."
It will be of more use to you than to be able to read Latin.

Charles H. Spurgeon

TIP

*Here's a tip to help you better handle the situation when someone asks you for financial assistance. I learned it from Wayne Dyer's book, **Your Erroneous Zones**, 40 years ago, and it always works for me: Learn to say no <u>without guilt</u>. Dr. Dyer's point is that saying no, by itself, is insufficient. It must be connected with your feeling NO guilt about having said no, even when you say no to a loved one, a close friend, a boss, a salesperson, anyone at all. For some of you who regularly live in a place of guilt, it may take some time to feel comfortable saying no without guilt, but practice makes perfect. You'll get the hang of it ... or not. I recommend you become an expert at saying no without guilt. It will change your life for the better.*

How can saying "no" *without guilt* save you money?

Aah, yes, you were wondering what saying "no" has to do with your money, weren't you.

MISTAKES BABY BOOMERS CANNOT AFFORD TO MAKE

---

1.   DO NOT CO-SIGN FOR ANY FINANCIAL OBLIGATIONS OF OTHER PEOPLE

In this time when money is in the forefront of Baby Boomer's thoughts, the subject of co-signing for a financial obligation of someone else seems to be popping up everywhere. Baby Boomers are regularly co-signing for their children's student loans, credit cards, mortgages, apartment leases, and car payments to name a few, and are finding themselves in financial trouble as a result.

It is understandable that parents want to give their children a financial boost at the beginning of their young adult lives, but in today's economy, it can be a death knell for the financial life of the parents. Baby Boomers face many years when they will need money not necessarily earned from employment, and so they must protect what money they do have.

Financial advisors and everyone from Suze Orman to Judge Judy say NEVER co-sign for anyone for any amount for any reason: not a parent, a sibling, a child, your best friend. No one. Oh, I know how much you want to help someone in need, and that the banks make it sound so simple, but it is really important to protect yourself financially in today's world, especially if you are a Baby Boomer.

Do you understand the legal and financial consequences of co-signing for the financial obligations of someone else? If you are ever asked to do it, speak with a lawyer and/or a financial advisor before signing anything. Don't feel pressured to obligate yourself without getting all the information you need to make a responsible choice.

If you have already co-signed for someone, did your instincts tell you to say "no," but you said "yes" anyway? Why did you ignore your instincts? Why didn't you just say no? Oh, right, I forgot … you feel guilty when you say no. Remember, this is business, not personal. This is about YOUR money. You have the right to say no, *even the obligation to say no,* in order to be true to yourself. That's not the same as being selfish. It's being smart.

While co-signing, by itself, may feel like an act of love and generosity, there are other emotions to be considered in obligating yourself this way, not the least of which is financial integrity. Ask yourself why *you* are being asked to back someone for a financial obligation. Is it because they have bad credit or no credit history? Can they afford to repay the debt on their own? What are the chances they will default and you will be stuck paying off their debt? Could you afford to have that happen? What happens to your FICO score when they default? Do they have a history of making promises and not keeping them? Can you afford to have your wages garnished, or a judgment placed upon your house, or your good credit ruined?

How would you feel about the person for whom you co-signed, after they defaulted, and when the financial institution came after you for the money? Can you see that a relationship can be permanently damaged by this kind of transaction, no matter how well intentioned.

Serious conversations are essential in a situation like this. Parents don't want to say NO to their children, but sometimes, it is the best thing to do for them. Young adult children should already know they cannot always have what they want when they want it. Isn't that the demand level of a 3-year old? Sometimes, the very act of waiting and earning their own money can benefit young adults who are accustomed to having "everything" given to them by parents who have been historically willing to place themselves in debt for their kids. Well, remember that "everything" includes debt. So, let them have their own debt, and figure out how to deal with it. *Or not.*

And, if you were to personally assume someone else's debt, and you were to die owing all or some portion of that money, your estate would be obligated to pay it back. Is debt the legacy you want to leave your family? *I don't think so.*

What I suggest is that before you co-sign for any financial obligation of your children, you speak with a qualified financial planner to evaluate your own financial situation and protect your assets before you even think about co-signing. I'm pretty sure the advice you will receive will sound something like this:

On a Suze Orman show in early January 2012, there was a family faced with the question of how to pay for the college education of their two daughters.

The older daughter was only investigating colleges that cost $40,000/year for tuition. Later, she admitted that she had no real career direction … she just wanted to go to an Ivy League college. The younger sister, in two years, planned to follow in her older sister's footsteps. When you do the math (arithmetic), if you multiply $40,000/year times 4 years, times 2 daughters, you get a total of $320,000 for college tuition. Suze asked the father how he planned to pay for that tuition.

The father proudly announced, on national TV, that he would happily mortgage his house 7 times over to give his daughters the tuition money for whatever schools they wanted. Upon closer examination, his statement did not withstand the test of reasonableness. He and his wife were 51, and would be looking to retire in fewer than 20 years. If they took upon themselves the student loan debt of $320,000 for 30 years at 8.5%, they would be looking at payments of about $2,000/month for 30 years over and above all their other expenses.

Suze asked the father where he saw himself in 30 years, and where he figured to get the money to make the monthly payments on that kind of debt, considering that he would be living on retirement income for many of those years.

> *She reminded him that the debt was not dischargeable in bankruptcy. He said he didn't know where he would get the money, but that he would figure it out. What? Was he kidding? Unfortunately, he was not.*
>
> *The family, in a vote of 3-1, voted that the parents should NOT go into that kind of debt and that the girls could attend less expensive colleges. Guess who cast that one lone vote?*
>
> ***College is optional, retirement is not.***

There are many ways to finance college education, but using your retirement funds is not one of the better ways. It is up to you to save your own money for your own retirement. I know you want to pay for your children's education, but don't do it at the expense of your retirement money. As hard as it may be, this is one place you must seriously consider saying NO without guilt.

**DO NOT CO-SIGN FOR A LOAN
FOR ANY PERSON,
FOR ANY AMOUNT,
FOR ANY REASON WHATSOEVER.**

2. DO NOT LOAN MONEY TO ANYONE UNLESS YOU CAN AFFORD TO LOSE IT.

Before you choose to loan money to anyone, you must first determine if you need that money yourself. You don't want to loan money if you have serious debt, or if you do not have a 1-year emergency fund, or adequate life insurance, or money set aside for your children's education, or if you have not fully funded your retirement fund. If these things are not in place for yourself, you cannot afford to loan money to anyone, in any amount, for any reason. This is where saying "no without guilt" will come in handy, because that is what you must do.

If, however, you do give in and loan money, require that person to sign a promissory note that states the terms of the repayment, and the deadline for repayment. Be sure the note is signed, witnessed and dated. If the person does not pay you back according to the terms of that note, there is the possibility the amount can be deducted from your income tax returns at some point in the future. You need to discuss this with your accountant. I don't know what the rules are, but I do know that, although it will not get your money back, it might at least give you some kind of financial relief.

If the person who asks you for money is a loved one or a close friend, do your best to separate your emotions from your decision-making while saying a firm no with a smile on your face. Be prepared for them to say (or imply) that you are selfish. Keep in mind that the transaction is business, not personal. You might actually be doing them a favor by saying no, although they might not see it that way.

And, if you have already loaned money to someone close to you, and they have made no effort to repay you, think of the money as having been a gift, because chances are you will never see the money again. Consider that money as the cost of tuition in the school of personal finance, especially if the other person will continue to be a part of your life. If your relationship with that person is important to you, put the relationship first, and forget the money. It's gone. And, after all, it's only money.

Polonius: *"Neither a borrower nor a lender be."*
Suze Orman: *"First people, then money, then things."*
Judge Judy: *"When you loan money to a friend, you lose both your money and your friend."*

3. DO NOT TAKE BACK A MORTGAGE

Most of my legal career, I worked for tax lawyers, so I often heard that taking back a mortgage was considered a good investment that offered certain tax advantages, the benefits of long-term payout, etc. That is not necessarily true anymore.

Recently, I heard Suze Orman say to forget about financial advice from the last 5 or 10 years. Things have changed so radically around the subject of money, that the old rules don't apply any longer.

- **SPENDING IS OUT.**
- **SAVING IS IN.**

If someone asks you to take back a mortgage, flashing red lights, bells and whistles should be going off in your head! Your instincts should begin to kick in as you wonder why <u>you</u> are being asked to do this, and why the person asking doesn't get a mortgage from a bank or mortgage company? Why indeed?

Asking questions would be a good start toward protecting yourself from what could turn out to be the biggest financial mistake you ever made. The chances are good that the person asking has bad credit and cannot get a mortgage elsewhere. The long-term negative consequences of this particular financial transaction can be dire, and if you don't believe me, read the following true story.

Once upon a time, a lovely woman, a widow, wanted to sell her big house and move into a smaller home. She hired a realtor, and stressed the importance of having a quick sale and no aggravation. And, besides, the realtor agreed to only a 4% commission for the sale. She was happy.

In a short time, the realtor brought her a potential buyer. The buyer agreed to pay the woman's asking price of One Million Dollars if she agreed to take back a mortgage of $900,000. The buyer would then pay interest only for 5 years, followed by a balloon payment for the remainder of the outstanding balance. The realtor was very good at "pitching" the deal to her, assuring her that he knew the buyer, and that she had nothing to worry about. The realtor was a nice man, and the woman had no apparent reason to think he could not be trusted.

In fact, when he asked her not to get any lawyers involved in the deal, she agreed. That was her first in a long series of mistakes. At that point, she should have seen flashing red lights to alarm her, but she did not. So, she did not retain a lawyer to review the Agreement of Sale, and although I am not a lawyer, I stand behind my statement that no lawyer I know would ever have given her the go-ahead on the transaction. But, she didn't ask. And besides, she didn't want to pay a legal fee.

Common sense, instinct, and a little arithmetic might have suggested that in this economy, it was not reasonable to think that any individual buyer could honor the obligations under that agreement, which called for the buyer to make monthly payments of $6,000 and still come up with the balance of $900,000 at the end of the 5-year term. Does that sound do-able to you?

The buyer defaulted in a very short time, continued living in the house, and did not pay real estate taxes or utilities for more than two years. The woman ended up having to buy her own house back at Sheriff's Sale, incurring enormous legal fees and back taxes.

But that wasn't the half of it. Before the buyer finally moved out, he nearly destroyed the interior of her beautiful house. Before she could put it on the market again, she had to pay for all sorts of major repairs, and she had to replace all the kitchen appliances and bathroom fixtures, which the people took with them when they moved out.

Oh, and one more thing. The value of the house in today's market is hundreds of thousands of dollars less than it was on the date of the original sale transaction.

Although the buyer put down $100,000, the woman walked away from the settlement table with less than $60,000 after closing costs, and after payment of the realtor's $40,000 commission.

The long and the short of it ... although, it's been more long than short ... is that she has been involved in 6 years of expensive, exhausting, stressful litigation and near financial ruin. And has paid lots and lots of money for her lawyer's fees.

Wouldn't it have been better for her to pay a lawyer $500 or $1,000 to review the Agreement-of-Sale beforehand? Are there lessons to be learned from this transaction? I certainly hope so.

And what about the questionable ethics of the realtor, who stood behind his buyer when he knew the buyer was a bad risk, who had a long list of judgments against him, beginning with the IRS. What did he care? He got his 4% commission right up front.

4. DO NOT USE A HOME EQUITY LOAN (or line of credit) TO PAY FOR CREDIT-CARD DEBT.

Credit card debt is "unsecured" debt, which means that you owe the money, but the credit card company has few options to force you to pay. Of course, they can always harass you until you buckle under the pressure to pay, and they could damage your FICO score. They can sue you and get a judgment against your house, but they cannot force you to sell your house to pay the debt. They will only get paid if or when you sell the house.

A home-equity loan, on the other hand, is "secured" debt, which means that not only do you owe the money, but the bank can take your house to pay the money back. A home-equity loan is, in fact, a second mortgage on your house, where your house has been put up as collateral for the loan. Don't be fooled by the appealing suggestion that you can deduct home-equity loan interest from your taxes. You could also lose your house! Why would you exchange "unsecured" debt for "secured" debt? DON'T DO IT. And, if anyone suggests this, RUN in the opposite direction.

If your home is your safe place in the world, you cannot afford to lose it to pay off debt that you incurred through lack of understanding, or a spending addiction, or honorable intentions. If you have to say no to someone, say no, even if that person is YOU, yourself. Do not put your home in danger. How would you feel if you lost it because you spent so much money buying "stuff?"

5.   DO NOT RAID YOUR IRA, 401(k), 403(b), OR OTHER RETIREMENT FUNDS TO PAY OFF DEBT, COLLEGE TUITION, OR LIVING EXPENSES.

If you find yourself in the shark-infested waters of financial damage, it is tempting to think you can "borrow" from your retirement accounts "just for the time being," and that you will repay it in the future. DON'T DO IT! If you think you are having money problems now, while you are still young and healthy and can still work, think what the problems could potentially be when you are in your middle 70s, when you are no longer employed, and you are quickly running out of money. Once that money is gone, it will most likely be gone forever. It is so easy to deceive yourself into believing you will repay it, but the chances are good that you will not be able to do that, no matter how sincere your intentions.

There are ways to rescue you from your financial mess, but this is not one of them. Rather than touch this money, seek the advice of a qualified financial professional. Together, you can find your way again. And DO NOT be so impatient and desperate that you will surrender to the high-pressure tactics of persons wanting to sell you some financial product that they guarantee will solve your problems.

The money you have accumulated in your retirement accounts are for your retirement and for that purpose only. You will need that money someday. In addition to the fact that the money in those accounts will be increasing over time, these accounts are protected against bankruptcy. That means that were you to find yourself going into bankruptcy, that money will not be taken from you to pay debt.

6.   PROTECT YOURSELF AGAINST SCAMS and IDENTITY THEFT

As for advice about scams, there isn't much to say that you don't already know, except this:

Don't transact any kind of business with the scammers in the first place!

That being said, it is easy to be scammed, and it has happened to lots of other people. If it should ever happen to you, don't beat yourself up thinking you are stupid or weak. Do your best to chalk it up to one of life's unsuccessful, unpleasant lessons, and move forward. As hard as that may sound, it may also not be impossible.

Don't give out your Social Security number, your bank account numbers, or any other kinds of personal information that can give scammers access to you. Don't respond to phone calls, emails or letters that say things like, "Congratulations! You have just won a foreign lottery. Send us $500 to cover costs." If someone calls and says he is your grandson and is stuck in a far-away place and needs you to wire him some money, don't do it unless and until you have verified that the person is legitimate. If someone calls, allegedly from a bank, asking to verify your Social Security or bank account numbers, hang up. If any one caller continues to contact you with unwanted solicitations, notify the law.

Shred every piece of paper (*euphemistically known as "junk mail"*) that comes to you to solicit your business if you are not interested in it. Shred old bank statements, credit card statements … shred every piece of paper that has specific information about you once you no longer need that paper. As bizarre as it sounds, there are people who are paid to go through your trash to collect papers that have your personal information on them. If you think you can't afford a good shredder, think how costly it could potentially be if you were to be scammed or to have had your identity stolen.

People who do this sort of thing (that is, scamming and identity theft) are creative and seem to keep coming up with new, enticing ways to separate people from their money. Stay abreast of news about the latest scams. Read about them in periodicals. AARP publications are especially good at publicizing information about scams.

The people most often intentionally targeted by scammers are not Baby Boomers, but their parents. This is not to say that Boomers couldn't get caught by an irresistible salesperson, but Boomers are not the people with the money. Seniors have the money. That is why seniors are so frequently the targets of scammers, who know that seniors are often alone, frequently alienated from their family, generally uninformed about their own financial situation, and seriously afraid of running out of money. They are also lonely, and they enjoy socializing, even if it is for a few hours spent in their own home with that nice young salesman. Seniors are so afraid of running out of money that they are easily persuaded to "invest" large sums of money into financial products about which they know nothing, but which they believe will be safe and produce future income.

So, Boomers, while you are busy protecting yourself from scammers, try to keep your eye on your parents' financial situation if you can. *More about that later ...*

You may find scammers in groups in which you may participate: the garden club, a fraternal organization, or your church, for example. They seem like such nice people, don't they? They are friendly, they smile, they seem genuinely interested when they ask about your health and your family, and then they ask if they can spend some time with you to talk about a business (financial) opportunity that is perfect for you. Well, what can I say? Invite them into your home at your own risk, serve them coffee and cookies, thank them for their time, and then say no without guilt.

If you know you are vulnerable to persuasive salespeople ... *you remember that nice young man in the business suit who seemed genuinely interested in your money* ... just remember that he was interested, all right ... for himself, not for you.

And, at the first suspicion that you [or your parent(s)] have been <u>targeted</u> for a financial scam, call your local police department and file a complaint, and then file a complaint with every possible regulatory agency or law-enforcement agency that may be able to assist you in getting your money back. But, don't count on getting the money back. Scammers have either spent it already, or they have put it in some untraceable off-shore account. If you are scammed, chances are good that you will never see your money again. While there are cases where the scammers have been caught and prosecuted, the money is seldom if ever recovered. They are very good at what they do ... separating people from their money. Be careful.

If there is even the remote possibility that someone is trying to convince you to buy something that sounds too good to be true, it just may be. There are two things required in order for a scam to be successful: (1) A highly skilled, high pressure salesperson; and (2) a person who is vulnerable to that kind of pressure. If one part of that equation is missing, the scam may fail. And, that must be your priority ... to make it fail.

In this economy of 2011 and 2012, scams are popping up like dandelions in your lawn in April. They look so pretty, but upon closer examination, they are weeds, not flowers. Such is the reality of a scam. They do not hold up under close examination.

If you believe that some financial investment you are looking into could be a scam, do your homework. Check with the Better Business Bureau and the local law enforcement authorities to see if there are any complaints on record, or if there is any questionable (illegal) activity in your local area from the organization trying to sell you something. Check it out with a financial professional or on the Internet at www.finra.com. But, don't sign anything until you know, for a fact, that your money will be safely invested as promised, something you cannot know for sure unless and until you do some serious fact-checking beforehand.

There is a lot of scamming that takes place on the Internet, particularly from dating sites. In order to meet new people, you may have revealed a great deal about yourself, and scammers will use that information against you if you give them the opportunity. Be careful of the romantic connection you recently made with that very nice woman or man, who says sweet things to you, makes you feel comfortable and happy, and then asks you to borrow a few dollars. I think you know what you should do when that happens, but maybe not.

Real people often show up on the Judge Judy show to try and collect money they lost to a very nice person they met on the Internet. It is important to remember that that money was not stolen from the Plaintiff without that person's permission. I'm not suggesting you go and live in a cloistered community to avoid people and money problems. All I'm saying is to BE CAREFUL who you trust with your heart and your money.

<u>TIP</u>

If a person presenting themselves to you as a financial advisor asks you to make a check payable to them personally, individually (that is, as opposed to making your check payable to a reputable financial institution), run quickly in the

---

opposite direction. This is something that people who make their life's work scamming innocent people do. It appears to be a simple request, but it is one of the ways for you to tell if they are legitimate or not. Be smart. Be careful.

Keep apprised of financial "scams" by reading your newspapers and/or watching TV news. AARP publications regularly publish scam alerts. Before signing with questionable people, you might want to check with your local police department to see if there are any scams in your local area that you need to know about. Go to the website www.finra.com and look up the person or organization by name. Ponzi schemes have popped up in the last few years, and many people have lost their life savings by trusting someone who was using their money for their own purposes. If a financial "scheme" sounds too good to be true, it probably is. Bernie Madoff is not the "only" Ponzi scammer.

- In addition, AARP has published an informative book, **_Outsmarting the Scam Artists_**, by Doug Shadel. It is available at aarp.org/bookstore or in bookstores. And, for more tips on avoiding scams and identify theft, refer to **_Scam-Proof Your Life_**, by Sid Kirchheimer. The book is published by AARP Books/Sterling.

IDENTITY THEFT

Identity theft is to be avoided in every way possible. But, how? Above, I recommended that you don't speak with scammers in the first place. What about when you are dead? That's right, I just said "dead," because identity thieves have targeted the assets of the deceased. It isn't as if there aren't enough living people to steal identities from, identity thieves deliberately target deceased persons to fraudulently open credit card accounts, apply for loans, and transact other forms of financial business (according to the AARP/Bulletin; March 2013). Unfortunately, the dead are easy targets.

Identity theft is insidious, and it can happen when you're least expecting it or when you're not paying attention to your personal business. It is an equal opportunity thief, and doesn't care if you are young or old, rich or poor, male or female, living or dead.

It often takes six months or more for anyone to discover that the deceased person's Social Security number, their bank and investment accounts have been stolen. Why so long? Because it takes that amount of time for credit-reporting bureaus and the Social Security Administration to receive, share, or register death records. This leaves lots of time for the thieves to practice their craft.

Criminals even file tax returns under the identities of the dead, collecting refunds from the IRS that totaled $3.2 billion in 2011 (according to AARP/Bulletin; March 2013). Fortunately, members of the family of the deceased are not generally responsible for such charges, but before such a mess is cleaned up, the family may suffer major personal upset and/or financial loss, and be forced to pay a tax attorney to resolve the situation.

- One of the favorite places for thieves to glean information about the deceased is from obituaries. With the name, address and birth date of a deceased person, thieves can quickly and easily illicitly purchase that person's SS number on the Internet for as little as $10. In an obituary, list the age of the person, but not their birthdate, or not their mother's maiden name, or other things that can identify the deceased person for the thieves. Also, do not list the home address of the deceased so as to reduce the possibility of home burglaries during funeral services (*it happens*).

- Another place thieves scour for information about the deceased is court records. Papers filed in the probate process, especially Inheritance Tax Returns, contain all kinds of financial information. Anyone can go through public records, even thieves. Thieves know that in the probate process, it takes time from the death of the person to the appointment of an executor or administrator to officially and legally take over the operation of your assets, and it is during that tiny window of time that thieves do their job.

- Consider using a Revocable Living Trust as the legal vehicle by which you pass your assets to your loved ones because ownership of those assets transfers immediately upon your death to your successor trustee ... that is, there is no time delay that occurs in the probate process. *Something else to thoroughly discuss with your lawyer...*

- Using ONLY the U. S. Postal Service certified mail/return receipt requested, send death certificates to each of the credit-reporting bureaus (Equifax, Experian, and Trans-Union), asking them to place a "deceased alert" on the credit report of the deceased.

In Chapter III – Funerals and Burial Instructions, I recommend that you buy at least 10 death certificates from the funeral director at the time of the death of a loved one. I just changed my mind. You should buy at least 25. Ignore the cost; it is miniscule when compared to the potential financial loss that can occur when an account is targeted by a thief.

- Similarly mail death certificates to banks, insurance companies, brokerages, credit card and mortgage companies … to every place where the deceased had an account. For every account you are closing, request that the financial institution mark the account "*Closed: Account Holder Deceased*" as the reason for the closing, and request that written verification of this fact be sent to you.

- If you are the joint owner of any financial accounts with the deceased, request that the name of the deceased person be removed, and also request verification of the completion of that transaction.

- Report the death to the Social Security Administration (800-772-1213). Report the death to the organization that provided a pension to the deceased, and to the holders of the decedent's retirement accounts.

- Contact the Department of Motor Vehicles to cancel the deceased's driver's license to prevent duplicates from being made by thieves.

- A few weeks later, check the credit report at annualcreditreport.com to see if there has been any suspicious activity. And do it again in several months.

- And, it bears repeating that if you believe you or a deceased loved one have been the victim of identity theft or loss of assets by virtue of a scam, immediately notify local law enforcement agencies. You may never get back the money that was taken, but you may stop the thieves before they can do it again.

7. DON'T USE BANKRUPTCY AS YOUR "GET OUT OF DEBT" FREE CARD

Bankruptcy is not something anyone wants to get involved with. People often say it just happened. Well, bankruptcy isn't like spontaneous combustion or lightning. It happens at the end of a series of financial transactions that were not handled well, or where something went terribly wrong. Bankruptcy should be only used as a last resort, because it has long-term negative consequences on your financial future, not the least of which is ruining your FICO score.

Before you go into bankruptcy, examine every other common-sense option first. Don't make an appointment with a lawyer and tell him/her to file bankruptcy papers for you. There may be other options better suited to your situation. If the lawyer you speak with doesn't thoroughly discuss those other options with you, I recommend you find another lawyer, or that you meet with a qualified financial professional to advise you of how bankruptcy can help you and how it can hurt you.

Suze Orman says there is a time to hold on and a time to give in. Sometimes, bankruptcy is the most reasonable thing you can do to rescue yourself from a financial nightmare. Bankruptcy sometimes carries with it a certain stigma of shame, embarrassment and humiliation. It may be caused by being betrayed by someone you trusted and/or loved. It happens. Just try to keep your emotions separate from your common sense when making financial choices.

> *Once upon a time, a woman had $20,000 of credit card debt for clothing that she had not yet worn. She shopped when she was bored, or happy, or unhappy, or upset … she was seriously addicted to the emotional high of immediate gratification that she got from shopping. There was a disconnect between her spending and the pleasure she thought she was getting from the experience.*
>
> *Her husband wanted a different kind of immediate gratification. In order to get rid of this debt, he was planning to go into bankruptcy. He wanted the debt "gone." The lawyer he consulted strongly suggested that bankruptcy was not the way to go because of the long-term negative consequences it would have on their financial future.*
>
> *Among other legal alternatives, the lawyer presented the man with a workable plan to contact every store, explain the circumstances, return as many items as possible, then establish a re-payment plan. The lawyer agreed to assist when and wherever necessary.*
>
> *The wife whined about having to give up her "stuff." So, to shut her up, the man caved in to the pressure, chose to ignore the lawyer's advice, went into bankruptcy anyway, lost his house, moved his family of 5 into an apartment, and has been miserable ever since about the bankruptcy decision.*
>
> *Did he ignore his lawyer's advice just to make his wife shut up?*

8. NEVER FORGET THE CONNECTION BETWEEN EMOTIONS AND YOUR MONEY.

By now, you know that three of the chapters of this book include Legal, Financial and Personal. You have just read about some of the legal and financial choices and consequences regarding your money. Now, let's look at some emotional choices and consequences.

The subject of money brings up emotions of all sorts, not always good ones, either. Money mistakes are often made when the emotions driving the action are excitement, fear, shame, or guilt.

Were you to win the jackpot in a lottery drawing, there would be <u>euphoria</u>, followed by simple <u>joy</u> of buying stuff, <u>happiness</u> at giving some of the money away, then <u>fear</u> of the tax consequences and <u>fear</u> of spending it too fast, and then the possibility of <u>regret</u> for not asking for professional advice on how to handle such a huge amount of money, and finally <u>regret</u> for spending all that money so frivolously, such that you have no money left. Don't laugh. It happens all the time.

And, then there is the fear at the opposite end of the pendulum, when you cannot pay your mortgage or rent or put food on your family's table, or when you lost your job and you have to say "no" to your children when they ask for the simplest thing. There is the upset that takes over because you don't know how to handle the situation and are afraid to ask for help from a professional because you think you may be perceived as stupid, or don't have money to pay his fee.

Fighting about money can lead to anxiety and worry, which can lead to depression, which can lead to more worry and anxiety, maybe even the break-up of your marriage, even illness, all of which will cost more money.

The best advice I can give you is to educate yourself about money. Read books, go to workshops at your local library, meet with financial professionals, ask questions, ask more questions and take notes, and watch Suze Orman on TV. OK, by now you know that I am a fan of Suze Orman. I watch her TV show every week and am continually amazed at the mistakes people make with their money, and the upsets money causes in their lives. Suze Orman says that fights are never just about money; there is always an undercurrent of a personal nature. Think about it.

All of the mistakes described have some kind of long-term effect upon your personal future. I want you to THINK about how you handle your money, avoid some of these mistakes, and keep as much of your money as possible for the rest of your life.

- Think of how you would feel if you lost your house to a mistake you made, but which might have been avoided if you had some professional advice beforehand.

- Think how you will feel 20 years from now, living in retirement, cash poor, maybe having to give up your house to live in a tiny apartment. It may have been because of some mistake you made or just circumstances beyond your control. Add to this scenario the possibility you would have to give up a beloved pet because the apartment won't allow pets, and besides, you can't afford their care and food any longer.

- Think how you will feel if you are burdened, years into retirement, with the repayment of a student loan that still has 15 years to go, and you find you can no longer afford the monthly payments. Then what?

- Think how you would feel toward a family member or close friend who defaulted on a loan for which you co-signed, and they left you holding the bag? What would that do to your relationship with that person?

- Think about how you would feel if you raided your retirement account(s) to pay credit card debt (immediate gratification), and now that you are in your early 70s, you have run out of money. What will you do then?

Don't fool yourself into thinking none of these things could happen to you. They happen to real people every day. Just try your best not to be one of them.

9. DON'T GIVE IN TO HIGH-PRESSURE SALESPEOPLE. LEARN TO SAY "NO."

Let's also give some thought to the pressure that is daily put upon people to spend money, often money they don't have. Stores have sales that are not really sales. TV commercials bombard you with pictures and words about how your life will be improved if you buy this car or that phone or some other thing you can easily live without. The ads are designed to convince you that you cannot live without those things.

Pressure like this can come in all forms, including those free-lunch seminars. What about the nice woman who came to your house to sell you long-term care insurance you don't need? What about the good-looking, polite man who tried to sell you a reverse mortgage? What about that nice couple from your church that wanted you to invest in some swamp land in Florida (*you get the idea*)? They seemed so trustworthy.

Take a look at why you are vulnerable to the soft sell? Just because the person doing the selling appears so nice does not mean they are. They are looking to make a commission selling you something, and, believe me, those commissions are huge. They will keep up the pressure until you either cave in or walk away. Sometimes, they are not even polite when you finally tell them NO. Oh, well, too bad. It's not their money.

Once upon a time, we received an ad in the mail about a time-share at a vacation resort in the Pennsylvania Pocono mountains. The ad stated that we would receive a free TV for just listening to their sales pitch. What started out as a pleasant day for a drive, turned out to be a horrible experience I have never forgotten.

When we arrived, we were driven by someone to another location than the one advertised. The route they took was full of twists and turns, and I don't think I would ever have been able to find our way back to our car, even though I have a near perfect sense of direction.

We were invited into a room with a conference table, a screen for slides, etc., and the "fun" began. They showed us pictures of a lovely mountain resort, happy people, beautiful guest rooms and restaurants. We sat through the whole presentation, said no thank-you and got up to leave. Not so fast. Another salesperson came in and started all over again. Again, we said no thank-you, and got up to leave. Another and another salesperson came into the room, and each had a more aggressive style. This went on for hours. No coffee. No water. No lunch. No bathroom breaks. Just high pressure from salespeople who really wanted to cinch the deal.

I was so hungry and exhausted that I would have signed anything just to get out of that room. I don't even like the mountains. I would never have wanted to stay at that resort. I also know that time-shares are not good investments. We only went for a pleasant day and a free TV.

At some point, my husband realized I was caving in from the pressure, and he actually threatened to beat up one of the men if they didn't immediately take us back to our car. (I knew, of course, that he would never do that, but it explains the level of our desperation.) When they finally realized they had been unsuccessful in selling us the time-share, they reluctantly gave us this tiny black-and-white TV, and we were driven back to our car. Believe me when I tell you we didn't need a TV that badly. And, we certainly didn't need or want a time-share in the mountains.

See what can happen if you believe there is something free in the deal. Remember TINSTAAFL (there is no such thing as a free lunch), or in this case, a free TV.

10.   DON'T BUY A TIME-SHARE

And, while I'm on the subject, don't buy a time-share. They are not the good investment the salespeople want you to believe. Once you own a time-share, you will find there are all sorts of (hidden) fees and costs you didn't know about in the beginning. Besides, how often will you really use it? And, I dare you to sell it. I personally know several people who have given them to one of their adult children just to get rid of them. *Excuse me? Did I miss something?*

And, if you own a time-share in a state other than your resident state, when you die, your executor may have to begin probate proceedings in that other state, too. Don't sign any papers until you discuss the pros and cons with your lawyer and financial planner.

11.   STAY AWAY FROM SALESPEOPLE

It is a good thing if you know that you are vulnerable to a (high pressure) sales pitch. If it's already too late, and you have found yourself paying for something you don't need or don't want, but bought anyway, I urge you to THINK about your behavior, and do not put yourself into situations where you could be persuaded by a person who stands to make a commission from your vulnerability.

When you invited that widget salesperson into your home, were you lonely? Were you looking for company, someone to sit with for an afternoon or evening, share conversation, coffee and cookies?

After 4 hours, were you induced by guilt to sign papers to buy what they were selling (reverse mortgages, insurance, windows and siding, annuities) because, after all, you had used up all that time with them. Keep in mind that time is what salespeople have on their side. Time and words. They count on your feeling guilty, and will use it against you to induce you to buy something from them you don't need or want. They are very good at using guilt to separate you from your money. Remove guilt from the business of money ... your money.

12.   DO NOT PRACTICE DO-IT-YOURSELF FINANCIAL PLANNING

You may recall in the Chapter I - LEGAL, I told you about two elderly sisters who wanted to save a lawyer's fee of $75 each to write their Wills, and the disaster that resulted. That was the legal side of do-it-yourself planning. Do-it-yourself financial planning is also a losing game, and I don't recommend it.

MISTAKES SOME BABY BOOMERS HAVE ALREADY MADE

- They believed there would always be time to save money **LATER**, ignoring the possibility that they could run out of money before they ran out of time.

- They believed that they could keep up with all the changes in financial regulations by themselves. If you ever saw the IRS Tax Code or the IRS rules about IRAs, you might change your mind.

- They failed to consider the effects of inflation and taxes, for example. What will that $1 million retirement fund be worth after taxes? Maybe $750,000, maybe less, depending on the tax rates and laws in effect when the money is needed in the future.

- They retired too early, without the assistance of a financial professional to determine their actual financial needs in their retirement years.

- They prematurely took money from their IRA or other retirement fund and incurred big penalties and taxes.

- They filed for Social Security at the age of 62, which means they will be receiving less than if they had waited a few more years, and they will most likely incur higher Income Taxes when the Social Security is added to their income.

- They believe in the concept of LATER. They don't think they will ever run out of time, so they leave important things go until later. Well, HERE IT IS … "*later*" has arrived.

Is this the same as believing you will live forever? *Just asking ...*

WHILE THE FOLLOWING MAY NOT EXACTLY QUALIFY AS MISTAKES, THEY ARE SITUATIONS THAT CAN CAUSE BOOMERS PROBLEMS AS THEY RETIRE.

Many Baby Boomers:

- do not have traditional pensions.

- counted on the value of their homes as available equity to finance their retirement.

- have mortgages that exceed the value of their houses, both on their residence and on their vacation house.

- have car payments.

- spent way beyond their means most of their adult lives.

- continue to spend with no regard for the future.

- are in serious credit card and/or home equity debt.

- are suffering the financial effects of a divorce (a particular problem for women).

- are in debt for their children's education, weddings and divorces.

- have failed to adequately save money during their highest earning years.

- have little or no cash available for emergencies.

- are financially assisting elderly parents (or adult children).

- will not be receiving that big inheritance they were expecting.

- have no budget for their present life.

- have no budget for retirement, and/or underestimated living expenses in retirement.

- have lost assets through divorce (without the protection of a PreNuptial Agreement).

- have not consulted a financial planner to determine how their Social Security income will affect their Income Taxes.

- have not consulted a financial planner to determine how much money they will need until they are 95 years of age.

- are hiding their heads in the sand, believing their financial problems will go away if they ignore them.

- are caught up in a vicious spending cycle of euphoria one day, remorse the next.

- are playing "do-it-yourself" financial planning.

- have not done any estate planning (Will; Powers-of-Attorney; Living Will; Revocable Living Trust).

- need to review all of their insurance, including life, health, long-term care, disability, longevity, auto, flood, homeowners' and renters'.

- have not historically kept their personal records organized.

- have not done any funeral or burial planning, and have no money specifically designated for payment of the expenses.

- have had their financial situation damaged by the expenses of illness.

- failed to consider the financial implications of inflation, taxes, emergencies, illness, disability, or death of a spouse or close family member.

- overestimated how much can be withdrawn from retirement accounts.

- over-managed retirement portfolio.

- accumulated money without consideration of <u>preserving</u> it for your future.

- took too much risk.

- relied upon questionable information sources.

- failed to diversify investments.

- underestimated life expectancy.

- failed to calculate potential healthcare expenses.

- and last but not least is a really big one! Focused on your money to the exclusion of all else; *e.g,* YOUR LIFE.

**Did you even ask a financial planner or a lawyer
for information, direction or guidance in making those decisions? If not, why not?**

WHAT FOLLOWS ARE SOME MORE FINANCIAL MISTAKES TO LOOK OUT FOR

If you have already made some of these mistakes, take a deep breath, wait a few minutes, and forgive yourself for not knowing what you didn't know. If you find yourself feeling guilty for having made a big mistake, get over it right now. Guilt will not help. What you need instead is information and education, and the willingness to do what is necessary to (a) clean up the situation you find yourself in right now, and (b) avoid the mistakes in the future.

It is entirely possible that you have already made one or more of these mistakes while under the pressure from a very nice, highly skilled salesperson doing his best to convince you that what they are "selling" is exactly what you need. They are not bad people. They are just trying to earn a living at doing what they are really good at – influencing people to part with their money.

You may have been influenced to make one of these mistakes by a loved one or a close friend who expressed what appeared on the surface to be a genuine need for your financial assistance. While it may have been true that their need was genuine, what was not necessarily true was that *you* were the person to rescue them. I know that it is much harder to say no to a loved one or close friend than to a salesperson, but saying no might be the most generous act of love you can give to them, particularly if they are inclined to have repeated financial crises.

This one I know … my father was an expert at living on OPM … that is, other people's money. He was an amazing person in every area of his life except the handling of money. He had no problem separating someone from their money. There are lots of people like this; they may even be people you love. Just remember to keep your feelings for them separate from your money.

If you have already made some of these mistakes, give serious consideration to seeking professional help to recover financially, legally, and even emotionally. Don't forget that there is a very large emotional component connected to money. Appropriate recovery actions may help, and they may not. But, you deserve to give yourself the opportunity to investigate as many possibilities as you can, including involving law enforcement if you have been scammed. You may already be feeling the negative effects of your generosity. And, believe me, there can be negative effects that will have long-term consequences for you.

TIP

If you have suffered a financial loss such as those described here, from which you have no hope of recovering, ask your accountant or tax lawyer if it is possible to take a tax write-off on your annual Income Tax Return. There are IRS rules that permit this under certain circumstances. I know nothing about the rules, except to say that they exist, and it is worth asking. Do what you can to recover, even if you never recover the actual dollars you lost.

And, if you have NOT yet made any of these mistakes, don't make these serious, long-term decisions alone. Seek professional advice <u>before</u> making a choice of whether to involve yourself or not. There is much at stake, including your house, your retirement money, and your peace of mind. All I can say is take your time and to be careful.

When a person co-signs for a loan or takes back a mortgage, it is often done out of genuine concern for the person who says they need your help. But, without a full understanding of how your generosity will affect your financial future, you could be making one of those Humpty-Dumpty mistakes … you know, the kind where you cannot uncrack the egg.

When the other person defaults on the loan or the mortgage, YOU'RE IT! The lending institution will come after you with a vengeance. They want their money back, it's that simple, and they really don't care who pays it back to them. If you cannot afford to make the payments, have your wages garnished, have your FICO score damaged, or even lose your house, do not get yourself involved in these kinds of transactions, no matter how genuine the appeal for your help, no matter how much you love the person asking for your help.

And, when you co-sign for a student loan, remember that student loans are not subject to discharge in bankruptcy. Once you are committed to repaying the loans, there is little (if anything) you can do to get out of the debt.

In the Philadelphia "Inquirer" in 2010, there was a story of a family plagued by the fact that their college-age son was on life-support and not expected to live, and he was being aggressively pursued by a bank that wanted to be paid back $50,000 for his student loans. Rather than apply for government-assisted student loans, the family chose to pay for his education by a bank-financed loan co-signed by the son and his father.

It is my understanding that had the son gotten loans from the government, and had his family advised the government of their son's terminal condition, the loans would probably have been forgiven. Not so, however, with the bank.

In fact, the bank refused to even discuss the matter with the boy's father, although they were thoroughly apprised of the boy's condition. In their eyes, the father did not have his own son's permission to discuss the matter without his son's formal Power-of-Attorney. Forget about the fact that the boy was in a coma and unable to speak. The bank was taking a hard position and doing what it believed necessary to collect money it was due.

It was only after the son died that the bank was even willing to discuss a repayment plan for the loan. Do you see the potential for problems? Co-signing for a student loan. No Durable Power-of-Attorney. No consultation with a lawyer or financial planner before making the financial transaction. In short, a mess.

This situation may be repulsive to you, but it can happen. Before you commit yourself to borrowing for your children's education, get the facts and know the consequences of the choices you make.

And get your lawyer to review the bank documents before you sign them. It would also be a good idea to talk about education financing with a financial planner so you never find yourself in a mess like this.

> *The bad news is that the bank refuses to forgive the loan. The young man's parents continue to make payments on their son's outstanding student loan. The bank gave them no other option.*
>
> *Could this mess have been avoided? What do you think?*

Why do you suppose this family chose this method of financing their son's education? Why did the father co-sign for the loan? Did the father really understand the consequences of that decision? Was this man one of those do-it-yourself people? Why didn't he consult with a lawyer and a financial planner before committing to that bank loan? Why did the father not require his son to execute a Power-of-Attorney, a Living Will and a Healthcare Power-of-Attorney when he went to college? After all, the boy was over 18 years. *[Oh, yes, I forgot. That's my rule, not theirs.]* More questions than answers. A very sad story.

COLLEGE EDUCATION AND MONEY

In providing for others, including your children, have you deprived yourself of money you need for retirement. I recently read this headline of a newspaper article that says it all:

COLLEGE IS OPTIONAL. RETIREMENT IS NOT.
(Think about that for a moment before you react.)

Follow this scenario:

Baby Boomer couple, well employed for many years, have incurred significant debt educating their children and otherwise assisting them financially. In addition, their children have other student loans. None of the student-loan debt can be eliminated in a bankruptcy action. These people have spent beyond their means for most of their adult lives and have saved little. Husband and wife each have a small employer-sponsored retirement account. They have a mortgage and a home-equity loan, no significant emergency fund, minimal retirement and investment assets, little life insurance on the husband, and none on the wife.

Fast Forward 20 years:

Baby Boomer couple are now in their mid-80s, haven't been employed for most of the previous 15 years, but have somehow managed to keep paying their living expenses and those student loans. While paying those loans, they have been unable to save retirement money for themselves and their future, and they can see themselves quickly running out of money. Now they need money to live on. Their well-educated children have not earned the salaries they anticipated when they graduated from college, are still paying off their own student loans, have mortgages, car payments, living expenses as any young couple with children might have. They are in no position to help their Baby Boomer parents financially.

What is the couple supposed to do now?
Could this scenario have turned out differently? Maybe. Maybe not. What do you think?

At the beginning of the Financial Section, I referenced *Rich Dad, Poor Dad*, by Robert Kiyosaki and Sharon Lechter as an example of two different approaches to selecting a lifetime career. The poor dad's advice was to go to college, graduate, get a job that will pay you a decent salary, and years later, retire on a pension. The rich dad's advice was to find a different way to earn money doing something you loved, something that suited who you are as a human being.

The time has come to re-think the guidance given to young people about their post-high school education. For years, people have followed the advice of the poor dad, and it is costing young people and their parents dearly. Young people are going to college by the hundreds of thousands every year, and graduating seriously in debt, finding themselves doing work they may not like, which may not even be in their chosen field. Why would anyone do that in today's economy (January 2012)?

Many of these young people discover, too late, that they are seriously unhappy in their "chosen" careers, yet are obligated to continue just to pay off the student loan debt? Is that anyway for a young person to begin their adult life? Seriously in debt and working in a career that does not satisfy them? So, why go to college in the first place, if that's where you are going to end up? Think a moment before you come up with a quick and easy response to the question.

In my opinion, what was missing was in-depth conversations with their parents and guidance counselors to determine the best career options for each young person. It didn't happen when I graduated from high school a long time ago, and it isn't happening now. Wouldn't you think someone would have noticed what is missing by now? (*Seems like a big hole in the guidance counseling process, but, that's a story for another day.*)

Although they are given a college diploma, are these young people really being educated? Elsewhere, I told the story of a college graduate, an accountant, who has $95,000 in student-loan debt, and doesn't know how to get out of that debt. Did I miss something? If she is a financial professional who cannot get herself out of a financial mess, what kind of advice does she give her clients? Did she learn nothing in college? *Just asking ...*

What are these young people qualified do after they graduate? They apparently don't know anything about money. I certainly hope the career they chose will pay them well, because they are entering adult life with an enormous debt that will hang over their head for years. Often, it is the parents who are obligated to pay for their children's education. "*Isn't that what parents are supposed to do?*" you ask. I'm not so sure any longer. I think there needs to be a serious evaluation of the cost versus the outcome. In other words, is the price of that education worth it?

I enjoy reading the engagement and wedding announcements in the newspaper. It strikes me as very interesting when I read that the woman graduated *summa cum laude* with a degree in something lofty like sociology or European history from a high caliber university, and works as an Administrative Assistant. Where I come from, that's a "secretary." (*I know, I know ... that word isn't used anymore, but you know what I mean.*) She sits at a desk and maybe earns $35,000 if she's lucky. The point I'm trying to make is that this young woman probably has $25,000 to $50,000 or more in student loan debt, and the best she could do was to get a job as a secretary? Are you kidding me? She might have been able to get that desk job without first going to college. And, besides, what secretarial skills did she learn while studying sociology or European history? *A rhetorical question.*

Add that to the young man's student loan debt, car payments on their two cars, living expenses for an apartment, condo, or house, plus food, clothing, insurance, etc., and you can see they are headed for a financial crisis sooner or later. And, what happens when baby makes three? Somehow, I don't think college is intended for the purpose of sending young people out into the world with that kind of debt.

Once upon a time, there was a man who chose to become a tax lawyer so he could read and understand the Internal Revenue Code in order to build wealth, and that is exactly what he did with his education and his life.

When he got his first job in a law firm, he realized that "old lawyers don't die, they just fade away," to paraphrase Gen. Douglas MacArthur. He saw that they never retired, and that is not what he wanted for himself.

His vision was clear. I doubt that is the case for many young people today, who say they want to go to college, even law school, but they don't know what they want to do with all that expensive education.

I must be missing something, because I can't figure why a young person would put themselves into such enormous debt doing something that offers them only a vague promise of a lifetime career (job?). And, what about their parents? Did they say, "*Of course we'll pay for your education?*" OK, I realize that graduating from college has become a necessity today, just like graduating from high school was years ago. But, at such a high price with such minimal rewards?

And, what about college? What do you do when a young person wants to attend a $40,000/year college, but who has no clue about what courses to take because she has no idea what career she wants for herself. Earlier, you read about the man who bragged that he would mortgage his house seven times over to give his daughter the $40,000/year education she wanted, but when asked, he had no idea how he was ever going to pay for it. Aren't parents supposed to be smarter than their children? I'm talking about Baby Boomers sending their children to college and putting themselves into debt for years, sacrificing their retirement money. This is no minor decision. Before you agree to pay for your kids' college education, you better get the opinion of a qualified financial advisor to see if you can actually afford this act of generosity and love.

BEFORE YOU SEND YOUR CHILD TO COLLEGE …

*ask yourself if they have shown mature, responsible handling of their money so far? Have you taught them how to handle their money wisely? There are people on the campuses who will encourage your child to get one of their credit cards, saying that the interest is and will remain low … blah, blah, blah. And, the first thing they know, your child will have incurred $5,000 in credit card debt **for what?** While it is true that college students (especially freshmen) will need to feel financially secure when they are away from home, be certain that there are limits imposed upon their spending. This is an important conversation for you to have with your financial planner and your child … all together in the same room at the same time.*

And, while you're thinking about your child going to college, don't forget to get them to sign a Durable Power-of-Attorney, a Living Will, and a Healthcare Power-of-Attorney. You read about this in Chapter I – Legal, but have you taken care of this aspect of your child's personal business yet?

WHY COLLEGE?
WHY NOT SOME OTHER EDUCATIONAL OPTION?

Let's begin by asking: "What is the purpose of higher education?" Well, for one, it could be to prepare young people for adult life and employment that will allow them to pay for that life. How about a career that not only pays a good salary but offers them the opportunity to do something they love? Higher education could help young people decide what type work they really want to do and what they are well suited to do. But, does it do that? Higher education could be a way to satisfy a desire to achieve certain professional status. It could be to expand their minds with higher learning, and prepare young people to live mature, responsible lives as adults. But, realistically, who, at the age of 18, can possibly know what they want to do with their time for the rest of their working life?

Is it even possible to say "college" without also saying "debt?" Well, I suppose if you are wealthy and you plan to pay for your child's education out of your own money, college can happen without debt. But, for the majority of young people attending college, either they and/or their parents will incur significant debt that will take many years to pay off, debt that cannot be excused in bankruptcy, that might not even enable the young person to earn a decent living in their chosen field after graduation.

So, what exactly is it that makes college worth going into debt for? Could it be that "college experience" that so many parents want their children to have? Oh, you mean time spent partying and drinking, joining fraternities and sororities. Things like that? *"Well, yes."* Are you willing to incur debt so your children can party for four years? *Really?*

Elsewhere, I wrote that college is optional, retirement is not. When looking into educational possibilities, mention alternative educational opportunities such as tech school, community college, or business school, and many people (both students and parents) turn their noses up. *"What, are you joking? Send my children to one of those schools? My kids are going to college even if it means I'll be in debt for the rest of my life."* Well said! Not so well thought out, however.

If you are a Baby Boomer and have not yet committed your retirement money to educating your children, I recommend you give serious consideration to alternate ways to educate them. Not every young person should go to college. Not every young person should study to become a doctor/lawyer/accountant, even when they believe it is the path that leads to high earnings. Maybe they are not personally suited for one of those careers. I didn't know that there is a personality profile for a secretary. No one in high school or business school ever mentioned it or tested us for it.

I had to find out the hard way that who I am, as a human being, is not well suited to being a secretary. I can't be the only person who chose the wrong career! In fact, I know many others who made the same mistake … that is, they chose a career that does not match who they are as human beings.

The point of considering tech school, community college and/or business school as a viable educational option is that it is an **in**expensive education that can offer good-paying successful careers doing something you love. Often, the education credits from those schools can be transferred to a college if the student needs further education to do something that calls to them. Wouldn't that make the investment in time and money worthwhile? From my perspective, it is a win-win situation.

And, still, people continue to jeopardize their retirement by going into long-term debt to send their kids to college because it has become the thing to do. It doesn't seem to even be connected to finding the perfect career. It's just what young people are doing, and it is costing them and their parents huge amounts of money … for what?

- Excuse me. Did I miss something? Do I correctly understand that people are willing to incur debt into the 6 figures, only to end up with a mundane sales (marketing) or administrative or business job sitting behind a desk all day, a job that maybe pays $30,000 or $50,000 per year? I obviously missed something. Explain to me how that makes good common sense, let alone good financial sense.

> *On February 2, 2013, on the Fox News TV channel, there was a show with panelists discussing the situation many young people are finding themselves in today … they have a college diploma, but they are unemployable, unemployed below the college level, often in a field other than that of their education, and find themselves seriously in debt. Unable to live independent lives, many have moved home with their parents. What does their future look like without money? The panelists pointed out how this whole college/student loan situation is damaging the middle class. Young people are suffering financial hardship and parents are risking their own retirement money to send their children to college. Why?*
>
> *The panelists went on record as saying that most of those young people should not have gone to college in the first place, considering the jobs they hold that will not enable them to pay off that student loan debt. They pointed out the value of tech-school education or community college education … even on-line college … as viable alternatives for ways to provide career opportunities that will enable these young people to have good lives.*
>
> *Who is going to stop the madness?*

What if a young person attends a tech school or a community college just long enough to figure out that they love to cook, and then decide to attend a culinary institute where they can get further education to enable them to do what they love? What if another young person learns from tech school that they love fixing cars, are naturally gifted at mechanical tasks, and then they become a repair technician for Porsches or Rolls Royces? I've heard they can earn a lot of money if they are really good at it. After all, somebody has to fix them, right? And, does it always have to be a person of the male persuasion? *Just asking …*

What if a young person attends tech school and discovers they are very good at hair-styling, enjoys the people and the work, and ends up opening a successful salon which becomes their life's work? Would that be so terrible? A young man or woman who becomes a hair stylist, for example, will always be able to earn a good living. And, yet, it is one of the education categories that most young people would frown upon as too insignificant and dreary. Women can do it from their homes and not have to put their children in day-care centers, and not have student loan debt. I see huge financial and personal freedom and advantages there. And, what if those women actually love what they are doing, enjoy being with people, enjoy the opportunities to be creative? Wouldn't that be like the cherry on top of the sundae?

> *Once upon a time, there was a young man who decided to skip college and all the debt that goes with it, and instead he went to beauty school. When he finished, he opened a salon. That was 30 years ago. Today, he owns and operates two successful salons, he owns and operates a restaurant, he owns five pieces of real estate (including a home in Florida), and he drives a BMW convertible. He had no student loan debt. He worked hard and made a good life for himself doing work he loved. It can be done. It helps to know who you are and what you want to do with your life.*

I went to business school to become a secretary and that's what I did (*a story for another book*). A friend went to business school with me and opened a successful travel agency, which has become her life's work. She had a drive and a vision I did not have. But, then I must remember that had I not been a legal secretary, this book might not have been written.

If you live long enough, you will retire from your job, hopefully with enough money to last for the rest of your life, and with a long list of enjoyable activities awaiting you in the time you have **between now and then.** But, how can you expect to do those things if the cost of your children's education has put you into debt that will last well into your retirement years?

If you children have not yet begun college, maybe a serious family discussion is necessary. Tell your children about the cost of their education … or the cost of their partying for 4 years. Try to keep the emotions out of the discussion. Focus that discussion on real numbers. Show them what the monthly payments would be on a student loan debt of $50,000 for 30 years at 8.5%. Ask them how they intend to pay for it, because <u>you</u> cannot afford it. Telling your children the truth won't kill you, and it won't kill them, either. Say NO without guilt.

If your children have already graduated, are they earning enough money to justify that educational expense? Be honest! There is nothing to be gained by kidding yourself.

> The best advice I ever heard about helping children select a lifetime career was this:
> **Figure out what you love to do, and then find a way to earn a living doing it.**

If this advice were to be given to children from the time they were very young, they would know there would be no financial help from their parents for college tuition. As a result, the children would became industrious and good at earning and saving money in ways that were uniquely their own. This was probably the best career advice and preparation for life a child could get.

> *So, what did I just say? Don't follow the crowd. Don't do what everyone else is doing just because everyone else is doing it. Give serious thought to the cost of educating your children such that they get the most education for the least amount of money. Help them figure out what they love to do and how to pay for their education without your money, because you're going to need your money for retirement. No kidding.*

I think it would be wise for young people to work for 3-4 years right out of high school to get a sense of what it's like to have to show up every day at a job, to be answerable to a boss. Let them find out that their earnings during that time will be limited and won't stretch very far. Whether or not they like the job is not the point. The point is to commit to the job and to save as much money as possible for their education in the near future. It shouldn't be too difficult if they continue to live at home, with limited expenses. The expenses you would incur from having your young adult child living at home for a few more years are tiny when compared to the cost of college. Do the math and see for yourself.

Nay-sayers will tell you that if young people did that, they would get a taste of earned money and wouldn't want to go back to school. I disagree completely. They would quickly come to see the salary limitations. You don't have to be a genius to figure out that a young person working in a retail store or an office, earning $12/hour for a 40-hour week would only earn an annual salary of about $25,000 before taxes. That is not enough money to live on, especially if they want to marry and have a family. So, seeing the numbers on paper might motivate them to keep working until they have enough money to pay for their own post-high school education. Why does everyone make it so difficult? It's plain to see that we're talking *arithmetic* ... not rocket science.

Those 3-4 years are a time of enormous personal and intellectual growth for a young person. It is a time for them to begin to think about who they are as human beings, to learn how to make intelligent choices, and figure out what they want to do with their lives. As they work during those years, their focus should be on saving money for education once they finally decide on what career they really want for themselves.

The two years during which I worked after high school as a supermarket cashier were some of the happiest years of my life. I worked a revolving schedule, such that I never had to be at the same place at the same time every day. I had a lot of free time. I earned enough money to buy my clothes, buy myself a car and keep the tank full of gas (at 25¢ a gallon) and still save all the money I needed for business school tuition. I made new friends and earned a high salary for the times. There have been days over the years when I thought I should have continued working in that supermarket rather than becoming a secretary, because it was a union job and I would have gotten benefits that were not available to me as a secretary. But, again, had I done that, this book would not have been written.

But, you say, they might not get to go to college until they are 25 or older, because it will take them that long to earn the money. So what? They will get to be 25 whether or not they earn that money and go to college; so, they might as well set their sights and stay on course until (a) they figure out what they want to do, and (b) they figure out how they're going to pay for their advanced education. There is tremendous pride in achieving their personal goal without financial aid or debt. I did it, and it made my life easy.

If your young adult children have no focus and want to go to college because that's what everyone else is doing, you need to have serious conversations with them. You need to point out that you cannot afford to pay for their college education, and together figure out a way for them to pay, or for you to work with them to pay a portion of it. But, whatever you decide to do, don't co-sign for any student loans. It is a choice you may live to regret.

SOCIAL SECURITY

What can I possibly say that you don't already know about Social Security and Baby Boomers? Not a day goes by when there isn't some TV news update about Baby Boomers and Social Security, or some magazine or newspaper article talking about them. Social Security is a subject of great interest and importance to Baby Boomers, and it is essential that they educate themselves about how it will affect their lives. In fact, Social Security touches the lives of most people in one way or the other.

How is anyone supposed to figure it all out? There are so many questions, so many choices, so few answers, and the answers are not always straightforward. Take it early. Take it late. Stop working. Keep working. Is it taxable or not? Will Social Security still be there when I retire, or not? Will it be sufficient to cover my living expenses in my later years, or not?

To find answers to your questions, I recommend *Retire Early? Make the Smart Choices*, a book written for Baby Boomers by Steven Silbiger, MBA, CPA. When he could not find a book that clearly answered his questions about Social Security, he decided to search for answers himself, and then he wrote about them for others.

During the course of his research, he discovered that many financial planners cannot answer your questions because they are focused on saving and investing their clients' money. When it comes to assisting their clients in deciding when to begin collecting Social Security, many admitted to Mr. Silbiger that they need his book as much as their clients need it. [*If you have difficulty finding his book in a book store, it may be available on Amazon.com.*]

I also recommend that you seek the advice of a financial professional who will help you navigate the often muddy waters of the Social Security system in the best way possible for you ... including ways to avoid having all of that Social Security income taxed. And, before deciding whether or not to work with a particular financial planner, ask whether he is knowledgeable in answering the question, "*Retire Early?*" or not. Social Security is another one of those places where you cannot uncrack the egg if you make a mistake.

Sign up at 62. No, wait! But, what if ...

Don't jump right in and apply for Social Security Benefits the minute you turn 62 (or 66). Even if you are eligible, there are many things to consider, and the best way to decide is to sit down with a financial planner well in advance of your birthday, and look at the numbers, decide what you want to do in your retirement years, and give an educated guess at how much money you will need until the age of 85 or 95! Yikes! Yes, people are routinely living that long, and living costs money. Make sure you have enough for the entire journey.

You can, of course, make the choices yourself, but be prepared for the possible consequences of making mistakes. What harm can possibly come from seeking professional help in making one of the most important financial decisions of your entire life?

EMPLOYER-SPONSORED RETIREMENT PLANS

This is an issue that is of enormous interest and importance to Baby Boomers as they come to the end of their working years. Many Boomers do not have fixed pensions; instead, they have IRAs, 401(k)s and other such employer-sponsored retirement plans. They are valuable tools for accumulating funds for your retirement years, especially when you consider that many employers contribute a certain additional amount to your account. On the other hand, these funds are not liquid, and they are taxable. It is extremely important that you determine how these financial vehicles can work for you, and not against you.

The subject of taking money from an employer-sponsored retirement fund is complicated! All sorts of tax laws and loopholes exist that can trip you up and cause you to make mistakes if you don't know what you're doing. You should see the book of IRA Regulations, if you don't believe me. It is huge!

The company has employees responsible for your retirement funds, and while they may be helpful in answering "simple" procedural questions, it is doubtful whether they can (or even should) give you financial advice.

When you retire, your employer will give you two choices about the money in your retirement plan. They are:

- TAKE IT <u>or</u>
- LEAVE IT

YOU ABSOLUTELY CANNOT AFFORD TO MAKE ANY MISTAKES ABOUT THIS CHOICE.

When you think about making a mistake right here, think of two things:

(1) what happens to film when you accidentally open the back of a camera; and

(2) what happens to an egg after you have cracked it.

In both cases, the damage cannot be undone. Such is the case with the choice to take your money or leave it. I'm not trying to frighten you. But, without good financial advice, the possibility is very likely that you could make a mistake that cannot be corrected when taking your retirement fund and moving it elsewhere.

If you have never before used the services of a financial planner, you need one now, before you make any decisions about your retirement account.   Mistakes at this point in your life can have long-term, possibly disastrous financial consequences, and you must be informed in order to successfully navigate the complicated waters of retirement funds.

Don't take the easy way out and leave your retirement funds with your employer just because it seems too hard to figure out all those papers you were given when you left the company. You may be thinking it would be so much easier to simply leave the money, rather than making your own choices. Not usually a good idea without having an understanding of the consequences of that choice.

- Have you ever seen the huge stack of papers employers give to retirees about their retirement plans? No wonder people choose <u>not</u> to make a choice? Who can read all that stuff, and who can possibly understand it all? After all, your money has been in your employer's plan all these years, what can possibly happen? What, indeed? It's so much easier not to think about it. Be very careful. This is no place to use Scarlet O'Hara's philosophy of "*I'll think about it tomorrow.*"

There are things you need to know if you leave your money with your employer. For instance, know that the person(s) in charge of your employer's plan don't even know you, let alone care about your financial goals and needs, interests, lifestyle, etc. They are just employees doing a job. Are they the people you want taking care of your money? If you have reason to call them about your money, they may or may not be knowledgeable. Besides, you probably shouldn't be asking them for financial advice in the first place! They are not qualified to give you such advice.

In the alternative, you can transfer your funds (rollover) using the services of an experienced financial planner you know and trust, with whom you may have worked over the years, who knows you and your family, and the needs and goals you have set for yourself now and in the future. Doesn't this sound much better? And, even if you don't know the financial planner on a personal level, know that he has the expertise to assist you in making this important transfer of YOUR money in ways that will allow you to avoid paying penalties and tax wherever possible. Allow him to guide you through the process of preserving your hard-earned money.

Before you decide to take your retirement fund, and manage it by yourself, understand that you will have only a very short window of time in which to roll it over (that is, invest the funds elsewhere).

- Do you know how easy it is to let that deadline slip by while you are thinking (*agonizing*) about where to put the money, discussing it with your friends, reading the Wall Street Journal and financial magazines, and checking the Internet to find out how to do it?

  <u>This is one egg you cannot un-crack.</u> **If you take your retirement funds yourself, and if you fail to reinvest them properly within the time allowed, you will incur taxes and penalties that will make you really unhappy!**

ISN'T THE WHOLE IDEA OF A RETIREMENT FUND
TO <u>PRESERVE</u> YOUR MONEY FOR YOUR RETIREMENT YEARS?

WHY WOULD YOU RISK LOSING HUGE AMOUNTS OF MONEY TO TAXES and/or PENALTIES
JUST BECAUSE YOU HAVE AN ALL-CONSUMING NEED TO "DO IT YOURSELF?"

But, wait a minute, there is still that big package of information you got from your employer when you retired. What should you do with that? Give it to your financial planner. It won't be the first such package he has seen

---

A Little Humor

A man was meeting with his financial planner who said,
> *"Quite frankly, your finances are a mess. Why haven't you put a little something aside for your retirement?"*
The man replied,
> *"To be honest, I was counting on being dead by now."*

IN THE "OLDEN DAYS"

In the olden days when our fathers and grandfathers lived, worked and died, they faced a very different life after retirement than the life that is before Boomers. In those days, retirement began on a specific date when the man actually stopped going to work. He may have been given a party, a gold watch, and a pension. His anticipated life expectancy may have been 60 years. Maybe less. The day after the party, he woke up wondering what he was going to do that day, and the day after that, and the next.

Our mothers and grandmothers, on the other hand, generally did not work out of the house, and certainly few (if any) ever retired, *per se*. The work of women was in the home, and would remain just about the same in their golden years as when they were young, except that her husband would not be going to work anymore. Many women dread the prospect of having their husband at home, all day, every day after he retires, because they instinctively know he will sit around the house and do nothing. How do women know this? *Just asking ...* Some men actually feel entitled to sit around and do nothing in their retirement years because they feel it is a sort-of payoff for all their working years.

Yet, even with their children grown with families of their own and living elsewhere, the house still needs tending, the meals need preparing, the laundry needs to be done. A woman's job will never be over, and she will never get to retire or collect a pension.

THINGS ARE DIFFERENT NOW

Both male and female Baby Boomers are quickly coming to the place in their lives when they thought they could stop working (also known as "retirement"). Sadly, it's not going to turn out that way for many of them for many reasons, some of which are within their control, many of which are not.

During their working years, Baby Boomers were very self-indulgent, and spent their adult years working, living life, and having fun. **Isn't that what people are supposed to do? Well, yes and no.**

Boomers have always had a very young mindset, and that is a good thing ... except when the people who feel "young" are really 65 years old and facing old age, with all the prospects of possible financial shortage and illness in front of them. Then, maybe they don't feel so young anymore.

Boomers generally recognize that they have not saved enough for retirement. How could they, the way they spent money? The good news is that their spending kept the economy in great shape. They bought and bought and bought. Now what? Now they wonder what they're going to do with all that "stuff." Did they even need it in the first place?

Baby Boomers either thought that by the age of 62, they would be set for life, or at least relatively debt free. For many, it has not turned out that way. Along the way, Boomers have incurred huge debt for several reasons, including (but surely not limited to) educating their children, taking out second mortgages (a/k/a home-equity loans) on their homes to finance a fancier lifestyle; buying vacation homes; and buying and buying more and more stuff, such that, in their 60's, they find themselves with high credit-card debt, mortgages, and a house full of "stuff."

As Baby Boomers face retirement, there are many decisions to be made. If you asked every 62-year old if the years went by quickly, they would be in complete agreement when they said a loud collective YES! Some planned for their retirement. Others did not. Both groups had their reasons.

Anybody who thinks money will make you happy, hasn't got money.

David Geffen

WHEN _____ **HAPPENS, THEN I'LL BE HAPPY.**

(fill in the blank)

For you, what words should be inserted in the blank line? Will you be happy …

- When you get married (divorced)?
- When you pay off the mortgage on your house?
- When your children graduate from college?
- When you are debt free?
- When you have more free time?
- When you have $1 million safely invested?
- When you move somewhere else?
- When you retire?
- Other? _____ (fill in the blank)

STOP RIGHT THERE!
How are you planning to retire when you never made a "plan" for retirement? *Just asking …*

Money brings some happiness, but after a certain point, it just brings more money.

Neil Simon

Retirement! Isn't that the time when you no longer go to work every day, and when you are no longer earning a paycheck, and when you have saved and invested enough money to pay for your living expenses for 20-30 years?

- *"Oh, you mean, that retirement?"*

I hear you whining already [I thought we agreed there would be no whining].

- *"Oh, yeah, saving for retirement. I never planned for retirement. It just sort of crept up on me when I wasn't looking."*

Nope! You can't get away with a weak excuse like that! You knew you would be 65 someday, that is, of course, unless you planned on dying before you retired. Dying would certainly make it unnecessary to save for retirement, wouldn't it?

Do you think people who died <u>before</u> they retired thought it was such a good idea? *Just asking …*

If you have made no plan for your retirement, and if you have not saved enough money to sustain you 'til the age of 85 or 95 years, how do you plan to pay your bills? How does living on Social Security, in a tiny apartment, eating dog food sound to you?

- Let's do the math. If you retire at 65 and you live until 85, you will need 20 years' worth of money to sustain you. At $50,000 per year, which is the approximate amount of money you will need to sustain a decent quality of life, that means you will need $1,000,000. One million dollars! Where do you expect that money to come from if you have not planned, saved and invested wisely?

- One thing that is so often overlooked is the effect of inflation on that $50,000. Pay attention to the numbers, because they don't lie.

168

If nothing else, you can see your immediate need for advice from a financial professional. Time is no longer on your side, and you know it. I hear you: you don't know any financial planners? Not a good reason. What is <u>really</u> stopping you from making that phone call today?

YOU NEED A WAKE-UP CALL

Try the following exercise just for the fun of it:

      (1) Write down the 10 problems you have today because you think you don't have enough money.
      (2) Write down the 10 problems you would potentially have if you had $10 million.

If you take the time to think about the questions and honestly answer them,
I think you may be surprised.

WHY ARE BABY BOOMERS IN THIS FINANCIAL SITUATION?

There was both a level of entitlement and addiction to the shopping habits of Baby Boomers, and their sense that more is better: more clothing, shoes, purses, golf clubs, a new car every 2 years, more and more and more. Add to that the mistaken ideas that shopping will make you happy and you're going to live forever. Can you see the problems? I sure hope Boomers got a lot of personal satisfaction from buying all that stuff, because I doubt they get any happiness from paying the monthly bills, that it assuming they <u>do</u> pay their bills on time. If you were to ask anyone with a high credit card balance what they have to show for it, what do you suppose their reply would be?

Lots of Boomers bought houses they couldn't afford, indulged themselves in luxury that may have been well above their basic living standard and necessity. That was all working beautifully until the bottom fell out of the financial market. Now here is the day of reckoning, and Baby Boomers are finding it painful. **What is needed now is learning to live below your means.** Wow, that's a new concept for Baby Boomers to think about. Money may not be everything, but it sure comes in handy when there are bills to be paid.

Unlike people who grew up in the Great Depression of the 1930s, Boomers never truly understood nor experienced genuine "want" such that they could distinguish between wants and needs. And, besides, they were making good money. Why shouldn't they spend it?

Here's another interesting intellectual exercise for you. Make 2 lists:

      (1) things you need;
      (2) things you want.

You may be surprised at your answers.

On the Dr. Phil show of April 26, 2011, he said that what you buy should have nothing to do with what you need **_or_** what you want. He said **you should only buy what you can afford!** A really quaint idea, don't you think? Might be fun to try.

Well, how do you feel today? You don't have a pension. You don't have a 1-year liquid emergency fund. You have a mortgage and a home-equity loan on your primary residence, you have a mortgage on your beach house, you have lease payments on two new cars, and high credit card debt. And, don't forget the cost of that divorce settlement, and the big chunks of your savings that went for your children's education, weddings and subsequent divorces. And, remember that inheritance you were anticipating from your parents' estates? It has been spent helping them pay for their own living expenses and needs, and most of it is gone. And, let's not forget about the basic need to buy food, pay taxes, maintenance and utilities on your house(s).

IT ISN'T FAIR!
Who said anything about "fair?"

Could you have done things differently. Of course. You know that. Looking back, you can see that maybe you could have made different choices, and let me remind you once again that you have an unlimited number of choices to make in your life.

TIME TO GET OUT YOUR CHOICE TICKET!

Don't stop making choices now because you are worried. Just try to think about the consequences a little harder, and make the choices that will benefit you beyond the momentary pleasure.

In December 2010, articles appeared in the Philadelphia "Inquirer" and the AARP Magazine about "credit card bullies."

That is the term that was used to describe employees of collection agencies that use storm trooper tactics to get people to pay their credit card bills. In both situations described, the collection agency was WRONG! Big Time Wrong! They bombarded the credit card holder, their relatives, friends, and even their employers with repeated threatening phone calls, emails and letters, going so far as to threaten to put them in jail if they didn't pay up. The article in the newspaper said that for a $4,000 debt, the collection agency demanded more than $250,000,000! What?

The articles acknowledged the terrible upset at being the target of such attacks, and encouraged people not to be intimidated by such unprofessional, irresponsible actions by collection agencies.

It was further recommended that when the very first such contact from a collection agency arrives, the person immediately send a letter to the agency, via <u>certified U.S. mail with return receipt requested</u>, so there will be proof that the agency did, in fact, receive the letter. (You do remember the U. S. Postal Service, don't you?) At least, give this a try before you incur legal fees to resolve this dispute.

And, if the harassment continues, contact your local police department. Or put it out on the Internet for others to see (be careful of this choice, however).

The people who were mentioned in those articles are planning to sue the respective collection agencies, who claim "they did nothing wrong."

BE CAREFUL about using debt recovery businesses that are advertising all over the media these days. Some are genuine; many are not; some are scams preying on people who are anxious to get out from under the burden of debt, mostly from credit-card spending.

Debtors are vulnerable and may listen to advice that is not only inappropriate, but potentially dangerous or even illegal. Elsewhere, I mention how Suze Orman was outraged at a question a caller presented to her about taking out a home-equity loan to pay credit card debt. The caller's advice was obtained from a debt-recovery business. Suze went so far as to say it was the worst advice she ever heard.

IS YOUR HOUSE AN ASSET OR A LIABILITY?

This question is answered clearly in *Rich Dad, Poor Dad*, by Robert Kiyosaki and Sharon Lechter. They point out that if your house is not earning any money, but is costing you money, and if you house is not increasing in value, but is decreasing in value, it is questionable whether your house is an asset.

A house has, for many years, been thought of as an asset that can be tapped when and if necessary. Lots of Baby Boomers "tapped" the equity in their houses when they took out home equity loans. When you combine the amount of money owed on two mortgages with the serious decline in real estate values, you can see a serious financial crisis. A 55-year old who takes on a 30-year conventional mortgage had better plan to have a good job to be able to pay off that debt <u>early</u>, because jobs are hard to come by in your 80s!

In 1990, 1 in every 6 households headed by someone 65 or older had a mortgage. In 2004, it was 1 in 4. What this means in 2011 is that more and more people reaching retirement age are less likely to own their homes free and clear than their predecessors of less than a generation ago.

How would you answer the question: "IS YOUR HOUSE AN ASSET?"

There is no one right answer, and no easy answer, either, and there are many variables.

It depends on who you ask.

> A realtor, a banker, and a mortgage broker might say YES.
> An accountant, a financial planner, a tax lawyer, may say NO
> An older homeowner and an unemployed person may say NO.

It depends upon when you ask them.

> In the early 2000's, the answer would have been YES.
> Today (2012), the answer will probably be NO.

Does your house generate any money?

> Unless you live in a house that has rental space that is generating an income to you every month, the answer is NO. [This is spelled out in the book, *Rich Dad, Poor Dad,* which I mentioned earlier.] Even if it were not a rental property generating income, there was a time in the not-too-distant past when a house significantly appreciated in value, so it could be said that, in that respect, a house generated money; however, that is not the case right now.

Does your house cost you money?

> You bet! Every house has expenses. Fixed expenses include things like utilities, real estate taxes, homeowners' insurance. It is difficult to reduce fixed expenses.

> Many houses have variable expenses that include new furnishings and renovations for decorative purposes, that really expensive riding lawnmower, repairs, maintenance, a landscaping service. These are places where you can reduce your expenses because these things are not always necessary right away, if at all

WHAT DO YOU WANT FROM YOUR HOUSE?

Is your house your sanctuary, your place of comfort and peace away from the stress and noise of the outside world, a place you can easily afford?

When you bought your first house, did you intend for it to be your home for the rest of your life? Or, did you look at it as your "first" house where you would live until you were financially ready to buy a bigger, more expensive house?

Or did you go for the big house first, not wanting to wait until "later," and now you find yourself in serious debt beyond your ability to repay it because of your impatience, your need for immediate gratification?

An article in the Philadelphia "*Inquirer*" of June 26, 2011, stated that **a house is a shelter, not an investment**. Technically, that is true. But, in the heady environment of the housing boom, people who sold their homes for huge profits might disagree. It was also a time when the equity in a home was so great as to enable homeowners to borrow against their primary residence to buy another house or a car and finance their children's college education. But, things have changed.

As the years passed, did you believe your home had increased in value, such that it would provide a nice nest egg for you?

- When 55+ communities began to spring up around the country, did you contemplate selling your present house and moving into one of them? Or have you already sold your big house and moved into a 55+ community? They are really nice, you know.

- Did you even think you would skip over the move to the 55+ community and make the big move to a Continuing Care Retirement Community (CCRC) in case one or both of you became ill or disabled? Five years ago, you even visited one in particular that you really liked, but believed you "weren't ready yet."

> A few years ago, I attended a luncheon sponsored by a local CCRC. During the sales presentation, it was mentioned that many people balk when they face the moment of decision of whether to move there or not,

usually saying, *"We're not ready."* The salesperson said that all too often, when you _are_ ready, they may be unable to accommodate you.

And, then, after a few years, when you and your spouse make the joint decision to move to that CCRC, thinking it can provide you both with the best possible long-term living advantages, what happened? Now, <u>you</u> can't afford it! WHAT? *Are you kidding?*

That's right. Not only has the cost of moving into the CCRC **in**creased significantly in the past few years, but the value of your house has **de**creased significantly, such that, *even if you can sell your house,* the money you get from the sale of your house will not be sufficient to pay the entry fee to the CCRC. OUCH!

How did that happen? It is OK for you to blame the politicians and the economy and the weather and your mother if it makes you feel better. But, wouldn't it be more honest to take a look at how you make choices? What was it that kept you from moving into the CCRC five years ago?

- The people already living there were **_so old_**. We're not *that* old.
- Neither of us is disabled or ill.
- We're not ready.
- It's too hard to down-size our present home.
- What if we don't like it after we get there?
- I want to make the move but my wife doesn't, or vice versa.
- What if we run out of money?

The reality is that if the two of you don't make this move together, one of these things will happen:

- One of you will become ill or disabled and have to go to a nursing home;
- One of you will die and the other will be left alone to ultimately make the move by themselves;
- You will never move anywhere else except to the cemetery.

Once upon a time there was a couple married to each other for 53 years. They reside in a small, but very nice house in a part of town that has experienced a decline in real estate values.

During the last 10-15 years of their marriage, the wife's health declined. Her prescription medicines cost them $6,000/year. The husband believes there may come a time in the not-too-distant future when he will be unable to care for her by himself, and that a move to a CCRC would be best for both of them, considering they are both 80 years old.

Five years ago, they investigated the possibility of moving to a CCRC. The husband was ready to move, but the wife began whining that "she wasn't ready yet." She was basically afraid she wouldn't like it, and they allowed <u>her</u> fear to make <u>their</u> decision. And, so they didn't move.

They recently looked again at that same CCRC, and discovered a very unpleasant truth. Now, they can't afford it because of the decrease in the value of their house ... they, like so many others, were relying on the equity in their house to pay for their retirement. What are they supposed to do now?

- How do you suppose the husband feels now?

- Can you see him building a resentment against his wife for holding them back?

- How do you think the wife feels knowing that her fears were the reason they didn't make the move a few years ago?

- Should the husband have "insisted" they move then?

- What if they got there and the wife was *really* miserable?

- What if the husband has a sudden massive heart attack and dies, leaving behind a disabled wife?

- What would you have done?

<u>Here's what Dr. Phil says</u>: Everything in a marriage is negotiable. Maybe these two people never learned how to negotiate constructively. Maybe the husband, early in their marriage, developed a pattern of always giving in to his wife's wishes (her NOs) just to make her shut up? I realize what I just said sounds harsh, but you and I both know it happens.

Interestingly, many CCRCs are realizing that people who want to move there cannot, because they are unable to sell their house quickly or for the amount of money they would need to pay the entrance fees. So, the CCRCs are becoming creative, because the truth is, they need to have their facility close to 100% occupancy, and with the economy the way it is now (2011), that has not been happening. Some facilities are even waiting for payment of the entrance fee until after the people's house sells. If you want to move to a CCRC, ask about the various ways to finance the move. Be proactive and creative yourself. Who knows?

IN SIMPLE LANGUAGE, HOW DID THE SUB-PRIME MORTGAGE MESS HAPPEN?

I once heard a Certified Financial Planner speak to a group of Baby Boomers about how and why the real estate market crashed. He talked about No-Doc Loans (no documents required to prove income and employment or taxes), and NINJA loans (stands for No Income No Job No Assets). In a nutshell, mortgage companies were giving mortgages to people for whom there was no expectation of their ever being able to pay the mortgage over time. So much for truth in lending!

Why didn't anybody figure this out? There are some answers to that question in the book, ***How We Decide***, by Jonah Lehrer. The author stated that 55% of all 2/28* mortgages were sold to homeowners who could have gotten prime mortgages (that is, as opposed to sub-prime mortgages), but who did not. Regular mortgages would have saved them lots of money over the long term, and might have kept them living in their houses (that is, as opposed to losing them to foreclosure). Their emotions tricked them into making a foolish (actually, disastrous) financial decision (mistake). [*A 2/28 mortgage has a low, fixed interest rate for the first two years, and a much higher adjustable rate for the next 28 years. Sort of like a new credit card, don't you think?]

WHAT HAPPENED TO COMMON SENSE?

If you can't afford the house, don't buy it! It's really very simple … except when it isn't.

And, don't forget all that realtor doublespeak about "comps," and market shifts. I find it very interesting that in all the discussions about how and why the real estate market went bust, there is no mention of the realtors having been complicit in the mess. "*Don't worry, I can get you that house*" they said. True. They got the people the house they wanted. But, how were the people expected to pay for it? What independent research did the buyers do to educate themselves about the financial and legal documents they were about to sign to buy a house they couldn't afford under any circumstances? None is most likely the answer to that question.

It is as if people forgot how to add and subtract. Once the real estate closing was completed, it was not the realtor's problem. They had done their job, had earned their commissions. They were happy. So what if the transaction ruined the lives of people who trusted them? Not their problem.

Let's do some arithmetic (because, it doesn't take an Einstein to calculate the numbers).

- Your income is $30,000.
- Your wife's income is $25,000
- You have $19,000 in credit card debt.
- The husband still has $63,000 in student loan debt
- You have car payments of $350/month for another 3 years.
- Your new house cost $250,000.
- You put down ZERO dollars.
- Your mortgage debt is $250,000.
- You were granted a 3-year Adjustable Rate Mortgage (ARM) at 6% with a balloon payment after five years.
- The 3-year period expired, and now you have to refinance almost the entire amount at a much higher rate.

HOW DID YOU THINK YOU WOULD BE ABLE TO AFFORD THE MORTGAGE PAYMENTS AT THE HIGHER RATE?

Or did you simply not THINK about it because you were caught up in the excitement of buying a new home? You are not a real estate or financial professional. How could you be expected to anticipate that this transaction had predictably disastrous consequences? A little knowledge of arithmetic would have been helpful. Or common sense could have kicked in. Or you could have consulted with a lawyer or a financial planner before agreeing to buy that house? Choices and consequences.

ARE YOU COLLECTING ANY KIND OF FINANCIAL ASSISTANCE?

Have you lost your job? Have you lost your home to foreclosure? Have you filed for bankruptcy protection to try to recover from your debt? Have you tapped into your retirement funds, for which you incurred both taxes and penalties? Are your savings (if you had any) gone? Are you using credit cards to pay for the basic necessities of life?

It is an unfortunate consequence of many kinds of financial situations coming together that have brought Baby Boomers to a place in their lives where they never expected to find themselves: collecting Unemployment Compensation, Food Stamps, Welfare, or the like. One might even call this *"the perfect storm"* of finances, where several situations came together simultaneously to create a furor of unprecedented proportions.

GO AHEAD, FEEL GUILTY or ANGRY IF YOU MUST. BUT IT WON'T HELP.

The first thing I'm going to say to you is that you cannot allow yourself to feel guilty or angry about being in this place. Oh, all right, if it makes you feel better to say you feel this way, go ahead, but don't indulge yourself in those feelings for very long. What good it is going to do you?

There is no shame in being laid off from your job, or finding yourself in foreclosure or bankruptcy. It's not generally good, but these things happen. What you must do next is find your way out of this situation. And, if it makes you feel any better, think of all the other people who find themselves in the same situation or worse.

CAN YOU SEE OPPORTUNITY IN THIS SITUATION?
"What opportunity? Are you kidding? I don't see any opportunity?"

> *We are continually faced by great opportunities brilliantly disguised as insoluble problems.*
>
> Lee Iacocca

FORCE YOURSELF TO SEE OPPORTUNITY EVERYWHERE.
WAKE UP EVERY MORNING EXPECTING A MIRACLE!

I know it may be hard for you to see opportunity ... *even possibilities* ... when things look so gloomy, when you are struggling to make ends meet. But, give it a try, anyway. Sometimes, when opportunity knocks, it is unrecognizable, especially if you are accustomed to seeing things only one way.

Today, you might meet someone in the supermarket line who can open a door for you, or meet someone who can make a connection that will make all the difference in the path you are walking. Maybe someone will call you, and in the most casual conversation, mention that there is a job opportunity that might be just right for you.

Allow me to ask you this question <u>again</u>.

Question: **What's the single most important thing you need to know when you are lost?**

Answer: **Where you are.**

So, where are you? Are you still in good health? Are you still able to work? Are you intelligent, resourceful? Are you willing to ask for and accept help, not in the form of a hand-out, but as coaching or guidance?

By now, you are beyond the feelings of guilt, anger and shame for allowing yourself and your family to get into this mess. It sounds to me like you are not completely lost, and knowing the place where you find yourself today, you should be able to find your way home again. It may not be an easy trip, but it may not be impossible either.

NO WHINING ALLOWED!

Whining is for 3-year old children. I know you are upset, and justifiably so, but the best way to get back on your feet is to reach deep down inside yourself, find the mature, responsible person you know you are, and hold on for dear life.

Don't spend your days wallowing. And, do not sit around watching TV, especially the financial news. It may only make you feel worse. Get off that couch and **do something**! While opportunity does occasionally "knock," don't expect it to knock on your front door while you're changing the TV channel.

And, for heaven's sake, don't WHINE.

Opportunity does not knock, it presents itself when you beat down the door.

Kyle Chandler

BUT, WHAT CAN I DO?

If your wife is working and you are not, do things for her to lighten her load. It will make you feel good about yourself to be contributing to the wellbeing of your family. Do the grocery shopping (ask your wife to make a list). Run the vacuum without being asked. Do the dishes and the laundry, and fold the clothes afterward. If you don't know how, ask her. Imagine how happy that would make her.

Once upon a time, I was working long days at a very stressful full-time job and, although my husband was also employed, he realized that I needed help around the house. He volunteered to do the laundry, but needed me to show him exactly how to do it correctly. I told him it was easier to do it myself, but he insisted. So, I decided to write a procedure for how to do the laundry. It took me two weeks of writing and editing until I got it perfect to my satisfaction, and guess what? My husband did the laundry ever after. I was glad he asked.

Be creative with the time you have. Think about this: when was the last time you had so much time on your hands? In all your working years, wasn't one of your big complaints that you never had enough time to do the things you really want to do? Remember that saying: *"So many books; so little time."* Now you can finally read for pleasure.

Half our life is spent trying to find something to do
with the time we have rushed through life trying to save.

Will Rogers

NOW THAT YOU HAVE THAT EXTRA TIME YOU WISHED FOR,
WHAT ARE YOU GOING TO DO WITH IT?

Ask yourself what have you wanted to do for many years that you can now do <u>without</u> <u>spending</u> <u>money</u>? Only you know the answer. So, figure it out!

Of course, I'm not suggesting you take an expensive vacation; I'm talking about those little things: clean the garage once and for all; build those shelves your wife has been asking you for; take your kids or grandchildren to watch little league games; go to the library; volunteer someplace where you can make a difference; plant a vegetable garden; learn a foreign language by listening to CD's in your car; organize your personal papers; learn to cook (all it takes is reading recipes); join a book club; get together with friends just for the sake of being with people whose company you enjoy, without the need for expensive food and drinks.

Maybe you could form a community group of people in similar situations to share tips on how to save money, or barter for services (I'll cut your grass if you groom my dog). You know how bartering works … I don't have to tell you. Be creative!

I THINK YOU GET THE IDEA.

You have found yourself in a place where you need financial assistance, and you need it now.
That is the reality.

Don't get all emotional about it, or you may lose sight of your goal, which is to hold on 'til things get better for you, for your family, and for the economy, so tied to one another are they. Try very hard not to allow fear and desperation to guide you. Remember common sense? If you were ever going to need common sense, it is now.

The thing to do is to **maximize the benefits** you are receiving to the point of being ridiculous. One way to do that is to eliminate everything in your life that you don't absolutely NEED:

- Stop drinking Starbuck's coffee; make your own.

- Stop the magazines and newspapers. You can read the paper online or at the library if they are important to you.

- Sell what you don't need and won't miss: have your own yard sales, or set up at a local flea market. You know you have too much stuff anyway. Turn it into cash.

- What about all those kids' toys that are not being played with anymore? Tell the kids if they allow you to sell some of their unused "stuff," you will use the sale proceeds to take them to see a movie. Ask the kids to help out at the yard sale. Make it a family day of fun.

- If you have two cars, can you manage with only one? If the answer is yes, sell the one that is costing you the most in payments, insurance and upkeep.

- If you keep the older car, contact your insurance company to change your coverage to only liability, and ask them to increase your deductible, thus reducing your car insurance payments.

- If you find you are unable to make credit card payments, contact the credit card company, tell them your situation, ask them for some assistance until you get back on your feet.

- Don't go to the movies as often, and when you do, don't eat their food.

- Examine your cable TV bills to see where you can make cuts.

- What about those things called "phones." How much of those monthly payments can you eliminate?

- Cut your own grass.

- Wash your own car.

- Women, stop getting your nails professionally done, and wash and color your own hair, and get your hair cut less frequently.

- Cut back on your electric and water usage. See if it makes a difference in your bills.

- Cook your own meals. Did you forget how to cook? Learn to read a recipe. Try new low-cost recipes that will provide you with several meals each week.

- Stop eating out, especially at fast-food places.

- Sell your unwanted and unused gold and silver.

- Read the supermarket ads to see which store has the best prices on the foods you regularly eat. Use coupons, buy only things on sale, and buy only what you need.

- If you have young children, explain your situation to them, and address any fears they may be having about your family's financial situation. And, teach them about saving money and eliminating waste.

- If you must buy clothing, shop at thrift stores or consignment shops. You'd be amazed at what you can find.

- You can sell your excess clothing and household furnishings at consignment shops. Look for high-end shops where you can get the most money.

- Treat yourself to a bunch of flowers or an ice cream cone (with sprinkles) every now and then. These small expenses won't break the budget. They are about comforting yourself at a time when you need to be comforted in little ways.

> *To save money, some people are giving up their pets as they face financial difficulty. Some people think it's all right to surrender them to a shelter or the SPCA. Others drop them by the side of the road, to fend for themselves ... those wonderful animals you loved so much, and who trusted you to take good care of them, now have to forage for their own food. Some people simply move out of their house or apartment and leave the pet(s) behind.*
>
> ## ARE YOU KIDDING?
>
> *My opinion of this is very strong, and you might not like it: You can NEVER give up your pet for financial reasons. You must find another way to have the money it costs to have a pet(s) in your life. You chose to have the pet. Now, it's your responsibility to care for it until the end of its' natural life. Figure it out!*

A WORD OF CAUTION

Do <u>not</u> begin taking money from your IRAs or 401(k) or other retirement accounts **unless it is absolutely necessary**. Some plans allow for "hardship withdrawals," but there are all sorts of conditions that must be met before they hand over the money.

And, DO NOT make this decision by yourself. Seek the advice of a qualified financial professional before making a mistake that cannot be corrected and could end up costing you a lot of money you won't be able to get back. There may be other options you don't know about. Ask questions. Be patient.

THERE IS HOPE

Have you ever tried paying yourself first?

> *"What, are you joking? Pay myself first? There's barely enough money to go around, and you're asking me to pay myself first?"*

Well, yes I am.

> *"It is a concept I have read about, but it sounds hard, even impossible"*

> *The 40-year old daughter of one of my close friends just called me to say that she wanted to add something to this book about how she handles money. She does two things every month: (1) She pays herself first; and (2) She pays her credit-card bill in full every month so she never pays interest.*
>
> *As a young adult, when she received her first credit card bill, she sent a check for the minimum required payment. When the next month's bill arrived, she noticed that interest had been added, and asked her mother about it. When she found out that the bank was always going to charge her interest every time she didn't make payment in full, she made a decision right then and there to pay every credit card bill in full from then on.*
>
> *She decided that if she cannot afford to pay for something in full at the time of purchase (or pay her credit card balance in full every month), she either will wait until she can, or decide not to buy it. As a result of this basic money philosophy, she owns her own home, has traveled extensively, and has money in all the right places.*

Paying yourself first can provide amazing results if you stick with it. Money is simply a tool, and it's value is as a medium of exchange: you give money in exchange for some particular thing or service. A simple transaction. Can you see that?

Do you ever handle your money (that is, do you touch it)? If you regularly pay with PLASTIC, you may feel disconnected from your money, as if you're not really spending money after all. This is a problem.

In addition to worry and fear, there is an element of bitterness about how the government could have put us in this position of having worked so hard for so many years, only to find that our hard-earned money may not be there when we need it, and may not be enough to sustain us in our golden years.

While you should be concerned about your finances, and committed to doing whatever it takes to accumulate and preserve your money for your retirement years, don't let your emotions take over. Keep your head on straight, don't believe everything you read and hear on TV, and be open to advice from learned professionals. **And, stop trying to do it all by yourself!** There is no shame in asking for help.

HOW DO YOU SPEND YOUR MONEY

Do you shop to make yourself happy? Is the momentary euphoria worth it when the credit card bill arrives? How happy are you when you pay the bill, that is, assuming you <u>do</u> pay the bill.

Do you get depressed when you look at all your stuff? Do you wonder where it all came from? Do you ever return any of that stuff you needed so badly in the moment, but which you know you will never use? Do you give your excess to charity?

Do you spend money you don't have for things you don't need? What about those 2-for-1 items you bought, when you didn't even need the first one? What about all the things you buy to give as gifts someday, but never do.

Do you buy things just because they are on sale? Do you make excuses to justify the purchase because you may need it later? I know a man who bought a pair of shoes that was the wrong size just because they were on sale. *Excuse me?*

Do you know when a sale is not a sale? When the seller puts a sale sign on a product knowing it is the same price as last month? Gotcha! And, how good is that "sale price" when you add on the 20% interest you are paying on your credit card?

Do you comparison shop for groceries? If you read the grocery store ads before you go to the store, over time, you will recognize when a "sale" item is not really on sale. I spend time every week perusing the ads from 3 grocery stores, making a shopping list, gathering coupons. If a product isn't on sale, and if I don't really need it, and if I don't have a coupon that will be, at the very least, doubled by the store, I don't buy it! Unless the sales in all 3 stores are terrific, I only go to one of those stores. It's not worth my time to be shopping at 3 stores every week.

A Little Financial Humor

Wife:	*Darn. All these coupons are expired. We could have saved 50 cents on 9 cans of dog food.*
Husband:	*But, we don't have a dog.*
Wife:	*Still...50 cents is 50 cents.*
Husband:	*No wonder we're going to die broke.*

Do you waste gas driving around looking for the cheapest price of one or two items at the grocery store, or a savings of one or two cents at the gas station? Give it up? Unless the prices are significantly different, save yourself time, aggravation, gas, and money, and shop at only one or two stores.

Do you use coupons? I hear you whining already: it takes too much time; it's boring; it doesn't really save money anyway, and on and on and on. If you don't believe you can save money using coupons, you should see my savings at the bottom of every grocery slip? And, in July 2011, there was a TV show called "*Extreme Couponing.*" It <u>*was*</u> extreme, and personally I'm not sure there was any real money being saved, but someone apparently thought shopping with coupons was important enough to have made a reality TV show about the subject.

Do you keep an exact list of what you spend every day? every month? "*Are you kidding? Who has time for that?*" Try it for a while. You might be surprised to see where your money goes.

Do you shop at the Home Shopping Network and QVC? Do you have piles of unopened boxes from places like that? Are you watching those TV channels because you are bored? Find something else to do instead. Where is your impulse control?

Do you order products from "paid programming" on TV? *"Well, you sometimes get two for the price of one?"* Do you really?" What about the shipping and handling costs? Question yourself about whether you really need the product in the first place. Oh, yes, I know, you'll keep one item for yourself and give the other to someone for a gift? Right.

Do you shop from catalogs you receive in the mail? It's almost irresistible, isn't it? So many lovely things in those colorful books, and you think you have just the right places in your home for them. Over the years, I have spent time carefully looking through a catalog and actually filling out the order blank for things I wanted, but I have never once mailed the order to the company. Why not? When I saw how expensive the shipping and handling costs were, I threw the order form in the trash. (a) I didn't really need the stuff in the first place; and (b) I wasn't about to pay S&H costs that are based on how much I spent, not how large or heavy the shipping box was going to be. Did you know that those companies make huge profit on the shipping and handling fees they charge?

Do you buy things that came from a telemarketing call? Things like replacement windows and siding? Chimney cleaning? Bathroom replacement? Have you ever heard this line: *"We're going to be in your neighborhood on Tuesday. What time is good for you to meet with our representative?"* If you are going to spend a large amount of money for things like this, contract only with a company with a very good reputation for actually completing jobs to the satisfaction of customers, preferably a local company for which you can obtain genuine references. How many times have you read or heard about people's being scammed by unscrupulous contractors who took the people's money in advance, and never showed up, or worse, began the job and never finished, and then went out of business. Be careful how you spend your money.

Do you send money to every charity that calls you on the phone? *"But that young man on the phone sounded so nice, and the charity seemed worthy."* Are you sure? Did you know that man was calling from a company that may or may not be doing the soliciting for the charity itself, and that that company is being paid a large fee for their services (that means that all your contribution is not going directly to that charity). Consider the possibility that you may need the money more than they do. And, besides, how legitimate is that charity, anyway?

> *When I worked for the CEO of a company, the receptionist called me and said there was a man from the police department who "insisted" on talking with my boss. Well, it was my job to screen such visitors, and yes, this man was "insisting" on speaking to my boss about "a police matter." He refused to give me any more information.*
>
> *My boss reluctantly agreed to see the man, who turned out to be a solicitor for a questionable "police" fund of some sort. My boss told the man to leave, and was furious (a) that the man had been less than honest about his reason for being there, and (b) that he had lied to me, who was responsible for keeping people like this away from my boss.*

Do you send money to every non-profit or charity that mails you a free tablet or address labels? If you keep and use the tablets or labels, do you feel *guilty* if you don't send money to "pay for them?" That is exactly what the non-profit company is counting on. Keep them or toss them, use them or give them away, send money or don't, but don't hide behind your all-too-ready excuse about feeling guilty. Whatever you decide, it doesn't matter. You are not required to send them money because you didn't order the tablet or labels in the first place. If it is a charity you wish to support, send them a donation. *[I've often wondered how much more money the charities would have if they stopped sending all these "free" labels and tablets.]*

Do you shop at those big box stores like Sam's Club? Costco? Wal-Mart? If you are young and raising a family, it may be wise to buy large quantities of non-perishable things. But now that it's just the two of you or yourself, do you really need all that stuff? Do you have any idea how much effort is put forth by those companies to make you believe a "sale item" is really "on sale?" They know your spending habits and they want your money, and they know how to get it. Is that OK with you?

Do you incur high credit card debt for Christmas shopping? Do you <u>complain</u> <u>every</u> <u>December</u> about how much shopping you have to do, of how busy you are buying and wrapping, how much money you are spending? I once suggested to a woman as she "whined" about this that maybe, just this once, she forego the shopping and exchanging of gifts (that nobody wants in the first place), and instead, just have a nice holiday dinner and enjoy the time together with her family, without increasing her credit card debt? The woman yelled at me, and told me I just didn't "understand."

Do you have lots of brand new clothes hanging in your closet that still have the price tags on them? Why did you buy them? (*They were on sale*). Why haven't you worn them? (*I gained weight*). Why haven't you returned the ones you haven't worn? (*I'd be too embarrassed*). <u>Who's in charge of your life?</u>

Do you have credit card debt from this kind of shopping? Pay it off as soon as possible. And, be very, very careful about companies and agencies that offer "credit consolidation services." I'll say no more than this, except that you need to pay your debt, one way or the other, so you might do better consulting a financial planner or an accountant in order to handle this kind of serious debt.

How much do you spend buying gifts for people who don't want the stuff in the first place? Give money ... for birthdays, weddings, anniversaries. Everyone already has too much stuff. They would much prefer money. If you don't believe me, ask them sometime.

> *To each of my nieces and nephews and their children, I give them money inside a book for their birthdays and Christmas. They have come to expect this from me. I select the books carefully in relation to the children's ages and interests at the time. I buy books in perfect condition, at "used book sales" rather than pay top dollar at a book store. After all, used books have exactly the same words as a new book and they cost so much less.*

Are you well on your way to becoming a "hoarder?" Only you know the answer to this question? If your answer is an honest "yes," get appropriate help right away to organize your stuff (which will include getting rid of much of it), and maybe even some counseling to look into why you are inclined to "hoard," how you can stop, and how you can keep from repeating this behavior. And, here's the hard question: How much money did you spend buying all that "stuff" that you didn't need in the first place, and which you now have in piles in your home?

Do you carefully examine your credit card bills each month to see where you money went? If the answer is NO, why not? *"Oh, no. It's way too scary. I never look at where I spent the money. I just look at the minimum and pay that amount."* Do you know what the interest rate is on your credit card? That should be the scary number.

How many credit cards do you have? Do you carry around one of those wallet-type credit card folders that hold 15 or 20 credit cards? Be smart and carry only 2 of those cards. And, stop carrying that thing around with you. What if you lost it? It happens.

Maybe you could reduce the interest rate on your credit card(s). Call the credit card company and ask for a lower interest rate, but if your FICO score is low, they may say NO.

Do you know the amount of money that is available for you to charge on each credit card? I know a woman who thinks that if her available credit is, for example, $20,000, it is like her own personal savings account and she can spend all that money. Where did she get that idea?

> **ARE YOU ABLE TO RESIST TEMPTATION WHEN YOU KNOW YOU CAN'T AFFORD IT?**
> **I repeat Dr. Phil's suggestion that you should only buy what you can afford!**

What do all the above shopping experiences have in common?

- They are purchased with plastic.
- The sellers want your money .
- The sellers don't care about your debt.
- The sellers know that you have low impulse control .

SO, I ASK YOU: WHO IS IN CHARGE OF YOUR SPENDING?

FINANCIAL INFIDELITY

How much explanation do you need to understand the term, financial infidelity? Somehow, I don't think it's very much. If you have read all the items in the above section, you can see areas where financial infidelity may exist in your life.

The Dr. Phil show on April 26, 2011, was about financial infidelity. He said that money is only arithmetic. Either the numbers add up or they don't.

- How much lying have you done about your money?
- Do you tell the truth about where you spend money?
- Or how you pay your bills (or don't pay your bills)?
- Or the excessive amount of shopping you do?
- Or the credit card(s) your spouse doesn't know you have?
- What about the clothes that still have the price tags, that you bought a few years ago and have never worn?
- Do you shop to make yourself feel good? Is your shopping an addiction? Be honest with yourself.
- If you handle the money in your family, does your partner know the amount of your joint debt, or that your FICO score is low?
- Do you have a substantial amount of debt that you never mentioned to your partner?
- Does your partner know that you don't pay your bills on time, and do you lie about phone calls you get from bill collectors?
- Do you hide bills when they arrive? Put them in piles without opening them? Does your partner know you do that?
- Do you have a Post Office box that your partner doesn't know about, so that bills and other financial papers can be sent to you privately?
- Do you trust your partner and his/her spending habits? Does he/she trust you and yours?

Previously, you said you didn't need a Pre-Nuptial Agreement because you want a relationship based upon trust. How much trust do you have with your partner if you discover they are lying about money?

Whether or not you are married to each other or in a committed relationship, do you share expenses? Do you share ownership of your house? Is your money jointly owned? Did you come to this relationship with debt you have not told your partner about? Did you know your partner's FICO score before you committed to this relationship?

You will remember Suze Orman's words that arguments about money are the primary cause of divorce. How much arguing do you and your partner do about money? Can you discuss your finances quietly, honestly, in a non-confrontational manner? When a problem arises, can you quickly, respectfully and successfully solve the problem? Are you able to confess your financial sins to your partner, with remorse and intention to do better in the future?

If you are guilty of any kind of financial infidelity, you need two people in your life:

1. A financial planner to closely examine your spending habits, and put a budget in place to get you back on track.
2. A psychologist to examine why you need to be dishonest with your partner about your money and spending habits.

Don't think you can keep lying your way out of the mess you created. If you are guilty of financial infidelity, get the help you need before you need the help of a bankruptcy attorney, and before your lying becomes truly pathological and you end up in jail.

> Remember Willie Sutton, the bank robber from the 1950s, who was asked why he robbed banks.
> His reply was simple: *"Because that's where the money is."*

Willie Sutton was a thief but he wasn't a liar. He told the simple truth as he saw it. He admitted that he stole money and had no intention of stopping. He didn't feel the need to lie about it. He didn't feel guilty about what he did, he wasn't sorry he took it, and he had no intention of ever paying the money back. He was no model citizen for you to try to emulate. But, he did have a certain (small) degree of honesty and integrity, while at the same time being a thief.

If you must go into bankruptcy because you spent money way beyond your means, such that you are unable to pay for the goods and services you bought, are you no better than a thief? Technically, you stole the money because you cannot pay it back. So, how are you different from Willie Sutton or Bernie Madoff, except by degree?

IF THAT FRIGHTENS YOU, GET HELP FOR YOUR FINANCIAL SINS.
DON'T WAIT ANOTHER DAY.

DO YOU PAY YOUR BILLS ON TIME?

Do you know your FICO score? FICO is an acronym for the Fair Isaac Corporation, (the creators of the FICO score), named in 1956 after its founders, Bill Fair, an engineer, and Earl Isaac, a mathematician. It is a complex credit-scoring formula that assesses the risk of whether or not a borrower may default.

The use of FICO scores really took off in 1995 when Fannie Mae and Freddie Mac (which purchased almost 2 out of every 3 real estate loans) recommended that lenders use FICO stores. It has become the standard adopted by the three main credit bureaus: Experian, TransUnion, and Equifax.

FICO scores range between 300 and 850. If you have a FICO score between 750 and 850, businesses will be quick to loan you money at a low interest rate. Above 600, you have a good credit history. If your score is below 600, you may find it substantially more difficult to obtain financing at a favorable rate. Your FICO score is essentially made up of the following:

- Payment history: 35%
- Total amount owed: 30%
- Length of credit history: 15%
- New credit: 10%
- Type of credit in use: 10%

If you choose to pay your bills late, you will not only be incurring late fees and penalties, but your FICO store will be negatively affected. This is no small matter, and it can have the effect of causing you to be unable to get a low interest rate on a mortgage or car loan. If you are looking to improve your credit score, work on your payment history and how much debt you actually have. In short,

- **pay your bills on time**
- **eliminate debt as quickly as possible**

If you have been paying your bills late for much of your adult life, know that your ability to borrow money in your later years may be seriously compromised by your low FICO score. Increasing your FICO score is not easy, and it doesn't happen quickly, but with commitment and good financial advice, it is possible to repair that score. Speak with a financial professional to see what you can do to improve your score while you are still earning wages. This is not something to put off until later?

- But, be very careful of companies that offer you a quick fix for your bad credit.
  Sometimes, they make it worse. Rely only on qualified, experienced professional professionals.

I think I finally found a way to balance my budget. Now, all I need is a Time Machine.

Author unknown

Why some people don't pay their bills on time?

- There are sometimes legitimate reasons for a person's not paying bills on time, such as serious illness or disability, or long-term unemployment, especially if you have a lot of credit cards and keep using them to pay regular living expenses because you are running out of money.

- There are other, less important, reasons why some people don't pay their bills on time; for example, they're too busy; they didn't get around to it; they're not organized; it's too upsetting; they don't have the money because they spent beyond their means.

- It could be that they never learned how to establish a reasonable budget for themselves and their family, or simply never took the time, and even if they did establish a budget, they didn't stick with it over time.

- It could be that they were never taught, or were never inclined to recognize the importance of saving money "for a rainy day." Well, for some folks, it's raining really hard today.

- There are other people who simply don't pay their bills, on time or otherwise. Such a person has a disconnect with their sense of responsibility. Somewhere in their mind, they don't feel they owe the money. I'm not going to get into the psychology of this, but it is a pervasive problem that will cause problems for your entire life. It can damage a marriage or friendships. It is often the cause of bankruptcy … even more than one in a lifetime. It can even cause you to end up in jail.

People in this category feel no remorse for cheating people out of money they owe to them, whether it be a family member, friend, or a large company. They are generally "judgment proof," which, in simple language, means you can sue them from now 'til next year, and never collect.

BUYING LOTTERY TICKETS IS NOT FINANCIAL PLANNING

How much money do you spend every week on lottery tickets? Have you noticed that the lines of people waiting to buy lottery tickets are generally seniors, the very people who are in need of money in their golden years? Where else could those seniors use that $25 each week that they spend (waste?) on lottery tickets?

Do you suppose they ever did the math? Let's say, for example, that in 52 weeks, a person who spends $25 each week on lottery tickets, parted with $1,300. Do you think they won that much or more? Maybe. Maybe not. It would be worth the time to track your lottery ticket spending habit and see if it is paying off for you.

Why do so many seniors buy lottery tickets? For all the obvious emotional reasons, even, one could say, for all the wrong reasons. Desperation. A yearning to take a risk, hoping against hope that they will win. They know the odds are stacked against them, and they buy the tickets anyway. Their defense is, *"Well, someone has to win, so it might as well be me."*

I always find myself annoyed when there is a particular lottery drawing that is worth many millions of dollars, and only one winner! What is that person going to do with all that money, especially if they have never before had such a huge amount of money?

If the lottery were worth $200,000,000, wouldn't it make more sense for everyone (including the economy in general) if 200 people each won $1 million, rather than having one person win it all? That would mean that 200 people would each buy a new car, go on a cruise, and spend that money ... which would be pumping the economy. There would be plenty left over for each to save for later. A win-win situation. Just another one of my opinions ...

I wonder if the people who buy lottery tickets took all the money they spent on lottery tickets every week and put it away (even into a jar on their kitchen counter), wouldn't they be financially better off?

RISK IS NOT TO BE AVOIDED – IT IS TO BE MANAGED.

On a scale of 1 to 5, what is your risk tolerance?

1 means you would be extremely conservative
5 means you would be inclined toward high risks

If you can't answer that question right now, give it some serious thought, because it is important to know your risk tolerance before you invest money. It is a question a financial planner will ask you, so you might as well think about it now.

It is also important to factor in your age. If you are young, still earning money, you can afford more high-risk investments because you have more time to recoup losses should you incur such loss. But, if you are a Baby Boomer facing retirement in the very near future, and you lose a large chunk of your money, you don't have much time left to recoup your loss. Be careful, but be open to possibility, too.

Many people are so afraid of risk that they will avoid it at all cost, and will refuse investments that are only moderately risky, but which at the same time, offer some degree of safety. But, know this: all financial risks are not necessarily equal or bad, and risk can usually be minimized with some serious thought and consultation with appropriate professionals, especially if you have clearly defined goals.

People who take action to bring about a desired result are people who know what they want, they do their homework, and they go after their goals. They take steps to calculate the anticipated risk of their choices. Here again, it's all about choices and consequences.

You can have only 2 out of 3 of the following things when you're speaking about investing your money:

- SAFETY
- LIQUIDITY
- RATE OF RETURN

- Let's say, for example, you put your money into a high-risk investment that promises you high return on your money. What one thing have you sacrificed in this transaction? <u>Safety</u>.

- Let's say, for example, you put your money into a long-term bank CD that pays a steady 3% interest. What have you sacrificed? <u>Liquidity</u>.

- What have your sacrificed if you put your money into a money-market account earning very low interest, because you are afraid of the stock market or other investments you don't understand? <u>Rate of return.</u>

See how that works.

Of course, things happen in life without planning, and those may not be things you would have chosen. Because we live in a global economy that is subject to the financial happenings of other nations as well as our own, it is entirely possible to lose your money due to events that are completely out of your control. Natural disasters like those which happened in Japan in early 2011 have an enormous ripple effect on money around the world.

Events that happen in your own life or far away, may be completely unpredictable and unexpected and can completely alter the direction in which you were headed. No matter what happens, even if you don't achieve your every goal, it is good to have a plan that is workable and suits your needs and personal style, and which has a certain amount of built-in flexibility for unforeseen events.

Even if you don't reach your intended goal, you will be a whole lot closer to your goal than if you had never taken the first step. You must take the first step to financial security. But, you already know that, don't you?

The journey of a thousand miles begins with a single step.

Lao Tzu

Why did the tortoise beat the hare? Because he never stopped putting one foot in front of the other ... slow and steady, right to the finish line. You don't have to drop out of the "financial race." You just have to keep on keeping on ... getting educated, getting solid advice from a financial professional, being smart about your choices and the consequences of each. And don't believe everything you read on the Internet.

Of course, you can avoid risk altogether by stuffing your money in your mattress.
And, if you do that, be sure to increase your fire insurance?

BEHAVIORAL FINANCE

It could, instead, be called the science of immediate gratification.

Within the financial planning field is a relatively new sub-specialty known as "behavioral finance" to better understand and explain how emotions influence investors and decision-making. It is part financial planner, part psychologist. Why? Because so many people handle their money based on their feelings.

When it comes to making decisions about whether to purchase something now or later, the emotions shout: *NOW, NOW, NOW. I don't want to wait!* Does this remind you of the behavior of a 3-year old child? *"I want it now"* they cry! Do you really enjoy behaving like a child? *Come on -- you know better.*

It's not easy for the brain to choose a long-term gain over an immediate reward. Such a decision requires cognitive effort, which is why getting rid of anything that makes the choice harder (cutting up your credit cards, for example) is so important. Sometimes, you just have to say NO to yourself.

Our emotions tend to overvalue immediate gains at the cost of future expenses. This is where the "emotional high" comes from shopping. We'll worry about paying for it later. It is sort of like Scarlett O'Hara's line: *"I'll think about that tomorrow. After all, tomorrow is another day."* It's OK with me if it's OK with you ... I'm not the person paying your credit card bill.

I again recommend that you read a book titled *How We Decide* by Jonah Lehrer, which explains how different areas of the brain react to the opposites of immediate gratification or waiting. A very interesting read.

Some people's emotions overpower rational thinking during times of stress, whether that stress is a result of euphoria or fear. These people then experience regret and overreaction when it comes to potential gains or losses of their money. Emotions got all mixed up with financial business.

Prof. Meir Statman (*What Investors Really Want*) an expert in the behavior known as "fear of regret," states that people tend to feel sorrow and grief after having made an error in judgment. He believes that investors avoid selling stocks that have gone down in order to avoid the pain and regret of having made a bad investment. They don't want to think about it, let alone talk about it. They are embarrassed to have to report the loss to the IRS, their accountant, their financial planner, their family and friends. Try to imagine the regret that people who invested their family money with Bernie Madoff feel now that their money is gone. What does it matter to them that Bernie Madoff is in jail? All they know is that their life has been radically altered by a thief who couldn't care less about them.

Many people have a hard time accepting some facts despite solid mathematical proof. Others are sometimes under the mistaken belief that they know, better than the professionals, how to deal with their own money. Still others who seek advice from professionals choose to ignore that advice. Many people regularly buy high and sell low, and when it turns out badly, they search for a reason or some particular person or thing to blame rather than consider the possibility that they made a mistake. Mistakes happen all the time. Don't let a mistake in the past cause you to avoid seeking financial advice now.

Once upon a time, a Certified Financial Planner had a client who, although he was retired, was heavily invested in the stock of his former employer, a well-known and highly reputable firm. The financial planner strongly recommended that this client significantly reduce the amount of company stock he owned because certain market indicators pointed that the value of the stock would soon decline. The client refused. What do you think happened to that stock soon after?

The client based his decision on the emotion of loyalty, rather than predictable facts. It was his choice to do so, and it cost him a huge amount of money that he will be unable to recover, and which he will need in his retirement years.

Do you think this man experienced regret at not having taken the advice of his personal financial adviser. Maybe not right away, maybe not until he runs out of money.

What would you have done?

Be patient for the long term. Americans are notoriously impatient. **We want patience, and we want it now!** When you make a plan, stick with it and change it only when circumstances suggest it is the right thing to do, or when your goals or your life situation changes. It would be good to get counseling from a financial planner before you make the change. Don't get caught up thinking you can be a day-trader. You probably will lose. And, forget that DO IT YOURSELF stuff!

ARE YOU READY TO GIVE UP WORKING FOR RETIREMENT? *Are you sure?*

Who makes the best transition from working to retirement? TEACHERS! Why? Because each year, during their summer break, they spend 2-3 months living life, relaxing, doing things they can't do when working full time, things like reading for pleasure, traveling, getting another degree, taking painting classes, learning another language, writing a book, and visiting friends. They have "practice" at not being at work.

THINK OF RETIREMENT AS 30 YEARS OF NOT GOING TO WORK.

What will you do with all that time *between now and then*? Vague answers like "*some travel, some work, some play*" can be just as debilitating in the long run as vague financial goals. Remember when your financial planner asked you the question, "*What do you want your money to do for you?*" and you didn't have an answer? When you retire, the question becomes, "*What do you want to do with all that time between now and then?*" Do you have an answer yet?

Have you made any plans for what you will do with all that time? Getting up every morning, reading the paper, eating breakfast, taking the dog for a walk. THEN WHAT? That's a lot of hours to fill between 10 a.m. and 11:30 p.m. (that is, after you watch the late news on TV) every day for 20 or 30 years!

If you are, and have always been, a self-motivated person, you already have a long list of things you want to do with all that time. You may not have had the time to actually contemplate what those specific things are, and may not have yet committed those ideas to paper. If this is true for you, chances are good that you are a woman. Why? Because men so closely identify who they are with what they do, and don't know who they are after they stop working and retire. It's a mistake to think that way, but you couldn't tell them that 25 years ago, or before they had a heart attack.

Dr. Bernie Siegel is a well-known author and heart surgeon. In one of his books, he talks about the day he realized that he was no different than an auto mechanic, who was called in to change the spark plugs or install a new battery. He realized that he never spent any time talking with his patients to learn about their lives before he opened them up and fixed their diseased hearts.

On the spur-of-the-moment, one day he asked a man, "Why did you have a heart attack?" And, to Dr. Siegel's absolute amazement, the man had a very quick reply: "I didn't know what else to do?" What?

It turns out the man lived in a poverty stricken area of the country, his company closed, he lost his job and his house, he and his family had to move in with his wife's family (a less than desirable situation). He went to another town so he could work, and for 5 days and nights every week, he lived alone, in a small, furnished room. He was riddled with guilt and shame and embarrassment at not being able to support his family. So, not knowing what else to do, he had a heart attack?

Do you think he is the only man to whom this has happened?

Now, in their 60's, Baby Boomers are getting a painful wake-up call! Let's just hope it is not a wake-up call like the one described above. This is not where they expected to be at this time in their lives. But, honestly, how could it be otherwise, considering their lifestyle and high level of spending?

IT ISN'T <u>WHAT</u> YOU KNOW THAT MATTERS.

IT'S <u>WHAT</u> <u>YOU</u> <u>DO</u> WITH WHAT YOU KNOW.

BENEFICIARY DESIGNATIONS

Beneficiary designations are necessary for all insurance policies, all IRAs, 401(k) and other retirement accounts, and bank accounts and investments that are designated as POD (Payable on Death) or TOD (Transfer on Death) accounts. Such designations allow for the immediate transfer of your assets upon your death. Although not absolutely required, it is also equally important that you name a <u>contingent</u> beneficiary just in case the originally named person predeceases you. It happens, you know!

If your named beneficiary should predecease you, and if you have not named a contingent beneficiary, the asset may pass into your estate. This is not generally something you want to happen, and it is a subject for you to fully discuss with your financial planner and/or your Lawyer.

If you designate more than one person as your primary beneficiaries, you must state how much each person is to receive. You could simply say that the proceeds are to be divided in equal shares, or you could specify the percentage each person is to receive. Just be sure the total adds up to 100%.

There are ways that your IRAs and other retirement accounts can be passed to your designated beneficiaries for many years into the future, such that the money they get upon your death passes with the best possible tax advantages, and will grow to very large amounts if the funds remain untouched by them until their own retirement. This is an extremely complex subject, and what I just said is a very abbreviated version of what can take place with your retirement accounts.

In order to educate yourself about the workings of your retirement accounts, speak with both a financial planner who is well versed on the subject of IRAs and your tax attorney. The laws on the subject of IRAs is extremely complex. Make no assumptions. Ask questions until you have at least a basic understanding of how they will work for you.

And, for those of you who are waiting until LATER to do the work of estate planning, if you do nothing else, at the very least, take care of the beneficiary designations of your investment accounts and insurance policies. If there is even a remote possibility that one or more of your beneficiary designations could be incorrect, check it out, and make the change NOW.

What follows is a story about a woman who had her lawyer draft a Will the way she wanted it to be. She believed she was being fair with her children in dividing her assets equally after her death. After all, isn't that what her Will said? Unfortunately, she apparently didn't understand the meaning of the words, "*assets that pass outside of your Will*" and that the beneficiary designation on her IRAs would basically cause her estate to fail.

Once upon a time, a widow asked her lawyer to prepare a new Will for her. She always told her three children that it was her intention to divide her estate equally among them, although the way she went about it prevented that from happening.

In her Will, she named her daughter as Executrix, and directed that her estate be divided equally among her three children.

The woman's money was in three IRAs, and her daughter was the named beneficiary of all three accounts. When the accounts were opened, the woman's intention was simply to put her daughter's name on the accounts "for convenience." (This "just for convenience" is something to question and look out for ... something bank clerks suggest all the time, and which frequently causes problems. Makes me wonder for whose convenience ... but that's just me.)

What this widow didn't understand (and, which may or may not have been clearly explained to her by the attorney who wrote her Will), was that the money in her IRAs could not, in fact, be divided among her three children by virtue of her Will, but would instead go directly to her daughter as the beneficiary of the IRAs. The money in her IRAs would "pass outside of her Will." This woman may even have heard her lawyer say that the money in the IRAs does not pass under her Will, but, if she didn't understand what that meant, she apparently didn't ask, either, and I'm pretty sure this woman did not know what was meant by the words "pass outside of your Will." She never intended to give all her money to her daughter and none of the money to her sons, but that is exactly what happened.

Can you see that her intentions did not match her actions? Now that she has passed away, she cannot explain to her sons how it happened. They feel cheated and angry. They say that their mother's Will said her estate was to be divided equally among her three children, and they don't understand how and why the IRAs don't pass under their Mother's Will. Fair or not, it is the law.

> *Maybe if her brothers are nice about things, this daughter might consider sharing that money with them. But, as often happens in families, they are not only <u>not</u> being nice, they are being horrible, bringing threats of litigation against their sister as Executrix. They actually believe their sister conspired with their mother to get all the money. See how easily things can become "messy?"*
>
> *The daughter, as Executrix, is left to clean up the mess her mother left behind, and has been incurring legal fees for her mother's estate which would not be ordinarily warranted, just to satisfy her brothers' need to understand how it happened this way. What had been a distant relationship with her brothers, has turned hostile. I doubt this is what their mother wanted.*

Do you see what can happen when people don't know what they're doing, don't ask questions, and when lawyers don't make a point of determining if the client understands or not. All the woman's three children know is that their mother said she intended to share her estate equally among them, and that's not how things worked out. If a Will says a person's estate is to be divided equally among their children, they not only *assume* that is what will happen, but they *expect* it to happen. So do your children. They probably don't understand what *"assets that pass outside a Will"* means either.

When you meet with your lawyer to draft your Will, don't assume the lawyer knows what you want. If your lawyer asks you about your money, don't assume the lawyer is being nosey. Don't make assumptions. Ask questions. It is essential that you and your lawyer talk about ALL of your assets, so that the lawyer can write a Will that is appropriate for you and your family, and which accurately, honestly, and legally expresses your intentions. If you don't understand why you are being asked certain questions, ask the lawyer to explain. You are paying the fee. You are entitled to know what you're paying for.

I believe that everyone who writes a Will believes they are doing what is right for their heirs. I believe that most people trust their Wills to carry out their intentions. Often, that doesn't happen. As I see it, the best solution to this kind of problem is to have honest, complete communication among all the people concerned, including your lawyer.

INSURANCE POLICY BENEFICIARY DESIGNATIONS

All insurance policies require that there be named beneficiaries. The naming of contingent beneficiaries is equally important, although often forgotten.

> *Once upon a time, there was an intelligent, very successful man ... a doctor ... who was in the process of completing his estate planning with his lawyer, but no documents had yet been signed. For several years, he had been encouraged by his personal financial planner to take care of his personal legal business, and he chose to ignore the suggestions. After all, he was still young and healthy and had no expectation of a premature death.*
>
> *But, the unthinkable happened. He died suddenly in a biking accident. At the time of his death, he had no Will, and the $250,000 life insurance policy on his life went to his <u>former</u> wife from whom he had been divorced for some years. She was the <u>last</u> person he wanted to have all that money, but he didn't do what was necessary to take care of his personal business.*
>
> *Because this man never signed a Change-of-Beneficiary form, combined with his attitude that there is always more time, his estate plan failed. It happens all the time.*

It is important and necessary for you to review all your beneficiary designations every few years, and especially when there are changes in your life that may affect these designations, including (but not limited to) death, marriage, divorce, remarriage, birth or adoption. If you are uncertain as to who is currently the beneficiary on your various policies, call your insurance agent right away. If you are uncertain as to who is currently the beneficiary of your other financial assets, call your financial planner right away. And if changes are required, make them now.

- Don't forget to check with your employer's human resources department to verify that your beneficiary designations on any company insurance policies or retirement accounts are up to date and exactly as you want them to be.

I recommend that you <u>schedule a specific date every year</u> to check on this very important aspect of your financial planning. Write it on your calendar ... in ink ... and do it without fail.

> *Once upon a time, two men bought a company with money they borrowed from a bank. They each took out separate life insurance policies for $1 million, naming the bank as beneficiary. Their intention was that, until they repaid the entire amount of the loan, the insurance policy would remain that way; and then, when the loan was completely repaid, each man would name his wife as beneficiary. In a few years, the loan was repaid, but they forgot to change the beneficiary designations.*
>
> *One day, a man called their office, and when the secretary asked the caller to state the reason for his call, his reply was, "Insurance." She gave the messages to her bosses, who immediately put them in the trash. No senior executive wants to be bothered by an insurance salesperson. Even when the same man called repeatedly, the men continued to ignore the calls ... that is, until one day when their secretary politely asked the caller to be more specific in his reason for calling, saying that if she could give her bosses more information, they might be inclined to return his call.*
>
> *It turned out that the man was calling to remind the men to change the beneficiary designations on those $1 million insurance policies from the bank to their wives. You can believe that the men were interested in speaking to him then.*

There are two sides to this story.

    1.   If you are an insurance representative attempting to contact a client for a purpose of this importance, at the very least, state the specific reason for your call. Learn how to communicate fully, especially with the assistant to a senior executive who relies on his/her assistant to carefully screen calls. Everyone will benefit.

    2.   If you are the person being called, don't automatically assume the insurance representative is trying to sell you something. The reason for the call could turn out to be something important.

WHAT ABOUT BENEFICIARIES OF EMPLOYER-SPONSORED RETIREMENT PLANS?

> *This matter of beneficiary designations is so important that the U. S. Supreme Court heard a case about it as recently as 2009. The matter had been in litigation for several years before it ultimately ended up in the Supreme Court. In* Kennedy vs. Plan Administrator for DuPont Savings and Investment Plan, *the Court unanimously held that a divorce decree that included a waiver of one spouse's rights in the other spouse's retirement benefits under a qualified retirement plan subject to the Employee Retirement Income Security Act (ERISA) was insufficient to cancel or change an existing beneficiary designation.*

OK, skipping past the legalese, what does this mean for you? Simply stated, it means that if you are in the process of getting a divorce, or if you are already divorced, you had better speak with your divorce lawyer, your tax lawyer <u>and</u> your financial planner to see if all your ducks are in order regarding designations of beneficiaries under your employer-sponsored retirement plan(s). THIS IS NO PLACE TO MAKE A MISTAKE!

It is clear that if the U. S. Supreme Court heard the case, it must be important. And, if this matter was in litigation for several years, and ended up in the Supreme Court, who do you think made a lot of money out of it? *Just asking ...*

> ***A lawyer with his briefcase can steal more money than a hundred men with guns.***
>
> Mario Puzo

BANKRUPTCY

Bankruptcy is a legal situation in which a person or an organization cannot repay the debts it owes to its creditors. As such, it is both a legal and a financial matter. And, don't forget about personal consequences of bankruptcy. I chose to include bankruptcy here in the FINANCIAL chapter because the root cause of the situation is money, but it is another one of the situations that is intertwined among legal, financial and personal matters.

In most cases, bankruptcy is initiated by the debtor (a voluntary bankruptcy), although creditors may file a bankruptcy petition against a business or corporate debtor (an involuntary bankruptcy) in an effort to collect at least a portion of what they are owed. An involuntary bankruptcy petition may not be filed against an individual debtor who is not engaged in business.

Some assets are considered exempt from bankruptcy proceedings and will not be lost in the bankruptcy transaction. The law allows you to keep basic possessions and assets to enable you to move forward. Exempt property cannot be used to pay your creditors' claims. If you are contemplating bankruptcy, I recommend you retain the services of a lawyer who specializes in bankruptcy. Be prepared to discuss with your lawyer a list of each item you will be claiming as exempt, including a description and the fair market value of each item. The list will be included in your Bankruptcy Petition, and will allow the court, the trustee, and your creditors to evaluate your case. If no one objects to the items on your list within a specific amount of time after the meeting with your creditors, the property listed will be declared exempt and will therefore be excluded as an asset with which to pay your creditors.

There are six types of bankruptcy under the Bankruptcy Code, located at Title 11 of the United States Code, although Chapters 7, 11 and 13 are the most well known.

In **Chapter 7**, a debtor surrenders his/her non-exempt property to a bankruptcy trustee who then liquidates the property and distributes the proceeds to the debtor's unsecured creditors.

In exchange, the debtor is entitled to a discharge of some debts. Chapter 7 relief is available only once in any 8-year period. Generally, a trustee will sell most of the debtor's assets to pay off the creditors; however, certain of the debtor's assets are protected to some extent, including Social Security payments, unemployment compensation, and limited values of the equity in a home, car, truck, household goods and appliances, trade tools, and books. These exemptions vary from state to state.

Chapter 11 is generally known as corporate bankruptcy, used primarily by business debtors, but sometimes by individuals with substantial debts and assets. It allows for financial reorganization in order to continue to function while debt repayment plans are followed.

Chapter 13 is wage-earner bankruptcy, rehabilitation with a payment plan for individuals with a regular source of income, which allows them to develop a plan to repay all or part of their debts. Chapter 13 relief is only available to individuals with regular income, and whose debts do not exceed prescribed limits. The debtor retains ownership and possession of all of his/her assets, but must devote some portion of his/her future income to repaying creditors, generally over a period of 3-5 years, generally not to exceed five years. The amount of payment and period of the repayment plan depend upon a variety of factors.

If you plan to use bankruptcy as the legal avenue to clear up debt, don't do it until you consult with your financial planner and/or attorney. There are financial, legal and personal consequences of bankruptcy, so don't look at bankruptcy as a "get-out-of-jail-free" card that will allow you to go right back into debt. And, remember, you cannot have student-loan debt excused in a bankruptcy action.

If your good name and credit are important to you, and if you hope to be able to buy a house or other large item in the future, your FICO score will be seriously damaged by bankruptcy. Know that there are often other, better, ways to eliminate debt.

DON'T TRY TO FIGURE THIS OUT ALL BY YOURSELF.

And, don't walk into a lawyer's office and say you want him/her to represent you in a bankruptcy action until you have thoroughly investigated every other possible option. Unfortunately, there are people who live a life of almost continuous overspending, and use bankruptcy as the means to get out of repaying their creditors. They are often people who are referred to as being "judgment proof" … that is, they own no assets in their own name, so they don't really care if the court or creditors threaten to take away their assets because they don't have any assets in the first place.

Bankruptcy Fraud: Bankruptcy fraud is a white-collar crime, and is a federal crime. It typically involves concealment of assets or destruction of documents, conflicts of interest, fraudulent claims, false statements and fee-fixing for redistribution agreements. Falsification on bankruptcy forms constitutes perjury.

SIMPLY PUT, DON'T DO IT.

ANNUITIES

I once asked an annuity salesman how he determines which annuity to sell to each person. His answer may shock you. He said:

"The one that pays me the biggest commission." OUCH!

An annuity is an investment contract between you and a life insurance company. You invest money (either a lump sum or a premium payment) with a life insurance company, and in exchange for your investment, the insurance company promises to make payments to you at some point in the future (for example, when you retire). Notice that I said <u>insurance company</u>. While an annuity is, in fact, an investment product, it is not an investment product like stocks and bonds, and it is not regulated by the SEC. An annuity is only as good as the insurance company that issues it.

<u>Annuities vary greatly when it comes to the details.</u> You probably shouldn't consider buying an annuity unless you're already contributing the maximum to your IRA or 401(k) every year. Unfortunately, that doesn't keep some people from being influenced to buy an <u>in</u>appropriate annuity, often at one of those "free lunch seminars."

There are both advantages and disadvantages to annuities, and it is important that you know which is which. And, don't buy an annuity without first consulting with an experienced financial professional who can explain the benefits and problems with annuities in such a way that you have a basic understanding of how they work. It isn't the same as buying stock. Be careful.

FAMILY MONEY

- Did you pay for your children's college expenses and weddings, buy them cars, give them trips to foreign destinations to help them grow into well balanced adults?

- Did you ever co-sign for a loan for anyone in your family, only to find they have defaulted and you are left holding the bag?

- Do you, now in your 60's, find yourself financially *"sandwiched"* between your children and your parents, and as a result, short of money for your own needs?

- Do you have one or more of your young adult children living with you since they graduated from college because they cannot find jobs and they have no money of their own?

- Have you had to financially assist your now-elderly parents in order for them to maintain a good quality of life as their assets have dwindled?

- Do you now find yourself financially assisting your young adult children as a result of their own poor money management and absence of planning about money?

- Is your daughter now divorced, with a baby, only a few years after the big wedding you are still paying for? Are you assisting her financially? Are she and the baby now living with you on a more-or-less permanent basis? Are their living expenses cutting into the money you were planning to use for your retirement?

- Are you the primary child-care person(s) for your grandchild because your children cannot afford day-care?

- If you were to find yourself financially destitute in your old age, will you be able to move in with one of your children? Will they be able to financially assist you in a time of need?

> So, you ask, ***"Isn't that what people are supposed to do for family, help each other out,***
> ***out of love and concern and respect?"***
>
> Maybe. Maybe not. What do you think?

Is it too late for Baby Boomers to catch up?
Probably not.
But, there is no time to waste. When you are in your 60's, time is the enemy.

So, now that you have been generous with your loved ones, what's left for you? In financially assisting your family, out of love and the very best intentions, have you ignored your own financial needs for your retirement, *always believing you will have more time*, that you will take care of it **later**? After all, retirement is still years from now, isn't it?

- And, then, it hits you! You are 62 and not ready for retirement, and you suddenly (how suddenly?) discover that you are not financially and emotionally prepared for your retirement years. You did what you have always done … you took care of others before yourself, you ignored the reality of your situation, made some questionable choices, and put things off until later.

I urge you to quickly consult with a financial professional to take a good look at
where you've been,
where you are,
and where you are going
in terms of your money and your life.

By consulting with a financial professional, you can determine exactly where you are right now. In addition, *and this is important*, you must also know where you want to go from here. This is where the name of this book comes from: You must know (or at least begin to think about) what you want to do with your life *between now and then*.

I strongly recommend that you don't put off making this appointment until LATER, (*when is "later?"*)**, or until you get around to it** (*you can't use this excuse any longer, because I already gave you your own personal ROUND TUIT*).

You may come away from that appointment upset or exhilarated, anxious or excited to begin a plan for your future; or you may feel a combination of all those emotions. In any event, you will come away knowing where you are and thinking about where you want to go. At least, you will be better informed and educated, and with the beginnings of a plan for the rest of your financial and personal life.

WHAT COULD POSSIBLY BE MORE IMPORTANT?

YOUR PARENTS' MONEY

If your parent(s) live long enough, whether they remain healthy or not, whether they continue living independently or not, and if they are unprepared for their healthcare and living expenses, you may find yourself assisting them with their financial needs … oh, you may not be legally responsible, but morally and ethically. Only you know your personal family situation, so, if your parent(s) are still living, take a close, hard look at your relationship with them.

> *On the Suze Orman TV show of March 3, 2012, a caller asked a question relating to his 60-year old parents' debt of more than $300,000 from a mortgage and credit cards. He asked if he will be responsible for paying any of their debt after they die. Suze's answer to him is no. If his parents die with debt, they will probably have insolvent estates, and the debt will not be repaid. Suze pointed out that his chance of inheriting anything from them is jeopardized.*
>
> *Suze also said the problem is if they don't die. She asked him what will he do if they continue spending at their current level, and if or when they come to him for money to pay their living expenses. What will happen if one or both of them become ill or disabled? What will happen when they retire and run out of money? The mother is already retired; the father wants to retire in 3-5 years. Then what?*
>
> *(Why do Baby Boomers want to retire so young? Just asking …)*
>
> *Suze told the caller that he must sit down with his parents, assure them of his love and concern for them, and tell them in plain language that he will not give or loan them any more money. They are still young enough to be employed doing something, but in 10 or more years, they most likely will not be able to earn money by way of a job. It is time for them to give up spending and figure out how and where they will get money for the rest of their lives.*

What Suze did <u>not</u> say, *but I am adding*, is that the son needs to quickly get his parents to a professional financial advisor who can help them figure out their financial needs and how to deal with all that debt at the age of 60. He should find out if they have all of their estate-planning documents signed and safely filed away. And, at the same time, he needs to begin planning for his own future.

You know that inheritance you have been counting on receiving "when the time comes," money that should rightfully be yours when your parents die, money you were counting on for your own retirement years, and money you were planning to use to pay off your mortgage and credit card debt -- you should probably forget about it.

YOUR INHERITANCE MAY ALREADY BE GONE.

It is entirely possible that your parents have spent much (if not all) of their money by virtue of their having lived a long life. How old were your grandparents when they died? Today, the senior generation is living well into their 80s and 90s. Not all of them are still healthy and vibrant, but they all have one thing in common:

THEY NEED THEIR MONEY TO LIVE ON.

What if the financial mistakes were made by your father, and you find yourself paying for his mistakes?

> *Here you are, in your mid- to late 50s, and your father is single, barely surviving on his Social Security check, his only source of money. He has no pension, no savings, no retirement funds, no investments, NOTHING ... and he can't make ends meet. You have been giving him money for a couple of years, and you are now beginning to fear that he has been spending your money frivolously, and by giving him money, you are jeopardizing your own retirement years and retirement funds. Duh!?!*
>
> *This was the scenario on a recent Suze Orman TV show when a woman asked for Suze's help so she could stop subsidizing her father. He had ignored all her advice through the years to provide for his own retirement, and he is now leaning heavily on his daughter. She loves her father and has been doing her best to help him, but she has reached the end of the road with his need for her financial support.*
>
> *Suze's advice was to give him no more money. She suggested, for example, that this woman go to the grocery store with her father and buy him only the most basic necessities, and that she personally send checks to her father's landlord. Suze told this woman to be brutal, and require her father to live without a phone or cable TV if he couldn't afford it, and hope that he comes to his senses and realizes what he is doing before it is too late.*

Who is the parent and who is the child in this scenario? Isn't the child supposed to learn good money habits from a parent, not the other way around? *Just asking ...*

Even if it was always their intention to leave you a nice inheritance, it may turn out to be impossible because of their own financial needs. I don't have to go into detail about what they need the money for. You already know the kinds of things their money goes to pay.

Often, elderly parents don't talk with their children about their money, particularly widows. Sadly, they have many fears about their money, are embarrassed about some financial mistakes they made in the past, and have some family baggage that gets in the way of honest, complete communication that allow them to put their trust in the wrong place.

> *In the Philadelphia "Inquirer" of April 17, 2011, there was an article about a widow who had $1.2 million when she appointed a lawyer as her agent under a Power-of-Attorney.*
>
> *What happened? He put all of her assets into an **ir**revocable trust, named himself Trustee, and proceeded to take nearly all of her money. The irrevocable trust placed all that money beyond the reach of anyone but the lawyer. [Pay careful attention to that word "irrevocable" – it means just what you think it means - that it <u>cannot</u> be changed.]*
>
> *The woman was very vulnerable. She had an unhappy relationship with her children about her money, so much so that she threatened to leave all her money to charity. When she finally agreed to appoint this lawyer and to the establishment of the trust, her family believed that her money would be protected for the future. They could not have been more wrong. They simply didn't know what they didn't know. He was a lawyer, after all. It only seemed obvious that they would trust him. They were not about to consult another lawyer to check-up on this lawyer. That's ridiculous. Oh, yeah?*

> *The lawyer diverted all but $270,000 of her money for himself. The woman's family has spent years and thousands of dollars in lawyers' fees attempting to get their mother's money back -- in vain, as is often the case, because the person who stole the money has a long history of fraudulent financial transactions. He has many judgments against him, and no one has been able to get anything back from him because he has no assets.*

The article goes on to say that stealing from the elderly is the perfect crime. Millions of elderly Americans are defrauded by lawyers and other trusted advisors or even their own relatives, who will argue they are just doing what is best for the person. One of the reasons the elderly are so vulnerable is because they suffer, to one degree or another, from cognitive decline, and are not always fully aware of details, choices, consequences, etc. The hard reality is that they are "easy targets.

WHERE ELSE MIGHT YOUR INHERITANCE HAVE GONE?

There is one other place where your inheritance may have gone that you may not be thinking about. If one or both of your parents are in a second marriage (or fourth, as was my own father), that inheritance you were counting on may be going to the new spouse. And, don't for a minute assume that spouse is going to feel like sharing that money with you! Maybe. Maybe not. When it comes to money, all bets are off. They may have children of their own from a previous marriage who would get priority.

I know, I know, there are people in second marriages who draw up "mirror" Wills, and agree that they will write the document such that their respective estate will be divided equally among the total number of their children. RIGHT! The day after the first spouse dies, the surviving spouse can change that Will and leave you out! It's been done. It's not illegal.

What they needed was a PreNuptial Agreement, but it's too late for that now.

It is, however, entirely possible for your parent and new spouse to execute a PostNuptial Agreement (that means, an agreement made after the wedding date). *Possible, maybe, but not likely.*

Getting parents to talk about their money in a situation like this will be way beyond difficult, bordering on virtually impossible. But, if you think you can mention it carefully, respectfully, lovingly, go ahead; just don't expect it to go very well. The financial arrangement your parent has with their new spouse may not satisfy you, and it may not even satisfy them, but it is what it is ... that is, until they see a good reason to make changes. That ship has probably sailed.

This is where COMMUNICATION becomes necessary and important, that is, if you can get your parent(s) to even talk about their money and their death. Good luck with that one!

Can you have, or have you already had, the hard conversations with your parents? You know the ones I'm talking about:

- What have they done in the way of estate planning?
- Where are their estate-planning documents?
- Who is their lawyer? Do you know him or her? Do you have their address and phone number?
- Have they signed a Living Will and a Healthcare Power-of-Attorney? Are you their Agent?
- If not, why not? And, who is?
- Do you know that person and the relationship your parents have with that person?
- Who is their Agent under a Durable Power of Attorney? Do you know the person personally?
  (a critical question related to scams)
- Do you know the name and phone number of their financial planner? Do you know him?
- Do you know where your parent(s) keep all the papers related to each money transaction?
- Have your parent(s) been meeting with financial planner(s) and/or insurance salespeople you know nothing about?
- Have your parent(s) shared information with you as to how their money is invested, where it is located, who has access to it?

194

- Do you know the details of the life insurance your parents have? On your father? On your mother?

- Do you know their insurance agent, and have his/her address and phone number.

- Do they have long-term care insurance? If so, where is the money coming from to pay for it? What is the exact coverage? Where is the policy, and what are the details about the issuing company?

- Have they made any funeral plans yet? Do they own a cemetery plot? Where? Where is the Deed?

- Do you know what they want for their funeral and burial?

- Where is the money to come from to pay for their funeral and burial?

- Are you and your siblings in agreement about such things? Do you ever talk about it?

- Are you and/or your siblings assisting them financially? Is there general agreement among your siblings about this arrangement, or is it now or later going to cause family problems that may require legal intervention? Learn to negotiate win-win situations rather than fight about money.

- Are your parents keeping up with their bills?

- Are their tax returns filed on time? Do they have the money to pay their taxes?

- Do you and your siblings take turns having your parent(s) stay with you on some kind of rotation basis?

- Do they have enough money for current living expenses?

- Can they look forward to independent living for the remainder of their lives?

- How is their health?

- Do you know the details of health insurance they have over and above Medicare? Or Medicaid?

- Are they taking their medications properly? Do you know what medications they take, the name of the prescribing physicians, the dosages?

- Do you know their total out-of-pocket expenses for prescriptions and other medical care each year?

- Do you have a current list of the medications they presently take so if you are asked that question in an emergency, you would have a ready list?

- Have you ever gone with them to doctor appointments?

- Do you have the names and phone numbers of all of their medical professionals?

- Are they taking good care of themselves? Eating well, personal hygiene, housecleaning? If not, how can you assist them with these daily needs, either personally or financially?

- How do they get to the grocery store? pharmacy? doctor? hair dresser?

- Have they shown any signs of cognitive decline or disability of any sort?

- Is it time for them to make a change in their living arrangements? A move to a CCRC? A nursing home?

IT IS A MISTAKE TO THINK THESE QUESTIONS CAN BE PUT OFF UNTIL LATER.

If you think there is even the slightest possibility that your parent(s) have money hidden in their house, it would be a good idea to try to get them to talk about it and show you where they have hidden that money or other valuables. It will do you no good if they die and you never find out, and then, some years later, their house is sold, and the new owners decide to renovate and find money or jewelry hidden in the walls, in the back yard, or under the rafters. It's worth a try to get your parent(s) to share this information with you before it's too late.

Before you learn that your parent(s) have parted with their hard-earned savings to some "get rich quick" scheme, or if you believe that they have no estate planning, or if they are remarried and have a living spouse, you may want to discuss their situation with a financial planner and/or an estate lawyer to get some understanding of what you may be up against financially caring for your parents. Do I hear you whining again? *"Oh, but, that will cost me money for the fees!"*
Maybe. Maybe not.
You haven't even asked yet, so the truth is that you don't really know.

So, tell me this: Even if the financial planner charges a fee (which he may not), would you rather **invest** a few hundred dollars for his fee now to protect your parent(s)' money and to educate yourself about possible scenarios, or is it just easier to throw up your hands and forget about it until the time comes. This one I know … sometimes, it's just easier not to bring up the subject if and when your parent(s)' reaction is strong and negative. Give it your best, and don't beat yourself up if your parents refuse to discuss these things with you. It happens. Just remember two things:

1. THAT MONEY COULD BE YOUR INHERITANCE
and
2. IT'S ONLY MONEY.

COGNITIVE DECLINE

There is a growing body of evidence suggesting that the brains of aging people are not well suited to making financial decisions. Many seniors suffer from some degree of cognitive impairment that will affect how they manage their money. Keep in mind that time is of the essence, and you may encounter strong resistance from your parent(s) who may accuse you of being nosey, or worse, of trying to steal their money. Firmly but lovingly assure them you are just trying to be prepared for any situation that may happen in the future.

Of course, chances are good your parent(s) will refuse to have the conversation with you in the first place, and will deny that they need help. Even so, you must do whatever it takes to help them with their money so it will be there when they need it, if only to pay their funeral bill. And, if your attempts fail, it may be necessary to let the situation be as it is, for better or for worse. Your parents need your love and support, even if they choose to do things which you know are not in their best interests.

Following are some suggestions for you to pay attention to as your parents age:

1. Get them to have a financial check-up. After all, they have regular medical check-ups, so why not examine their finances. Both are vitally important to their future.

2. Do you know the names of their personal financial planner and lawyer? Have you ever met them? You might want to get to know them before a crisis happens in your parents' lives so that you will feel comfortable consulting with them now and in the future.

3. If your parents will allow it, take the time to examine their estate-planning documents to be sure that they are current and exacting, and determine if your parent(s) have a good understanding of what the documents will do for them now and after their death.

4. Are you their Executor? If not, why not? Do you know who is? Did they name a Substitute Executor?

5. If they have no documents, or if their documents need updating or revising, a consultation with a lawyer is required as soon as possible. You should be present at that meeting. There could come a day when one or both of your parents would be unable to sign their name because of physical, mental, or legal incompetence. Do not procrastinate and think it can be done later.

6. This might be a good time to include a discussion with your parent(s) and their lawyer about executing a Revocable Living Trust if they have not already done so. The process of establishing such a trust has a particular benefit in that it requires an examination of every account and asset so each can be retitled. This presents not only an opportunity to take a serious look at the existing accounts in order to retitle them, but allows their financial planner to look at everything they have to see if their investments are appropriate and producing the desired results.

7. Find out if your parents have Durable General Powers-of-Attorney for assets, and if you are their designated Agent. And, if not, why not, and who is? This is a conversation best had with your parents, their lawyer and you, all being present at the same time.

8. While you're at it, check into who they have named as Agent under their healthcare documents, too. If it is necessary and appropriate to make changes, don't delay. If you are the person designated for these various responsibilities, have the hard conversations with your parents so you can know what they want and don't want for healthcare in the future. And, if you are not their designated Agent, why not? Who is? Do you know that person? Do you trust them to handle the extreme medical situations that can happen to your parents in the future?

9. Find out where your parents keep their estate-planning documents and other important papers. Ask if they have a safe deposit box at a bank, and get the details.

10. After close examination of their present accounts, it would be wise to simplify them. Have a discussion with their financial planner about putting their investments into "cruise control" mode to reduce the need for your parents to actively participate in the decision-making process about their investments. By the time your parents are in their late 70's, they should at least have given up the idea of "day trading" in favor of accepting professional guidance. Some of their investments could be put into financial vehicles that will give them money that shows up on a regular basis without their having to do anything to make it happen.

11. See that all of their money comes to them via electronic deposit, including Social Security checks. Prepare a list of all their money that comes to them automatically, including sources, dates, and amounts.

12. Ask about how much money they spend every week buying lottery tickets? Some parents will argue that it's none of your business, that it is their hobby, that it gives them a little pleasure to scratch off those little cards in the hope of winning a few dollars. Some parents will be very annoyed that you even asked. Just feel your way around the subject in a way that is sensitive and respectful.

13. While it may not be entirely possible, do your best to protect them from scams. The elderly are especially vulnerable to a soft-sell approach. While they are afraid of losing their money, they often settle for get-rich-quick schemes without first asking or telling you. And, if they are victimized by scam artists, they are ashamed and embarrassed, so they might not even tell you until their money situation becomes a crisis.

14. Be aware that your parents will often deny that they are losing cognitive capacity. They will not easily accept your questions, your suggestions, your coaching, or the transfer of responsibility from them (as parents) to you.

15. Work only with a financial planner who is a fiduciary. Look for a financial planner who is somewhat younger, who is current on the laws, and who will still be in business when needed the most. I say this with all due respect to older financial planners and/or lawyers with whom your parents may have worked for years, but it is also true that they may not be as sharp as they had been years before, and may not be current with laws relating to investments. *Just one more thing to think about ...*

16. It may be necessary for you to put some formal, legal safeguards in place in their bank and investment accounts to prevent them from withdrawing large amounts of money.

17. Whether your parents have long-term care insurance or not, it is important that you talk with them about the kinds of care they want and how that care will be paid for. Nursing home expenses will eat up their assets in a hurry if there has been no effort put into preserving those assets. Consult with a financial professional you trust to examine their present situation and provide guidance for their future.

18. Try to ascertain how much they regularly spend for food, transportation, prescriptions, out-of-pocket medical expenses. Ask them if they need help writing checks and if their bills are current. Look around their house to see if there are piles of unopened mail (bills).

19. Assess your parent(s)' living situation to determine if they are finding it hard to live by themselves. Don't expect this to be an easy conversation. Ask them if it is time to move to a continuing care retirement community. Ask yourself what <u>you</u> think about it. This kind of change in living arrangement will cost money, so you will need to have a general idea of their financial situation. And, if it is decided that they are going to move out of the house they have lived in for many years, be ready, willing, and able to assist them at every step of the way. Are there others in the family willing and able to help?

20. DO IT NOW. If you are a Baby Boomer and your parents are living, that means they are probably older than 80 years of age. There is no more time to procrastinate.

---

1. There will come the day when it's too late for the conversations.

2. There will be many people who have not done what is necessary because it is easier to ignore it all.

3. You've heard all this before.

YOUR CHILDREN'S MONEY

If you are a Baby Boomer, most of your children are young adults by now. How are they doing financially?

1. If your children learned how to handle money from observing how you do it, there could be problems. You know that you spent too much and saved too little. Are they doing the same thing?

2. You asked very little (if anything) from them in exchange for your financial generosity. So, if they have a sense of entitlement, where do you think they learned it?

3. Did they earn their own money to pay for college? Or did they do what so many others have done, which is to incur student loans that will take years to pay off? Whose idea was that, anyway? Did you and your children just follow the crowd to the student loan office? How much time and effort did you and your children spend investigating other financial and educational opportunities for their education?

4. Did you buy cars for your children? Who paid for them? Who paid for the insurance and maintenance? Whose name is on the title?

5. Did your children have jobs when they were young? Did they cut grass or shovel snow? When they were old enough, did they have a part-time job to pay for their own expenses, put gas in the car, buy their own clothes?

6. Did you ever find yourself in the terrible, heartbreaking position of having to post bail for one of your children who broke the law (DUI, for example)? Retail theft? Drugs? Did you require them to pay you back? If not, why not?

7. Do you have a disabled child with huge financial needs? Have you explored every possible avenue for resources to assist you with all the expenses associated with the child's disability? If not, why not? Get help. It's out there ... you just have to find it, because it won't come knocking on your door any day soon.

8. Have you provided for financial security for your disabled child after your death? This is not an easy thing, but one that must be addressed before it is too late.

- Let me tell you a very sad story about a man who believed he had done what was necessary to take care of his adult special-needs son when the father died. This will make you sad and mad at the same time. I have repeated this story from the LEGAL chapter because I think it is so important.

> *Once upon a time, there was a man, a widower in his middle 80's, who had a son who was in his 50's. The son had severe learning disabilities, and the father and son were inseparable, lifelong pals, especially after the man's wife passed away. This was the man's only child, and he wanted to be assured that his son would be personally and financially secure after he, himself, died.*
>
> *So, he consulted with financial and legal advisors to put into place an extremely safe, very original estate plan to care for his son after he, himself, died. The father's estate plan gave his home and all of his money, in trust, to a local organization that provided group housing for disabled adults, with the agreement that his son would continue to live in the family home for the remainder of his life, and upon the son's death, the organization would then become the sole owner of the house and any money that was left over.*
>
> *You see, although the financial planner came up with the plan, he could not prepare the documents. Only the lawyer could do that. Despite the repeated urgings of the financial planner to his client to keep reminding the lawyer to put the plan on paper, the client always said, "Oh, I don't want to bother him. He's a busy man." He apparently lost site of the fact that the plan was only an idea until it was committed to paper. He thought there would always be more time. The man also apparently lost sight of the fact that he was then 80 years of age, and his son was 50, and that time was of the essence.*
>
> *It doesn't really matter why he didn't <u>insist</u> that the lawyer prepare the documents; the fact is that the man died without the plan ever having been formalized. The son ended up living in an assisted living residence (also known as a nursing home), which is exactly what the father did NOT want to happen. The son did not adjust well to the unfamiliar surroundings without his father, and was obliged to move to a different facility once or twice. Neither the son nor the organization ever got the opportunity that the father intended. The son died only a few years later.*
>
> *What happened to the plan, you ask? Nothing. Absolutely nothing. Why? Because the father's Lawyer never prepared the documents necessary to bring this plan into being.*

Whose fault was this?

---

9. Did you pay for your only daughter's wedding (or all of her weddings)? How much did it cost you? Did you have any say in the wedding expenses?

10. If you have more than one daughter, did you pay for the weddings of all of them?

11. Did you contribute financially to the wedding(s) of your son(s)? If not, why not? Oh, right, there is that old-fashioned idea that the bride's family pays. *Time for that myth to go away forever.*

12. Did you pay for any one or more of your children's divorces? *How much did that end up costing you?*

13. Did you ever take the time to have a financial-planning meeting with your children to educate them about earning their own money, balancing a checkbook, saving, budgeting, etc? *No, I didn't think so.*

14. Did your child marry a person with a similar financial background and situation, such that they are already behind the financial 8-ball early in their adult life? Do each of them have student loan and credit card debt? Do they both have car payments? Do they have jobs that pay them salaries in proportion to their education, jobs that will enable them to keep up with their debt payments?

15. How do they expect to be able to pay for the big house they bought? *Where did they learn that one?*

16. Do they know what it costs to maintain a big house?

17. Is their mortgage on that big house under water, to the point of possibly losing it to foreclosure?

18. And, now, in your "golden years," do you find yourself raising another family? *What do you mean?* I'm talking about the fact that your adult children are in such a financial bind that both of them must work full time just to pay the bills, and their children are in need of day care, and they can't afford it, so you have become their primary child-care person? How does that feel? Do you feel that your children are taking advantage of you? I know you love your grandchildren and you love spending time with them, but every day, all day? *Not what you expected, is it?*

19. If your children are in their early 30s and already heavily in debt, married with children already, what kind of financial future do you see for them? Arguing about money is often the cause of divorce. Have your adult children taken too big a bite out of the apple? Do you see your adult children being mature and responsible enough to have the painful conversations about money and still have their marriage survive? Be honest, now, if only for your own peace of mind.

20. Are any of your children married to spouses who had been previously married, who have children from that first marriage for which they are obligated to pay court-ordered child support? How are they working out their respective financial obligations? Have they even talked about it?

21. Did your children have PreNuptial Agreements in place before the weddings? What did you think of that possibility? Did you ever talk about the document with your children? Did you arrange for them to consult with your lawyer about the benefits of having a PreNuptial Agreement, and the consequences of not having one?

YOUR MONEY AND PARTNERS

Money (and other assets) can be owned jointly with another person. That person could be your spouse or a person with whom you live in a committed relationship without benefit of clergy, whether heterosexual or homosexual. A partner could be a child, a friend or relative, or someone with whom you entered into a business partnership.

You will remember that elsewhere, I stated that the five parts of this book are inter-connected. Well, this is one of those situations where joint ownership of assets with a partner could have an effect on the legal, financial, funeral/burial, record-keeping, and personal aspects of your life. I had to make a choice about which section in this book to write about this matter, so I chose to put it Chapter I – LEGAL.

OTHER PEOPLES' MONEY

Sometimes, this is referred to as OPM. There are people who manage very nicely living off other peoples' money, almost like the way a parasite lives off another living thing. People who do this are usually very likeable, fun to be around, appear to be living the good life. It is not usually obvious that they don't have money, because, on the surface, it appears they are well off financially.

Their (dirty little) secret is that they are living a lie. Some of them worry that their problems will come crashing down on them one day; others don't even worry. They just keep borrowing money from other people, always with the promise to repay the "loan," but never actually paying it back. I suppose they believe their own lies, not actually aware they are not telling the truth.

In a Frank Sinatra song from the 70s, he asks, *"Why do some people make promises they never intend to keep?"* I don't know. I would not presume to analyze the psychology of this kind of behavior. I just know it causes hard feelings (even financial hardship) among family and friends who loaned money to such a person.

When some people who live on other peoples' money are pressured by one person to repay a debt, they will "borrow" money from someone else, then repay the first person, and round and round it goes. I'm not sure that when the person makes the promise to repay the money, they even mean it. This kind of financial behavior works well until it doesn't.

Mingling your money and your relationship with people like this can get complicated, and the relationship could be destroyed, or at least negatively affected, by such financial transactions. If you enjoy their friendship, keep the relationship separate and don't loan them money. That way, they won't be put in the position of making promises that will not be kept, and you won't be disappointed by their behavior and lack of financial and personal integrity. It is possible to enjoy the person and not their behavior.

GIFTING

Consider the option of "gifting" money to your children today. As of 2013, you can "gift" $14,000 to *anyone*, including each child, each child's spouse, each grandchild ... every year. Know that the amount you are permitted to gift changes over time, so before you start giving your money away, check with your accountant or financial advisor to determine the accurate amount.

And, if your assets are large enough that you can afford to gift some of your money to your family members, it will have the effect of reducing your taxable estate, thus reducing the amount of inheritance and/or estate tax due upon your death, and leaving more money for your beneficiaries. They're pretty good reasons to consider "gifting," don't you think?

> *"Money, pardon the expression, is like manure.*
> *It's not worth a thing unless it's spread around ..."*
>
> Mrs. Dolly Levy in "Hello Dolly"

BUT, BE CAREFUL not to give away so much money that you find yourself short of money for your own life, especially when you consider you might live to be 90 years old. And, if you give more than the $14,000 to any one person, you will incur Gift Tax expense. Know also that the rules periodically change regarding gifting, so don't make any decision without first consulting with a tax lawyer and/or a financial planner.

Why would you want to give some of your money to your heirs now, rather than making them wait until after your death? Because that money, given today while they are younger and struggling to build a life for themselves, may mean more to them now than many times that much later when they may not really need the money. And, besides, you will be alive to watch them enjoy your gift.

NOTE: There is another aspect of gifting I want you to think about. Everyone knows that people enjoy receiving gifts of money, but if you don't have money to give, give the gift of your time and knowledge, and the gift of yourself, your family stories, your family photographs. Take your loved ones to places that don't cost very much money … the library, the zoo, fishing, the beach, museums. You know what I'm talking about. Give the gift of yourself while you have time to share the experience. Someday, it will be too late.

HAVE YOU MADE GIFTS or LOANS TO YOUR CHILDREN?

One mistake that can seriously diminish your own retirement money, although made with love and the very best of intentions, is your making large gifts or loans to your children. Follow this scenario:

- One of your sons asks you to loan him $100,000 to start a new business. *"Sure,"* you say.
- Then your other son asks for the same amount to put down on a new house. *"Sure*, you say.

You feel good that you are in the financial position to assist your sons. Yet, in those two personal financial transactions, you have reduced your nest egg by $200,000.

"What? Not to worry, they'll pay me back," you say.

Oh, yeah? When? How? Under what terms and conditions? Do you have it in writing? Did you ask them to sign promissory notes?

Did you even talk about it with them? Did you say to them? *"Here is $200,000 that is not to be returned. It is my gift to you."* Or, did you say, *"Here is $200,000. When may I expect you to pay this money back to me?"* Or, did you just give them the money without any conversation about repayment?

CAN YOU SEE THE POTENTIAL PROBLEMS?

- Did you consult with your financial planner or lawyer before giving your sons the money?
- Did you ask either (both) to sign some kind of writing wherein they agreed to pay you back?
  An Agreement? A Promissory Note?
- Did you establish a plan for repayment of this money?
  (monthly payments, interest rate, length of the loan, for example?)
- Did you intend the money to be gifts or loans?
- Did you specifically state whether it was a gift or a loan?
- Did you expect any of that money to ever be repaid?
- Did you think about and/or pay Gift Tax?
- Do your sons assume the money was a gift?
- Did your sons express intent to repay you?
- Did either or both of your sons misinterpret your generosity; that is, if it was a loan, did they think it was a gift, or the reverse?
- Do either or both of your sons have bad credit, or a history of not paying their bills on time?
- Do either of your sons live from paycheck to paycheck?
- Do either of your sons have a partner (wife, fiancé, girlfriend) who has incurred credit card debt because she shops to make herself happy? Has your son assisted her financially on a regular basis?
- Are either of your sons paying child support for his children in one family, while raising a second family?

- What if your son's business fails and he can't pay you back?

- What if your other son gets a divorce, or goes into foreclosure or bankruptcy, loses the house and can't pay you back?

- What if one son pays you back and the other does not?

- Do each of your sons know about the money you gave to your other son?

- If so, did they express any unexpected emotions (surprise, for example)?

- What if you need that money for your own life in retirement?

- Will your sons give you financial assistance in your retirement years if/when you run out of money?

- If either or both of your sons agreed to pay you back, have you ever seen any of that money?

If there comes a place in time when you can see that they cannot ever pay you back, or worse, have no intention of paying you back, you must declare that money as having been a gift. Hard as that may be, you must do it for yourself and for your relationship with them. In addition, you must clearly <u>tell</u> them (or the one who has not paid you back) that you have decided that the money is to be thought of as a gift and not to be repaid, even if that was never your intention. (After all, you know now that you won't ever see that money again). Once you have told them that the money is a gift, you must <u>never</u> again bring up the subject of that money. The subject is to be considered closed forever.

There may be emotional upset when you discover that your son(s) will not be paying you back the money you so generously gave to them when they asked. Keep in mind that if you did not specify repayment terms, you are partially responsible. But, try your very best to forgive yourself if you feel you were taken advantage of, for being a "nice guy." At the same time, try your very best to forgive your son(s) for their lack of integrity in the transaction.

If you tell him (or them) that the money is a gift, you do it so that the transaction doesn't control you. You must never allow money to exercise control over you, no matter what. If it's going to be a block between you and a loved one, either declare it a gift, or drop the subject entirely and let it go, the same way you would let go of a string holding a helium balloon.

First people. Then money. Money and family usually don't mix well.

Can you see how you may have financial problems in your retirement years because of the way your family handled money?

- The inheritance you were anticipating may be gone.

- You gave your children a great deal of money through the years, and now you find yourself with little for yourself in retirement?

So, you can blame the government, or your former employer, or your parents, or the weather for your lack of money in your golden years, but you know that part of that blame belongs to you. And, I don't see what you will gain from playing the blame game.

NOW WHAT?

NOW IS THE TIME TO DO SOMETHING ABOUT YOUR FINANCIAL SHORTFALL. Do what, you say? I don't know, but I recommend you meet with a qualified financial professional and figure it out before it's too late.

- Question: Did you ever pay for your adult children to meet with a financial planning professional to get a good, financial head start in their adult lives? No, I didn't think you did that either? If you are a Baby Boomer with young adult children, you might consider giving them the gift of professional financial planning. It could make all the difference between their financial success or failure in their adult lives.

Your children needed financial education before they went to college or before they got married. But, it's not too late. The one thing young people have going for them is TIME! Time to recover from mistakes of the past. Maybe some of those mistakes were yours. What you don't want to do is point fingers or assign blame. You want to assist your children in the best way possible, and you might even learn something yourself.

You know that your children's future financial situation is uncertain, considering the economic situation of the world. Who knows what will happen? No one. But, a good place for them to begin their adult lives is to consult with a financial planner who can be their own personal GPS … to guide them along the route to financial security in their later years. Wouldn't this be a better gift than something you bought in a store?

LIFE INSURANCE

One of the first things to know about buying life insurance is that the man (husband) will usually do his best to resist buying it, even when he knows his spouse and family want and need the financial protection insurance will offer them after his death, even though he knows that statistically, women outlive men. Men selfishly figure that they, themselves, will never see the benefit of all those premiums, so there is no need. Wrong!

A man's unwillingness to talk about his own death often keeps him from buying life insurance to financially protect his family after his death. If your spouse and/or children count on you for their financial survival, and if you leave them no life insurance, are you saying that you are willing to leave your widow in such a bad financial position, that she will need to marry another man … *any man* … just to help her pay her bills? Know this: The more important you are in the life of another person, the greater the void you will leave behind for them to contend with after your death. If your family counts on you to take care of them now, you must also do it after your death, and life insurance is one way to ensure your family will be financially protected.

> *Once upon a time, a 70 year old man had a fatal heart attack while driving. He had been retired for many years, and was living off the proceeds of a small pension and Social Security. The man never felt obligated to even get a part-time job to supplement their income, and was content to let his wife, also in her 70's, work hard operating a small business. She knew they needed more money for their living expenses, but the man seemed oblivious to the reality of their situation.*
>
> *When he died, he had no life insurance because the inexpensive term policy which he had, had lapsed a few years before his death, and besides, by that time, he had become uninsurable because of his age and poor health.*
>
> *His widow was forced to sell her home, give up her business and live in a low-rent apartment. Why? Because her husband made very bad decisions about life insurance in particular, money in general.*

How do you think this man would feel were he alive today to see the financial struggles his wife is experiencing? They had a good loving relationship and family except for the shortage of money, mostly due to his financial choices. Couldn't he have foreseen the possibility of this happening to the woman he loved for more than 50 years? Or did he not even think about it at all?

How do you think the woman feels about her husband's having caused the financial hardship she has experienced since his death? About her inability to live a nice, peaceful life in her older years, without the every-day worry of running out of money, just because he refused to get adequate life insurance to protect her? Angry? Disappointed? Resentful?

More questions than answers. Were their adult children included (welcome) in the discussion about their parents' money? Many parents don't include their adult children in conversations about their money. Each person and family situation is unique, of course, so including your children in every conversation may not be appropriate, but you might want to ask them how they would feel if the couple described above were their parents. How would they feel watching their mother struggle financially at this place in her life.

And, while we're on a roll here, ask your mother if she has life insurance? It's a fair question, don't you think?

- Don't think you can SAVE enough money so that you won't have to buy insurance. How long would it take you to save $100,000? If you had an insurance policy in that amount, and even if it had a brief waiting period until it went into effect, the minute you die after the expiration of that waiting period, the entire amount would be payable to your beneficiaries, tax free.

> There are people who actually believe that they don't need life insurance, that their assets are and will be sufficient to pay for final expenses and death taxes and still have some left over for their loved ones. It

would be a mistake for you to think this without having a thorough discussion with your financial advisor, because you just might be wrong.

- If you own a business or have significant assets which might be liable for death taxes, speak with your financial advisor and lawyer about the possibility of an **ir**revocable life insurance trust. They are not for everybody, but in the right situation, can make an enormous difference to the family you leave behind.

- Don't wait until it's too late to buy affordable insurance. There will come a day when you are uninsurable because of health problems or your age.

- If both spouses are well employed, and the salaries of both are needed to cover their living expenses, it is wise to also insure the life of the wife. If the wife dies before her husband, especially if there are young children, he may find himself without sufficient income or assets to pay for her funeral, pay for childcare and a housekeeper, and maintain his lifestyle, and may be forced to make major changes.

> **Life insurance is an investment, not an expense.**
> **It passes directly to the beneficiary, usually tax-free.**
> **And, no, I don't sell insurance.**

- Thoroughly discuss life insurance needs and options with your financial planner. Appropriate financial plans regularly include life insurance, but not always. Many wealthy people have assets sufficient to rule out life insurance as a viable financial planning tool for themselves and their families. This is not the case with most people, however. It is a subject that requires conversations with your loved ones.

> On Public Television, during their fund-raisers, a financial advisor named Ed Slott has a show about retirement money. He is a serious advocate about the financial and personal benefits of life insurance. I recommend that you watch his TV shows and/or buy his books for more information.

- Don't buy the cheapest policy. You get what you pay for. A friend of mine, many years ago, said, "*It never costs more to go first class.*" He, of course, was referring to the cost of aggravation by choosing to go the least expensive way, believing you were saving money. Maybe you saved a few dollars, but what did that choice *really* cost you, especially if, by choosing the least expensive option, you sacrificed peace of mind, comfort, safety and/or satisfaction.

- Always check the rating of the insurance company. You want to be certain that the company will still be around when the time comes to submit a claim for death benefits. Your financial planner can assist you with this.

- The proceeds of life insurance policies are paid to the named beneficiary or beneficiaries immediately upon the death of the insured, outside of probate. Life insurance passes outside of your Will … the terms of your Will do not include life insurance. The insurance proceeds may not be taxable to your estate or to your beneficiaries.

- When the claim is filed and the check received for the proceeds of the life insurance policy after the death of a person, no one questions if it was a good decision to buy the insurance in the first place.

- If you have a very small estate, with very limited assets, life insurance may be a way for you to provide a nice "inheritance" for your family, or to pay for your funeral.

- Are your beneficiaries listed correctly on your insurance policies? The circumstances of many peoples' lives change over time, such that the people originally named as beneficiaries may no longer be appropriate. If you need to make changes, do it immediately.

- If you are divorced and your former spouse is your primary beneficiary, be sure to change the policy as part of the divorce proceedings unless you want her to get the proceeds when you die. If you do not, make the change right away.

- Even if your beneficiaries are correctly listed, be certain your insurance agent has their correctly spelled names, addresses, and phone numbers. You may also be asked to provide Social Security numbers.

- Have you named <u>contingent</u> beneficiaries on your life insurance? These are the people who will claim the right to the life insurance if the originally named beneficiaries are no longer living at the time of your death. If your original beneficiary predeceases you, and if you have not named contingent beneficiaries, the proceeds of your life insurance will go directly into your estate and be divided according to the terms of your Will (or by the intestate laws of your state). I doubt this was your intention.

- Keep your eye out for changes in your family situations that might affect your life insurance. For example, if your daughter were in the midst of a messy divorce, you might not want her to benefit from an insurance policy on your life in the event of your death; so, instead, you might consider passing the proceeds to her children (your grandchildren). And, something else to consider about giving the money to your grandchildren is the possibility that it could affect their ability to get student loans. And keep in mind that because minor children cannot inherit money, some kind of trust fund or account will have to be arranged for the money they will inherit. This is a serious conversation worth having with your financial planner.

- Never cancel an old policy until you have received your new policy in your hand. It may be tempting to save a few dollars by canceling your old contract as soon as you apply for new insurance, but what if the new company turns you down for health reasons? Or worse, what if you were in a car accident and died before your new policy was issued?

- Once you have received your new life insurance policy and you have verified that all of the information on it is correct, you may want to shred the old policy. At the very least, write something on the front of the policy to indicate that it has been superseded, then sign your name and date. Of course, the insurance company that issued that old policy will have removed it from their records. But, years later, if your executor comes upon that old policy among your personal papers, and if there is nothing written on it to indicate that it is void, it will be his/her responsibility to actively investigate whether or not that policy is in effect at the time of your death. If you replaced it with a new policy, and if your executor does not know this, it will cost your estate money for the time it takes to write to the insurance company. Pay attention to the details of your personal papers.

- It is entirely possible that your financial planner will recommend that you <u>not</u> have life insurance. There are valid reasons for this, and this is a discussion you should have to determine whether or not life insurance will benefit your family and if it fits into your complete financial and estate plans.

- Do you know where the original insurance policies are located? Do your family members (or your executor) know where you keep your life insurance policies? Could they find them on short notice?

    - Prepare a list of every insurance policy, including policy numbers, face amounts, cash values, beneficiaries, contingent beneficiaries, agent's name, address and phone number, etc., and put such information in your 3-ring binder. (See Chapter IV – Record-Keeping.)

    - If you know that the name of the life insurance company changed over the years, be sure to indicate this information in your records. If the company was called ABC Life Insurance Co. when you bought the policy, and since then, it has changed names twice, such that today it is called XYZ Life Insurance Co, if you don't put some kind of notation on the policy about this name change, including the new address and phone number, and new agent (if any), your executor will go on a scavenger hunt in order to put in a claim for the insurance proceeds. Scavenger hunts by executors increase legal fees. *Just one more thing for you to think about.*

- Many life insurance policies are never claimed because family members don't even know the policies exist. Don't let this happen to your family. When you bought the policy, you intended for the insurance proceeds to go to someone in your family, so, at the very least, be sure they know the policy exists and where you keep it

---

On her TV show on July 30, 2011, Suze Orman told of a situation where a woman believed she was buying insurance that provided both a death benefit and a lifetime income. The woman put up $25,000 and received a promise of a 400% increase over time. Shouldn't that have raised a red flag?

After initially speaking with the woman, Suze investigated the insurance and discovered that it had NO income provision, that it was strictly a life insurance policy with a death benefit. The insurance agent had lied.

Suze contacted the insurance company, which, by the way, she stated was reputable (it was the agent who was not), and got all of the woman's money back for her.

What lessons can be learned from this situation?

- Don't part with a large sum of money without knowing exactly what it is for.

- If it seems too good to be true, it probably is. Pay attention to your instincts if they are shouting at you.

- Do your homework about anyone trying to sell you an insurance product for something other than its original purpose.

- Sometimes, you cannot get out of a bad investment. Don't count on Suze Orman to bail you out of a bad deal.

LONG-TERM CARE INSURANCE

For Baby Boomers, it is time to consider whether or not to purchase long-term care insurance. It is often recommended for anyone over 50, who has significant assets to protect in the event of a chronic illness, a desire to maintain independence of care, as well as peace of mind. <u>It is important to be aware of the fact that the laws concerning long-term care insurance change over time and may vary from state to state.</u>

Also know that whether or not you are insurable depends largely upon your health and your age. So, if you think you want or need long-term care insurance, investigate the costs, what it can and cannot do for you, and analyze your personal financial situation with a professional experienced in both insurance and finance.

Long-term care insurance is complicated, and there are no easy, right-or-wrong answers about whether or not you need it. A person who sells long-term care insurance will, of course, tell you that you need it, but don't be fooled. That salesperson stands to earn a very large commission by selling you insurance coverage you may not need. They are not bad people, just people trying to earn a living. But, the fact is they may not be qualified to accurately assess your needs. This subject is too important to discuss only with an insurance salesperson. You need to also discuss it with your financial planner.

If you decide to become a resident of a Continuing Care Retirement Community (CCRC), they may require that you have long-term care insurance. Verify this before selling your house and making the move.

<u>Good news</u>: Long-term care and long-term care insurance are expensive, so there is a movement in the insurance industry to encourage people to convert their life insurance to pay for long-term care as an alternative to abandoning their policies. This is something that could make a big difference in your life, and I urge you to discuss it with your financial planner and insurance professional to learn about the benefits of this financial opportunity.

LONGEVITY INSURANCE

Just when you think there can't possibly be another kind of insurance, the industry creates still one more. I'm referring to what is called Longevity Insurance, which has grown out of the fact that many Baby Boomers will live to 85 years of age or older, and will run out of money.

This insurance product is new, and sounds like a life preserver for Baby Boomers who are afraid of running out of money before they die. But, before you call your insurance agent and buy some, remember that Reverse Mortgages were also sold as life preservers, too. In fact, Reverse Mortgages in the right circumstances, can be valuable, the operative words here being "in the right circumstances," but they can also create problems you could not have anticipated. I believe the same thing applies to this new Longevity Insurance.

- Keep in mind that I don't sell insurance. I don't get a commission from anything relating to insurance. I'm just passing this new information to you to investigate for yourself in case it will be of benefit to you and your family.

Longevity insurance is an annuity. Annuities have a less-than-sterling reputation, mostly, in my opinion, because they are often sold by people who are interested in making a big commission, and who are not qualified financial professionals acting as fiduciaries (that is, in your best interests).

Here's how it works. You give a sum of money to an insurer (say $50,000 or $100,000) when you are in your 60s in exchange for monthly payments that begin coming back to you at age 80 or 85 and continue for the rest of your life. Now, doesn't that sound like it has possibility?

If you have no pension and if your own investment/retirement account has been diminished by the economy, it might be good for you to look into. But be diligent in your research. Be patient before signing anything. Check it out.

OTHER INSURANCE

While you are discussing insurance with your financial planner, take the time to look into other types of insurance coverage that may or may not be necessary and appropriate for you and your family, depending upon your circumstances, including (but not necessarily limited to):

- Automobile (other vehicle) insurance
- Disability insurance
- Flood insurance
- Health insurance
- Homeowners' insurance
- Liability insurance
- Personal Unemployment Insurance
- Renters' insurance if you are a tenant
- Travel insurance (when appropriate). More about this in Chapter V – PERSONAL LIFE.
- Vacant house insurance and other appropriate insurance if you are a landlord

Review your insurance needs periodically, as market values change, and as your life circumstances change. When your insurance agent or financial planner calls you to schedule an appointment to review your insurance coverage, don't automatically assume he is just trying to make a commission. You may be surprised at what you will find out about new products and new coverage that can benefit you and your family.

**If you don't like paying for insurance,
think about the replacement costs of everything you could potentially lose if you didn't have insurance.**

VIATICALS

Technically, this name refers to viatical life insurance settlements. The word viatical comes from the Latin word *viaticum*, which means to be given a stipend or a living expense for your journey or your travels. Translated, it means that you will be given money to sustain you for the rest of your life.

Here's how it works. A person, who may or may not be terminally ill (known as the seller/owner of a life insurance policy) sells his/her policy to another person (buyer/investor) for a price less than the face value of the policy, for which the seller is paid cash. The buyer/investor, looking upon the transaction as an investment, is gambling that the seller/owner won't live long, and then, when the seller/owner dies, the buyer/investor is paid the full value of the policy by the life insurance company.

Why would anybody do this? For the money. The seller/owner needs the money, and the buyer investor hopes to profit by the transaction.

> **A WORD OF CAUTION**. Viaticals are another one of those financial products that are presented to seniors as a be-all/end-all solution to financial problems. If you have elderly parents, be on the look-out for any hint that they have contracted for this kind of "investment." It could turn out to be a financial mistake that cannot be corrected.

It is often seen as a win-win situation for both seller and buyer. Sometimes, however, the seller doesn't die quickly, and the buyer/investor has to wait a longer-than-anticipated amount of time to collect on his/her investment. Even so, he will eventually collect the death benefit of the policy.

One category of people can be seen as losing in the deal: the beneficiaries of the life insurance policy. They will never collect the amount originally intended for them by the seller/owner of the policy. For this reason, viaticals are often arranged by people who have no beneficiaries. If you are considering selling your life insurance policy, you may want to discuss this matter with them beforehand. If your family sees that you are in a serious financial position, they may actually encourage you to sell in order to obtain cash to continue living at a reasonable standard of living. Don't assume anything, however. Have the "hard" conversations.

When a person sells his/her insurance policy for cash, they are often doing it because they really need money to pay medical bills or living costs until their death, which, as said above, is expected in the not-too-distant future. The person who sells his/her insurance policy is often terminally ill and not expected to live much longer. Other times, the seller may not be terminally ill, but is up in years and in desperate need of cash for medical or other living expenses.

Viatical settlements gained popularity in the early 1980s when AIDS became well known as a disease that brought death relatively quickly. Some AIDS patients sold their life insurance policies for less than face value in order to get cash to pay their medical bills and/or living expenses. Later, the industry expanded to include other terminally ill people, especially cancer patients.

Viatical settlements probably aren't right for the majority of people, whether a buyer or a seller. If you are considering investing in this kind of transaction, or if you are thinking about selling a life insurance policy, don't do it without first consulting a financial planner and/or a tax lawyer.

A down-side of receiving the cash payment is that the amount of money may be taxable, so be sure to verify this with your tax adviser; but, realistically, if the person needs the money and is soon to die anyway, taxes may be the least of his/her worries.

And, if you are planning to sell your policy, know that there is a history of fraud and misrepresentation, as some dealers in viaticals seriously misrepresent the expected returns. There are no recognized national standards for this kind of transaction, and not every state regulates the investments.

It is not necessary that you be dying to sell your life insurance policy this way. Take for example the 85-year old man whose $500,000 term life insurance policy was set to end in 2 years. He was able to sell it for $350,000, pocketed the money, and has since outlived the term of the policy, which means that the buyer (investor) got nothing. And, even though his beneficiaries will not receive the entire proceeds of the insurance policy, having the cash enabled this man to live out the remainder of his life in comfort, and the money he left behind went to his heirs anyway.

BE CAREFUL AND DO YOUR HOMEWORK.

This is not an investment to jump into without knowing the facts.

CASH SETTLEMENTS

If you anticipate receiving a large settlement from an insurance company or a law suit, but you know that settlement is years away, it is possible for you to obtain a portion of the anticipated settlement funds early. There are companies that "buy" the settlement funds from you. They are sometimes referred to as life settlements.

The company will evaluate the net present value of the settlement and offer you a portion of the whole settlement. When the case is settled, they will get the difference. The company is willing to wait, but if you don't want to wait for the money, or are strapped for cash, it may be something to look into.

In the insurance industry, such transactions are frowned upon … as are the viaticals mentioned above. But, if you believe in freedom of choice, what is so terrible for a person to sell something that is theirs to someone else who wants to buy it, if the terms and conditions are agreeable to both parties, and if the "buyer" (the company) is legitimate? *Just asking ...*

There are legitimate firms that buy insurance and law-suit settlements in situations described above. Just do your homework, and ask for guidance from a reputable financial professional before signing anything.

Be careful to whom you are "selling" your insurance or law-suit settlement. There are scammers who are hungry for your money. Just be sure that you are not so hungry that you will make a **"ready-fire-aim"** decision. *What?*

- *Read that again. Shouldn't it be "ready-aim-fire?" Well, yes, it should be, but sometimes, people fire before they aim, and the consequences can be most unsatisfactory.*

HOME EQUITY LOANS

Let's not forget those parasitic financial transactions known as home equity loans. Here is my personal definition of a home equity loan:

A financial transaction whereby you pay money to the bank
for the "privilege" of borrowing your own money.

OK, so that's just my personal definition of this type of money transaction. In 1990, I wanted to open a flower shop. The mortgage on my house had been paid in full for 7 years. Seeing that we had no mortgage, the bank was eager to give us a $50,000 home-equity loan to open the business. It seemed like a good idea at the time.

OUCH! It makes me nauseous to even remember it.

Today, even though I no longer have the flower shop, I still have a mortgage. I've refinanced that mortgage three times since 1990 in order to reduce the interest rate. The monthly payments are low, and we get the interest as a deduction on our US Income Tax Return, but if I had really understood the consequences of a home equity loan, and if I knew then what I know now, I may have figured out another way to finance the flower shop. Oh, the benefit of 20-20 hindsight. *And I have not changed my opinion of home-equity loans.*

As I stated earlier, never borrow money (that is, take out a home-equity loan) against your house to pay off credit card debt.

Never borrow money against your house to buy growth-related investments, no matter how good the idea sounds. It's very easy to lose that borrowed money in a bad market, and there you are, in debt to the bank with nothing to show for it.

Not long ago, people looked at their homes as their own personal ATM machines. Need money for a new car? Get it from the home equity line of credit. Need money for a new kitchen, or that new addition to the house, or college education or weddings for your kids? Get it from the home equity line of credit.

That financial stream has pretty much dried up. And, what does it leave you with? A second mortgage on your house, which, in your 60's, is not a good thing. If you can, pay it off as soon as possible. You may have an investment that is not doing well, and it could possibly be liquidated to pay the balance of that home equity loan. But, don't make this decision without a consultation with a financial professional.

One way or the other, sooner or later, you will have to pay it off, even if the debt is paid from your estate after your death. A financial planner can help you determine if and when you should do it, how to do it, and where the money can come from. And, don't forget about the tax consequences of taking money from one place to use it to pay somewhere else. Ask your financial planner and/or tax attorney to guide you. **Choices and consequences.**

Believe it or not, I recently saw a sign outside of a bank that invited people to investigate the option of a home equity loan to pay for their children's student loans? *Are they kidding?* I thought people understood why that is not a good idea, yet there was the bank, promoting the idea, just as they did in the past, just as they promoted sub-prime mortgage loans. Let's never forget that the business of a bank is to make money for the bank. You are the vehicle that makes it happen for them.

AUTO TITLE LOANS

Have you seen the TV ads for auto title loans? Smiling, happy people holding cash after they surrendered the title to their vehicle in exchange for that cash? Don't do it.

What if the minute you get that cash, you pull out of the driveway of the loan office, only to have your car totaled in an accident? You can kiss your money good-bye.

People in desperate financial situations often do desperate things. They are vulnerable to "deals" like auto title loans. They need the immediate satisfaction of getting cash in hand, forgetting about long-term consequences.

Don't make quick decisions that may come back to bite you. Educate yourself. Ask questions. Try not to get into a situation that would cause you to do something you will regret.

PAY-DAY LOANS

I repeat paragraphs 3 and 4 from the above section about Auto Title Loans.

REVERSE MORTGAGES

Since 1988, much has been written about Reverse Mortgages. If nothing else, the headline stories present inconsistent information: One year, they're seen as a life saver; the next year, they will lead you to financial ruin.

When first introduced, reverse mortgages sounded like a wonderful way to take the equity out of your house and provide you with cash you need to live comfortably in your "golden years." But, now, the equity in homes of many seniors has been seriously reduced due to the housing bust of recent years.

Reverse mortgages are complicated and are subject to debate. They are generally sold by "salespeople" who stand to be paid large commissions, and who may or may not be qualified to analyze your financial situation now or in the future.

Reverse mortgages are often presented as the remedy for many financial problems, and are a breeding ground for taking advantage of seniors. Yet, the seniors went for them with a vengeance, often failing to see the devil in the details. But, isn't that what many seniors do? They focus on the sales pitch (the messenger) and not the message. Who wouldn't believe Robert Wagner when he pitches reverse mortgages on TV? People don't seem to remember that old adage:

"If something looks too good to be true, it probably is."

What is a reverse mortgage? A reverse mortgage is a special type of loan that enables people 62 or older to convert some of their home's equity into tax-free cash.

How does it work? Unlike standard home-equity loans, no repayment is required until the home is no longer the principal residence ... that is, until the owner dies or sells the house (or, in the case of married couple, when the second spouse dies). The homeowner(s) must occupy the property as their principal residence. The home must be owned free-and-clear or have a small outstanding mortgage balance that can be paid off with the reverse mortgage. No income, employment, or credit requirements are necessary.

How much cash can someone receive? The amount that can be borrowed is based on a HUD formula that factors in the age of the youngest homeowner, the interest rate, appraised value of the home, and the location of the property.

What are some of the benefits?

- The reverse mortgage customer always retains ownership and continues to live in their home.
- Cash advances can be used for any purpose.
- Loan proceeds are not taxable.
- Loan proceeds will not affect Social Security or Medicare benefits.
- Heirs can keep the house once the reverse mortgage is paid off when the second owner (in the case of married owners) dies.

Interest rates? A reverse mortgage is an adjustable rate loan linked to the 1-year Treasury Security Rate.

What are the tax-free cash options?

- Lump-sum cash advances make cash immediately available.
- Line-of-credit makes cash available upon request (as needed).

<u>What about costs?</u>   Closing costs can be financed into the loan (origination fee; title insurance; appraisal; mortgage insurance premium; attorney fees, for example).   Fees are generally high, and generally cost thousands more than a conventional mortgage.   Be sure you understand how much this mortgage will be costing you.

<u>How is the loan repaid?</u>   A reverse mortgage is due and payable when the property is no longer considered the customer's principal residence, to be paid in one payment – either from the sale of the home or through other resources; translated, that means when the homeowner(s) sell the house, or when the last one dies (in the case of a married couple).

CAVEAT EMPTOR

Do not get a reverse mortgage without first consulting an accountant, a tax attorney, and/or a financial planner ... preferably ones who personally know you and your financial situation.   Do not fall for a sales pitch!   Even the government requires you to talk it over with a counselor before finalizing the transaction, which is complicated and not necessarily easy to understand.   Older homeowners are urged to weigh all options carefully before tapping home equity values.

Reverse mortgages can be a good financial fallback under appropriate circumstances, and work best as a last resort if all other income options fall short.   And, the older you are, the more money you can get.   It is important to weigh the costs and risk against other viable alternatives.

And, if the reverse mortgage salesperson tells you what a good idea it is to get the cash out of your home equity in order to put the cash elsewhere (for example, into some kind of high-commission financial product he is selling), **RUN!**   In this situation, the salesperson would collect one commission on the reverse mortgage placement plus a second commission on the financial product sold to you.

Keep in mind also that the laws regarding reverse mortgages change periodically.

Under the right circumstances, a reverse mortgage can be the perfect vehicle to provide needed cash for seniors, but it has to be under the right circumstances.   Don't think you can successfully live large on the money you took from your home equity to pay for a beach house or a cruise or a new car.

Oh, well, that's not true.
You absolutely are free to live large and spend your money any way you wish.
But, be careful.   You just might run out of money.

AND HERE'S THE LATEST NEWS ABOUT REVERSE MORTGAGES

In the spring of 2011, it came to light that many seniors who got reverse mortgages are losing their homes to foreclosure! *WHAT?   Didn't they say that couldn't happen?*

It happened because the people who find themselves in this terrible financial position did not carefully calculate and/or budget for their anticipated living expenses in retirement.   They did not plan for inflation, or emergency repairs to the house, or illness or disability expenses, or funeral expense for the death of a spouse, or the loss of income after the first spouse passes away.

A person who gets a reverse mortgage is only required to keep paying their real estate taxes and homeowner's insurance. OK!   That's easy enough.   But, the people who didn't plan well for their financial needs in retirement are running out of money paying for upkeep and unanticipated expenses ... and worse, finding their house isn't worth what it was when they got the reverse mortgage in the first place.   So if they had to sell their house (that is, **if** they could even sell it in the current real estate market), it would probably be at a loss.

You need the advice of learned professionals before taking on a financial transaction as complicated as a reverse mortgage. Actually, I recently heard a financial planner say, in reply to a question about whether or not a couple should get a reverse mortgage: Her reply was immediate and firm: "NEVER."   She had her reasons.

BE CAREFUL.
This could be another one of those eggs you can't "uncrack."

ELECTRONIC MONEY

In *The Philadelphia Inquirer* of September 9, 2012, there was an article titled, "Are All Your Electronic Affairs in Order?" The article states that in a recent survey by the BMO Retirement Institute, more than half of the survey respondents believe it is important to make plans for their personal and financial online assets, yet 57 per cent have not made any such provisions. Those people say either that they didn't think about it, or don't believe it's necessary.

Excuse me? Some people say (brag?) that they do many (if not all) of their financial transactions online, yet don't see a need to provide a means for their family or executor to figure it all out after they die? *What did I miss?*

According to this article, as but one example, Yahoo's Terms of Service refer to "no right of survivorship and non-transferability." The other search engines probably have similar terms. To adequately protect your rights will require careful examination of their rules to see that your survivors will have access to your account information in the event of your disability or death. And, if you want your online information transferred to your heirs, I suggest you consult with a lawyer thoroughly knowledgeable about the subject of electronic information as it relates to your estate. It's complicated. Much (but not all) depends upon the laws of the state in which you reside.

If you don't take care of this one aspect of your personal financial business in an appropriate legal way (that is, by way of your Will or Trust), your family might miss out because they might not (a) know these accounts exist, or (b) be recognized as your personal representative. And, worse, your family might have to spend money to retain a lawyer to go to court to gain access to your information. Do your best to see that you don't burden your family this way.

> NOTE: The article states that if you value your photographs, put them on a CD such that they can never be lost to fire or flood. I stress the importance of this in Chapter V – PERSONAL.

- Do you pay your bills online?

- Do you shop online from places like eBay, QVC, HSN, Amazon, etc?

- Do you order magazines, clothing, etc., online?

- Do you do your banking and investing online?

- Do you transfer money between accounts online?

- Do you have a "stash of cash" in your home in the event of a power failure when you would not have access to your bank account at the ATM? Who besides you know where it is?

If you do any of these things, it is essential that you prepare a very complete PRINTED list of all of the places where you transact your electronic financial business, because someday, someone else will be responsible for closing all those accounts. They will need your User ID's, passwords, and all other relevant information, including the names of all the financial institutions or businesses with which you transact your business, their addresses, phone numbers, account numbers, etc. Don't leave anything off this list. More is better.

And, if you change any of this information, you must then change your list accordingly. It is important to keep the list accurate and up to date, and easily available to someone you trust in the event of your disability or death, which means, printed on PAPER. Who do you trust with this information? Your spouse? Your executor? You must trust someone with it, even if you put your list in a sealed envelope, marked "to be opened upon my disability or death," and keep it with your Will.

PASSING YOUR MONEY ON TO YOUR HEIRS

Ask yourself: **How much money do you *really* want to leave to your children?**

Opinions vary greatly for many reasons.

- Some people will say they want to leave every possible penny to their kids, even if it means that they themselves will have to do with less.

- Others will say (sometimes humorously, sometimes not) that they are spending their children's inheritance.

- Others say they need their own money for their old age, and there won't be any money left for the kids.

- Warren Buffet says: *"Enough money so they feel they could do anything, but not so much that they could do nothing."*

IT'S YOUR MONEY, SO THE CHOICE IS YOURS.

You know your children's strengths and weaknesses. You can even intentionally leave no money to a child if you believe you have good reasons.

To disinherit one of your children requires the assistance of a good estate lawyer to write your Will or Revocable Living Trust to clearly and accurately spell out your intentions. Be prepared to have your lawyer suggest that you leave some money (maybe $1,000, for example) to that child because it will make it harder for him/her to contest your Will. And, if you really don't want one or more of your children to inherit from you, a Revocable Living Trust may be better than a Will, because the trust is more difficult than a Will to contest. One more conversation to have with your lawyer before you sign any documents.

NOTE: If your intention is to disinherit one of your children, don't forget to pass that child's portion on to his/her children or to your other children in equal shares.

Here is a true story of what happened when a woman unintentionally disinherited her daughter. It is one more example of what can happen when a person does not understand the consequences of their choice.

Once upon a time there was a divorced woman in her mid-50s who had two adult children, a son and a daughter. She was in poor health, and had virtually no money. Her only asset was her house which was in poor condition, and, at the time, may have been worth $250,000. I believe that today, it would be worth substantially less. She lived from Social Security check to Social Security check, and was generally unable to pay the bills on her house.

Because she was cash poor, she asked her single adult son to move in with her to help out (whatever that meant to her), and she sold her house to her son for $1.00. Did she ask for, and then ignore, the advice of a lawyer who might have told her what a bad idea that was?

I don't know what conversations the mother had with her son about the exact financial assistance she expected from him, or what else she expected him to do for her while living in that house. I only know that she trusted him to help her pay the bills on her house so she could remain living there.

Did she know and understand that her son's financial and life obligations elsewhere could have a negative impact upon her situation? What if he did not (could not) pay for the expenses of the house as he promised? What if he lost the house in bankruptcy or other debt? Where would she then live? Did he have children to support? Did he have a good job that provided steady income? Did he have debt of his own or a bad credit history? What if he wanted to move a woman into the house with them, whether it be a wife or girlfriend? Questions, questions, and more questions.

Some years later, it was pointed out to her that by giving her house (her only asset) to her son, she had entirely disinherited her daughter. She never intended to disinherit her daughter, but that is exactly what she did. It had never occurred to her what the consequences of her actions were. All she wanted was to be able to stay in her house and have some help paying the bills. But, she chose a method that had potentially negative consequences of which she was apparently unaware.

> *Do you think that woman's son will give his sister money equal to one-half of the value of that house after their mother dies? He could sell the house, and divide the net proceeds equally between his sister and himself. But, what if he plans to continue living in that house … where would he get that money to give to his sister?*

And, I remind you that if you want your money (your assets) passed to specific people at the time of your death, you must take all of the steps necessary to have the appropriate legal documents signed, sealed, and delivered! *Or not …* You may remember that if you don't have an estate plan, the state in which you live has one for you, and I'm pretty sure you and your heirs will not like it.

DEATH & TAXES

> *… "but in the world nothing can be said to be certain except death and taxes."*
>
> Ben Franklin

By now, you can see the intertwining and overlap of the five chapters of this book:

- Legal
- Financial
- Funeral and Burial Planning;
- Record-Keeping
- Personal Life Planning.

No one section exists entirely by itself … and each somehow contributes to and depends on the others.

Why did I begin a section with the sub-title, "Death and Taxes?" Why, indeed. Because both are part of life and estate planning. One can be avoided. The other cannot. There are lots of life choices and consequences to be considered regarding death and taxes … some easier than others, of course … but they are choices nevertheless. Let's begin with taxes, and (legal) ways to avoid paying them.

1.   **WHAT IF YOU DON'T PAY THEM:** You may choose _not_ to pay taxes that you rightfully owe; of course, you will not like the consequences. But, hey, this book is all about choices and consequences, right? Remember that it was the IRS that ultimately put Al Capone in jail for tax evasion when other law enforcement agencies knew he was guilty of other crimes, but were unable to prove it. Just figure that if you don't pay taxes, the taxing authority will catch up with you sooner or later. Is that OK with you?

2.   **WORK WITH A TAX LAWYER:** There are many ways to avoid paying taxes that are in keeping with the law, the Internal Revenue Code, and other taxing authorities. The subject of tax is extremely complicated. For some reason, people lump the many taxes into one category they simply refer to as "tax." It is not that simple, because there are many taxes for many reasons: for example,

- Ad valorem tax
- Bank tax
- Capital Gains Tax
- Consumption Tax
- Corporate Tax
- Currency Transaction Tax
- Environment Tax
- Estate Tax
- Excise Taxes
- Expatriation Tax
- Financial Activities Tax
- Financial Transaction Tax
- Gift Tax
- Income Tax

- Inflation Tax
- Inheritance Tax
- Local, Township, State and Federal taxes
- Luxury Tax
- Per Capita Tax
- Poll Tax
- Real Estate Tax
- Sales Tax
- School Tax
- Social Security Tax
- Tariffs
- Transfer Tax
- Value-added Tax
- Wealth (net worth) Tax

NEED I GO ON?

If you think you know a lot about taxes, or if you are inclined to lump them all together as if they were one tax, think again. Tax law is complicated, and if you don't believe me, go to a library and ask to see a copy of the most recent edition of The Internal Revenue Code.

Some people will pay some of these taxes. A few will pay all of these taxes. A small number will pay none. Consider that most of you will never pay most of these taxes. It depends on many variables, and decisions regarding taxes are not for the faint of heart or the uninformed. While you don't need to know the details of most of these taxes, you need to know <u>when</u> to consult a tax lawyer and/or an accountant.

There are various ways that you can use to avoid paying certain taxes ... maybe not all, but some. I recall hearing the reactions of certain people when the subject of "gifting" was suggested to them as a way to reduce their own personal taxable estate. If you "gift" the proper amounts of money at the proper times, under the proper circumstances, there is no Gift Tax to be paid.

- Unfortunately, what was told to them is <u>*not*</u> what they heard. *"What? Gift Tax! Are you crazy? What are you talking about? Are you saying that if I give my money away while I'm still alive, I have to pay Gift Tax. Oh, no, there will be none of that!"* And then they stop listening. See how the words a speaker says are not always the words the listener hears!

  If your lawyer suggests "gifting," take a deep breath, sit back, relax, and pay attention. It's really not as bad as you think! ASK your lawyer or your financial planner about the benefits of "gifting" for your children and grandchildren and for you, yourself. It could save you money you might otherwise pay in taxes at a later date. Do not immediately react negatively to the word "tax."

And, take advantage of tax credits at every opportunity. I would not presume to explain anything to you about tax credits except to say that they exist and can offer you a distinct tax advantage if you and the circumstances qualify. ASK your tax advisor! Don't miss this opportunity to save yourself a few dollars.

3.   **CONSULT WITH A FINANCIAL PLANNER**. And, I'm not referring to one of those persons SELLING investments. I'm talking about a genuine professional financial planner who will act as a fiduciary.

While a financial planner can and will not give you tax advice, *per se,* he can help you set up your assets in ways that can minimize, or even eliminate, taxes, especially when you take your 401(k) or IRA when you retire, and upon your death, so that your hard-earned money can pass to your heirs as tax-free as possible.

It's complicated. Don't try to figure this out by yourself.

To all of this, you may say, *"Why should I care about estate taxes or cashing in my IRA, because I'll be dead."* Believe me, your loved ones will care.

Ed Slott, CPA, financial advisor and well-known author of several books, has this to say on his public television fundraising shows:

> **"The government wants ALL your money, and they're very patient ... they will wait 'til you're dead to get it."**

Estate and Financial Planning are complex subjects that require the services of professionals to guide you through the maze of regulations and laws. To the average person, the Internal Revenue Code may appear to be written in hieroglyphics, but a good tax lawyer can translate the Code for you, and show you how to make it work for you.

Many investment products include stocks and bonds which are governed by the regulations of the SEC. At the same time, there are investment products sold by insurance companies that are <u>not</u> governed by the SEC. Did you know that? Do you know which is which? What each can do for you?

It is entirely possible (actually, quite easy) for the uninformed person to make choices about their money that will result in serious, negative, and possibly long-term consequences, when they choose to move their money without the tax advice of an accountant, a financial planner, and a lawyer

> **How many times have I already said that it's generally a bad idea to practice do-it-yourself financial planning?**

> *Once upon a time, there was a man, age 75, who wanted to buy a new house and have no mortgage. In order to pay for the house in cash, he took money out of his IRA and incurred large penalties and taxes. He also sold some of his investments and incurred huge Capital Gains Tax. His reasoning was that he needed cash to pay for the house because he didn't want a mortgage payment every month. Technically, he got what he wanted: he paid cash for his house and had no mortgage. But, at what price?*
>
> *Why do you suppose he did not consult with an attorney and/or a financial planner before he made those financial choices? <u>Because he didn't want to pay their fees!</u>*
>
> *He thought he knew what he was doing. Sadly, he now knows that he did not, and that there were serious, expensive, and long-term consequences for his practicing do-it-yourself financial planning. So, OK ... he has no monthly mortgage payments; so what? True, he got what he wanted, but he also has a whole lot less liquid money! If he runs out of cash, he can't take the deed to his house to the supermarket or gas station.*
>
> *Before taking all that money out of his accounts without professional advice, and losing huge sums for taxes and penalties, would it not have been better to pay a few hundred dollars to consult with a tax lawyer and/or a financial planner in advance? Just asking ...*

It's a shame that so many people think of fees for professionals as "expenses" rather than as "investments." Picture "Dagwood Bumstead" trying do-it-yourself plumbing, and you'll get the idea!

It would be a mistake for you to consider what I just said as tax advice.

It is not! It is just a story about what happened to one man as a result of choices he made without thoroughly considering the consequences. What I am saying is, go ahead and make choices all by yourself if you know what you're doing, but be careful! And if you are not certain, ASK! There is no shame in asking for assistance in an area about which you know very little.

There *are* ways for you to save your money and avoid paying taxes, and, if you want to reduce or eliminate your tax liability, work with a tax lawyer and/or a financial planner. And be willing to pay for that advice. Your lawyer and your financial planner are not running charities!

<u>ONE MORE THING ABOUT DEATH AND TAXES.</u>

Keep your tax returns and all associated documentation for no less than seven (7) years. It would be wise to put a note with instructions to your executor about where your tax returns can be found after your death, because you executor will be responsible for filing your final tax returns.

> *Once upon a time, a man was the executor of his brother's estate. Before his brother died at the age of 92, the executor repeatedly asked him about the status of his taxes, including the whereabouts of his tax returns. He was assured that everything was all right. Turns out that was not true. His brother had not filed tax returns for 3 years. It wasn't as if there was any kind of intentional tax evasion going on. His cognitive abilities had simply declined to the point of his not remembering details about his money or tax returns. The executor needed to retain the services of a tax attorney to recreate tax returns for the final 3 years of his brother's life, which increased the legal fees to administer his brother's estate. Just another one of those expenses of probate that people so dislike ...*

WOMEN AND MONEY

I once read an article in a magazine for financial planners entitled "*What Women Want.*" Really? In a financial magazine? I found that interesting and at the same time peculiar, because what women want goes way beyond anything having to do with money, even as they recognize their basic need for enough money. Which brings up that question again: "How much money is enough?"

I suppose it was easy for the writer to direct the article to financial planners, because Baby Boomer women need financial planners, and they need them NOW. It is good to educate the financial planners about some of the needs of women, which are different than the financial needs of men.

Women also know that money won't buy happiness, or do they? Ask a compulsive shopper if money can make her happy, and what do you think she'll say? Except, that it isn't the money that makes her happy, it is the experience and the adrenaline rush she gets from selecting and charging things she wants in the moment. Money is completely removed from the transaction, because of those little plastic things called credit cards.

Many of the things women want are tied to money, that is, having enough money for the basics, like a safe, comfortable place called home (and all the expenses related to home), transportation, food, employment, an occasional vacation, retirement security, health insurance.

There are other women who understand, at a deep level, that the things they <u>really</u> want will not necessarily come to them by way of money. Things like (in alphabetical order):

____	Abundance
____	Acknowledgement
____	Adequate, safe, affordable transportation
____	Creative expression
____	Financial freedom
____	Freedom from worry
____	Friendship
____	Fun
____	Good Health
____	Good Memories
____	Grace
____	Help
____	Hobbies
____	Legacy for their children
____	Leisure-time reading (so many books, so little time)
____	Less Responsibility
____	Love
____	Meaningful Education, Information, Knowledge
____	More Energy
____	More Time for themselves
____	Occasional Escape from the rat race
____	Opportunities
____	Peace and Quiet

	Peace of Mind
___	Peace of Mind
___	Places to articulate their dreams
___	Purpose
___	Respect
___	Rest and Relaxation
___	Retirement assurances
___	Secure home environment
___	Sense of Financial Security
___	Solitude
___	Time to day dream
___	To be heard
___	Trust
___	Unconditional love
___	Understanding
___	Vacations

The items listed above do not necessarily relate to money except, of course, if you don't have enough money and time to enjoy them. Women also understand, at a deep level, that they must do whatever it takes to survive ... for themselves and for their families ... even if it means sacrificing many of the things listed above.

**BABY BOOMER WOMEN, ESPECIALLY IF THEY ARE SINGLE,
HAVE SPECIAL FINANCIAL NEEDS AND FEARS FOR VARIOUS REASONS.**

Are your fears about money genuine, based on some personal event (illness, loss of job, bankruptcy, foreclosure, divorce, death of a spouse) that threw you into the financial abyss you see before you, or maybe, quite simply, it is a breakdown in your arithmetic skills? Or is your fear imagined because you are a chronic worrier?

- One reason women worry about their money is that women who have worked all their lives have not generally been paid the same amount that has been paid to men. (*Will that situation never be corrected? Just asking ...*)

- Many women dropped out of the working world to raise children, and so have been unable to save money or to contribute the maximum allowable amounts to their IRAs or retirement funds.

- Some Baby Boomer women, because of divorce, find themselves financially disadvantaged.

- Other women relied on their spouse to handle their jointly owned money, and now, whether single by virtue of the death of a spouse or divorce, those women do not handle their money well, are not confident about their ability to handle their own money, and sometimes they make financial mistakes that cannot be corrected, leaving them financially destitute in their old age.

- The husbands of other women have passed away, and because the husbands were the breadwinners, those women now find themselves without his income, and often have to go to work for the first time in many years.

- Some husbands died, leaving their wives unprotected by having inadequate (or no) life insurance and other monies. Often, the husband's pension stops as of the date of his death, and if the wife is collecting Social Security of her own, after her husband's death, she will receive only the amount he received.

- Some husbands always took care of their money, thinking that they were doing their wives a favor, and they never bothered to educate their wives about their marital assets. This leaves a woman uninformed and uneducated about her own money.

Women, especially Baby Boomer women, need to put retirement planning at the top of their personal To Do List, whether they are married or single. They need some kind of financial guidance to help them determine if they will have enough money for the remainder of their lives, and if not, how to establish a workable financial plan for their future. Since women are generally willing to ask for directions, it shouldn't be too hard for them to establish a working relationship with a seasoned financial professional. Whatever they do, they should not ignore the sometimes harsh realities of their financial situation. If you need help, go get it while you still have time.

BAG LADY SYNDROME

How is it possible that so many Baby Boomer women have reached the age of 62 and know so little about managing their own money? If you have read what I've written earlier, you know some of the reasons why. OK, I get it. The years just flew by; nevertheless, Baby Boomer women, in particular, are running out of time. It is essential that they begin to take a hard look at where they are (financially), where they want to go, and where they expect to be in 20 or 30 years.

Do you or anyone you know suffer from "Bag Lady Syndrome?" That is the name coined to describe the condition of women's fear of running out of money before they run out of time. And, for some women, the fear is genuine.

Sadly, there is no pill or medical procedure that can be prescribed to lessen the symptoms, unless, of course, you count cutting up your credit cards as an appropriate surgical procedure. And there is no vaccination you can get to keep you from getting the syndrome, unless, of course, you count good financial planning.

Statistics are not on the side of women, either. They continue to earn less money than men, many married women don't have any money of their own, others allowed their spouses to handle the money and find themselves uncertain as to how much money they do have and where it is. Many women do not receive a pension, and receive Social Security at a rate lower than that of men. Add to these numbers the fact that most women outlive their husbands by an average of seven years, and could be widows for many years. I know several women who outlived their husbands by more than 35 years. It happens.

Let's throw divorce and remarriage into the mix, and women lose there, too. Everyone knows that more than 50% of first marriages fail, but do you know that more than 60% of second marriages fail … within as few as six years. Divorce among middle aged people has increased by large numbers in the last few years. Divorce is expensive, no matter how amicable the parties are in negotiating their separation. And, I'm not just referring to legal fees. If you mingled your assets with your new spouse, you will have to split them one way or another.

The fear of running out of money is genuine, particularly for single women. What is needed to alleviate the fear is a committed effort on the part of women to educate themselves about their money … *that is, every aspect of money, from saving, establishing a liquid emergency fund, eliminating frivolous, addictive spending, getting out of debt, living below their means, saving for retirement, budgeting, investing, Social Security, IRAs and 401(k) accounts, long-term care financing* … and then do whatever it takes to establish some degree of financial freedom for themselves. And remember to review your finances every year.

You know the drill. Could it be that, even though you know what is required to avoid "catching" Bag-Lady Syndrome, you have never taken steps to prevent it from happening?

Do you believe Bag Lady Syndrome is contagious?
It must be if so many women find themselves suffering from it.

You know that there are many articles, financial magazines, and "how-to" books to advise Baby Boomer women about money, but I'm not sure that reading those books has helped if there are so many 62+ year old women in fear of outliving their money. Reading about money is good, but taking action is better.

A truly good book teaches me better than to read it.
I must soon lay it down, and commence living on its hint.
What I began by reading, I must finish by acting.

Henry David Thoreau

NO PLACE FOR BLAME

If it will make you feel better to feel guilty of being so "*stupid*" (I prefer "uninformed") about money, go ahead, feel guilty. You could choose to blame your (ex-)husband, or your parents, or the economy, or the weather, but it won't help. Taking responsibility and action are what is needed, and as uncomfortable or unfamiliar as that may feel for you, you must do it if you want to outlive your money.

A friend recently told me that it is only now, 15 years after her divorce, that she has begun to relax about money. For those 15 years, she has lived in daily fear about how she will survive with the money she earns, considering how the cost of living has increased during this time. Maybe she would have benefited from consulting with a financial planner years ago to alleviate some of her financial worries, but she is a woman who doesn't like to be given advice; so, she just kept on worrying. Women are known to be worriers. Worrying will not help. Taking action will help.

It is no sin not to know the intricacies of money management, which is often complicated. Mostly, however, it is just simple arithmetic. You <u>can</u> do arithmetic, can't you? If you earn $45,000 and you spend $80,000, you can pretty much anticipate a problem sooner or later. $45,000 subtracted from $80,000 leaves you $35,000 in the hole. Now, how hard was that to figure out?

This is the time for you to be honest with yourself if you expect to dig yourself out of the financial hole you find yourself in, and begin to take steps to protect yourself from having insufficient funds for the rest of your life. It doesn't matter how you got to this place; what matters is what you do ***between now and then.***

YOU NEED TO ASK FOR DIRECTIONS

Come on, now, you're a woman. You're not afraid to ask for directions when you're driving and you are lost. So, how is this different? You are on your life's journey and you are lost. So, ask for directions. And, if necessary, keep asking until you have found your way to your personal destination known as financial freedom and security.

Remember also that the single most important thing you need to know when you are lost is exactly where you are, so that you can find your way again. This kind of journey is best taken in the company of a knowledgeable guide ... I'm speaking about a financial planner who will make you have conversations you may not want to have, require you to do certain things you may not want to do, and seriously look at the hard facts that you are facing if you think you could run out of money before the end of your life ... that is, the financial planner will <u>work</u> **with** <u>you</u> to create a PLAN for your money for the rest of your life.

Many Baby Boomer women are facing retirement age alone, either by choice, by death of a spouse, or by divorce. Some women have been well provided for. Other women are afraid of outliving their money. What is the best thing to do with fear? Get busy doing the thing you fear the most, and the fear goes away.

> ***You must do the things you think you cannot do.***
>
> Eleanor Roosevelt

- Some women are fortunate enough to be receiving a pension from years of employment, or have faithfully saved money in an IRA or employer-sponsored retirement plan.

- For some women, the death of their husbands provided them with money that will last for the remainder of their lives.

- Other woman may have received a generous divorce settlement that will provide them with assets that will last for the reminder of her life.

- Still other women have either already received an inheritance from their parents, or anticipate receiving one. But, be careful about counting on the inheritance ... your parents may outlive their money, too

- There is always Social Security.

If you are one of the fortunate women who has money at this time in your life, it is essential that you **preserve** it for your retirement years. And, preserving your money is more than just having it invested in the right places; it means not spending beyond your means, it may mean saying NO to family (and friends) who wish to "borrow" money; and it means exercising caution if you plan to marry or remarry at this age to protect your assets by either a PreNuptial Agreement or a Co-Habitation Agreement.

It also requires your consulting an experienced estate-planning lawyer who can provide you with the important documents you need for your life *between now and then*, and which will provide for the orderly transfer of your assets after your death.

DO NOT SKIP THIS STEP and DO NOT DO IT YOURSELF!

And, don't wait until after you are finished with the financial planner. Wise women will work with the lawyer and their financial planner simultaneously in order to get the best possible protection for themselves.

THINGS COULD BE WORSE

Those same events I mentioned earlier, however, could have left some women financially damaged, sometimes in the short term, other times for many years, even for the rest of their lives.

- The death of a spouse who passed away before collecting a pension, and who had been the primary wage earner, can leave the widow desperate and in fear about how she is going to survive the rest of her life with very little money.

- A single woman who has been working for her entire life may have lost her job through no fault of her own, and may find that she will not be able to collect that pension she expected. She cannot make ends meet without her salary, and she finds it hard to get another job earning the same salary as before.

- A divorce can put a woman in a very uncertain financial position from which she may never recover, especially if her divorce settlement favored her ex-husband. If he got to keep his pension and retirement accounts, and because she was not the primary wage-earner of the family, she may be without financial resources of her own. At the very least, the standard of living of a divorced Baby Boomer woman may be significantly diminished.

  - Often, their children have not yet finished their education, and so some of their money is being spent for the children's expenses. Divorced women often lose the big house, and find themselves and their children living in smaller houses or apartments that are not equal to the living situation to which they had been accustomed.

  - If their "ex" may still be well employed and living in a big house with his trophy wife, the children complain all the time that it is so much more fun at daddy's house, which is large and has a pool, and where daddy promised them a new car when they graduate, etc. But, the kids don't know that daddy isn't paying the court-ordered child support, and forget that you're doing your best to make ends meet. They are resentful that you require them to participate in the new frugality of your current living situation. They are angry, *as are you*, and it just makes your situation seem that much worse. What's important is to turn that anger into action.

Talk with your children about your new situation. If they are old enough to have an understanding of what is happening, ask them to help reduce your stress by doing more things around the house. Ask them how they feel about the new arrangement and about their fears and anxiety. Even while you are hurting, do your best to quiet their fears. They didn't cause the situation, but they will believe they did, and it is up to you to assure them that things will be all right in a little while, even if you aren't exactly certain how that will happen. If necessary, fake it 'til you make it. Your children need to know that you are safe and their life is secure.

As the child of parents who had an ugly, expensive divorce in the 1950s, I understand what these women are going through. And, at the same time, a divorced woman in a difficult financial situation will either find her way out of the mess she was left with … or not. In my mother's case, it was *"or not."* Divorce was uncommon in the 1950s, and the world was not sympathetic to a woman trying to raise children by herself.

IT'S A NEW DAY

Times have changed. Women today have many options available to them to support themselves and their children, even if (or while) their "ex" is living the good life. They may not even know what options are available, but they can begin to educate themselves. If you are afraid you will run out of money before you run out of time, it is up to you to investigate every possible avenue to educate yourself about money. NO ONE ELSE CAN DO IT FOR YOU.

Women are no longer without the power to live life without a man to support them. It's just that, if you never had to do it before, it can be scary and dark some days. But, every night ends with the dawn and the bright sunlight of day.

> **Never forget!**
> **YOU ARE A BABY BOOMER, one of the movers and shakers of the last 50 years!**
> **You can do this!**

Find yourself a financial planner with whom you feel comfortable working. There are many qualified females in the financial business if you are more comfortable with a woman. Read Suze Orman's books and watch her TV show for good advice on how to be a powerful woman around the subject of money, and how to survive a financial crisis. I like her "no nonsense, in-your-face" style. She'll tell you what your need to hear, and she doesn't sugar coat it. Suze is not interested in what you want to hear. She's interested in giving you facts to empower yourself and your financial future.

And, one more thing about Suze Orman. There are women who say they don't like her style and her haircut. I've heard others say she's too aggressive and pushy [*sort of like the things women say about Martha Stewart ... and strong women, in general*]. In my opinion, the way Suze wears her hair has nothing to do with her competence in giving financial advice. And, even if you don't like her style, DON'T KILL THE MESSENGER. She has valuable input for women willing to listen to the message.

> **AND, AS WITH EVERYTHING IN THIS BOOK,**
> **YOU CAN CHOOSE TO FOLLOW MY RECOMMENDATIONS ... OR NOT.**

RECOVERY MAY BE DIFFICULT, BUT NOT NECESSARILY IMPOSSIBLE

If you are in dire financial straits through no real fault of your own as I have discussed earlier in this book, now is the time to consult with a financial planner to help you find your way to financial security. And, for once in your life, be willing to listen and learn. Stop thinking you know it all and can do this by yourself. You need help, and you need it now.

If you are guilty of the sin of shopping to make yourself feel good (addictive shopping), then it is time to stop shopping and sell things you no longer need; and, if you cannot stop by yourself, consult with a therapist specializing in addictions. You cannot continue spending like you have in the past and hope to have your money last.

Women tend to use shopping as their "therapy of choice" and often justify the addiction as being "better" than drinking or drugs. Well, yes, maybe. Maybe not. Have you ever thought about how you will ever pay for all that stuff? If bankruptcy is your solution of choice, you might want to think again.

This is, no doubt, not the place where you expected to be at age 62. You anticipated an easy transition from your middle age into retirement, and it isn't going to turn out that way. Go ahead, acknowledge all the emotions you feel, but don't wallow in your upset. This is the time for complete honesty with yourself about what happened that caused you to be in this position. If much of it is because of your own bad habits and choices with money, then take responsibility, fix the mess, and move on. It can be done.

It is an unfortunate consequence of many kinds of financial situations coming together that have brought some Baby Boomers to a place in their lives where they never expected to find themselves: collecting Unemployment Compensation, Food Stamps, Welfare, or the like. It happens. Don't wallow in your situation. Be always open to possibility and sound advice. It may be cloudy today, but the sun will shine again. Maybe even tomorrow.

Once upon a time, in the checkout line of a supermarket, I was speaking with a woman about 65, whose husband had just lost his job for the first time in his life. She was shopping with Food Stamps, and was unfamiliar with how they worked, and was visibly embarrassed.

I suggested to her that there are ways to stretch those food stamps to enable her to buy more groceries. My first suggestion was to buy the Sunday newspaper ... and I barely got the word "newspaper" out of my mouth when she angrily cut me off, saying: "What are you talking about? My husband just lost his job. I can't afford newspapers!"

When she finally took a breath, I pointed out to her that the newspaper only costs $1.50 and there are sometimes hundreds of dollars' worth of grocery coupons in the paper, and with the store's policy of doubling the value of coupons, she can get more for her money. I even got to suggest that she only buy things that are on sale, which, when combined with double-value coupons, should make her food stamps go farther, and her shopping less stressful.

Do you think she followed my suggestion? I don't know, but I doubt it. She was in a place of fear and (over)reacting, not listening, not being open to possibility. In my opinion, she was so afraid of this new situation in her life, that she was closed off to hearing suggestions of any kind. Just my opinion ...

There is no shame in being laid off from your job, or finding yourself in foreclosure or bankruptcy. It's not generally good, but these things happen. What you must do next is find your way out of this situation. And, if it makes you feel any better, think of all the other people who find themselves in the same situation.

HIDDEN MONEY

GOLD

It is possible you have money you forgot about, or assets that could easily be turned into cash. In Chapter V - YOUR PERSONAL LIFE, I have made many suggestions for getting rid of your excess "stuff," many of which will allow you to get cash for the sale of them, and/or get a tax deduction for donating them.

Gold has been selling for all-time high prices. You may be in possession of gold jewelry that you don't care about any longer, even gold jewelry that belonged to others in your family who may have passed away.

Caution: Do not **SEND** your jewelry to any company that offers you this chance to "get rich quick." Not by FedEx, UPS, or the Postal Service. Only deal in person with reputable jewelers or other businesses that will pay you cash on the spot for your gold. And before you actually sell it, check to see what gold is selling for on that date.

Silver is also selling for an all-time high. My sister recently asked me if I had any objection to her selling our mother's sterling silver flatware. When I told her it was all right with me, she sold it to a reputable dealer for $1,200 and divided the cash among her three children. Our mother would have liked that.

On the Suze Orman TV show on January 30, 2012, she spoke about "hidden money," with a focus on selling and buying gold. Rather than buying gold bars, she recommended that if you want to invest in gold and other precious metals, you do so through an exchange-traded fund that deals in those commodities. One reason for her suggestion is that if you want to sell your gold bars, the dealer will take a commission, and your net gain will be less than if you were dealing with investment funds. I am just passing this information on to you. It is not necessarily my recommendation, because I am not a financial advisor or a dealer in precious metals, but, with the high value of gold right now, it is something to consider ... *or not.*

CAUTION: There are websites that claim to help you find hidden money. Be careful, because some of them are scams, operating in order to collect information about you and your money. It continually amazes me how clever thieves are at ways to separate you from your money. If you are interested in locating "hidden money," you might be better to check with the Department of Revenue in the state in which you reside. I'm pretty sure the process of *escheat* takes place everywhere. I think this kind of search has a better chance at being legitimate. BE CAREFUL!

> *Once upon a time there was a woman about 45, who was having a conversation with her father shortly before his death. They had been very close all their lives, and they were spending important time sharing with each other before it was too late. Toward the end of their conversation ... almost humorously ... he said to his daughter, "Don't throw the encyclopedias away until you first check between the pages."*
>
> *With those softly spoken words, he gave his daughter the gift of several thousand dollars that could easily have been tossed into a dumpster with the encyclopedias, which no one seems to want anymore. While he did wait until nearly the very end of his time on earth, at least he did make a point of mentioning his secret hiding place for some of his money.*

UNCLAIMED MONEY (and other assets)

In *The Philadelphia Inquirer* of October 12, 2010, there appeared a full-page notice from the Pennsylvania Treasury's Unclaimed Property Division, stating that in 2009, the Pennsylvania Treasury returned over $107 million of unclaimed property. (The list appears every year.) The list of things that would fall to *escheat* includes (but is not necessarily limited to):

- Abandoned bank accounts
- Forgotten stocks
- Safe-deposit box contents (jewelry, coins, family heirlooms, stock certificates, old bank books)
- Certificates of Deposit
- Unclaimed insurance policies
- Uncashed checks
- Unclaimed pension benefits
- Unclaimed accounts with a previous employer

> *Escheat* is the forfeiture of all property to the state treasury if there are no heirs, descendants, or named beneficiaries to take the property upon the death of the last-known owner. Any business that finds itself holding any property belonging to someone else that is unclaimed after a specific period of time, must remit that property to the state, which then has the obligation to find the legitimate owner or heir. If, after a certain statutory period of time, no one claims the money, it passes into the state treasury.

The *escheat* process applies to all unclaimed property, including the contents of your safe deposit box at the bank that no one even knows you have. It doesn't matter that you put valuables in the bank box for safekeeping. **What matters is that no one in your family knew about the box when you died,** and so, the state's Treasury Department eventually became an heir of your estate. I'm pretty sure that was never your intention.

The $107 million was only the dollar value of unclaimed property that was <u>actually returned to the rightful owners or their heirs</u>. There are still many millions of dollars of **un**claimed property. Although the Pennsylvania Treasury Department is self-supporting by virtue of selling unclaimed property, the state is always trying to get these assets back to their rightful owners where they belong.

What followed that full-page newspaper ad were pages and pages of tiny print, containing approximately 6,000 names of individuals and other entities that had unclaimed property being held by the state, just waiting to be claimed. How many people do you suppose read that list?

The published list generally represents assets that no one in the families knew about when a loved one died. What does that mean for you? It means that you must keep good personal records so that, after your death, your family does not lose out on your assets that you want them to have, but which they will not get because your records were incomplete or disorganized. (See Chapter IV – RECORD-KEEPING.)

> In *The Philadelphia Inquirer* in February 2011, there was a brief article about unclaimed property that was the subject of the local news TV Channel **CBS-3** series titled *Claim Your Cash*. The station claimed to have helped 12,233 people recover $5.8 million. The viewers were encouraged to look themselves up online. One woman found she was owed $40,000. The $5.8 million is just a tiny part of the $1.6 billion in unclaimed money and property.

IF SOME OF THAT MONEY WERE YOURS, WOULDN'T YOU WANT TO GET IT BACK?

I actually enjoy perusing those lists. Several years ago, long after his death, I saw my father's name on that list, and put in a claim that was worth $118. It was a small amount, but had I not read the list, I would not have seen his name, and that $118 would have eventually ended up in the state treasury by virtue of *escheat*.

> *This is an example of why it is good to get extra Death Certificates when making funeral arrangements. In order to verify my right to claim that $118, I needed to prove that not only was my father deceased, but that I was, in fact, his daughter. You never know when you'll need an extra Death Certificate and Birth Certificate.*

If a bank account remains untouched for a period of years (the time period may vary from state to state and bank to bank), such that the *escheat* process takes over, some banks may deduct a small fee before turning over the money to the state.

WHERE IS YOUR MONEY?

I strongly recommend that you prepare a very complete list of where all your money can be found. Include names of financial institutions, phone numbers, addresses, and account numbers, for every financial and insurance account you have, of every sort (checking, savings, CD's, U.S. bonds, money-market, IRAs, 401(k) accounts, insurance policies, investment accounts, and all on-line account activity). Include any safe deposit boxes you rent. Don't leave anything out. Someday, someone will be responsible for closing these accounts, and you don't want them to miss any of them, do you? You see what happens to unclaimed assets.

If you change any of this information, you must then change your list accordingly. It is important to keep the list accurate and up to date.

Who do you trust with this information? Your spouse? Your executor? You must trust someone with it, even if you put your list in a sealed envelope, marked "to be opened upon my disability or death," and keep it with your Will.

Do you have a stash of cash hidden somewhere in your house for safekeeping? I absolutely understand your wanting to hide some money for an emergency (or other reason), but, at the same time, be smart about it. Who knows about it besides you? If you don't tell somebody, some day, you will die, and no one will ever know about that money? Is that what you want?

LAST MINUTE MONEY THOUGHTS

- Before leaving the section about finances, I want to remind you of the importance of appropriate estate planning so that you can pass your assets to the people you want to get them. You will find estate planning discussed at length in the Chapter I - LEGAL.

- And, don't forget about Pre-Nuptial Agreements. They are about money, although they fall somewhere inside legal, financial and personal transactions.

- In all of this planning, do not leave out possible discussions with a tax lawyer and/or an accountant about the taxability of inheritances, life insurance proceeds, liquidation of assets, etc. Making the wrong choices regarding taxes can cost you big time!

- Do your family members (or your executor) know the name, address, etc., of your financial planner? Your lawyer? Your accountant? Could they locate this information on short notice, if necessary?

- Do your family members (or your executor) know where you keep information and documentation about your assets and investments, and could they locate it on short notice?

- Do you have a significant amount of money hidden in your house in the event that you are unable to get cash from an ATM? Electronics and money don't always mix well. Be prepared.

- If you have decided to financially contribute to the education of your grandchildren, ask your financial planner about a 529 Plan specifically for this purpose. Take the time to investigate and discuss all options for paying for their education.

- If you have set aside (or designated) money for the specific purpose of paying for your funeral, don't forget to let your family know about it well in advance, especially where they can find this money.

- Photocopy everything you carry in your wallet, especially credit cards. And, carry only 1 or 2. Use them sparingly, if at all, especially if you cannot control your habit of paying with plastic.

- If you are still working, do your absolute best to pay down debt, especially credit card and home-equity debt. You don't want to carry them into your retirement years, when your earnings may be significantly lower than now.

- If you are still working, continue contributing the maximum amount to your 401(k) Plan and/or your IRA.

- Ask your financial planner about whether or not you will benefit from converting your IRA to a Roth IRA.

- Never use margin. All it is, is borrowing against your securities to buy more securities. It's great while it lasts, but it never lasts, and when you receive that margin call request, you had better be ready to pay that money back. A perfect example of what can happen in margin situations is in the Eddie Murphy movie, *"Trading Places."*

- If you are still working, always pay yourself first. It's an old idea, but a good one. If you don't pay yourself before everyone else, it won't happen, and there will come the day of reckoning.

- If you have a Revocable Living Trust, is it fully funded? If you don't know what that means, ask the lawyer who drafted the document for you in the first place. A trust that is not completely funded will fail, and will not do the things you intend it to do, not the least of which is to avoid probate.

- Review and possibly rebalance your investment portfolio at least annually with your financial planner. Things change, sometimes quickly, and you don't want to be caught unprepared.

- Review the beneficiary designations of all your insurance policies and other financial instruments for which there is a named beneficiary and contingent beneficiary. Do it on the same date every year. Mark your calendar … in ink.

- As terrible as it sounds, I'm going to ask you if you have quickly accessible money available for a sudden death in your immediate family; for example, a child killed in an auto accident from drinking and driving? or a child who has died from a long illness? or even you or your spouse? Would you have to put such funeral expenses on your credit card?

A very, very sad story, indeed.

In The Philadelphia Inquirer of April 6, 2011, there was a small article about a local family who buried their 16-month old baby in their back yard because they didn't have money for a funeral and burial elsewhere. They were $30,000 in credit card debt for extreme medical treatments the child required since birth.

The parents had been cited by their township for violating zoning laws, and had to retain a lawyer to help them resolve the matter. Ultimately, it was decided that they would be allowed to leave their baby rest in peace, and the township would reimburse them for the legal expenses they incurred because of the citation.

I AGAIN REMIND YOU THAT YOU DON'T HAVE TO DO ANY OF THESE THINGS ...

as long as you know that when you die, someone else will have to do them, and if that someone has your information easily accessible, it will save your estate money that would be spent for lawyers trying to locate assets and insurance policies. Also, if that someone cannot find an asset, or an insurance policy, or other financial account of any sort, that money could ultimately be lost to your heirs. Be smart about this. I think it's important. What do you think?

FINANCIAL CHECK-LIST

1. Do you know for a fact that you have enough money to last for the remainder of your life?

2. If you are not sure, have you consulted with a qualified Financial Advisor (not a salesperson) to get some direction? If not, why not? When do you plan to do it?

3. Do you balance your checkbook every month?

4. Do you pay your bills and handle your investments on-line? Who else knows how to do this if you were to become disabled? What are the terms and conditions relating to those accounts if you become disabled or when you die? Do you have a printed copy of those terms and conditions? If so, where is it?

5. Have you ever made any serious mistakes by practicing do-it-yourself financial planning? What were the consequences?

6. Have you taught your children how to handle money? If they are young adults, do they handle their money and debt wisely?

7. Do you have a wait-and-see attitude about your money? How long can you continue that way before your face financial disaster?

8. How much debt do you have? What kind of debt is it? (student loan? credit card? under-water mortgage? home equity loan?)

9. Have you ever been in bankruptcy? Did you use it as a get-out-of-debt-free card? Why did you make that choice? Did it provide you the financial relief you were looking for?

10. Do you expect to receive an inheritance in the next 10 years?

11. Do you have a Will or a fully funded Revocable Living Trust?

12. Have you hidden any money in your home? Who else knows about it?

13. Do you have valuables (cash, jewelry, stock certificates) in a bank safe deposit box? Who else knows about it?

14. Do you pay your bills on time? If not, why not?

15. What is your FICO score?

16. If you are married, do you know your spouse's FICO score? Did you find out what it is before or after the wedding?

17. Did you enter marriage with a pre-nuptial agreement to protect your assets for yourself and your children?

18. When you married, did one of you have significant debt and/or significant assets that made your financial relationship unequal? How have you handled this situation?

19. Do you have adequate life insurance? How do you define adequate?

20. Are your beneficiary designations current and exactly as you want them to be?

21. If you are married, do you have life insurance coverage for both husband and wife?

22. Do you have enough of other kinds of insurance to protect you and your family from financial disaster? Disability insurance? Homeowner's and Auto insurance? Renters' insurance? Long-term care insurance?

23. Does anyone owe you money? Do you have it in writing? What is your expectation of ever being repaid?

24. Do you file your Income Tax returns on time? If not, why not? Where do you keep the copies?

25. Do you shop to make yourself happy? To show the world something about yourself?

26. Do you have valuables that you could easily and quickly turn into cash (gold, for example)?

27. Are you unemployed? How have you managed your money without a regular paycheck? How much longer can you survive this way?

28. Do you have sufficient investment funds to provide you with money to enable you to live at your current lifestyle? What is your plan if you run out of money during your retirement years?

29. At what age do you plan to retire? Why that age? How did you make that decision? Is it reasonable considering all things relating to your personal finances and the economy?

30. Do you have a 12-18 month emergency fund? If not, how much do you have? If you have no emergency fund, how can you immediately begin saving money for emergencies which are bound to happen sooner or later?

31. If you have children, how do you plan to pay for their education? Have you consulted with a qualified financial advisor about the best way to do that? If not, why not? This is not a do-it-yourself project. Remember that college is optional, retirement is not.

32. If you are married, are you and your spouse on the same page when it comes to your money? How you save it? How you spend it? Buying gifts for each other and others? Do you fight about money? How do you resolve those disagreements? Do you have financial integrity? Who is in charge of your money?

33. Do you and your spouse have joint credit cards? Do you have another credit card just for you? Does your spouse know about this "other" credit card?

34. Are your assets jointly owned? If not, how do you and your spouse hold ownership of your assets?

35. In whose name is the ownership of your house? If it is not jointly owned, why not? Do you understand the consequences of joint ownership vs. single ownership?

36. Do you have a special needs child who requires a great deal of your money? Have you made adequate financial and personal provisions for that child for the time when you are no longer living?

37. Do you trust your Will? Are you sure?

38. Are you afraid of money such that you bury your head in the sand and ignore warning signs that things are not going well? Do you know what some of the warning signs are that indicate you are in financial trouble?

39. Did you ever borrow money against your house to pay off other debt?

40. In what order should you prioritize payment of your debt? If you don't know the answer, consult with a financial planner before making a decision.

41. Have you ever used a credit consolidation service that caused you more problems than you had before? How can you fix that mistake?

42. Have you ever chosen to ignore good advice given to you by a financial professional, to your own detriment?

43. What is the biggest financial mistake you ever made? How did you resolve the problems it caused? Or did you?

44. Did you ever co-sign for a personal loan, a student loan, a real-estate or auto lease, a mortgage? What were the consequences of that act of generosity?

45. Have you ever been the victim of a scam? What did you do about it after you realized the mistake?

46. Do you have adult children living with you? Do they pay rent? What is your arrangement with them for this living condition? What is their financial contribution to the household expenses? Do you have a win-win plan for gently pushing them out of the nest?

47. Do you financially subsidize your adult children so they can make ends meet? Do you give them cash or checks, or directly pay some of their bills? Do you pay for their child care? Can you really afford to keep this up into your own retirement years?

48. Why are your adult children in a financial situation they cannot afford? How do they plan to resolve the problems so that you don't have to continue supporting them and your grandchildren when you need the money yourself?

49. Did you put your house in the joint names of yourself and your son? Did you do it on your own, or did you consult with a lawyer and/or a financial advisor first? Do you have a plan for when things go bad as a result of this choice?

50. Do you still buy too much stuff that you don't need? Why? What can you do to turn that stuff into cash?

51. Are your personal papers organized in such a way that someone else can find an important document in a moment's notice? Who would that someone else be? Do they know it?

52. Have you designated some money or a particular asset for the specific purpose of paying your funeral expenses?

53. Did you ever loan money to someone? Was the loan documented in writing (such as a promissory note)? Has the money been paid back? If not, have you left information about this transaction with your personal records so your executor can try to get the money for your estate?

54. What financial questions did I leave out that you would like answered?

IN CONCLUSION

There are some good suggestions in this section about money. Some of them will be very helpful to you and your life situation. Others, less so. Always remember that you are not required to do anything in this book. The choice is up to you. I do, however, ask you to THINK about your money, learn about ways that money can help you live the life you want to live, the way you want to live it, so that it will last for the rest of your life, for all your days *between now and then.*

And, if your heirs are lucky, you just might even leave a little money for them.

YOU'RE RUNNING OUT OF TIME, AND YOU KNOW IT.

REMEMBER THAT YOU SAID YOU WOULD DO WHATEVER IT TAKES.

NOW IS A GOOD TIME TO BEGIN.

Now and then it's good to pause in our pursuit of happiness and just be happy.

Anonymous

I wish for you
> **love,**
>> **abundance,**
>>> **peace of mind,**
>>>> **good health,**
>>>>> **good friends,**
>>>>>> **long life,**
>>>>>>> **and time and money to do things you want to do** ... *between now and then.*

And, I leave you with Suze Orman's words of wisdom:

FIRST - PEOPLE

SECOND - MONEY

THIRD - STUFF

Tempus Fugit

FINANCIAL THINGS TO DO   *   IDEAS   *   FOLLOW-UP

#	A,B,C	Description	Start Date	Completion Date
1				
2				
3				
4				
5				
6				
7				
8				
9				
10				
11				
12				
13				
14				
15				
16				
17				
18				
19				
20				

Chapter III

FUNERAL & BURIAL

No matter how rich you become, or how famous or powerful,
when you die, the size of your funeral will still pretty much depend on the weather.

Michael Pritchard.

> **The only thing people really have in common is that they are all going to die.**
>
> Bob Dylan

Parts of this chapter are directed to the people inclined to make advanced arrangements for their own funeral and burial. Other parts are written for the people who will be making arrangements for someone else. The information is valuable no matter in which position you may someday find yourself.

Most of what I have written about funerals and burials comes from my own experience: from having made funeral arrangements for my Mother, my Father, and my former Husband; from attending funerals of family members and observing how things were done and not done; from attending funerals in the church where my Mother was the organist; from attending many funerals of friends and extended family members; and from being a Sales Counselor at a cemetery.

My writing is limited to information I know about Protestant and Roman Catholic funerals. I have not described funeral and burial traditions and practices from other religions, nationalities, and ethnic backgrounds because the subjects are too vast to be included in this book.

It is a known fact that death will touch the life of every person, sooner or later. Whether or not the death is sudden or long expected, and, even if you choose not to think about it until it happens, some kind of funeral arrangements will have to be made.

It is also safe to say that most people understand that there are lots and lots of things to do to arrange a funeral, even if they don't know what those things are. Considering that funeral arrangements must be made in an unreasonably short time, everyone will benefit from having knowledge of what's required. The information in this chapter will prepare you to meet with a funeral director, and can put you well on your way to knowing what is required so that if you are ever called upon to arrange the funeral for a loved one, you won't be so overwhelmed by the details that you cannot focus on the loss of a loved one.

Previously, I stated my opinion that everything in this book requires conversations and some kind of advanced planning. I restate that opinion here. Some conversations are relatively easy. Others, not so easy. Conversations about your funeral and burial obviously revolve around the subject of your death, and I know you don't want to even think about it, let alone talk about it, even though, at some level, you know that the mortality rate for human beings is and always will be 100%. Knowing that fact, however, doesn't seem to motivate people to have the "hard" conversations about this very sensitive subject. If we can agree, then, that death is the only certainty in life, wouldn't it make sense to at least talk about it before it's too late?

Simply stated, there are four basic steps to funeral and burial planning:

1. Research your options
2. Determine what you want and do not want
3. Preserve your wishes in writing
4. Tell someone about them

If you learn nothing else from this chapter, learn this: your funeral will take place, with or without your input. It doesn't matter whether or not you previously made your own choices/decisions, whether or not you documented those choices/decisions, and whether or not you communicated that information to your family. If you don't do these things, you are saying that it is all right for you to leave them to be made by someone else who may feel completely unprepared, at a time when they may be overwhelmed with grief from losing you. Most people already know this, but have a way of ignoring the reality for all the obvious reasons. If I repeat myself on this one point throughout the text, I apologize in advance.

Have you ever had conversations with your family about planning for your funeral and burial? If not, why not? What are you waiting for? Even though people really do know that conversations will have to take place sooner or later, even if that time turns out to be at the time of your death, most people will avoid the conversations as long as possible. And, in so doing, those same people are merely postponing the inevitable. It is painful to contemplate the loss of a loved one, but won't those conversations be more painful at the time of death of a beloved family member?

It is all right with me if you make the choice to avoid this whole subject ... that is, if it's all right with you. But I have to ask: *"What about your family? Did you ask them if it is all right with them?"* Have there been times when you seriously *attempted* to have the conversations, and your family members got all squeamish and refused to talk about it with you. Did they say something like, *"Oh, Dad, we don't have to talk about this now. There will be plenty of time later?"* Is that what they said to you? Of course, they didn't happen to say when "later" is, did they? And they haven't brought up the subject since then, have they?

Forgive them, for they are reacting to their own fear associated with losing you, while you are attempting to handle your personal business. Two very different topics. As you begin to see and understand that their fear is keeping them from talking about your death, as difficult as it may be, be patient but persistent. If this conversation is important to you, you must make the effort to enroll them in the possibilities of having this conversation with you (sooner) rather than about you (later). Point out the benefits of having the conversations before your death, and the consequences of avoiding them.

Try your best not to force them into having the conversation. The time to talk about funeral arrangements is when you and/or your family are healthy, calm, relaxed, thinking clearly, sharing your thoughts, questions, and intentions, everyone willingly participating in the "hard" conversations, without the emotional pain of your death. And, even if you think it may be a stretch, it *is* possible to inject some humor into the conversation ... and that can only happen when talking about this in advance of the actual event.

Even if you are relatively young, it would be good to at least think about and write down your preferences and give that writing to someone in your family who will be able to see that your wishes are carried out. Everyone knows that accidents and sudden deaths happen every day, so why not be prepared. Every day in the news, you read about the sudden, unexpected death of someone who was in the wrong place at the wrong time. Do you think those people were prepared? What about the teenager who crashed his car while speeding? What about the jogger he killed with his reckless driving? What about the families of the people who died? Do you think they were prepared? These things happen every day.

This conversation with your family, no matter how "hard" it is, may be the only opportunity you ever have to express yourself, to have your family members express themselves and to ask questions, to begin to see things from each other's perspective, and recognize how important it is for you to talk about these things with them now. Help your family to understand your wishes, and get them to agree to honor your request that they follow your instructions. Ask them to do it for you, even if they can't see that you are really doing it for them.

I realize that talking about your own death may be difficult and very emotional, even painful, for you and your loved ones. But, didn't we agree that death is a part of life? If you can think of it that way, it may make it easier to have the conversations with your family. I've made funeral and burial plans several times, each with a combination of pre-planning and final arrangements that had to be made at the time of death. I also sold cemetery property, so I've seen the planning process from both sides. I recommend some planning, but not all. *More about this later.*

The point I'm trying to make is the necessity and importance of timely, appropriate CONVERSATIONS.

If your children refuse to have the conversation with you, or, once having begun the conversation, "drop out," then it will be up to you what you do next:

1. you can acknowledge their upset, and do your best to keep them engaged in the conversation; or
2. failing that, you can continue with your own research, and
3. then you can decide what kind of funeral arrangements you want, and,
4. then you can put all of your decisions (choices) in writing; and,
5. then you can tell your family what you have decided, and where they can find your instructions, and,
6. you can decide whether or not to make and/or pay for the arrangements you want for yourself; or
7. you can succumb to their upset and do nothing.

> **Love is the only thing that we can carry with us when we go, and it makes the end so easy.**
>
> Louisa May Alcott

PHONE CALLS TO FAMILY and FRIENDS

Long before the time of need, there is something you can do. Someday, it will prove to have been a very good use of your time. I'm talking about filling in the form I call PEOPLE TO CALL. An actual form is included at the end of this chapter.

I believe it is important that your family know the names and phone numbers of all the people you would want to be contacted in the event of an emergency, injury, illness or death. You would want that, wouldn't you? As much as you don't like talking about it, remember that we agreed earlier that the day will come, so you may as well be prepared.

I recommend that you create a list or chart to include four columns as in the sample below. I created my list on my computer so I can easily change it when necessary. The form is best created in **Landscape** format because it allows for additional spacing. Below is a sample to give you the idea.

Name	Phone Number	How I know this person	Email address
Jane Doe	1-234-567-8900	We worked at ABC Co.	
John Doe, MD	408-678-9100	My doctor	
ABC Company	256-234-5678	My employer	
Lions Club	104-237-9645	I am a member	
Mary Smith	104-239-5678	High School Alumni	
etc.			

There is nothing wrong with creating the list in your own handwriting or printing on a tablet if it is easy for you to create and keep up to date, as long as it is always legible, and not filled with inserts, cross-outs, and Wite-Out. Do take the time to make this list and keep it current.

Put this PEOPLE TO CALL list with your Funeral & Burial Instructions, and give a copy of the list to the member of your family you trust to carry out this request when the time comes. And when you revise the list, shred the old one, replace it with the new one, and give this person a revised copy.

Prepare your list with only 10 names on each page. If your list includes 100 people, you will need to create 10 separate pages. Why? Read on.

- When the time comes to make the calls, if each page has only 10 names on it, it would not be burdensome for any one person to make those 10 phone calls. Going one step further, you might ask someone if they would make more than 10 calls, because you'd like everyone on your list to be contacted. Chances are very good that they will gladly take on more calls or even suggest others willing to help.

Be certain to include the names and contact information for all organizations of which you are a member, especially if the organization might be participating in your funeral service. It will make contacting them easy. Also, include names and contact information for people from you past – school friends, people from the old neighborhood, co-workers through the years, EVERYONE you want to know. And, don't forget the names of professionals in your life who have the need to know (doctors, lawyers, accountants, insurance agents, financial advisors, clergy). Everyone! More is better.

- A PEOPLE TO CALL list can also be the place to find the names of people to call to help you care for a loved one who is ill, injured or disabled … particularly if you find yourself in the position of being that person's caretaker and you need a break. Complete the list before it is too late.

> ### REMEMBER:
>
> No other person knows <u>all</u> the people you know ... not your spouse, your children, your parents, your friends ...
>
> ONLY YOU.

Making phone calls is no small task. Remember that your family will be upset and, without your list, they may not remember to contact all the people you want to know about your situation. They may not even *know* some of the people on your list. You may have friends, former co-workers, and family members who live out of town, people who would have no way of knowing of your death if no one calls them. Also keep in mind that your obituary may be published in the local newspaper too late for some people to see it; and others who live elsewhere might never even find out because no one called them.

Someday, your family will thank you for being so organized.

> *OR NOT ...*
>
> *I recently asked 7 people if they have filled out the form yet, and all 7 said no. Why do you suppose that is? One person suggested that I call the form something else, mmm ... something that did not carry with it the connection with illness and death ... something more pleasant. Excuse me? Did I miss something? Isn't that the whole point of the form?*
>
> *I could call it "My List of Friends" or "My Happy List" or something else equally happy and pleasant, but the purpose of the list would remain the same. If I changed the name, would that motivate people to fill in the form? Would it satisfy the need of some people to ignore the fact that they will die someday?*
>
> *Every person told me they were very busy. Maybe those words should be carved on their tombstones:*
> *"Here lies John Doe. He was very busy."*
>
> *Include the completion of this list on your "Bucket List" of things to do before you kick the bucket. Give it a high priority. I am not kidding. Fill out the form, already. Stop making excuses. No one else knows all the people you know.*

Here are some true stories about why I believe this list is important.

> *1.*
>
> *Years ago, the husband of a friend of mine died. For years, he had been the best friend of a man I'll call Harry. They had been best men in each other's weddings. They had vacationed together many times. But as time passed, they lived in different towns and were no longer in regular contact with each other.*
>
> *When my friend's husband died, Harry didn't show up at the funeral. Nor did he send a card or flowers. My friend never heard from Harry because he lived out of town, where he had no access to the local newspaper obituary about her husband. And, no one called him. How was Harry supposed to know that his friend died if no one called him?*
>
> *The fact that no one had called Harry made two people upset: first, my friend, who remains upset and bitter years later, about the fact that she never heard from Harry; and second, Harry himself, for never having been given an opportunity to attend his friend's funeral had he known. But he didn't know. There were hurt feelings on both sides.*
>
> *2.*
>
> *Another example of the use of this form was when my former husband died in 2009. Several months before his death, I asked him to fill out the form, and he did it right away. I only asked him at the time because I was asking "everyone" I knew to do it. In retrospect, I was surprised that he did at all, because it wasn't in his nature to talk about serious matters like illness and death. But, looking back, maybe he knew the extent of his illness and didn't tell me.*
>
> *Anyway, when he got his final diagnosis, and was told that he only had a short time to live, I began calling the people on his list. So, for the last 3 weeks of his life, he was well enough to enjoy the visits of his friends and relatives, some of whom he hadn't seen in a long while, all of whom were generous and interested and happy to be visiting. It provided an opportunity for everyone to share fond memories, a few laughs and some tears, and a chance to say one last good-bye.*

> *3.*
>
> *When my Mother died, hers was the first funeral where I was responsible to make the arrangements. Among all the other things that had to be done, I spent hours making phone calls to people she knew and who knew her. I know that I missed some people, and I regret that, but my Mother's A-Z book was not complete. I did the best I could, and I would have called many more people if I had had a complete list.*
>
> *4.*
>
> *A lawyer I know likes this form so much that he includes it in his discussions with clients about estate planning.*

What Can I Do To Help?

I'm sure you have experienced a time when there was a family emergency, illness or death, and people asked what they could do to help. When people ask that question, that would be the perfect time to ask them to make phone calls. I would be surprised if anyone refused the request, because, after all, they *did* ask how they could help.

> *When my Father died, a close friend asked what she could do to help me. I said that she could send me flowers. Well, for most people, that would have been an ordinary request; but, you see, at that time, I was the owner of a flower shop, and because of this fact, I was pretty sure no one was going to send me flowers, and I really wanted someone to send me flowers. She said she would feel "funny" doing that, and gave me a macaroni casserole instead.*
>
> *If you ask what you can do to help, unless you make a specific offer to do a specific thing, be prepared to do what you are asked, or at least have a very good reason why you cannot honor that request. Remember: you asked.*

WHERE SHOULD I KEEP MY FUNERAL AND BURIAL INSTRUCTIONS?

I recommend putting all documentation regarding your Funeral & Burial Instructions into a 3-ring notebook, to be kept in your safe with all your other important papers.

Use page protectors to keep things organized and together. Include all relevant information, receipts, insurance policies, and purchase documents, as well as your written instructions and requests ... safeguarded all in one place.

Having made your decisions about what you want and do not want for your funeral and burial, and having written them down, and placed them in a 3-ring notebook in your safe, let's take a look at two places where your Funeral & Burial Instructions should <u>NEVER</u> be:

- WRITTEN IN THE TEXT OF YOUR WILL
- IN YOUR SAFE DEPOSIT BOX AT THE BANK

Why not? After all, you want your instructions to be safe. Aren't they safe places?
Well, yes. Maybe *too* safe. Here's why.

- Your Will may not be read until **after** the funeral.

- The Safe Deposit Box is not generally opened until **after** your funeral.

- **By then, it will be too late ...** especially if the instructions you wrote are different than the way your family did things. *Remember, that egg you can't uncrack ... ?*

If you have written letters to be opened after your death, place each in a separate envelope and place them with your Funeral & Burial Instructions until the time comes.

If you have written a list to direct your executor in how to distribute your possessions after your death, include that list.

And, don't forget to tell someone where to find this notebook well in advance of your death so they make the arrangements you want. Remember, they are not mind readers.

MISTAKES HAPPEN

If you have made pre-need funeral and/or burial arrangements, your family must know about them so that they can follow your instructions and so they don't duplicate them? Consider the following scenarios:

- What if you have an insurance policy with a funeral director to pay for all of the arrangements which you, yourself, have made in advance; and, you have selected and paid for a burial plot at a local cemetery and have even gone so far as to have your tombstone bought, paid for, and installed. **Did you tell your family?**

- What if, being a thoughtful planner, you prepared detailed instructions and information about all of your plans, and put the information into a nice notebook, and put it away for safekeeping. You included the cemetery deed (also known as a certificate of ownership). **But you never told anyone in your family where to find it? Your family doesn't even know it exists.**

  - What's the big secret? Your Funeral & Burial Instructions are not important to national security?

- And, then, when you die, because your family is completely unaware of your planning, what if they go to a different funeral director and bury you in a different cemetery? Worse, what if they cremated you? All your plans and all your money were wasted because your family made other arrangements, and spent a duplicate amount of money for the simple reason that you never bothered to tell them ... *all because of a conversation that never happened.*

WHOSE FAULT WOULD THIS BE?

MEETING WITH THE FUNERAL DIRECTOR

Previously, I have said that one of the main purposes in my writing this book is to prepare you to meet with professionals in all of the five categories of this book. If you have never sat down with a funeral director to make arrangements, you may not know all the questions you will be asked and all the information they will need from you. The text of this chapter will prepare you for such a meeting.

Some funeral directors offer Funeral Planning Booklets that they will give you at no cost. It would be a good idea to get one or two to familiarize yourself with the necessary things for planning a funeral, whether it is your own or that of someone else.

Before you get into talking about the actual funeral arrangements, the funeral director will need certain specific information from you about the decedent. Be prepared with a written list that includes the following information about the deceased and his/her family:

- Name, address and phone number of decedent
- Social Security Number
- Armed Services Number (copy of military discharge papers)
- Birth Date and place
- Cause of death if you know it
- Name of attending physician
- Father's name and birthplace
- Mother's maiden name and birthplace
- How long the decedent lived at his/her current address
- How long he/she lived in the state of permanent residence
- Occupation and employer
- Workplace address and phone number
- Cemetery Deed (if you have one)

- Funds to pay for the funeral
- Will you (or the family) be providing clothing for the your loved one?
- The deceased person's instructions.

If you make a special request of the funeral director, do your best to make it understood how important the request is to you, and that you <u>expect</u> it to be honored. Remind him, if necessary, that you are paying him, not the other way around. And, if you are a funeral director reading this, do not assume you know better what the family wants, especially if they have expressly told you what they want, and you took it upon yourself to change their request because it is "unusual," as you define unusual.

You and the funeral director will also need to talk about the following important details:

1. Location of Funeral & Burial Instructions of the deceased person (any unusual requests?)
2. Source of Money
3. Organ Donation or no Organ Donation (have arrangements already been made?)
4. Does the deceased have a pacemaker or other device implanted in their body?
5. Viewing or No Viewing? Where?
6. Cremation or No Cremation (disposition of cremains?)
7. In-ground Burial or Mausoleum (cemetery deed or certificate of ownership?)
8. Limousines (how many?)
9. How many Death Certificates will you want? (at least 25)
10. Disposition of flowers after the ceremony?
11. How many chairs do you want set up at the gravesite? Do you want a tent?
12. To whom should the American flag be presented (if there is one)?

13. <u>Transportation</u>: The funeral director will also want to know if you anticipate a large number of people attending the services, whether in the funeral home or the church. Arrangements need to be made for the funeral director to provide adequate staff to handle the parking of cars and organizing the vehicle procession from one location to another. As you talk about the number of people, you and the funeral director may see that some police presence will be necessary to adequately and safely assist with the vehicle procession. If there is a significant geographical distance between the funeral home, the church and/or the cemetery, that distance has to be discussed when making the funeral arrangements.

> <u>Note</u>: If it turns out that a police escort will be provided, it would be good to make a donation to the local police association. The funeral director should be able to provide you with details.

14. <u>The Weather</u>: Are funerals ever postponed due to inclement weather? You might want to talk about the predicted weather on the day and/or evening of the viewing and/or church service. It is entirely possible that extreme weather conditions can significantly alter the best plans, for better or for worse. Think excessive heat warning, hurricanes or ice storms, for example. When I worked at the cemetery, I only assisted at one funeral during a heavy rainstorm, and it was not a pretty sight. Thankfully, the thunder and lightning didn't start until the last person drove out of the cemetery.

> - As inconvenient as it may be to have to postpone a funeral (or at least a burial) because of extreme weather, in addition to other factors, it may be necessary because of legal liability. Someone could slip and fall and be injured on a muddy lawn or icy driveway. I recall the pallbearers carrying my grandmother's coffin to the top of a hill on snow-covered ground and wondering, *"What if they slip and fall and drop the coffin?"*

> - If there are to be any extreme weather conditions on the day(s) of the funeral, who will be responsible for making the final decision of whether or not the funeral can proceed, and by when? How will that decision be communicated to the people in need of that information? What arrangements will there be at the cemetery in the event of heavy rain or snow?

> - Ask if there is an indoor chapel where a service could be held instead of at the gravesite in case of bad weather, and how much extra it will cost to use the chapel. Ask also if the fee to use the chapel because of bad weather can be waived. *It can't hurt to ask.*

15. Some people are very upset at seeing the casket of their loved one lowered into the grave; so, if it is important to you, you must make the specific request that the casket not be lowered and the grave not be closed until everyone has left the cemetery, and get confirmation that your instructions have been communicated to the cemetery personnel and/or your funeral director.

> - Additionally, it is extremely upsetting to some family members to see the cemetery workers sitting nearby, talking, eating (or worse, laughing) while your loved one's graveside service is taking place. If this is important to you, please discuss it with the funeral director so it can be passed on to the cemetery staff. Such

behavior is in extremely poor taste on the part of the grounds crew, and is something that should be reported to the cemetery management to address.

16.   Theme Funerals: If you will be making special requests of the funeral director to arrange a theme funeral, you will have to determine if the event is to be a dignified celebration or a riotous party. The funeral director may not want a loud party on their premises, but may be willing to assist you in making the arrangements for another location, or suggest where else you might have the celebration. There is a trend toward personalizing funerals (lately, called life celebrations), and the funeral industry is trying to keep up with the ideas and imagination of Baby Boomers by building designer caskets and urns. Google "theme funerals" for more on this subject.

- Baby Boomers have been re-arranging the rules (*that is, as opposed to breaking the rules*) for their entire adult lives. If you are a Baby Boomer and you are either planning your own funeral or the funeral of another, a theme funeral would not be an unlikely choice for celebrating the life of a loved one. It could be said that such an event is only limited by (1) your imagination, (2) your available funds, (3) the amount of time required to arrange such an event, (4) the family's sensibilities, (5) the weather, (6) the cooperation of the funeral director and/or (7) the church. If it is decided that a traditional funeral is **in**appropriate for the person recently passed, the arrangements could be dignified, yet still keeping with that person's life interests. But, pay attention to see if someone close to the deceased is seriously opposed to the idea, and if so, might there be room for compromise? If the arrangements include services in a house of worship, determine in advance if the unusual arrangements are permitted.

ORGAN DONATION

The funeral director will need to know the details of this donation right away. Once the funeral director has finished with a body, there is no going back. Remember my philosophy of getting it right the first time? Here is one place where there are no do-overs.

If you intend for your organs to be donated, or for your body to be donated to science, there are steps you must take before you die to formally and legally document your intentions.

• These may include checking the box on your driver's license indicating your intention to donate your organs, or making pre-arrangements with a medical school for your body to be donated at the time of your death.

• If either of these choices is your intention, document all the details of the organization that will be receiving your organs or body, including names, addresses, phone numbers, contact persons, terms and conditions of your agreement with them, etc.

• Keep this documentation with your Funeral & Burial Instructions, and be sure your family knows of your intentions and your actions. Put a photocopy of a Driver's License with your Instructions so your family can see that you checked the box for "organ donation." You might even want to let your physician, your executor, and your lawyer know what you have done.

The opposite is that you absolutely, under no circumstances whatsoever, wish to donate your body parts to anybody! If this is something you feel very strongly about, you must also communicate this to your loved ones, in advance, preferably in writing. *Another one of those "hard" conversations ...*

If you have no strong feelings one way or the other, you might tell your loved ones that, should you die under circumstances that would allow for your vital organs to be donated to save someone's life, give them written permission to make appropriate arrangements for such organ donation at the time of your death.

No matter what you decide, your loved ones, doctor, lawyer, executor, must know about your plans well in advance of your death and funeral. **This is no place for a failure to communicate!**

- Oh, yes, one more thing. I recently read that medical devices implanted in the body must be removed, especially before cremation, and can sometimes be donated for use by others in foreign countries ... things like pacemakers, TENS units, and defibrillators. Don't have the details as of this writing, but you may want to discuss this with your physician and your funeral director.

ADVANCED PLANNING

Gail Rubin, in her book, *A Good Good-bye*, writes: *"Just as talking about sex won't make you pregnant, talking about funerals won't make you dead – and your family will benefit from the conversation."*

Be prepared for this. Men don't like to talk about their death. They often sabotage all efforts to make funeral and burial plans for themselves and you. Be ready for a man's refusal to participate in the process. A man who sabotages end-of-life planning is afraid, plain and simple. But, can he clearly state what he is really afraid of? *Oh, I suppose he could just be selfish, but let's give him the benefit of doubt.*

Men, in their own defense, will say that they, themselves, will never personally see the benefits of the money spent for such things, so why bother? OK, I see their point of view, but I don't agree with it. What about your family? If you love them as you say you do, can you at least consider the possibility that making funeral and burial arrangements in advance is a loving gift you can give to your family?

The fact that women live longer than men means that the probability is very high that the wife will be the person making arrangements for her husband's funeral. Why should she be left to make the decisions alone, just because her husband refuses to ***talk*** about making plans for his ultimate death, let alone actually make the plans in advance? I would really like it if husbands could get in touch with how selfish this behavior is, how very inconsiderate they are being when they refuse to talk with their wives about the one single event that is going to happen to everyone, sooner or later.

There are things a man can do to alleviate some (all) of his fears if he is willing to (a) admit to the fear; (b) ask questions; and (c) try new things.

- Could it be that there are religious questions and fears that he has never resolved?

    If this is the case, he could seek counseling from a member of the clergy of his chosen religion, or for that matter, from another religion, in order to talk about these matters which are obviously of great importance to him.

- Could it be that he is afraid that if he admits to his fears, he will be considered weak, and no man wants to be perceived as weak?

    Could he contemplate the possibility that he only <u>thinks</u> people will think that about him. Often, others see you entirely different from how you see yourself. At least consider the possibility.

- Could it be his level of discomfort talking about his own death, which may be many years in the future or it might be tomorrow?

    Would he be happy if he knew the date of his death? Well, get over that one ... it's not about to happen. And, don't sit around worrying about it. Live for today and let tomorrow come in its own good time.

- Could it be his refusal to accept the fact that there will come a day when he is no longer living?

    *Remember that elsewhere, I said that once you "get it" that you will die someday, you will experience a new-found freedom to live your life to the fullest degree possible ... for the rest of your life **between now and then** ...*

- Could it be that he is afraid he won't be remembered?

    This is an easy one. There are so many things a man can do so that his loved ones and friends will remember him – think good things only. No one wants to be remembered for having done bad things. So, if you make a mean stack of pancakes for your grandchildren when they visit, they will remember you for that. They will remember fabulous tomatoes you grew every summer, and the ball games you took them too, the stories you told them, the dogs you had and how much you loved them. If you don't believe me, go to some funerals and listen carefully to the things people say about the deceased person. You might be very surprised at the lovely things people remember. And, be sure to leave behind lots and lots of photographs.

- Could it be that he knows he has not taken care of his personal business, and that he might be leaving a mess behind?

This, too, is easy. Just do it! Straighten out your personal papers. Sign the estate-planning documents, share your last wishes with your family, put them in writing, keep them in a safe place, and tell someone about them. What are you waiting for?

- Could it be that he is afraid of what lies *between now and then?*

    *This one I get completely. It is one fear that we have the least amount of control over. Who knows what will happen **between now and then**? Nobody. So, all you can do is be prepared to the best of your ability. Take care of your health the best way you know how. Give thought to the kinds of care you want for yourself if you become ill or infirm. Clearly state your wishes in writing, especially in a Living Will. Share your intentions and desires with your family. Ask them to honor your wishes so you can have some peace of mind. And, then live out the remainder of your life doing at least some of the things that make you happy.*

Do you think women are less afraid?

Even if a wife is afraid of all the things named above that are involved with dying, she is generally much more willing to talk about her fears than is her husband. Women know that they can solve problems by talking them out. Men are hesitant to talk about their fears and upsets. Women know what's involved for them if they are left alone to make funeral arrangements for their husband. Wives want, need, and understand the protection that pre-planning offers, including the emotional comfort, financial protection, and assurance that she won't be left alone to make all the decisions by herself.

> *Somebody should tell us, right at the start of our lives, that were are dying. Then we might live life to the limit, every minute of every day. Do it, I say. Whatever you want to do, do it now. There are only so many tomorrows.*
>
> Pope Paul VI

Pre-planning is best done **together**, the way most husbands and wives have lived their lives ... making plans together. Well, maybe **not** together.

- Maybe I just assumed this is how most couples live their lives because I think it works best this way.
- Or, maybe the husband has all the say, and the wife surrenders because it's easier than arguing with him.
- Or, maybe it's just the opposite.
- Maybe they never learned how to negotiate win-win resolutions to disagreements.
- Maybe their way of making decisions is to make NO decision. Ouch! *I could tell you stories ...*

WHY DOES THE "NO" ALWAYS WIN?

I don't know why. I wish I did. The first time I heard this statement, I was really annoyed. It doesn't seem fair! *Excuse me, who said anything about fair? Oops, my mistake. Sorry.*

I've had conversations with many people over the years about this "NO" thing to find out what their opinions are, and I still am not satisfied. Why does the NO always win? Who benefits? Who is inconvenienced? If you don't believe that the NO always wins, pay careful attention to your interaction with your spouse, friends, co-workers, and relatives for a while, and test the theory of how the NO determines even simple choices. Are there people in your life who say NO automatically?

Elsewhere, I wrote about the NO; that is, the use and misuse of this tiny little word that has so much power. I point out the benefits of learning to say NO *without guilt* in situations that would ultimately protect you from something that was not in your best interest; for example, saying NO to people who want to borrow money from you, or in some other way, take advantage of your good nature.

The NO in that situation has a different context than the use of NO when planning for a funeral or burial. A person who says NO and holds fast to that position will generally create a situation in which no funeral plans are made. They may become argumentative or belligerent because they simply don't want to talk about funeral planning, and you may have a hard time convincing them to change their mind.

<u>MEMO</u>

To: All Husbands
From: Jeanne C. Hoff
Subject: Funerals and Burial (yours)

Please be advised that NOW is the time when you must take care of your personal business, which includes at the very least, seriously discussing your desires for your funeral and burial. NOW is the time to talk with your wife about her emotional and financial needs on that terrible day. Your wife needs your help and input to make decisions about your funeral and burial while you are both healthy and vibrant. It is your responsibility to support and protect her from having to make those decisions by herself on the worst day of her life … *the day of your death.*

Do not avoid the subject by thinking the kids will help your wife when the time comes. Children do not always agree with their Mother's decisions. Factor in the emotions they are experiencing over your death. Factor in the spouses of your married children, and you may have a complex family dynamic that can cause problems well into the future.

Do you want your family fighting over your funeral arrangements? Your heart and your head both say, "*NO!*" yet this could very well be what happens if you don't make plans now. And, stop saying, "*just put my body in a plastic bag and put it out with the trash.*" It isn't even original, and it isn't funny! <u>We're talking about your *death*, here</u>! Those words, even spoken in jest, are selfish and mean-spirited, and inflict pain upon your loved ones. Why would you so disrespect your family with those words?

Your family loves you and respects you and wants you to have the dignity that a well-planned funeral can provide. They also want your ideas and suggestions. Stop thinking only about yourself. Making funeral plans will not bring about your sudden death!

You can avoid this if you disagree with me. You can keep avoiding it until one day, it will be too late. On that day, your wife will have to make your funeral arrangements by herself. Is that really what you want to happen?

Most people would die sooner than think; in fact, they do.

Bertrand Russell

WHAT HAPPENS WHEN THE WIFE DIES FIRST?

Husbands generally don't handle making funeral arrangements very well. Alone, thrust into the most painful decision-making process of a lifetime, they are ill prepared … even men who make major decisions in their business and personal lives every day. Their refusal to accept the reality of death paralyzes many men, and the result can be a lot of emotional upset, over-spending, and family disharmony.

Men will often rely on their children to assist them in making funeral and burial arrangements, and the more people who are involved in the decision-making process, the harder it is to come to agreement. You know that management by committee never works.

Once upon a time, there was a woman who was in a very bad marriage of many years. She had the opportunity to purchase two mausoleums at a very low pre-construction price, so she bought them and never told her husband because she knew he would have said NO in very unpleasant ways. It is not for me to judge whether or not her decision was good, but she believed it was the right one for her at the time, and it did allow her to have the comfort and assurance that it was taken care of for when the time came.

This woman died in the middle of a week that had been very hazy, hot and humid. I can't imagine how terrible it would have been for her children to have to "shop around" for a cemetery plot with that man who just happened to be married to their mother. She knew him well, and that he would have made their lives hell when it came to making burial decisions for her, so she took care of her own personal business without his input or money to save her children from

243

having to deal with him on one of the worst days of their lives ... the day of her death. Her advance purchase of that mausoleum was an act of generosity and love for her children.

And, it turns out she was right. Right after she died, her husband began whining about how much it was going to cost him to buy a cemetery plot. When he learned that it was already bought and paid for, he was equally angry that his wife hadn't told him.

Sometimes, you have to do things yourself, at the right time, for the right reasons,
knowing you can't please all the people all the time.

The woman was my Mother.

Can you see the benefit of pre-planning for both surviving spouse and children?

By now, you know that I encourage advanced planning for many areas of your life, including funerals and burial, and, while I do recommend certain aspects of advanced funeral and burial planning, I do, however, hesitate when it comes to actually making and paying for all your funeral and burial arrangements in advance. You will read about my reasons in the following pages. If, however, you do choose to make and pay for your own advanced funeral and burial arrangements, keep a few things in mind:

• First, ask yourself why you are making the arrangements by yourself, why you are not including your family in your plans? Are they unwilling to have the conversation with you? Are you certain they would want to be excluded? Will they be hurt when they find out you have made the arrangements without them?

• Before you sign any papers, you might want to check with your financial planner and lawyer.

• You must specifically and legally sign all papers and do everything necessary for the transactions to take place at the time of your death, and then leave all that information in your Funeral & Burial Instructions which you keep with your Will and other important documents such that the papers could be quickly and easily located by the person who will be making the arrangements at the time of your death.

• Remember to safeguard the original receipts, signed original documents (cemetery deed, certificates of ownership, for example), and associated literature with your Funeral & Burial Instructions. Your loved ones will need those papers some day.

• You could put your instructions in a sealed envelope marked "to be opened at the time of my death," but be sure that someone else knows that these instructions exist, and where you keep them. Do NOT put funeral and burial instructions in your Will, or in your bank safe deposit box where no one will have access at the time of your death

• I recommend that you give someone very specific, written details regarding your payment of the expenses of your funeral. That someone can be your spouse, your executor, and/or your children ... someone you trust. You don't want the funeral director and/or cemetery telling your family that you never paid. (More about payment options follow.)

• Your writing might include a personal request, *signed and dated in your own handwriting*, that your loved ones do their very best to honor you and your wishes.

• Even if you do, in fact, make all your arrangements and pay for everything in advance, understand two things:

1. Your family can only make those specific arrangements if they know the details; and,

2. Following your instructions is a moral obligation, not a legal obligation

What If I Change My Mind?

You are certainly permitted to change your mind, but be careful when you do it. There could be legal and financial consequences you might not have thought about or understood at the time of purchase. If you actually do alter your pre-arrangements, be sure to understand the cancellation documents before you sign them. You might even want to have them reviewed by a lawyer beforehand.

If, after careful thought, you are absolutely certain you want to cancel the arrangements you have made and paid for, then you, yourself, will have to do what is necessary to cancel the plans with the funeral director and the cemetery, or change the financial vehicle you have in place to pay for everything. Although it may not be possible to get all your money back, you won't know until you investigate.

If you do change your mind, be sure to also change your instructions to your family. Do so in writing, and be sure to sign and date the paper. Give a copy of the revised instructions to the person(s) who have your original instructions. Remember to put both the original instructions and any changes in your notebook containing your Funeral & Burial Instructions, and always keep the original and altered instructions together in one place. (More on the Notebook later.)

Already, you can see how funeral plans connect to your legal, financial and personal choices.

WHAT ARE THE BENEFITS OF ADVANCED FUNERAL PLANNING?

- The choices are your own.
- There is time to make payment arrangements in advance.
- There is money to be saved, discounts to be had.
- Time for discussion with your loved ones in advance.
- Time to change your mind.
- Time to investigate options.
- Time for comparison shopping.
- Time to consider and establish priorities.
- A huge burden is lifted from your loved ones.
- Few (if any) regrets.
- More time for your family to celebrate your life.
- Few (if any) hurt feelings.
- Peace of mind.

There are several steps to take to begin the process of investigating and/or making your own funeral and burial arrangements:

1. Shop around. This would be time well spent, because you would then have a basic understanding of funeral and burial details and expenses.

   - Spend time (months, maybe), driving through cemeteries to determine what kind of burial space satisfies you emotionally and financially. If there is time, visit cemeteries in different seasons. Meet with cemetery representatives to discuss options and costs.

   - Meet with several funeral directors. Become familiar with the selections available to you for your funeral. Find out what selection and payment options are available to you and what each costs in terms of today's dollars and future costs.

2. Gather as much information as possible regarding your selections. Organize it and keep it all together with your Funeral & Burial Instructions.

3. Write down all your decisions and instructions and put them in the notebook with your Funeral & Burial Instructions, where they can be found by the person(s) who will ultimately be making your funeral arrangements.

4. Tell someone else (your spouse, your executor, your children, your lawyer) about your decisions, and where your written instructions (your Notebook) can be found.

Without direction from you, your family will have to rely on each other and the funeral director to make suggestions and arrangements. Funeral directors are experienced and can provide guidance, but they may not be able to spend time assisting with the choice of a cemetery, or comparison shopping, or making luncheon arrangements or flower and music selections. You need to express yourself completely if you want things to be done your way. Funeral directors are not mind readers.

WHAT ARE THE CONSEQUENCES OF MAKING NO ADVANCED PLANS?

- Burden of making decisions without direction from you.
- Emotional over-spending.
- Possible financial burden for your family.
- Important things overlooked or forgotten due to lack of time.
- Mistakes and decisions that cannot be corrected/changed.
- No cost savings; no discounts.
- No time to comparison shop.
- No time to look around for a cemetery.
- No time to investigate and consider burial options.
- No time to change your mind.
- Possible hurt feelings among survivors.
- Regrets for decisions made under time pressure.

I HEAR YOU ALREADY:

"Our loved one is dead and didn't specify what he/she wanted, so what does it really matter?"
It only matters if it matters to you and your family.

PAYMENT OPTIONS

*Disclaimer: Before you begin reading this section, know that the information provided
is for basic educational purposes only. I cannot guarantee it as being factual, and ask
that you consider this as you make your arrangements.*

There are several options available to pay for funeral and burial arrangements in advance, and as I said above, long-term payments are <u>not</u> available at the time of a death. If you are arranging a funeral, be prepared, one way or another, to pay for the funeral ... *in full* ... at the first meeting with the funeral director.

I strongly recommend that, before making any payment arrangements in advance, you have completed your visitation to funeral homes and cemeteries, have gathered information about your options, and that you have met with your financial planner before making the final decision, and certainly before you sign any papers. Your financial planner might know of other payment options that will be safe and offer you peace of mind. *See how these things interconnect?*

1. **Paying in advance.** If you were to have paid the funeral director in advance, your money would be put into a state-guaranteed escrow account to be used at the time of your death. Should you wish to later change to another funeral home, the funds could be designated accordingly. Rules and regulations about such things may vary from state to state. Be sure to get complete documentation of the transaction and safeguard the record of this payment for the future so it can be produced at the time of need. And, let your family know about this pre-need arrangement. This is another one of those things that your family must know about.

- **An alternative to paying in advance** would be to determine exactly what you want for your funeral, and then document your decisions in writing, but <u>then make **no** arrangements</u>. You will have investigated your options, decided what you want, you will have told someone else about your wishes and where they can find the papers, but you will not be committed to any plans, financial or otherwise. This way, your family will be able to follow your instructions, and will find it relatively easy to make your funeral and burial arrangements at the time of your death.

2. **Paying over time.** <u>This option is **not** available at the time of death.</u> Many funeral directors will establish a payment arrangement whereby you can pay over time (often, as many as 10 years) if you are making ***pre*-arrangements. It is also possible that, were you to die before that 10-year time period expired, the balance of your outstanding bill would be forgiven. Ask about this option. But, remember that there is no such financial advantage at the time of need.

3. **Paying at the time of death (cash or credit card)** If a family member pays the funeral bill with their own money or credit card, they should later be reimbursed in full from the decedent's own money, that is, of course, assuming the decedent had sufficient funds to reimburse the person who paid for the funeral. They could also be reimbursed from the decedent's estate if there will be an estate to administer and assuming the estate has sufficient funds. The person who made

the payment should submit verification documentation to the executor of your estate in order to be reimbursed. Reimbursement will not happen automatically.

- If you are the person who offers your own money or credit card to pay for the funeral of another person, it would be useful for you, personally, to have some clear understanding of when and how you will be reimbursed … that is, unless you are in the financial position to pay the expenses without the need to be reimbursed. *One more important conversation.*

4. **Paying from a decedent's estate.** Assuming that the decedent's estate has sufficient funds, the funeral director may agree to submit the funeral bill to the executor of the decedent's estate (or to the successor trustee of your revocable living trust) with the understanding and expectation that the bill will be promptly paid in full.

5. **Saving and designating money for the funeral bill.** If you have set aside money for the payment of your funeral bill, you must let your family know where to find this money so it can be used for the purpose you intended. Who other than you has access to that money? Where do you have that money? In the mattress? In a fire-proof box in your house? In a bank safe deposit box? In a separate bank account? In an investment account? Whose name is on that account? Details, details, details. Your written instructions should include all this information, too, plus your signature and the date. Once again, I remind you that these things do not happen automatically. They require planning and conversations with the appropriate people in your life.

6. **If you were to have funds in a joint bank account**, which you have designated for the specific purpose of paying your funeral bill, you must make it understood that the money in that account is, in fact, your money, and that the other person's name was put on the account for "convenience" only. *Whose convenience, by the way?* [See Chapter II – FINANCIAL for a discussion about joint bank accounts.] You must understand that upon your death, that other person becomes the sole owner of the money in that account by right of survivorship … unless you make it perfectly clear to that person (and any others who might have input), in a writing signed and dated by you, that you have specifically designated the money in that account for payment of your funeral expenses. Be aware that your instructions could potentially be ignored and the person could choose to keep the money. This is not your best option for payment of your funeral expenses.

7. **An insurance policy payable directly to the funeral home**. If you have purchased an insurance policy through the funeral home, the insurance proceeds will be used for the purpose of paying your funeral expenses. Funeral homes operate under the guidelines of the Federal Trade Commission. This protects the consumer. Money you pay to a funeral home in advance is 100% guaranteed because your money is put into a state-approved savings account or insurance program through the funeral home. Funeral directors who provide this insurance protection must be licensed to sell insurance.

- Ask questions.
- Verify information.
- Get it in writing.
- Safeguard the paperwork.
- Tell someone about it.

8. **A payable-on-death account.** You could establish a savings, money-market or investment account which you designate as POD (that is, payable on death) to the funeral director.

- Another word of caution: If you designate money to be paid to a specific funeral home, there is always the possibility that at the time of your death, the funeral home will no longer be in business. So, think long and hard before making a decision about this option.

9. **An insurance policy payable to a named beneficiary.** If you were to take out a life insurance policy on your life, and the named beneficiary is your spouse or one or more of your children … and, it is your intention that the proceeds of this policy are to be used to pay your funeral expenses … you must make it clear to your family that the insurance proceeds are, in fact, for the specific purpose of paying your funeral bill.

- Keep in mind, however, that the beneficiary named on that insurance policy is under no legal obligation to give up that money to pay for the expenses of your funeral. The proceeds of that insurance policy are technically to be his/her/their money. Remember, that is how **you** set it up. If you anticipate a problem, make other arrangements. You do NOT want your family to fight about this. Or else, include this insurance in your conversation with your family so that they understand what will happen at the time of your death, and will not fight with each other.

10. **If you have appointed an Agent under your Durable General Power-of-Attorney**, that person could pay your funeral bill in advance of your death. This would only be a good idea if your death is imminent and there is no question that you have run out of time. It is important to know and understand that the appointment of a person under a

power-of-attorney ceases upon your death … which means that immediately after your death, your agent no longer has access to your money for the purpose of paying your funeral expenses.

In each situation, I recommend you discuss the sources of money with your financial advisor and/or your lawyer.
THIS IS NO TIME OR PLACE TO MAKE A MISTAKE.

$255 SOCIAL SECURITY DEATH BENEFIT

Let's take a look at the one-time $255 Death Benefit (which amount, by the way, has not changed in many, many years). It is available for a surviving spouse or minor children under certain conditions that must be met in order to receive the payment. It is not an automatic payment; *i.e.*, someone must apply for it.

My husband and I were sitting in the waiting room of the local Social Security office one afternoon, behind two men discussing the $255 death benefit. They were quite animated in their conversation about how or why the government figured a person could pay for a funeral with only $255. Where did people get the idea that this one-time payment was supposed to cover the expense of a funeral? I don't know the answer to this question, but it is a very popular conversation among seniors that the government is letting them down by paying so little toward a funeral which, everybody knows, will cost thousands of dollars. There are even commercials on TV saying how the government funeral benefits are insufficient. Of course, the commercial is trying to sell you life insurance which, by the way, is expensive.

Several months ago, I heard that the U. S. Government could save *billions* of dollars if they simply stopped paying out this $255 Death Benefit. $255 or no $255, the government (*that is, we the people*) will not be paying for your funeral, no matter how many people feel entitled to this "benefit." Come on, now, you already know that, when compared to the actual cost of a funeral, $255 won't even make a dent!

Be careful

> On December 11, 2010, my husband received a mailer for a "Government Benefit Supplement Policy." The mailer stated the company is "proud to announce a Senior Final Expense Program to help pay what Social Security does not pay for your final expense." Interestingly enough, the name of the insurance company was nowhere to be seen. The mailer did, however, say, in very small print at the bottom, that it is not affiliated with or endorsed by any government or Medicare program. The return address is only "Information Processing Center."
>
> The mailer goes on to say it will pay up to 100% of all funeral **expenses not paid by Social Security**, up to $15,000 for each Senior Citizen covered."
>
> What they **say** they want you to do is return the mailer and schedule an appointment for a representative to come to your house to provide a "FREE" service to you. What they **really** want to do is sell you insurance. True, if you buy enough insurance, it will cover the expense of your funeral, but the insurance is expensive. You will have to weigh the costs vs. the benefits before signing on the dotted line.
>
> There are questions you must answer before committing yourself to such a financial transaction that is advertised this way. It could be a scam. It could cost you thousands of dollars, although it was advertising as being "affordable." What if the insurance company is not highly rated? Be cautious. If it sounds too good …

The truth is, either your funeral will be paid for by you, personally, or by your estate, or by your family. Technically, if your estate pays for your funeral, that *is* your money, so you will ultimately be paying for your own funeral. That's just the way it is. There are payment options to be investigated and considered, but I wouldn't count on the Social Security benefit of $255 doing much good.

HERE ARE SOME POSSIBLE PLACES FOR REDUCING FUNERAL EXPENSES

- You don't need to buy the most expensive casket, grave marker, or cemetery plot.
- You don't need a fancy urn for your cremains.

- You don't need limousines.
- You may be able to select inexpensive (but still beautiful) flowers.
- The funeral luncheon doesn't have to be expensive and elaborate.
- You don't have to purchase a tombstone immediately.

QUESTIONS

I recently asked someone, "**What is the first thing you would like to know about funeral planning?**" and their answer was that they wanted to know what to do immediately after a person dies. So, here is where you can begin:

1. If someone dies at home, dial 911. The police will respond, and then it will be determined where the person's body can be taken. Someone will have to "pronounce" ... which means to officially state that the person has actually died ... and that may require having the presence of a medical professional who can do that. If the person died from natural causes, things should go smoothly. If the reason for person's death cannot be immediately or easily determined, the medical examiner may have to do an autopsy. If the person's death was murder, suicide or some other extreme cause, other arrangements may need to be made as determined by the authorities at the time. If the person's body does not have to go to the medical examiner, the funeral director can be called and will come to remove the body to their facility.

2. Remove and safeguard all jewelry from the deceased person's body before transporting.

3. Notify the funeral home. If the death was expected, someone may have already been in contact with the funeral home of choice to make some pre-arrangements, and all that is required to begin the process of making final arrangements is that phone call. If no such pre-arrangement conversations took place, soon afterward, someone will have to meet with the funeral director in person to make the actual arrangements.

4. Call friends, family, co-workers. (See the PEOPLE TO CALL form below.)

5. If the deceased has already written his or her own obituary, take it with you to the funeral director. If not, gather all the information necessary to write an obituary as hereinafter described. In most cases, the funeral director will submit the obituary to the newspapers of your choice. Also take all the information the funeral director will need about the deceased.

6. Locate the decedent's Will and Funeral & Burial Instructions.

7. Secure the home of the deceased. It may mean calling a locksmith. Remove and safeguard all valuables from the home (if necessary). If the home of the deceased is a crime scene, the premises may be sealed by the police.

8. Select and ask someone to house sit (if appropriate).

9. Forward mail to the executor, next-of-kin, or to the lawyer who will be handling the decedent's estate.

10. Cancel newspapers.

11. Notify the decedent's executor, lawyer, accountant, insurance agent, physician (and all other medical providers), clergy, fraternal, military, civic organizations ... hopefully, their names will be on the PEOPLE TO CALL list.

Think about what you want and do not want before you decide how to respond to each question. For each question, there are three major responses that are possible:

1. You absolutely DO want it.
2. You absolutely DO NOT want it.
3. It doesn't really matter to you.

What follows are some questions that require answers, either now or later, either from you or from someone who will be making your funeral arrangements.

DO YOU WANT A VIEWING OR NOT?

Before you answer this question, consider your family. Some people have very strong opinions on this subject. I believe there are valid reasons for having a viewing. Mostly, viewings are for the living, as a way to say a final good-bye and have some degree of closure with the deceased person. While you are discussing the matter of your viewing with your family, give them permission to override your choice if it feels right for them at the time of your death, and if it will give them closure and peace of mind. For others, the decision will be made that, because of serious illness or injury, it would be best not to have a viewing.

NOTE: You can have a viewing and still be cremated afterward.

And, when arranging for a viewing, <u>plan for sufficient time</u> for family to greet visitors and guests. It may require two separate viewing times: one in the evening; one the next morning before the funeral service.

- If a person is 90 and has lived in a nursing home for years, there may be very few guests.

- If a person has been active in his/her community and many organizations, and/or has a large family, there may be hundreds.

- If there will be people coming from long distance, you might want to extend the time for the viewing to allow for their arrival.

Be Prepared for the Unexpected

When my Mother died, I discovered something I never knew before ... that a viewing is a social event. I saw people I hadn't seen in years: friends of my Mothers' from her high-school class, the old neighborhood and her church; people I worked with, people my sister and my husband worked with. So many people. Do not deprive your family of this occasion unless you have extremely strong feelings against it. I was surprised at the satisfaction her viewing brought to me and to the people who attended.

DO YOU WANT CREMATION OR NOT?

Let's say, for example, that you absolutely **do not** want to be cremated under any circumstances whatsoever; but, because you never told your family you didn't want your body cremated, and because your family is upset at your passing and having trouble coming to an agreement, and because they don't have money for your funeral expenses, they make the collective choice to cremate you. It will be less expensive and easier for them than having to make all those other decisions.

Remember Humpty Dumpty? This is one egg you can never uncrack.

How could this have happened? You didn't want to be cremated. Easy. You have no one to blame but yourself.

(1) you failed to make your own arrangements; and/or,
(2) you had made your choices, but never bothered to tell anyone in your family

---

What about your expectation that your family would honor your wishes?
Too bad! They did the best they could.
After all, they didn't know what you wanted because you never told them!

If you want your body cremated, you could join The Cremation Society and make all arrangements in advance, including payment for their services. If you make this choice, safeguard all of the paperwork you receive from the organization (including a receipt for payment) in your notebook with your Funeral & Burial Instructions, and tell your family, well in advance, what you have done so they will be prepared at the time of need. You could also make pre-arrangements for cremation with your local funeral director.

If you have no particular preference about cremation, let you family know that they are free to make the decision at the time of your death.

Although cremation is a popular option, there are many people who have very strong opinions on the subject. Whether you want your body cremated or not, you must tell your family in advance. And, should you choose cremation, what do you want to happen to your cremains? *Oh, no, not more questions ...*

WHAT DO YOU WANT DONE WITH YOUR CREMAINS?

It seems that when I asked people about their purchasing a burial plot, people regularly said:

"Oh, I don't need a cemetery plot. I'm going to be cremated" ...

as if that's the end of it. Maybe it is. Maybe not.

There are many things that can be done with your cremains:

- They can be buried in your cemetery plot, even if there has been a prior burial in a casket.
- Or scattered in a location you designate.
- Or placed in a single container for your family to keep.
- Or divided among several small containers to pass out to family members.
- Or in an urn and placed in a niche at the cemetery.
- Or in a mausoleum at a cemetery, even if there has been a prior entombment of a full casket.
- Or in an upright granite grave marker designed to hold cremains of several people.
- Or in a granite bench for the same purpose.
- Or placed into a stuffed animal.
- Or buried at sea.

> ***Did you even know there were so many choices?***

While each of these dispositions is best made by some kind of advanced planning, of course the decisions can be made in the time of need. The costs will naturally depend upon the choices made as to where the cremains will ultimately be placed.

The Los Angeles Times reports that more and more bodies are going unclaimed because relatives simply cannot afford to pay for the costs of a funeral and burial. Even a basic cremation costs about $1,000, and there is always the question of what to do with the "ashes."

IN-GROUND BURIAL or MAUSOLEUM?

Beyond the obvious differences between in-ground burial and entombment in a mausoleum, there is a cost difference, as well as personal preferences to be considered. Generally, mausoleum entombment is more expensive, but not necessarily. In-ground burial requires a concrete over box, and either a flat bronze grave marker or a granite tombstone, which cost money. The only way to know the actual costs is to shop around while you have time.

> *In 1980, my husband and I paid $2,500 for two full-casket mausoleum spaces at a cemetery that was selling mausoleums at a pre-construction price. Today, they could cost between $10,000 and $14,000. Such a bargain! We could probably not have gotten such a good return on a $2,500 investment from the stock market!*

Cemetery Trivia

In *The Philadelphia Inquirer* of May 29, 2012, there was a small article stating that Elvis Presley's original granite and marble mausoleum at Forest Hill Cemetery in Memphis, TN, is going to be auctioned to the highest bidder later in the month. Elvis and his mother, Gladys, had originally been buried there, but they were relocated to Graceland in the early autumn of 1977 soon after Elvis died.

Some people believe funeral pre-planning is morbid. You could choose to see it that way; on the other hand, I simply see these decisions as part of planning my own personal business *between now and then.*

I have even had conversations with people on the subject of funerals where we found a great deal of humor and fun by stretching our imaginations. I'm sure you have heard stories of people who wanted to be buried sitting upright in their favorite car. Imagine the cost of *that* burial? Of course, humor is only possible when you are <u>not</u> planning a funeral for a recently deceased person.

Life does not cease to be funny when people die
any more than it ceases to be serious when people laugh.

George Bernard Shaw

Whether your make the decisions and/or pre-arrangements yourself, or you leave them to be made by others at the time of your death, is completely up to you.

Because of indifference, one dies before one actually dies.

Elie Wiesel

Don't forget that upset, stress, and emotional anguish surrounding the death of a loved one may cloud the judgment of the person(s) making the arrangements, possibly causing them to spend too much money, make poor choices, or worse, render them unable to make decisions at all.

Do you really want to leave all the decisions to a loved one on one of the worst days of their life …
the day of your death?

What follows is a story about what happened when a widow was unable to make decisions for her husband's funeral. This woman's husband was my Father.

My Father died suddenly at 3 a.m. on a Friday. At 11 a.m., my sister and I went with his wife (who was not our Mother) to the funeral home to arrange for the service. What my sister and I did not yet know was that arrangements had already been made to cremate our Father's body, and there was to be no viewing. No discussion.

There was no real reason <u>not</u> to have allowed time for a viewing; he had been perfectly healthy before his death, and had not been injured in any kind of accident so that his body was disfigured. It was simply that his wife did not want a viewing. We asked her to reconsider her decision. She said, no, that she couldn't handle it … it was too much for her. We asked if she would allow us to arrange for a viewing and not attend herself, that we would take care of everything. She said no. She forbid me to make any flower arrangements, even though at the time, I was the owner of a flower shop.

I was very upset that the decisions had been made without including us. The funeral director repeatedly told us that his wife got to make this decision "under the law" and that we, as his only children, had no say in the matter. In retrospect, I probably should have challenged this, but I acceded to her wishes against my better judgment in order to keep peace.

252

Our Father had been a prominent physician, a life-long active Boy Scout, and a Mason, active in his church and community, and we believe, to this day, that he would have wanted a viewing ... he was always a bit of a show-off. And we believed that many people would have attended his viewing.

What was going on for our Father's wife was that our Father was her second husband to die suddenly in the middle of the night. She was totally distraught at this having happened twice in her life, and really wasn't thinking clearly. She insisted that our Father wanted to be cremated without a viewing. We do not believe it. But, he never wrote down his wishes for his own funeral.

And, even if we were certain of his wishes by having had conversations with him, the funeral director was having no parts of it. He deferred to our Father's wife on every decision, even though she was clearly too upset to make reasonable decisions, because he was protecting himself legally. Our wishes were of no concern to him.

You see, my Father didn't expect to die suddenly at the age of 75. He always jokingly told us he was going to live to be 100. Well, even if he had lived to be 100, he still should have written down his desired funeral arrangements so that my sister and I might have been able to give him a proper funeral.

As the person "legally" making all the funeral arrangements, my Father's wife was responsible for paying the bill. Guess what? She never paid the bill, and made no arrangements for burial or scattering of our Father's cremains. Two years later, my husband and I paid the bill and brought his cremains home with us. His wife had just left them at the funeral home. Don't ask ... because I don't know.

If you are in charge, stand your ground. Do not be bullied or intimidated by others who insist that things be done in ways that go against your better judgment or your wishes, <u>especially if you are the person who ends up paying the bill.</u>

SELECTION AND PURCHASE OF A CEMETERY PLOT

LOCATION, LOCATION, LOCATION
The 3 most important words in buying real estate.

Try to imagine buying a house and closing on the sale in fewer than 4 days! Outrageous! Not possible, you say ... that is, unless the "house" and land you are buying are for your burial.

How much thought have you given to where you want your final resting place to be? You know how exhausting it can be to shop for a new house ... days and days of driving around, meeting with salespeople, reading real estate ads, searching for just the right place. Well, when you remember that the cemetery plot will be your residence forever, it may take on a higher degree of importance; and, if you haven't taken the time to decide where you would like your body buried ...

- you will be leaving this decision to someone else who may care very deeply about you,
  but who is exhausted and upset, and having difficulty focusing; or,

- to someone who doesn't care one way or the other.

Picture This Scenario

Your husband just died unexpectedly. You are out of your mind with grief and exhaustion, and now, you find yourself walking through a cemetery, trying to decide where he (and ultimately, you) will be buried.

What if it's very hot and humid?
What if it's raining?
What if there is snow on the ground?
What if you are not physically able to go to the cemetery to select a space? *Then what?*

"But, how," you ask, *"can I decide? There are so many choices, and I'm so upset, and it's so **hot**!"* When you finally reach your limit, and cave in, you may say, *"Oh, just pick a spot and let's get it over with."* Not the best way to select a cemetery plot, but under the pressure of the moment, it happens.

You may find yourself annoyed, even angry, at your husband for refusing to discuss this matter with you years before. It is all right if these are the emotions you are feeling. You are thinking that this decision should have been made by <u>both</u> of you long ago, while you were still young and healthy. But, the thought passes, and you find the cemetery representative still standing beside you, patiently waiting for your decision, because there is no more time to think about it. You have run out of time. Today is the day.

Keep in mind that the choice you make will be permanent (and, while we all know that people do, in fact, relocate deceased, buried loved ones, it may take a court order and a lot of money to do it), so I recommend you get it right the first time!

If it matters to you where your final resting place is to be located, then it is up to you to spend time visiting cemeteries and memorial parks, and make your selection, IN ADVANCE. Why leave it up to someone else whose opinions and priorities may be different from yours? On the other hand, if it doesn't matter to you one way or the other, keep putting it off until you get around to it, or, exercise you option to do nothing.

---

*Gee whiz, do I have to give you another **ROUND TUIT**?*

This is not a decision for a surviving spouse to make alone, but many times, that is how it happens. It is a decision that you and your spouse or partner should make <u>*together, in advance.*</u> You <u>***can***</u> see that, can't you?

And if you absolutely refuse to talk about your funeral and burial plans, then go ahead and make your spouse or partner select the place for the two of you at the time of <u>your</u> death! It's all right with me if it's all right with you, but maybe you should first ask your spouse or partner what they think. Don't forget to think about his/her feelings or suffering or inability to make important decisions on one of the worst days of their lives … the day of your death.

Can you see how selfish it is for you to think this way?
Can you see how you are only thinking of yourself in this situation?

<u>Let's take this scenario one step further.</u>

What if you are single because of divorce, and you die without having first made burial arrangements for yourself, or without documenting your wishes? Picture your children driving through a cemetery on a hot, humid summer day, trying to select a nice place for you to be buried.

- But which cemetery?
- What if they cannot even agree on which cemetery, let alone which plot?
- What if, in their grief, they cannot agree on anything, and they fight among themselves?
- What if they have never really gotten along, and are now forced to come together to make this difficult choice?
- What if they decide to cremate your body because it is less expensive, and you never wanted to be cremated?
- What if they overspend and later find that there is insufficient money to pay for your funeral?
- Did you provide any money for your funeral, or do you have sufficient assets in your estate to pay for it?
- What if they don't have the money to pay for your funeral?
- What if, at some point, without agreement among them, they cave in and say, *"Oh, let's just get this over with."* It is at that point when poor decisions are often made.
- What if the arrangements they ultimately make, turn out to be arrangements you would <u>never</u> have made for yourself, had you made any.

Remember, you could have made all these decisions yourself, but you made the choice to keep putting it off until LATER, until you got A Round Tuit, until you were READY. Now it's too late! "Better late than never" doesn't apply here.

> Does it <u>really</u> matter? I don't know. Maybe. Maybe not. What do you think?

DO YOU SEE THE POTENTIAL FOR PROBLEMS?

People from various nationalities have very specific preferences about where they want to be buried in a cemetery. It is necessary that you know this information before purchasing burial ground.

For some families, funerals and burial are taboo subjects, never to be discussed. In those families, you simply don't talk about these things until the time comes. And, of course, those same people certainly don't buy cemetery property in advance. *What an outrageous idea? Who would do such a ridiculous thing?* Well, if you don't make the decisions yourself, who do you think is going to take care of this, and when? On the day after you die? Oh, I guess they figure that if they don't think about it, it will go away. Bad idea!

> *Some families consider burial spaces important places for them to honor the memory of their loved ones. I once sold a single cemetery space to a man whose Father had died and was already buried in Florida. This man wanted a space for his Father in the veterans' garden of a local cemetery, where he and his wife and children could pay their respects to his Father on his birthday and other special occasions. You might think this was a ridiculous thing to do, or was a waste of money to buy a cemetery plot and a bronze plaque. If you had met the family, and seen how important it was for them and their children to remember their father and grandfather this way, you might see it differently.*

FINALLY, HERE IS THE LIST I TOLD YOU ABOUT
You thought I forgot about it, didn't you?

This list will give you some idea of the many decisions and choices to be made to arrange a funeral in a really short time.

1. Selection of a funeral director.
2. Selection and purchase of a cemetery plot.
3. Selection of a cemetery monument or plaque.
4. Do you want cremation or in-ground burial?
5. Do you want to donate your organs or your body?
6. Do you want a viewing or not?
7. Selection of casket or urn.
8. If you don't want your cremains buried, do you want them scattered, and if so, where?
9. Where do you want the *urn* kept? In-ground burial; niche at the cemetery; on the mantelpiece of a loved one?
10. Limousine or no limousine? Who gets to ride in the limousine?
11. Formal church service, informal service at the funeral home, or graveside service at the cemetery? None?
12. Services by a fraternal organization?
13. Clergy or no clergy?
14. Music selections.
15. Musicians (organist; soloist; bag-piper, etc.).
16. Flowers?
17. Readers?
18. Presenters?
19. Who do you want to give your eulogy?
20. Clothing for you to wear?
21. Pallbearers?
22. Your obituary?
23. Newspaper notices.
24. Luncheon/reception/Shiva? Where? Where is the money to pay for it?
25. Who will make phone calls to friends and family?
26. Possible transportation or housing needs for people from out of town?
27. Designation of person(s) to house-sit during the viewing, funeral and luncheon.
28. Child care or care for elderly or disabled persons and/or pets.

29. Thank-You notes.
30. And, last but not least, where will the money come from?

DID I MISS ANYTHING?

SO MANY DECISIONS, SO LITTLE TIME
If all you do is <u>read</u> the list, it may confuse and stress you. Relax and take a deep breath.

IT WILL HELP TO ASSIGN PRIORITIES.

If you are reading this list so that you can consider what arrangements you want for your own funeral and burial, and whether or not to make those arrangements in advance, you will have time on your side to investigate the options. But, at the time of a death, decisions absolutely must be made right away; some can wait a little while, but not for very long. Remember, the funeral is only a few days away.

If you have strong opinions one way or the other about your own funeral and burial, it is up to you to express yourself clearly and in a timely manner. Your loved ones are not mind readers, and they cannot know what you want unless you tell them.

In this book, I have expressed my opinion that advanced planning in many areas of life generally produces the results you want. You will read about situations when that is not always the case. Advanced planning for funerals is no different; it requires a lot of thinking and conversation. [There's that word again.] Better late than never doesn't apply here. Neither does he said/she said.

You can run and you can hide, and you can avoid thinking and talking about your funeral until your last day if you want to … but you know that if you don't make your own decisions and clearly state your wishes about your own funeral and burial, someone else will make the plans for you. Be assured of this one fact: plans <u>will</u> be made, one way or another, with or without your input. So, pay close attention to your own private thoughts and feelings about this very sensitive, very important subject – your funeral and burial.

---

*I hate funerals, and would not attend my own if it could be avoided,
but it is well for every man to stop once in a while to think of
what sort of a collection of mourners he is training for his final event.*

Robert T. Morris

No doubt, you know of a family where a loved one died suddenly, unexpectedly, either by natural causes or otherwise, and they had never talked about funeral plans. Do you remember how hard it was for them to make all the decisions and arrangements under the pressure of time and while suffering a terrible loss? Most people in a situation like this don't have money set aside for "funeral expenses," so on top of their emotional suffering, there can be a painful financial loss as well. *Just something else to think about ...*

- Do you remember that at the beginning of the book, I warned you that you might have to have conversations you don't want to have and spend money you don't want to spend? Well, this is one place where those two things come together.

As you read through this chapter, you will also see how funeral planning is connected to legal, financial, record-keeping and personal matters.

WHERE TO BEGIN?

SELECTION OF A FUNERAL DIRECTOR

It is not uncommon for families to use the same funeral director through several generations. The members of the family personally know the owners of the funeral home, and trust them. Be careful, though. Times have changed.

> *The old neighborhood has changed.*
> *Hurley Brothers Funeral Home is now called <u>Death 'n' Things</u>.*
>
> Elmore Leonard.

I recall seeing a "60 Minutes" TV show several years ago about how the funeral business has changed over the past few years - - while many funeral homes have the same name as they had for the past 50-75 years, they may have new owners: Big corporations operating in the "death care" industry. When they purchased the various mom-and-pop funeral homes, they agreed to retain the former owners' names, because name recognition in the funeral business has always been extremely important.

There are still some funeral homes individually owned, but not many. If this matters to you, check out who really owns the business in advance of any need, to see if you will be able to feel comfortable working with them when the time comes. Some people recognize this change in the funeral business, other do not. Ultimately, what is important is the service the funeral director provides, not who owns the business.

In many towns where there were people of various nationalities, their funeral home of choice may have historically been the one that was popular with people from similar backgrounds. It was simply how it was done years ago. I'm not so sure that people follow that example anymore.

Have you ever wondered why so many funerals are just like most other funerals? I think it could be that funeral directors are not in the habit of offering interesting, creative alternatives, even though such alternatives are available. It may also be that because people wait until a loved one dies, there is no time to be inventive or creative. Faced with the reality of all that must be done in a few days, everyone just wants to get it over with.

I want to point out something from my own experiences. Funeral directors, with few exceptions, are not people who usually think "outside the box." I mean no disrespect toward funeral directors, because I know they are doing their best to provide an absolutely necessary service while dealing with emotionally distraught people every day. It can't be easy. Nevertheless …

> *When arranging my Mother's funeral, I made the very specific request that the funeral director invite all the guests to the reception while everyone was still in the church, not from the gravesite, which is how it is usually done. The cemetery, the church, and the catering hall were geographically far apart, and I figured many people wouldn't want to do all that driving, and would go directly from the church to the reception hall.*
>
> *Since I had cried so much during the entire service, I hadn't noticed that the funeral director did <u>not</u> do as I specifically requested. I didn't notice it until I saw how few people were at the gravesite, which is when the funeral director invited the people to the reception. He chose to ignore my specific request. I was outraged, and told him so, but it was too late. The damage had been done.*
>
> *We planned and paid for a luncheon for 125 people, and only about 50 people showed up. The others, because they didn't go to the cemetery, and because they didn't hear any invitation at the end of the church service, thought there was no reception, and simply went home. I was very upset that everyone had been deprived of the opportunity to be together with our Mother's friends at the luncheon just because the funeral director was not comfortable doing something that he considered out of the ordinary. It was not HIS Mother's funeral. It was OURS, and he had no right to go against my specific request.*
>
> *Be prepared for the funeral director's "this is how it is always done" speech. I say this not as an accusation against funeral directors, per se, but so that you will be aware of how they think and speak, and be prepared to stand your ground if the arrangements you want are different than the norm, whatever that is.*

> *One year later, I was still upset about this, and wrote the funeral director a strong letter, telling him not to do that to someone else ... that we had paid him for a service, and he failed to provide the service as requested. His response was typical of people who operate under the square-peg/square-hole theory, and said that my request was not usually how things were done, and he had done his duty. He was unconcerned about how he deprived our family and friends. Excuse me? Just because my request was "different than the norm" was no reason for him to have ignored it.*

Every day, funeral directors meet with people who are in great emotional distress, often unable to think or make the simplest decisions, people who are suffering greatly at the death of a loved one. The job of a funeral director is hard enough when you consider the huge amount of guidance they provide for people in painful situations. Generally, however, I see that the way funeral directors do things is the way they have always done them, and it has been my experience that they will do their best to keep to the tried and true ... that is, unless you require them to do otherwise.

I began to wonder why most people are content to "settle" for choices actually made by the funeral director. I concluded it is because people, in general, have no experience in planning funerals, and they have received no direction or requests from their recently departed relative. It is simply easier ... *even necessary* ... for the funeral director to take the lead.

And, most people never took the time to investigate options and make their own decisions. Besides, who wants to be experienced at planning funerals? No one ... unless you are a funeral director. Oh, I suppose there are people from really large families who have been responsible for the funerals of many family members over the years, and I suppose that counts as experience, but it is not something most people are happy to be doing.

It is said that you cannot know how to do something you have never done before. This fact alone should inspire people to ask questions and for direction in making decisions. Stated another way, if you have done something at least once, you have some idea of how to proceed; but, funeral planning, for most people, doesn't fall into the category of having ever done it before, let alone very often. If you have never before planned a funeral, allow the funeral director to guide you through the maze of decisions that must be made in an impossibly short time, and allow the above lists to prepare you.

By the time your loved one meets with the funeral director to plan your funeral, they are exhausted, possibly financially drained, very upset at your passing. The funeral director must take the lead and provide your family with direction. There is no time left, and so they do that which they have always done ... they take the safe, usual, sometimes boring route.

Wouldn't you do the same, if you were a funeral director? I know I would.

> How can you expect a funeral to represent who you were in this life if your funeral is just like the funerals of everybody else? If you want your funeral to say something special about you, something about who you really are as an individual, YOU WILL HAVE TO DECIDE ON THE ARRANGEMENTS YOURSELF.

Some people, after the funeral, are unhappy (even critical) about decisions that were made at the time of death of a loved one, and felt the arrangements should have been different, more thoughtful, loving, appropriate, less expensive. I'm not even thinking about the cost – I'm thinking about the choices that were made or not made. A family in the throes of strong emotions at the death of a loved one will do the best they can, with what they have to work with. They need your compassion, understanding and forgiveness. They probably did the best they could under the circumstances.

(Having said this, you will find that I am particularly critical about funeral arrangements for members of my own family.)

DEATH CERTIFICATES

When arranging a funeral, you will be asked how many Death Certificates you want. Order as many Death Certificates as you think you may need to close every bank and investment account, sell cars, real estate and stock, plus at least 5 or 10 more. If, however, a person dies with virtually no assets, only a few Death Certificates are needed.

Death Certificates are inexpensive when obtained at the time of making the funeral arrangements. They cannot be legally photocopied, and do not expire. You would be surprised at the times in the future when you might need a Death Certificate.

Because it takes time to get new ones, it is good to have a few extras. After all, you may have just spent thousands of dollars for funeral costs, so what's a few more dollars for Death Certificates. This is not the place to pinch pennies.

If you run out of Death Certificates, you may be able to order more from the office of your local state representative. They may have a daily courier service between their office and the state offices, and can expedite the process for you. You may also be able to order additional Death Certificates at a later date from the funeral director, but know that Death Certificates are less expensive when ordered through the funeral director at the time of making funeral arrangements. If you need to order additional certificates at a later date, not only is the cost higher, but it could take as long as 18-24 weeks to get them. Consider that if it takes that long to get a Death Certificate, the delay may extend the probate process of the decedent's estate, and could interfere with the sale of real estate or other assets.

There are various reasons why Death Certificates could be required in the future. So, be safe rather than sorry, and get extra Death Certificates right away from the funeral director. They are non-perishable, don't cost much, and don't take up much space. Protect the original Death Certificates you don't immediately use the same way you protect all of your other important documents and records … in your safe.

- Among my family records, I have original Death Certificates for my parents and some of my grandparents and great-grandparents. I consider them an important part of my family history and am happy to have them.

When the funeral director gives you the Death Certificates, check them to be sure that all the information is correct, and if corrections are required, notify the funeral director immediately so that the changes can be properly and legally made. Do not write on the original Death Certificates. The funeral director will have them corrected and then give them back to you.

WHAT DO YOU WANT TO WEAR?

It's your final performance.
This is no dress rehearsal.
The show closes today.
There is no encore.
You have to get it right the first time.

This is the last important social event of your life, and you say you have nothing to wear! A common complaint among women! After all, you want to look good.

> *I told my husband that if he ever buries me in a pink dress, I will haunt him through eternity. I never wear pink. I look terrible in pink, and certainly won't look good in pink after the funeral director has finished with my body.*
>
> *I want to be buried wearing black, not because I think it's the color of death, but because, in life, I wear a lot of black, I look good in black, I feel good wearing black, and believe it or not, black is my favorite color. No kidding!*

You may recall that I stressed the importance of getting things right the first time. Well, here is a perfect example of when that is necessary.

If it matters to you, tell someone you trust the exact clothing you want to wear, and tell them where it can be found. Ask that they see that your wish is carried out. If you don't specify the clothes you'd like to wear for your funeral, or at least the color, you could end up wearing pink! *Oh, no, not that!*

Be very specific if you want to wear a certain uniform or ceremonial garb for military or fraternal services. If you are a member of a fraternal organization like the Masons or a Knights of Columbus, you may want to be buried wearing a tuxedo and ceremonial ribbons, aprons, or jewels. If you wish to be buried in military uniform, specify exactly what clothing you want to wear. I know a man who was buried in his work clothes, because he was a well-known builder, and people knew him best in his work clothes. Be sure to include the location of your desired clothing and ceremonial regalia with your Funeral & Burial Instructions.

If you wish to wear jewelry for your viewing, specify the exact jewelry. Select wisely, and only have jewelry placed on your body if it is very important to you. Be very specific with instructions that the pieces of jewelry you wear for your viewing, must be removed from your body before burial or cremation. As you make your selection, keep in mind that a lot of jewelry is stolen by cemetery and/or funeral workers … an unfortunate reality, but sometimes true.

- *Maybe you might consider giving your jewelry to family members during the years before your death.*

If you wish a specific portion of that uniform dress to be given to a member of your family before your burial or cremation, you must be very specific with your instructions about this, preferably in writing to be kept with your funeral instructions. For example, if you had been the Master of a Masonic Lodge or the Grand Knight of the Knights of Columbus, you may want your ring or jewel given to your son or daughter. This sort of thing may not happen without your specific written instructions. Both the person who makes your funeral arrangements <u>and</u> the funeral director need to know this information.

I want to tell you about the burial clothing of 4 people, three of whom were members of my family.

1.

Once, in a casual conversation, years before her death, my Mother said she would like to be buried in the dress she wore for my sister's wedding. We weren't even talking about funerals that day, but I guess the idea just popped into her head. And, when she died, we saw that she was buried in that beautiful dress she, herself, chose.

2.

My maternal grandmother, who always wore black or navy blue, was buried in a PINK dress purchased from the funeral director. Never in her life did she wear pink! She looked terrible in pink. This happened because the people in charge of her funeral made that decision; they disrespected her in life, and did the same when she died.

3.

The next story about burial clothing relates to my other grandmother. Her husband, my grandfather, had a huge, showy funeral he planned for himself. He did not, however, bother to make any plans for my grandmother's funeral. She was a widow for 5 years, and when she died, her 3 sons made the funeral arrangements, making selections that were expedient and inexpensive, and in no way reflected the lovely woman who was their Mother.

My grandmother's sons (including my own Father) buried my grandmother in an old dress of her own, but no one knew it because they had specified a closed casket. When I questioned them as to why they didn't give her a more appropriate, loving, respectful funeral, they said it was because they didn't buy her a new dress. Excuse me! Why not?

So, my dear little grandmother was buried wearing an old dress, with a closed casket, no church service, no flowers, no music … just a minister saying a few words at the funeral home. It was a very sad funeral for lots of reasons, but I never forgot that her sons wouldn't buy her a new dress.

4.

I once heard Leo Buscaglia, noted author and speaker, tell a story about a woman who, for many years, wanted a red dress. Each time she mentioned it to her husband, he criticized her for wanting such a "ridiculous" thing. One day, she found out that she had cancer, and she soon died. The husband then asked Leo Buscaglia if he thought it would be all right to bury his wife in a red dress.

<u>As for your eyeglasses</u>, some people have very strong opinions about whether or not they want to or should have their eyeglasses placed on their body. Some people believe that it is ridiculous because it is as if they are sleeping, and no one wears glasses when they sleep. Other people think that because, in life, everyone knew them wearing eyeglasses, they should wear their glasses in death. Again, this is a strictly a matter of personal preference.

If it matters to you, you must let someone know how you feel.

LIMOUSINES

The use of limousines costs extra. I do, however, think it is a very nice, thoughtful gesture to provide comfortable transportation for grieving family members from the funeral home to the church and then to the cemetery, especially during inclement weather.

How many limousines you need will depend upon how many people you want to ride in the limousines. For example, you would most likely choose people closest to the deceased person during their life, including (but not necessarily limited to the following people):

- the spouse of the deceased
- young children of the deceased
- elderly and disabled family members close to the deceased

The decision as to who rides and who doesn't ride in a limousine can be difficult for some families, and some kind of priorities should be established for making the choices. This is another one of those decisions that may cause people to express hurt feelings at being left out. If you anticipate any squabbling among family members, the safe way would be to use no limousines and do your best to arrange other transportation.

I personally believe that who rides in a limousine is not a place where anyone should fight or expresses hurt feelings; I do, however, know of such situations, and it is best that they be avoided whenever possible.

WHAT HAPPENS TO THE OWNERSHIP OF A CEMETERY PLOT IF YOU DIVORCE?

The ownership of a cemetery plot (or mausoleum) between husband and wife after they divorce is a matter to be discussed and finalized at the time of the divorce, along with the separation of all their other marital assets. It is, however, regularly overlooked.

If you and a spouse purchased cemetery property while you were married, and you later divorce, there are important papers to be signed by both of you at the cemetery to indicate the change of ownership. You must decide who gets the cemetery property, and the decision should be memorialized in the Property Settlement Agreement between husband and wife. As I said before, it is usually overlooked. Here is a scenario describing what can happen if the matter has not been handled previously.

> *Once upon a time, a married couple purchased a burial plot in joint names, and forgot about it during their divorce proceedings. Some years later, the wife remarried. Ten years after that, her second husband died, and she went to the cemetery to arrange for him to be buried in that plot.*
>
> *The problem was that her former husband, who was still living, remained joint owner of the plot. The woman needed him to sign a release, whereby he would be giving sole ownership of the plot to her. After that, she would be free to bury her present husband there. Fortunately, this woman's former husband agreed to transfer his share of ownership to her without any problems.*
>
> *If, for any reason, she had been unable to locate him, or if he refused, she would either have to buy another cemetery plot or make other arrangements. The reality is that she and her former husband remained the joint owners of that cemetery property until they executed appropriate documents saying otherwise.*

RETURN OR EXCHANGE POLICY

If you think it possible that cemetery property you buy now may not have the same appeal when you are older, don't buy it.

While it is technically possible to purchase cemetery/burial property (that is, a cemetery plot, a niche, or a mausoleum) and change your mind later, do not think of this purchase as you would think about buying and exchanging clothing, for example – that, if you don't like it, you can simply take it back and get a refund. It is not quite that simple, and if anyone tells you it is, make sure you ask them to thoroughly explain your rights of exchange and to give you a written guarantee.

Cemeteries generally don't buy back property. If you want to sell cemetery property, they can give you the name of a broker who may or may not be able to find you a buyer. Or, you can run an advertisement in a local newspaper, or sell it to someone you know. In any event, don't expect to sell the property in a short time, or for a profit, or even fair market value.

> Some years ago, my aunt and uncle moved from Pennsylvania to California, expecting to live out their lives in California. Years before, they had purchased plots at a local Pennsylvania cemetery, and when they moved, they gave me Power-of-Attorney to sell them on their behalf.
>
> I contacted the cemetery to see if they would buy the plots, and the answer was no. Over several months, I ran ads in local newspapers for the sale of the plots, at a seriously discounted price, and got no replies. At the time, I didn't know about cemetery brokers, but from what I know now, it probably wouldn't have mattered.
>
> The Power-of-Attorney my aunt and uncle granted to me was for the specific task of selling the cemetery plots, and had an expiration date of two years. In all that time, I was not able to find a buyer for their plots.
>
> My aunt and uncle have since died and were buried in California. Upon their death, my cousin, their only child, inherited their cemetery plots in Pennsylvania. Several years ago, he, too, unsuccessfully attempted to sell the plots.
>
> Now, he, too, has died, and was buried in California, and his daughter is trying to sell those Pennsylvania cemetery plots. She and I have recently talked about her donating the plots to a veterans' or charitable organization.

It is not <u>im</u>possible to change your mind, but it may not be easy, and you may run out of time deciding. Again, I remind you not to put the decision off for too long.

ONE MORE THING ABOUT EXCHANGES

If you were to move from one state to another, where you intend to reside for the rest of your life, and if you had already purchased property in a cemetery owned by one of the national companies that own and operate cemeteries, the company might allow for transfer of the funds you paid to one cemetery to be credited to another which they own in your new residence state.

If such a transfer is not for the cemetery of your preference, they may arrange for a monetary exchange that will assist you in purchasing burial property in your new state at the cemetery of your choice. And, while this transfer of funds may not be an exact dollar-for-dollar exchange as it applies to the kind of cemetery property you originally purchased, at least you won't be losing all your money.

WHAT HAPPENS TO UNUSED BURIAL LOTS?

It may not be the best idea to actually *purchase* cemetery property in advance unless you are absolutely certain you and/or your family will want to use them when the time comes, or if you will never relocate or change your mind.

If you own cemetery plots that you know will never be used by anyone in your family, (and if you have not been able to sell them as mentioned above), ask the cemetery to assist you in making arrangements to donate those plots to a church, a charitable organization, or a veterans' organization. I know a man who, years ago, inherited 24 cemetery plots from his uncle's estate. He has been unsuccessfully trying to sell them all this time. As long as he owns them, they are considered assets of his estate, which is something he doesn't want. Ultimately, he decided to donate the spaces to a local veterans' organization.

If you donate the plots, you will then be able to take a tax deduction for a portion of their then-current fair market value. Timing is important in making such donations. You do not want to make mistakes that could increase you taxes or trigger an IRS audit, so it would be in your best interests to talk with your accountant or tax lawyer before making such a donation.

> *When I worked at a cemetery, I arranged the burial of an elderly man whose executor was his former secretary. He was an only child, never married, had no children and no living relatives. He was buried with his parents in a family plot that included burial space for 20 people.*
>
> *Many years ago, before people married and began moving away, families lived and died geographically near each other, and it was common for a father to buy large cemetery plots for his future generations. At the time, it was considered a good investment. I'm sure this man's father thought there would be more children and grandchildren in his family as the years passed, but it didn't turn out that way.*
>
> *We talked about ways to dispose of the remaining spaces, and that it would probably not be easy. I even suggested that the executor and her husband might want to buy some burial spaces for themselves from the estate of the deceased. I don't know what ever happened to the remaining 17 spaces, but chances are good they will remain unused forever.*

It is much less expensive to pay for burial space well in advance, than at the time of need. <u>But be very careful!</u> You want assurances that the purchases you make today will be honored at the time of need in the future. Safeguard your purchase documents and receipts together with your Funeral & Burial Instructions. <u>Weigh the options against the risks and the expense,</u> especially the predicted expense in 5, 10 or 20 years.

SPEAKING OF BUYING REAL ESTATE

(*were we?*) … you know that term, "cemetery deed?" Well, technically you will not receive a deed, representing ownership of the real estate, but a <u>certificate of ownership</u> of the right to use that real estate for the sole purpose of burying your body when you die.

Why the distinction? Because, during the Great Depression, when people were rendered homeless, many camped out on the family burial plots, thinking that they owned the land. After all, they had a "deed," didn't they? So, the law was changed to give people the right to use the land for burial, but not as a place to live.

HOW MANY ROOMS?

Cemeteries plots have different configurations. It's sort of like houses: how many rooms, and where are they located in relation to each other?

- For example, you could purchase one plot that has space for 2 burials side-by-side, or

- One plot with space for 2 burials, one on top of the other; or

- One plot with space for 4 burials, 2 side-by-side, each with space on top of each of those two; or,

- One plot with 2 side-by-side spaces, both with burial space for two more on top, and space for two cremains. If you were keeping count, that plot allows for the burial of 6 people.

It's confusing. Keep your wits about you when the salesperson is describing the plots, and know what you are buying and whether it is what you really want. Ask questions. Ask the salesperson to draw you a diagram if it will help you understand what you are buying. You can see how it would be easy to make an unsatisfactory decision about this at the time of the death of a loved one, when you are emotionally exhausted and unsure of all that needs to be done. It's important to get it right the first time.

Imagine trying to figure this out on the day your loved one dies?

A Little Cemetery Humor

A journalist was speaking with the owner of a cemetery to inquire about the varying costs of funerals and burial, specifically asking why it costs so much more to bury politicians than it does to bury regular folks. The funeral director's answer was that *"politicians have to be buried three times as deep, because, deep down, politicians are good people."*

FAMILY CEMETERY PLOTS

Before you go buying some big "family plot," talk with your family to see if that is what they want for themselves. Otherwise, you would be wasting your money and buying cemetery property that may potentially never be used.

If your family already has a "family plot" in a local cemetery, where there are still spaces available, that may be your first choice for a cemetery. If it is, you must first locate the Cemetery Deed (or certificate of ownership), and have it available at the time of making the burial arrangements. If you cannot locate the ownership documents, contact the cemetery management staff, and get duplicates as soon as possible.

Cemeteries owned by Churches:

Many families choose burial in a family plot in the cemetery operated by a church, where other loved ones have been buried for generations. If this is your choice, carefully <u>investigate their policies and fees for perpetual care</u>, or whether or not they even have perpetual care, because churches are often short of funding to care for their cemeteries. Some church cemeteries are not well cared for, and have a very sad, untended look about them. If this is not what you want, keep looking.

Other churches have designated gardens on the church property for the specific purpose of burying cremains. *Something else to look into ...*

FAMILY MAUSOLEUM

If you have lots and lots of money, and want to spend the rest of your life in a *"little house in the cemetery,"* you can arrange to have your own family mausoleum built. They are very beautiful and very expensive.

Definition of Mausoleum: noun.
The final and funniest folly of the rich.

Ambrose Bierce

I personally love the architectural beauty of family mausoleums! When we were children, my sister and I spent warm summer days walking through graveyards near our grandparents' house, peering in the little windows, seeing the sunbeams shining into the interior, wondering about the people buried there.

Years ago, family mausoleums were popular. You will see many in older cemeteries, some quite large and elaborate, marked with the names of wealthy, prominent families. If you ever have the opportunity to visit a large, historically well-known cemetery, if you only drive through, you will see some exquisite examples of granite architecture dedicated to the memories of deceased loved ones. (Remember that the Taj Mahal is a mausoleum.)

VETERANS OF THE U. S. MILITARY

Veterans have several burial options available to them. You can check with your local Office of Veterans' Affairs to see where Veterans' cemeteries are located in your area. If it is your wish to be buried in a Veterans' Cemetery, your funeral director can make the arrangements for you. Under certain circumstances, some veterans can be buried at Arlington National Cemetery in Virginia, but it will be necessary to contact the U. S. Army, which owns and operates the cemetery, to determine their requirements. Your funeral director or local Veterans' office can probably direct you.

Many cemeteries have separate areas dedicated to Veterans. At the time of purchasing cemetery property, you can visit that area and decide for yourself.

If you are making burial arrangements for a Veteran, you may want to ask whether Taps can be played at the graveside service, if the cemetery makes the arrangement for the musician, or if you have to do it. Maybe the funeral director can arrange it, but it will not happen without pre-arrangements. You will have to ask. And don't forget to ask who is responsible to pay for the musician.

Generally, the funeral director, or members of the military who conduct the graveside service, will present the flag that was draped over the coffin to the next-of-kin (spouse or child, usually). However, if you would like the flag presented to someone else, you must specify this in advance.

SELECTION OF A TOMBSTONE OR BRONZE PLAQUE

Whether you want a granite tombstone or a flat bronze plaque, know that the choice may <u>not</u> be up to you:

- If you are buried in a <u>cemetery</u>, your grave can be marked by a tombstone (usually granite).
- If you are buried in a <u>memorial park</u>, your grave will be marked with a flat bronze marker.
- Certain cemeteries allow both.

The cost of the granite tombstone is generally (but not always) higher than the cost of a bronze grave marker, depending on the size, style and color of the granite. As I understand it, tombstones are not generally made of marble, but of granite, which does not suffer the negative effects of acid rain. A 100-year old granite tombstone might look as perfect today as it was the day it was installed.

There are many choices when selecting a tombstone. If you don't know what you want, there is no rush to make a decision. It is possible to delay the selection of the grave marker if funds are short, or if you are having trouble deciding. This time delay can give you a welcome breather from all the hectic decision-making and running around that was necessary to arrange the funeral and burial. It also gives you time to shop around for the best selection and price. Feel free to delay your selection for a while, but set a time limit for yourself, or it may not ever happen.

I am a firm believer that when a person dies, their grave should be marked with their name, birth date, and date of death. Some people believe it doesn't matter. Apples and oranges! Sorry … but to me, it is important that a person's grave be appropriately and lovingly marked if it is possible.

> *Once upon a time there was a little girl whose all-too-short life turned out badly. There were many reasons for this, and she sort of "fell off the edge of the world" with her family. She was a lost child, who ended up dying alone, somewhere far away from her family who had lost touch with her over the years.*
>
> *The fact is, they didn't like her very much, so they never made gestures to remain in touch with her. And, then one day, her Mother got a phone call saying that this young woman had died, and asking where her ashes should be sent.*
>
> *Her family buried her ashes in the cemetery plot with her grandparents (because it was <u>much less expensive</u> than having to purchase a separate plot for her). Her name was never even inscribed on the tombstone below the names of her grandparents, and in death, she remains as she did in life: invisible, lost forever.*
>
> *I know people who say it doesn't matter that her name isn't on that tombstone. I disagree. What do you think?*

In making those arrangements, I believe the family not only showed a lack of love and respect for their departed family member, but they made a public statement about the kinds of people they, themselves, are.

PERSONALIZE YOUR MARKER

Some people want very specific images or emblems to indicate facts about them during their lives that they would like remembered: for example, if the deceased was a member of a particular military or fraternal organization, or if they loved cats, or if they were a musician or a doctor, etc. It may cost a little extra, and these images can be put on either a granite tombstone or a bronze plaque, although the space on the bronze plaque is limited.

Some tombstones and bronze plaques have complete date of birth and complete date of death. Others have only the year of birth and the year of death. How it is determined usually has to do with the cost: the more letters and numbers, the more expensive.

- <u>Consider this for the future</u>: For people who are doing a family genealogy study, complete dates are very helpful.

There are new options available because of advanced technology. I recently saw a flat bronze grave marker on which appeared the replica of photographs that memorialize the life of the deceased, including a picture of the man, his dog, a golf club, and other things that told you about his life. Double markers are also available for husband-and-wife. The cost is high, but if you can afford it, it is a beautiful tribute to a deceased loved one.

> *I know of a tombstone where the names of the deceased, and the dates of their births and deaths, are followed by the word, "HELLO!" The man who arranged this for himself and his wife figured that it was their way of greeting people who passed by their tombstone!*

ONE LAST THING ABOUT GRAVE MARKERS

Whether flat bronze marker, flat granite marker, or granite or marble tombstone, THEY SINK!

Laurel Hill Cemetery in the Fairmount Park section of Philadelphia, has begun a program of restoring grave markers that have fallen over or which have sunk into the ground. Presently, there are many thousands of graves in the cemetery in poor condition. It is an expensive, enormous task to reset them, and will take a long time to complete. There are many other cemeteries where that same situation exists. It really can't be prevented. Monitoring it is difficult and often doesn't happen unless someone from the family makes a formal request.

Pay attention the next time you drive past a cemetery and notice how many of the tombstones are sinking, crooked and falling over. This is a natural occurrence because they are set into soil which is eroded by the weather.

> *I once went out into the cemetery with a family to help them select a burial place for a loved one that had just passed away. They wanted a space that was nearby others in their family who died before. As we walked around the area where the family was certain their loved ones' flat bronze grave markers should have been, we found that <u>they were not there!</u> The family was confused, so we checked the cemetery records, and sure enough, we were in the right place. But, the markers were missing! How could that be?*
>
> *The Head Groundskeeper was called and he walked around the area with a long metal rod which he poked into the earth until he struck metal. It turns out that four family bronze grave markers had been completely buried in soil 4-6 inches deep. The burial spaces were on a slight incline, not even what I would call a hill, and years of soil run-off had completely covered them.*
>
> *The grounds crew removed the soil, unearthed the markers, and reset them at no expense to the family. Who knows how long they would have gone unseen?*

The moral of this story is that you, yourself, have to monitor the condition of the tombstones and bronze markers when you visit the grave sites of your loved one. If you notice that there is some sinking taking place, call the cemetery office and put in a request that it be fixed. There will most likely be no cost to the family.

While it is possible that a member of the grounds crew might see a particular marker that is sinking and arrange for it to be raised, it is highly unlikely, because there are thousands of grave markers in most cemeteries.

- Even if the markers or tombstones you see that are in jeopardy are not of your own family, it would still be a nice gesture to report it to the cemetery office so the situation could be remedied.

If you should ever find that the bronze marker on the grave of a loved one is missing (see below), notify the cemetery office immediately, and the marker may be replaced at no cost to the family as long as the marker was purchased through the cemetery at the time of burial.

- Here is a good reason not to shop on the Internet … if you had purchased a bronze marker from somewhere else, the replacement cost would be yours alone.

Be Aware: Bronze is a metal that can be melted down for cash. As recently as February 2011 in the Philadelphia area, 24 bronze grave markers were ripped off their concrete bases and stolen. There is supposed to be a law in place that makes it a crime for anyone to accept bronze that is obviously stolen from a cemetery, but once the metal is melted down, who's to know?

And again, in June 2011, a woman stole hundreds of brass military flag holders from Philadelphia area cemeteries and sold them for cash. The buyer then contacted the police, who were able to recover the flag holders. Chances are good that it will not be possible to put the holders back where they belong.

A FEW MORE THINGS TO KNOW ABOUT CEMETERY PLOTS

Flowers: Many people regularly place flowers on the graves of loved ones. Some people actually plant flowers if the cemetery permits it. Other people never visit graves. It's a matter of personal preference and tradition.

> *Again, when I worked for the cemetery, a dear little old woman, who lived in Chicago, came to the cemetery in suburban Philadelphia to put flowers on her husband's grave once every year. She came alone, by train, taxi, and on foot.*
>
> *Once, while walking from the nearest train station (approx. 5 miles from the cemetery), a local Police Officer saw her walking alone by the side of the road, gave her a ride to the cemetery, stayed with her the entire time, and then drove her back to the train station for her return trip to Chicago. Now that's true dedication and love.*

There are people who might say that her actions were ridiculous, even dangerous and expensive. It doesn't matter what others think. What mattered is what this woman thought and did. Her actions came from a deep place of love and respect for her deceased husband. Who would dare criticize that?

Cemeteries have policies about what can and cannot be placed on graves, and when they will remove flowers after a holiday such as Christmas, Easter, and Mothers' Day. Usually, the rules are published and available for all to see. The management is simply trying to keep the cemetery from appearing cluttered and unattractive, not infringe on your freedom to honor your dearly departed relatives and friends. The job of a cemetery grounds crew is hard work, subject to weather conditions and available staff, so don't get all upset with the cemetery management about this. You will appreciate the care of that space each time you visit.

> *When I worked at a cemetery, a grief-stricken woman came into the office, sobbing that someone had cut down all the flowers she had planted on the grave of her recently-deceased young son. She was sure the grounds crew had cut them down when they were cutting the grass.*

267

> *The Head Groundskeeper checked the grave site, and reported back that the flowers had not, in fact, been cut down, but had been eaten by deer which freely roam the cemetery at night. He gave the woman a list of flowers that deer will not eat, and suggested she only put those on her son's grave.*

If you ever have a complaint about the way the grave site of a loved one is being cared for (or not being cared for), don't hesitate to speak with a representative of the cemetery. It is not possible for them to have knowledge of every grave site, so you will be doing them a favor by bringing legitimate complaints and requests to their attention.

Flags are in great abundance in many cemeteries, especially on holidays honoring the military dead. On Memorial Day (which used to be called Decoration Day, and which was specifically designated for the veterans killed in the Civil War) many local veterans' organizations put flags on the graves of every person who had been in the military service of the United States. This is a huge labor of love and respect.

INTERNET SHOPPING

Caveat Emptor

When I worked at the cemetery, I occasionally heard a person (usually a husband) tell me that he could buy a bronze grave marker for less money over the Internet. Well, I recently checked it out for myself, and it is absolutely true. You can even buy caskets and granite tombstones ... even pet caskets ... over the Internet.

Are the prices lower, as advertised? You may remember my saying that not long ago, I arranged my former husband's funeral, and afterward, I compared his casket price with those on the Internet and saw almost no difference. I did _not_ find that the prices for caskets, for example, are 80-85% lower than funeral home prices, as advertised.

> I was particularly amused by one of the Internet ads for caskets that said:
> "Hassle-Free Returns."
> *EXCUSE ME?*
> How do you go about returning a casket, especially if you have already opened the shipping container, without hassle?
> Of course, you would have opened it!
> How else could you have known it was _unsatisfactory_ and needed to be returned.
> **Do you see what I'm getting at?**

So, if all you are shopping for is a cheaper price, go for it!
But, give it some serious thought first, and be prepared to pay the price of aggravation.

Remember: LIFE (and death) ARE NOT ALWAYS ABOUT MONEY.

What I am saying is that there are many very personal, very interesting choices available for the remains of a loved one when they die. These options are best considered in a relaxed environment, when there is time to thoroughly consider and discuss options, not the least of which is the cost. And, besides ...

what would you plan to do with the casket or the tombstone or bronze plaque
from the day it is delivered to your front door until the day you die?

Somehow, I can't picture a casket sitting in your living room, used as a coffee table until the time of need, although I understand it happens. (*see "Green Burials" on the following pages*)

You can have caskets delivered directly to the funeral home at the time of need. The ads say "guaranteed" delivery. Does that mean they guarantee that it will be delivered sooner or later, or "someday," or on time? And what about the shipping charges? Will it cost more for overnight delivery? What if the casket doesn't arrive on time? Keep in mind that you are working with a short deadline? Is this really the place where you want to cut corners?

I recently asked a funeral director if he will accept a casket from the family of a loved one who just died, which had been purchased elsewhere? He said yes, but the family must make arrangements for, and pay to have it delivered to the funeral home **in time** for the funeral. Duh!

> Do you really think you'll have time to comparison shop on the Internet just to save a few dollars, considering all the other things you have to do to arrange for a funeral? And, why would you trust an anonymous seller from the Internet versus a reputable local funeral director? *Just asking ...*

It is my opinion that at the time of the death of a loved one, you will have more than enough things to do besides worry about a casket being delivered to the funeral home on time. Among other things, that's what funeral directors do ... they sell caskets and they provide personal service at a time when you really need someone to do things for you. Some people actually complain that funeral directors make money selling caskets. So, what did you think, they were running a charity?

Keep in mind that, at the time of need, chances are that the person(s) arranging for the burial will be very busy and upset, and may have difficulty making wise choices in the short time before the funeral.

Some families overspend out of a sense of guilt, or a need to show the world that they have plenty of money, or that they really loved their family member who just passed away. There are much better ways to show the world you love someone than by overspending for a casket. Try very hard to see your selections as common-sense personal business decisions, and do your very best to keep the emotion out of the decision-making process. I know it is not easy, but try your best.

GREEN BURIALS – An Ancient Idea

A small number of people are choosing to go green, even in death. The Green Burial Council sets standards, and counts more than 300 approved providers in 40 states. A March 2010 survey by the International Cemetery, Cremation and Funeral Association found a quarter of those polled like the concept of environmentally friendly burials.

A trend that is starting to gain momentum, although in a very small way, is burial on private property, using the minimalist approach of a plain wooden box, no embalming, etc.

While I realize it sounds peculiar, some people are actually having cabinetmakers construct coffins for themselves, and using them alternatively in their homes until the time of need (*e.g.*, as coffee tables, book shelves, entertainment centers). Check out www.lastthings.net for interesting, creative funeral ideas.

If you are relying on your family to see that your private burial plans are carried out, keep in mind how they fight among themselves at Thanksgiving. They may not want to be bothered with your body after your death.

As in so many other areas of life, if you want this kind of burial, you should probably make the arrangements yourself. It may not, however, even be possible. Check with your homeowners' association and local zoning officials first.

ANOTHER TAKE ON GREEN BURIALS

While this may not exactly fit into the category of green burials, it seems a good place to describe a memorial burial garden in a church yard. Before the church could establish the memorial garden, the church had to comply with many rules and regulations of various local and church authorities. The church charges a minimal fee for this burial.

The memorial garden is attractively but simply fenced in, about 20' x 20' in size, with capacity to bury the cremains of approximately 200 people. The names and other information about persons whose cremains are buried there are preserved in the church records, along with a grid identifying the location of each person's cremains. There are no markings of any kind on any of the plots. None! The people who want to be buried there want it that way. To the uninformed eye, it looks just like a peaceful grassy yard.

The burial spaces can be one on top of another, or side by side. During the commitment ceremony conducted by the clergy of the church, the cremains of the deceased person are poured into a round hole. No urns. No wooden boxes. No bags. Nothing but "*ashes to ashes, dust to dust.*"

WHAT KIND OF FUNERAL SERVICE DO YOU WANT?

- formal service in a house of worship?
- informal service at the funeral home?
- graveside service at the cemetery?
- some other place (be specific)?
- none?

My family and I attended an Episcopal church, where the minister absolutely refused to preside over a funeral service in a funeral home or at the grave site because he believed funerals, like other rites of the church, were properly conducted in church. For many people, a funeral service in their house of worship is as important as a christening, baptism, confirmation, and wedding. For other people, a church funeral doesn't matter. Decide what you want and do not want and let your loved ones know.

I believe that some kind of funeral service is an important part of life. I know people who disagree with me. If you don't care one way or the other, you can let your loved ones decide at the time.

Once upon a time, a man died, and his wife gave him a Quaker funeral. She was a Quaker. Although he, himself, was not a regular church-going person, he was also not a Quaker. He was, however, a Christian and a 32nd degree Mason. His funeral service was held in a Friends' Meeting House, in the plain tradition of the Quakers: no flowers, no music, very little speaking of any kind, and there was no service provided by his Masonic Lodge.

Whether or not this service was appropriate for the man is not a question for me to answer. I'm sure that from his wife's Quaker perspective, it was genuine. But, I couldn't help thinking that he, himself, would not have wanted a funeral service in a house of worship that was not his own.

I personally believe that, in making funeral arrangements, it is important to arrange dignified, respectful funeral services that are in keeping with the lifestyle and personal and religious beliefs of the deceased person. This, of course, is just my opinion, and not an absolute. It is just something else to think about when making arrangements. Decisions like these deserve the utmost respect, discretion, and sensitivity from the people making them.

CLERGY OR NO CLERGY?

Anyone in particular? If there is a particular member of the clergy who you would like to conduct your funeral service, you must specify this to your loved ones. Sometimes, a house of worship will allow only their resident clergy to conduct the service; others welcome the participation of others, even those of different religious faiths.

If you do not want ordained clergy to officiate at your funeral, you must specify who you want to officiate, and make this wish known to the person(s) who will be making your funeral arrangements. Don't forget to give the clergy the appropriate gratuity. It may be included in the bill from the funeral director, or it may not. Be sure to ask.

PRINTED PROGRAMS FOR THE SERVICE

Many times, printed programs are given to people who attend a religious service or a service at a funeral home. The programs can be printed by the funeral home, or by the church, by yourself, or by someone else. I think it's a nice gesture and a very nice keepsake.

If you want to have a program, ask the persons making the arrangements at the church and funeral home if they will be printing the programs or not. You don't want to duplicate them, but you also don't want to have no programs because you didn't ask. And, don't forget to ask about the cost.

And, remember to include the details of when and where the funeral luncheon or Shiva will be held after the services.

MUSIC and MUSICIANS

If there are specific pieces of music and hymns you would like played at your funeral, write them down and keep the list with your Funeral & Burial Instructions. Especially if your funeral is in a house of worship, beautiful music, appropriate to the occasion, adds to the solemnity and beauty of the service. If you don't specify musical selections, the person making your funeral plans will have to make the selections, or the church organist will make them.

Some houses of worship are very particular about certain music's not being played, others are more liberal, but the idea is to use music to enhance the beauty and significance of a funeral service. It is common at some Catholic funeral services to have a bagpiper play "*Oh, Danny Boy*." When I was arranging my former husband's funeral, the priest told me that the music was permitted, but not the actual words to "*Oh, Danny Boy;*" there were, however, alternative words that were approved by the Church. Check with the clergy before making your final selections.

If you are making funeral arrangements for someone else, do you know what kind of music they would want? Some people have very specific preferences, but you won't know them if you don't talk about them. It is a worthy conversation to have well in advance.

If you don't know exactly what pieces of music you would like to be played at your funeral, have a conversation with the organist at the church where your funeral will be held, tell them your favorite selections, and/or ask about the various pieces that are appropriate. Ask the organist to play them for you so you can hear them, and make a selection that pleases you. After all, it's your funeral. Give this some thought. Whether or not you specify certain music depends upon how important music is to you.

A Little Funeral Humor

Once upon a time, a bagpiper was asked by a funeral director to play at a graveside service for a homeless man. The man had no family or friends, so the service was to be at a pauper's cemetery. The bagpiper, who was not familiar with the area, got lost on the way, and in typical male fashion, didn't stop to ask for directions.

When he arrived an hour late, he noticed that the funeral director was gone already and the hearse was nowhere in sight, but there were still a few cemetery workers left, and they were eating lunch.

The bagpiper apologized for being late, and went to the side of the open grave and looked down to see that the vault was already in place. The workers put down their lunch and began to gather round the bagpiper.

Later, he said that he played his heart and soul out for the homeless man, in fact, he believed he had never before played so well. When the bagpiper played "*Amazing Grace*," the workers began to weep.

As the bagpiper was preparing to leave, he heard one of the workers say: "*I never seen nothin' like that before, and I've been putting in septic tanks for twenty years.*"

I told you there is humor in conversations about funerals and burial.

Organist? Soloist? Choir? String quartet? Bag-piper? If it is important to you that certain musicians participate in your church service or at grave side, you must tell your loved ones so arrangements can be made in time. If you want Taps played at your graveside, you must tell your family so that arrangements can be made. If you know the names and phone numbers of the musicians you want, write them down, and include them with your Funeral & Burial Instructions.

Don't forget to pay the musicians. Their gratuity may be included in the bill from the funeral director or it may not. Remember to ask.

FLOWERS

I really don't like reading obituaries that say: "*In lieu of flowers ...*" How did it happen that people began making requests for no flowers? As a person who loves flowers and who owned a flower shop and also worked at a cemetery, I believe flowers are an important way for people to express their sympathy and pay tribute to a departed loved one. Allow people the opportunity to send flowers if it is their choice to do so.

Have you ever been to a funeral or viewing where there are no flowers? It's very bleak and sad, even depressing. Flowers are for the living, not the dead. They make everything more beautiful. They are tangible evidence of the sense of loss of a loved one. *But, again, that's just my opinion.*

The Case of the Missing Flowers

The night before my fraternal grandmother died, I had a dream that she died. It was a beautiful dream scenario, where she was dressed in a long, peach-colored chiffon dress with a picture hat ... the outfit she had worn for my parents' wedding. In my dream, she was carrying a bouquet of flowers.

After my Father called me the next morning to tell me of my grandmother's death, I called a florist and ordered a bouquet of gardenias to be placed by her hands in the casket. It was very important to me that she have these particular flowers. When the florist delivered them to the funeral home, he was told, "There are to be no flowers." I was certain there had been a mistake, and called the funeral director, who said there was, in fact, no mistake, that when my Father and his two brothers made the funeral arrangements, they specified <u>no flowers</u>.

When I asked that the bouquet nevertheless be placed in the casket with her body, I was told that there was to be a closed casket (no viewing). I told them I didn't care about that; I just wanted my grandmother to have these exquisite flowers for her last journey. They reluctantly agreed to place the flowers in the casket, although not without a lot of pressure from me.

In addition, 27 people sent flowers when they heard of my grandmother's passing, not knowing about the edict of "no flowers." Those 27 flower arrangements were placed on the floor in another room because of my family's instructions. A friend recently asked me why I didn't move the arrangements into the room where the casket was? The honest truth is that it never occurred to me.

See how things can easily slip by you when you're upset? If details like this are important to you, you must be firm and stand your ground with people who don't have your vision. How do you suppose the people who sent those 27 flower arrangements felt when they didn't see them there? Just asking ...

Close family members and friends of the deceased may simply wish to buy some personal flowers, and for the casket and the church. Other people will send flowers, too. Many people say that because the flowers are only going to die, why spend money for them? *Did they forget the reason for the occasion?*

I told my husband that I want a casket cover of gardenias like the one at the end of the movie, "Imitation of Life." It will cost a fortune! What do I care? I'll be dead, and besides, gardenias are my favorite flowers.

DONATIONS IN LIEU OF FLOWERS:

If you would like friends and family to make donations to a specific charity in lieu of flowers, offer it as an option, not an absolute. Be sure that you make it known to someone you trust to see that your wish is carried out, and that the obituary published in the local newspaper gives specific information about the intended charity. Or ask that people make donations to their own favorite charity, in memory of the deceased person.

- Interestingly, I saw a recent obituary that requested that the funeral guests send flowers to someone they loved, in memory of the person recently departed. I think this is a lovely idea.

Keep in mind that by the time your death notice appears in the local newspaper, it may already be too late – many people will have already ordered flowers. I recommend that you don't make a big deal of this. Many people really do want to send flowers as an expression of sympathy.

Besides, it's bad for business for the local flower shop owners. I like lots and lots of flowers, and I'm not sure there could ever be too many flowers. *But, hey, that's just my opinion again.*

As I said, I attended many church funerals during my lifetime because of my Mother's being an organist. I saw many exquisite flowers, and have very strong preferences and opinions about flowers and funerals. I know I am not the only person who wants beautiful flowers at funerals. I once made 11 arrangements for a funeral during Christmas week, all with poinsettias as specifically requested by the family.

What do you want done with the flowers AFTER the funeral?

The funeral director will customarily take all of the flowers from the funeral home and church to the grave site unless you request, *in advance*, that certain specific flower arrangements be kept for you. If the weather is especially hot, rainy, or snowy, the flowers will be seriously and quickly damaged outside, so you might want to keep some of them or pass them out to relatives and friends. It's best not to wait until you are standing around the grave site to ask the funeral director to see that certain flowers are saved. By then, it will be too late. The flowers will already be out at the gravesite, and may even have been damaged in transit.

- Some people may want to take one or more flower arrangements home with them, or to the home of a person who was unable to attend because of illness or disability … particularly if that person is in a hospital or nursing home. It is a very loving, thoughtful thing to do.

- Some people may request that one or more arrangements be placed on the nearby graves of other loved ones.

It used to be that if a family requested it, funeral flowers would be donated to local nursing homes or retirement communities, where the arrangements would be taken apart and remade into smaller arrangements to be passed out to the residents. I think it is a wonderful idea, but it seems that two things are keeping this from happening:

1. The nursing home does not have adequate staff to do the work.
2. The residents don't like getting the flowers because they know they come from funerals.

It is something I always wanted to do, but still haven't found time. *Maybe someday …*

A FEW MORE THINGS TO THINK ABOUT AS YOU MAKE ADVANCED PLANS

There are certain tasks to be done as part of your funeral planning that involve other specially selected people, including readers, presenters, pallbearers, people who get to ride in the limousines, the person you would want to give your eulogy. The selection of these individuals frequently causes hard feelings in families because of the people who were asked and those who were not asked. The best way to avoid such hard feelings is for you, yourself, to select the people … *in advance* … and include their names in your Funeral & Burial Instructions, rather than to leave the decisions up to the people who actually make your funeral arrangements.

And, once having decided, it would be a very nice gesture for you to write a personal note to each person, telling them why you selected them for each task. This is something to think about because, at the time of your death, people will already be suffering from your death, may be very busy, and may be very sensitive to perceived slights. Tell them why you selected them. It would be so much more meaningful to the individuals than simply to be asked by someone else.

And, if you are a person who is inclined to get hurt feelings from perceived slights such as these, I seriously recommend you don't do it. I've seen way too much of this in my life, and it is a waste of time and energy, and causes additional upset. This is a time when families should come together, not be torn apart by petty grievances. *Just my opinion ...*

READERS

Do you have a preference of who you would like to read the scripture at your funeral? Some churches allow you to select the persons who will do the readings; others do not. If you have certain specific people you would like to read, make your wishes known. Otherwise, other people will make the decisions. The clergy in charge of the funeral will generally suggest a few appropriate readings; but, if there are special Bible passages you want to be read, make your wishes known in advance, in writing. In addition to, or instead of, Biblical or scriptural readings, you may want certain poems or classical passages read. Check with the clergy beforehand to see if the selections are permitted.

> *When I was making the arrangements for my former husband's funeral mass, I asked the Pastor of the church to do all of the readings himself so there would be no squabbling among his family members as to who should have read and who was left out. The priest was very understanding in accommodating my request. Sometimes, when you are in charge, it's best to take the easy way out!*

PRESENTERS

Some church funeral services includes communion. At one point in the service, two (or more) persons walk up the center aisle of the church with the wine and the host, and present them to the officiating priest. Selection of the persons to present these gifts is often looked upon as an honor, and of sentimental importance; so if there are people you would like to so recognize, specify their names in your Funeral & Burial Instructions for the person who will be making your funeral arrangements. Write them a note also.

WHO DO YOU WANT TO GIVE YOUR EULOGY?

- Who do you want to speak about you?

- Some churches only allow one person to speak.

- Some churches set a moderate time limit for the person giving the eulogy.

- Other churches, depending on the rules of their particular church and the preferences of the clergy, will invite people to come forward to talk about the person who has passed away.

> *When making arrangements for my Father's funeral, the minister said he would be inviting people to come forward to speak about him. I said that he should absolutely <u>not</u> call upon me because I don't do public speaking. My sister also asked that he not call on her, but if she was so moved, she would offer a few words, which she ultimately did.*
>
> *The whole time people were speaking, my brain was racing back and forth: "I should really say something; this is my last chance. But, what would I say? I don't do public speaking. I will embarrass myself. But, I <u>have</u> to speak ... if I don't speak, I will regret it forever ... this moment will never happen again ..." back and forth in my head.*
>
> *Finally, after nine people spoke about my Father, the minister stood up to proceed with the service, <u>and then I stood up</u>. My family was shocked, nervous about what I would say. I went to the front of the church, walked up the steps to*

the pulpit, and looked out upon a sea of color ... one half of the church was filled with adult Boy Scouts wearing full-dress uniforms! [My Father was a life-long, internationally honored Boy Scout.]

I began by saying that my Father, who loved camping, had no sons ... only two daughters who hate camping! Everyone laughed, and from that point on, I was able to relax and briefly say what I wanted to say. My sister and I are beach girls! One of the worst weeks of my life was spent at Girl Scout Camp. Speaking at my father's funeral was one of those moments in time that will never happen again. I am proud and happy that I made the choice to speak. No regrets.

I just heard comedian Jerry Seinfeld say that, in general, people fear public speaking more than death! He said what it means is that you are better off in the casket than giving the eulogy.

WHAT DO YOU WANT SAID ABOUT YOU?

A Presbyterian Minister I know is regularly asked to officiate at the funeral of a member of his church. He is also the sponsor of the Senior Group in his church, which has a large number of elderly members. Several years ago, he created a form which he passed out to the group, wherein he asked them what they would like him to say about them when the time came ... what did they want to be remembered for? Only 3 or 4 people filled out the form and gave it back to him. The others ignored it.

This sometimes puts the Minister in the difficult position of saying only the things he personally knows about the person who just passed away, (... *"just the facts, ..."*) when there are probably many other things to be said. Why can't those people see that they missed a wonderful opportunity? He really cares about telling what they want others to know. So, if there are things you want said about you and your life, it would be very useful for you to have written those things down and given them (in advance) to either the Minister or other person(s) who may be speaking about you. What would you have done with the form? *Just asking ...*

YOUR OBITUARY

So many obituaries remind me of the 1950's TV show, *"Dragnet,"* with Det. Joe Friday saying,
"... just the facts, ma'am."
Boring!

If you write your own obituary, you get to say what you want published about your life. It is another aspect of getting things done your own way, as opposed to having someone else do it who may not get it just right, who may just be going through the motions. You can make it *"just the facts"* or you can add some humor or other interesting facts about your life.

It is even possible to have the writing of your own obituary be an enjoyable experience for you as you reflect on your life and the things you want people to know about you. Don't miss this opportunity. I even recommend that you write several versions of your obituary:

- one version to be published in the local newspaper, and
- another version just for your family, and
- another version to be read at your funeral luncheon/celebration.

If you actually do write your own obituary, be sure that every version is kept with all your other Funeral & Burial Instructions.

A FEW THINGS TO KNOW ABOUT OBITUARIES.

For starters, an obituary should include (at least) the following information:

- Exact name of the decedent (including any other names by which the person may have been known)
- Decedent's maiden name (if a married or divorced female)
- Date of birth and birthplace*

- Mother's maiden name and birthplace*
- Father's name and birthplace
- Survivors and the decedent's relationship to each (including former spouses)
- Family members who preceded them in death
- Occupation(s) and employer(s)
- Hobbies and special interests
- Schools attended and educational degrees
- Significant accomplishments in life (including awards and honors)
- Military service (branch, rank, where the decedent served)
- Preferred charity for donations (if appropriate)

*NOTE: It has been recently pointed out that your mother's maiden name and your complete birth date should be LEFT OUT of your obituary because identify thieves look for and use that information for their own purposes. I don't see any reason that these two facts about your life need to be published if to do so would put your assets and family in jeopardy. *Just one more thing to think about ...*

If the funeral information is not submitted by the funeral home to the newspaper by their printing deadline, it may not appear in time for people to know about the times and locations of the viewing and funeral service. **People really do want to know.** So, it is up to you (or the person making the arrangements) to find out how and when to get the obituary published in time for the services. There isn't much point in having the obituary published after the funeral.

This is another appropriate time to use the PEOPLE TO CALL list. You have filled it out, haven't you?

If your loved one is originally from another town or state, consider also having an obituary published in the local newspaper in your loved one's home town. There will be people who appreciate it, and will reach out to contact your family to express their condolences. It was too late when it occurred to me that I had not published my Father's obituary in his home-town newspaper, and to this day, I regret that oversight.

I recommend that you publish the obituary at least twice to give the greatest number of people the opportunity to read it. Some people don't want to pay the cost of more than one publication, but I say it is not the place to skimp on money.

Are you kidding? You just spent $15,000 on the funeral!
Why would you skimp on this important step just to save a few dollars?

Also, it is my understanding that many newspapers will only publish obituaries submitted to them from the funeral director. In fact, I just recently read a disclaimer in my local newspaper that states that all obituaries are submitted to the newspaper from funeral homes, and the newspaper is therefore not responsible for any mistakes that are printed.

- There is an unfortunate trend in newspaper obituaries where incorrect words are being used. For example, a man's military medal was spelled "metal," and a woman's membership in the Red Hat Society was spelled Red "Hot" Society. The newspaper in question blamed the respective funeral homes for the mistakes. *Excuse me?* These are not "spelling" mistakes; they are mistakes in word usage. Had these mistakes been made in the obituaries of any family member of mine, I would have refused to pay for the obituary until it was corrected and republished at no cost. Just last month, I received a call from a friend who had just read the obituary of a man we both know. She was distressed because they (who?) got his name wrong! *Excuse me?* How hard is it to get a person's name correct in an obituary? *Just asking ...*

If it matters to you that the obituary is accurate, here is what I recommend if the published obituary is incorrect. If the newspaper is not accepting responsibility for mistakes, ask your funeral director to submit a corrected obituary to be published again at their expense. You have most likely already paid for the cost of publishing the obituary in the bill you got from the funeral director, and you may or may not have to pay for the publication of the corrected obituary, but even if you do have to pay again, I think it is important that the obituary be correct. *Just another one of my very strong opinions ...*

A recent obituary for a 96 year old woman stated that "she was a retired looper." EXCUSE ME? What is a looper? (Turns out she worked in a garment factory.)

Why would someone write this about a woman who had not been employed for more than 30 years? As I was reading it, I thought it was insensitive, even disrespectful. I doubt that is how she would want to be remembered. But, again, that's just me.

This kind of thing can be avoided if you write your own obituary. And, keep in mind that if you are a Baby Boomer, it may very well be that you were retired for many years before your death, so how do you want to be remembered?

PALLBEARERS

Who would you like to carry your body to your final resting place? Your sons? Your brothers? Your nephews? Friends? Members of the Military? Think about this, and if there are specific people, list their names in your Funeral & Burial Instructions. Without such instructions from you, other people will make the selection. This is another one of those places where people's feelings get hurt by the selection. Even if it seems important at the time, this is no place to express hurt feelings over something like this. If necessary, you can ask the funeral director to supply pallbearers. And be sure to ask if there is a fee to be paid for those professional pallbearers, and whether or not it is included in the funeral bill.

LUNCHEON/ RECEPTION/ WAKE/ SHIVA

It is always nice to have family and friends gather together after a burial to celebrate the life of their loved one.

How do you want people to celebrate the gift of your life? If it is important to you, state your wishes for the funeral luncheon, celebration, wake, or Shiva, including the name and location of the place where you want the celebration to be held after your funeral. And, if possible, provide funds for the expenses of such event … not necessary, but a nice gesture nevertheless.

- Large or small?
- Casual or Formal?
- Sit-down or Buffet?
- Private or Public?
- Simple or Expensive?

This was one of my former Husband's favorite jokes (he, of course, was 100% Irish):
What's the difference between an Irish wedding and an Irish wake?
There's one less drunk at the wake.

It is often easier to hold the celebration at a public venue rather than in someone's home, where it may be necessary to borrow or rent chairs, arrange for food preparation, clean-up and delivery, etc. Of course, it is always possible to have a caterer rather than having loved ones do all that work. Sometimes, the decision must be made based upon available funds.

And, unless you have a specific preference of where your funeral luncheon should be held, you can just leave it up to your family.

I have noticed a recent trend where the printed program for the funeral service includes an invitation to tell people where the luncheon will be held and where the family will be receiving friends and family. I like this idea a lot!

Another Of My Family's Funeral Stories

After the brief funeral service for my fraternal grandmother, the members of my family went back to her house … that is, all 8 of us. We sat in the living room making small talk for a long time, and the subject of a funeral luncheon never came up. My grandmother had lived in a nursing home for about 6 weeks prior to her death, so there was nothing to eat in her house.

Well, I sat there as long as I could stand it, all the time complaining that my headache was getting worse. I needed food! I needed coffee! No one suggested food of any sort, and, so, my sister and brother-in-law, and my husband and I left and went out to dinner by ourselves.

What we didn't know was that there <u>was</u> a luncheon waiting for the others of my family and friends elsewhere, and we (that is, my sister and I) were not invited. It wasn't until years later that I found out this tacky piece of family history.

<u>Back story</u>: At the time, my Father was dating the woman who broke up our parents' marriage many years before. My sister and I were not invited because no one had the nerve to tell us that she would be there.

My sister and I were furious when, years later, we learned about this ridiculous charade. They had decided to leave us out, without explanation. I only found out about the luncheon from a friend, who, years later said, "We didn't know what to do!"

Excuse me! Open your mouth and say the words. <u>Communicate</u>! My sister and I were adults, capable of making our own choice of whether to go to that luncheon or not. Because they all assumed we wouldn't be able to handle being around "the other woman," they made the decision for us. I do not like people making decisions for me.

In truth, my sister and I were deprived of a possible opportunity to make peace and begin the healing process with our Father and that woman. They never thought about that, did they?

Hurt feelings? You're darn right!

TRANSPORTATION OR HOUSING FOR PEOPLE FROM OUT OF TOWN.

It is entirely possible that there will be family or friends coming from out of town, even long distances, to attend the funeral of a loved one. Someone has to be in charge of making living accommodations for those people, either in individual homes or at hotels.

Have clear communication with all parties about who will be making and/or paying for these travel plans and accommodations. Some people will be unable to attend because of personal reasons, illness, employment responsibilities, or the expense. If this happens, don't take it personally! Give people permission to grieve in their own way, even if it is by long distance.

It is also possible that you request a certain member of the clergy to participate in your funeral, and that person will be coming from a long distance. This is one place where very thoughtful arrangements should be made to accommodate that person, including paying for their trip expenses.

HOUSE SITTER

Arrange for someone you trust to house sit during <u>all</u> of the funeral services, receptions, etc. <u>This is no small request</u>, and is very important. There are unscrupulous people who read obituaries for the sole purpose of burglarizing the homes of recently deceased persons. Be prepared, and be careful! Anyway, someone should be at the house to receive visitors, flower deliveries, and phone calls.

It may also be necessary to provide for care of infants, minor children, pets and/or elderly or disabled family members during viewing and funeral services if they will not be attending

MAINTAIN LISTS

Designate someone to be in charge of keeping lists of visitors, people who phone, all sympathy cards, emails, flowers, mass cards and other donations. These lists will be the source for names of people to whom thank you-notes will be sent after your funeral.

THANK-YOU NOTES

Writing thank-you notes seems to be a dying art … that is, for those who don't want to write them. For those who receive a thank-you note, the words speak loud and clear that someone is grateful for an act of kindness, a gift, a pleasant dinner. Thank-you notes for funerals can be mostly for flowers, mass cards, or donations to charities. You also may wish to send special cards to clergy, musicians, and all people who helped you in various ways before, during and after the funeral, and to those who participated in the funeral service itself.

Funeral directors usually provide simple thank-you notes, so it may not be necessary for you to spend more money buying them. If, however, there are people you wish to thank in a special way, you may want to buy thank-you cards that are a little bit more personal. But, in my opinion, it is not the card, itself, but the thought behind it that makes people happy to receive it.

Many people who give mass cards put a little note in them that says it is not necessary to send them a thank-you note.

If there are many cards to be written, it may take a "team" of volunteers, and if no one volunteers, you might ask some of those people who, when the person died, asked, *"What can I do to help?"*

FOOD

Just one more thing to think about … The night of the viewing for my father-in-law, my husband and I, and his immediate family, had not eaten dinner beforehand. The viewing began at 6 p.m., and by the time it was over at 10 p.m., we were all really hungry, so we went to a local restaurant and ate dinner. It probably wasn't the best idea to eat a big meal that late, but that's what happened.

So, remembering this, the evening of my mother's viewing, we went to dinner first. That way, we could go right home after her viewing and get some sleep before the day of her funeral.

This may seem like a tiny thing, but if you are feeling faint from not having eaten, or have a headache for lack of caffeine, or any other condition that can be *"cured"* by eating, don't forget to eat.

WHAT IF YOUR FAMILY DECIDES NOT TO HONOR YOUR WISHES?

OK, you have done your part of planning for your own funeral. You have researched your options and documented your wishes for others to follow, but, what if your family collectively decides not to honor your wishes? What if someone gave their word that they would follow your instructions, and the family's decision would mean that that person is breaking a promise? In your opinion, what is the moral and ethical thing to do when a family chooses <u>not</u> to honor the wishes of their departed loved one? What then?

Well, I suppose the most obvious comment must be that you will have already passed away and won't know. There are people who will say it doesn't matter. What do you think?

The only thing I can say is that it depends on circumstances ... there are no general rules to guide you. This is a situation where the wishes of the departed loved one must be carefully, lovingly weighed against the opinions (and ultimately the choices and finances) of the family making the funeral arrangements.

Once upon a time, a single man, a widower with no children, but with a large family otherwise, age 69, died. His body was interred in the cemetery where his wife had been buried several years before.

Before his death, he had insisted that his family make no fuss over his funeral and burial. He didn't even want an obituary published in the local newspaper because people would then find out about his death. So, his sister being the person in charge of making his funeral arrangements, honored his request ... in part. She chose to call a few members of his family, but not all of them. She arranged for a mass of Christian Burial at a local church, but not the church of which he was a member, because she felt that his death notice would have been published in the church bulletin, and she didn't want that to happen. All along, she believed she was doing the right thing in honoring his last wishes.

What she wasn't counting on, however, was the publication of his Estate Notice in the classified section of the local newspaper. Many people saw it, and were upset to learn that he had died six weeks earlier. One who was especially hurt was his Godchild.

By honoring the wishes of a man who lived a very reclusive life, his sister denied people who loved him the opportunity to pay their last respects. Many people were upset at her for her choice to exclude them.

Would you have honored this man's wishes? Or, would you have overridden his wishes and held a dignified, but quiet, funeral where others were given the opportunity to pay their last respects to a man who was much loved, even though he didn't feel it? Can you see the conflict?

WHAT IF YOUR FAMILY CANNOT AFFORD TO HONOR YOUR WISHES?

It happens all the time ... families short of funds to pay for a funeral, or left with debt paying for the funeral and burial of a loved one. Funeral and burial arrangements cost big money. It is not unreasonable to expect a funeral, burial, and luncheon to cost between $10,000 to $15,000 ... *or more.*

What if you have done your homework, completed your research with funeral directors and cemeteries, have written down all of your intended selections, and have put that writing with your Will and other important papers, have told someone else what you want ... but, you made no payment arrangements for your funeral and burial, and your family cannot afford them? What then? Well, by that time you will already have passed away, and won't be available to discuss the money. Now what? What is your family supposed to do in this situation?

You may be thinking, *"Why should I bother with any of this? They'll figure it out one way or the other when the time comes."* Do you really want to leave someone in serious debt paying for your funeral expenses? Oh, I know your family doesn't want to think about your death, and surely doesn't want to talk about it, but if these things are important to you, you'll figure out how to have those "hard" conversations before you run out of time. If there are things you can do and say now, to prevent upset among your loved ones later, why not do what you can to prevent discord among them before it becomes a problem?

Do you expect your family to honor your wishes even if there is no money? Can you see how you would be placing both a financial and emotional burden on your family if you have made no payment arrangements for your funeral and burial you want? This being said, don't you think it is reasonable to discuss your funeral and burial expenses with your loved ones way in advance of your death so you will have the opportunity to talk about the money, where it will come from, who will be responsible to pay for your funeral? Isn't that just plain common sense?

Once upon a time, a man was very ill and knew he would die shortly, and yet, he was busy winding up his affairs. In discussing things with his executor, it became clear that he had very little money, and certainly no money to pay for his funeral. What he did was change the beneficiary of a $50,000 life insurance policy from his sister to his estate. He told his *sister (his sole heir) what he was doing, and she respected his decision. By this one simple transaction, he provided money to pay for his funeral, burial, funeral luncheon and any miscellaneous expenses of his estate, and what was left over from the $50,000 went to his sister as part of the man's residuary estate under the terms of his Will.*

Why did I tell you this true story? To point out that there may be ways to come up with the money needed to cover the expenses. It can be done. Ask questions. Get answers. Figure it out before your loved one passes away.

As you read through the payment options, you will see more examples about how funeral, burial, legal, personal and financial matters are interconnected.

- And, before we get too far into the conversation about funerals and money, if you are considering advanced payment and planning, I recommend you discuss it with your financial advisor before you make any purchases. If this is something you really want to do, and if you have the money, don't be easily talked out of it if your advisor doesn't believe in advanced planning. But, take your time. Listen and learn. Maybe your financial advisor will have good reasons for you, in your personal and financial situation, to make different arrangements.

- If you had a revocable living trust, your Successor Trustee would have immediate access to your money, and could pay for your expenses, that is, of course, assuming there is sufficient money.

- But, if you had only a Will, no one would have immediate access to your money until after your executor is appointed by the Register of Wills and the probate process begun. Nevertheless, if you had sufficient liquid funds in your estate, in a short time, your executor could pay the funeral and burial expense from your estate funds.

- What if your family simply didn't have the money, no matter what kind of legal document you had? Then what?

- Would they feel morally obligated to honor your wishes, no matter what?

- Would they be racked with guilt if they did not honor your wishes?

- Would they be willing to go into debt to honor you wishes?

- Is there someone in your family who would have enough money to assume the expenses and not need to be reimbursed?

- What if they have the money, but don't want to spend it paying for your funeral and burial because they are angry at you for something or other from the past or for not having made payment arrangements before your death?

- What if paying for the things you want for your funeral and burial creates a serious financial (and emotional) burden for your family? What are they supposed to do now?

As you are mulling over these questions, don't lose sight of the fact that the funeral director is sitting across the desk from your family, waiting for direction from someone about what is to happen with your body, waiting to hear how the funeral bill is going to be paid.

- At that point, there is little time left to make decisions. Often, it is at that point that people make mistakes:

  1) Emotional over-spending is one reaction of family members when they have no direction from the decedent. They select the most expensive things to "show the world" how much they love you. You can prevent that from happening if you do what is necessary to make your own plans.

  2) What if someone in your family says, *"Oh, let's just get it over with and cremate him?"* but, cremation is something you absolutely do not want. Of course, you do know that cremation costs much less than the choices you made for your funeral and burial, so you can see how your family would be inclined toward that choice, can't you?

- If someone steps up and agrees to pay for your funeral and burial out of their own money, will there be sufficient assets in your estate to reimburse them? If this is the payment option you were thinking of all along, it is essential that you state as much in your Funeral & Burial Instructions, and tell your family about this plan. There would be no real harm if someone wrote a check or used their personal credit card to pay for the various expenses (including the funeral luncheon), if that person would soon be reimbursed from your estate. There would be a short time delay until they got the money from your estate, but at least there would be funds there for them.

- What if you did not have any assets or any estate? Who do you think will pay for your funeral expenses? Because you did not make the effort to designate money for the payment of the expenses, who did you expect would be generous enough to incur a possible debt of $10,000 to $15,000 for your funeral? Are there people in your life who love you that much? Wouldn't you think some members of your family might be angry that you left your loved ones with such a mess?

- What if someone cares enough about you and your memories that they are willing to incur credit card debt for all the expenses of your funeral, burial, and luncheon? If they were to charge $10,000 on their credit card that charges 20% interest, do you know how many years it would take them to pay off that debt, a debt they took upon themselves, but which was rightfully yours? If you were still living, would you even think of asking someone to do this for you?

- What if someone went so far as to take the money out of a home-equity line of credit? Well, you may be thinking, it _is_ one way to pay for your funeral expenses. It is not a good idea. In Chapter II - FINANCIAL, you read about the problems with using a credit card or home-equity line of credit for paying debts like these. The worse of the two would be the home-equity loan, because it is debt that is secured by a house. Should that generous person ever be unable to pay back the money to the bank for this loan, the bank could put a lien on his/her house that could force him/her into foreclosure. *Once again, take a hard look at how interconnected personal decisions are with legal, financial and funeral situations.*

- What if your spouse or a child does not have the money to pay for your funeral and burial expenses, and they want to take out a loan, but their credit is bad, and then someone else offers to co-sign for that loan. Do you really want your loved ones putting themselves in such financial jeopardy? If all they can afford is cremation, then so be it. Let them know it would be all right with you if that is how it ends up. (You already read about the danger of co-signing for a loan in Chapter II – FINANCIAL.)

- What if, for example, you stated that you want to be buried with a former spouse in another state? Transporting your body and casket is very costly, and may not be the best option. Cremation offers one option that will cost less money, and will allow for your ashes (cremains) to be easily transported.

- What if your family comes up with the money to give you a "decent" burial, no matter how they came up with the funds, but they run out of money before they can purchase a tombstone? Technically, legally, there is no need to have a tombstone at all. It is just something that families do if it is important to them. A tombstone or a bronze plaque can be installed at your gravesite at a later date, even if it takes a year or more to save the money. If someone volunteers to pay for the marker out of their own money, they can submit a bill to your estate, requesting reimbursement, assuming your estate has sufficient assets.

- What if you should pass away while traveling in a foreign country? Not only might the cost of returning your body to your home be exorbitant, but there might be laws that prevent transportation of your body. If you do that kind of traveling, always get a travel insurance policy that includes transportation of your body back to your home (what the insurance companies call "repatriation") if you should die while on a trip outside the country. If you can afford the trip, be sure you can afford this insurance, too.

What you DO NOT want to do is create a financial hardship for someone who really cannot afford to pay for your funeral.

On the TV show "60 Minutes" in early May 2012, Anderson Cooper interviewed a young adult woman who was searching for her father's grave. She stated that because it was so important to her mother to see that her father's grave was properly marked with an appropriate tombstone, she and her siblings went without food many days because of the money her mother spent for the tombstone. This mother inflicted suffering on her children just so she could buy a tombstone for her deceased husband.

Was that a good choice? Maybe. Maybe not. I don't know. What do you think?

**All of these things can be worked out in advance, but they will not happen automatically.
It is essential that you have the appropriate conversations and
take the actions necessary to see that these things happen ...** *if they matter to you.*

**Are you up for the "hard" conversations?
Are you up for taking care of your personal business in advance?**

Think before you answer the questions.

WHAT IF YOUR FAMILY DOES NOT WISH TO HONOR YOUR FUNERAL REQUESTS AND INSTRUCTIONS?

What if your family absolutely does not agree with your choices, and simply doesn't want to do what you have asked of them? Then what? Here's an example of such a situation:

> *In the movie, "The Bridges of Madison County," you may remember that Francesca left specific instructions to her children, that her body be cremated and scattered under the Roseman Bridge. Her son took a hard and fast position that his Mother's body was not to be cremated, and insisted that she was to be buried with her husband (their father), in spite of her specific directions.*
>
> *She explained her reasons in a letter to her daughter and son. Ultimately, her children agreed to honor their Mother's wishes after they read her letter. If you want certain funeral arrangements that your family might squabble over, write them a letter explaining your reasoning, and asking them to honor your wishes.*

So what am I saying to you? If it really matters to you, it is your responsibility to

- (a) have the "hard" conversations with your family well before your death; and/or
- (b) write down your specific instructions; and/or
- (c) write a letter to your family, explaining the importance of your selections, your reasons why, and asking them to honor your last wishes.

Because they may not know these things are important to you, or why, it's up to you to tell them.

Does it <u>really</u> matter? I don't know. Maybe. Maybe not. What do you think?

A LITTLE HUMOR CAN WORK WONDERS

OK, it's a stretch, but it <u>is</u> possible.

> ***Do not take life too seriously. You will never get out of it alive.***
>
> Elbert Hubbard

One way to bring up the difficult conversation about your funeral and burial is to use humor. If talking seriously about such matters is way too hard for you and/or your family, see if you can't find some way to stretch your imagination using humor to bring up the subject. You will see that I have inserted humor in a few different places. I urge you to look for funeral/burial cartoons in the newspapers or magazines and have them ready. And, I'd be willing to say that you can find humorous quotations and/or cartoons on the Internet that just might enable you to connect with your family on this important subject. *Just an idea...*

- Elsewhere, I humorously mentioned that if my husband buries me in a pink dress, I'll haunt him for eternity. *What, you thought I was kidding?* You could use your clothing selection as a good starting point for a humorous conversation. What about your eyeglasses? I have often heard people joke about whether or not to have their glasses on their body for their viewing. I'm only mentioning humor as a possible vehicle for opening up a discussion that may be hard to talk about. Think about it before you dismiss the idea as ridiculous.

The point is that the "hard" conversations might be made easier with humor.

Question:	HOW WILL EVERYTHING GET DONE IN SUCH A SHORT TIME?
Answer:	BE PREPARED WITH INFORMATION, ASK A LOT OF QUESTIONS, and ASK FOR HELP

Considering that most people have been to at least one funeral, and know there are lots of things to be done, why are so many people unprepared for the whirlwind of decisions and activities necessary to make all the arrangements in such an impossibly short time? *Just asking ...*

Some Pre-Arrangements Can Save Time and Stress

When my former husband was in the end-stages of his illness, we talked about the things he wanted for his funeral. Afterward, and following his direction and requests, I got the cemetery deed from his safe, and then I called the following to discuss arrangements in advance:

- *Funeral director*
- *Cemetery (advised them of his impending death)*
- *Church (Priest arranged for church and musicians)*
- *Florist (selected flowers)*
- *Restaurant (selected menu)*

We also discussed how all these things would be paid for when the time came.

When he died, all I had to do was make a few follow-up phone calls to people who were already expecting to hear from me, because of our pre-arrangement conversations.

If you have the opportunity to make some pre-arrangements, do it. It will save a lot of time when your loved one passes.

If you were planning a wedding, *which you definitely are <u>not</u>,* you might hire a wedding planner -- but, you are planning a funeral, and there is technically no such thing as a funeral planner. Now what? Like it or not, you are that one person. There is no time for comparison shopping, no one to keep track of the finances, <u>no one person who is not directly involved in the emotions of the loss of a loved one</u>.

I found myself in a difficult situation when I was making arrangements for my former husband's funeral. All of the plans were exactly as he wished them to be. A friend suggested that I share the arrangements with his brothers and sister so they wouldn't feel left out. It seemed like a good idea at the time.

Remember that my former husband and I had talked about the arrangements at length, and the plans were exactly as he requested. This fact did not seem to matter to his family members, who refused to get past the subject of who was to stand beside the casket, and in what order. They were also very clear that they felt I should not be the person making his funeral arrangements because I was his former wife. It didn't matter to them that I was the person he asked because I was the person he trusted. I was subjected to much verbal abuse, which surprised me because I thought that the idea of sharing the arrangements, in advance, was a good one. I did not anticipate such a venomous personal attack.

Why did I tell you this? To prepare you for anything. People say and do "odd," sometimes even nasty or cruel things, when they are upset. If you are the person responsible for the arrangements, just do your best. No one can ask more of you than that.

BE KIND TO YOURSELF & OTHERS

First, Consideration For Others

I am about to ask you to do something that you may find very hard (if not impossible) to do if you are the person making funeral arrangements:

- While you are nearly consumed with grief and stress from all that has been, and remains to be done, try very hard to think about other people who are also grieving, people who may be sensitive to perceived slights that can ultimately create long-lasting hard feelings. I know full well what I am asking.

As you begin to ask people to participate in the funeral arrangements and service (*and you must ask for help, because you cannot do it alone*), it would, of course, have been great if you had some direction from the person who just passed as to who he/she wanted to participate. Because <u>chances are good that you do not have that direction,</u> you must make the decisions on your own.

- Some people quickly volunteer to help any way they can.

- Some people are happy to be asked and willing to participate.

- The person you ask to give the eulogy at the funeral service will need some time to prepare, unless they want to speak extemporaneously. Be sure to ask which way they would prefer.

- Others are reluctant, even nervous, but may be influenced to participate.

- Some people say they will help, but in the end, do not.
  Be prepared with an alternate plan, and don't expect too much.

- Some people will refuse. Give them permission to say no, and ask someone else.

- Some people will be very ***un***happy they were <u>not</u> asked.

- Others will be very ***un***happy about the people you did ask.

- Be prepared for some people to be so caught up in their emotions that they may criticize your choices.

- Try very hard not to take it personally.

If you know you did your best,
<u>forgive</u> yourself for things you may have overlooked, and
<u>ignore</u> the criticism of others who did not walk in your shoes.

Consideration For Yourself

I'll tell you what I did for ME to help me stay focused and deal with my former husband's last illness, funeral and burial.

- **<u>First, I REdiscovered donuts!</u>** Not exactly nourishing food, but definitely comfort food at a time when I needed comfort. I had all but given up donuts for more than a year. When Bill was in the hospital the last week of his life, I surrendered to temptation when a nurse asked me if I would like her to order a breakfast cart. Considering that I arrived at the hospital every morning around 7 a.m., it sounded like a good idea. I didn't know that the "breakfast" cart included only coffee and donuts. But, that was OK by me! I declared donuts to be "health food" for the duration.

- **<u>Second, I got a massage every week or so for a while.</u>** A person must do what they must do in order to survive difficult times. I wasn't able to carve out time for a massage before Bill's death, but in the months afterward, when I was closing out his home and administering his estate, those massages were much more than comfort for me … they saved me!

Even though I was able to comfort myself with donuts and massages during Bill's illness and funeral, and even afterward as I administered his estate, I held tightly onto my emotions, and I paid a price for being so controlled. Don't do it. Cry. Talk. Soothe yourself with flowers, good music, the company of people who love you. Be good to yourself. You will survive!

If you were the person making all the funeral plans … *and even before that, if you were the person caring for a loved one during his/her last days* …. you may have been too busy to have expressed your emotions. You may have been afraid you would lose control if you did, and there were so many things that had to be done, and you were the person who had to do them. I get it. Nevertheless, it is important to remember that stress can make you sick.

Give yourself permission to feel the feelings you are feeling, and express yourself fully and appropriately. Don't feel a need to apologize for your emotional outbursts. Even though you may not believe me, they will lessen in frequency and intensity over time.

- If it means that you need a particular exercise routine to burn off the unexpressed emotion, stick with it.

- If it means that you cry a lot, then cry.

- If you find that you need to eat comfort food for a short time, do it. You can go on a diet soon enough.

- If you need to listen to certain music to soothe yourself, then surround yourself with it.

285

- If you find that you need to meditate or pray, then do it.

- If you need "alone" time for a while, even 30 minutes a day for a while, do whatever it takes to set time aside. A bubble bath or a hot shower can do wonders to restore your body and spirit.

- If it will help you to look at photographs, keep the photo albums (and the Kleenex) close by. Spend time looking at the pictures with other people who loved the person, too.

- If you need to speak with a counselor, do it.

- Get a massage as often as you can.

- Take stress vitamins and try to eat well.

- Get enough sleep. Go to bed one hour earlier every night.

- Try very hard not to depend upon medication for relief.

- If it helps to talk about your loved one who just passed away, do it with others who will understand your feelings and not try to talk you out of feeling them.

- If you feel the need to join a bereavement group, then do it.

WAYS TO MEMORIALIZE YOUR LOVED ONE

How you and your family decide to memorialize a loved one who has died is a very personal decision and there is no right or wrong way to do it. The options are many. If you were to do a search on the Internet for Memorials for Deceased Loved Ones, you will find many ideas of how you could create a permanent memory of a deceased loved one, including, but certainly not limited to:

- plant a tree in Israel through the Jewish National Fund (800-542-8733).

- plant a tree through Lofty Oaks (800-533-7554).

- plant a tree in a U. S. National Park through an organization known as The Trees Remember.

- donate a bench on the boardwalk of a beach town, or in a park, or in a cemetery.

- donate religious items, including clergy vestments, altar cloths, hymn books, memorial windows and pews, candlesticks or chalices, choir gowns.

- donate funds for air conditioning to your church (if it doesn't have one already), or an elevator or a ramp for disabled persons to have better access to the church.

- donate books to a library or to a children's ward in a hospital.

- donate funds to a local animal shelter.

- donate a painting to a public building in your community.

- donate a wing to a hospital, school, library, etc.

Think about how best to memorialize your loved one. The places and organizations that would be very pleased to accept a donation are endless, and you are only limited by your imagination and your funds to determine where and how to memorialize your loved one.

MAKING FUNERAL ARRANGEMENTS IN A BLENDED FAMILY

As if decisions and arrangements for funerals are not hard enough, consider the problems that can arise when making funeral arrangements in a blended family. What if there are current spouses and former spouses who don't get along? What if they live far away? What if there are different religious traditions to consider? What if there were no instructions left by the deceased to guide the decision-making process? What if there are major disagreements among family members that will cause hard feelings? What if some members of the families don't get along, and could cause a fuss during the services? Who will be in charge? Who will pay?

The following story is an example of the problems that can occur when people don't take the time (or don't insist) on having the hard conversations with their loved ones.

> *Once upon a time, there was a 60-year old man, the oldest of 3 children, whose mother died 6 years ago. His mother had been married to her husband (this man's stepfather) for about 35 years. The relationship among her children and her husband was and remains extremely close and very good in every respect.*
>
> *The man has 4 children by his first marriage. While he kept in touch with them at some distant level, there was never any friendship among his children and his wife's children, and they didn't celebrate family events together. When it comes to holidays and family get-togethers, he spends the time with his stepchildren and their families, not his biological children.*
>
> *Now, the man is in his 90s, and fortunately, is a healthy, active man whose own father lived to his mid-90s. He lives alone in a small house in a 55+ community which does not have a healthcare facility.*
>
> *So, what is the problem, you may be asking? The problem is that he is unwilling to discuss important matters with his stepson who could very well turn out to be this man's primary care giver, and the person who will be responsible for making decisions and arrangements of all sorts if the man becomes ill and/or when he dies. Does this man have a Living Will and a Healthcare Power-of-Attorney? A Will? If so, where are they? Is the stepson the agent under those documents and the man's executor? Lots of questions ... but no answers.*
>
> *His stepson wonders what will happen when this man dies. What kind of funeral does he want? Who will be responsible for making funeral plans in the absence of any direction from the elderly man? The step-family, or his biological family? What if they don't agree?*
>
> *This man refuses to talk about any of these matters, saying he'll do it <u>later</u>?*
> *Excuse me? When you are in your 90s, WHEN IS LATER?*
>
> *What would you do if you were the stepson?*

Do you see the potential for problems that could be solved by the simple act of having conversations while there is still time? You won't die from the conversations, but you will die eventually! But, then, you already know that, don't you?

WHO WILL CARE FOR YOUR PETS AFTER YOUR DEATH?

This is a subject of extreme importance to me, personally. I have no sure-fire ways to offer you about how to handle the care of your pets in the event of your disability or death. I get upset just thinking about it. But, I present it here for your contemplation and so that you will remember to designate the person and the funds to take care of your pets the same way you would if you were here to do it yourself.

One thing is pretty certain: No one will ever love your pets as much as you do.

I believe that our commitment to our animals is sacred. They are completely helpless without someone to care for them. This becomes a very real problem when you have to think of who will take care of your pets if you are disabled for a long period of time or after you die.

Erin's Tale

During the last three weeks of his life, my former husband and I made plans for his funeral and burial and took care of his personal business. Several times, he said to me, "Take care of my cat." He knew that if anyone was going to take good care of his cat, it would be me. I promised him I would do just that. He knew it was not possible for me to bring Erin into my home with my two cats.

Erin was born to a mommy cat that belonged to his brother. The mommy cat had died several years before, and I asked his brother if he would give Erin a good home during the few remaining years of her life (she was already 13). He refused ... repeatedly.

So, my sister and I went about finding a no-kill shelter where Erin could live comfortably and safely. In his Will, Bill made provisions for a substantial donation to whatever shelter where Erin would live. Happily, my sister reported that she had found a good one near my home. And, so, I confidently but sadly gave Erin to the woman who ran the shelter. I also gave her a check for the amount of money that Bill specified in his Will for the person who would be giving his cat a home.

Six months later, this woman's home was raided by Animal Control and SPCA personnel because she was a cat hoarder who had 115 cats, most undernourished and diseased, living in filth. Oh my God! What about Bill's cat? The woman was a complete fraud! And, what makes this story worse, and what makes me so mad, is that I actually knew this woman ... she came from a good family. I never suspected anything like hoarding. Why would I? I moved heaven and earth to find Erin, but to no avail. I will always be heartbroken that I wasn't able to keep my promise. And I will always feel sad, wondering what happened to Erin.

As executor of Bill's estate, I wrote to this woman and demanded that she return the money. Surprisingly, she did.

IF YOU HAVE PETS, YOU MUST GIVE SERIOUS THOUGHT TO WHO WILL CARE FOR THEM WHEN YOU CAN NO LONGER DO IT YOURSELF.

HOW DO YOU GO ABOUT SELECTING THIS PERSON?

First, you must select the person who will promise to take care of your pets and lovingly care for them for the remainder of their natural lives. Before you designate the person to care for your pet(s), you must have a conversation with them to determine if they are willing and able to do this for you, so that you will get a sense of how committed they will be in taking on this responsibility. If you have the slightest doubt, pick somebody else.

I realize this is asking a lot. Taking your pet(s) into their household might cause an upset where other pets already live, or where someone has a pet allergy, or even where they don't have enough financial resources for food and veterinarian costs.

If you are asked to care for someone's pet and you feel that you cannot, you MUST say no immediately. One of the worst things that can happen, at least in my opinion, is that the person you designate says "yes," finds that they can't handle the added responsibility, and then takes your beloved pets to the local shelter or SPCA, possibly to be euthanized. This would cause terrible suffering to your animals, which are already stressed at the loss of you. Remember Erin's story. My heart breaks every time I think of the promise I made, and how badly things turned out.

You must be absolutely certain that you can trust this person to do as you ask, specifically if you request that your pets not be separated if you have more than one.

If you leave pets behind, leave some money for their care. There are trust funds that can be established for this specific purpose. Discuss this with your lawyer or financial advisor, and if it appears feasible, ask your lawyer to prepare all the legal papers for you to sign. Keep them with your Funeral & Burial Instructions, and give a copy to your executor and the person(s) who will be caring for your pet(s).

If your lawyer or financial advisor make even the smallest joke about it, get somebody else who takes it seriously. You do not want any slip-ups.

It would be a good idea to write a letter to the person who will be caring for your pets, and include the following and any other details you want them to know.

- Tell the person about your pet's personality, their favorite <u>foods, toys and sleeping arrangements.</u>

- If you have a cat that is declawed, <u>you must specify that the cat never be let outside.</u>

- Give instructions for any medications your pet takes, the cycle of when their shots are due, plus the name, address and phone number of your veterinarian.

- If your pet doesn't like children, don't put the pet into the home of people with children in the hope that it will all work out. <u>It probably will not.</u> Your pet will be just as stressed in this situation as the children, and you don't want to have your pet bite a child and have to be put down. What a horrible thought!

- Give clear instructions of what the person is to do with your pet when the pet dies. You could pre-purchase a plot in a pet cemetery, or leave written instructions and funds for burial of your pet. If you do this, be sure to specify to this person where to find the cemetery deed, where the cemetery is located, etc. In the alternative, you might designate that the animal is to be cremated and include instructions of what you'd like done with the ashes.

- There are pet cemeteries where you can bury your beloved animal(s).

- Some general cemeteries have specific areas designated for this purpose.

- Other cemeteries do not permit animal burial.

One of my Mother's dogs was buried in a pet cemetery which has tombstones, and if you want to spend a sunny afternoon walking through a cemetery, you will be amazed at the words on the tombstones. It is clear that many people loved their animals more than their relatives.

- If there comes the time when your pet must be euthanized by your vet because of terminal illness or injury, this person must have the strength of character to stay with the animal until the end, holding the animal, soothing and comforting it. Can and will this person do this for you? If you're not sure, pick someone else. Talk about it well in advance until you are comfortable and satisfied that this person will do what you are asking them to do.

    NOTE: There are unscrupulous vets who will sedate the animal on the pretense that they are putting them down, only to later sell the animal to a pharmaceutical firm for animal testing once the animal wakes up again. You didn't know this??? Well, it is sad-but-true. If you don't want your pet used for animal testing, you must take responsibility to see that it never happens.

Once upon a time, there was a woman who had two dogs that she loved very much. They gave her companionship and comfort every single day, and she cherished their very existence. Both dogs were getting old; one, blind, the other, deaf. She gave instructions that if she were to die while owning these beautiful animals, she would want them to be euthanized and their cremains buried with her. If you ever agree to do this for someone, be sure you keep your word.

CHECK LIST
(in no particular order)

Since there are only a few days in which to accomplish all that is necessary to make funeral arrangements, the following Check-List may be useful for anyone who is planning a funeral. Just skip over the tasks that are not appropriate.

Asking for the opinions and approval of others may <u>not</u> be the best way to make these decisions. Sometimes it's best to make clear statements about what you want and do not want for your funeral and burial. You may never get everyone to agree or approve, and besides, whose funeral is it, anyway?

_____ Have you **told** your loved ones what you want? (notice I did not say "discussed," *I said "<u>told</u>."*)

_____ If you have made pre-arrangements, does your family know that you have made them? If not, why not?

_____ Have you at least put it in writing? If not, why not?

_____ Does your family know where they can find your written instructions? If not, why not?

____ Selection of a funeral director.

____ Donation of organs arranged.

____ Made all financial arrangements to pay for funeral, cemetery, flowers, clergy, musicians, etc.

____ Met with funeral director and made all selections and arrangements.

____ Gave funeral director all necessary information about decedent.

____ Obituary completed and submitted for publication.

____ Arranged for persons to make phone calls.

____ Decedent's clothing delivered to funeral director.

____ Arranged for limousine(s).

____ Met with clergy and arranged for funeral service.

____ Made arrangements for all musicians.

____ Arranged for printing of program for funeral service.

____ Ordered flowers.

____ Directed that certain flower arrangements be delivered to places other than the cemetery.

____ Selection and purchase of a cemetery plot (if none already owned).

____ Cemetery Deed located for cemetery plot already owned.

____ Made and paid for all cemetery arrangements.

____ Selection of a cemetery monument or plaque.

____ Made all arrangements for a viewing.

____ Contacted fraternal (or other) organization to provide service at viewing.

____ Made all arrangements for cremation after viewing.

____ Cremains will be buried in cemetery plot.

____ Cremains will be disposed of as decedent directed.

____ Made arrangements for readers.

____ Made arrangements for all pallbearers.

____ Made arrangements for all presenters.

_____ Met with clergy to arrange funeral service, select appropriate music, and passages for readers,

_____ Made arrangements for person(s) to give eulogy.

_____ Made arrangements for funeral luncheon.

_____ Money is available for luncheon.

_____ Made arrangements for house-sitters.

_____ Made arrangements for care-givers for children, elderly, disabled persons, and/or pets.

_____ Transportation arranged for out-of-town guests.

_____ Housing arranged for out-of-town guests.

_____ Arranged for volunteers to write thank-you notes.

> ***Show me the manner in which a nation cares for its dead, and I will measure with mathematical exactness the tender mercies of its people, their respect for the laws of the land, and their loyalty to high ideals.***
>
> William Gladstone

IN CONCLUSION

I have strong opinions about funerals and burial, many of which you have read about in this book. I believe that a funeral is a rite of the church, just like baptism, confirmation and marriage. But, remember, I was raised in the Episcopal church, so I like a formal service in the church sanctuary. Even if you don't want a formal church service, and all you want is for your ashes to be thrown to the wind at the beach, keep dignity, love, and respect foremost in your mind as you go about making the arrangements.

Lots of people disagree with my opinions, even people in my own family. If you anticipate disagreements among your family members about making your funeral arrangements, then it's up to you to set things straight either with conversations, written instructions, or pre-arrangements. A funeral is not supposed to be an event where family members fight. I know. There has been way too much fighting in my own family about such things. Again, this is where communication is essential.

If you are put into the position of having to plan a funeral and burial for a loved one, the best possible scenario would be that you know what your departed loved one wanted for his or her own funeral, and then follow those instructions. And, in the absence of that information, just do your best.

> ***Knowing how to die is knowing how to live. What is death anyway? It's the outcome of life.***
>
> Jeanne Moreau

Tempus Fugit

THINGS TO DO   *   IDEAS   *   FOLLOW-UP

#	A,B,C	Description	Start Date	Completion Date
1				
2				
3				
4				
5				
6				
7				
8				
9				
10				
11				
12				
13				
14				
15				
16				
17				
18				
19				
20				

In the event I become ill, injured, or when I die, these are the
PEOPLE TO CALL

_____
(insert your name)

Date _____

- List the names, phone numbers, email addresses, and your relationship to ALL the people you would want to be notified if you became ill, injured, or when you die.

- Complete this form NOW – TODAY. Don't put it off until it is too late.

- Don't forget anyone who is important to you (even people from years ago).

- Give a copy of the completed form to the person(s) who will be in charge at the time of need.

- Make sure that someone knows where to find this form when it is needed.

- Update this form periodically by adding names (try not to remove any names if you think there is even the vague possibility you would want them to know about your situation).

- Shred the original form.

- Every time you revise the form, give an updated copy to the person who has the other copy, and request that the original be shredded.

- To streamline the process of making the calls when the time comes, please ask certain people to call approximately 10 people each (that is, one page) … more if they think they can manage more.

- Let them know if it is all right to pass the information along to others, or if it is not all right.

- Keep a current copy of this form with your Funeral & Burial Instructions and other estate-planning documents.

Only put off until tomorrow what you are willing to die having left undone.

Pablo Picasso

NAME	PHONE NUMBER	EMAIL ADDRESS	HOW I KNOW THEM

(please print legibly)

(attach additional pages as necessary)

Chapter IV

RECORD-KEEPING

Organizing is what you do before you do something,
so that when you do it, it is not all messed up.

A. A. Milne

RECORD-KEEPING

Don't put off until tomorrow what you are willing to die having left undone.

Pablo Picasso

Here are three good reasons to keep your personal records and papers organized. You will save:

- Time
- Aggravation
- Money

ORGANIZING YOUR PERSONAL BUSINESS PAPERS

Record-keeping? *"Isn't that the same as filing?"* Well, yes it is. I know you dislike filing ... in fact, I'm not crazy about it either ... but I do it because I know the benefits of keeping good records and the consequences of not putting the effort into it. Keeping your important papers in **PILES** on your desktop or your dining room table or kitchen counter does not qualify as good record-keeping!

Maintaining your family personal business records is just as important as maintaining records of a business ... after all, it is YOUR PERSONAL BUSINESS we're talking about! It is not necessarily an easy task, especially if you have never taken the time to set up even the simplest filing system, but it is not impossible either.

The loss of personal papers may not have the same degree of negative consequences as might happen in the business world; nevertheless, the misfiling and disorganization of your personal files can create upset and personal or financial loss for you.

Think how comforting it will be to know that all of your personal records are organized and safe, and can be easily and quickly located when needed

---

Once your personal records are organized, you may find that other things will more easily fall in place. You may find that you have a little bit more time for more desirable activities, or that you are less stressed because you will not find yourself wasting time looking for documents and papers anymore.

Establishing and maintaining your personal records does not have to be a monumental task if you apply good common sense and establish a simple filing system (*emphasis on "simple"*) that works well for you, and will allow someone else to easily locate all the information they need in the event of an emergency or your death. The task requires discipline and a committed effort on your part to regularly do what is necessary to maintain your system once you have set it up.

Some people will argue that they are simply not organized people, and they have managed satisfactorily all these years, so they don't see any reason to change the way they keep their personal papers. That may be true, and that's all right with me if it's all right with you. Nothing says you have to organize your papers as long as you recognize the consequences of not organizing them. But maybe you should ask your family if your choice is all right with them.

One person's mess is merely another person's filing system.

Margo Kaufman

Here are some more good reasons for keeping an organized records management system, not necessarily the most sophisticated system, but one that is simple and easy for you to maintain and easy for someone else to understand:

1. Keeping your important papers all in one place so you would be able to "grab them and go" in an emergency.

2. Making your own life easier when you need to locate a particular piece of paper (save time, reduce stress).

3. Keeping your personal contact list (you're A-Z list) current and easily accessible when necessary, noting the people to be notified in an emergency, including the names of your medical and legal professionals.

4. Keeping your personal tax records all in one place so you can provide your accountant with all the papers necessary to prepare timely, accurate income tax returns.

5. Proving losses to insurance companies in case of fire, theft or other catastrophic event.

6. Disputing mistakes by banks, credit card companies, your medical provider, your investment companies, your insurance company ... all the people you do business with. Mistakes are made every day, and you must be able to produce accurate, timely records to protect yourself.

7. Keeping your children's school and medical records together so you can find them when you need them.

8. Keeping your own financial records all together and easy to locate when needed.

9. Keeping the records from every aspect of your personal life organized and safe (auto titles, deeds, insurance policies, Marriage Certificate, Divorce Decree, Pre-Nuptial Agreement, Passport, Social Security card, birth certificates ...).

10. Keeping your Living Will and Healthcare Power-of-Attorney together in one easily accessible place so that if you were to become injured or seriously ill, someone would be able to locate your documents in a moment's notice.

11. Keeping your Will, Trust, Power-of-Attorney and all other estate-planning documents safe and available when needed.

12. Keeping all your Funeral & Burial Instructions (including cemetery deed) together so that someone can find them when needed.

13. Keeping information about your entire life available to others after your death. Your executor can only follow the paper trail you leave behind, and it is expensive if you force him/her to go on a scavenger hunt to locate important papers.

14. Keeping the lawyer's fees for the administration of your estate to a minimum because your records are in such good condition.

COMMUNICATION

Again, here is that word, communication. Organizing your papers is only part of the job; the other part is telling someone about your system. You do <u>not</u> want to be the only person who knows the workings of your document management system.

While it is important to protect your personal papers and guard your privacy, it is also important that you provide information to others so that, in the event of your illness and death, they can quickly and easily locate the necessary documents, as well as the key to your safe deposit box, the combination to your safe, your computer User Id numbers and passwords, and any secret hiding places where you keep assets, important information, and documents.

Once again, I remind you that many things in this book require conversations in order to make them happen.

It is not what we intend but what we do that makes us useful.

Henry Ward Beecher

Scenario No. 1

You are in an accident and immediately hospitalized with multiple injuries, and unconscious, at least for the moment. You'll be laid up for months. Will the person you designate as your Agent under your Power-of-Attorney, Living Will, and

Healthcare Power-of-Attorney be immediately able locate these documents so they can take care of your medical, legal, and personal business? Will they be able to find your checkbook to pay your bills?

Does that person even <u>know</u> he/she has been appointed? I certainly hope so!
(refer to Chapter I – LEGAL)

You <u>do</u> have these documents, don't you?

Scenario No. 2.

You died, leaving PILES of papers all around your home: bills, checkbooks and bank statements, deeds, car titles, insurance policies, magazines, prescriptions, and junk mail ... several years' worth of papers, all mixed together. You never took the time to organize your important papers and information and put them in a safe place where they can be easily located and managed by someone else acting on your behalf.

Your executor may have to gather every paper he/she finds in your home, put them in a large cardboard box, and take the box to the lawyer who will be handling your estate. A paralegal will sort through your paper mess to make sense of it all and investigate <u>everything</u> you left behind, in order to determine if there is value to be obtained for your estate, or if you owe any money, etc.

Although many of the papers in the box were not current (bank books from accounts closed years before; expired/cancelled insurance policies; expired credit cards), each must be investigated. One or more could turn out to be valuable, and it is the responsibility of the lawyer and executor to be certain.

I believe in opening mail once a month, whether it needs it or not.

Bob Considine

If you regularly keep old, expired papers of all sorts, at least put some indication on them that they are no longer valid. Better yet, shred them. After your death, your lawyer will bill your estate for the time it takes to sort out the mess you left behind, and you know that legal representation (even the work done by a paralegal) is expensive. So, it is easy to see that if your personal records are in good shape, the attorney's fee will be lower than if your files are a mess.

Isn't that sufficient reason to keep good records?

Of course, you say, it won't matter to you, because you will already have passed away. But, it will matter to your heirs, because that legal fee will reduce the amount of their inheritance. Trust me, it will matter to them!

If the only immediate benefit from organizing your papers is to notice how lovely your home looks after you put away all those papers piled in places where they don't belong, you are on your way to successful document management. You don't have to believe me when I tell you how important it is. All I'm asking is that you compare the benefits if you do the work versus the consequences if you don't.

OK, OK ... I hear you.

"How am I supposed to organize all those papers? I'm not a secretary? (ouch!) And, besides:

- *What documents am I supposed to keep?*
- *And for how long?*
- *And where should I keep them?*
- *And why is it so important, anyway?*
- *And who should be responsible for all this record-keeping?*
- *And why should I believe you?"*
- *I'm very busy.*

The answers to your questions are in this book. Don't stop reading yet.

> **It is not enough to be busy; so are the ants. The question is what are we busy about?**
>
> Henry David Thoreau

The good news is that your record-keeping system doesn't have to follow any particular rules of filing, or be the way your parents kept records, or even the way a professional would recommend. In addition to knowing the basics of filing (that is beyond A, B, C ...), logic and common sense are very useful in setting up a filing system. All that is really necessary is that your personal record-keeping system must be such that, were you to fall off the face of the Earth today, someone else could find all of your papers and documents quickly and easily.

Are your records in that condition now?
Tell the truth!

Remember

The secret of good filing is not simply putting papers away.
The secret is that you (or someone else) can easily find those papers when necessary.

Once upon a time, a woman died owning liquid assets of $900,000. Included among those assets were two $25,000 Certificates of Deposit. Evidence of the CDs was found among her personal papers, which were reasonably well organized, but incomplete as it turns out.

From the office of the attorney handling the estate, an inquiry letter was sent to the bank which issued the CDs. Turns out that the bank had been sold three times since the date on which the CDs were issued. The investigation into the whereabouts of the missing CDs went as far as the Federal Reserve Bank for purpose of tracing the changes in ownership from one bank to another. Still, the banks could not produce evidence of those CDs.

Although it is entirely possible that the woman had cashed in the CDs when they matured, she had no papers to document such transactions, and neither did the bank. It was never determined whether the CDs were cashed in sometime in the past, lost in the maze of changes in bank ownership, or lost among the woman's personal papers.

Isn't that a shame for her family? Maybe they got the money before she passed away ... that is, if she cashed in the CDs ... but maybe they did not. One thing is certain: every hour of the lawyer's and paralegal's time was billed to her estate.

FILING IN THE BUSINESS WORLD

In the business world, accurate filing is essential. Although a great deal of filing today is done electronically, the requirement is always the same: Put the files away in such a way that someone else can also find them quickly and easily. Sounds simple enough. Yet, most people find it difficult, if not impossible, to do. Still, it must be done.

Once upon a time, a secretary was looking for the file for ABC Corporation in the "A" section, where it rightfully belonged. But, it was not there. So, she asked another secretary where it might be, and her ready reply was, "It's filed under "S" for John Smith. He owns the corporation." (Excuse me!) When it was pointed out to her that corporations are separate entities from the person who owns them, and need to be filed under their own individual names, she said, "That's not how we do it here."

Can you see the importance of filing in such a way that others can also find documents?
What if there had not been anyone else around to ask where the file was kept?

Do you remember years ago when computers were introduced to the business world? We were told that computers would reduce or eliminate papers. <u>Did not happen!</u> While it is a huge understatement to say that computers have streamlined many aspects of the business world, it must also be acknowledged that there are still many reasons for paper copies. If you don't believe me, take a look at the walls of files in your doctor's office.

Loss of files in the business world has serious consequences. It could mean loss of your job, your employer could lose his company or be sued. Loss of someone else's money can put you in jail. Loss of a classified document can mean a breach of national security. Loss of a lawyer's client file can mean the loss of a case or even malpractice. Loss of a financial planner's file can mean the loss of a client's money. Cemetery documents get lost or misplaced through the years, and, for the person needing to bury a loved one or attempting to trace their family tree, that loss can be very distressing.

If you agree that it is important to establish and maintain good record-keeping systems in the business world, why, then, would you assign less importance to keeping your own personal business records?

ELECTRONIC RECORD-KEEPING

As I write this, I am aware that many people transact much of their personal business electronically. If you are a person who stores your records electronically, at least leave some kind of (paper) trail for others in your family to follow in the event that you are ever ill or disabled. It is especially important for you to leave a trail for your executor, who may or may not have immediate access to your electronic accounts, depending on the rules of the various Internet sites.

Electronic filing of your personal records adds an entirely new dimension to the process. Have you set up your electronic files on an iPod, or a Blackberry, or some other electronic gadget? What happens if you lose it? On a recent TV show, one of the characters told a police officer that his computer had been stolen from his car, and that he needed it back immediately *because his whole life was in that computer.* I don't think that's such a good idea, although many people do it because they don't like paper files.

In the summer of 2012, there was an article in *The Philadelphia Inquirer* regarding the topic of storing your legal and financial affairs electronically ("*Are your Electronic Affairs in Order?*") There is an entirely new, complex and ever-changing specialization in the law to address the issues associated with records stored electronically. Suffice it to say that if you are storing your vital personal information electronically, you must be very careful to see that it is protected, that someone you trust will be able to access that information when and if necessary during your lifetime and after your death, and that anything you don't want people to know about you shouldn't be there in the first place.

Eventually, someone will have to get access to your electronic accounts and close them out. But, the law is out of step (time wise) with the Service Agreements of the various Internet providers. I recently read another article in a local newspaper about the mother of a young man, as she fought to get access to his Facebook account after his death.

People who work in the information technology field may say that they can retrieve almost anything, and while that is probably true, I think that having a paper back-up file is also necessary. The best advice I can give you is to leave an adequate paper trail for your family to follow and consult with an attorney specializing in the field of information technology for guidance in handling these matters.

WHO SHOULD BE RESPONSIBLE FOR ALL THIS RECORD-KEEPING?

Someone has to be responsible for family records. Who will that be?

- If you are single, you're it!

- If you are married or in a committed partnership, you must decide which of the two of you is best suited to this kind of responsibility. In fact, maybe it should be a shared responsibility, with each one taking charge of certain parts of the process. In any event, both of you must understand the workings of your filing system.

- If you have children who are old enough to understand, they should know that you have a system for keeping family records, how the system works, and how to easily locate information.

- And, remember that the person in charge of your records should <u>not</u> be the ONLY person who knows the workings of the family's files.

I recommend that you develop a regular schedule for paying bills, balancing your checkbook, filing the paid bills. Once you have a system in place, the routine will actually reduce the amount of time needed for this task. It will also eliminate the possibility that you could pay a bill beyond its due date, and incur late fees. Decide if you want to pay your bills online, or write checks every month. No matter what your choice, it is still necessary to keep records current and organized.

SAFE DEPOSIT BOX

I RECOMMEND THAT YOU

DO <u>NOT</u> PUT THE **ORIGINALS** OF THE FOLLOWING DOCUMENTS

INTO YOUR SAFE DEPOSIT BOX AT THE BANK*

1. Cemetery Deed
2. Funeral & Burial Instructions
3. Your Estate-Planning Documents including:
   - Will
   - Living Will
   - Durable Power-of-Attorney
   - Healthcare Power-of-Attorney
   - Revocable Living Trust (other trusts), if any

You are, of course, free to ignore this suggestion. I only make it because I have seen situations where time was of the essence, and the document that was needed at that moment was not accessible. I'm asking you to think of what could happen in the time it would take to get the document. It is not wrong or illegal to put your documents in the safe deposit box. It just may make it hard to get to the document.

1. **Cemetery Deed**. What if you specified that you be buried in a specific plot at such-and-such cemetery, and had even placed the cemetery deed in the bank box, but no one opened the box until after the funeral … that is, until after your family had purchased another plot in another cemetery? What if your family didn't even know about the box? Then what?

2. **Funeral & Burial Instructions.** What if you put your Funeral & Burial Instructions in the box at the bank, and you specified that under no circumstances do you wish to be cremated, but your family went ahead and cremated your body because they didn't open the box until after the funeral. Then what?

3. **Estate-Planning Documents.** While it is absolutely essential that you keep these records safe, it is not a good idea to put *originals* of the above documents in a bank box because it is difficult for anyone to gain access to the box in an emergency, or at the time of your death. I said "*difficult*," but not impossible.

- Banks usually allow "Will searches" where a person can go to the bank immediately after your death, state that you died, produce identification, and request assistance to do a "Will search." A bank representative will be present during the search and will not allow anything to be removed from the box except a Will if it happens to be in there.

- If you put your other estate-planning documents in a bank box, you (or someone else) may not have immediate access to those documents at a time of need, and time may be of the essence.

  - What if one of your documents (for example, your Living Will) is needed on a Sunday or at night, and the bank is closed?

  - What if you cannot go to the bank yourself (because of illness or injury, for example)?

  - What if the only other person who could open the bank box had to be someone else who was listed as a signer or a co-owner of the box, <u>except that you only listed yourself?</u>

  - What if that other person is unavailable for any reason whatsoever?

- What if the only other person who could have access to your bank box is the person you named as Agent under your Durable Power-of-Attorney, and your original Durable Power-of-Attorney is in the bank box, so your agent cannot get to it?

Can you see the potential for problems?

WHO ELSE KNOWS ABOUT YOUR SAFE DEPOSIT BOX?

While this may immediately seem like an unnecessary (*even ridiculous*) question, believe me when I tell you that many safe deposit boxes are never opened for the very reason that the only person who knows about the box is the person who opened it in the first place. If someone else (your spouse, partner, executor, lawyer, for example) does not know about the box, and therefore the box remains closed for years, eventually the state in which you reside will take possession of the contents of the box by the process known as escheat.

- *And, don't you think it is the owner's responsibility to let their family know the existence and location of that bank box? Once again, here is a situation that requires timely conversations with the people in your life who have the need to know.*

> *Once upon a time, there was a young man, an only child, who was executor of his widowed mother's estate. He encountered a problem locating his mother's bank safe deposit box. He knew she had one, because she spoke about it regularly, but he could find no information or documentation to prove it.*
>
> *His attorney contacted several local banks, and was never able to locate her bank box. This is very sad ... because whatever she left behind in that box was obviously meant for her son, and all of it could eventually become the property of the state if he is never able to locate the bank box. He will never know what was in the box, and what should rightfully have been his... unless he eventually finds the box or reads the list of Unclaimed Property from the state Treasury Department years later.*
>
> *Who knows why this woman didn't tell her son about the bank box? What was the big secret, anyway?*

Some banks only allow their own customers to have safe deposit boxes, and the box fee is paid annually by an automatic debit from the customer's bank account. At the time of a person's death, the existence of the box would then become known to a family member or an executor when they go to close out the bank account. This makes perfect sense. Unfortunately not all banks tie the payment of the box fee to an existing account, and so some families may never know about the existence of the bank box.

If you do not want that to happen, tell someone you trust about the box before it's too late. They need to know the name and address of the bank branch, the box number, and the whereabouts of the key. It might even be good if you arrange for another person you trust to be a signer (signatory) on the box. This is just another one of those places where communication is required. Besides, what are you keeping in the box that is so important that no one else should know about it? *Just asking ...*

*EXCEPTIONS TO MY RULE

It is my opinion that a bank safe deposit box is not the best place to store your original documents. I stand by that opinion *in general*, but I also acknowledge that there may be exceptions where a bank safe deposit box makes perfect sense. When you see houses that have been destroyed by extreme weather events, the first thing you think of is probably not their personal papers ... but, chances are good that those papers may be lost or destroyed.

In Chapter V – PERSONAL, I point out the benefits of a bank safe deposit box if you live in a place where the possibility of extreme weather events is significantly higher than in other places. I'm talking about hurricanes, tornadoes, earthquakes, wildfires, or floods. If you live in such an area, it becomes even more important that you protect your personal papers.

While I am generally in favor of keeping *original* documents in a water-proof/fire-proof safe in your home, it would still be a good idea to keep photocopies of your important papers in a bank box, including (but not necessarily limited to) credit cards, financial accounts of all sorts, birth certificates, marriage/divorce certificates, every document you would never want to lose. In an emergency, a bank box would provide a safe location for your important papers away from your home, such that if your home were to be destroyed, you would be able to go to the bank and retrieve papers you need after the emergency passes.

In the alternative, you could copy the originals to a CD, and place the CD in the box. It is also wise to put negatives or electronic copies of your family pictures in the bank box, because if your actual photographs were to be destroyed, you could always reprint them. Put as much information on each photograph as possible, including at least the full names of the people and the date of the event in the picture.

Either the actual photos of the contents of your home (or an electronic copy) should be kept in the bank box as well, and when you get new furniture, etc., take new pictures and put them in the box. On each photograph, write information about the purchase, including the date, purchase price, where you purchased it, etc. It will be of enormous assistance in documenting your possessions for an insurance claim.

UNCLAIMED ASSETS

Many assets go unclaimed because of poor record-keeping, not the least of which includes the contents of many safe deposit boxes.

In Chapter II – FINANCIAL, you read about an article in *The Philadelphia Inquirer* of October 12, 2010, that included a full-page notice from the Pennsylvania Treasury's Unclaimed Property Division, stating that in 2009, the Pennsylvania Treasury returned over $107 million of unclaimed property. A similar article is published every year.

IF SOME OF THAT MONEY WERE YOURS, WOULDN'T YOU WANT IT BACK?

I have been told that life insurance companies know and actually count on the fact that many paid-up policies go unclaimed. Why? Because they are in the bank box no one else knows about. That means that someone paid the premiums for insurance they intended for their family, but which the family will probably never get. Somehow, I don't think that was their intention.

DO YOU GET THAT?

**If you make the choice to keep poor records and files,
and then don't tell anyone about them,
your family may be deprived of assets that were yours, and which you want them to have after your death.**

Is that OK with you?

WHY DO YOU SUPPOSE THE LIST OF UNCLAIMED ASSETS IS SO LONG?

Because a lot of people didn't talk about those assets with their families. Remember my stating that many things in this book require conversation? This is another one of those situations. Some people did not store or record evidence of their assets in ways that allowed their family/or executor to even know they existed, let alone be able to locate them. If there are approx. 6,000 names on this Pennsylvania list, and there are 52 states that have similar lists of unclaimed property ... *do the math* - that equates to a whole lot of money that individual families lost because of poor record-keeping and poor communication.

Once upon a time, a 55-year old woman died in a fire that consumed her house, all her personal property, personal records and documents. Because of the extensive damage done to her property, the police and fire department were unable to determine, let alone locate, her nearest relative. A neighbor was later able to provide information about the woman's only known relative ... a son who lived 50 miles away.

At the time of her death, she was a single woman, an employee, a homeowner, who obviously had other assets in addition to her home (bank accounts, investments, car, etc.) This means that she left behind an estate that would have to go through probate. Did the woman have a Will or a Trust Agreement? Who knows?

Maybe those documents burned in the fire. Maybe they were in her bank safe deposit box, or in a lawyer's office, but without her personal records, how was her son supposed to even know about a bank box or the name and address of

---

her lawyer? What if this woman had kept perfect records? Who would even know? The one thing she did <u>not</u> do was safeguard her personal records in the event of a fire or other catastrophe.

That young man had a daunting task before him. Without information about his mother's personal business, he was put in the unenviable position of not only grieving for the loss of his mother under horrific circumstances, but he was left to piece together her life, with few clues, such that he can close out her estate. It may not be impossible, but will be extremely time consuming, difficult and expensive.

MORAL OF THE STORY:
Buy a fire-proof/water-proof safe, and put all your important papers in it ... before it's too late.

HOW CAN A BANK SAFE DEPOSIT BOX BE CLOSED?

To remove the contents of the box after your death, and to close it, will require a formal written inventory of the contents. In Pennsylvania, that Inventory had until recently, been done with the bank representative, plus a representative of the Pa. Department of Revenue, and your Executor. It is possible that the representative from the Department of Revenue may not have to be present any longer due to shortage of personnel; nevertheless, the Inventory must be done, and your Executor will schedule the appointment with the Bank representative, and together, they will prepare the Inventory. While <u>the rules and procedure may be different in every state,</u> Executors must determine how the Inventory should be completed, and take care of this matter in a timely manner as part of the task of administering the estate of a decedent.

- The purpose of this inventory is to determine if any of the contents are taxable. (*Remember Ed Slott's comment about the government wanting all your money, and they are very patient ... they will wait 'til you die to get it?*) Even if the box only contains papers, the inventory must be done. A copy of the formal written inventory must be kept by the Executor and given to the attorney handling the estate so the inventory form can be attached to your inheritance tax return.

IS IT ALL RIGHT TO STORE OTHER VALUABLES IN A BANK SAFE DEPOSIT BOX?

Of course it is all right for you to store other valuables in a bank safe deposit box ... as long as someone else knows about the box, including the bank location, where you keep the key, and some idea of what's in the box. In fact, <u>if</u> <u>you</u> <u>insist</u>, you can even keep your Will and other estate documents in your bank safe deposit box, as long as you know that you may be creating a problem in situations where time is of the essence. (*see above*)

Just use your common sense when deciding what to put in the box, and what to leave out.

Here is a true story about a man who stored coins in a bank safe deposit box.

Once upon a time, there was a man who collected coins for many years, and stored them in his bank safety deposit for safekeeping. He was always afraid of his home being robbed. He put thousands of dollars' worth of coins in his bank box, and he had never taken the time to prepare an accurate inventory which listed the cost of each coin, each coin's face value, year of issue, date of purchase, etc.

When he died, it was necessary for the bank box to be inventoried by a representative of the Department of Revenue. The resulting inventory had to be given to a coin appraiser to determine the value of every single coin as of the date of death of the owner of the coins. Why? Because every coin had to be accurately documented and given a <u>date-of-death</u> value so the value of each coin could be taxed for Inheritance Tax.

At that inventory, there were 5 people present for a day and a half: The Department of Revenue representative; the Lawyer for the estate; a bank representative; and the two adult sons of the deceased, who were Co-Executors of their father's estate. The estate was billed for the Lawyer's time for approx. 8-9 hours (do the math). Also, after the inventory, the appraiser charged a fee for his services.

> *Think of the consequences if no one in the family had known about this bank box. In as little as 5 years (depending on the laws in that jurisdiction and depending upon the rules of the bank), the state could have seized the coins and been the beneficiary of all that cash. Remember "escheat"?*

MORAL OF THE STORY:

If you have a bank box, be wise about what you put into it, and make sure someone else (a) knows that you have the box; (b) the name and address of the bank where the box is located; and (c) the whereabouts of the key. Of course without the key, the box could always be drilled for a fee. I'm talking about what if no one even knows about the existence of the box.

Might this man, instead, have put his coins in a safe in his home?

Remember that list in *The Philadelphia Inquirer* about unclaimed property? Much of it comes from contents of safe deposit boxes that no one claimed. Think of all the valuable possessions that go to the state because no one in the family knew about the box: jewelry, cash, insurance policies, bank books, silver and gold, family heirlooms, to name just a few. Don't make the mistake of thinking your valuables are safe UNLESS SOMEONE OTHER THAN YOU KNOWS ABOUT THE BOX!

Well, technically, they will be *safe*, all right ...
safe, that is, until the state revenue agent comes to claim them.

IS THAT WHAT YOU WANT TO HAPPEN?

It seems that, years ago, it was customary for people to store their valuables in a bank safe deposit box. While there is nothing inherently wrong with this practice, think about what you keep in the box? If it is only papers that could be kept in a fire/waterproof safe in your home, you could close the box and save the annual fee it is costing you. So many times, after a person dies, a family member or personal representative finds nothing but worthless papers contained in the box. The box had not been used for its obvious purpose, and the person wasted years' worth of annual fees paying for a box that was not needed.

DON'T KEEP EVERYTHING

It is as important to know which documents to keep and for how long, as well as which ones to dispose of and when. If you were to keep everything, you will run out of storage space sooner or later. You have to be able to sort out the important papers from the junk. As soon as you receive every piece of paper, determine if you want to keep it (file it), toss it (shred it), or act upon it and/or send it to someone.

Shred every piece of paper that you don't want to keep, especially those on which your name and/or account information are printed ... all those applications for new credit cards, or some kind of insurance ... you know the "stuff" I'm referring to. It is important that you don't throw this kind of mail into your regular trash, because, believe it or not, there are unscrupulous people who actually pay others to go through your trash for just this kind of information so they can steal your identity.

And, you know all those inserts that come with credit card bills and advertisements of every sort that come with your various statements -- throw them away, right away! And, when you file papers, don't save the envelopes, too, unless you think you might need the postmark at some time in the future, or unless you use them for scrap paper.

Invest in a good quality shredder, and immediately shred papers that you don't want to keep. Don't wait until you have a big pile. I actually gave up trying to shred everything myself because the shredder gets jammed and makes a mess with little pieces of paper everywhere. So, instead, I look for local events where a shredding truck will be present to shred large quantities of papers. Townships, service organizations, local elected officials, churches, or other groups provide this service at no cost to the public. I accumulate everything that needs to be shredded in a large plastic tub until the day when I can take it to the shredding truck, and then off it goes.

I actually bought a pair of "shredding scissors," thinking that I would cut up each individual piece of "junk mail" as it came into our house, but I'm not that disciplined. Now, I just toss the stuff in the plastic tub mentioned above.

I once reduced the volume of papers in a decedent's estate by 50% simply by disposing of those junk inserts and the envelopes which the decedent had kept. Naturally, the estate was billed for my time, money that the estate could have saved had the decedent done timely, accurate paper management.

WALLET STUFF

I recommend that you photocopy everything you carry with you in your wallet ... both sides. *I'm not kidding!* All those credit cards, your driver's license, your ATM and debit cards, your health insurance card. Everything! Put the photocopies in your Big Book or other place of safekeeping.

> *If you think this is a ridiculous waste of time, consider that whatever time it takes you to photocopy the contents of your wallet will be a whole lot less than the time it would take to replace and duplicate those items if your wallet were lost or stolen.*

I don't have to tell you how hard and time consuming it is to replace all that stuff you carry with you. If you take the time to photocopy all that stuff, should your wallet ever be lost or stolen, you will have all the information you would need to get replacements.

And, women, why you are carrying so much stuff in that enormous purse? I don't care if it was made by the most famous designer in the world, or how many thousands of dollars you paid for it ... fill that purse with bubble wrap if you have a need to make it look full, but stop carrying "your life" around in that purse.

> *A place for everything and everything in its place.*
>
> Samuel Smiles

PRE-FILING

For many years, my sister (also an executive/legal secretary) and I have used a system we created and call "Pre-Filing." It is really no big deal, but it has saved us a lot of time and aggravation.

A pre-filing system would be very easy to use in your home for personal filing. A pre-file operates as a "holding place" that keeps papers organized until you have time to do your actual filing. The system allows you to quickly and easily put your hands on to certain papers if necessary before you have filed them in permanent places. Here's how the system works:

- My sister always used one of those big accordion-pleated folders that comes pre-marked A-Z. Into the appropriate section, she temporarily placed papers that would be eventually put into more permanent files. For example, bills for MasterCard would be put into the "M" section. Investment account statements might be placed in the "I" section for investments. You get the idea.

- I don't like those accordion-pleated files, so, instead, I use individual manila folders. Using a fine point black marker, I hand print the name of each individual company on separate manila folders ... plus one more folder marked "Miscellaneous." For example, my bank statements from ABC Bank go into the folder marked ABC Bank. My American-Express bill goes into a folder marked American-Express. You get the idea.

And, when you have time, you can easily transfer the papers into the permanent files where they belong. Until that time, however, if you were to need one particular paper in a moment's notice, you could easily locate it.

WHERE IS YOUR CONTACT LIST?

I believe it is important to have a personal contact list PRINTED ON PAPER. Call me old-fashioned, but I know the benefits of the printed list.

Many people today are keeping their contact list (a/k/a A-Z List) on electronic devices. While this may work beautifully for them, individually, it may present a problem in an emergency, when it might be difficult for someone else to locate the names of people to contact by way of that little device.

I believe that a good workable system for creating and maintaining your personal contact list is to put all that information on a table in your computer, so you can periodically edit the list and then print revised hard copies. It really doesn't matter where you keep the printed list as long as it is easy to find, and someone else knows where you keep it.

Your Contact List should contain, in alphabetical order, the names, addresses and all other pertinent information about everyone in your life, including (but certainly not limited to) family, friends, neighbors, your bank, doctor, lawyer, accountant, plumber, lawn service, credit card companies, the utility company, the library, your insurance agent ... EVERYBODY!

- I realize that most this information is available on the Internet. Nevertheless, I keep one copy of my list in my kitchen. If I am downstairs in the kitchen and need a phone number, I do not want to have to go upstairs to my computer just to get a phone number; and (b) phone books are generally not published anymore. I am not a patient person, and in this instance, my contact list gives me the immediate gratification of being able to find the phone number I want right now.

Your Contact List is a place where MORE IS BETTER.

- Be sure to include one highlighted and capitalized item in the name column titled ICE (that is, **I**n **C**ase of **E**mergency), and then list the information about people you would want contacted in an emergency.

- I don't recommend that you permanently remove any names of people from your list. Even though you may not be in contact with certain people right now, you might want to get in touch with them in the future.

- I do not recommend that you separate the names by category (*i.e.*, all your family members together, then all your friends, and finally, businesses) because, sometimes the names overlap (*e.g.*, you may do business with a friend, so which category do you list it in? Can you see the problem?) Keeping this list by category will only cause confusion in an emergency. KEEP IT SIMPLE. ... everybody, strictly A-Z.

I suggest you print at least two hard copies: one to be kept by your home phone (if you have a home phone), or on your desk or kitchen counter; and the other should be kept in Your Big Book (if you have one). I actually print 4 copies: I keep one each in my kitchen, TV room, home office, and my Big Book. I put 3 of them in brightly colored term-paper folders.

I created my Contact List (that is, my A-Z list) on a table in my computer, set up **ALPHABETICALLY**, in **LANDSCAPE** style. Frequently used names are **HIGHLIGHTED** and **CAPITALIZED**. The list includes (at least) the following information about each contact:

Name	Address (home and business)	Phone Numbers (all)	email address (home and business)	Misc.

If you don't have a computer but you do print legibly, there is absolutely nothing wrong with hand-printing your own list, although, revising it will involve cross-outs and additions that can make the list messy and ultimately difficult to decipher. If your present address list is in your own handwriting, with lots of cross-outs and inserts, it would be good to start over. Your handwriting might be perfectly clear to you, but not so to someone else, especially not in an emergency.

If you have a different way of creating a contact list, especially if you use some electronic device, I say "just do it." Keep in mind, however, that (a) electronic devices can get lost or broken, (b) are regularly replaced by newer, better models; (c) not everyone knows how to use them; (d) in an emergency, someone might be unable to find it, let alone figure out how to get access to your list. There may be no time to waste looking for phone numbers on electronic devices. *But, hey, that's just my opinion.*

If you don't like the idea of the computer list, don't use it.
Just keep in mind that the object is to create a workable PRINTED list that can be easily located in your home.

A Surprise Party

When my sister planned a surprise birthday party for me, she took one of my printed lists from my house so she could use the list to get the names and addresses of my friends to invite to the party. Because I have 4 lists in my house, I didn't even miss the one she borrowed.

Needless to say, I was pleasantly surprised by some of the guests, many of whom I hadn't seen in years! Their names were on my list, my sister recognized them, and sent them invitations. My A-Z list made her job easy, and made my party a real treat for everyone who attended.

ONE MORE THING.

Do not confuse this list with the PEOPLE TO CALL list described in Chapter III – FUNERAL & BURIAL, which is a separate, abbreviated list to be used for a very specific purpose.

Don't agonize. Organize.

Florence Kennedy

TIPS ON WAYS TO SET UP YOUR FILES

I'm going to tell you how I keep files for my husband and myself. Not only did I learn specific filing rules in business school, I also learned the necessity for filing precision in my jobs. To some of you, it may seem ridiculous that I am going into this kind of detail about a filing system, but maybe it will inspire some of you to begin the process of organizing your own papers in a way that satisfies you. I believe in having hard copies of important papers, so, if my advice about files sounds "prehistoric," I apologize.

I have set up two kinds of files:
- ACTIVE
- PERMANENT

ACTIVE FILES

These are the day-to-day files where I put paid bills, etc. I keep them in the drawers of a large file cabinet. While it may seem to duplicate some of the contents of My Big Book (mentioned later on), remember that this is an active file, and the Big Book is more or less a permanent file.

I use both hanging file folders (Pendaflex) and manila file folders. I use **only** the dark green hanging files and **only** plain manila folders, NEVER multiple colors. I don't believe this is the place for colorful creativity. I stick to the basics. It makes it easier to find things … if you don't believe me, just trust what I say. I have many years of experience keeping complicated files.

When I am making the tabs for the hanging files, I hand print them using a fine black marker. Of course, you can choose to be much neater and print labels on your computer, but I take the quick and easy way out and use black markers.

I ALWAYS put the files in the drawer in alphabetical order, with <u>every</u> tab either in the left, middle, **_OR_** right position of the folder. I NEVER put the tabs all over the place because it makes it more difficult, <u>visually</u>, to quickly and easily locate a particular file. *Again, trust me on this.*

In the file cabinet drawer, the hanging folders are placed alphabetically, by <u>category</u>, and include tabs that say things like BANKS, CREDIT CARDS, MEDICAL, PHONES, RECEIPTS, HEATING/AIR CONDITIONING, SUBSCRIPTIONS, TRASH, UTILITIES, HOUSE, etc. Your will set up your file drawers to include whatever files are appropriate for you.

I don't always put the individual names of service providers on the manila folders, because sometimes they change. For example, in a file folder marked TRASH, I keep paid bills and other correspondence from whatever company picks up our trash. The name of the company has changed several times over the years, and as far as I am concerned, it doesn't matter what the name of the company is, as long as I have all the receipts and documentation about the individual companies, all in one folder. All that really matters to me is that I can easily find the folder when I need it. Printing TRASH on the folder seems to do that for me.

Inside each hanging file, I place one or more manila folders, also identified with a black marker. For example, I have one tab on a hanging file that says CHRYSLER, and another that says VOLVO. Inside each hanging file folder, I have individual manila folders with tabs that say, for example, Purchase Documents, License and Registration, Car Payments, Inspection and Repair bills, etc. I think you get the idea.

Set up one hanging folder titled RECEIPTS, and keep receipts for all <u>major</u> purchases in the event you want to return something, or you experience a loss by fire, theft, etc. These receipts, along with photographs, will assist you in establishing values.

In another hanging folder marked TAX RECEIPTS – (year), you will keep all the papers, receipts, etc., which your Accountant (or tax preparer) will need to prepare your Income Tax returns. Keep them together (by year) until it is tax time. In this folder, you would also keep receipts for contributions to charities and thrift stores.

- There is a new scanner available in office supply stores, that enables you to scan small receipts and organize them electronically. If you are "electronically inclined," you may wish to keep your records this way. Although I haven't tried one myself, it sounds like it has possibilities. If you choose to file this way, be sure that someone other than yourself knows how to get access to your records under appropriate circumstances.

Periodically go through your files and remove papers that are out of date or no longer needed. If you have the file space, it's probably good to keep records for at least two (2) years unless there is a specific reason to keep some for a longer period of time. <u>This does not include tax returns</u>, which should be kept for at least 6 full years, as described elsewhere. And, after cleaning out your files, be sure to shred all those unwanted papers.

PERMANENT FILES – THE BIG BOOK

For storing and protecting your personal files, especially PERMANENT FILES, I recommend a file system that is about as basic and simple as it could possibly be: The BIG BOOK! The book provides simplicity and ease. It is a 3-ring notebook that is at least 6 inches deep. Notebooks like these are expensive (sometimes more than $30) in an office supply store, but very _**in**_expensive in thrift stores and yard sales. (I have found them for as little as $1). Whenever I find one, I buy it for future use or to give to someone I know who is working this system for themselves.

The ultimate goal of putting The Big Book together is to create and leave behind a filing system that will:

Be easy for you to maintain.
Provide a "grab and go" book to take with you if you ever have to evacuate your home.
Be easy for your family and executor to understand and deal with at a time of need or at the time of your death.
Reduce the legal fee to administer your estate.

Do you need any other reasons?

310

> ### *The perfect is the enemy of the good. Just get it done already.*
>
> Author unknown

If, after reading the following description, you don't like the idea of a Big Book, and if you have created a workable system for yourself, that will, at the same time, allow someone else to locate your documents when needed, then you have succeeded. Go for it! While there are all sorts of filing systems, folders and cabinets in office supply stores, and many books on the subject of organizing your important papers, you don't need to invest in expensive or complicated filing systems, as long as you:

- Keep your papers safe from theft and loss by water or fire damage.
- Can locate a given document on a moment's notice.
- Keep the records/files current.
- Periodically shred out-of-date papers.
- Remember that in the end, you're trying to keep the legal fee for administration of your estate as low as possible.
- <u>Keep it simple.</u>
  - Do you have any idea how many men die, leaving behind women who know nothing about their personal filing systems? Who ever said that men are better at record-keeping than women? After all, isn't it women who have been secretaries all these years? Oh, well, maybe there is no easy answer to the question. I just thought I'd give you something else to think about.

> ### *Discipline is the bridge between goals and accomplishment.*
>
> Jim Rohn

Putting the Big Book together is no small task, and it requires discipline and a commitment to do what it takes to keep it up to date. If the Big Book is too overwhelming for you to consider as <u>your</u> method of record-keeping, ***don't do it***. I agree that the finished product is BIG and it can look really intimidating. The point of my describing My Big Book is for you to see it as an example of one way to keep your personal records. It may give you an idea of how you can organize your own records in other ways, always staying focused on the idea that you are creating a filing system that will be easy for someone else to decipher someday in the future.

NAYSAYERS ARE EVERYWHERE! I recently heard the following comments about the idea of using such a Big Book for personal record-keeping:

- *"My important papers are already in my safe, so why do I have to put important documents in a Big Book and then put the book in the safe?"*

  YOU DON'T! It is just my opinion that having your documents organized in the book can make it easy to locate your important papers … and easy to "grab and go" in an emergency.

- *"Even if I did put my own Big Book together, I probably won't keep it up to date!"*

  Maybe. Maybe not. But, why would you go to all the trouble of creating the Big Book in the first place if you have no intention of keeping it current? *Just asking…*

- *"It's **too** <u>BIG</u>!"* Duh!?!

Whether you keep your important papers organized this way (or some other way), or whether you don't even try to keep your papers organized, remember that someday, someone else will have to organize them. So, if you agree that this last statement is true, why not do your part and keep your records in good shape.

My Big Book is a more or less permanent place for safekeeping original documents. We keep the book in our safe, and I don't have any reason to look at it on a regular basis.

When you put your own Big Book together correctly, it will contain information about your entire life **all in one place**. This will not only make your own life easier, but certainly will make things much easier for those who come behind you after your death and have to try to recreate and document your life. For every one of your documents they can't find, there is a price to be paid, calculated in monetary terms (*e.g., legal fees*), or in headaches, stress and aggravation.

OUR BIG BOOK

In our big book, in individual page protectors, I have placed every important paper that relates to our life, including birth certificates, diplomas, military discharge, deed, cemetery deed, death certificates for my parents ... *everything*. Once again, more is better.

I created a Table of Contents in my computer so I can easily revise it. The Big Book is divided into sections with <u>over-size</u> tabs that are necessary because regular tabs will not stick out beyond page protectors, which are larger than 8-1/2" x 11" pieces of paper. While I say the completed book is HUGE, keep in mind that ...

THE BOOK WILL NEVER REALLY BE COMPLETED ...

because it is <u>an evolving document</u> that changes as things change in your life. I update the book periodically, removing pages that no longer apply, inserting new pages as appropriate.

It took me months to gather and <u>photocopy</u> the various documents, and put the book together. I just recently spent another 3-4 hours to update the book. I am committed to keeping this book current, because, some day, when my husband and I have passed away, it will be easy for our trustee or executor to handle every aspect of our estates.

OUR OTHER BIG BOOKS

We have <u>two</u> other (smaller) notebooks that we also keep in our safe.

- One containing our original ESTATE-PLANNING DOCUMENTS.
- One containing our FUNERAL & BURIAL INSTRUCTIONS.

WHY DO I BOTHER?

If you are wondering why I go to all this trouble, it is because I was a legal secretary who sorted through the messy boxes and piles of papers other people left behind, and I do not intend to leave behind a similar mess. AND, because, someday, someone (our trustee or executor) will have to come behind us and close out all those business accounts and contacts, and their job will be so much easier with this Big Book than it might be otherwise.

Do yourself and your family a huge favor, and begin keeping your records in such a way that if you died today, your family and executor would be able to find everything they need to administer and close your estate. If nothing else, it will help to reduce the legal fees for administration of your estate.

While examination and handling of that paperwork for the administration of your estate will be time-consuming, usually done by the lawyer's paralegal and billed at a rate lower than that of the attorney, nevertheless, the billing time of the paralegal is one of those "costs of probate" that can be significantly reduced by your keeping good records <u>now</u>. Just as accountants are happy to be given organized, complete records for preparation of tax returns, so lawyers are equally happy to be given organized, complete records for the administration of a decedent's estate.

God put me on this Earth to accomplish a certain number of things.
Right now, I am so far behind that I will never die.

Bill Watterson

HOW TO CREATE YOUR OWN BIG BOOK

I recommend that you begin today to put together your own Big Book. When you finish setting it up, it will be large and heavy, and it will contain all the important facts and information about your life … *all in one place*.

IT IS A MARATHON, NOT A SPRINT!

I said earlier that putting this notebook together does not have to be a monumental task, but keep in mind that preparation of this book is not a one-time thing or a project for a rainy Sunday afternoon. I give you notice right here that it is a big job that could take you a few weeks … *even months* … to complete, depending on your available time and level of commitment. You have to be in it for the long term, until the job is done.

"Begin at the beginning," the King said gravely, *"and go till you come to the end; then stop."*

Lewis Carroll
(Alice's Adventures in Wonderland)

LET'S BEGIN

If the project appears too daunting, break it down into small, manageable tasks that you can complete in short periods of time. You could begin by gathering the supplies you will need, including:

(a) one five- or six-inch 3-ring binder that holds 8-1/2" x 11" paper.

(b) two or three thinner 3-ring binders that hold 8-1/2" X 11" paper.

(c) large box of page protectors.

(d) 8-1/2" x 11" paper.

(e) a paper punch for 8-1/2" x 11" paper.

(f) file labels (if you are so inclined).

(g) <u>over-sized</u> divider tabs that are large enough to stick out beyond the page protectors. Get enough so that you will have one tab for every category. The Table of Contents of my Big Book includes 64 items, and your Big Book may have more or less. The tabs are sold in packages of 5 or 8, depending on the size of the tabs, so figure out how many you will need. You may have to special-order them. <u>Regular-size tabs will **not** work with page protectors</u>.

(h) Colored term-paper portfolios, that will accept 3-ring punched 8-1/2" x 11" paper (as many as you need to print sets of your personal A-Z list).

(i) A small copy machine. You may already have a printer attached to your computer for making copies, but if you do not, you can buy a small, multi-purpose copier for approximately $100 in an office supply store. Trust me, you will need a copy machine in order to do this job well and completely.

(j) If you do not already have one, buy a safe that is fire-proof and water-proof, and **large enough to hold your Big Book** and all the other valuables you would want kept in a safe! This is no place to skimp! <u>A small fire-proof box will **not** do</u>!

(k) A good shredder.

In every section, I recommend you include as much information as possible relating to each particular subject, including (but not limited to) the name, address and phone number of the provider, your account number, and any terms and conditions that are specific to that account.

Keep in mind that the accumulation of documents and creation of this Big Book is not for every-day filing. It is for the (permanent) storage of <u>original</u> documents.

WHERE SHOULD YOU KEEP YOUR BIG BOOKS?

Your Big Books and their contents must be safeguarded, but how and where should you store such large notebooks?

IN YOUR SAFE.

Your other notebooks containing important documents should also be kept in your safe, along with other valuables. Put the safe in a place in your home that is free from potential water damage, and is hidden yet accessible. Also, write down the combination where you can easily get to it. You may also want to give a trusted family member the location of the safe and the combination.

NOTE: For several reasons, as I explained previously, I do not recommend using a bank safe deposit box for storage of your <u>original</u> documents ... in fact, I don't think this notebook, if you complete it as I suggest, would even fit in a bank box.

If you don't put this notebook together or create some other workable filing system for yourself, you will always have to deal with the annoying, stressful process of searching for some particular document in a time of emergency or need. Or, worse, someone else will be searching for an important document related to you and your life and be unable to locate it.

Can you easily and quickly find your Healthcare Power-of-Attorney?
What about your Passport, Automobile Titles, Social Security Card, or Birth Certificate?
If you answer is NO, then you know what you must do ... or not!

GRAB AND GO

In the event of an emergency, it is essential that you take your important personal papers with you in a way that would keep them safe and dry. Your "completed" Big Books can be the quick and easy solution. They would be easy to "grab and go," and should be No. 3 on your list of things to take with you if you were forced to leave your house in an emergency ... behind (No. 1) your family members, and (No. 2) your pets.

In order to make it easy to grab the books and go, I bought a large suitcase at a yard sale for $1.00 specifically for this purpose. It is large enough to hold all three of our Big Books, and I keep the suitcase right beside our safe. The suitcase has no other purpose except to sit there and be ready if the time ever comes.

HOW TO NAVIGATE YOUR BIG BOOK

At the beginning of the book, insert a Table of Contents that matches all the tabs. I don't think it matters if you list the contents alphabetically or categorically. The point is to make it easy to locate a document in a moment's notice. When you add or delete something from the book, revise the Table of Contents accordingly. It will be easy to maintain if the Table of Contents is created and retained as a file in your computer. If you do not use a computer, just keep the list neat and current.

PERMANENT RECORDS

The following items, in more or less alphabetical order, are suggestions of things to include in your Big Book, and are presented here to get you thinking about the kinds of things to include in your book. Of course you will add or delete things that do or do not apply to your life.

In each category, put as much information as possible as it relates to each category. MORE IS BETTER. When you have finished, everything about your life will be all in this one book, all in this one place.

1. Appraisals: for example, if you have printed appraisals of any of your possessions (jewelry, paintings, antiques, sterling silver flatware, furniture, cars, etc.), put each original appraisal in its own page protector. Include the exact name and contact information for every appraiser.
2. Appliance insurance
3. Auto club
4. Auto insurance
5. Bank accounts
6. Bank safety deposit boxes
7. Baptism and christening certificates
8. Birth certificates
9. Boat slip(s)
10. Boat(s)
11. Cemetery deed or certificate of ownership
12. Child Custody agreements and Child Support information
13. Children: (natural born, adopted, step-child, or foster child)
14. Credit card insurance
15. Credit cards
16. Credit reports
17. Death certificates
18. Deed(s)
19. Divorce Settlement Agreement and Divorce Decree, plus information about your lawyer
20. Drivers' licenses
21. Family (information about living members)
22. Family (information about deceased members)
23. Family pictures (indicate where they are kept)
24. Health insurance
25. Home equity loans and line-of-credit
26. Homeowners' Association Agreement
27. Homeowner's insurance
28. Income tax returns (There will not be room for your actual U. S. IncomeTax returns in your Big Book; but include a section titled INCOME TAXES that identifies the location of where you keep your original tax returns, plus the name, address and phone number of the tax professional who prepares your tax returns. You should keep all income tax records for at least six (6) years, in a fire/waterproof safe.
29. Insurance (life and all others)
30. Internet (all passwords, User ID numbers, and all other relevant information)
31. Investments (all of them, kept separately in page protectors)
32. Leases for real estate that you are renting
33. Leases for real estate you own
34. Location of your original Will, Powers-of-Attorney, etc.
35. Long-term care insurance
36. Marriage documents (including Prenuptial Agreements)
37. Mortgages that you owe
38. Mortgages that you hold
39. Other tax information
40. Passwords and other computer information
41. Pets (including medical insurance, pet sitters, dog walkers, veterinarians, microchip information)
42. Pharmaceuticals
43. Phones (house; cell)
44. Photographs of contents of your home
45. Real estate taxes
46. Recreational vehicles
47. Religious affiliation
48. Renter's insurance
49. Service agreements (vehicles, heating & air-conditioning systems, etc.)
50. Social Security and Medicare
51. Special needs of members of your family
52. Vehicle payments
53. Vehicle titles

54. Warranties on major appliances, roof, and all other major purchases.

BY NOW, IF YOU HAVE READ THE LIST, YOU PROBABLY HATE ME.
Hey, I'm only trying to help!

Even if this information-gathering process appears impossible, once you have it together and you see the benefit of maintaining good records, you will thank me. People in your life will likewise thank <u>you</u> for making their life easy some day in the future.

OK! OK! I hear you shouting: *"Why do I have to do this?"*

I remind you again that you don't have to do any of this. I do, however, continue to suggest that if you don't like the idea of creating your own Big Books, you could at least create a workable record-keeping system of your own, but you really don't have to do that either. There is no penalty for NOT keeping good records ... *except* ...

- _____
- _____

(fill in the blanks)

YOU CAN TAKE YOUR TIME, BUT YOU MUST BEGIN, AND YOU MUST FINISH.

Even if you are a person who procrastinates about organizing your personal records, I nevertheless suggest that you begin today. Don't use that excuse that you'll do it later, when you get around to it. You will recall that I already gave you your own personal ROUND TUIT. Now would be a good time to use it.

You don't have to finish today; in fact, it is impossible to complete this book in one day! And the task won't be finished until you have an easy-to-follow, easy-to-manage filing system for every single original document and paper pertaining to your personal business. Think how good you'll feel when you have completed your own filing system.

ASK FOR HELP

If you feel you cannot organize your personal records <u>by</u> yourself, you may want to retain the services of a professional organizer.

If you are not interested in completing this notebook <u>for</u> yourself, then complete it for your family and anyone else who would be in a position to handle your personal business in your absence ... including your executor after your death.

Organizing your documents and papers is a gift to yourself and your family. Were anyone to ever need to know details of our personal life or household, all the information is together in one place: in a very large, heavy, 6-inch, 3-ring notebook in our safe.

Don't struggle with organizing your personal records.
Just do it.

An ounce of action is worth a ton of theory.

Friedrich Engels

IN CONCLUSION

You can run, but you can't hide from this responsibility. Well, technically, that's not true.

You are <u>not</u> required to do any of this. Or you could do it half-way, skipping steps you think are not important or necessary. There are many choices available to you. You can always continue living your life exactly as you have been doing, and someday, after your death, having left behind a big mess, someone will come and clean it up.

Is that really the legacy you want to leave behind?

Whether you think you can or think you can't, either way you are right.

Henry Ford

Even after reading this chapter … *maybe, especially after reading this chapter* … you may still be resistant to the idea of keeping good records. You may think it's an unpleasant activity or a complete waste of time. You know that there will always be things you have to do, but don't want to do … all those things you keep putting off until later, because you don't feel like doing them now. It's more exhausting to resist doing the things you know you "should" do, than to actually do them. You will feel so much better once you have finished the task of getting your personal papers in order.

Again, you'll have to trust me about this.

Do your best to make this a worthwhile, enjoyable project.

Take a break every now and then. Don't put pressure on yourself to hurry and finish.

As you see yourself coming to the completion of the project, give yourself credit for a job well done.

The secret of happiness is not in doing what one likes, but in liking what one has to do.

James M. Barrie

Keeping your personal records organized, safe and accessible provides rewards for you and your family for years to come, and especially at the time of your death. And, I know how you dislike thinking about that day, but you have already agreed with me that the day will come. So, you might as well leave behind a clean slate.

In the end, you don't have to LIKE any of my ideas or suggestions.

You don't even have to DO any of them.

The record-keeping police won't come knocking on your door
with a warrant for your arrest on charges of keeping messy files.

"Whew! That's a relief!"

(You were worried there for a minute, weren't you?)

You may never know what results come from your action,
but if you do nothing, there will be no result.

Mahatma Gandhi

Tempus Fugit

317

<u>RECORD-KEEPING TO DO LIST</u>

#	Priority A,B,C	Description	Start Date	Completion Date
1				
2				
3				
4				
5				
6				
7				
8				
9				
10				
11				
12				
13				
14				
15				
16				
17				
18				
19				
20				

Chapter V

PERSONAL PLANNING

Dream as if you'll live forever.
Live as if you'll die tomorrow.

James Dean

PERSONAL PLANNING

Scenario: two old men sitting on a park bench. One man says:
"At our age, there are only two questions:
1 - How much time do we have left?
2 - What will we do with that time?"

That just about sums up this book.

- The answer to the first question is and will remain unknown until your last day.

- The answer to the second question is completely up to you.

Elsewhere in this book, I stated my opinion that CONVERSATION is the single most important thing that is required if you want to accomplish all the things you want to do *between now and then.* And, having come this far, I repeat that assertion. I apologize if you are tired of reading about the importance of conversation. I know how hard it is for some people to speak their own truth, yet I also know of the miracles that can result from having had those "hard" conversations. If you have been avoiding them, now would be a good time to learn how to say the things that matter to you before it's too late. If you are uncomfortable expressing yourself deeply, remember the quotation by Harriet Beecher Stowe:

"The bitterest tears shed over graves are for <u>words</u> <u>left</u> <u>unsaid</u> and deeds left undone." (emphasis supplied)

LIVING YOUR LIFE WITHOUT REGRETS SHOULD BE YOUR PRIMARY GOAL AS YOU CHOOSE HOW TO SPEND YOUR TIME FOR THE REST OF YOUR LIFE.

What would your life look like if <u>YOU</u> were the only project on your To Do List?

What would your life look like if <u>YOUR</u> interests and activities were at the top of your priority list?

Now is the time to begin to figure out what you are going to do with the rest of your life *between now and then.*

This chapter is about your <u>personal</u> **life**. The previous chapters were about your <u>personal</u> **business**. Let's proceed on the assumption that your finances are in good shape now and for your future, that you have completed your estate planning documents, have made your funeral and burial preferences known to your family, and have all of your personal documents and important papers perfectly organized.

Whew! That wasn't hard, was it?

Now, I want you to think about <u>YOUR</u> LIFE for a while.

What do you plan to do with *your* time … that is, the time you have left *between now and then?*

There is no cure for birth and death save to enjoy the interval.

George Santayana

WHAT IS YOUR RELATIONSHIP WITH TIME?

How do you relate to time? Do you think about time? Doesn't everybody? Some people think in terms of minutes, and if you don't believe me, ask a lawyer. Other people, in terms of hours, days, and years. Still others, in terms of the time it takes to accomplish certain tasks. Thinking about time can be a problem on the job as you watch the clock, or it can generate excitement when you think there are only 3 more days until you leave for your vacation in Hawaii. Time relates to what happened in the past, what is happening now, and what will happen in the future.

Do you find yourself worrying that you will run out of time before you do all the things you want or need to do ... things that are so important that, on your last day, you would regret not having done them? Do the 24 hours in every day seem insufficient? Well, if so, that's a problem, because there are and will always be only 24 hours in every day. So, how can you make time work for you? Thinking about how you use your time is one way. Planning is another.

Can you easily remember what you were doing 5 years ago? What about one month ago? What about yesterday? Does time seem to fly for you, or does it drag? Do you seem to notice the passing of time based upon the seasons or holidays, or the growth of a child, or the death of a parent? What do you use as your basis for telling time other than a watch or a clock? But, that's not what I'm talking about here; I'm talking about a lot of time, as in 20 or 30 years.

I once took a time-management course entitled "More Time." The presenter started by saying that since we were all there to get more time, he was going to give us an immediate 5-minute break, saying, *"There, I just gave you more time."* He pointed out afterward that we wasted those 5 minutes doing nothing, and that there is no such thing as time management, although I'm pretty sure there are many business people who would disagree with that statement. The course was designed to show us how to get the most out of our time by using a Day-Timer style book. Today, time is "managed" on electronic devices, although I still love and use my Day-Timer. The object remains the same: to plan for and keep track of how you spend your time.

> *This ideal of simultaneous accomplishments fuels the favorite fantasy of the decade: that if we were only more organized, and blessed with all the proper electronic helpers, we would be able to squeeze at least two lives into the time for one. Instead of making choices, we think we can make time.*
>
> Excerpt from *Value Judgments* by Ellen Goodman

Each day, there will be things you must attend to and for which you must show up: doctor appointments; pick up your dry-cleaning; take your car for inspection; get your hair cut; go to your grandchildren's softball game or school play. It helps to have these things planned for, *by priority*, rather than having to scramble to get them done ... squeeze them in between other things. Some people will tell you they thrive on chaos. *I don't believe it, but hey, that's just me.*

Planning how to spend your time allows for relaxation, reduced stress, and the peace of mind and sense of accomplishment that come from getting everything done with a little time to spare. How does that sound? It is important for Baby Boomers to begin looking at how they will spend their free time, because they are about to face 20-30 years of "free time." And, so, we come back to the question that this book keeps asking:

"What do you plan to do with the rest of your life _between_ _now_ _and_ _then_?"

It's a reasonable question, and one that suggests a lot to think about. It is so easy just to allow time to pass with no notice, to live one day at a time until that final day. Or, is it? People in prison live day to day, crossing each day off on a calendar or on the wall. Is that how you intend to live out the remaining days of your life?

I know a man who was really looking forward to retirement, so much so that he had a 3-inch cube-style tablet made that had, in reverse order, the numbers 1,000 to 0, representing the number of days left until he could retire from his job. Each day he tore off one page until there were no pages left. For him, it was sort of a joke ... but it did represent the reality of his time remaining on the job.

How much busywork are you capable of doing in a given day? week? month? year? How many TV shows can you watch every day? How many newspapers can you read? How many times a day can you walk around the block? How much free time would equal boredom for you? I don't know. What do you think?

Having just said that, I thought about neighbors who walk through the development <u>many</u> times every day. They don't follow the same route each time, and they never speak to each other. When I used to walk my other neighbor's adorable little white dogs and we would pass that couple on the sidewalk, they wouldn't even nod or say hello ... not even to the sweetest little dog that just wanted them to stop for a moment to say how cute she was. So, I wonder, is that what they do all day, every day? They walk? I guess they're healthy from all that walking, but they certainly aren't friendly. And they don't look very happy. Just my opinion ...

Time is a gift. How you use it is up to you.

WHAT DO <u>YOU</u> PLAN TO DO WITH YOUR FREE TIME *between now and then*?

Are you a person who wastes time? How do <u>you</u> define "wasting time?" Are you one of those people who must always be busy <u>doing</u> something? Do you think that reading a book is doing nothing? Do you constantly complain that there isn't enough time in each day to do the things you want to accomplish? Are you generally late or always early for appointments and social events? Does it even matter to you? Are you always saying you will do things "later?" Have you ever taken time to figure out when "later" is? Are you aware of how you use time (or lack of time) as an excuse for not doing things? Do you complain that you use all your time doing for others, and that leaves no time for yourself? Isn't it time for you to begin to <u>choose</u> how you will spend your time?

When you realize that you may be nearing 70 years of age, can you actually get in touch with that number and all that it represents in relation to time ... all that you have seen and done in those years? In 5 years from today, will you look back at the time that passed and think, *"Where did it go?"* ... *"What did I do with all that time?"* ... feeling that you wasted those 5 years, 60 months, 1,825 days ... or will you be pleased with yourself for filling that time doing things that are important to you, knowing that you will run out of time on some unknown day in the future?

- Did you ever notice that some people spend their money like they spend their time ... that is, they find that they have run out of it, but don't know how it happened, or where the money went? *Just asking ...*

In the same way that people regularly cannot answer the question that financial planners ask them (*"What do you want your money to do for you?"*), people are generally unable to answer the question about what they plan to do with all the free time they are facing. To answer these questions requires thought. Up until now, life has had a certain predictability and structure that originated in the responsibilities of education, employment, and marriage and family obligations to name a few. Baby Boomers' are facing years of freedom to choose what to do, without the obligations that limited them in the past. Sometimes, having too many choices can paralyze you. That is when it is time to focus on the things that are important to you.

Women are good at busywork: cleaning the oven, changing curtains, straightening up closets and drawers. Women see busywork everywhere. Men, on the other hand, do not, and too often are content to do nothing.

A little end-of-life humor

Wife:	*Honey, what are you doing?*
Husband:	*Nothing.*
Wife:	*But you did that yesterday.*
Husband:	*I wasn't finished yet.*

Retirement means twice as much husband and half as much money.

Anonymous

Once upon a time, I met a lovely woman at a yard sale she was hosting in her brand-new home in a 55+ community. She had quite a few objects for sale relating to cats, and naturally, she and I struck up conversations about her cats. (In case I haven't mentioned it already, cats are my favorite thing in the world.)

She had 3 absolutely gorgeous long-haired Himalayan cats which she entered in cat shows, and she asked if I would like to see them. Yes! Absolutely! So, she opened her front door, and out came the 3 most amazingly beautiful cats!

We began to talk about how she began raising and showing cats, and she said she was "forced" to do it after her husband retired. What? Turns out he was a lawyer who worked in a firm that required the lawyers to retire at the age of 72. Since that day, he had been sitting around their new home, feeling sorry for himself, bossing her around, criticizing her every action, whining, complaining about being bored, unwilling to engage in any activities in his new community, and generally making his wife's life miserable. He was one of those men who had become what he did. If he wasn't a lawyer, then who was he?

She told me ... a stranger ... that she couldn't stand to be with him in their beautiful new home, so she found something to do which keeps her busy and away from him. She has a reason to get up every day, she travels, meets new people, gets to spend her life doing something she loves. She is excited about her life. Isn't that what life's supposed to be, whether before or after retirement?

What does he do while she's away at the cat shows? He watches TV.

Health, Money, and Time

Question: Will Baby Boomers remain physically healthy and financially secure enough to enjoy all that time?

Choices must be made in relation to your health, your money and your time. There appears to be a disconnect between the way Baby Boomers manage their health, their money, and their time. Have you noticed that many people put a lot of time and effort into their physical health, but do not put an equal amount of time and effort into their financial health? They go to the doctors for annual physicals, take prescription drugs, exercise, try to eat right, do everything their doctor tells them to do, and, as much as possible, do everything to assure themselves that their health will hold out until that last day. Are you one of those people?

Do you put the same amount of effort into taking care of your money that you put into taking care of your body? When did you last have an annual "financial physical?" When did you last consult a financial professional to evaluate the health of your finances? Do you do everything your financial planner tells you to do? Are you confident that your finances are in good health, and, if not, why not? And, if you are <u>not</u> confident about your money lasting for the rest of your life, you know there are things that you need to be doing, and that the time to begin is now. What are you waiting for?

As you begin to think about all the time you have left on earth, determine how to use that time wisely. Remember to include some time for fun things you love to do, things like travel, possible volunteer activities or educational opportunities you always wanted but for which you had no time or money to pursue. What about those painting classes or music lessons you always wanted to take? And what about all those books you want to read?

What you do <u>not</u> want ... *at least, I don't think you want* ... is to look back at your life 20 years from now, from the perspective of knowing you COULDA, SHOULDA, WOULDA done so much more with all that time, would have put forth so much more effort to remain physically and financially healthy, but you didn't ... and you are left with regrets and the knowledge that you are quickly running out of time. Will it matter at the end of your life? I don't know. Only you know your own truth.

> *Life is a journey that must be traveled*
> *no matter how bad the roads and accommodations.*
>
> Oliver Goldsmith

And, while you're doing all that thinking, it is important to remember that you don't even have to make any of the suggested choices. Your life will go on, one day at a time, until your very last day.

> *It's only when we truly know and understand that we have a limited time on earth –*
> *and that we have no way of knowing when our time is up –*
> *that we will begin to live each day to the fullest, as if it (were) the only one we had.*
>
> Elisabeth Kubler-Ross

"My dear friends, death is the only certainty of life." These were the opening words spoken by a priest at the funeral of a friend who died suddenly and unexpectedly at the age of 54. He was going to retire in 3 months. He had lived a very busy, active, happy life, and was looking forward to his "retirement" years as a time of doing many things, especially with his family.

This man was not here to walk his daughter down the aisle at her wedding. He was not here to see his grandchildren born and growing up. His death was way too soon for all those who loved him. But, that's how death will happen... *unpredictably* ... to each of us, on some unknown day in the future. If you agree with this statement, it is up to you to decide what you will do with the time you have left on earth.

His funeral services were attended by many hundreds of people from the various organizations and groups he touched with his generosity of spirit and good humor. I believe that he lived his short life to the fullest, and that he had a lot of fun. He probably had regrets also, but doesn't everyone? I doubt, however, that if given a choice, he would have chosen that particular day to be his dying day. At the graveside, that same priest said, *"Only God knows the hour of your death."*

I learned to appreciate and treasure each day,
because you don't know how many you're going to be given.

Sandra Day O'Connor

Death is as natural as birth.

Everybody knows they will die someday, don't they? It just won't happen to you.

It is, after all, *"the only certainty of life."*

People do think that if they avoid the truth,
it might change to something better before they have to hear it.

Marsha Norman

WHAT IF YOU <u>KNEW</u>, WITH ABSOLUTE CERTAINTY,
YOUR DEATH DATE JUST AS FACTUALLY AS YOU KNOW YOUR BIRTH DATE?

This is a big question and requires a lot of thinking to come up with an answer. Keep in mind that there is no "right" answer. There is only "your" answer, and if you want to make changes, think about how you will go about making those changes before you run out of time, and whether or not you will die with regrets for *"deeds left undone."*

If you knew that date, in advance, would you be living your life differently?

- Would you be going to the same job?
- Would you be married to the same person?
- Would you live in the same place?
- Would you belong to the same religion?
- Would you have the same friends?
  ... all the while wishing for changes,
          remembering lost opportunities,
                  dreaming of a different future?

You have a choice. Live or die.
Every breath is a choice, every minute is a choice, to be or not to be.

Chuck Palahniuk

It is my opinion that answers to these questions <u>give you power</u> because they offer you opportunities to look at your life as you are living it today, consider what is working or not working, and determine what, if any, changes are needed, and then go about making the changes you believe are necessary and important.

325

- Would you change the direction of your life to follow your dreams?

- Would you begin to take advantage of opportunities you casually dismiss because you think you will live forever?

- Whether or not you choose to use or ignore opportunities is completely up to you. You don't have to change a single thing – your life is perfect as it is today. *Or is it?*

- No matter what you decide, you will die anyway

Progress is impossible without change,
and those who cannot change their minds cannot change anything.

George Bernard Shaw

On the occasion of her 70th birthday (August 4, 2011), Martha Stewart is quoted as saying,
"My new motto is, 'When you're through changing, you're through.'"

ARE YOU HAPPY WITH YOUR LIFE CHOICES SO FAR?
or, ARE YOU LIVING SOMEBODY ELSE'S LIFE?

- The life your parents wanted for you?

- Did you marry the first person who asked you just because you were afraid no other person would come along?

- Do you hate your hair, or your over-all appearance?

- Do you want to move to a different place?

- Are you working at the job your high school guidance counselor told you would earn you big bucks,
  that you hate more and more every day?

  If you could do it all over again, would you choose the same career?
  (61% said NO; 39% said YES, according to a poll in Parade magazine on January 9, 2011.)

- What do you <u>really</u> want to change about your life?

- Are you serious enough to do something about it?

- What do you plan to do during your retirement years?

It's a nice fantasy to consider that as-yet-unknown date … you know the date I'm talking about. You could consult psychics or clairvoyants who might predict a date, but I doubt they would guarantee it, so you still would never know for sure. The fact is that you <u>*do not*</u> know that date and you never will. All you know … *if you are really honest with yourself* … is that it could happen today, or tomorrow, next week, next month, or next year, but it will happen eventually.

You say, *"Oh, don't be ridiculous. I have lots of time left to do the things I want to do. Why are you bugging me about this?"* while you languish in a job you hate, a marriage that has gone stale, living in a place of steel and concrete when your soul longs for the pristine clear air of the mountains or the beach.

ARE YOU WAITING FOR PERMISSION FROM SOMEONE ELSE
TO LIVE YOUR OWN AUTHENTIC LIFE?

I already gave you a <u>PERMISSION SLIP</u>.

NOW WOULD BE A GOOD TIME TO USE IT.

WHEN YOU RETIRE, WILL YOU BE LEAVING A CAREER OR A JOB?

It may be too late for you to change careers or jobs if you are still working and have quite a few years left to work before you retire. If that's the case, I strongly recommend that before you retire, you find something to do that you LOVE, if it means to volunteer at an animal shelter, join a chorus or the art league, a non-profit organization that needs help but cannot pay, a library, a National Park, or take classes that interest you … you get the idea. Keep your day job, but find something to fill that hole in your soul that was created by many years of working in an unsatisfying job and ignoring your own needs.

If you begin looking for (or trying) activities while still working your full-time job, you may be able to eliminate some you thought you would like, only to find out that you don't like them so much after all. Finding this out in advance of retirement can save you time, money and aggravation. If you find the right activity for you, it can help you make an easier transition between working and not working.

> *Once upon a time, there was a successful lawyer who was the chief counsel for a corporation. He had been in private practice when he was young, but preferred working in the corporate world.*
>
> *Several years before his retirement date, he decided to learn to play a musical instrument and to paint. Turns out that he was not only good at both of these activities, he loved them both. So, when he retired, he was able to happily fill his life with music lessons, concerts, painting classes, art exhibitions, all in addition to the other social activities in which he and his wife were engaged.*
>
> *Although he was a lawyer by virtue of his employment, he had not "become" lawyer in his persona. He recognized that there was, for him, life after retiring from the practice of law.*
>
> *Before he retired, this man actually took the time to think about what he wanted to do with the rest of his life **between now and then**, and when the time came, he actually did those things. He is to be congratulated for finding ways to fill his life with meaningful, life-affirming activities.*

If you are close to retiring, give serious thought to what you want to do NEXT! Maybe it will be a job that pays you; maybe not. Closely examine your options (including your finances), and for once in your life, pay attention to what you love to do, what you want to do, not what others expect of you.

Some people spend years doing work they don't love until the pressure builds up and they have a heart attack. Is that how you want to live your life … waiting for an emergency to catapult you into doing what you really want to be doing? While the heart attack could turn out to be an opportunity for you to evaluate your life priorities and make new, different, more appropriate choices, wouldn't it have been better to have made the conscious choices for yourself, in advance, rather than waiting for your body to break down and scream, *"Save me?"*

- And don't forget all those "hard" conversations you have been avoiding for years. The pressure and stress that build up over time for all the conversations you chose <u>not</u> to have can likewise give you a heart attack.

What kind of wake-up call are <u>YOU</u> waiting for (besides a heart attack) before you make the changes necessary to live your own authentic life?

- A divorce?
- Death of a loved one?
- Loss of a job?
- Financial ruin?
- Illness?

WHAT IS THIS THING CALLED RETIREMENT?

Retirement could be defined as the time period between your last day at your job and your death. It could also be said that retirement is at the heart of the question which is the basis for this book:

"What do you plan to do with the rest of your life *between now and then?*"

Retirement is not a once-in-a-lifetime event. It will not happen on a specific day. The first day of your retirement won't be like the first day at a new job, where you may experience excitement for new responsibilities and meeting new people. If it means that you won't have to get up early to go to work, that may feel wonderful ... for a while ... like a vacation. But it also means that you have no specific things to do every day in the same way that you had when you were working.

Retirement, if it is to serve you well, requires thought and planning. It is a process over time...hopefully a lot of time. If you are a Baby Boomer who is serious about taking charge of the rest of your life, one of the challenges you face is the question of how to fill the days during those retirement years. Twenty years is a long time if you don't have a plan. What will you do with all that free time?

> *Now that it's all over, what did you really do yesterday that's worth mentioning?*
>
> Coleman Cox

ARE YOU FINANCIALLY PREPARED TO RETIRE?

The focus of this book is to help you figure out what to do with all that <u>time</u> *between now and then.* I don't want you to overlook one of the most important elements of retirement: YOUR MONEY! People are inclined to believe they will spend less during retirement ... *especially in the first few years* ... than they will spend later on; however, financial planners will tell you that is not true. If you simply pick an arbitrary date to retire and then take the plunge, hoping (believing, trusting) that everything will work out, that is not a plan. Remember, this book is about planning.

How much thought have you given to <u>your</u> retirement? Do you anticipate years of fun, or years of worry about money, illness and diminished capacity to enjoy life? The questions about your retirement relate not only to what you will do with all that time, but how you will afford the cost of your living all those years. Life may not be all about money, but it sure comes in handy to pay the bills.

> *It takes as much energy to wish as it does to plan.*
>
> Eleanor Roosevelt

One way to prepare yourself is to participate in a retirement boot camp. Some large financial organizations offer such events to help people identify their needs and misconceptions about their own retirement, and to make a plan for their future, including an accurate budget.

- In the alternative, you could put forth the same effort by working closely with an independent financial planner who is highly qualified to assist you ... not the "financial advisors" who just want to sell you something. There is much to consider in planning for retirement, and there is no one quick-fix product. The financial planning process requires focus, commitment and discipline. And, if you think it will be too tough for you, think how tough it will be well into your retirement years when you run out of money.

RETIREMENT IS NO JOKE

Anyone who is living in that place in time known as "retirement" and has run out of money is not laughing. You can run and you can hide from the statistics, but you had better take a long, hard look at the numbers before you jump headfirst into retirement without a plan. You do not want to run out of money before you run out of time. If you have not already begun taking charge of your finances, now would be the time to begin. Not tomorrow or next week. NOW! (See Chapter II – FINANCIAL.)

How is it possible that retirement and Baby Boomers can be spoken in the same sentence? Where did all those years go? Well, honestly, 65 years is a long time, except when it seems to have passed by so quickly. Are you facing retirement with anticipation or dread? There is much to contemplate as you think about your future and what you'll do for the rest of your life. You probably know that you won't be doing all the same things you did in the first two thirds of your life, and that being said, what else is there for you do? What else do you *want* to do?

The real truth is that there is so much for you to do, that if you were to live another healthy, vibrant 30 years, you still will not have tried everything. Let you imagination soar. Remember how to day dream again. Read travel magazines, even if you never even leave your hometown. Do all the things you wanted to do during your working years but were too busy at your job.

You know that old line about being careful what you wish for, because you just might get it. Well, Baby Boomers, you wished for more free time; and here it is, in the form of retirement. Whew! Finally. Now what?

YOU ARE A BABY BOOMER.

YOU CAN DO ANYTHING YOU PUT YOUR MIND TO!

Philosophy is perfectly right in saying that life must be understood backward.
Then one forgets the other clause – that it must be lived forward.

Soren Kierkeggaard

Baby Boomers are probably the first large group of people who, collectively, will be looking forward to many years with very little time structure … that is to say, they will not be living within the time constraints and discipline of a job. The one thing working people have in common is that one day, their work life will come to an end. It may already have ended by virtue of a job loss or lay-off, or a forced (early) retirement. Those people will be left with a huge block of time to fill **between now and then.** Some people think about what they will do with all that time; others don't even give it a thought.

Never before have so many people faced so long a period of time without some structured activity, some place to be, something to do every day. Technically, a person could retire from their job on a given day, and find that they have nothing to do for the rest of their life. How does that sound to you today? How do you think it will sound to you after 10 years of *doing nothing*?

You will no longer need a note from a parent to explain your absence from school. It won't be like being AWOL in the military where you could be sent to prison for not showing up. You will no longer need a doctor's note to explain why you didn't go to work today. Nobody will come looking for you because you didn't show up at your job.

So, the question remains: what are you going to do with all that time? Twenty or thirty years! Wow! There is not enough TV in the world to watch for 10 hours every day for 20-30 years. There are definitely enough books to read, but the inactivity of sitting around reading all day and night will eventually get to you.

If you are financially sound enough to live out the rest of your life without the struggles of insufficient money, you will, of course, have fewer problems than people who didn't bother to save, or who lost money in the stock market, or whose company did away with the pension fund, or people who have spent themselves into serious debt. But, I'm not referring to money right this moment. I'm talking about TIME … lots and lots of time … *your* time.

YOU MUST FIND SOMETHING WORTHWHILE TO DO WITH ALL THAT TIME.

Once upon a time, there was a woman about 65 years old. She had had many jobs (careers) during her adult life. She was a multi-talented woman with a good business mind combined with an extraordinary gift for the creative arts. She had a very high energy level and a genuine excitement about life. She loved being actively engaged in something worthwhile and fun, not just being busy (as in "busywork").

Her "real job" for many years was as a paraprofessional accountant. She also waited tables in the evenings after her day-job. In addition, at different times, she sold real estate and later, cemetery property. She bought and operated a bridal shop for several years. She took many, many craft courses. She was an accomplished seamstress, and loved to try new recipes. She and her husband together designed and built their own house and managed to find time to travel.

> *When the subject of retirement came up, her words were always, "I can't retire. What would I do all day?" And, then one day, a light must have come on in her head, and she retired. Just like that!*
>
> *After that, you needed a date book to keep track of her if you wanted to speak with her or get together. She was never in one place for very long, and found many ways to stay busy. She volunteered everywhere – Red Cross Blood drives, at a National Park, and at a local historical movie theater. She delivered Meals on Wheels. She taught Reading to inner-city grade-school children. And on and on. Her days were filled with activities, one in the morning, a different one in the afternoon, and then a different set of activities the following day.*
>
> *She worried there would be nothing for her to do after she retired from her day job. Turns out she worried for nothing. And believe me when I tell you she was never bored.*

Oh, darn, I keep forgetting. You really <u>don't</u> have to follow my suggestion to find something worthwhile to do. You *can* do nothing, just as you can ignore my suggestions elsewhere. Doing nothing is absolutely one of your options … as long as you understand and agree to the consequences of such inaction.

> ***He that leaveth little to chance will do few things ill, but he will do very few things.***
>
> Lord Halifax

When our grandfathers retired, usually on a specific date, they may have been 65 years of age, with the expectation of living 5 more years, maybe less. But 20 or 30 more years? People did not generally live to be 80 and 90 years when our grandfathers retired. Times and people have changed.

I'm asking you to THINK about what you want to do ***between now and then***? I don't have any easy answers, because I don't know you and what you like to do. Only you can answer the question, and my suggestion right now is that you find something to do with all that time.

> ***Two per cent of the people think;***
> ***three per cent of the people think they think;***
> ***and ninety-five percent of the people would rather die than think.***
>
> George Bernard Shaw

RETIREMENT IS A NEW BEGINNING

**THINK OF RETIREMENT LIKE GRADUATION,
WHICH, TO MANY, IS THE END OF THEIR SCHOOL LIFE,
BUT WHICH, IN REALITY, IS A NEW BEGINNING, THE START OF ANOTHER LIFE ALTOGETHER.
<u>THAT'S WHY IT'S CALLED COMMENCEMENT!</u>**

At graduations, young people are frequently asked where they see themselves in 5 years? or 15? or 25? So, now, at this second commencement, I ask you: Where do you see yourself in 5 years, or 15, or 25? Will you use this time wisely or will you waste it?

Retirement can give you the gift of free time. Are you excited about this new opportunity to live every day YOUR way? Isn't that what you wanted and dreamed about for so long? So, why are you feeling so anxious? Is this how you felt when you graduated from high school or college … anxious? If that was true then, was it because you didn't know what you were going to do next? But, that was then, and this is now, and here you are, older, wiser, more in touch with who you are as a person. You figured out what to do after graduation.

YOU ARE A BABY BOOMER. YOU WILL FIGURE THIS OUT, TOO!

What frightens you about this new beginning? Would you feel better if you had a plan for what you will do ***between now and then***? Without a plan for how you will use all your newly gained free time, boredom might set in. Oh, maybe not right away, but sooner or later. Then what?

GET READY, GET SET, GO!

With regard to making plans for your future, there are some important things that require your immediate attention. Other things can wait, but not indefinitely. Now is a good time to begin.

1. **Your Emergency Fund**: Have you saved an amount of money equal to one-year's income which you have in an accessible account? I realize in this economy this may be asking a lot I'm not referring to your investment money or your 401(k) account. Money in those places is <u>not</u> to be used for emergencies. The money I'm referring to should be someplace like a money-market account that would give you immediate access to your money in an emergency. I don't think I need to tell you how valuable that money would become in an emergency. And, if you have not saved enough in your emergency fund, begin now to contribute to it regularly, and keep on saving until you have one year's income. I know that "saving" is a foreign concept to Baby Boomers, but you are strong and resilient and you can do it if you set your mind to it. If you need assistance from a financial planner to figure out how to do it, make the appointment today.

2. **Your Estate-Planning Documents**: Next, if you have not already done so, make an appointment with your lawyer to have your estate-planning documents drawn up immediately. They include:

   - Last Will and Testament
   - Durable Power-of-Attorney
   - Living Will (a/k/a Advance Directive)
   - Healthcare Power-of-Attorney
   - Revocable Living Trust (optional)

   [You can read more about these "To Do" items in the Chapters I and II]

3. **Your Bucket List**: It's time to begin your own personal "Bucket List." You know what I mean … the list of all the things you want to do with the time remaining ***between now and then.*** Try things that immediately appeal to you, and if you find you don't like them, cross them off your list and move on to the next item.

A Little Humor

Mother, speaking to young adult son: *"What are you writing?"*
Son: *"I'm making my bucket list."*
Mother: *"Don't you think you're a little young to be thinking about such things now?"*
Son: *"Mom, do you want anything from KFC or not?"*

---

4. **The Hard Conversations**: There is much you need to talk about before and during retirement. Now is the time to have some of those hard conversations … *you know the ones I mean* … those conversations you don't want to have, that you keep putting off until later. Assuming you have any plans for retirement, have you talked about them with your spouse or partner? Or if you are single, at least have you given serious thought to what you want to do with the possible 20-30 years of retirement? You know you have been thinking … *actually, dreaming* … about having more free time. Well, here it is -- right in front of you, waiting for you to move into the next phase of your life.

> In the *Introduction*, I listed several books that offer guidelines and insights
> into ways to have successful conversations. If you haven't read them yet, now
> would be a good time. The books by Deborah Tannen and John Gray are especially
> enjoyable and informative. I think you will enjoy reading them. I also recommend
> *Last Wish* by Lauren Van Scoy, M.D., for a look at of end-of-life medical situations
> and treatment.

Beyond Conversation ...

In addition, I recommend you read *New Passages* by Gail Sheehy. I think you will find her insights and stories very interesting and timely as you take a look at where you've been, where you are, and where you're going as you continue on your life's journey. In my opinion, she has had her finger on the pulse of the lives of Baby Boomers for many years, and her writings follow Boomers from their early 20s until the present time.

In *New Passages*, the author talks about retirement from the perspective of the actual passage from one phase of life into another. This transition is a major unknown, because few people know how to live without having any place to go every day and without having anything that must be done every day ... that is, living without a job. She writes about how retirement affects people at the personal level, how some people thrive, others sink into despair and ill health. She also speaks briefly about money.

She writes about both men and women, from the perspective of those who are encouraged to retire (I don't like to say *forced*, although sometimes that is the reality) and those who can hardly wait to retire. The transition from being a working person to a non-working person (in terms strictly about employment) is very hard for some people, especially men. For others, retirement is a welcome passage, notably for people who have a long list of things they want to do **between now and then.** For years, the people eager to retire have been making (mental) lists of things they plan to do and can hardly wait to begin. More often than not, these people are women.

Men often equate retirement with failure. Not all men, of course; many blue-collar workers who had physically demanding jobs are happy to give up that kind of work. But after they stop working, they, too, don't know what to do with the time on their hands. Many sit around and watch too much TV. Some drink and gain weight. Others become depressed to the point of having the depression lead to serious illness of one kind or another. I can only ask them, *"Is this what you waited for all those years while you were working so hard?"* Really? I don't believe you.

What about the white-collar workers near the top of the ladder? They, too, often see retirement as failure. They strongly identify who they are with what they do, and wonder who they will BE when they stop DOING.

Oh, of course, there are the few who planned well for their retirement, as the lawyer I mentioned previously. Some working men make a successful transition into consulting in the industry with which they are familiar, while others feel out of the loop as a consultant. Give it a try if the opportunity is available to you, and if it doesn't work, find something else to do.

If you are a teacher at any level, from first grade to college, you may have the opportunity to continue doing what you love. You haven't lost your love for teaching, have you? Oh, I can see how it could happen, but it *is* possible to get excited about teaching in a different environment. You may have a fixed pension which will enable you to eliminate the worry about money. There are so many places begging for what you have to offer. If you were an English language, art, or music teacher, think of all the opportunities where your talents would be so welcome. Use your imagination and creativity.

YOU ARE A BABY BOOMER! Remember!
You will figure it out.

The greater danger for most of us is not that our aim is too high and we miss it,
but that it is too low and we reach it.

Michelangelo

One category of working men who suffer are the very rich. *Uh, oh, I don't hear a lot of sympathy.* Agreed, they have lots and lots of money, but that's not where the problem lies. They are often unable to figure out the answer to the question of what to do **between now and then.** Many are smart and have accomplished great things. Since they graduated from college, they have been on a treadmill that has been on high speed for 40+ years, their goal being to make money and keep on making money. If you asked them why they keep doing it, they may say they never gave it any thought ... it's just what they do.

Now that they have accumulated great wealth and a lot of stuff, they are beginning to wonder why. Some have lost their families through divorce and find themselves deeply unhappy. They might even admit to having way more money than they will ever need or spend for themselves and their loved ones. Many are frightened about what the future holds for them, yet confused at the same time. Wasn't all that money supposed to make them happy? They have probably made few if any plans for their retirement years. They have money, but don't know what to do with it. More's the pity. And, like many other Baby Boomers, they are wondering, "NOW WHAT?"

COUPLES' RETIREMENT

I just asked my husband what he thinks is the most important thing for a couple to consider as they retire. His easy response was to talk about their money. Amen.

Considering how long I have been writing this book, I now wonder why I didn't ask him the question long ago, but yesterday was the day. He continued by saying that the two people have to talk about things as they come up. He has been retired for nearly 4 years at this writing, so he has some experience on the topic. He and I are among the fortunate people who can happily spend 24/7 together without getting on each other's nerves too much.

He and I have known each other for a very long time, and long before we ever married, what we had together was conversation. It is one of the things I always appreciated about him. We know lots of couples who cannot talk about the little things without arguing, picking at each other, blaming the other person. How do those couples handle the really important stuff? One way is to ignore them, hoping they will go away by themselves.

If you are married or in a committed relationship, it is important that the two of you talk about what you, individually and as a couple, want and expect from your retirement years; that is, what do each of you plan to do with the rest of your life *between now and then?*

Retirement requires PLANNING, COMMUNICATION, NEGOTIATION and ACTION.

> ***Do you want to know who you are? Don't ask. Act! Action will delineate and define you.***
> Thomas Jefferson

It is essential that upon entering the retirement chapter of your life, you learn to talk with each other as never before. Every day, there will be decisions and choices to be made, from the simple ones (what shall we do today?) to the complicated ones (shall we sell this house and move elsewhere?). Can the two of you discuss things like these without fighting about them? Can you disagree without being disagreeable? *Just asking ...*

If you never learned how to negotiate differences between you, or if one or both of you is a right-fighter, or if one or both of you regularly criticizes the other, you can anticipate problems. You will both have to learn to be flexible on subjects about which you may have previously been rigid.

As you face retirement, never lose sight of the fact that you are two separate individuals who have come together to form a long-term partnership. Even though marriage vows often say "*and the two shall become one*," or words to that effect, when you retire, you do not become one person, surgically attached at the hip. You are still two separate people, with different needs and ideas that may or may not be compatible. It is the rare couple who can happily spend 24/7 together. Be prepared to handle the differences with compassion, patience, understanding, and the intention to negotiate and establish peace in your marriage and your life until your last day together.

At this time in your life, your basic personality differences may show up in ways that can cause upset. You may find that you are incompatible in unexpected ways. Being "thrown together" in retirement can bring to the surface hidden feelings of all sorts, not all happy, I'm sorry to say. People sometimes find that they don't even like each other, can't stand listening to the same music or watching the same TV shows. They may have lived together for many years, not really knowing each other very well.

Conversations about retirement might be some of the most difficult, yet important, conversations you ever have, because retirement is the beginning of a long period in your life when you may be spending a lot of time together. If being together 24/7 is something you have never done before ... *except maybe on vacation* ... there may be a period of adjustment for both of you individually, and for the two of you as a couple. If you are willing to compromise without feeling like you are selling out, together you can make this one of the most rewarding chapters in your life together.

You may benefit from counseling to be able to reach a place of peace and calm going forward into this new phase of your life; and if you need counseling, get it right away. Retirement is unfamiliar territory. Don't wait until things reach the point of no return when it might be too late to rescue your relationship. There is no shame in asking for direction from a professional; and for the men reading this, contrary to popular belief, asking for directions will not kill you!

Do you have plans for your retirement, or do you simply "plan" to let your days go by, one at a time, like most people do: Get up, read the paper, take a walk, go to the doctor's, eat out, watch TV. Go to bed. Get up. Repeat. That's it? For 20-30 years? *Are you kidding?* Apparently not, because that's how many couples live their retirement years unless they have given it some thought, have talked about it, explored possibilities, and have made some plans to make those years happy, healthy and productive.

What do you/we want to do, where do you/we you want to live, and how will you/we spend our money are good beginning topics for discussion. Make this a period of learning about the many aspects of retirement. Attend seminars or workshops to learn about money and health. Spend time in the library, where you can read books at no cost to you.

> *Elsewhere, I may have given the impression that every free-lunch (dinner) seminar should be avoided. Let me re-state and clarify my position on the subject. Those seminars are only to be avoided if you are a person who cannot say no to high pressure salespeople trying to sell you something you don't need and don't want. But, those seminars offer you the opportunity to gather information about retirement, ask questions, enjoy a pleasant meal, meet new people ... at no cost to you.*

Look for local senior organizations hosting free information seminars. Join AARP ... their free monthly bulletin and magazine are filled with interesting information about retirement, especially in relation to Baby Boomers. AARP is no longer just for the "old folks." And, no, I don't work for AARP.

You may find that you and your partner don't share the same interests, but that your relationship is solid and will not suffer from your different activities. On the other hand, those differences could cause serious damage to what you had believed was a good relationship, but which had serious foundation cracks you didn't notice before. Sharing retirement years can be a real burden for a couple who lived busy, somewhat separate, lives for years, and find the togetherness of a 24/7 lifestyle doesn't work well for them ... maybe not at first, but maybe you can ease you way into it ... after all, isn't that what you waited for all those years you were working? Free time?

Have you talked about your individual and joint expectations of this period in your life? Do you even know what they are? Chances are good that you never talked about the important things before you got married, so why would you think you have to talk about them now? Like most people, you may have gotten married and just figured it out along the way. Not a good plan, by the way, but it is the way most people approach married life <u>and</u> retirement. But now, you are older, more mature, more understanding of the ways of the world, such that you know there are things you need to talk about before you retire.

- Of course, you could retire and never talk about any of the topics, and somehow you would survive together ... *or not.*

Retirement changes people in many ways. Having lots of free time, especially when they are not accustomed to having free time, brings problems to the surface that include fighting with your partner, boredom, anger, confusion, depression, and illness, to name a few. There are people who get sick soon after retirement and will actually say they were never sick when they worked because they didn't have time to get sick, or they didn't get paid for sick days. Are they saying that <u>now</u> they have "time" to be sick? *What?* I know people who say that if they didn't have a doctor's appointment every day, they would barely know what to do! Now, that is really pathetic.

In the alternative, people could approach retirement as an opportunity to get reacquainted, reconnected to the person they fell in love with so long ago.

A successful marriage requires falling in love many times, always with the same person.

Author unknown

Boredom

Boredom is insidious. If you let it creep into your life, a little bit at a time, pretty soon you will find yourself seriously depressed, unhappy, possibly even ill. Boredom tends to happen to newly retired people when they have no idea what to do with their free time. It also leads to increased dependence on drugs and alcohol for relief from boredom. Isn't that ridiculous, when you consider that the best cure for boredom is to keep busy doing things that interest you? Don't be tempted to rid yourself of boredom by using anything that can cause you to become addicted: food, drugs, alcohol, shopping. If you are bored, get off the couch and find something to do.

Boredom becomes a concern when it causes you to procrastinate and become unusually indecisive. If there comes a day when you realize you are really, really bored, try to figure out why you are bored and then take steps to remedy the situation. It's important to remember that boredom only exists in your mind and will go away if you use your mind to find things to do.

There are simple ways for you to overcome boredom, but they require you to take action. Boredom will not go away by itself.

1. Take up a physical activity you never tried before (walking, indoor tennis, bowling, swimming).
2. Try to accomplish one new thing every day.
3. Try to spend your time with interesting people.
    If your friends bore you, look for people who have the same interests you have.
4. Change your routine. You find life boring because of repetition in your daily activities.
5. Change your thoughts from worry and fear to possibility and excitement.
6. Set your imagination free. Daydream. Expect miracles.
7. Write a list of 10 things you want to do within the next year, and work from there.
8. Develop a sense of curiosity. Learn new things.
9. Join a club or group that is involved in activities that interest you.
10. Prepare a list of books you've been waiting to read, prioritize the list, and begin.
11. Find a new hobby that is not too expensive.
12. Learn how to use new technology (a computer, a digital camera, etc.)
13. Avoid boring people and situations, and if you can't walk away from them entirely, try to keep the time you spend with them to an acceptable, agreeable minimum.
14. Learn to cook. Try new recipes.
15. Volunteer someplace where your intelligence and interest will benefit others less fortunate than you.
16. Adopt a dog or cat (or two). Volunteer at a no-kill shelter.
17. Begin a personal journal, and write in it every day. In a year or two, you might turn it into a book.
18. Relax. Listen to music you love. If your partner doesn't share your musical interest, use headphones.
19. Learn to play chess, or pinochle or bridge … something that will stimulate your brain.
20. Join the "Y" and participate in the many activities offered there.

As children, my sister and I were never allowed to say we were bored because our mother would always find ways to keep us busy. But, you're not a child, and I'm not your mother. It's not my job to find things for you to do. That's your job.

Some Words of Caution

Over time, boredom can lead to depression, and depression can lead to serious physical or mental illness. If you choose the behavior, you choose the consequences. If you make the choice to do nothing until boredom and depression take over your life, expect your mind and your body (maybe even your family) to suffer one way or another. Do you want to live a happy, active, healthy life, *between now and then*, or settle for boredom and depression? The choice is yours. And I think you already know that one of the best cures for boredom is to actively engage in doing something you love.

It puzzles me why so many men are content to sit around and do nothing after they retire. Women worry about this for years before their husbands retire because we know that men become attached to the couch and the TV. They disengage their brains and their bodies for the mind-numbing effects of TV. Oh, of course, I know there are many men who are exceptions, men who couldn't wait to retire to do the things they really love to do. Remember that lawyer who retired to become a musician and a painter? Remember the woman whose lawyer husband's retirement literally drove her out of her beautiful new home because of his do-nothing attitude after retirement?

Which kind of person will you be? The active one, or the TV watcher?

Previously you read the little joke about the husband who said he wasn't finished "doing nothing." It seems to me that men like this regularly show up in cartoons, and if something shows up in cartoons, it represents some aspect of real life. In the newspaper of 11/13/12, a cartoon shows an old man saying, *"Fantastic! A whole day without anything to do."*

If a man becomes seriously ill, it is doubtful if his doctor will ask him what he has been doing every day since he retired. Doctors like to write prescriptions for pills or procedures to "fix" the symptoms and seldom look deeply into the cause. This do-nothing attitude that men have is a killer. You don't have to believe me. Just look around and pay attention.

I personally do not know what a woman can do to motivate a man to get off the couch if he doesn't want to. If his doing nothing leads him into boredom, depression and illness, it will be her job to take care of him. This is not what a woman bargained for.

All I can say to men (collectively) is, *"Did you work so hard all those years just so you could sit on the couch and watch TV until it was time to call the funeral director? What kind of a legacy is that to leave behind for your family? FIND SOMETHING TO DO before it's too late."*

Nobody can stop you but you.
And shame on you if you're the one who stops yourself.

Damon Wayans

You are a Baby Boomer! Open your eyes. Look around you.
FIND SOMETHING TO DO.
There is so much to do that you could never make a list that long!

Let's make every moment count and help those who have a greater need than our own.

Harmon Killebrew

What's for dinner?

For me, the worst three words in the English language are, *"What's for dinner?"* If I am doing something that is important to me, I do not want to stop to make dinner. It is the *every-day-ness* of it that grates on me. I don't want to eat out every meal for all the reasons why it's not a good idea; but, on the other hand, I also don't want to be the person fixing 3 meals every day.

One solution to this dinner problem is to begin cooking foods that can easily and quickly be turned into a second or third meal without much fuss. Learn to prepare meals in a slow cooker. Make soup. Cook roasts or turkeys. Figure out how to create spectacular left-overs. We sometimes joke about how terrific our left-overs are. You can do it, too.

If you have been together for a long time, chances are good that the woman has done much of the meal preparation, and if she is anything like me, she is sick of it already! So, what do you do now? Will the man prepare dinner for both of them at least a few times every week? Do they have the money to eat out regularly? What if he is hungry and she is not? Will he prepare dinner for himself? A snack for her later in the evening? *Just asking ...*

Now that he has retired, does the man expect breakfast, lunch and dinner to be prepared and served to him by his partner? Does he expect it served at 8, 12 and 5? [*I know men who do.*] Unless the woman absolutely loves cooking, unless it is her passion, this daily preparation of food will become a problem sooner or later.

Meal preparation requires conversations for possibility. So, decide on a reasonable, mutually agreeable plan for sharing the responsibilities of meal preparation, including after-meal clean up and grocery shopping. They are not necessarily female activities, so maybe the husband will shop if his wife will prepare a (very specific) list. If they can afford to eat out occasionally, then maybe the wife will be more inclined to prepare several dinners each week and the husband can clean up. Conversation. Negotiation. Agreement. You'll figure it out ... *or not.*

- And, while you're talking about meal preparation, come up with a mutually agreeable plan to divide household chores. Unless one of you is disabled or sick, if two people live in your home, two people are responsible for doing the chores.

WHERE WILL YOU LIVE?

- Your present home?
- An age-restricted (55+ community)?
- A Continuing Care Retirement Community (CCRC)?
- Move in with family?
- Other?

Do You Really Want to Move?

Why do you want to move? Are you really unhappy where you are presently living? Do have a genuine reason why you think you should move, or are you simply bored with your present living arrangement and want something new? Would a little re-decorating make you feel better? What if only one of the two of you wants to move? What if you cannot afford it? Whether or not you move requires serious conversations and research before you make any financial or legal commitments.

What if you move, and afterward, decide you made a mistake, will you be able to emotionally and financially afford another move?

Once upon a time, there was a couple in their late 70s. They had been married for 53 years, and had three highly educated, independent adult children. One of them lived in a nearby state, the other two lived in a state 2,700 miles away. This couple had visited that far-away state many times for brief periods of time, always happy to return home. They had no need, interest, or desire to move anywhere, yet their children influenced them to move, and the couple agreed to move.

What really happened, though, was that this couple surrendered to the pressure from their adult children who said that their parents needed to be closer to the two children who lived 2,700 miles away, although those two children were employed professionals with no time to take care of mom-and-pop should they ever require help ... which, at this point, they do not. Their children believed they knew what was best for their parents, but yet the three of them disagreed on what was best. Their voices were loud and demanding, and this couple surrendered and gave up the home they had lived in for 45 years and moved across the country ... just to quiet the voices of their children.

Their son made the arrangements for where they were to live, and the couple believed they were moving to a 55+ community, but it turns out to be a CCRC, where many of the residents are disabled, getting around on walkers or wheelchairs. They believed the child with the loudest voice, and now they regret moving and want to come back.

Why did this couple move? Because they did not do their own independent research; because they believed their son; because they did not stand up for their rights as competent, healthy, independent adults; because they did not say NO. So, having given up their home, their friends, their medical professionals, and their comfort zone ... everything they knew for years ... they found themselves living in a place where they were profoundly unhappy.

What happened to common sense? What happened to speaking your own truth? What happened to saying NO without guilt? What do you think the chances are of their ever moving back? I say they will never come back, but maybe I'll be wrong. When someone asks why they moved, what are they going to say? We moved to shut our kids up? Do you think that is a good reason? What would you do in a similar situation? Be careful with your answer ...

Before you commit to a move anywhere, compare as many features of your present living arrangement with your potential future living arrangement as possible to see which offers you the most in terms of peace of mind, financial protection, safety, and general satisfaction. This is one decision that leaves little room for error. Choose wisely. There is much at stake, not the least of which is money. And be honest about it ... don't try to gloss over the truth of your feelings or the reality of the numbers and facts. And, if you don't want to move, say NO without guilt.

If you long to live somewhere else, is it because of money or the weather ... or maybe your health? What do you expect from living elsewhere? New friends, lots of interesting activities, better weather, no outdoor maintenance? Do you require assistance for your daily activities? Has your health deteriorated? Do you have too many steps in your present residence? Have you become unable to maintain the outside of your property?

Have honest conversations with your spouse or partner … and your adult children … about moving or staying where you are. For the move to be truly successful, it helps if both parties are in agreement about everything that is involved in such a drastic, life-altering change. Things you cannot immediately agree upon, negotiate win-win solutions. If one party moves to please the other, you can expect problems sooner or later.

Your Present Home

If you are content living in your present home, if you have created it to be exactly the way you want it to be, if you can afford all of the expenses of living in your home, if it is your sanctuary, maybe you should stay there for the rest of your life. If it turns out you have insufficient funds to move, it may remain your home by default.

Whether or not you move from your present home requires a thorough analysis of your reasons for wanting to move <u>and</u> <u>your</u> <u>finances</u>. There may be resources available to you to enable you to keep living in your present home and to keep your finances stable or growing. I suggest that before you commit to any such thing (for example, a reverse mortgage), you get professional advice from a financial planner, not someone selling some vague financial opportunity that could turn out to be a scam, or will eat up your money in fees. Don't try to go it alone when there is help available.

- If it is your decision to remain in your present home until the end of your life, it would be wise to investigate home-health agencies NOW … well before the need arises … so that you will be fully informed if you ever need those services. Ask questions, take notes, gather information. Knowledge is power.

- You might also spend some time investigating those Life-Alert programs that provide you with immediate access to medical professionals in an emergency. Find out the costs and the services each program offers.

An Age-Restricted Community (also known as a 55+ Community)

Do you like the look of the houses in the new 55+ communities that are popping up everywhere: new, smaller, no grass to cut or snow to shovel, tennis courts, swimming pools, golf courses, new friends! Wow! What's not to like? They are perfect for Baby Boomers who think and feel young, who have no young children living at home any longer. But, there are things to consider before you sell your home and move into a 55+ community.

- Before you make the move, remember that they do not offer healthcare facilities. If one or both of you should become ill, it might necessitate another move to a Continuing Care Retirement Community (CCRC), where medical care is available. A second move in a short time would be doubly stressful and expensive.

- 55+ Communities remind me of cruises, where there is a cruise director offering daily activities. The fact is that for most communities, that is not the case. The activities are there for you to do or not, as you choose. Before committing to a move to a 55+ community, however, it would be good to decide if you are happy in group activities, or if you prefer a more solitary life. It is wise to have a thorough understanding of who you are, what you expect from living in this new home, and what the community offers and what it does not. This is no place to make a mistake, because this may be the last residential move you will ever make.

- Each 55+ community has a Homeowner's Association (HOA) to which you will pay a monthly fee that will cover things like trash collection, snow shoveling, and grass cutting. The fee may or may not cover the planting of small bushes and flowers. If this matters to you, find it out beforehand. Also, there are terms and conditions that state how much of your fee is committed to major repairs of the community (things like roads, sidewalks, roofs)

- I have heard horror stories of the Homeowners' Associations in these communities, where Association members and strict guidelines interfere with the personal freedom of the residents in favor of the general good of the community. Have you ever seen a Homeowners' Agreement? Those I have seen (probably 25) are on 8-1/2" x 14" paper, and pages and pages of "legalese." Even lawyers don't use paper that size any longer. If you plan to move into one of these communities, you had better read every word of the Agreement, make notes of questions you have, get answers to your questions, and pay a lawyer to review the document with you. Think of the legal fee as an investment in your future happiness and peace of mind.

- Inside those Agreements, you will find such things as stating the color of the lights you can use to decorate your house at Christmas, the exact manufacturer's color of paint for your shutters and front door, whether or not you can use curtains that can be seen from the outside, how many pets you can have, and where you can and cannot walk your dog. Sometimes, these issues can become matters of serious (sometimes legal) contention. Before you make this move, decide if you will appreciate the efforts of the HOA, or find their rules intolerable.

- While the Agreement is a legal document, the terms and conditions may or may not be legally binding. BUT, *and it's a big "but,"* whether or not the document is legally binding, it may not be in your best interests to challenge the HOA. After all, the members of the Association are your neighbors, and they are in a position to make your life miserable.

- Chances are good that you figured this would be your last move during your life, but if you find yourself sufficiently unhappy such that another move is necessary, it will be stressful and expensive. I know two couples who moved into 55+ communities and then found the HOA's rules so intolerable that they moved again to a single home. This is a costly move in terms of money and aggravation, and in order to avoid it, you will have to really know who you are and what you want for the rest of your life ***between now and then.*** This move could be one of those Humpty Dumpty situations.

Continuing Care Retirement Community (a/k/a CCRC)

If you jointly decide to move to a CCRC, it would be beneficial to personally visit and thoroughly evaluate several communities so you can have sufficient information to determine which one suits your needs, both personal and financial. Do your homework. Discuss this with both your financial planner and your lawyer. Talk to people who already live there. Have a thorough understanding of what the community offers and what it does not. This is no place to make a mistake, because this will probably be the last residential move you will ever make.

- Many CCRCs offer invitations to tour their facility and enjoy a meal there. That is your opportunity to ask general questions. If you really like the place enough to seriously consider moving there, make an appointment when you can meet with a representative and ask specific questions; for example,

> Is there a waiting list? How long?
> What are the entrance fees? Monthly fees? What is and is not included?
> How long has the facility been in operation? In what state is it licensed?
> How long have the Administrator and the Director of Nursing worked there? (Frequent turnover indicates problems.)
> Who is the house physician? How often is he/she on-site? Does he/she specialize in geriatric medicine?
> What hospital does the facility use for emergencies?
> Do they allow pets? What kinds? If so, how many?
> Who at the CCRC should be contacted if there are problems? What is their problem-solving procedure?
> What is their billing process?
> What happens if you run out of money?
> How is transportation provided if you no longer drive? Is there a fee?
> How is personal laundry handled?
> Is there a pharmacy on the premises? A hairstylist? A barber shop? A dentist? An eye doctor?
> How does a resident pay for these services?
> Is there a residents' council? Is there a family council? (you are looking for "yes" answers)
> Is there a chapel on the premises? Are regular religious services held there? Is it available for funeral services?
> Does the facility have an Alzheimer's Unit?
> How does a resident report an emergency? Who should they call? What is the phone number? How does the facility contact a family member in the event of an emergency or death?
> Ask about the activities available to residents? Swimming (indoor and outdoor pools)? Library? Wood shop? Crafts and Painting? Gardening? Exercise classes? Dancing? Billiards? Bowling?

- Many CCRCs are founded and run by religious organizations. Some are non-profit. Others are not. Some communities will allow you to remain in residence even after you run out of money. Others will ask you to move out.

- CCRCs usually have three levels of admission fees. The highest level is the most expensive, provides healthcare, and may allow for a portion of it to be returned to your heirs after your death. The middle level cost less and proportionately allows for less money to be returned to your heirs after your death, and the lowest level is the least expensive, and will probably return little or no money to your heirs. The third (least expensive) is often the choice of people who have no children.

- Determine how the community provides health care. Is it covered in your monthly fee? Would you only pay for health care if you need it? What is a covered expense? What is not? Will you need to have long-term care insurance before moving in?

- CCRCs usually require that you have your estate-planning documents complete and up to date.

- Ask if you will be required to have your funeral pre-arranged and pre-paid before you move in.

- Some retirement communities are now allowing people to visit for a week-end to get a sense of the environment. I think it is something to consider, if only to help select or eliminate a particular place from your list of possible communities. Give yourself every opportunity to make this enormous life transition as happy and stress-free as possible. Once, an 80-year old woman told me how hard the recent move had been for her and her husband, and cautioned me about waiting too long. For you, how long is "too long?"

- Get complete information about how the community handles emergencies in general, power outages in particular. I recently learned that one of the finest CCRC communities in the geographic area where I live in SE Pennsylvania was without electricity for several days during hurricane Sandy, and their emergency generators provided no heat and only minimal light in the hallways. Considering how high the monthly fees are, it would seem that they should be able to provide adequate back-up power. Be sure to ask about meals and other amenities that require electricity, and how long they allow people to reside in their buildings without electricity, and what alternate arrangements they would make if there is a power failure of long duration. Ask how "long duration" is defined.

- Before you move to a CCRC, inquire as to whether or not the community has insurance to cover the replacement cost of your personal possessions in a fire or some such extreme occurrence. If not, you will need to have renters' insurance. If the representative of the retirement community says that their insurance would cover the loss of your personal possessions, ask to see it in writing. If you don't understand the document, ask questions, and maybe even have a lawyer review all the papers before making such a huge commitment of your life and your money.

- Before you move into a CCRC, ask if they allow pets. Some do. Some don't. And, if they allow pets, ask about the number of pets you are allowed and what their requirements are for walking dogs. Do your best not to put yourself in the position of having to give up your pets in order to make this move. If your pets are important in your life, find another place to live, or in the alternative, find a loving home for your pets to live out the remainder of their lives.

- Don't forget about the meal plan. I'm inclined to say that many women will love not having to cook dinner every evening. In fact, if I never cooked dinner again, it would be great; however, I'm not sure that I would enjoy the dinner arrangements at the retirement communities. Maybe you would. Do you think you would enjoy getting dressed up for dinner every evening (some retirement communities require it)? Would you enjoy eating in a restaurant-like setting every evening? Would you enjoy dining with other people, some of whom you may not know or like, some of whom may not like you? I have heard "horror" stories about dining room cliques, rules, and situations, which sound like junior high school to me. *Just one more thing to think about ...*

Move in with Family:

> NOTE: *Moving in with family can happen in one of two ways:*
> > *(1) one (maybe both) of your parents move in with you; or*
> > *(2) you are the person moving in with a family member.*
>
> *The following information will be helpful in either situation.*

There was a time in the past when multiple generations of people lived under one roof. It was understood that the younger family members would take care of the older family members. Times have changed, and that is not generally the case now ... except when it is.

Baby Boomers have been looking forward to retirement for years so they can finally have time for themselves, to do the things they have put off until "later," to relax and have some fun. And, yet, Baby Boomers are sometimes sandwiched in between the needs of their parents and their children.

They were not necessarily thinking about having to take care of their parents ... except that it happens. An important question to ask yourself and your family is whether or not you will be prepared for all that is involved for you if one or both of your parents were to move into your house in the long term ... or, if you are the person who would have to move in with one of your adult children and their family. Either way, there is much to be considered ... in advance, if possible.

There are many factors to be discussed and agreed upon before family members actually begin sharing living space, especially if one or two of the people are elderly, possibly disabled to some degree. Here again, the necessity of honest communication rears its ugly head, like it or not. Whether or not this living arrangement can sustain itself in the long term depends largely on the understanding of every person involved.

One of the factors that can make or break the situation is whether or not the move was planned and thoroughly and happily agreed upon, or whether the move was in reaction to a sudden event; e.g., the death or disability of one of the parties.

For purposes of this section, I've created a scenario that makes some broad assumptions. Why? To make you aware of some things you may face that you may not have expected, and to provide you with questions to ask and some suggestions of how to handle the situation.

Scenario

Elderly widow in fragile health (although not suffering from any specific illness) is no longer physically or financially able to remain living independently in her own house. The decision has been made to have her go to live with her Baby Boomer daughter and family, which consists of a wife, husband, and two teenagers. The elderly woman has one other daughter and one other son who stated they were unable to take their mother into their respective homes. They had their reasons.

The woman who will be having her mother live with her will have much to deal with as time goes on. She did not take the time to investigate every possible option to help her mother because decisions were made in a short time, and so, now she has lots and lots of questions and few answers.

While the questions directly relate to the widow (or the elder person living in your home), they also relate to the wellbeing of the Baby Boomer and her family who will be taking care of her mother. Being able to answer the questions will allow for the caregivers to have some degree of peace of mind that can be gained by information and knowledge. It also helps to have an enormous amount of compassion and generosity of spirit to be up to the task of taking care of an elderly parent, who will resist your efforts to treat her like a child. The elderly do not make an easy transition from their being the parent into your being the parent. You might want to read some material on the subject, or even consult a counselor familiar with the situations in eldercare.

What follows is a list of questions, presented here in no particular order, to cause you to think before you make decisions and take actions that cannot be changed.

- How does your mother feel about moving into your home? Did you even ask her?
- What are her fears and concerns? Did you talk about these things in advance of her moving into your home?
- Is the person moving into your home your own parent or an in-law? What difference will it make? If it is an in-law, is your spouse able and willing to assist you in caring for their parent? *Don't skip this conversation ...*
- Do the people in your family (or in the family of your inlaws) have a history of getting along well?
- Before you made arrangements for your mother to live with you and your family, what other living arrangements did you investigate?
    - Did she express a desire to live elsewhere, including in a CCRC?
    - Does she have enough money to move into a CCRC?
- Honestly ask yourself: If she wants to live in a CCRC, and if she can afford it, why is she moving in with you, considering all the benefits of her living in a CCRC?
- Are you emotionally unable to let your mother live in a retirement community or nursing home? Even if that were in her best interests? Even if that's what she wanted?
- Are your siblings happy about the new living arrangement for their mother?
    - How was it decided that she would live with you? By default, or by happy agreement?
    - Do your siblings resent you for taking their mother into your home? Or are they relieved?
    - Do they think you will be benefitting financially by this new living arrangement?
    - Do they envy you ... and wish their mother had come to live with them instead?

- Have you and your siblings been able to work out an arrangement whereby your mother lives with you for some portion of the year, and with each of them for some other portion of the year? What if one agrees and the other does not? What if one or both live far away, such that your mother would have to fly to the destination? Would she be able to fly there by herself? If not, how would she get to their house(s)? What if this arrangement does not work out to the satisfaction of everyone?

- Have you willingly agreed to take this upon yourself and your family, or has it been "dumped" on you because others in your family are either unwilling or unable to help?
  - Do you resent this intrusion into your life and your home?
  - Can you put your own feelings aside until the right decisions have been made for your mother?

- Keeping in mind that she is your mother and deserves your utmost respect, be careful not to treat her as your maid.
  - Will your mother be able and willing to help out around the house? What specific chores do you expect her to do? Have you talked about it? Is there agreement among you, your family, and your mother about this?

- What plans do you have in place to take care of yourself during the time your mother lives in your home? Time alone every day? A bubble bath? A massage, or a mani/pedi? Keep in mind that stress can make you sick, and if your mother is counting on you, can you really afford the "luxury" of getting sick? I know, it sounds harsh, but think about it for a minute before you comment.

- Before you reach the place of serious overload, investigate options for respite care for your mother. Find out the names and locations of places that offer it, how much they charge, how much notice they require. Respite care for your mother can be your salvation.

- How do you intend to handle disagreements and upsets that are bound to occur?
  - Is your family supportive of this new arrangement or resentful? Did you even ask them?

- Do you and your spouse work full time?
  - Will your mother be able to be left alone all day while you and your family go to work or school? Or not?

- What if this new living arrangement seriously damages your marriage? Or your relationship with your mother? Or with your relationship with your children or your siblings? How will you address such problems?

- Are you prepared to have your mother living in your home for years? In sickness and in health?

- Will there be sufficient financial resources to sustain this living arrangement?
  - How much money does the mother have?
  - Does your mother have a personal financial advisor with whom she has worked for a long time? Do you know this person? Do you have their contact information?
  - How and where is her money held? (i.e., bank CDs, brokerage accounts)
  - Was the money jointly owned with her husband? With someone else (a sibling of yours, perhaps)?
  - Does she have money of her own (e.g., an IRA)? Who are the named beneficiaries?
  - Is she familiar with her money situation, such that she has a good understanding of her income and her expenses?
  - Does your mother have a regular income from Social Security, a pension (hers and/or her husband's), or money drawn from her investments as Minimum Required Distributions? Do you know the amounts?
  - Do you know the details of her money, including the sources, the amounts, where the money is, the names and addresses of her brokers, etc.?
  - Will you have access to her money if it is needed for her?
  - Do you or your mother have an accountant who will prepare her Income Tax returns every year? If her finances are complicated, don't try to "do it yourself" just to save a few dollars.

- Does your mother have any credit card debt or debt from unreimbursed medical expenses for her husband's final illness?

- Does your mother have a bank safe deposit box? At which bank (branch)? Where is the key?
  - Who are the signers on the box? If you are not, you should be.
  - Do you (does she) know what is in the box? It would be good to inventory the box at this time.

- Does she still need that box? If not, have her close it out.

- Has her home been listed for sale by a realtor yet?
    - Do you have knowledge of that transaction?
    - Were you present when your mother met with the realtor? When she signed the Agreement of Sale?
    - What are the terms and conditions of the sale agreement?
    - Can a quick sale be reasonably anticipated?
    - How much money is your mother expected to net from the sale of her home?

- Does she have an outstanding mortgage, home-equity loan or reverse mortgage that will significantly deplete the proceeds from the sale of her house?

- Have you and your mother together met with a financial planner to discuss the best way to preserve the money from the sale of her house?

- Are you the person who will be most involved in helping your mother break up her home, get rid of the "stuff" she no longer wants or needs?
    - Will your siblings voluntarily assist in the process, or will you have to ask for their help?
    - What if they cannot or will not help out? Will this cause hard feelings?
    - How will it be decided who among you and your sibling can take items from the house?
    - Do you anticipate any fighting among you and your siblings over "stuff?" (Don't do it!)
      Who will resolve disputes about your mother's "stuff?"
    - If there is no plan to handle the disposition of your mother's "stuff," it would be good to write a list of who wants what, who gets what, what items are to be sold, what things are to be donated to thrift stores or a charity.
    - Who will be responsible for the money obtained from the sale of her things? You? Into what account will the net sale proceeds be placed? Whose decision will this be?
    - Remember to ask the thrift store for a receipt to allow for a tax deduction on her Income Tax return.
    - Keep itemized lists of the distribution of your mother's things and how much money was obtained from the sale of such things … just in case you are questioned.

- Will your mother be financially contributing to the household operating expenses?
    - How much?
    - How was that figure determined?
    - Do your siblings know about this? Should they know? If not, why not?

- What if your mother runs out of money?
    - Are you in the financial position to provide for her indefinitely?
    - Have you investigated financial options by speaking with a financial planner?
    - Will your siblings help you to financially provide for your mother?
    - What if they cannot or will not?

- Does her husband have a probate estate that is currently being administered?
    - Who is the personal representative of the estate? Your mother? Someone else? Who?
    - Who is the lawyer handling the estate? Have you met with that lawyer to determine the status of the estate administration, and if there will be any money coming to your mother at the end of the probate process?
    - What are the approximate net proceeds from his estate? To whom are they payable?
    - If there is money coming to your mother from her husband's estate, what does she plan to do with that money? Has she consulted with a financial professional about how to preserve her money and how to provide her with an income from that money?

- Will you be financially compensated by your mother for allowing her to move into your home?
    - Have you discussed this with your tax lawyer, your financial planner, and your siblings?
    - Whose decision was it to compensate you?
        - Who decided the dollar amount? In cash or in kind?
        - Should you refuse?
    - Will your compensation be paid to you on a regular basis, or in a lump sum at the time of your mother's death through her Will? What if that never happens because she will have run out of money

343

before she died, and there will be no money in her estate to pay you? Discuss this with your financial planner and your lawyer before deciding.

- Is this a good plan?
- What will you be expected to do in exchange for this compensation besides allowing your mother to live in your house?
- Will your siblings be upset or angry at this financial arrangement? Will they be told? How and when will these "hard" conversations take place? Will you have to initiate them? What if this causes a serious upset in your family?
- Consult with a tax attorney to see what the tax consequences will be for such a financial arrangement. [For example, if you plan to take your mother as a deduction on your U. S. Income Tax return, will you then have to claim the money she pays you as income?] It's complicated, so don't try to go it alone and later find out you have made irreversible decisions.
- This is no place for "do-it-yourself" financial planning. Don't make the decisions about money without first consulting with a financial planner and a tax lawyer.

- Will your mother's living in your home, combined with the financial compensation, *enable* you to quit your job? Will her living with you *require* you to quit? What if you don't want to stop working? What if you need the salary and benefits from your employer more than you need the compensation from your mother?

  - Before you quit your job, consult with a financial planner to determine if it is even financially feasible to do so, keeping in mind that you are still working and saving to prepare for your own financial health during your retirement years, so be careful of the financial choices you make. Ask questions. Get answers.

- Do you have your mother's Power-of-Attorney? If not, you should take care of this immediately by having a lawyer experienced in elder law prepare the document.

- If your mother has a Power-of-Attorney, are you named as her agent? If not, why not? Who is? Do you know where the original document is, and how you could get it if needed in a moment's notice?

- Will you be responsible to write her checks and pay bills?
  - If you have siblings, do they trust you to do this, or can you anticipate problems and questions about how your mother's money is being spent?
  - Will you be writing checks for her under the authority of a power-of-attorney, or did she put your name on her bank account(s) as a joint owner? If so, remove your name immediately, and get her to name you as her agent under a Power-of-Attorney. These are two very different ways to handle <u>her</u> money. (more about this in Chapter II – FINANCIAL).

- Does your mother have a Will or a Revocable Living Trust?
  - Do you know the terms of the document?
  - Are you named as her Executor (Successor Trustee)? If not, do you know who is? Why not you?
  - It might be wise to consult an estate attorney to see if her estate plan should be updated.

- Does your mother have a Living Will and a Healthcare Power-of-Attorney?
  - Are you her Agent under these documents? If not, do you know who is? Why are you not her agent?
  - If your mother is living with you, you should be her agent, so arrange for her to have new documents prepared. When you so this, you, your mother, your lawyer, and you should all be present at the same time. And, it would be good if your lawyer specialized in elder law.
  - Do you know where the original documents are, and how to get them in a moment's notice?
  - Have you discussed and do you know what she wants in regular or extreme healthcare situations?
  - Do your siblings know what your mother wants? Are they in agreement, or can you anticipate fighting?
    - Remember that fighting about this sort of thing is expensive in more ways than money.

- Do you know what kind of health insurance your mother has beyond Medicare? Do you know the name of the insurance company, the policy number, contact numbers, what is covered and not covered by the insurance?

- Do you know the names, addresses, and all other contact information for all your mother's healthcare providers?

- Does your mother have long-term care insurance? Do you know the name of the insurance company, the details of the policy coverage, the amount of the annual premium?

- Does she have life insurance?
  - Do you know the name of the company and the details of the policy, including the name of her agent, the policy number, the whereabouts of the policy, the name of the beneficiaries? Is the policy paid up, or will there be premiums due every year?

- When she visits her medical providers, make sure she completes the HIPAA release forms to grant you access to her medical records.

- Do you have the information relating to all of her medical providers, how often she sees them, what medications she takes?
  - Will she be able to monitor these things by herself, or will you have to take on this responsibility, too?

- To what degree will your mother's living in your house disrupt the tranquility in your home?
  - Did you discuss this new arrangement with your family beforehand, or did you just announce that she was moving in?
  - What was the immediate reaction of your husband and your children?
  - Were you able to calm their upset? Answer their questions?
  - Will your children be resentful about having a grandparent living with them full time?
  - Will they be helpful in caring for your mother, or find ways to stay out of the house?

- Will you be required to make significant alterations to your home to allow for her to reside with you? For example, entrance ramps, bathroom safety devices? Who will pay for those things?

- What if her living in your home causes tension in your marriage such that a divorce is contemplated? How would you resolve this issue?

- Will one of your children have to surrender their bedroom to give your mother a room of her own which will afford her some degree of privacy? Will this cause hard feelings and resentment? What other room could be turned into a private room for her so that no one will have to give up their own room? Will she have her own TV in that room?

- Does she frequently wake up (and wander) during the night? If so, how will you handle that so she doesn't fall?

- Will you need to change your mother's clothing and bed linens? Or will she be able to do that herself? What happens when the time comes when she cannot do those things for herself?

- Is she capable of taking care of her own personal needs (bathing, for example)?
  - Does she have special dietary needs that will complicate meal planning?

- What will she do every day … all day … to keep herself occupied?
  - How is her vision? Is she able to read?

- Does she still drive? If so, is that wise, considering her age?
  - If she does not drive, who will be available to drive her to and from the hairdresser or doctor appointments, or to visit friends or attend senior activities?

- What arrangements will you be able to work out to see that your mother gets to religious services if she wants to attend? What if you yourself don't go any longer? Who will take her? Can you arrange for a friend to pick her up and go with her?

- Will she be permitted to invite her friends into your home to maintain those friendships which are especially important to her now that her husband has passed away? Will there be a room in your home that will allow for her to spend private time with friends (a den or separate TV room, for example)?

- What if you and your mother and your family don't get along? What if her living in your home becomes an emotional burden on everyone? How will you handle this to the satisfaction of everyone?

- Will having your mother living in your home limit your own personal activities? At what point would you begin to resent her intrusion? For example, will taking care of your mother's needs interfere with your personal time to go to the gym, have lunch with friends, invite people into your home? Will you have to be "always available" for her?

- If your parent has (or, in the future becomes) ill, have in-depth conversations with her medical professionals to learn about her illness and the anticipated trajectory of the illness. For example, if she has COPD, the classic trajectory of her illness suggests there will be a need for oxygen and/or limited activity in her future. Don't wait until her illness overtakes her, you, and your family.

- Will you be prepared to deal with the situation if/when your mother begins to display signs of cognitive decline (dementia, for example)?

- How will you prepare (in advance) for the time when your mother can no longer be left alone while you and your husband go to work?
  - Before the need arises, investigate options for home health aides and adult day-care, especially the costs. Don't put this off until "later" because, should the need arise suddenly, it is easy to make mistakes.
  - Know when it is time to ask for help (hospice, for example).

- If it becomes necessary to move your mother into a nursing home, will you be able to do it without too much upset and guilt? It will help to look at the benefits for her (and even for you).
  - Will you require agreement (approval?) among you and your siblings before you can make the change?
  - Do you anticipate agreement and cooperation from them, or conflict and upset if/when the time comes for making the decision?

- Have you and your mother discussed this at length, such that you know and understand her wishes. Have you communicated this with your siblings?

- Have you and your mother visited several such facilities?

- What financial arrangements will be necessary to provide for her to live in an assisted living facility?
  - Have you and your mother met and discussed this with a financial planner? If not, why not?

- Will you be the person making the funeral and burial arrangements for your mother?
  - Will your siblings be involved in making the arrangements, or will they defer to you?
  - Is there a burial space for her where your father is buried?
  - Do you know what kind of funeral your mother wants?
  - Will there be money to pay for it?
  - Familiarize yourself with Chapter III – FUNERAL & BURIAL so that when the time comes, you will be able to more easily make the arrangements and be prepared to meet with the funeral director.

- If it becomes necessary to have a lawyer intervene between feuding family members, where will the funds come from to pay the legal fee?

I realize this is a very long list, and I know there are people who have allowed a parent to move into their home without any kind of in-depth conversations. Sometimes things work well; sometimes, not. Having a senior parent move into your home will alter your life in many ways. If you anticipate this could be in your future, do you very best to be prepared.

As the parents of Baby Boomers age and become unable to continue living independently, hard choices will have to be made. Sometimes, it will be the Baby Boomers themselves who have to make the decisions for their parent. No matter who ultimately makes the decision, it will be painful for everyone concerned, but there are things that can be done and said to minimize the pain from the transition. (Remember "*words left unsaid and deeds left undone*")

The older family members would say, almost without exception, that they never want to be a burden to their children. Many adult children (Baby Boomers) would agree as they, themselves, age. They also would say they want to be there to help their parents should the need arise. But, life is not simple anymore. Much is involved in establishing a multi-generational home, much more than selling the parent's house and filing a change-of-address with the Post Office.

Once upon a time, there was a man whose widowed mother-in-law moved into his home. She was in her mid-70s, had lived independently after her husband died, and she was in reasonably good health. He and his wife did little talking about it in advance, and in retrospect, it seemed that his wife was going to do it with or without his consent.

At first, the woman's health was good enough that she could contribute to the household in small ways, but as the years went by, she became unwilling or unable to lift a finger, felt entitled to be waited on, even though her daughter and son-in-law had full-time jobs. Even though everything was being done for her, she expressed no happiness or gratitude; in fact, it was the opposite. She began to criticize everything and everyone, to the point that the grandchildren moved out of their family home because they were so unhappy about the living arrangements.

> *This man's wife knew how unhappy her husband was and that their marriage was in jeopardy, yet she refused to talk about any other living arrangement for her mother. She had two siblings who could have helped, but did not. As a point of pride, she regularly said she would never put her mother into a nursing home. She sacrificed the happiness of her husband and her children in order to have her mother live in their home, where she resided for ten years before she died. During that time, the husband's relief came from being at his workplace, where he arrived early and left late every day just so he didn't have to go home.*
>
> *Who benefitted from this living arrangement? What do you think?*

Was this the best choice for that family? I don't know. I can't answer that question because I was never faced with the situation. All I can say is that if you ever find yourself having to decide whether or not to have an elderly parent move into your home, you had better have the "hard" conversations sooner rather than later. If you think it will be hard to make arrangements for an elderly parent to live in some kind of retirement community, think what your life and your home life will be like if you decide they should move in with you.

There is no easy way to handle this situation. There can only be the arrangement that you and your parent(s) come up with after taking many things into consideration. These things require conversation. So many questions. So few answers.

Spending the latter years with a parent in your home could turn out to be a gift for everyone, an opportunity to complete your relationship, to forgive, to express gratitude and love for a life well spent. Or, it could be a living hell. There are choices to be made to determine which scenario will play out. I hope for you and your family it will be the first one, because the second one gives opportunities for regrets that may last a very long time. Remember, one of the goals of this book is to encourage you to make choices that will enable you to live a life without regrets.

The one thing I do suggest is to investigate every possible option for the living arrangements of your elderly parent(s) well before the need arises. This process will give you information you may not have known before. Making plans before the need arises may keep you from reacting to a crisis and possibly making poor choices that have unpleasant consequences. And, before such an arrangement is made, I recommend you consult with a financial planner about your money and about your parent's money, and consult with a lawyer specializing in Elder Law. Whatever their fees will be, think of them as an investment in your future. You cannot put a price on peace of mind.

BEFORE YOU MOVE

No matter what you decide to do, there is a lot to think and talk about before you move from your present residence. It may require that you sell your present home first, so that you will have the money to buy your new home. But, you say, your real estate market is depressed, and you won't get as much for your house as you might have several years ago. While that may be true, the housing market where your potential new house is located, may also be depressed, so you might be able to find the perfect new home for yourself at a reasonably low price.

Do you absolutely have to sell your present home before you can make a move? Even if you sell your present house for $350,000 and buy a new one for $350,000, it won't be an "even exchange" because you must deduct the realtor's fee and closing and moving costs from the sale of your house.

- But, you say, you plan to sell your house by yourself (FSBO), thereby avoiding the realtor's commission. Great, if you can do it! But, be very careful! This is another one of those places where you cannot afford to make a mistake, and, while the realtor's fee may seem high at first glance, I recommend that you look at it more as an investment than as an expense. You are paying for their expertise and assistance in what has become a very complicated process of paperwork, inspections, fees, etc. It is no longer as simple as getting a buyer to sign an Agreement of Sale, and you both show up at a settlement table in 90 days.

What about all the stuff in your house? Well, you'll have to get rid of much of it ... it's simply the law of physics! You can only get so much stuff in a given space, no more, no less. This can be an enormous problem. If you have family members who honestly want some of the things you no longer need or want, give those things away before you make the move to the new house. Yard sales are also a good way to get rid of stuff. You might be surprised how much money you can make while getting rid of a lot of unwanted stuff. You could also donate unwanted things to a thrift store or charity.

Realtors have all sorts of good ideas of what to do to improve your chances for a reasonably quick sale, and one of the major ones they recommend is getting rid of clutter. It may require that you rent a storage unit and move a lot of your stuff into it, but before you do that, you should sell or donate things you will not want or need in your new home.

Don't rent a storage unit in the long term. You don't want to be paying storage fees for "stuff" you will ultimately be getting rid of.

Don't buy the first house you see UNLESS IT CALLS TO YOU WITH SUCH POWER THAT YOU ABSOLUTELY CANNOT LIVE WITHOUT IT (assuming, of course, it is a house you can afford).

If you plan to relocate to a completely different geographical area, live there for a while to see if you like it. If the weather is significantly different, try to live there for an entire year to see how you like the change of seasons. I know of several couples that moved and moved and moved again once they sold their original home, because they were never again contented in the places where they <u>thought</u> they would be happy. This is expensive, exhausting and stressful.

- If you think you want to move to Florida or Arizona, rent a house, apartment or condo there for a month in the summer. Can you tolerate the humidity in Florida in August, or the hot, dry 115° summer days in Phoenix? Don't fall for that myth that it's 'cooler' in Arizona because the air is dry. Hot is still hot!

Be prepared to find new medical professionals in your new location. Ask your current medical providers for referrals.

Don't forget about money. Considering that you are in your 60s and facing a change in income because of retiring, it is appropriate to have conversation(s) with your financial planner to see if a move is financially feasible for you.

Do you have sufficient cash available for the costs of moving and redecorating? You absolutely do not want to start paying for such things with a credit card!

Is the cost of living higher or lower than where you presently live?

- Will you still have a mortgage? Will it be affordable 20 years from now?

- What about the monthly homeowner's association fees (if any)?

- What about real estate taxes and auto insurance?
    [For example, had we moved from SE Pennsylvania to the New Jersey shore, our real estate taxes and our auto insurance would have <u>doubled</u>.)

WHAT IF THE COUPLE CANNOT AGREE?

Making a move from the home you created and love to a new home in a continuing care retirement community (not a 55+ community) is not easy. It generally happens in one of three ways:

1. One person becomes disabled or dies, and the survivor, finding it too hard to remain in their house alone, moves to a retirement community. In this scenario, there is little if any time to "shop around." Sometimes, in a quick reaction to what has just happened, a decision is made that may turn out to be less than acceptable. Then what?

2. Over the course of several years, the couple talked about moving to a retirement community, especially one that has an excellent medical facility ... just in case one or both become ill or disabled. They talked and talked and talked. They even visited several desirable communities. Yet, they never came to an agreement. The only thing they agreed upon was to do nothing. Oh, yes, they also agreed that when something happened to one of them, the other would have to figure it out by themselves. They said they were comfortable with that decision. I don't believe it.

3. The couple researches and visits several retirement communities, sees what their options are, and makes a conscious choice to move <u>together</u> while they are still young and vibrant enough to enjoy the new life they chose to create for themselves, while they still have each other to make the transition less painful, even enjoyable.

More often than not, it is choice No. 1 or No. 2, because many couples cannot agree on where to go or when to make the move, so they do nothing. I'm not sure they understand that they actually <u>*chose*</u> to do nothing … it is just how some people live their lives.

It is my belief that in order to make a good transition from a home you love to a retirement community requires enormous understanding of who you are as a person, and who you are as a couple. By that time, you should know what you like and what you don't like, and what potential situations might cause you stress or unhappiness. This is where research becomes necessary and important … and includes having conversations with others who have already made the move to learn about their experience and things to do and things to avoid.

Making no choices leaves you in a place of no power, of self-doubt, of fear of the unknown, and fear of change. I'm not saying that any of this is easy. I am saying you must give it serious thought before things in your life fast-forward to the place where there is no more time left for research, for conversation. Making this move just might be one of the things you will have to do **between now and then,** like it or not. I know people who took the big leap and are so very happy they did. They have the comfort of knowing they did it together, they made new friends together, they are living in a place that can support a lovely way of life, including medical care if necessary.

Would you rather make the choice to do nothing, and then have to make the move by yourself?
Just asking…

> ***One of the greatest discoveries a man makes …***
> ***is to find he can do what he was afraid he couldn't do.***
>
> Henry Ford

If you subscribe to the philosophy of "when in doubt, do nothing," don't be surprised when things do not go your way, especially if you never defined "your way." There is great benefit that comes from speaking your own personal truth, even if it is upsetting, even if it makes someone else mad at you for a while. If you regularly choose to do nothing, what you are really saying is that you don't trust yourself enough to make a good choice, so you'll just sit back and let Fate make the decision(s) for you. To quote Dr. Phil: *"How's that workin' for you?"*

Not making choices enables you the opportunity to blame something or someone else for your problems, to never take responsibility for your situation. It seems to me that the opposite is that you can never take responsibility for your personal successes, either. Does that sound harsh? Maybe. Does it make you think about how you make choices? I hope so.

Dr. Phil also repeatedly tells people on his show that most situations require a hero … someone willing to step up and make the hard decision that others seem unwilling to make. If you, as a couple, cannot find it within your relationship to negotiate a peaceful agreement, or make the choice to move to a retirement community <u>*before*</u> one or both of you needs to, then one of you must do it for both … *before it is too late.* You know what I'm talking about, don't you?

If you have not yet learned the art of negotiating with your spouse or partner, now would be a good time to begin. Fighting is not the answer. Neither is doing nothing. There is always anger and resentment on the part of one party when there is no happy agreement between them. Is that what you want?

One of the things that keeps people from making the move is their standing behind the statement that they are not ready. To be "ready" requires that you understand at a very deep level that your life is headed toward its final days, and you don't want to deal with that possibility … although it is <u>not</u> a possibility. It is a reality. The only unknown is the date. After all, *death is the only certainty of life.*

I know a childless couple who moved into a single home on the property of a fine retirement community when they were in their early 50s. They figured by the time they needed the amenities of the community, they would have established a good life there for themselves, and that is exactly what happened. Twenty-five years later, the husband died after a long illness, but all along, the wife had the support and friendship of the entire community around her.

No one is ever really ready unless you do what this couple did … consciously choosing to move before the need arises. Once you understand that the decision to move is in your best interests, the two of you can do it together, and can then be able to share the experience the way you have shared your entire adult lives … together.

349

WHO WILL RETIRE FIRST?

Who will retire first? If one of you is older than the other, this may be the deciding factor. Who retires first may be decided by the companies you respectively work for, and what their policies are concerning retirement. Did you talk about it? If you are married or in a committed relationship, there is much to talk about before one or both of you retire. Don't skip over these important (necessary) conversations, no matter how difficult they may seem.

IF THE HUSBAND RETIRES FIRST

1. What is your PLAN for retirement? *[Plan? Are you joking?]*

2. How was it decided that the man would retire first?

3. Are you eager to retire, or are you dreading it?

4. Were you *forced* to retire by your employer who called it "downsizing" or some other euphemism?

5. How happy are you with this situation?

6. Were you given a substantial financial buy-out to retire early?

7. Have you and your financial planner discussed what to do with this chunk of money to preserve it?

8. Did you consult with a financial planner before you retired so that you can know if your money will last for the rest of your life? Or did you just take the plunge and hope for the best?

9. Are you obligated to retire at a specific age by virtue of your employer's rules?

10. Would you want to continue working indefinitely for that same employer if it was permitted?

11. How is your health as it relates to going to work every day? Do you still want to work every day?

12. Do you need to continue working at that job for financial reasons? For how long?

13. If you find that you are not well positioned financially to retire due to insufficient savings and serious debt, how do you plan to pay your bills during your retirement years? Have you even thought about it?

14. Will you be receiving a defined pension from your employer?

15. If the pension is tied to your having worked a certain number of years and having reached a certain age before you can collect that pension, will you be eligible to collect your pension when you are ready to retire?

16. Will you continue to work for that same employer until you do reach those milestones?

17. Is your money in an employer-sponsored investment plan [401(k), 403(b)]?

18. Have you discussed this money with a financial planner?

19. If you retire from your primary employer, would you want or need to get a part-time job to keep you busy or to supplement your income? Something else to talk about with your partner and your financial planner.

20. Would there be a significant loss of income as a result of your retiring? How would you make up for that loss?

21. Would you experience a reduction in lifestyle as a result of that income loss?

22. If in 5 or 10 years after you officially retire, you find yourself short of money, will you be able to go back to work doing something that will earn you additional income? If that is even a remote possibility, guard your health and stay in contact with people who may be your lifelines to future employment.

23. What about Social Security? When should you begin collecting?

24. Have you discussed the collecting of Social Security with a financial planner and/or a tax lawyer so that you can understand and avoid the tax consequences of simultaneously working and collecting?

25. Was retirement a happily anticipated life transition?

26. What do you plan to do to stay busy until your spouse retires?

27. If the first retiree was the husband, will he run the house while his wife continues working? Laundry? Dishes? Vacuuming? Grocery shopping? You know the things that need doing regularly.

28. Now that you will be having a lot of time on your hands, will your adult children want (*expect?*) you to take care of their small children?

29. Did you thoroughly discuss this with your partner or your children?

30. What if you do not want to be a primary day-care person for very young children?

31. Would you consider it a delightful opportunity to take care of your young grandchildren every day, or a burden? Keep in mind that you may not have enough energy to keep up with them at your age.

32. If you want to play golf or bowl several times a week, will you have the funds to pay for those activities? How would you feel if you find yourself short of money and cannot afford these activities?

33. People often say that they intend to travel after they retire. Will you have enough money to do the kind of traveling you want to do?

34. Will you get antsy or bored being home by yourself, and therefore put pressure on your spouse or partner to retire so you won't be lonely? Will your spouse/partner's retiring early reduce her retirement money just because you are lonely?

35. What about the opposite situation? If you are retired and your spouse is not, is your spouse going to rush into retirement just so they can stay home from work, too … forgetting the financial consequences of such a choice?

36. What if he/she doesn't want to retire yet, or is ineligible to retire because of age or longevity with his/her employer?

37. If you were paying people to care for your yard before you retired, will you be able to afford that yard service now?

38. If you take over the yard work now that you have the time, what if you find it physically impossible to do?

39. If you own a vacation home, will you be able to continue paying the bills on that property, or will you be forced to sell it (even at a loss) because you will be unable to afford it? Other than selling the home, what other options are available for you to consider? This is another one of those conversations you need to have with your spouse or partner and your financial planner.

40. How is your health? Your spouse's health?

41. Do you have adequate insurance of every kind you will need?

IF THE WIFE RETIRES FIRST:

1. Many of the questions that relate to the husband's retiring first relate to the wife as well, so read the above list again.

2. Will much of the work around the house continue to be her responsibility, just as it has always been?

3. Will she be the primary child-care person for a grandchild? Has she discussed this with her spouse or partner?

4. Will it cut into her free time and her finances?

5. Was there an agreement made between her and her adult children relating to this child-care arrangement before she retired?

6. What if she doesn't want to do it? What if you don't want her to do it because it will cut into your time to do things together that you have waited to do for years?

7. Will she have her own retirement income?

"in sickness and in health"

While it is not generally possible to plan for the time when a serious illness or injury will happen, it is possible to plan for such an event, and then hope it never happens. Planning is sort of like buying insurance: you have it in place in case you need it, all the while hoping you never do.

Whether or not you are in a committed relationship with another person by virtue of marriage or otherwise, those words from the wedding vows apply. People approaching retirement are generally anticipating a life of freedom and good health, but you know it doesn't always turn out that way.

One of the biggest issues to consider is what happens if or when one or both of you becomes ill and requires medical care. The need for medical care or household assistance can occur any time, no matter where you live. If sickness or injury happens in a moment's time (a stroke, heart attack, fall, or vehicle accident, for example), there will be no time to research your options. To be prepared for any such eventuality, I recommend that you investigate every option of this sort well in advance of your need, so that if or when the time comes, you will be thoroughly informed about the costs, services, and reputation of several retirement communities, health providers, home health agencies, and so you will know and understand options available to you. This, too, is part of end-of-life planning.

If you need assistance to manage your household or your health at home, who is there to help you? Of course, you will reply that your family will take care of you. While that may be true, people are busy and have their own lives, and may be unable to respond to your needs. There may be no one able and available to move in with you, or to provide the level of care you need. The person(s) you may be thinking of to help may not be suited for or be willing to take on the role of caregiver, and that is something to seriously consider before jumping into what could turn out to be an unpleasant situation.

Of course, there are home-health agencies to provide services for you. Home-health agencies are popping up like dandelions in April because of the huge need for their services as Baby Boomers age. Some of the agencies are reputable and provide excellent personnel and services. Others are not. The costs vary greatly, often based on the exact services which the agency will be providing. Before you commit to such services, you will need to thoroughly evaluate your needs, both medical and non-medical, as well as the health insurance coverage from Medicare, Medicaid or your own supplemental insurance. Much of the medical coverage is dependent upon your financial situation, so you might want to consult with a financial professional well in advance of need for these services.

If you decide that a relative (or friend) is going to move in with you to "help out," it would be good for you to have the hard conversations with that person beforehand to have a thorough understanding of why this person is willing to move in with you in the first place. What do you expect this person to do for you? What are their expectations for the living arrangement in your home? What if this person and you simply don't get along? *It happens, you know.* How will you handle conflict should it arise, especially if your health is fragile? If the arrangement turns out to be a total failure, will you be able to handle the changes necessary by yourself, or will you require personal or legal assistance to do it?

I recommend you talk with your lawyer before committing to such an arrangement. Do you want this person to have your power-of-attorney or not? Will this person be handling your money, paying your bills? Does the person have altruistic intentions, or are they, themselves, in a difficult (financial) situation and looking for a place to live and someone to help support them? The conversations will not be easy, but can make the difference between whether this arrangement succeeds or fails.

BEING A CAREGIVER

This is a time, if never before, that requires hard conversations between the two of you.
The partner who is ill needs to talk and be heard.
The partner who is the caregiver needs to talk and be heard.

If the two of you are unfamiliar and uncomfortable expressing yourself deeply, this could be a problem. Remember the quotation by Harriet Beecher Stowe:

"The bitterest tears shed over graves are for words left unsaid and deeds left undone."

This may also be the time to apply The Regret Test, which goes like this:

> If, on the last day of your life, there is something you always wanted to say, but have <u>not</u> said,
> will you regret not having spoken the words?
> If the answer is yes, then you must begin right away!

If one of you becomes seriously ill, is the other prepared to be a full-time caregiver, with all that is involved in taking care of another person whose health has deteriorated, or of being with someone who is dying? It is not easy, especially if you are not inclined toward the household and nursing tasks that will be required of you. If you find that you are absolutely not suited for the role of caregiver, you must say so. It would not be good to take over the role and then quit in the middle because you become overwhelmed. There will be much to do and think about. Maybe you could be the back-up caregiver instead of the primary caregiver. Think about these things and talk about them with your partner well in advance of need. Have a plan.

If you are the primary caregiver, arrange for a reliable back-up, someone you can call upon to give you relief when you need it. In the beginning, you won't know when you need it: maybe it will turn out to be one hour each day; maybe one day each week. But, sooner or later, you will get a sense of your own personal needs as you care for the needs of someone else. It is important not to ignore your own needs, because someone else is counting on you, and if you allow yourself to become exhausted or sick, you won't be able to fulfill your responsibilities as a caregiver. This is where conversations and planning become essential.

Investigate the places and agencies that offer respite care well in advance of need, so that when the time comes, you will have all the information you need to make the appropriate arrangements. It is one way to give yourself some breathing space and at the same time, allow for alternative care for your loved one.

Depending on the seriousness of your partner's illness, you may be called upon to do all kinds of domestic tasks with which you are unfamiliar (especially true for men). If you are still working, this could be a problem, so don't feel like you have to do everything by yourself. Ask for help. People want to help, but often don't know what to do, and don't know how to bring it up. You do the asking, and you may be pleasantly surprised at the love and generosity people express to you and your partner.

- In Chapter III (Funeral and Burial), you will find a form titled PEOPLE TO CALL.
  If you and your partner have done as suggested (that is, filled out the form), all
  you have to do is begin calling the people on the list if that is something you and
  your partner want to do. You need to talk about this before making the calls, however.
  Sometimes, a person does not want company right away, but maybe later, and maybe
  not at all. Keep the conversation alive without putting pressure on the person who is ill.

Elsewhere in this book, I wrote about my being a caregiver for my former husband during his last days. I'll tell you what I did for ME to help me stay focused and deal with my former husband's last illness, funeral and burial.

- **<u>First, I rediscovered donuts!</u>**
Not exactly nourishing food, but definitely comfort food at a time when I needed comfort. I had all but given up donuts for more than a year. When Bill was in the hospital the last week of his life, I surrendered to temptation when a nurse asked me if I would like her to order a breakfast cart. Considering that I arrived at the hospital every morning around 7 a.m., it sounded like a good idea. I didn't know that the "breakfast" cart included only coffee and donuts. But, that was OK by me! I declared donuts to be "health food" for the duration.

- **<u>Second, I got a massage every week or so for a while.</u>** A person must do what they must do in order to survive difficult times. I wasn't able to carve out much time for a massage before Bill's death, but in the months afterward, when I was closing out his home and administering his estate, those massages were much more than comfort for me ... they saved me!

- Even though I was able to comfort myself with donuts and massages during Bill's illness and funeral, and even afterward as I administered his estate, I held tightly onto my emotions, and I paid a price for being so controlled. Don't do it. Cry. Talk. Soothe yourself with flowers, good music, the company of people who love you. Be good to yourself. You will survive!

IT IS IMPORTANT TO REMEMBER THAT STRESS CAN MAKE YOU SICK.

You cannot afford to get sick when a loved one is counting on you.
This is why it is important to take care of yourself for as long as it takes.

If you are the person caring for a loved one during an illness and/or his/her last days .... you may have been too busy to have expressed your emotions. You may have been afraid you would lose control if you did, and there were so many things that had to be done, and you were the person who had to do them. I get it. Nevertheless, it is important, even necessary for your sanity and health, to give yourself permission to feel the feelings you are feeling, and express yourself fully and appropriately.

- If it means that you feel like crying, then cry.

- Don't feel a need to apologize for your emotional outbursts. Even though you may not believe me, they will lessen in frequency and intensity over time.

- If it means that you need a particular exercise routine to burn off the unexpressed emotion, stick with it.

- If you find that you need to eat comfort food for a short time, do it. You can go on a diet soon enough.

- If you need to listen to certain music to soothe yourself, then surround yourself with it.

- If you find that you need to meditate or pray, then do it.

- If you need "alone" time for a while, even 30 minutes a day for a while, do whatever it takes to set time aside. A bubble bath or a hot shower can do wonders to restore your body and spirit.

- If you need to look at photographs, keep the photo albums close by.

- If you need to speak with a counselor, do it.

- Get a massage as often as you can.

- Take stress vitamins and try to eat well.

- Get enough sleep. Go to bed one hour earlier every night.

- Try very hard not to depend upon medication for relief.

- If it helps to talk about your situation, do it with others who will understand your feelings and who will not try to talk you out of feeling them.

- If you feel the need to join a support group, then do it.

" 'til death do us part"

There will come a day when one of you passes away. Will the survivor be prepared to handle all that is necessary to arrange for a funeral and burial in 3 or 4 days? I recommend that you familiarize yourself with Chapter III (Funeral and Burial) well in advance of need, so that when the time comes, you will feel confident that you know what to do.

What you will do after the funeral is another story altogether. Have the two of you ever talked about what your life will look like after the first one of you passes away? Statistics indicate that it is often the man who passes away first. That being said, is the woman prepared to live alone? Does she understand your joint finances so that she can make a good transition into managing her own money by herself? Can she afford to remain in the home you established together? Is her health good enough to allow her to remain living alone, without the assistance of a healthcare professional?

What if the woman passes away first? Is the surviving man able to take care of the responsibilities that were historically handled by the woman? Does he even know what they are?

Have you ever talked with your adult children about their contribution to the wellbeing of the surviving spouse? Will they have to contribute time or money in order for the surviving spouse to manage alone? Will they even be in a position to help? What would you want them to do for you? What if they are unwilling or unable to help?

The questions above are barely the tip of an iceberg of topics to think about and talk about before the first one of a couple passes away. I recommend that you keep a running conversation going, ask each other lots of *"What if _____?"* questions. As long as you are having these conversations in advance, you have the opportunity to thoroughly examine your options. But, it is possible to wait too long, until one or the other of you is no longer able to actively participate in such conversations. What then? Begin talking about these things NOW!

RETIREMENT, DIVORCE, and RE-MARRIAGE

Each of these life events is the subject of many books. Each deserves its own book. That being said, let's nevertheless take a brief look at what can happen in each category.

Retirement and divorce are not necessarily connected, but sometimes they happen simultaneously. Retirement and divorce can sometimes lead to re-marriage, which has its own set of problems. Remember the importance of COMMUNICATION with the people in your life who matter to you. There is much to be discussed and resolved before you remarry. Think about what you learned from your first marriage that ended in divorce, and try to learn from any mistakes that were made then.

1. Are either (or both) of you marrying on the rebound ... that is, too soon after a divorce, relationship breakup, or death of a spouse?

2. What unresolved issues from your previous relationship will you be bringing into this new relationship? Are you willing to address those issues with a professional before you marry so you can begin your new life with a clean slate?

3. Do you know how to negotiate your way through marital disputes? Are you a right-fighter?

4. What if one of you has children and the other does not? What are the children's ages?

5. Have you told your children about your intention to remarry? What was their *immediate* reaction?

6. How well do your children know your intended spouse? Do they like this other person? Have they been honest in telling you what they think of this other person?

7. Do either or both of you have children who disapprove of your intended spouse, or even the idea of your remarrying? How do you plan to handle their disapproval?

8. Does it matter to you if your children disapprove? How important is it to you that your children give you their blessing?

9. Have your children met each other? Do they get along? What will you do if they seriously don't like each other?

10. Are you prepared for the possible problems of blending families? Have you thought about it, discussed it?

11. What if one (or more) of your children refuses to attend your wedding? Would that change your mind about marrying this person?

12. What kind of wedding do you have planned? Who will pay for it? What is the budget?

13. Do either or both of you have young adult children still living with you? How will you handle that situation after you marry?

14. Do those children pay you rent or otherwise contribute to the expenses of the household?

15. Are either or both of you financially assisting young adult children?

16. Have either or both of you previously given large sums of money to your adult children. Do you anticipate that money being paid back? If not, why not?

17. Have either or both of you co-signed for any student loans, auto purchases or leases, apartment leases, mortgages or other financial obligations for your children? Why did you do that? Do you know the consequences for yourself of that act of love and generosity?

18. Are you each willing to be honest with each other about your money (that is, every aspect of your money), such that you can discuss your money without fighting?

19. Who will be responsible for paying the bills and keeping your financial records organized?

20. Have you prepared a budget for your new life together? Will you be able to follow it? What if you don't?

21. What if one of you has lots of money, and the other has significantly less?

22. Do you know each other's FICO score? If you don't, you should.

23. Are either (both) of you in serious debt? Have you discussed how you will individually pay off that debt before your marriage? Or will you be carrying that debt into your new relationship/marriage? How do you plan to pay off your debt on retirement money?

24. Did you sign a PreNuptial Agreement or not? If the subject comes up, will it be a deal breaker?

25. Do you have compatible spending, saving, and investing habits? How do you know?

26. Do you have financial integrity? Do you have any "secret" accounts? Who else knows about them? What financial (little white) lies have you told each other about your money? Why?

27. Will you keep your money separate or will you combine it? How will you decide? Do you trust your intended spouse with your money? Do you know how much money each of you has and where it is? Will you have "his," "her," and "our" money? Did you discuss this with your financial advisor?

28. How is the health of both of you? Are you properly insured for long-term health matters?

29. How and where will you celebrate holidays? What about major family events (weddings, birthdays, etc.)

30. Where will you live? What will you do with all that stuff you each own? If you are each keeping your own furniture, will it blend well? What if you don't like your new spouse's decorating taste? How will you resolve this if it brings up serious disagreements between you?

31. Have you always paid your taxes on time? Will you be filing jointly or separately? How will you decide?

32. How will you decide the division of household tasks? Will you talk about it first, or just get married and figure it out later ... sort of like you did the first time?

33. What will you do if your spouse bosses you around or otherwise mistreats you after the wedding, especially if you are not accustomed to being treated that way?

34. Is one of you a solitary person and the other very socially active? Does one of you want to travel, and the other want to stay at home? Can you negotiate a win-win so each of you gets to be happy? Better to know these things sooner rather than later.

35. Is one a reader and the other a TV addict?

36. Do either of you have any physical problems that you should reveal to the other, including addictions?

37. How much do you each spend out-of-pocket each year for prescription medication?

38. Are either of you retired? Or just one? Or both? Do you each have retirement income other than SS?

39. Is one of you presently the primary child-care person for a grandchild? What if your new spouse doesn't want you to continue?

40. How will you decide how much money to spend on gifts for your respective family?

41. If you need to cut back on expenses, how will you decide where to cut?

42. What if one of you becomes seriously ill? What kinds of medical treatment do you want at the end of your life? Have you discussed it in detail, or are you just hoping never to have to think about it or deal with it?

43. Do you each have your individual estate-planning documents signed, or should you get in touch with your lawyer(s) to have new ones made? Will you use your own individual lawyer, or will you find one you can both work with? Will your new spouse and your children fight over your estate after your death?

44. Will you be appointing each other as the agents in your various estate documents, or will you appoint one or more of your children? Why did you make those decisions?

45. Do you each have a personal financial advisor? Have you met with those advisors recently? Alone or together?

46. Where are your important papers? Who else know where they are? Who else has access to them?

47. Do you have adequate life insurance? Who are the beneficiaries? Contingent beneficiaries? Are the beneficiary and contingent beneficiary designations exactly as you want them to be? And, if not, take care of this immediately.

48. Do you have long-term care insurance, disability insurance, auto and homeowners' insurance, renters' insurance?

49. Beneficiaries are not only on life insurance policies. They are also on IRAs, 401(k) accounts, etc. Check the beneficiary designations on these, too.

50. Have you talked about your religious affiliations? Church attendance? What if there is serious disagreement?

51. Do you love this person enough to spend the rest of your life with them? Do you believe that love is enough to maintain your relationship in the face of financial problems, serious debt, illness, abuse, infidelity?

52. Is your intended spouse strongly encouraging (forcing?) you to get rid of your cats(s) or dog(s) before you marry? That's a deal-breaker about to happen for anyone who loves their pets. This is something that will need to be carefully thought out and discussed. If someone wants you to give up a pet that you dearly love, what does that say about that person? *Just asking…*

53. What about the two cars on which you still have car payments? Will you be able to afford the payments, or should you sell one and get a nice used car? Can you live with just one car, or do you really need two?

54. What kind of funeral and burial do you want? Have you written it down? Where are those instructions? Who else knows where they are? Where will the money come from for the expenses of your funeral and burial?

55. Will you be buried together, or with your former spouse? Or elsewhere? Have you talked this over with your children? Will they follow your instructions? What if they don't agree? What if your new spouse and your children disagree about your funeral and burial arrangements?

WHOSE LIFE IS IT, ANYWAY?

Simply stated, it's *your own* life,

- the life you were born to live;

- the life you would be living if money were no object;

- the life you would be living if you made your own honest choices, free of influences from others
  (spouses, children, parents, teachers, friends, religion, neighborhood, etc.).

What we really want to do is what we are really meant to do. When we do what we are meant to do, money comes to us, doors open for us, we feel useful, and the work we do feels like play to us.

Julia Cameron

"What do YOU really want?" is a question many people can't answer easily or quickly. Some can't answer it at all. Others are puzzled – *even annoyed, startled or upset*– by the question. The usual response is, *"I don't know."*

Sometimes, the best way to figure out what you want is to first determine what you <u>don't</u> want. This frequently helps because it is so easy to find areas of your life that don't work … this list is sometimes very long and easy to prepare. And you may find that eliminating all the things you don't want helps you focus on things you do want.

"What do you <u>really</u> want?" is a question that may be very hard to answer because we long ago suppressed our deepest desires. Why did we do it? Well, when we were children, and we freely expressed our wishes, we were sometimes told

that we were selfish, that we were supposed to think about other people first and not about ourselves. And, so we learned to suppress our own needs and desires. But, they are still there, hidden deep inside.

Selfish is what we usually call someone who doesn't think of another's needs, only just about one's own. Part of being a mature, responsible adult is recognizing that one's obligation to one's self is of primary importance because it is only when we keep ourselves ... *body and mind* ... whole and healthy can we then meet our obligations to others. Actually, to always think of the needs of others first is backwards, but after a lifetime of thinking like that, it may take a little time to re-think the word "selfish" from the perspective that it is not necessarily bad.

On the other hand, a person who is self-ish is addressing the needs of their own higher self – the source of life, happiness, natural growth and contribution. This kind of care of your own self takes on the nature of an investment. To be self-ish is the best thing you can do for yourself.

Being self-ish also means being able to easily and comfortably answer the question, *"What do you really want?"* ... to not be so focused on what everybody else needs and wants from you.

Are you a selfish person?
Do you mostly think of others' needs before your own?
Do you put yourself and your own needs at the top or at the bottom of your To Do List?

Are these questions hard for you to answer? They shouldn't be. After all, it's YOUR life. Nobody else's.

- If you cannot answer these questions, why can't you?

- Is it because you never took the time to think about such things?

- Is it because you're very, very busy taking care of the needs of other people?

- Is it because you never considered your own needs and desires because you were taught it is selfish to do so?

This is no dress rehearsal. This is *your* life, the <u>only</u> life you have.
What are you doing with it?

What are you waiting for, planning for?

At the end of your life, whether it is next week or many years from now, will you be able to die peacefully, with no regrets, assured that you have done everything you wanted to do ... YOUR WAY?

- If your answer is NO, you have a lot of work to do.
- And I suggest you start NOW!

Remember that lovely song which Frank Sinatra sang in the 1960s, "*My Way.*" He understood.

Oh, dear, I can hear you WHINING again:

- *Where do I begin?*
- *I'm too old.*
- *I'm not smart enough.*
- *I don't have enough money.*
- *I don't know what to do.*
- *I don't know how to do it.*
- *I can't start now because (_____fill in the blank_____).*
- *People will laugh at me.*
- *I have to lose 25 pounds first.*
- *I'll think about it.*
- *All the other excuses people regularly use to avoid doing things they know they should be doing.*

These are just excuses for not living your own life YOUR WAY. They are not real. These excuses only live in your mind. Yet, they have worked for you most of your life, and you regularly use them when you are confronted with some activity that challenges your comfort zone.

I believe you really CAN answer the questions if you take your time and think about each one for a while, and give yourself permission to be honest. You really do know what to do.

I hereby give you permission to be your own authentic self.
[Remember, I already gave you a PERMISSION SLIP. Now would be a good time to use it.]

TAKE A FEW MOMENTS TO REVIEW

You are in good shape if:

1. you have already executed your estate-planning documents, and

2. you have your finances in good condition, taking the future into consideration, and

3. you have at least written down your funeral and burial wishes, and

4. you have all your files and important papers organized and safeguarded, and

5. you have done some of the things you want to do with your life regarding your family, marriage, career, travel, leisure-time activities, with a plan for accomplishing the things still remaining on your "Bucket List."

Notice that the things on this list match the five chapters in this book.

What, you think that's an accident?

The title of this book came from a question I've been asking for years:

What are you planning to do with your life <u>between now and then</u>?

"*now*," of course, means today and "*then*" means the date of your death.

If you were to die next week, have you done everything you want to do in your life?

Would you be able to die without regrets?

WHY ARE YOU SO TIRED?

If you are a person who is always stressed, tired, headachy, and irritable, can you give your family or your job the time they need, want and deserve from you? Of course, you want to do that, but *you're just so tired*! By addressing the source of your fatigue and taking steps to reduce your stress level, you may find yourself not only feeling better, but enjoying your time with your family and your job.

If your energy is being sapped from your job, speak with your supervisor to come up with ways you can alter your job description to make you feel excited about your work. There may be ways for you to tweak little things that annoy you, and make them less aggravating and stressful. *It's just a thought ...*

Take good care of yourself. If the source of your fatigue is not directly related to a medical problem, begin to address YOUR individual needs, a little at a time, and see if your energy level doesn't increase. Meditation, relaxing in a bubble bath, private time with a good book, a nice nap, a massage, good eating habits, and regular exercise all contribute to lowering one's stress level and increasing one's general well-being, and can be fitted into your lifestyle, if only in baby steps ... one at a time. And, if you are convinced you cannot afford the time or money for these personal "indulgences," ask yourself whether you can afford to skip them.

Once again: *"What do you want for yourself?"*

Well, as far as an answer goes, it's not as if there is one <u>right</u> answer, or the perfect answer, as if this were some kind of a test. <u>There **IS no** right answer</u>! What surprises me is that so many people don't have any answer at all. It makes me wonder who is in charge of their life?

If we're talking about <u>your</u> life, and you don't know what you're going to do with the rest of it, then who does know?

And, if <u>you</u> don't know, why don't you know?

As you begin to think about your answer to these questions, it's important to recognize that the rest of your <u>life is a journey over time</u> … the time *between now and then*.

Life is <u>*never*</u> about the destination. It is <u>*always*</u> about the journey.

It helps to begin looking at things from the past and the present, and then deciding how you want your future to be. What activities gave you the most joy and happiness? What did you always love to do? Begin to think about what things you want to do and what things you do <u>*not*</u> want to do with the time you have left. And, stop asking that annoying question children often ask while riding in a car: *"Are we there yet?"* Remember where your final destination is. What's your hurry? You'll get there soon enough.

I just saw a cartoon that shows a car plunging into an open grave.

The caption says, "The Inevitable Navigation System," with the car's GPS saying,

"You have arrived at your final destination."

ONCE YOU "GET IT," YOU ARE FREE.

<u>What is "**IT**?"</u>

- "IT" is the honest, complete understanding that you are going to die some day. I believe the most important step in embarking on this journey *between now and then* is for you to acknowledge that you are going to die on some unknown day in the future. Then, you can decide what to do with the time you have left on earth.

<u>Free from what?</u>

- Free from everything in your life that is keeping you from being true to yourself, everything that is holding you back, interfering with your happiness and peace, from doing things that matter to you, all those little things you want to do but keep putting off until "later," always believing there will be a time known as "later."

<u>Free to do what?</u>

- Free to do *everything* you want to do. Once you "get it," you are free to do all the things you want to do, and free also to <u>*not*</u> do things you don't want to do.

Have you started your own list of things you want to do *between now and then*?

MARRIAGE

Are you in a marriage that has grown stale, and is making you unhappy, afraid, even sick? Can you picture yourself married to this same person in 5 years? 15 years? Is your home a happy, safe, healthy environment in which you and your family can grow?

- Do you *really* want <u>out</u> of the marriage, and if so, what are you willing to do to make it happen?

OR

- Do you *really* want to re-define and re-focus your relationship with your spouse to accommodate changes in your ages, your health, your lifestyle, your financial situation, the empty-nest, retirement time alone with each other, and if this is what you want, how do you plan to go about making it happen?

> *I recommend a movie to you: "Hope Springs," with Meryl Streep and Tommy Lee Jones.*
> *It's about a couple married for 31 years, who lost touch with each other, and how they*
> *found their way back to love, romance, and happiness as they looked forward to the*
> *rest of their lives together. A very enjoyable movie.*

These questions can be difficult and painful to answer, and <u>require conversations</u>; but the answers may give you happiness and freedom you have never imagined, especially when you consider that the purpose of the questions in the first place is to help you THINK and DECIDE then ACT upon ways in which you plan to live the rest of your life *between now and then.*

DIVORCE

What about that dreaded "D" word: divorce. Baby Boomers are getting divorced in their retirement years. It is not what they expected, but it is happening in alarming numbers. For some, divorce is a welcome breath of fresh air, allowing them to get out of a relationship in which they had been smothering for years. For others, it comes as an unwelcome surprise. Sometimes, one person finds themselves in the embarrassing place of having to get a second divorce ... especially if that marriage to the "trophy wife" didn't turn out as expected.

The reasons for divorce in the retirement years are as diverse as the people getting the divorces. I wonder what would happen if people spent as much time, energy and money trying to rescue their relationship as they spend for the costs of divorcing? What may be missing in lots of those relationships is good, honest, complete communication, and a sense of commitment. Why is it so hard for people to speak their minds to the person who, by all standards, is the most important person in their life? *Just asking* ... [see the movie, "Hope Springs."]

If you have been unable to "recapture the rapture" of your marriage and if divorce is inevitable, do your absolute best to separate in a reasonably considerate, civilized way, with as little negative fallout as possible, such that each of you can live the rest of your life peacefully. I am completely aware of what I am suggesting, and I am not saying it will be easy. But it can be done. Remember,

YOU ARE A BABY BOOMER –
YOU CAN DO ANYTHING YOU PUT YOUR MIND TO!

While you are working through this painful event in your life, don't forget your children. No matter what their ages, they have watched and heard what was going on between the two of you; and, don't delude yourself into thinking they don't know what's going on, or that they have not experienced hurt and anger, too. Your bad marriage has damaged them, even if you think it has not. Trust me when I say this.

If you can manage it, amicably decide the terms of your separation agreement before you meet with your lawyers. Pay the lawyer(s) to do the legal work for you to get your divorce, but don't pay them to fight over your stuff. Remember, lawyers bill their time by the hour (minute?). It is less expensive in the long run to give up all your stuff to your spouse and buy new stuff, than pay your lawyer to fight over it.

Be careful if your divorce lawyer tries to persuade you that the separation agreement you and your spouse worked out with blood, sweat and tears is not equitable, and that the lawyer can get you a much better deal! I've seen the messes and unhappiness such legal advice can cause. Remember that all that generously offered advice comes at a price per hour. Ask yourself if you are both happy with the Agreement? Can you live with it in the long term?

All I can say to you is to trust your instincts, be honest and fair during the process, and decide if you feel your agreement with your spouse is right for both of you, such that it will allow you to separate with integrity, respect, and peace, and move forward into the next phase of your life.

And, remember, if you have children, that person (your "ex") will be in your life forever, so be generous and try to work through the negative emotions in a reasonably short time. Get help if you need it. **Don't stay angry and bitter for the rest of your life.**

And, remember to consult your Financial Advisor about your options as you separate your assets.

Get personal counseling if you and/or your children need it. You will go through the same steps of grief as if someone close to you had died: Denial, anger, bargaining, depression, and acceptance ... not necessarily in that order. Divorce is the death of a marriage; but, you can survive it if you don't surrender to your feelings of anger and bitterness in the long term. Give yourself permission to feel what you feel for a while, but not for the rest of your life. You <u>must</u> get over it. I say this knowing that our mother never got over it, and the price she paid was enormous.

Watch the movies, "*It's Complicated*" with Meryl Streep, Alex Baldwin and Steve Martin, and "*Something's Got to Give*" with Jack Nicholson and Diane Keaton to see examples of life after divorce for Baby Boomers.

AND

If (when) you plan to remarry, sign a Pre-Nuptial Agreement first. This is another one of those Suze Orman MUST DO's. Don't let "love" cloud your judgment. You can love a person who is financially irresponsible, and you can still marry them, but you also need to protect yourself from their personal financial mess. That love you feel in the beginning could quickly disappear along with your money. Be smart and protect your assets for yourself and especially for your children.

OH, AND, ONE MORE THING:

I apologize for bringing this up, but you may want to have both of you tested for STD's before entering a new relationship. *I know, I know,* it sounds terrible, but so are the consequences of not being careful and protecting yourself. Since Viagra became available, STDs among Baby Boomers and seniors are becoming common-place, even in retirement communities. Don't risk your health. You are no longer a teenager experiencing sex for the first time. Use your experience and knowledge to make wise decisions about how you plan to live the rest of your life as a happy, healthy adult.

ABUSE

Are you in an abusive relationship of any sort whatsoever? Does your spouse abuse you verbally or physically? Are your health and safety at risk? Is there any kind of sexual abuse from your past that has never been adequately addressed? Do you have someone in your life who constantly berates you and tells you you're not good enough, who makes you feel inadequate and imperfect? Are you the victim of some kind of harassment?

You do not deserve to be abused, and it's not your fault. You *do* know that, don't you? No one is entitled to inflict abuse on you ... either verbal or physical ... and you must free yourself of the abuse in ways that allow you to begin the healing process.

- Ask for help.
- Don't try to do it by yourself?
- Ask questions.
- Find answers.
- Set yourself free.

You goal should be that you can live the rest of your life "your" way, safe, happy, and peaceful.

ADDICTIONS

ALCOHOL AND DRUG ADDICTION

Many addicts are middle-aged, middle-class, and retired. Part of the reason for this new trend in addiction is that many Boomers are <u>bored</u> <u>with</u> <u>retirement</u>.

Isn't retirement what they waited for all their adult life?

Yet soon afterward, they complain they are bored.

Excuse me, did I miss something?

Many Boomers retired with no plan for what they will do for the next 20 or 30 years, and they are finding comfort and relief from drugs. Too many Baby Boomers who used recreational drugs during the Woodstock period of their young lives have transitioned into using prescription drugs as mood-altering substances. They don't seem to know how to deal with life without some kind of medication, legal or otherwise. When you consider that their bodies are no longer young, and may be damaged by injury or illness, their powers of recovery are significantly less than when they were young.

Historically, alcohol was the drug of choice among the elderly, but that has changed to stronger stuff. Some Baby Boomers are addicted to alcohol and/or prescription drugs, some to street drugs. It hardly matters. An addiction is an addiction. For many, what started out as pain medicine prescribed for a particular physical condition, has become, over time, an unmanageable addiction. Some people self-medicate in greater amounts than the original prescriptions, and combine those pills with other pills and alcohol, all of which exacerbates the problem … to say nothing of how much money the addiction(s) are costing.

And, who is getting rich by virtue of these addictive substances? The people selling the alcohol and the drugs and Big Pharma. Unless you are a drug dealer or a stockholder or a senior executive in one of those big drug companies, why would you be doing anything to make them rich, at the expense of the quality of your own life? *Just asking…*

In the January/February 2011 issue of AARP magazine, there is a feature article saying that millions of older Americans are confessing that they are addicts, and their addiction is tearing families apart. The article discusses the process of intervention, which is hard on the loved ones of the addict, but represents their level of desperation to "get their loved one back." These people are willing to do whatever it takes. The article also states that a lot of Baby Boomers are going into treatment programs with cocaine and heroin addictions.

Boomers are in significant denial about their addictions, yet there is a growing understanding that in the next few years, their collective need for alcohol and drug rehab will become so great as to cost in the hundreds of millions of dollars. Not only are existing rehab facilities gearing up and building additions to accommodate the growing number of people who will need their services, but new facilities are being built as well in anticipation of the need.

If you find that an addiction is causing you to live a life that is not true to yourself, does not provide you with the quality of life that you desire, give it up … whatever IT is. I know how brutal that sounds to someone suffering the effects of the addiction, but you must know that you and only you can give up the addiction. There are professionals who can guide you, but you are ultimately responsible.

And, why would you want it any other way? Why would you want someone else responsible for your life choices? Sure, you can blame it on your parents, or your friends, or society, or poverty, or the weather … but, ultimately, you chose the addiction in order to survive some particular situation, even knowing that it was not good for you. The addiction provided you with comfort you were not getting elsewhere in your life.

OK, OK, I get it. *"But you don't understand. I really need those pills."* I know you believe you can't live without them, but have you ever tried? Do you take a pill at the first sign of some anxiety or pain? Do you rely on pills to get you to sleep, and others to get you awake? Have you ever tried alternative approaches to the problems you say you have? I am trying to get you to <u>think</u> and take responsibility for your own life. Do you really want to be an addict? *I doubt it.*

**How many more days do you think you have remaining on this earth
that you are willing to waste being addicted to drugs?**

At your age, you should know better.

> **Live your own life, for you will die your own death.**
>
> Latin proverb

SHOPPING ADDICTION

(This subject is more fully examined in Chapter II – FINANCIAL.)

Do you go shopping to comfort yourself when you feel tired, or bored, or unhappy? Is shopping your mood-altering "drug of choice?" How much stuff have you bought that will never get used, things that still have the price tags on them? Are you coming close to hoarding? Are you a shopaholic? Tell the truth. You can't fix what you won't acknowledge, according to Dr. Phil.

How much credit card debt have you incurred comforting yourself with shopping? Oh, I heard you say how good you feel when you find that perfect pair of $600 shoes. Honestly, who <u>needs</u> shoes that cost $600? To that, I must ask you how good it feels when you get the credit card bill? Or, are you one of the people who doesn't even bother to open the bills, let alone pay them, because you know they will upset you.

Two sides to your shopping addition.

- Euphoria when you buy;
- Depression when the time comes to pay.

> **Too many people spend money they haven't earned,**
> **to buy things they don't want,**
> **to impress people they don't like.**
>
> Will Smith

Get rid of things you can't afford and do it now. If you can't afford the payments and the upkeep, do you *really* –

- *need* a 7,000 square foot house?
- *need* a $50,000 car to drive to work?
- *need* $600 shoes?
- *need* $2,000 purses?

How much more "stuff" do you need to make you feel good about yourself? Well, now that you have $30,000 in credit card debt from buying all that stuff, how do you feel?

- Stop the spending now.
- Pay the bills now.
- Get help to figure it all out now.

It's just arithmetic, not rocket science.

> **If your <u>INCOME</u>**
> **exceeds your <u>OUTGO</u>,**
> **your <u>UPKEEP</u>**
> **will be your <u>DOWNFALL</u>**

FOOD ADDICTION

What's eating you? Do you eat when you are lonely or bored? Do you comfort yourself with food because you are unhappy? How happy is all this eating making you? What does food provide for you that you're not getting elsewhere in your life? Answer: Unconditional approval and acknowledgement. This one I know all too well.

When did you begin overeating to comfort yourself? I know what my answer is. Do you know what YOUR answer is? Were you abused as a child (no matter what form the abuse took)? Did your parent(s) tell you that you weren't good enough? Was there verbal abuse, fighting, alcohol and/or drugs in your family? Are your parents divorced?

Overeating isn't the only problem with food addiction. There is the opposite end of the spectrum: anorexia and bulimia. Overeating can ultimately kill you, but it may take years; but anorexia and bulimia can kill you suddenly, while you are still young. Is that what you're trying to do: kill yourself?

WHAT ARE YOU TRYING TO SAY THAT ISN'T BEING HEARD?
Is your addiction solving your problems?

SPEAK YOUR OWN TRUTH FOR ONCE IN YOUR LIFE, KNOWING THAT YOUR DAYS ARE NUMBERED. TELLING THE TRUTH PROBABLY WON'T KILL YOU, BUT YOUR ADDICTION MIGHT?

WHAT'S NEXT?

Is it all right with you that you might die tomorrow, an addict to something that prevents you from being your own authentic self? Or, instead …

- will you <u>choose</u> to get the help you need?
- will you live in a story about why you didn't get help, or why you can't or won't?
- will you do whatever is necessary to beat the addiction?
- And then, will you proudly tell the story of how you did?

THE GOOD NEWS IS THAT THERE IS HELP FOR YOUR ADDICTION!

ASK FOR HELP. LOOK FOR ANSWERS. YOU WILL FIND THEM IF IT IS IMPORTANT TO YOU.

MORE ABOUT SAYING "NO"

I apologize in advance if this is a subject that sounds familiar, but I believe it is one of the single most important things a person can do in order to live a life true to one's own self.

Saying "no" without guilt might serve you well during your retirement years, when you will be putting emphasis on your own time and your own life more than ever before. Saying "no" without guilt may well be new to you, but it is not all that hard to learn.

Do you say "yes" when you really mean "no?" How often do you find yourself doing this? Is this normal behavior on your part because you find it hard to say "no" to even the simplest request? Whose feelings are you protecting?

"No" is a complete sentence. It requires no other letters or words to amplify or convey its meaning. It requires no explanation. "No" means "no." It doesn't mean maybe, or I'll think about it, or if you give me more time, I will probably change my mind and say "yes." Saying "no" skillfully can save you a lot of time, aggravation, upset, and money.

> *All the mistakes I ever made were when I wanted to say "no" and said "yes."*
>
> Moss Hart

If you believe that you are in charge of your life, responsible for your own choices, now is the time to re-learn how to say "no" *without guilt.* Do you think a 2-year old child feels guilty when they say "no?" Guilt is learned. It can just as easily be unlearned.

If it is said well, appropriately, *"without guilt"* and with intentionality, a polite "no," spoken with a firm voice and a smile on your face, can keep you out of many situations that can cause you to be really unhappy. I'm talking about both the big situations and the little ones.

Why have I pointed out the value of saying "no" *without guilt*? Because guilt is the emotion that people will use against you if they sense you are weak and easily persuaded to do something they want you to do, even if you don't really want to do it. I think a really good salesperson can "smell" guilt.

When you say "no," does the listener know you really mean it? Or do you say "no" in such a way that the listener believes (hears) that you are not really sure of yourself, especially if you give out signals that maybe the listener could change your mind. If you do that, salespeople will love you. Also, certain members of your family know when to push your "hot guilt buttons" to make you say "yes" when you want to say "no." Pay attention to how you respond to their requests.

There is an art to re-learning how to use this tiny word to your advantage. After all, you are no longer a 2-year old child expressing his/her unhappiness in the strongest way you know. You are an adult, and you have choices as to the words you use and how and when you use them. It is understandable that, at first, you may find it hard to say "no" to someone close to you. That being said, why do you struggle with saying "no" to a salesperson you don't even know? What do you care what they think of you?

You may have to start saying "no" in baby steps until you feel comfortable saying it, and soon, you will begin to feel confident and proud of yourself for standing in your own truth and no longer allowing people to take advantage of you.

If you find yourself regularly being pressured by certain people to do something you don't want to do, you have to ask yourself why you allow that to happen, and begin to examine your motives and intentions, not theirs. Family and friends ask you because they have an expectation that you will say "yes" sooner or later because you have a history of doing that, and they know that if they put enough pressure on you, you will cave in. What is your payoff for saying "yes" when you mean "no?" Do you think that other people's requests are more important than your protecting yourself?

It is important to examine how and when you use the word "no" in your life. Can you say "no" to the small stuff, but cave in to pressure if you perceive the request to be big, or if it comes from someone who, in the past, has been able to successfully exert pressure on you, or from someone you think is really important ... like a boss, or a doctor, or a salesperson? Can you say no to strangers, but not to loved ones or friends?

Let's look at some ways in which you say "no."

- Do you have a history of saying "yes" when you mean "no"?

- Do you believe something terrible will happen if you say "no," or worry that someone won't like you if you do?

- Did your parents teach you that it is not polite to say "no" or that if you say "no," you are being selfish?

- Do you say "no" and soon after, change it to "yes?"
  Do you know why? Do others know this about you and use it against you?

- Do you feel guilty when you say "no?" Why?

- Do you say "no" until someone pressures you to change your mind by inflicting "guilt" upon you?

- Have you ever been caught up in a scam because you said "yes" when you should have said "no"? How much money did you lose in the transaction? Did you tell your family or financial advisor?

- Do you think before you say "no," or do you say "no" automatically?

- After you say "yes" when you mean "no," do you experience regret? How do you deal with it?

- Do you have trouble saying "no" to friends and loved ones?

- Can you say "no" to your doctor? This is a big one. There are times when saying "no" to your doctor is the most intelligent thing you can do for yourself? Can you distinguish those times, or do you always say "yes" and sometimes regret it afterward?

- Can you say "no" when someone close to you asks to borrow money?

- Can you say "no" when someone close to you asks you to co-sign for an apartment lease, or a car loan, or a student loan? Do you know the consequences for you if you co-sign for something and the other person defaults?

- Have you ever said "yes" to something when you really wanted to say "no", and afterward, found yourself holding the bag (whatever that "bag" turned out to be?) … for instance, a loan on which you co-signed?

- When you say "*No I need some time to think about it,*" are you genuinely committed to investigating your options, or are you just putting off the inevitable time when you will cave in and say "yes?"

- Can you easily say "no" to salespeople attempting to sell you something you don't need, want, or even like?

- What about high-pressure salespeople attempting to sell you something you really like, but cannot afford?

- Can you say "no" to random phone calls from (alleged) charities?

- Are you able to say an easy "no" when your instinct kicks in and you feel something is amiss with an offer for something that sounds too good to be true, or have you become accustomed to ignoring your instincts?

- Have you ever said "yes" when your lawyer (or your doctor) asked you if you understand, when you mean "no" because you do <u>not</u> understand? Why did you do that?

- Can you say "no" to your mother when she asks you to drive her to the doctor's office tomorrow morning but you have a hairdresser appointment at that same time, especially after she reveals that she has had the appointment for a month and is just now asking you? What about when she says you are being selfish? What about when she says that her appointment is more important than yours?

- Can you say "no" to your daughter who needs you to be the primary child-care person for her pre-school age children?

- Can you say "no" to your daughter when she asks to borrow your fur coat (or your car, or money) and you know she is irresponsible with her own possessions?

- Do you say, "*Of course I don't mind, I'd be happy to (fill in the blank   ),*" when your mind is shouting "NO!"

- Do you say, "*Of course I would love to (fill in the blank   ),*" when it is the last thing on earth you would ever want to do?

- When you do say "no", do you have a compulsive need to go to great lengths to explain why, when no explanation is necessary?

- When someone asks you to do something you don't want to do, can you say, without guilt, "*No thank you, I have other plans,*" even if those other plans are to stay home, relax and read a book?

Once you have mastered the art of appropriately saying "no" *without guilt*, your life becomes your own. At first, people may say you are being selfish. That would be only natural, because you have taught them that your usual response is "yes." They will be surprised, possibly even angry, when you first say "no." Allow them this response, but don't cave in to their pressure, and don't feel obligated to apologize. As people in your life become accustomed to your saying "no", they may stop asking you to do things for them. It is, after all, your life, your time, and your money.

And, not to get too far into the psychology of this, if you have a long history of saying "yes" when you mean "no", have you enabled some of the people in your life? Have you weakened their ability to take responsibility for their own actions? *Just asking…*

It is entirely possible that for most of your life, when you said "yes" to things you didn't want to do in the first place, people who did the asking didn't even know you really wanted to say "no." How could they? They're not mind readers. If you said "yes" and you meant "no," is it any wonder people keep asking you.

After a while, as you begin to say "no" appropriately, your intentions will match your words and your words will match your actions. I think you will find it an enormous relief to feel what it's like to finally be honest with yourself and others. Wouldn't it be nice, as Suze Orman says, to live in your own truth.

AND, ONE LAST THING:

It is important that when you say "no," you do so with confidence that it is the right thing for you. Say it firmly but politely, with a smile on your face and consideration for the other person's feelings. You will not benefit from speaking the word harshly, with defiance or attitude in your voice. Think how you would feel if the situation were reversed.

SPIRITUALITY

This is about as individual and personal as any subject in the world.

- Do you attend the church of your parents or your spouse just to make them happy?

- Do you feel at peace with what you hear and observe there?

- Do you have questions that you'd like answered, but don't know where to begin?

- Have you been criticized by people in your life who don't even like the fact that you have questions, and so you've given up your inquiry?

- If you are dissatisfied with your spiritual life as it is today, change it before you run out of days.

When your last moment in time arrives, it will be you and you alone, embarking on your spirit's journey ... by yourself, without all those other people. They cannot go with you, so why should they have any say in how you choose to nourish your spiritual life on this Earth?

PROFESSIONAL SUPPORT

For some aspects of your life, you may find it beneficial to seek the support of professional counselors. Most people don't have any problems consulting a physician, so why are they reluctant to consult other professionals such as:

- Accountant
- Acupuncture Therapist
- Addiction Counselor
- Financial Planner
- Lawyer
- Nutritionist
- Personal Coach
- Personal Trainer
- Professional Organizer
- Psychiatrist/Psychologist
- All other possible qualified counselors

There is no shame in asking for help. Just try to ask the right people. You yourself can't know everything.

No one expects you to?
Or do they?
Or do you?

The people in your life all say how independent and self-sufficient you have always been. Do they know your real story?

- *Don't tell them if you don't want to, especially if there is nothing to be gained by including them in your life's troubles. Be careful to whom you bare your soul.*

If you don't feel comfortable with your counselor, get another. If you have any instinctive feeling that you don't trust a particular counselor, get another. Don't wait. Don't feel embarrassed. Don't feel the need to apologize. This is about taking care of yourself in a time of need, no matter how trivial it may seem to you or anyone else.

PEOPLE LOVE LISTS!

We anxiously wait for the list of Oscar nominations, the 10 best beaches, the top 5 vacation spots in the world, the best (and worst) dressed personalities, best schools, the best movies, best-selling books, restaurants. The lists are endless.

Next, you might want to list the enormous, *actually infinite*, number of possibilities that are open to you in this life from which to choose things to do *between now and then*.

WHAT KIND OF THINGS?
EVERYTHING IN THE WORLD!

I gave you a CHOICE TICKET. Use it.

MAKE LISTS.
READ, PRIORITIZE, AND REVISE THEM REGULARLY

I like making lists, because, for me, the process takes things out of my head and puts them on paper where I can contemplate them … slowly, one against the other, over time … and once the ideas are on paper, I won't forget them.

If you make a list and begin with the major aspects of your life … fun, creativity, future, career, family, marriage, abuse, addictions, health, spirituality, finances … you will have the beginning of a good list. As you examine each of these areas individually … and any others that are important to you … determine what you want from each category as well as what you don't want. It is sometimes in the "Don't Want" columns that you find the answers you are looking for.

Maybe your list should contain two columns captioned PRO and CON. Making a list like this can help you compare the good aspects of an idea with those that may not be so good. It really does help to see the ideas in writing.

I recommend that you prioritize your lists and set timelines for making your ideas happen. They might not happen otherwise.

For years, I talked about wanting to own and operate a flower shop. It was a vague idea, and I had given no real thought about how to make it happen. One day in December, a friend asked me, "So, when are you going to open that flower shop you keep talking about?" And, to my utter amazement, I replied, "August 14th." I had not given that date any prior thought; the words just came to me. Turns out, it was the anniversary of the date of my mother's death, and it seemed perfect. So, on August 14th the following year, I opened Blue Gardenia. Once I had spoken the date, everything fell easily and quickly into place. That's how it works.

Make your own list of all the things you really want to do *between now and then*, establish priorities and deadlines, and then relax and watch them happen. It's really a lot of fun to stretch your imagination when it comes to things you want to do in your own life. Have you ever given yourself permission to dream?

I gave you a PERMISSION SLIP. Use it.

An idea not coupled with action will never get any bigger than the brain cell it occupied.

Arnold H. Glasow

As you create your lists, look for patterns of areas in your life that may have been neglected, that are crying out for attention. It may not be prudent for you to give up your day job and devote all your time pursuing a hobby; but, if it is something you have always wanted to do, something that you long to do and that calls to you, it is important that you at least try it. If it is something you have been putting off "until later," later is today! And, if it turns out you don't like it, so what? Try something else.

You can add that hobby to your life in a committed way, to honor your own desire and need for self-expression, all without taking time away from your other obligations. By satisfying your personal needs in little ways, even a couple of different ways, you get to cross these things off your list of things you always wanted to do but never got around to doing.

You may also begin to feel better physically, have more energy, be more relaxed, because you will finally be doing something for yourself. *Imagine how good that will feel!*

It is time to use your ROUND TUIT!

THE REGRET TEST

In deciding what you want and don't want to do *between now and then*,
I recommend **THE REGRET TEST**. It goes like this:

If, on the last day of your life, there is something you always wanted to do, but have <u>not</u> done,
will you regret not having done it?
If the answer is yes, then you must begin right away!

DO YOU HAVE A LONG LIST OF THINGS YOU WANT TO DO *between now and then?*

It doesn't matter if the things you want to do are large or small. Either way, now is the time to begin making <u>your</u> own "Bucket List." But, you say, you wouldn't know where to begin. How about things like:

- Be a tour guide for whitewater rafting trips down the Colorado River.
- Volunteer for Habitat for Humanity.
- Live in Paris for 5 years and tour France extensively to paint and soak up the culture.
- Marry the girl or boy of your dreams.
- Establish a shelter for abandoned cats and dogs.
- Learn German, French, Russian, Japanese and Hebrew fluently.
- Play bassoon with the Boston Symphony Orchestra.
- Live in a house on the beach.
- Operate a bed & breakfast.
- Write a book (this was high on my priority list).
- Begin reading all those books you have been anxious to read.
- Get a dog and show it in the Westminster Dog Show.
- Adopt a child, or a cat, or a dog (or two).
- Redecorate your living room.
- Buy a convertible.
- Change the color of your hair.
- Anything else you long for in the deepest place in your heart.

Your list does not have to include monumental things like some of the items above. The things on your list can be little things you simply never took the time to do.

And, don't forget to share your "Bucket List" with your loved ones. They may be upset when you tell them what you want (need) to do, so speak softly and sincerely so they will hear and understand. Ask them if they, too, have a "Bucket List." Compare your ideas. It may even be easier to make things happen together. *Just my opinion...*

> **The indispensable first step to getting the things you want out of life is this:**
> **decide what you want.**
>
> Ben Stein

Once you have made your list, establish priorities and make a plan:

- For every item on your list, give each a priority designation representing the level of importance to you.
- Give each important item a deadline for when you will have accomplished it.
- Pick one task you believe you can accomplish within a reasonable time.
- Begin.

> **Many men go fishing all of their lives without knowing that it is not fish they are after.**
>
> Henry David Thoreau

I am not going to tell you that it will be easy to achieve all your goals:

- it may be difficult,
- it may cost you money,
- it may require you to have difficult conversations you would rather avoid,
- it may take time, maybe even more time than you imagined, and
- you may not finish your list, but it is important that you begin.

> **In the middle of difficulty lies opportunity.**
>
> Albert Einstein

On the other hand, maybe you only *think* it will be hard and take a long time, but you don't know for sure because you never really tried any of the things on your list. I thought it would be hard to open and operate a flower shop. Turns out, it was simple. All I had to do was give myself permission to do it.

Remember, if you don't even try, how will you ever know what you are capable of accomplishing?

While you are writing your list, there are a few more lists that may help you achieve focus, excitement, energy and satisfaction from your life. An exercise I really like from Dr. Phil's book, *Self Matters*, includes naming the:

- **10 Defining Moments in your life**
- **7 Critical Choices you made**
- **5 Most Pivotal People**

As you make these 3 lists, write notes about why you made each choice, and why each is significant for you. This exercise will cause you to think about how you got to this place in your life, who helped you, and who may have hindered you.

And, guess, what? The good news is that you made it this far, and I'm pretty sure you're going to make it the rest of the way.

Each new day is a new opportunity to live your life your way.

If you are a person inclined to make lists, I recommend a book titled, *List Your Self*, by Ilene Segalove and Paul Bob Velick. Every page has a specific topic. You can fill in the blanks for some or all of the lists, at your own pace. Let the topics inspire and guide you.

THINGS TO STOP DOING

And, as long as you are making lists, make a list of "Things To <u>Stop</u> Doing." Your goal is to stop doing things that are keeping you from living your own authentic life, or keeping you from spending time with people who are important to you, or doing projects and activities you really enjoy.

Do you want to stop smoking? Shopping? Overeating? Drinking to excess? If you need help to accomplish these goals, seek it. You might not be able to do these things without professional support and guidance.

Examine how you keep yourself busy (you watch too much TV, eat when you are bored, and attend social functions you really don't want to attend), and then establish new priorities for yourself once you have determined what is important.

FROM COMPLAINT TO POSSIBILITY

How does that statement sound to you? Some people think it is not reasonable. But, I recommend that, before you quickly dismiss the statement as ridiculous, you try the following exercise.

• Make a <u>list of all your complaints</u> -- in your personal life, in your family, your workplace, the world. Don't forget little things, like how you complain about traffic, and "rainy days and Mondays." Include <u>everything</u>.

• And THEN, try to turn each complaint into a possibility. That is the challenge and the fun. You'd be amazed at how creative you can be.

> *A simple example would be your daily complaint about potholes in streets. The possibility comes from your contacting someone who can fix the problem. It might only take a phone call or two. Your complaining, by itself, will not fix the problem. But, there is someone who can. Get in touch with that person.*

Apply this same theory to all of your complaints. Figure out if you are the person who can remedy the situation, or if there is someone else you need to contact to fix the problem, and then turn your complaint into a possibility. A complaint can be the source of progress. Some remedies are that simple.

And, don't be one of those people who believes all complaints are negative. Complaints offer infinite possibilities for improvement. If you are cursing the darkness, light a candle, to paraphrase one of Ben Franklin's statements. Every invention came out of a complaint, no matter how trivial. If you don't believe me, think of those yellow *Post-It* notes as an example of how a simple complaint turned not only into a possibility, but into a multi-million dollar invention.

Life isn't about finding yourself. Life is about creating yourself.

George Bernard Shaw

WHAT ARE YOU WAITING FOR?

What if you find yourself old and sick and realize it's too late?

Will you regret not having taken those piano lessons, when there was no <u>real</u> reason for not doing it?

IF IT'S IMPORTANT TO YOU, JUST DO IT!

You may find that in taking those piano lessons now, you don't like playing the piano half as much as you thought you would. That's terrific! Cross it off your "To Do" list and move on to something else.

Trying some of the things on your list is a great way to eliminate the things you only "think" you want to do, and which you may not actually like once you've done them. You can once and for all give up that story you've been telling yourself for years that says, "*If only I had taken piano lessons, then my life would have been better (different), etc.*" <u>Give it up!</u>

The idea is to try them all … *big things and small things* … fill up your life with activities that honor YOU for a change.

EMERGENCY PLANNING

For some emergencies, there is time to prepare, but more often than not, there is NO TIME. By definition, an emergency is something that comes to you out of the blue, suddenly, unexpectedly. This is why planning is so important and necessary. **Be prepared** was a life lesson taught to children in the Boy Scouts and Girl Scouts.

There are LITTLE emergencies that require only a first-aid kit; and then there are BIGGER emergencies, like your car breaking down on an unfamiliar country road; and then there are ENORMOUS emergencies. You know the kind.

What word is big enough to adequately describe the triple-blow that happened to Japan early in 2011 … an earthquake, a tsunami and nuclear danger all at the same time. What about hurricanes Katrina or Sandy?

I know that you can't plan for every eventuality, but being prepared for some of the obvious ones would make sense. Emergencies happen every day, somewhere, somehow. *Of course, they always happen to someone else, don't they?* Sometimes. Sometimes not. So, if an emergency of any kind should happen to you or your loved ones or anyone else in your life … *anywhere* … would you (would they) be prepared to handle the situation?

While you are taking your beginning steps toward living your own life, *your way*, I recommend that you give serious thought to planning for emergencies, all the while praying they never happen. Think of emergency planning the same way you think of auto insurance: you are prepared by having insurance coverage for something you hope never happens. <u>After all, this book *is* about planning</u>.

Before proceeding, I'm going to once again ask you if you have taken care of items of personal business I stressed in the beginning of this chapter:

1. Your Estate-Planning documents.
2. Your one-year Emergency Fund.
3. Your personal papers and documents organized in one easily accessible place.

I sincerely hope your answer is YES; and don't tell me you haven't done them yet because you've been busy, or you haven't gotten around to it, or you'll do it later, or you're still thinking about it. Those excuses won't work any longer.

> *One of the greatest discoveries a man makes …*
> *is to find he can do what he was afraid he couldn't do.*
>
> Henry Ford

Financial planners and lawyers, even Suze Orman, will tell you of the importance of these "To Dos." As far as Suze Orman is concerned, they are not optional. I agree.

Speaking of Suzy Orman, on her TV show of September 10, 2011, she asked her viewers if they had taken her advice from 10 years ago? What advice? It was advice she gave on her TV show immediately after the 9/11 disaster when she discovered that many people who died did not even have Wills. She told people to get their "documents" prepared, and to do it right away. On this recent show, she asked how many viewers had actually taken her advice? She speculated that the number was low. Do you think she was correct? Why is that?

She was, of course, speaking of a Will, a Revocable Living Trust, a Power-of-Attorney for Healthcare, and an Advance Directive (a/k/a Living Will).

- It's interesting to me that she does not include a General Durable Power-of-Attorney in her recommendation, but I believe it is because she recommends that the basic terms and conditions contained in this document be spelled out in the Revocable Living Trust (for example, an incapacity clause).

Once again, from the top ...

Have you had your legal documents prepared yet?

Have you been making regular deposits into your emergency fund?

Have you begun working on your "bucket list?"

Have you had some of those "hard" conversations yet?

Have you examined your insurance coverage lately?

And, once again, if not, why not? When do you plan to take care of these items of personal business?

WHAT CONSTITUTES AN EMERGENCY?

- Would it be a fire in your home?

- Loss of electric power for an extended period of time?

- Or would it be some other huge natural event over which you have no control -- the kind of natural disaster that insurance companies call "acts of God."

- Would it be a phone call in the middle of the night, telling you that a loved one has been injured, or worse?

- Would it be a life-altering injury from an accident, or some other medical emergency?

- Would it be the sudden death of a member of your family?

Some emergencies respond to good advance planning. Others do not. You cannot know if/when someone you love will die suddenly, or be injured in an accident. You cannot predict when a fire will destroy your home. For weather-related incidents, advanced planning can sometimes make the difference between whether you, your loved ones, your pets, and your home survive or not.

And even when the best planning fails, you can have adequate insurance coverage, and you can have a substantial emergency fund and an emergency plan, and you can have all of your legal documents signed, sealed, delivered, and safeguarded along with all your important personal papers and documents so that you will have some protection when events like this occur.

The question is: Do you have those things in place?

We live in an uncertain world in uncertain times. Not all terrorists are from foreign countries. There are terrible acts committed by domestic terrorists, too, including young people who go to school with guns and kill people, cop-killers, murders of family members. One might even say that Mother Nature is a terrorist.

Every day, we read or hear about a crisis (whether natural or man-made) that has seriously damaged people and places: floods, hurricanes, wildfires, a volcano, tsunamis, earthquakes, mud-slides, tornadoes, blizzards, droughts. The loss from such occurrences in the last few years is incalculable, for individuals and for the economy.

MEDICAL EMERGENCIES

While it is possible to prepare for many emergencies, preparing for medical emergencies is a different story. Most people know that taking good care of their bodies and their health can reduce the chances of some medical events that can quickly become real emergencies, but not always. There is little a person can do to predict, let alone, prevent medical emergencies such as injuries sustained in vehicle accidents, falls, fires, lightning, injury from gun-fire. So what is there to be done?

- Think about how you feel about extreme medical treatment, and determine what you would want and what you would not want.

- Be the person to open the discussion with your family about your decisions. **Tell** them what you want <u>and</u> what you do not what, in very clear, precise language. They are not mind readers. Do your absolute best to make them hear and understand you, and make them understand that you **expect** them to honor your wishes.

- Before you strongly announce that you want to be kept alive at all cost, that you want the full actions of the medical establishment to do everything possible to keep you alive, I recommend that you learn as much as possible about some of the major medical conditions and situations that can happen in a medical emergency; for example, what happens when you are put on a ventilator; what does "full code" mean; what happens if you are comatose for a long time, etc. This information will help you decide what you would want for care if you were ever to be in an extreme (possibly terminal) medical situation and to determine and clearly state your own personal limits to extreme medical treatment. (*think Terry Schiavo*)

- Research your options (medical professionals, hospice organizations, home health agencies, nursing homes, etc.) before the need arises. Create your own file of relevant information for future reference.

- The medical profession generally does not determine the treatment given to a patient based upon the cost. If you state that you want all sorts of extreme medical treatment, etc., determine whether or not the money will be well spent to save you, or will it be spent in a futile attempt to keep you alive in the face of medical evidence that you are near death? Will your choice put your family into financial ruin in the event of your eventual death? *Just something else to think about...*

- Know how you define quality of life for yourself. If existing in a hospital bed, attached to mechanical equipment for a long period of time does not fit into your definition of the quality of life you want for yourself, then you must tell your family how you feel.

- Before you make your selections on a Living Will, have a good understanding of what actually will happen to you and your body for each of those choices. Initiate conversations with your doctor about the realities of extreme medical situations. Ask questions and require answers. After all, how can you make an <u>informed</u> <u>choice</u> without all the facts?

- Have a clear understanding of your choices and the consequences of each, including the choice to do nothing.

- Consult with a lawyer experienced in estate-planning or elder- or healthcare law so that you will have a good understanding of what a Living Will and a Healthcare Power-of-Attorney can do for you and what they cannot do for you. Ask questions, and require answers. (More about these documents in Chapter I – LEGAL).

- Select the <u>right</u> person to act as your Agent under your Living Will and Healthcare Power-of-Attorney. Who would that person be in your life? It should be **the** person you would trust with your life … the person who will be prepared to hold fast to what YOU want, and not what everyone else in your family wants. Your failure to appoint an agent and to sign appropriate legal documents could eventually cause you to suffer more than you may want to, and if it is your choice to put these legal and medical decisions on hold until "*later*," know that someone else may have to make the decisions anyway, so it might as well be you. Without your written intentions and instructions and without your appointment of an agent, there can be huge conflict among your family members and the medical professionals, each of whom has an opinion about your medical treatment that may be significantly different than yours.

- Have your documents signed and safeguarded, and let people know where to find them. Make sure your doctors know your intentions. Give them copies of the documents for their files.

- Know to dial 911 in a medical emergency, even if you think the need is not catastrophic. You might be right, but then again, you might be wrong.

- Consider getting one of those Medic-Alert systems, especially if you live alone.

- Remember that there are worse things than dying.
  If you don't believe me, read *Last Wish* by Lauren Van Scoy, MD.

FAMILY PLANNING MEETING

This family meeting is to be separate from the meeting about estate planning. Although they, like many things in this book, overlap. the two topics are way too broad to be discussed at the same time.

What you CANNOT have in your family is a <u>failure to communicate!</u> Before an emergency occurs, you and your family members must have some kind of plans "just in case." I recommend a family meeting for the purpose of discussing and making emergency plans, and then agreeing upon them.

> ### *The greatest problem with communication is the illusion that it has been accomplished.*
>
> George Bernard Shaw

Oh, I hear you already, complaining that you can never get everybody together at one place at the same time. It doesn't matter if your kids don't want to be there, or if they whine and complain.

YOU MUST MAKE THIS MEETING HAPPEN, AND THEY MUST ATTEND.

When you finally get your family together to talk about emergency planning, <u>do not surrender to their usual complaint:</u>

"Oh, Mom, you worry too much. Nothing's going to happen."

And, make it understood from the beginning that everyone stays for the entire meeting. Nobody gets a free pass to make an early exit for any reason. What could possibly be more important than the safety and preparedness of your family? And, don't forget your kids who are living away from home, in college, or on their own, away from your family home. <u>They, too, must be included in this planning meeting, one way or another.</u>

- *If there are young children in your family, arrange for someone (not a family member) to provide care for the children during the time it takes to complete the meeting. Everyone must agree to this so that the purpose of the meeting can be accomplished quickly and without distraction.*

An emergency may not happen to your family ... *and I pray it never does* ... but it does happen to some families. Every member of your family must be made to understand that it is both important and necessary to be prepared for life's twists and turns to the greatest extent possible.

If there are young children in your family, do they know how to make a 911 emergency call? I mean, beyond dialing the numbers? Do they know how to speak with the operator to state where they are (their address)? Can they adequately describe the emergency situation to the operator, who will continue to ask questions, which I believe can be very upsetting to the caller, especially if the caller is a child. Maybe you could practice a few times to prepare your children to make such a call if necessary. You may also want to take time to educate your young children as to what to do in an emergency if you, yourself, become ill or injured, and you need the child to call for help.

Don't forget to talk about what your young children or grandchildren should do if they ever get separated from you in a crowd. Do they have some form of identification on them at all times? Would they know how to get in touch with you? Do they know your full name, your home, work and cell phone numbers, their home address?

- (If you were to ask many little children what their mother's name is, they would reply, "*Mommy*.")
  Just more things to think about ...

> ### And, while you're discussing emergency plans,
> ### don't forget to stress the importance of each adult's having a Healthcare Power-of-Attorney and a Living Will ...
> ### that is, every person in your family over 18 years of age.

If you can afford it, why don't you pay a lawyer to prepare at least these two documents for your young adult children. It would be a wonderful gift, and you might get some peace of mind from knowing they have the protection of the documents.

HAVE YOU EVER HAD A "FIRE DRILL" IN YOUR HOUSE?

A fire leaves no times for thinking. Instinct and preparedness must kick in immediately to save your lives and the lives of your children and pets.

- Do you have fire extinguishers for "small" fires?

- Do you check them periodically to see if they work perfectly?

- Does everyone in your family know how to use them?

- Does your family have an escape plan if there is a fire in your house?

- Have you ever had an actual fire drill?

- Do you have stickers on your windows to indicate to firefighters where the children are sleeping?

- Do you have stickers on your windows to indicate that you have pets?

- Do you have smoke detectors with good batteries? Do you replace the batteries at least annually?

- Do you have carbon monoxide detectors? Do you check the batteries periodically?

- Do you have your chimneys safety checked at least annually?

- Are all your important papers (including photographs of your possessions) in a water- and fire-proof safe in your home, or in the alternative, in a bank safe deposit box?

- Do you know where your "grab and run" suitcases and pet carriers are so you can get to them on a moment's notice?

- Do you have <u>enough</u> homeowner's and flood insurance?

- Do you have photographs of your home (inside and outside) and all your furnishings and valuable possessions? Where do you keep them? or did you take the cheap way out, not wanting to pay for sufficient replacement insurance coverage, saying there will never be a fire or flood? Insurance money can go a long way toward replacing your lost or damaged stuff.

- Maybe you should re-evaluate (and possibly increase) your insurance coverage to see if it is sufficient to replace damaged property.

- If you rent, do you have renters' insurance for the contents of your apartment? Your landlord's insurance will not cover the loss of your personal possessions. It is an **_in_**expensive investment to protect your possessions from loss.

- Have you safeguarded your family photos from fire and flood?

WHERE WILL YOU AND THE MEMBERS OF YOUR FAMILY BE WHEN THE EMERGENCY HAPPENS?
WHERE WILL YOUR PETS BE?

Chances are very good that if an emergency occurred during daylight hours, that was so huge as to involve your entire family, you would find yourselves in different places. If such an emergency happened at night, chances are good you would all be home together, but not necessarily.

Be prepared for either eventuality.

<u>HOW WOULD YOUR FAMILY MEMBERS GET IN TOUCH WITH EACH OTHER IN AN EMERGENCY?</u>

You must agree (in advance … preferably at the family meeting) upon a specific meeting place that everyone knows about, when each member of your family is in a different place when an emergency happens.

- You could agree to meet at a nearby hotel lobby or a public building. Pick two locations, and give one of them the priority, but if it is not available, then the second location would be the meeting place.

- Each person should have the address, directions how to get there and a phone number (if possible), and some means of transportation.

- Each person agrees to show up at that place as soon as they are able.

YOUR BEST LINE OF COMMUNICATION IS YOUR CELL PHONE!

- Everyone agrees to KEEP THEIR CELL PHONE WITH THEM AT ALL TIMES, FULLY CHARGED. Everyone also agrees to carry their chargers with them.

- Every member of your family either knows each other's cell phone numbers from memory, or has a written list of the numbers with them at all times, or has everyone's phone numbers stored in their hand-held cell phones.

- Each person agrees to have some sort of identification on their person, which includes the name of the person to contact in an emergency

- Each person agrees to keep in regular phone communication with each other;

This is no place or time for a breakdown in communication.

"What we have here is ... failure to com-MU-ni-cate!"

This line is spoken by the Captain of the Prison Chain Gang
in the movie, "Cool Hand Luke," starring Paul Newman.

COMMUNICATION CENTRAL

This is another topic for discussion during your emergency planning meeting with your family. Let's say, for example, you live in a place that is known for harsh winters, deep snow, storms that cause power outages of enormous magnitude, vehicles and people stranded on highways or in office buildings or shopping centers for hours or days, without heat, light, food, water, blankets, medicine.

Agree upon a specific person you all know, and who knows you, and who lives far away, in a geographical area that would not likely be struck by the same storm or other extreme weather situation ... for example, if you live in the north, perhaps select someone who lives in Florida or Arizona.

- Ask them if they are willing to be the center of communication for your family in an emergency.

- This person could be either a relative or a close friend, and would agree, in advance, to serve as the center of communication for your family if you were all separated by an emergency.

- Each person in your family would have the name, address and phone number(s), and email addresses of the designated person.

- Each person, as soon as they are safe and able to make a phone call, would call the designated person to say they are safe (or not), and to give their whereabouts, and to find out about the other members of their family ... who has reported in, and who has not ... the idea being to stay in constant communication with your loved ones through this designated person.

WHERE WILL YOUR CHILDREN (GRANDCHILDREN) BE?

What about your young children or grandchildren who may be at a Day-Care Center, or your children who are each in different schools, and your children living away in college?

- I recommend that you meet with the people in charge of the Day-Care Center and schools to find out what their emergency plans are, how they would locate and communicate with you, how they would provide safety for your children.

- You must do everything possible to see that your young child is never left alone, crying, waiting for you, afraid you forgot them. Assure them that you will come for them.

- Get information from your child's college about their plans for emergencies and how they would communicate with you.

- Get it in writing.

HOW WOULD YOU PROVIDE EMERGENCY ASSISTANCE TO A FAMILY MEMBER WHO WAS DISABLED, BEDRIDDEN, OR ELDERLY?

This is not an easy one. Every situation will require very specific plans, and the time to think about the plans and to discuss them among family members is NOW, before an emergency. Time is your enemy.

If a member of your family resides elsewhere due to infirmity or old age, you should meet with the administrator of the facility to learn about their plans for emergencies or evacuation. Ask for printed material containing names of contact persons and phone numbers, and give them all your contact information, too.

EMERGENCY MONEY

Do you have some cash put safely away in your home in case of emergency, cash that you could take with you on a moment's notice? How much cash would be enough? I don't know; it would depend on your circumstances, the number of people in your family, etc. You will have to make that determination yourself. Before you come up with a list of reasons why this is a bad idea, why don't you just do it instead? Get a small fireproof box and keep it in an accessible place. How hard is that?

- Keep in mind that bank machines (ATMs) will not work during a power failure; in fact, even the banks might be closed. But, you say, you can always cash a check at the supermarket, but what if they are closed, too? There will be no time to drive around looking for a place to cash a check, that is, of course, assuming it is safe to drive. And, it is doubtful if you could pay for gas and groceries with gold bars.

> *There are risks and costs to action.*
> *But they are far less than the long-range risks of comfortable inaction.*
>
> John F. Kennedy

- And, let's take a look at the benefits provided to victims of natural disasters from FEMA. That assistance usually comes in the form of low-interest loans, not cash to rebuild or restore your lost possessions. Without an emergency fund, how would you be able to pay back a loan? *Just asking ...*

The best suggestion I can give you is to figure out how to <u>save lots of money for a rainy day</u>. It's an old adage, but oh so true. And, it is probably a good idea to keep a reasonably large sum of money in your home. The problem is to decide where to put it so it will be both safe and accessible.

And, while you're contemplating emergencies, don't forget actual financial emergencies, like loss of your retirement fund for any number of reasons, loss of investments from someone like Bernie Madoff, long-term unemployment, bankruptcy, foreclosure, disability or illness that prevents you from earning a living. If you had an adequate Emergency Fund, you would have fewer worries than if you did not. Why am I even telling you this? You already know it.

> *Once on the Dr. Phil show, a young woman was **whining** about her wedding's being a "disaster" because something didn't go exactly as she wanted it. Oh, gee...*
>
> *Dr. Phil encouraged her to rethink the way she uses words to describe life situations, and that "disaster" did not even come close to describing what happened at her wedding when compared to the enormous natural and/or man-made catastrophes that happened in the world during the last few years.*

During the last few years, the world has endured some horrific natural events in relation to weather. Extreme wildfires in Arizona. Heat waves in Texas and the entire southwest. Weather as hot as 105 degrees in the far central northern states. Tornadoes in the central and eastern states. Hurricanes through the east that even devastated New Jersey and states as far north as Vermont, where covered bridges were washed away and burial caskets unearthed because of heavy rains. Power failure to hundreds of thousands of people, some lasting for days. So many people suffered unimaginable loss due to extreme weather.

Of course, this is not the first time such disasters have occurred. Nature has always done a lot of damage to the things of civilization (think Vesuvius and Pompeii). One must wonder why people keep on living in places that regularly flood or burn in wildfires? I've heard them say it is because they love it there. I get that, but I personally would not be able to tolerate more than one flood or fire that damaged my house and all my possessions. *But, hey, that's just me.*

I again recommend that you carefully check your homeowners' insurance policy (or meet with your insurance agent) to determine exactly what is a covered loss and what is not, especially in relation to damage from wind and water (flooding, hurricanes, etc.). Homeowners' insurance policies often do not cover such losses without riders. It's better to be safe than sorry.

SUGGESTED SUPPLIES YOU WOULD NEED IN AN EMERGENCY

In your home:

Do you have <u>in your home</u> at this moment, a sufficient supply of things you would need were you and/or your geographic region to be without heat and electricity for a week? For example:

- Appropriate clothing
- Battery operated lighting; extra batteries
- Bread, crackers, cereal, snacks
- Bucket(s) and sponge(s)
- Candles and matches
- Canned Goods and hand-held can opener or pop-top cans
- Cash
- Cell phones and automobile chargers
- Chlorine bleach with eye dropper to treat non-bottled water for drinking
  (8 drops of bleach per gallon; 16 drops if the water is muddy or cloudy)
- Face masks for dust, smoke, mold
- Fire Extinguisher
- First-Aid Kit (*)
- Flashlights and batteries and/or LED lights
- Food (bread, cheese, hard-boiled eggs, salads, snacks, fruit, peanut butter and jelly)
- Full tank of gas in your car

- ▪ Gloves (sanitary and heavy-duty work gloves)
- ▪ Medications (2-week supply)
- ▪ Milk, juice, coffee, tea, fruit (fresh or canned)
- ▪ Pet food
- ▪ Portable battery-operated radio
- ▪ Powdered Milk
- ▪ Tarps, plastic sheeting and duct tape
- ▪ Tools (hammer, screwdrivers, pliers, scissors)
- ▪ Towels (extra for flooding or leaks)
- ▪ Water for drinking and food preparation
  (1 gallon of water per person per day; 14-day supply)
- ▪ Water for dishwashing; flushing your toilet, bathing and personal hygiene:
  fill your bathtub(s) with clean water for these purposes (have a clean bucket ready).
  In the alternative, fill plastic gallon-jugs with clean water and put them in your bathtub.

(*) Your First-Aid Kit should be water-proof and be quickly and easily transported if necessary. A plastic tool box would be perfect. Basic necessities for your First-Aid Kit should include:

- • Antacid
- • Antibiotic ointment
- • Anti-diarrhea medication
- • Aspirin or other non-prescription pain relievers
- • Burn ointment
- • Eyewash (for flushing contaminants)
- • Hand-sanitizer
- • Hearing aids and extra batteries
- • Laxative
- • Multi-purpose pocket knife
- • Plastic bags in various sizes
- • Soap
- • Spare eyeglasses and/or contact lenses
- • Sterile dressings and adhesive bandages
- • Sterile gloves (2 pairs)
- • Thermometer
- • Toilet paper
- • Toothbrushes and toothpaste/mouthwash
- • Wipes

In your Vehicle:

I believe it is essential to belong to an automobile club (e.g., AAA, or an auto club provided by the manufacturer of your vehicle). Being out on the road is not always safe in many areas due to the dense population and the high number of cars on the road at the same time. And, then, at the opposite end of the spectrum, there are the back roads where you may be the only car for miles. In either scenario, you may need assistance and protection and the ability to immediately communicate with others.

Every driver knows that in a moment, something terrible can happen. [*If you don't believe me, watch the TV show, "Criminal Minds."*] You no longer want to change your tire yourself, or get a "jump" from the battery of someone else's car, particularly, if you are a woman. This is no time and place to prove you can do it by yourself.

If you regularly travel the interstate highways, and especially if you plan to take a long driving trip, have your vehicle checked for safety, and never get on the highway without a full tank of gas, even on your daily commute.

DO YOU HAVE IN YOUR VEHICLE EVERYTHING YOU COULD POSSIBLY NEED
IF YOU WERE TO BE STRANDED FOR A CONSIDERABLE AMOUNT OF TIME?

I realize that we cannot all have so many things in our vehicles as are listed below, all the time. But this list will get you thinking about what you would need in an emergency. There are extreme weather conditions that strand people in vehicles for hours, even a day or two. If you live in a place where a bad storm could force you to be stranded in your vehicle, at least consider having some of the items in your car if you head out on the road before or during a snowstorm. And, if possible, stay home until it is safe again to travel.

And, you know that you cannot keep your vehicle motor running continuously or you will run out of gas.

The auto clubs and auto stores sell emergency kits, some for very specific uses. If you don't want to spend the money, ask for one for your birthday or other occasion. Or, put together your own kit from things you have in your house. Actually, the following list includes more items than those ready-made kits, and maybe even more than you would need, but you have to begin someplace:

- A white towel to hang on your window indicating you need help
- Assorted fuses
- Basic tools (screwdriver, pliers, wrench, box cutter, scissors)
- Batteries
- Blanket(s)
- Brushes and/or broom to clean snow off your vehicle
- Bungee Cords (several in various sizes)
- Cable ties
- Camera (throw-away, kept in glove compartment)
- Cell phone and cell phone charger for use in your vehicle
- Duct tape
- Emergency information
- Face masks to protect you from breathing dust, etc.
- First-aid kit (as complete as possible)
- Flashlights (preferably one with a blinking light)
- Fresh drinking water
- Gloves (sanitary and heavy-duty)
- Hard candy
- Hats and gloves
- Headache remedy
- Ice scrapers
- Kitty litter (especially useful in snow)
- Kleenex
- Large candle in a metal coffee can
- Large umbrella(s)
- List of names and phone numbers
- Map(s) or a GPS
- Matches kept in a water-tight container
- Paper towels
- Pen and paper
- Pet supplies (carriers, food, blankets, identification, leashes, medication, etc.)
- Plastic bags (grocery store bags, and kitchen or large leaf bags)
- Poncho(s) for protection from rain
- Portable shovel
- Rope (clothes line works well)
- Sanitary Wipes
- Small amount of cash and coins
- Small towels and cloths for other uses
- Snacks (packaged crackers, power bars, etc.)
- Zip-lock bags

What if that vehicle emergency happens <u>today</u> and you are unprepared? WHAT THEN?

EVACUATION OF YOUR TOWN and/or YOUR HOME

Emergencies happen somewhere, almost every day, and many carry with them the possibility of evacuations of human beings and animals. Would you be prepared? What if you lost everything you owned to one of those disasters?

- What would you do?
- Where would you go?

Right before the New Jersey shore was badly battered by Hurricanes Irene and Lee in the summer of 2011 and Sandy in 2012, Gov. Chris Christie told the shore town residents to "*get the hell off the beach.*" When there is a hurricane coming, the ocean is magnificent to see, and people want to be there and experience and photograph it. Nevertheless, it is not a safe place to be. There were people who didn't like how the Governor said it, but were probably grateful that he did. *You can't please everyone.*

Some people refused to leave their homes, and they were told by the emergency management team that if they did not evacuate as instructed, they had to know that there would be no one to rescue them later. It is my opinion that the people were afraid they would never get back to their home again, and were unprepared to leave their things behind. Furniture can be replaced. Maybe all the people's important papers could be replaced, too. Maybe not. Why risk it? Do what is necessary to be prepared.

Is there anyone who will ever forget the horrific pictures of the residents of Louisiana and Mississippi during Hurricane Katrina, or scenes of the beach towns of New Jersey damaged beyond recognition? Such a terrible waste of life and property. Some people got out in time. Others did not ... *could not* ... for many reasons. It was heartbreaking to see pictures of houses turned to piles of boards; to watch pictures of people and their pets sitting on the roofs of their houses as they floated down the mighty Mississippi. So beautiful. So bad.

How do you prepare for natural disasters of such enormous proportions? One element of advanced preparation would be the decisions made at your family meeting. Another is to be aware of what is going on by staying tuned to your local radio station and the broadcasts of the local emergency team. Gather your "stuff" and get out, ASAP! Communicate with your loved ones. How? You'll have to figure it out for yourself, based on where you live and upon your life situation, but you must figure it out.

If an evacuation is about to happen ...

In a moment's notice, could you put your hands on everything you need to take with you were you ordered to evacuate your home?

Would you have a portable emergency kit(s) you could "grab and run" with? Would you have your important documents and records in one place, such that you can grab them and run (for example, in a Big Book)? That's a really tall order, and for most people, their answer would probably be NO. But putting such an emergency kit and Big Book together way in advance of need is a good idea, especially if you live in an area that is prone to extreme weather conditions. It will take a commitment on your part to complete the kit(s), but the effort may be worth your time if/when an emergency occurs.

- *I bought a very large canvas suitcase on wheels at a yard sale for $1.00, and would use it for this purpose. I mention "on wheels" because you would not want to have to carry a heavy suitcase for any time or distance. Depending on the number of people in your family, you might want to prepare more than one such suitcase – maybe one for adults, one for children, another for pets.*

What about your important papers? How would you be able to gather all those papers if you were forced to leave your home in a moment's notice? The answer is to grab your BIG BOOK and take it with you. If you followed the guidelines in Chapter IV - RECORD-KEEPING, your Big Book will contain everything you need ... all in one place, ready to go. And, if you made the choice to not organize and protect your records as suggested, take a moment to think about how you would duplicate them if they were lost in an emergency?

In my "grab and go" emergency suitcase are things I would absolutely have to have with me, including:

- Another pair of comfortable shoes

- Camera (digital or phone-camera or film camera) and film (plus water-tight container)
- Can opener
- Canned tuna, fruit, juice
- Cash (safeguarded from loss or theft)
- Cell phone and charger
- Checkbook and pen
- Clothing appropriate to the season or circumstances
- Credit Cards
- Drinking Water (3-day supply sufficient for every person)
- Eating utensils
- Emergency contacts (names, phone numbers)
- Extra underwear and socks
- Family photos
- Feminine products (if appropriate)
- Flashlights (and batteries)
- Gloves (plastic and heavy-duty work gloves)
- Headache remedy
- Laptop Computer(s)
- Medications for people and pets (and written prescriptions for each in case you run out)
- Paper and writing instruments (black markers, too)
- Paper plates and cups
- Personal hygiene products (toothbrush, deodorant, etc.)
- Personal papers (photo ID, driver's license, passport, etc.) (in plastic zip-lock bags)
- Pillows and blankets
- Playing cards, computer games, etc.
- Raingear
- Reading material
- Snacks in waterproof plastic containers/bags
- Special needs as appropriate
- Tape (clear packing and/or masking tape)
- Terry cloth and paper towels
- Toilet paper

This list will at least give you a place to start to make your own list. Of course, if you are traveling with a baby or young children, and pets, your list will include the things they need for such an unexpected journey. And, if you are traveling with a person with disabilities or an elderly person, you would adjust the list to their specific needs.

WHERE WILL YOU GO?

This is a big question for which there is no easy answer. Do you have family who could let you stay with them for a short while? How short?

But, what if you had experienced total destruction of your house, such that there was no place to go home to? Then what? I don't know. No one in our family has a home that could accommodate the two of us and our three cats. Then what? I think a hotel would be the best place for us for a few days, and we would just have to pay the room rate on a credit card.

A public shelter set up in a local school or firehouse would be better than nothing. But, know that there is no space for your stuff, and pets are generally not allowed.

There are also apartment complexes that rent fully-furnished apartments if this is an option which you can afford. It would be a good idea for you to investigate such places <u>well in advance of need</u>, and hopefully, you will never need them. Ask if they allow pets and children.

Just in these few paragraphs, you can see a need for an emergency fund.

HOW WOULD YOU GET THERE?

I just asked my husband if we were ever forced to evacuate (we live near a nuclear plant), would we take both cars or only one. He quickly said both, filled to the windows with our stuff and our cats. This is where "grab and run" kits fit in. Have you ever taken the time to prepare such a kit? One for each person? And one for your book containing all your important papers? Be sure to grab you're printed A-Z directory. You will want to have all that information in your possession, safely secured in some kind of waterproof container or zip-lock bag.

And if you take pets with you, take carriers for them so they cannot escape. They are not prepared to live on the streets if they have been your pampered pets.

Our family pictures are also in 3-ring notebooks inside large, very heavy plastic tubs with lids. We would fit as many as possible into the cars.

Forget clothing except the most basic. We can always buy new clothing, but we can never replace the pictures.

> In *The Philadelphia Inquirer* of January 30, 2012, there was an article about a photo album's being retrieved from a trash can in Norristown, a suburb about 25 miles west of Philadelphia. The album contains photos of African-American people going back many years. Many of the pictures were taken in Europe during and after WWII. Nowhere is there any identification of the names of the people in the pictures.
>
> The person who found the album gave it to the Montgomery County Historical Society for safe-keeping until (and if) they find the rightful owners. The Society deemed it a valuable historical collection, and wonders why the pictures ended up in the trash. Maybe they were thrown away after a fire or some other catastrophe in someone's home. No one has yet been able to locate the owner (as of Nov. 2012).
>
> My husband's mother actually threw away all of his family's pictures. I personally know of three other situations where someone in my family was about to trash family pictures, and my sister and I were able to save them at the last minute. We cherish those pictures, and don't understand why people throw family photos in the trash.

WHEN WOULD YOU DEPART?

This is another question for which there is no easy answer. Timing, as they say, is everything, and in an emergency evacuation, timing can mean the difference between whether or not you survive.

When an evacuation is ordered by law enforcement agencies, most people rush to get on to the highway. This creates bumper-to-bumper lines of cars moving at the pace of a snail. The cars are using gas and going nowhere. I'm sure you've seen pictures on the TV news channels about traffic jams of several miles.

So, it is our opinion that it would be best to wait a while. I recently heard someone say that they waited to leave their Jersey shore home until most of the people had already gone, and they were able to drive through to their destination without delay. You will have to use your best judgment.

POWER FAILURES

Many natural disasters cause people to be without power for days. Being without power for days goes way beyond a minor inconvenience. I think the people who work for utility companies to restore power under horrific conditions are miracle workers.

There are many things to think about, especially if someone in your home has special needs. And what about all that food in your refrigerator and freezer? Keep the doors closed. If you open and close the doors frequently, the food inside will not last very long. And, there is a danger from bacteria in meats that have thawed and been refrozen. Besides, how would you cook the food if you only had an electric stove? Dry ice is a possibility for keeping foods cold. Find out where to get it in advance of an emergency.

Some people, after experiencing a power failure, invest in an **emergency generator**. Stores like Home Depot and Lowes regularly sell out after a power failure. I don't know whether it's a good idea or not if you only ever experienced one power failure, but if you live in a region that experiences frequent power outages, it is something to think about. And, if you get a small generator, pay close attention to the instructions regarding adequate ventilation to avoid carbon monoxide poisoning.

- After hurricane Sandy on the East Coast, people were stealing emergency generators from the outside of homes. Isn't it amazing? You get one thing that offers a positive benefit (the emergency generator), and then you must weigh the benefit against possible consequences such as theft and vandalism, or as extreme as death? *Doesn't seem fair, does it?*

In some places, an electric pump provides running water from a well into homes. Keep a quantity of bottled drinking water on hand at all times. When the electricity is out, there is no running water to drink, to flush a toilet, or bathe. If you have time to prepare before a storm, you could fill a bathtub with water for everything but drinking. I'm not so sure that a bathtub full of water is a good thing to have in your house if you have young children or pets, but you could fill gallon jugs with water and put the jugs in the bathtub.

TIP

If you experience a power failure, and if it lasts into the night, you could bring in the solar lights from your garden as well as those that line your front sidewalk and driveway. Put them in every room where you require light, and in the morning, put them outside again to recharge. Hey, it's better than sitting in the dark.

Sump Pumps

Another situation that can occur during a power failure is that your **sump pump** will not operate. We have two sump pumps in our home, one of which always had a battery back-up. During a recent storm, we were without power for 5 hours. The pump with the battery back-up performed perfectly; the other did not work at all. Fortunately, we did not experience any major water damage, but we have since had a battery back-up installed in the second pump. It was worth the price for the peace of mind.

I know people whose sump pump needs to be manually turned on if it is to work. Excuse me? What if you are not at home to turn it on? Then what? Water in the basement, I suppose. You could choose to think of upgrading your sump-pump system as an investment in your home, your possessions, and your peace of mind, particularly when you consider that many homeowners' insurance policies do not always cover water damage. *Just one more thing to think about ...*

PETS

Your pets rely on you to protect them, feed them, and keep them safe and close by you. Are you prepared to do whatever is necessary to protect your pets and keep them safe at all cost? If not, you will have to live with whatever decision you make at the time.

In every extreme act of devastation (whether manmade like 9/11 or by Mother Nature as in hurricanes Katrina or Sandy), there are pets lost or left behind. There are organizations that do their best to save the animals and reunite them with their owners, and they would be grateful for your donations of cash, food and supplies, or your time. It is not an easy job, and requires commitment, compassion and hard work.

In the events of 9/11, people went to work in the morning, in complete faith that they would be returning home at the end of the work day. No one leaves their home in the morning thinking they will not return at day's end. Your pets are expecting you to return. They need you to return. So, what happens to them when you don't?

You could designate one person to be responsible for your pets in an emergency, preferably a neighbor you know and trust. Make arrangements for this person to check on your pets if you are absent for any *unusual* length of time other than for a planned vacation or similar planned event. Your neighbor should either have a key to your residence, or some other authorization to gain access if there is any question of why you haven't returned within a day or two.

Generally, cats do well for several days IF YOU LEAVE THEM ENOUGH DRY FOOD, WATER and KITTY LITTER. Dogs must go outside. Cats know how to pace themselves with water and food. Dogs, on the other hand, do not. Dogs will eat it all at one sitting. All these things must be taken into account when you do your emergency planning.

- Breaking news! There is a now a product on the market called "dog litter." Good idea!

In some emergency situations, especially evacuations, people are forced to abandon their pets. THIS IS AN ABSOLUTE NO-NO FOR ME! My pets go where I go! There has been some change in the rules and regulations of shelters where people go during emergencies. The general rule has been "no pets," but after Katrina, rescue people began to understand the connection between people and their beloved pets, even in emergency and life-threatening situations. So, some shelters allow pets. While you are preparing your own "grab and run" kit, prepare one for each of your pets at the same time.

- You could put all your pet's needs into a secure carrier, including pet medication, collars and leashes, pet identification on their bodies, pet food, blankets, towels, some provision for kitty litter. One carrier for each pet. And, if they have a microchip in their body, have the information about the company with you in case your pet gets away from you. Be sure the carrier has a secure Id tag on it.

VEHICLE SAFETY and PETS

It is your job to protect your pet(s) from dangerous situations, and jumping out of the car into moving traffic qualifies as a dangerous situation.

Cats and Cars

When you take your cats in the car with you, do you secure them in a pet carrier? I hear you shouting *"NO! Kitties don't like it!"* to which I say, *"So what?"* [By now, you have probably guessed that I am a serious pet lover.]

Scenario No. 1
Your cat doesn't like to be in a cat carrier in the car and howls the whole time, so you let Kitty sleep on your lap while you drive. You're calmly sitting in traffic at a red light, and your car is struck from behind by another vehicle. You didn't even bring a cat carrier with you, because, remember, she doesn't like it! Now what? What do you think the cat will do when you open the door?

Scenario No. 2
What if you were stopped by a police officer for a routine traffic stop, and you would have to open your window to give the officer your driver's license? What do you think the police officer's reaction will be to your allowing your cat to sit on your lap while you drive? What do you think the cat will do when you open that window? Do you suppose the officer will help you get your cat back if it bolts? What if you're in the middle of noon-time traffic in a busy intersection and your cat is killed right in front of you?

Scenario No. 3
You have a service dog you love. Your very existence depends upon your dog, to which you trust your very life. Your dog has identification on his/her collar, and has a microchip. While driving in a vehicle, the dog is not restrained, and in a vehicle accident, the dog bolts and runs away. That dog is not prepared to live on its own. What will you do without that dog? Why would you not restrain that magnificent animal on whom you rely for so many things? Just asking ...

Have you ever seen a frightened cat bolt? I have, and it's not a pretty sight. Their fear propels them into harm's way, which, in these cases, would be directly into traffic. If the cat isn't injured or killed by another vehicle, chances are it will run off and you will never see it again. IS THIS WHAT YOU WANT TO HAPPEN, just because you want the cat to be happy? What about your cat's being SAFE? That's your responsibility. The cat doesn't get a vote! *But, hey, that's just my opinion ...*

Does your cat have a microchip in the event that someone finds the cat, dead or alive? If not, get one! Keep the information with your other important papers.

Dogs and Cars

Anyone who has ever owned a dog knows how they love riding in the car. They love putting their heads out the window to feel the breeze on their faces (which, by the way, is a really bad idea – if you don't believe me, ask your vet).

- Have you ever seen photos of dogs wearing goggles ... dogs riding on motorcycles, or hanging their heads out of cars. I think they look very cute. Nevertheless, I believe it is important that you get them used to wearing goggles when they are very young in order to protect their eyes from debris that could injure them. They won't enjoy the ride any less with goggles than without.

While riding in the vehicle, does your dog have a leash attached to its collar, such that, in a traffic emergency, you could grab hold of the leash so that you dog cannot get away. *"No, he doesn't like that."* Again, I say, *"So what?"* WHO IS IN CHARGE?

You could also put your dog in a large crate in your car. No matter what you do, the object is to keep your beloved dog safe in an emergency or accident.

A Frightening Scenario

I once saw an unrestrained golden retriever jump out of the back of a pick-up truck in the middle of a very busy intersection at lunch time. The dog apparently saw something and went after it. When the dog realized it was in the middle of traffic, it panicked and began running this way and that. Fortunately, EVERYONE stopped their vehicles, such that the dog's owner could get out of his truck and get his dog. What an absolutely irresponsible person to allow that gorgeous dog to ride, unrestrained, in the back of that truck! Thank goodness, this scenario had a happy ending. Some do not.

In the local newspaper on August 10, 2011, and again on August 29, 2012, there were lengthy articles about using restraints for your dog while traveling in your vehicle. A similar article appeared in the AAA magazine. So, apparently, I'm not the only person who is concerned about the safety of dogs riding in cars. In the autumn of 2012, New Jersey legislators were trying to pass a law requiring that dogs be restrained in vehicles to keep them from distracting drivers. Although the Governor has said that the state has more important things to do other than pass laws like this, it is nevertheless a good idea ... just don't make it a law. There are already too many unenforceable laws on the books of every state. *Just another one of my opinions ...*

- I have mentioned the use of such restraints for dogs riding in their cars to several friends, and without exception, every one rejected the idea as "stupid." Excuse me? Did I miss something? Isn't your dog one of the most important living things in your life? You put children in restraints in your vehicle, so why not your dog? *Just asking...*

Pet stores carry all sorts of vehicle restraints for dogs. Get one. Put it your car. Make your dog wear one. It would be easier if you had trained the dog that way from the time it was a puppy, but it is not too late to protect this animal from the dangers of traffic.

Does your dog have a microchip in the event that someone finds your dog, dead or alive? *Just asking ...*

- In the local newspaper of November 13, 2012, there is a Dear Abby letter from a man who experienced the injury of his beloved Golden Retriever because he was a distracted driver. As the driver was texting, he ran into the car in front of him, which engaged the airbag. His dog was so freaked that he jumped out into traffic and ran away. Fortunately, the dog was found and taken to a vet, who was able to identify the dog by way of his microchip. The dog was seriously injured, but survived. The dog paid the price for his owner's mistaken belief that texting while driving is all right, and that a dog does not have to be restrained in a moving vehicle.

Whatever decision you make on this subject, you will have to live with the consequences. The writer of the above letter said that he can never forgive himself. Don't put yourself and your pet(s) in harm's way.

OK: This is my last try to get you to realize the importance of restraining your dogs in vehicles. In the newspaper of December 29, 2012, there was an article about a traffic incident in Santa Ynez, CA, where two women pulled over on a highway, and when they opened a car door, their small dog jumped out into traffic and was struck. As the women attempted to get their dog before it was too late, all three of them … that is, the dog and the two women … were killed.

SAFE DEPOSIT BOX and/or BIG BOOK … in emergency situations

Whether or not you should have a bank safe deposit is one of those grey areas of life planning, because there is no right or wrong answer. I would say "it depends" on situations and circumstances of your own life. I believe, however, that there is a distinction to be made in relation to safe deposit boxes if you live in a place where there have been major natural disasters … *not just one* … but enough to make you want to protect your important papers. So, after reading the following, you will have to decide for yourself.

There is nothing inherently wrong with having a safe deposit in a bank, as long as someone other than you:

1. knows the name and branch office location;
2. knows where you keep the key.
3. has access to that box, either as a signer, a joint owner, or under your Power-of-Attorney.
4. knows what you keep in that box
    (for example, your Will, your burial instructions, your important papers, jewelry, cash).
5. can have immediate access to the box in an emergency.

Elsewhere, I stated my opinion that certain <u>original</u> documents that should not be placed into a bank safe deposit box:

4. Cemetery Deed
5. Funeral and Burial Instructions
6. Your Estate-Planning Documents including:
    - Will
    - Living Will
    - Durable Power-of-Attorney
    - Healthcare Power-of-Attorney
    - Revocable Living Trust (other trusts), if any

… the reason being that it might be difficult and take time for someone else to be able to retrieve these documents from your bank box if you, yourself, are unavailable, and especially if time is of the essence.

But, as with many things relating to life planning, these rules are not always black-and-white either. As I said above, **I make an exception to the bank box if you live in a geographic area where extreme weather events are known to happen.** I believe it is in your best interests to rent a large bank box today if you have not already done so. Leave it empty if you want to, but at least it will be there and ready if you ever need to safeguard important papers on a moment's notice.

Unless all your important family papers are in a Big Book [as described in Chapter IV (Record-Keeping)], which you could "grab and go," it might be impossible for you to take the time necessary to gather all your important papers in the event of an evacuation, fire or flood. And even if you did, there would be the possibility they could get lost or damaged. But, those papers would be safe in the bank box until the emergency passes.

Try to think ahead of the emergency whenever possible. If you ever find yourself in a situation where evacuation seems possible, but not yet certain, I recommend that you take all of your important papers to a bank and put them into the safe deposit box which you have previously rented. If there is an extreme weather prediction that allows you time to take your papers and valuable to the bank box, don't wait until the last minute. What if the bank were closed when you got there?

While I am still not in favor of everyone's keeping <u>*original*</u> documents in a bank safe deposit box in the long term, it would at least be a good idea to keep <u>photocopies</u> in a bank box, along with copies of all your other important papers, credit cards, financial accounts of all sorts, birth certificates, marriage/divorce certificates, etc., etc. I think you get the idea.

In recent years, homes were destroyed all over this country by horrific events. If you lost your home and had left your important papers in your house, they would be gone, too. And, remember what I said elsewhere about what people miss the most: their family pictures.

- In an emergency, a bank box would provide a safe location for your important papers away from your house, such that after the emergency passes, you can go to the bank and retrieve papers you need.

- It is also wise to put negatives or CD's of your family pictures in the bank box, because if your actual photographs were destroyed, you could always reprint them.

- Photos of the contents of your home should be kept in the bank box, and when you get new furniture, etc., take new pictures and put them in the box as well. It will be of enormous assistance in documenting your possessions for an insurance claim.

- Additionally, you could document all of your possessions, assets, bank accounts, insurance information, family and personal information, etc., in your computer and copy the information to a CD, and place the CD in the box.

- Also include your A-Z contact list in the box. It would be very difficult to recreate your list if you lost it in a fire or flood. Of course, if you have it in a hand-held electronic device, it would be safe; but not everyone operates out of such devices. You could always put your list on a CD and put that into the bank box.

- And, if it would be possible, you could also take your Big Book with you if you had to leave your house in an emergency. That's why I keep a big suitcase right beside our safe where I keep our Big Book.

- Ideas, suggestions ... I'm sure you have your own, and they might be better than mine. Begin to think about what you would do in an emergency. If my writing does nothing but get you to think, make plans, and take action, I will have succeeded.

IDENTIFICATION

Anything you would take with you in an evacuation should have identification on it that could not be damaged by water, and that would not become detached. This may take a little planning and a small expense to get such ID tags, but it would be a good investment. Luggage stores are a good place to begin looking for such tags ... some are even plastic with imprinted information, much like a credit card. You would want to put:

- identification tags on handbags, suitcases, computer cases, cameras, pet carriers, and other valuables

- identification on your person and on every member of your family, especially children. It is possible to have metal tags (similar to military "dog tags") made for every member of your family, but do it well in advance of an emergency.

- identification tags and a microchip on your pets.

And, while we're on the subject of identification ... If you pay attention to the world around you, you may have noticed a human tendency to respond AFTER a crisis ... that is, as opposed to planning and being prepared. Why do you suppose that is? The illusion (*delusion?*) that if you don't talk about a problem or think about it, it might not happen. The choice to ignore a problem in the present, only to be faced with it at a later date, isn't exactly avoiding a problem, is it?

- In The Philadelphia Inquirer of November 26, 2012, there was an article about this very thing. It was about a New Jersey next-of-kin registry that adds teen ID cards. This law came out of a situation where a young girl was fatally injured in an automobile accident, but because she did not carry sufficient identification, her parents could not be notified until after the girl died. A woman was quoted as saying that she was delighted at this new law, which will give her peace of mind. Why should anyone expect the government to issue ID cards. Isn't it the parent's job to see that a young person carries identification? SHOULDN'T EVERYONE CARRY IDENTIFICATION? *Excuse me. What did I miss?*

  So, if you do not already carry an ICE card in your wallet (that is, **I**n **C**ase of **E**mergency), make one up right now. It doesn't have to be fancy. All it needs is accurate information about you.

- And, remember the story of Jane Doe from Chapter I? Her situation would have been made much easier for everyone concerned if she had had some kind of identification with her when her medical emergency occurred.

ARE YOU PREPARED FOR EMERGENCIES WHEN YOU TRAVEL?

Travel Insurance

All sorts of things can happen while you are traveling, whether on vacation or for business, whether in the continental USA or elsewhere? There are things you can and should do to protect yourself and your possessions while traveling.

Travel insurance is something many people either reject or forget. It may show up as just one more expense for your already expensive trip, and an expense you can easily avoid. *"Who needs it,"* you say. <u>You</u> <u>do</u>. Buying travel insurance may seem like an odd kind of planning, but one that can pay huge dividends in a time of loss, whether that loss is just your stuff, or your life. Like any other kind of insurance, you buy it hoping you will never have to use it. And no, I don't sell travel insurance.

There are stories in the media every day about extreme travel accidents and emergencies. Are you one of those people who quickly and regularly reject the notion of being prepared? Do you hear your mother's voice reminding you to take your jacket in case it rains? I'm talking about serious emergencies with potential life-altering consequences. What, you think it only happens to other people? What harm would there be to be thoroughly prepared? *Just asking ...*

OK, I realize that if you are fortunate enough not to have suffered injury, and you only lost your "stuff," nevertheless that "stuff" has a replacement cost, and that's where travel insurance comes into play. Travel insurance can provide you with much greater benefits if you purchase the correct policy for your circumstances. Such a policy can include financial and other assistance during a medical emergency while traveling. It can include something the insurance companies call "repatriation," which means that if you die while traveling, they cover the expense of returning your body to your home. If you are traveling "on a shoestring," where would the money come from to return your body to your home should the unthinkable occur? When I was on a cruise on the QE II in 1994, someone died. It happens, and it's expensive.

The next time your travel agent suggests that you purchase travel insurance, and you are inclined to say, *"No thank you. I don't need it because nothing's going to happen,"* be prepared to sign a Release, indicating that you were invited to get the insurance and you chose not to. This relieves the travel agent from liability in case some unforeseen event happens to you on your trip. Remember to think of travel insurance as an investment, not an expense. And when you get safely home, don't forget to cancel the policy if it does not cancel automatically.

> ***Life is a journey that must be traveled no matter how bad the road and accommodations.***
>
> Oliver Goldsmith

During Your Trip

OK, so now you have taken care of the travel insurance aspect of your trip. While traveling, how prepared are you otherwise?

1. How do you protect your credit cards, your passport and other identification cards, currency or travelers' checks?

2. If you are traveling with a spouse, do each of you carry only a portion of that currency, so that if it is lost or stolen, you would only lose that portion?

3. If you are traveling with a spouse or companion, do you carry information about that other person with you at all times in case you get separated? Do you include cell phone numbers, email addresses, where you are staying, etc?

4. Do you carry detailed information about your entire trip, so that, in the event you get lost or separated from your spouse, travel companion, or travel group, you would be able to be safely, quickly reunited? Does your list include their cell phone numbers and email addresses?

5. Did you make arrangements such that you will be able to be reached by cell phone or internet access by people at home? Such communication is not <u>in</u>expensive, so tell your family and friends not to call to chit-chat.

6. Do you carry appropriate, current photo identification, protected from water damage?

7. Do you carry a list of people to contact in an emergency? This would include the person(s) on the trip with you, as well as the person(s) at home who you would want to be contacted.

8. Do you carry evidence of your Living Will and Healthcare Power-of-Attorney, including detailed information about the person(s) who are your Agents under those documents and where the original documents are located in case they would be needed in an emergency?

9. Do you carry a list of prescription medications you regularly take?

10. Do you have a written prescription for each medication with you in case you lose your pills?

11. Do you carry a card in your wallet that gives all personal medical information that might be needed, including your blood type and any diseases or conditions you might have during the time you are away from home? If you usually wear medic-alert jewelry, don't leave it home.

12. Do you carry the name, address, and phone number of your primary care physician?

TIP
I recommend that you buy a travel pouch that allows you carry this important information on your person ... that is, as opposed to carrying it in a purse or suitcase that could be stolen or lost.

Did you leave sufficient important information at home?

1. Did you leave behind a detailed list of your exact travel itinerary, including dates, addresses, phone numbers, contact persons, including all the places where you will be staying?

   - Have you left exact information about the plane, train or boat schedule, or if you plan to drive, some indication of the rental car information, the route you will take, etc.?

   - Did you leave at home a complete listing of where you will be at all times when you are away ... just in case someone at home needs to be in touch with you in a moment's notice?

2. Where is that list? Who has it?

3. If your home has an alarm system, who, besides yourself, could get into your home if necessary? Did you notify the local police that you would be away? If the local police are needed to gain access to your home, who knows it is necessary to contact them first? Who has their phone number?

4. If you are traveling without your children who you left at home with someone you trust, does that person know all the details about your trip?

5. Did you leave behind detailed information about the care and feeding of your pets in your home while you are traveling, including complete information about your veterinarian, including name, address, and phone number.

   - Does your list include what to do if your pet(s) become ill or injured? What to do if they should die while you are away?

   - If your pets have a microchip in them, leave the information about the company that provides the locator service in case your pet should get lost.

   - If your pets are elsewhere (in a kennel or staying with family or friends), have you left detailed information about the whereabouts of your pets while you are away, including the contact information for the person responsible for their care?

6. In your home, have you left in a visible location, information about your Living Will and Healthcare Power-of-Attorney, including the whereabouts of the original documents, and the name, address and phone numbers of your Agent(s)? Primary care physician? Lawyer? Clergy? Who else has that list?

Extraordinary Circumstances

If you are traveling with young children, the elderly, or a person with special needs, you will, of course, be required to pay particular attention to details to accommodate their respective needs and to protect them in every situation. For each of these persons, the most important thing is for them to have, on their person at all times, complete identification as to who they are, who to contact in an emergency, what their immediate needs are, and how to find you in the event you become separated. Beyond that, you know better than I what their needs are and how best to deal with them. Do whatever is necessary to protect those people who are counting on you.

MOST ACCIDENTS HAPPEN IN THE HOME

Who besides you has a key to your house or apartment? Just the other day, our neighbor (a widow who lives alone) locked her keys and cell phone inside her purse inside her car inside her garage. She came to our house to ask if we would call the police, and within minutes, they arrived and "rescued" her. Things like this happen all the time. In a situation like this, it would have been wise for her to have had an extra key outside her house in a safe, hidden-but-accessible location, or to have asked a neighbor to keep a key for emergencies such as this.

One way to keep yourself in communication with the outside world is to <u>keep your cell phone on your person at all times.</u> I hear you already, complaining that this is ridiculous! *Oh, yeah?*

- Let's say, for example, you are <u>not</u> living alone, that your husband is at work, and you are home by yourself and fall down the cellar steps and are injured such that you cannot get to a phone. It may be hours until your husband comes home.

- What if you actually do live alone, and are seriously injured in a fall?

- In both cases, without a phone, how could you call for help? The answer is simple: You couldn't!

Remember the TV commercial showing a woman who says, "I've fallen and I can't get up?" This happens way too often, when a person is alone and is injured and cannot communicate to the outside world that they need help. Situations like these generally happen to a person who lives alone, whether elderly and disabled, or not. And there are many statistics that say that most falls occur in the home.

One remedy is to purchase one of those Life-Alert devices the woman on the TV commercial advertises. This device is connected to a service that will respond to you simply by pushing a button in a time of need. Keep the device (and your cell phone) on your person at all times. These things won't do you any good if you don't have them with you in an emergency. Check out the various companies offering this service to compare costs and services.

How many times do you hear about a person who is injured or dying when they are alone, and they are not found for hours, even days? My answer to those questions is, "*Way too often.*" Ask any Emergency Medical Technician (EMT) who has shown up at a location where there is "suspicious activity," only to find that person had died several days before.

There is a monthly fee for this service, but it is not so high that it should not be considered a viable option for your safety.

- *You may be thinking that you don't need it, because you have friends and family who check on you every day. Still, if you live alone, there are many hours when they are not with you and when anything could happen.*

A cartoon shows an old lady who slipped and fell on her icy driveway as she went to get the newspaper. She says to herself: "*I don't think I can get up. I'd better use that medical alert beeper that my son got me. Darn, it must be in the house. I told him that thing was a waste of money.*"

IF YOU ARE A BUSINESS OWNER:

If you are the owner or operator of a business on which others depend, whether as employees or customers, have you in place a set of emergency plans to get everyone through a crisis situation?

- Do you have sufficient legal structure, estate plans, and insurance coverage in place to shelter the financial health of your family from any disaster your business incurs?

- Do you have sufficient insurance to cover damage to your building, equipment, supplies and inventory?

- Do you have adequate Workers' Compensation insurance in the event an employee is injured?

- Do you have adequate liability insurance in the event someone other than an employee is injured on the premises?

- Do you have a plan for your employees' safety, both physical and financial? In the short term? In the long term?

- If a fire were to destroy your entire facility, do you have an emergency fund to cover your living expenses until you can get the business up and running again … that is, if that is even a possibility?

- Do you pay Unemployment Compensation so that if your employees lose their jobs as a result of the destruction of your business, they would at least have some income?

- Have you checked with the laws of your state to see what specific forms of disaster planning you must have?

- How would you serve the customers who depend upon your products or services during a lengthy business interruption?

THERE IS A LOT TO THINK ABOUT.

Know what is required. Talk with your lawyer, your insurance broker, your financial planner BEFORE the need arises.

IT'S TOO MUCH TO THINK ABOUT

I agree. But what is the alternative? To do nothing? Somehow, that doesn't seem a viable option. Planning for emergencies is much the same as planning for your life and your death, and I already know you don't like talking about any of it. I get it.

If you believe that planning for all these emergencies is upsetting and exhausting, and way too much for you to think about, let alone do, remember the words of *Scarlett O'Hara*:

"I can't think about that now! I'll go crazy if I do. I'll think about it tomorrow …"

You can choose Scarlett's way, or you can make plans. Every family … *every situation* … needs a hero. It just might be you. If you are a responsible, organized person, the planning might fall into your hands whether you want it or not. But, ask yourself this question: If planning has to be done (and it appears that it must), would you be the best person to do it, or would you prefer to leave it to someone who is more tuned **out** to such things, the people who always say, "*You worry too much,*" or "*That will never happen.*" Just asking...

So, make your plans.
Have your family meeting.
Investigate every option you might need.
Make notes and lists.
Gather your stuff.
Complete your documents.
Establish your emergency fund.
And be ready … *just in case.*

ARE YOU TAKING GOOD CARE OF YOUR BODY?

- Do you see your dentist at least once a year?

- Do you have your eyes checked at least annually?

- Do you have regular medical check-ups?

- Do you have a health problem that you are ignoring?

- Do you exercise on some kind of regular basis?

- Do you give yourself "down time" to alleviate stress?

- Do you use therapeutic massage or acupuncture to relieve health problems?

- Do you eat well? Take vitamins?

- Do you get enough sleep?

- Do you take prescription medications? What for? (*)

- Could you find alternative ways to eliminate the need for them?

- Do you work with a nutritionist and a personal fitness trainer?

- Do you know your families' medical histories.

- Give up soda and cigarettes.

- Reduce fast food, sweets, and packaged frozen dinners.

(*) An article in *The Philadelphia Inquirer* the week of November 15, 2010, stated that Boomers generally consider themselves very healthy, yet they take the top 10 classes of drugs prescribed for people age 45-65. In descending order, they are (1) noninjectable opiate pain relievers; (2) Statins for high cholesterol; (3) Antidepressants; (4) ACE inhibitors for hypertension; (5) Beta-blockers for heart disease; (6) remedies for acid reflux; (7) thyroid drugs; (8) drugs for anxiety, insomnia, etc.; (9) medications for seizure disorders; and (10) anti-inflammatories for arthritis. I notice there is no medication listed for diabetes? I wonder why not, considering how many Baby Boomers are diabetic. *Just curious ...*

Many Boomers are taking several of these medications. DO YOU REALLY NEED THEM ALL? Maybe you should give some serious thought to investigating the consequences of taking all these drugs ... individually, or in combination. ... to see if the risks outweigh the benefits. *Just a suggestion ...*

DO YOU NOURISH YOUR SPIRIT?

- Do you watch too much TV, especially the news?

- Do you participate in group activities that you enjoy?

- Do you read books?

- Do you watch movies you love?

- Do you go to concerts or listen to music you love?

- Do you have pets that give you unconditional love?

- Do you treat yourself to flowers every now and then?

- What would you love to be doing right now, but are not doing? Why not?

- Are the people in your life really friends or just acquaintances?

- Do you take a walk or exercise on a regular basis?

- Do you attend religious services that nourish your spirit?

- Do you grow things (plants, herbs, flowers)?

- Stop making mountains out of molehills.

- Write a list of all the things you love.

- Do you stay in regular communication with people who matter to you?

- Look around and find beauty everywhere.

- Smile often. Feel the joy it can bring to you and others.

- If you gossip, give it up.

- Stop saying, "*What if*_____?"

- Do you express your creative side, whatever that is?

- Some things I really appreciate about myself are _____.

Small deeds done are better than great deeds planned.

Peter Marshall

HERE ARE SOME SUGGESTIONS
FOR YOUR OWN PERSONAL "TO DO" LIST
(in no particular order)

Watch the movie, "The Bucket List" and other uplifting, joyous movies you love.

Research and document your family's genealogy.

Stop buying "stuff" you don't need.

Save the money you didn't spend on all that stuff.

Start a "rainy day" fund and keep adding to it.

Eat ice cream on a cone, with sprinkles.

Write letters to people who have special meaning in your life

Connect with people you have "lost" through the years

Put together photo albums. *Saving pictures on the various kinds of technology may be all right for right now, but what about 50 years from now? In my family, we have photographs that go back to the late 1800's. To us, these pictures are sacred. If you are now saving pictures on some kind of technological device, at least print some of them out so they can be placed in an album. Years later, your family will thank you.*

Stop doing things you don't want to do. *Say NO. Be nice and polite, but be firm.*

Learn to say NO without guilt. *Remember: "No!" is a complete sentence.*

Tell people you love them. *Say it often, and mean it. You have an unlimited supply of love inside you to give at every opportunity. Don't "hoard" you're love. The more you give, the more you get!*

Write a list of your favorite possessions, and tell the story about why they are so special to you.

Use coupons and buy sale items every time you grocery shop. *Look at the bottom of your cash register receipt and see the large amount of money you saved. If you can, put that exact amount of money into a big jar, and when it is full, treat yourself to something you really want!*

Stop saying you are bored. Find something interesting to do. *When I was a little girl, I regularly complained to my mother that I was bored. Her response was always the same: "Find something to do, and if you can't, I'll give you something to do, and you'll probably like your choice better than mine." To this day, I am never bored. Her words worked for me my whole life.*

Collect popular family recipes and share them with others before it's too late

---

The Case of the Missing Shoo-fly Pie Recipe

Our mother had a recipe for what we consider the world's greatest shoo-fly pie, and for several years, we believed she took the recipe with her when she died. But, thankfully we were wrong. Here's what happened.

My mother was not Pennsylvania Dutch (that is, of German ancestry), but she made a very fine Shoo-Fly Pie, a classic Pennsylvania Dutch recipe. She always made it from memory, and I have no idea where she got the recipe. She would occasionally give the shoo-fly pies to my sister and me, so we never bothered to learn how to make them.

One day years ago, while I was watching my Mother make a Shoo-Fly Pie, I asked her to tell me the ingredients she used and the amounts, and how she put them together. As she spoke, I wrote her instructions in Gregg Shorthand on the back of an envelope, and put the envelope in a shoebox where I keep recipes I cut out of magazines.

When my Mother died, my sister and I were saddened when we realized that we had lost her Shoo-Fly Pie recipe forever. We tried several recipes from books, and none satisfied us. Shoo-Fly Pies from bakeries never satisfied us either.

A few years after my Mother's death, I sorted through the shoebox and found the Shoo-Fly Pie recipe I had written in shorthand, and fortunately, I could still read it. I made my first shoo-fly immediately, and called my sister and her family to come to my house for a surprise. Mom's Shoo-Fly Pie!

Now, my sister and I both can make Shoo-Fly pies exactly the way our Mother did for so many years. And, we have passed this recipe on to my niece. Mom's recipe has become a family heirloom. In fact, for many years, Shoo-Fly Pie was "birthday cake" in our family!

[You'll find the recipe at the end of this Section.]

Put together a photo album of every one of your pets, and write a story about each.

Begin writing a family history. *This is not the same as genealogy ... this is about the people and their stories. Of course, this is not to say that you might not also want to trace your family tree, but that takes years and a huge commitment.*

Family History

I now find myself in the position of being the oldest person in my family. I am the person with the memory. So, I spent 18 months writing our family history. I wrote it by category: Mom, Dad, Mom & Dad, Mom's parents, Dad's parents, Aunts & Uncles, Cousins, Brothers and Sisters (individually, by name), Pets, Schools, Christmas, Vacations, etc. (you get the idea). The final product is 900 pages. which includes many cherished photographs. I loved every minute of the process, and I am very proud of the final product. I hope my nieces and nephews will appreciate it someday.

Organize a family reunion. *Have a theme for the party. Let your imagination go! Invite others to participate in every way possible. HAVE FUN!*

Buy a supply of greeting cards for all occasions. *You may get away with sending email birthday cards, etc., but **don't send email sympathy cards.** It is just my opinion, but they say that you really don't care all that much and are way too busy to take the time to shop for a card. Even if you don't have money for a card, a hand-written note on a piece of paper is more meaningful than just one more email. Think about it.*

> *Keep a variety of greeting cards on hand. You don't have to buy expensive Hallmark cards; Dollar Stores sell very nice cards for 2 for $1.00. The idea is to send your greetings through the mail. I enjoy sending cards to the people in my life who are important to me and I look forward to receiving cards on my birthday. I am blessed with people who remember me this way.*
>
> *I spent a fortune on greeting cards during my life because I LOVE sending cards, I LOVE selecting just the right one for the right person for the right occasion. Even if I find the perfect card for an occasion 6 months in advance, I buy it.*
>
> *I once had everyone in a Hallmark store laughing with me as I found the perfect Father's Day card for my father. (It was the comic strip character, Lucy, from the "Peanuts" cartoon strip, making one of her usual wise-cracks.) He had been estranged from my sister and me for many years, and a really sentimental, mushy card would not have done! He loved the card.*

Start doing things you always wanted to do, but have been putting off. *It can be something small, or something really big, but make it just for you. And it doesn't have to be expensive.*

Start doing everything that is <u>important</u> to you, so that, as you lay dying, you will have no regrets for not having done these things.

Always send thank-you notes when someone gives you a gift.

> *You don't even have to like the gift! You do, however, have to express thanks for their thoughtfulness in remembering you. And, you don't really have to hand-write the thank-you if you find it too difficult -- an appropriate store-bought thank-you note will be sufficient - but it says some very good things about you if you take the time to express yourself in your own handwriting. Sorry, NO email thank-you notes! (another one of my opinions).*
>
> *There were only 15 kids in my 6th grade class. We had a small party on each kid's birthday. Everyone gave the birthday child a present ... and there were two rules about this gift. (1) It could cost only 5¢, and (2) the birthday child had to hand write a thank-you note for every gift. In retrospect, it is clear that the entire process was a learning exercise for us, in addition to one of celebration. Here is a sample thank-you note:*
>
> *Dear Bobbie: Thank you very much for the pink pearl eraser. The one I have is worn down, and I am happy to have a new one. Each time I use this eraser, I will remember your thoughtfulness in helping me to celebrate my birthday. Sincerely,*

Celebrate your birthday every year. *For one day, one week, or one month. The day you were born was a blessed happy occasion for your family. Why would you want to discount such an event with negative comments like, "I don't celebrate birthdays anymore?" On your birthday, people send you cards, give you cakes, visits, dinners, gifts? What's so terrible about that? After all, if you're not celebrating birthdays anymore, you're dead!*

Express yourself fully – both verbally and in writing.

Host a dinner party, *even if you have to hire a caterer or buy prepared trays at the deli. The food is irrelevant; the point is to get together with people whose company you enjoy.*

Tell people what you need from them. *They cannot know if you don't tell them. People aren't mind-readers.*

Hire a housecleaning service. *Schedule them regularly as you can afford it, even if only once every year.*

If you are planning to buy a new(er) car, consider donating your old car to a charity. *First, be certain the charity is legitimate. In most cases, the car doesn't even have to be in running condition. The charity will provide you with a receipt for the fair market value of the car and you can take that amount as a tax deduction. It's a win-win!*

Get a cat or dog or two. *Get them from a shelter.*

Have nothing in your home that is not useful or beautiful.

Use correct English when you speak. *Using sloppy, careless words when you speak says volumes about you (mostly bad). It might even kill your chances of getting a job, or a promotion, or a partner. Who knows?*

Buy some "forever" stamps from the Post Office. *At less than 50¢, they are one of the few bargains left! Stop complaining about the increase when stamps go up in price. Could you deliver an envelope to California for 50 cents? I don't think so. When you hear that the rate of a stamp is going to increase, immediately buy a large supply of "forever" stamps at the lower rate ... you can continue to use them "forever." That's the point.*

Begin a "Gratitude Journal" to write down, every day, some of the many blessings of your life.

Reconcile with people while there is still time. *Pick up that phone and be first the person to offer the olive branch. They could die before you do, and then it will be too late.*

Get a face lift. Change your hair style (color?)

Once upon a time, 54-year old woman had a heart attack and was taken to the hospital. While on the operating table, she had a near-death experience. Seeing God, she asked, "Is my time up?" God said, "No, you have another 43 years, 2 months, and 8 days to live."

Since she had so much more time to live, she figured she might as well make the most of it. Upon recovery, the woman decided to stay in the hospital to have a face-lift, liposuction, breast implants, and a tummy tuck. She even had someone come and change her hair color and brighten her teeth.

After her last operation, she was released from the hospital, and, while crossing the street on her way home, she was killed by an ambulance. Arriving in front of God, she demanded, "I thought you said I had another 43 years? Why didn't you pull me from out of the path of the ambulance?" God replied: "I didn't recognize you."

Did you think this was a true story?

Create a CAVE for yourself inside your home ... *[man or woman, it doesn't matter]. Every person needs one special place, even if it is only a chair in a corner, that they can call their own, to meditate, contemplate, listen to music, read, relax ... alone! Make it known to your family that the space belongs to you, and when you are there, you are not to be disturbed. Establish your own rules about your "cave," communicate your rules to your family, and let them know that you expect them to respect your privacy. They're not mind-readers.*

If there is some place you want to go, figure out how to get there.

If there are questions you would like to ask your parents about their lives, about the lives of *their* parents, ASK THEM NOW before it is too late. *Generally, parents won't offer you details about themselves unless you ask. My sister and I did have the chance to ask our parents a few questions of importance to us, but we find that we still have a long list of questions that we wish we had asked. And now it's too late.*

Eliminate the word "*should*" from your vocabulary.

Get a massage once a month.

Volunteer somewhere, anywhere. *In tough economic times, all sorts of organizations are looking for volunteers, from food kitchens, to animal shelters, to libraries. Let your imagination go! You'll find something that is just the right fit for you.*

Collect and donate new socks and underwear for the homeless.

Read cartoons. Laugh out loud if you find them funny. Put them into scrapbooks. Send them to your friends when one is particularly appropriate. *Read Anatomy of an Illness by Norman Cousins.*

Stop taking everything so personally. It's probably not about you! *Read The Four Agreements by Don Miguel Ruiz.*

Forgive everyone who has wronged you, even if you don't do it in person. *Maybe it wasn't intentional.*

Forgive yourself.

Forgive your parents.

Take your time. *What's the big hurry ... in traffic, for example, or in the supermarket line? What does it really matter if you get where you're going one minute sooner?*

Write a love letter to each of your children. *Don't forget to sign and date it!*

Read all those books you've been saving for <u>later.</u> *"So many books; so little time."*

Be patient with yourself and others.

Schedule lunch with your friends *... you know who they are ... they're the ones you're always saying you want to get together with ... and don't.*

Take that cruise you've been talking about for years.

Go to bed 1 hour earlier.

Peruse flower and bulb catalogs in the winter.

Spend more time outdoors, no matter what the weather.

Plan and execute a reward for yourself for work well done.

Browse through a big-box craft store *and buy something that you've wanted to do for a long time, or get in touch with a particular craft/art you did when you were young, something you enjoy doing, and that will bring back sweet memories.*

Drop that extra 20 pounds once and for all ... the right way.

Give yourself permission to sleep late occasionally. Enjoy it!

Tell your spouse how important they are to you.

Fill in the blank: Something I really love doing is_____. *Explain why.*

Tell your children how proud you are of them, and how much you love them

Sign up for art classes (or dancing, aerobics, yoga, tai chi, or music lessons).

If you have children, be a good parent. *If you don't know how, get counseling and read books so you don't damage your kids. They are exposed to more than enough negativity out in the world; they don't need it from you, too.*

Learn to swim.

Park a long distance from the stores in shopping centers *so you can get some extra exercise.*

Change your shopping habits. *Discover the joy of "shopping" at yard sales and thrift stores. The prices are low and there is often amazing stuff there that won't break your budget.*

Get excited about something. *Your favorite sport team? A new hobby? A worthy cause?*

Have a family photo taken yearly (include your pets)

If there is one thing that, if you do <u>not</u> do it before you die, will cause you to regret <u>not</u> having done it, set a deadline and JUST DO IT! *I don't know how, but you will figure it out if it is important enough. What are you waiting for?*

Plant flower bulbs in pots in your house in the winter for a touch of early spring.

ARE YOU GETTING THE IDEA?

GET RID OF YOUR STUFF

I hear your brain already shouting: *"Easy for you to say, but what am I going to __do__ with all this stuff?"* Let's agree that at some point in time, Boomers will likely down-size; i.e., move from the big house to a smaller house that better suits your new lifestyle.

Downsizing <u>requires</u> that you get rid of a certain amount of stuff because it simply will not fit into your new residence, be it a smaller house in a 55+ community, or a condo, or an apartment in a CCRC. No matter where you choose to live for the rest of your life, your stuff will probably not fit. So, choices must be made. Trust me when I tell you it is easier to make the choices slowly, over time, with some serious thought about what to do with those things you have accumulated, especially the things you love, than to have to make a fast move under some kind of pressure, especially if that pressure comes in the form of disability or death. It is also easier to get rid of your "stuff" while you are still vibrant and healthy ... don't wait until it's too late. I suggest you begin with your children (or other family members) to see what they want. You may be surprised!

    *a. **Have yard sales**, as many as you need and can manage, as many as your township will allow. Know that you will have to price your stuff very low, but keep in mind that the point of the sale is to get rid of your stuff, not to make a profit. Put out legible signs to direct people to your sale. Advertise in the local paper. Some people even advertise their yard sales on Craig's List. Put a price sticker on every single item if you don't want to be hassled all day with people asking prices. Some people are shy or embarrassed and will not ask, thus causing you to lose potential sales. If it rains, let it be known through your advertising when the rain-date will be. You can make hundreds of dollars at every sale, and afterward, you may discover you don't even miss the stuff you sold.*

    *b. **Sell some things on eBay.***

    *c. **Sell some stuff at local flea markets.** My husband and I got "hooked" on selling at flea markets for a few years. We didn't make much money, but we did get rid of stuff. And, we had a lot of fun doing it.*

    *d. **Auctions are good ways to get rid of your stuff.** The auctioneer does all the work, and after the auction, writes you a check. Sounds pretty easy to me.*

    *e. **Give certain things to certain specific people yourself.** No doubt, you have at least a few personal possessions which you cherish, and which you would want some particular person to have after your death. The best way to see that this happens is to give the things to them yourself. You can do it on the occasion of their birthday, or some holiday. Explain the significance of the item and how happy it makes you to personally give this gift to them.*

    *f. **Put stickers on the bottom of each item you want to be given to specific people <u>after</u> your death.** Things like your Lladro pieces, or your grandmother's cut-glass bowl, things that are in your china closet now, pieces of furniture you really don't want to part with at the moment. You may even want to have conversations among your family members to ask which pieces they want, so there is no squabbling over "stuff" after your death. Keep in mind that if your family is going to fight over your stuff while you are still alive, think of how they will fight if you don't have a plan for distribution of your possessions after your death. If you can see that the disagreements among them are serious and beyond reconciliation, give your stuff to a charity. Make it clear to them that you will do this if they continue to fight. Believe me, it's not worth fighting over stuff. Try to impress upon them that a loving relationship among family members is much more important than any tangible item of personal property.*

    *g. **If you have things (clothing in particular) that you want to give away, there are many worthwhile charities** that will be happy to accept your donations. They will even pick up the things at your front door. Many operate thrift stores, so you can not only donate your "stuff" to them, you can get a tax deduction for the value of the donated "stuff," and you can shop at their stores, too, thus supporting the organization two ways.*

    *h. **I have shelves and shelves of books I love. What shall I do with them?** People who read look everywhere for used book sales ... at libraries, yard sales, thrift stores, etc. As I see it, a used book has the exact same words in it as if the book were brand new, so why should I pay $25 when I can get it for $1? Libraries have lost much of their funding, so they are very happy to accept donations of your used books which they will then sell several times a year. It's a win-win-win! You get rid of the books you don't want anymore, the library makes money, and people get bargains by finding books at good prices while supporting the library!*

    *i. **If you have very valuable possessions (art, silver, jewelry, furniture, antique cars, etc.), do your research now about how to dispose of these articles in order to get the most money.** I know, I know, you don't want to part with these cherished possessions right now, but keep in mind that if you have enjoyed owning them, someone else will likewise enjoy* owning them afterward. Find those other people. Yard Sales and Thrift Stores are NOT the places for your valuable possessions. Remember that if you don't do this now, your executor will be responsible for getting rid of your cherished possessions by the easiest, quickest way possible.

j. **Consignment shops** *are another option for getting rid of stuff, especially good quality clothing. There are also consignment shops that deal in good quality furniture, lamps, pictures, etc. Know that consignment shops have rules that are not very flexible, and that "they" usually set the price without your input. If you don't expect to make a profit or have your possessions sold for then fair-market-value, you won't be disappointed. Last year, I consigned some of my best, most expensive clothing (suits, coats) which I had decided I wouldn't be needing anymore. I was paid $53 from the sale. I was outraged, but there wasn't anything I could do about it ... I had signed their consignment agreement. They also have rules about how many days they will keep your items, and after that, you must come and take them back, or they will keep them and sell them. Remember they are operating on a zero cost basis, and everything they sell is at a 100% profit for them, less the small percentage they pay to you. You can also shop there and find wonderful bargains. I know women who buy and sell at consignment shops all the time. So, do not discount this possibility. Just decide if it is right for you.*

k. **If you have collectibles (stamps, Hummels, old baseball cards, dolls, books, etc.),** *do your homework and find places where you can sell or otherwise lovingly dispose of your possessions. Remember, your executor probably does not love your things, and will do whatever is necessary to get the monetary value as soon as possible.*

l. **If you have possessions of historical value,** *research the many avenues for donating or selling your things. This kind of research may not be easy and may be very time consuming. It's completely up to you whether it's important enough for you to put forth your effort to find "good homes" for your historical possessions. If you ever watch "Antique Roadshow" on PBS, you will know that there has been a lot of valuable stuff saved over the years in families or found at yard sales, auctions or junk piles.*

m. **You can also donate things to the local historical society.** *My former husband had been active in a local service club, and he put together a very complete scrapbook of the activities of the club during the year in which he was President. Our local historical society happily accepted the donation for their archives. They may also be interested in scrapbooks that include old photographs and newspaper clippings from years past. It's worth asking.*

n. **Church missions** *are always happy to accept donations of gently used clothing and other items.*

o. **Clean out your files** *and get rid of old papers that are no longer relevant: old bank statements, old credit card statements (unless you need them for tax purposes), papers you have been saving for a long time but don't know why. If they don't pertain to your present life in a meaningful way,* **shred** *them.* <u>*Do not simply put them into your trash.*</u> *Find a local shredding event if you have too much paper "stuff" to shred yourself.*

p. **Local organizations and churches** *periodically have flea markets for the purpose of raising money for their good works, or to send children to camp, etc. Read the newspapers and find out about these events. You will be getting rid of stuff you don't need or want any longer, and the organization will be making a little money to support their activities. It's a win-win!*

q. **Habitat for Humanity** *has a new thrift store in my area. They accept donations of old appliances in good working condition (stoves, refrigerators, washers and dryers, dishwashers), and supplies that builders no longer need (bathroom sinks, tubs, and toilets, wood, tiles, etc.) ... all at bargain prices, with the sale proceeds going for a good cause.*

r. **If you have gold or silver you no longer want, sell it ...** *especially if the things you own are no longer sentimental or necessary, and especially if no one in your family wants them later on.*

s. **What about all those video tapes and all those 33-1/3 rpm records?** *I donated lots of each to the local senior center, and they were happy to get them. The center regularly shows movies, and I had a wonderful collection of the old classics and musicals, etc. Also, the records were classic music that the seniors love to dance to. The senior center will give you a tax receipt for your donation. Another win-win!*

t. **Local little theaters generally accept out-of-style and out-of-date clothing, both men's and women's, including old ties, tuxedo's, hats, furs, coats, gowns, gloves, shoes.** *Think of all the plays that little theatre groups put on, and all the costumes they need. They may even accept donations of some small pieces of furniture for stage sets. They may even give you a receipt for a tax deduction.*

u. **What about formal gowns? Bridesmaids dresses? Prom dresses?** *A local church accepts donations of gently used formal gowns and dresses for girls who are financially unable to pay the high price for new prom dresses they will probably only wear one time. And, don't forget about donating those unwanted dresses (or tuxedos) to thrift stores.*

v. **What about business clothing you can no longer wear because you gained/lost weight?** *There are groups who collect and either sell or donate business clothing (especially for women).*

w. ***Don't forget about shelters for abused women starting over.*** *It is entirely possible that some women walked away from their every possession in their search for safety for themselves and their children, and they may need just about everything to start over.*

x. ***Soup kitchens and homeless shelters would welcome donations of non-perishables and extra vegetables and fruit from your gardens.*** *If you find you have overstocked your home pantry, consider donating the excess before its expiration dates.*

- You could do <u>some</u> of these things; or,
- You could do <u>all</u> of them; or,
- You could do <u>none</u> of them; or
- You could make your own list.

And, in case you can't bring yourself to part with any of your personal possessions, when you die, someone else will get rid of your stuff, and you won't be around to direct them. That's just how it works.

IF THERE IS SOMETHING YOU ABSOLUTELY MUST DO ***between now and then***, JUST DO IT!

- Starting today, determine the date on which it will be finished.
- Even if you don't know how to do it, you'll figure it out if it is important enough.
- While you're making lists and choices, forget about the limits of money, time, distance, education, etc.
- Let you imagination take over for once in your life … ***stop being so practical.***

SUGGESTIONS FOR MAKING YOUR OWN LIST OF THINGS YOU WANT TO DO

<u>Step 1</u>: On sheets of lined paper, write numbers from 1 to 100 down the left-hand side.

<u>Step 2</u>. Read through <u>my</u> list one time, without comment and without making notes.

<u>Step 3</u>. Read through my list a second time. This time, put a check-mark beside suggestions you like, or which interest you. Jot down notes, ideas and comments that come to you as you are reading. Cross out things that don't apply or that you don't like.

<u>Step 4</u>. Begin your own "To Do List" by writing them on your 1-100 sheet of paper. (Of course, the list can be longer or shorter -- *I think longer is better*.)

<u>Step 5</u>: Establish priorities for everything on your list. Without priorities, a "to do" list, by itself, will scramble your brain and leave you frustrated and mentally exhausted, and at that point, you will probably give up. So, if it is important that you do some of the things on your list, it is necessary to think about what things are of the highest degree of importance, and work down from there.

The point of all this is to

BEGIN DOING THINGS FOR YOURSELF

before you run out of time.

IN CONCLUSION

By now, you may hate me for stirring up so many things for you. Or, just maybe you have been inspired to begin taking care of some aspects of your personal business while you still have time. I apologize if you have read some of these things more than once, but I believe they are important enough to mention again.

Keep in mind that it will take the rest of your life to accomplish all the things you want to accomplish, and you probably will never complete your "To Do" List. <u>The point is to begin.</u>

THIS IS THE TIME, AND IF NOT NOW, WHEN?

Go confidently in the direction of your dreams! Live the life you've imagined."

Henry David Thoreau

Tempus Fugit

SHOO-FLY PIE

Pre-heat oven to 300 degrees.

1. **Crust**: (Use only deep-dish glass pie plate)
   Make regular pie crust by your usual recipe…OR
   use a Pillsbury refrigerated pie-crust

2. **Crumbs**:
   Combine the following ingredients to make crumbs:
   - 2 cups flour
   - 1 cup sugar
   - ¼ lb. (1 stick) softened butter

3. **Goo**:
   In a 2-cup size <u>glass</u> (Pyrex) mixing cup or small glass mixing bowl, stir together until blended:
   - ½ cup dark Karo syrup
   - ½ cup unsulphured black-strap (dark) molasses (e.g., Brer Rabbit or Grandma's)
   - 1 cup hot water (not boiling)

   Stir in 1 teaspoon of baking <u>soda</u>. Mixture will foam.

4. Immediately pour molasses mixture into pie shell.

5. Pour crumbs evenly into molasses mixture a little at a time. Let them settle by themselves.

6. To collect any overflow of molasses during the baking process, put a piece of aluminum foil on oven rack and then place pie plate on the foil. NOTE: Make the foil larger than the actual pie plate and curve the edges up so as to collect any drips.

7. Bake at 300 degrees for 1 hour (and possibly 10 minutes longer if pie doesn't seem done)

**It is absolutely <u>essential</u> that you make this shoo-fly pie in the order listed above.
Do <u>not</u> make the molasses mixture first, and then let it sit while preparing the crust and/or crumbs.**

MY "BUCKET LIST" of things to do
between now and then

#	Priority A,B,C	Description	Start Date	Completion Date
1				
2				
3				
4				
5				
6				
7				
8				
9				
10				
11				
12				
13				
14				
15				
16				
17				
18				
19				
20				
21				
22				
23				
24				
25				
26				
27				

CONCLUSION

> *People do not like to think.*
> *If one thinks, one must reach conclusions.*
> *Conclusions are not always pleasant.*
>
> Helen Keller

> ***We die only once, and for such a long time.***
>
> Moliere

When you hear your name called … *and you will, you know* … you must obey. Will you be ready to answer the call? Or will you plead for more time …

- because you're not ready,
- because you don't have your house in order,
- because you have so many things left to do before you go.

Sadly, you will not be the first (*only?*) person ever to have wanted more time? The truth is that when you hear your name called, you will have run out of time. There will be nothing more to do.

Does this knowledge frighten you or spur you to action today? If that list of things you want to do is long, then start today; and, again, again, I ask you, "***If not today, then when?***"

> ***Do one thing every day that scares you.***
>
> Eleanor Roosevelt

It is my hope that you have read this book and learned things you may not have learned elsewhere, some subtle, some not so subtle, but important nevertheless. I hope you have learned some questions to ask about people, things and situations that matter to you, so that you will have knowledge and information to help you make wise choices.

> **REMEMBER THAT YOU ARE
> STRIVING FOR EXCELLENCE AND COMPLETION,
> NOT PERFECTION.**

What follows is a check-list to help you evaluate what you have accomplished so far, and to take a serious look at what remains to be done **between now and then.** Use this check-list as a guide over time. As you complete each item, write the date in the margin. Review it periodically to see how far you have come.

**DON'T JUST READ THE CHECK-LIST ONCE, GET UPSET, and QUIT.
KEEP GOING.**

CONGRATULATE YOURSELF FOR YOUR ACCOMPLISHMENTS TO DATE.

**DON'T BEAT YOURSELF UP FOR THE THINGS STILL TO BE DONE.
JUST DO THEM!**

> ***Choice of attention – to pay attention to this and ignore that – is to the inner life what choice of
> action is to the outer.
> In both cases, a man is responsible for his choices
> and must accept the consequences.***
>
> W. H. Auden

CHECK-LIST

<table>
<tr><td>

THIS IS NOT A TEST!

There are no right or wrong answers. Only <u>your</u> answers.

All that is required is honesty. Check only the blocks that are true.

There are no grades. It isn't even a Pass-Fail!

BEGIN NOW!

</td></tr>
</table>

_____ I have (___ do not have) a lawyer I trust and can work with to achieve my goals.

_____ I have (___ do not have) a certified financial planner I trust and can work with to achieve my goals.

_____ I have (___ have not) actively begun to review and revise my financial situation with the goal of having adequate retirement funds.

_____ I have (___ do not have) a 12- month easily accessible emergency fund.

_____ I have (___ have not) signed a Will.

_____ I have (___ have not) signed a Revocable Living Trust.

_____ My Revocable Living Trust is completely funded.

_____ My Revocable Living Trust is not completely funded, but it will be completed by _____.

_____ I have (___ do not have) adequate life insurance, but will take care of this by _____.

_____ I have (___ have not) recently reviewed the beneficiary designations on my life insurance, and they are satisfactory.

_____ I have (___ do not have) the beneficiary designations in my life insurance exactly as I want them to be, and will contact my insurance agent to make the necessary changes by _____.

_____ I have (___ do not have) long-term care insurance (if appropriate).

_____ I have (___ have not) recently reviewed the coverage of my homeowner's, renters' and auto insurance but will do that by _____. If changes need to be made, I will do that by _____.

_____ I have reviewed the coverage of my homeowner's and auto insurance and determined they are satisfactory.

_____ I have (___ have not) designated the beneficiaries in my IRAs and all my other retirement accounts exactly as I want them to be.

_____ I have (___ have not) signed a Living Will appointing an Agent and a Successor Agent.

_____ I have (___ have not) signed a Healthcare Power-of-Attorney (HC/POA) appointing an Agent and a Successor Agent.

_____ I have (___ have not) given copies of my Living Will and HC/POA to my primary physician.

_____ All my original documents are in the safe in my house, and my spouse and/or executor know (___ do not know) how to locate them.

_____ I have (___ have not) given copies of my Living Will and HC/POA to my spouse or other family member(s) who have the need to know.

_____ I have (___ have not) had a meeting with my family to talk about my wishes for end-of-life healthcare.

_____ I have (___ have not) had a family meeting to discuss my estate plan.

_____ I have (___have not) had a family meeting to talk about emergency planning.

_____ I have (___have not) had the "hard" conversations with the people in my life.

_____ I have (___ have not) told my spouse or other family member(s) where to find my Living Will and HC/POA

_____ All (___ none) (___ some) of my children (and their spouses) over the age of 18 years have signed a Living Will and a HC/POA.

_____ I have (___ have not) signed a General Durable Power-of-Attorney appointing an Agent and a Successor Agent.

_____ I will review all of my documents periodically and will make changes as appropriate.

_____ I have (___ do not have) a well-stocked emergency kit in my car.

_____ I have (___ do not have) a "grab-and-run" emergency kit in my house.

_____ I have (___do not have) all of my important papers/documents in a place where I could grab them and go in an emergency. I plan to have that task completed by _____.

_____ I have (___ have not) taken all appropriate steps to donate my organs at the time of my death.

_____ I have (___have not) made my wishes regarding organ donation known to my family.

_____ I have (___ have not) prepared a list for my executor, designating who is to get certain of my possessions after my death.

_____ I have (___ have not) given that list to my executor.

_____ I have (___ have not) made the location of my bank safe deposit box and key known to my family and my executor.

_____ I have (___ have not) made it known to my family (and executor) what I want to happen to my pets after my death.

_____ I have (___ have not) made provisions to care for my pets in an emergency.

_____ I have (___have not) provided funds for the care of my pets after my death.

_____ I drive (___ do not drive) without properly securing my pets in my vehicle (leashes, crates, seat harnesses, etc.).

_____ I have (___ have not) made my own funeral and burial arrangements.

_____ I have (___ have not) prepared a written statement of my intentions for my own funeral and burial to ease the burden of making all the decisions at the time of my death.

_____ I have (___ have not) talked with my family about what kinds of treatment I want in extreme medical situations but I plan to do this before _____.

_____ I have (___have not) written out specific things I want and do not want in extreme medical situations so there can be no mistakes or misunderstandings if the time comes, but I plan to do this before _____.

_____ I have (___ have not) told my family what I want for my funeral and burial.

_____ I have (___ have not) provided funds for my funeral and burial, but I intend to look into the matter by _____.

_____ I have (___ have not) gone through files and piles of papers in my house and have thrown away (shredded) all unnecessary ones.

_____ I have (___ have not) begun the process of organizing all my own personal papers, records, documents, and will be finished by _____.

_____ I have (___ have not) begun the process of getting rid of my "stuff," but I will do it before _____.

_____ I have (___ have not) gone through my stuff and have given certain things to other people now, before my death.

_____ I have (___ have not) started the process of improving my lifestyle (stopped smoking, exercise regularly, lost weight, eat better, etc.).

_____ I have (___ have not) stopped doing things I don't want to do anymore.

_____ I have (___ have not) made a list of the things I intend to stop doing.

_____ I have (___ have not yet) learned to say NO without guilt, but I'm working on it.

_____ I have (___ have not) set aside time every day (even 15 minutes) just for me.

_____ I have (___ have not) signed up for a class.

_____ I have (___ have not) begun investigating possibilities of where I would like to volunteer my time after I retire.

_____ I have (___ have not) eliminated credit card debt.

_____ I am (___ am not) working a plan to reduce my credit card debt.

_____ I have (___ have not) written a list of things I want to do **between now and then.**

_____ I have (___ have not) organized family photos.

_____ I have (___ have not) begun reading books I always wanted to read.

_____ I have (___ have not) made contact with friends and/or family members with whom I have lost touch over the years.

_____ I have (___ have not) begun investigating possibilities of where I/we should live for the rest of our lives: In our own home? In a 55+ community? In a continuing care retirement community? With family?

_____ I am working hard to live the rest of my life in such a way as to have no (or very few) regrets when I die.

_____ If I were to die tomorrow, I would have (___few) (___ lots of) regrets.

_____ I have made a list of all the things I have to do as a result of reading this check-list, and will begin doing those things by _____.

SO, WHAT DO YOU THINK?

ARE YOU ON COURSE, OR NOT?

AND FINALLY ...

Most people have never learned that one of the main aims in life is to enjoy it.

Samuel Butler

Be patient with yourself and others.

Give yourself credit for your accomplishments, whether large or small.

Don't quit.

Get it right the first time.

Savor each hour.

412

Express yourself clearly.

Give out love, not anger, hatred and negativity.

Be creative in every aspect of your life.

Be generous with your love, your compassion, and your forgiveness.

Remember that money isn't everything.

Don't live your life out of fear.

Take good care of yourself.

Surround yourself with beauty.

Strive for excellence in all things.

Take time to smell the flowers.

Always give it your best!

Do your absolute best to live by the Golden Rule.

Go and live a wonderful life.

BE HAPPY!

**THIS IS WHERE MY STORY ENDS
and
YOURS BEGINS.**

---

*The purpose of life is to live it, to taste experience to the utmost,
to reach out eagerly and without fear for newer and richer experience.*

Eleanor Roosevelt

Remember that this book is NOT a textbook or a "Do It Yourself" manual for estate planning, financial planning, funeral planning, or personal planning. It is not intended to be a substitute for appropriate professional advice.

This book is designed to educate you about things you should know before you speak with the professionals, so that you can engage them in meaningful conversations, ask the right questions, and come away from meeting with them fully informed about the options available to you. With this information, you can begin to make wise decisions for yourself and your family.

- You do not have to <u>agree</u> with the anything I've written.
- You do not have to <u>like</u> what you have read.
- You do not have to <u>do</u> any of the things I've suggested.
- You can choose to do nothing.

Nevertheless, I invite you to begin …

- <u>thinking</u> about these topics,
- <u>deciding</u> important things for yourself,
- <u>talking</u> about them with your loved ones and appropriate professionals,
- <u>making wise choices</u> for the rest of your life,
- <u>taking action</u> to achieve your goals.

Do not be afraid to speak your own truth, because, one of these days, it will be too late.

> *... The woods are lovely, dark and deep,*
> *But I have promises to keep,*
> *And miles to go before I sleep,*
> *And miles to go before I sleep.*
>
> Robert Frost

Tempus Fugit

ACKNOWLEDGEMENTS

I have had the privilege of learning from many excellent teachers, and have worked with some very talented people, each of whom has taught me something of value which I bring to this book. Lawyers and financial planners I worked with were generous in teaching me intricacies about estate and financial planning and estate administration. Many people have contributed to this book in ways they may not know. I wish I could put the names of all these people in the order of their respective importance in my life, but that is not possible. Every one of them would be in No. 1 position. I especially thank the following people for their incalculable contribution to this book and to my life:

- the teachers I had in the 1950s, who stressed attention to detail, getting it right the first time, accuracy in the use of, and a love for, the written and spoken English language, and the pursuit of excellence in all things.

- Erle Stanley Gardner for creating the fictional characters of *Perry Mason* and *Della Street.*

- James J. Heffernen, Esq., for allowing me to be his *"Della Street."* With Jim, I got a taste of the practice of estate law, and fell in love with it.

- the late Richard A. Stern, Esq., who taught me, by his every word spoken through a Dictaphone, how to do the work of administering a decedent's estate … the legal work I love the best.

- Stephen H. Frishberg, Esq., for letting me be myself, and who understood me in so many ways, who taught me so many things that relate to estate planning and administration. And, we had tremendous fun working together!

- Stanley J. Lieberman, Esq., as we shared the experiences of The Forum and personal coaching, and ultimately working together. He was always generous in answering my seemingly endless legal questions.

- Jean White E. Jones, Esq., who brings together her amazing knowledge of health care, the business world, and the practice of law. She brings humanity to the profession of law as no other lawyer I have ever known.

- Dr. James J. McKeown, Jr, a former lawyer, reborn as a university English professor and writer, for his friendship and his never-ending encouragement and support in writing this book.

- Richard Bank, Esq., lawyer, professor, writing coach, for his guidance and encouragement as my book moved from my computer to a publisher, and ultimately into the hands of readers. I took one of his writing/publishing classes years ago, and that class may have been the impetus I needed to seriously consider writing this book.

- Alfred T. Benelli, CFP®, for introducing me to the world of investments and money. I got to see the connection between the practice of estate law and finance, and learned so much from him about life, as well. I thank him especially for offering to write the Foreword.

- E. J. Long, financial advisor who encouraged me to keep writing and to share what I know with others.

- Donald A. Young, a kindred spirit I found in a corporate wasteland. As much as anyone else, he was responsible for challenging me to open my flower shop, *"Blue Gardenia."* I thank him also for reading portions of my manuscript and offering suggestions for improvement.

- Kim Cherry, L.Ac., M.Ac., Dipl.Ac., my acupuncture therapist, for her understanding, support, guidance, and enthusiasm, all of which kept me focused on the completion of this book, and, without her unending generosity of spirit, this book might still be languishing in my computer.

- MaryLou Nicholas, RN, my massage therapist, Reiki Master, my counselor, for all her healing support and guidance during some very rocky times.

- My friends, Sherrie Schoen and Susan Anderson, for reading drafts of sections of my manuscripts, and for offering valuable comments and suggestions to help me make this book the best it could be.

- Donald Moore, Funeral Director, whose opinion I value greatly, and for his interest in my writing about funerals and burial.

- Christine Hickson, the manager of the cemetery where I was employed. Not only did she teach me what I needed to know, but she did it with enormous grace, intelligence, sensitivity, and a profound sense of humor ... especially considering the surroundings and the circumstances.

- My sister, Cheryl, my lifelong companion, my friend, my shoulder to cry on. We shared good and not-so-good family times, and, together, we survived.

- My former husband, the late William E. Moran, Jr., for his support, love and generosity, and for putting up with me and my lifelong need for mental stimulation and change, even when he didn't understand.

- All the people who have expressed interest and kept the conversation about my book alive, as they have been asking me for the past several years, *"When will your book be finished?"*

- And, as the saying goes, *"the first shall be last, and the last shall be first,"* – with this in mind, I thank my husband, William R. Hoff, my first love, my friend, my lover, my dear companion, for completing me in ways that most people would find hard to understand. My life would have been unimaginable without him.

CPSIA information can be obtained at www.ICGtesting.com
Printed in the USA
BVOW05s2338260713

327023BV00006B/11/P